KU-107-113

NAZI EUROPE

NAZI EUROPE

CAVENDISH HOUSE

Published by
Marshall Cavendish Books Limited
58 Old Compton Street
London W1V 5PA

ISBN 0 86307 172 4
Printed and bound in Hong Kong
by Dai Nippon Printing Company Limited

CONTENTS

SEPTEMBER 1939

WARTIME

...IT IS SUNDAY MORNING, 3 September, 1939. The British are listening to the radio at 11am. There is one last minute delay before Britain's premier, Neville Chamberlain, speaks... another rumour that Göring is ready to fly in on a peace mission.

Then Chamberlain tells the world: there has been no reply to Britain's ultimatum...The war begins...

BUT WHY? What happened to make it necessary? Why did this conflict spread to engulf the world in flames?

WARTIME is the story of this huge drama, told in a way never attempted before. Each week, from now, you will live through one whole month of the war, sharing the experiences of those who fought, suffered and endured the six most extraordinary years of our century. You will read eyewitness accounts, still fresh from that time of trial. You will discover the smell and feel of wartime itself. Here too is the most detailed encyclopedia of the war ever created. Wherever a word appears in bold type, you will find the person, machine or place explained in the **War Notes** at the chapter's end. And, as you turn these pages, you will discover the story of those years in colour—as filmed at the time, or recreated now from meticulous research in archives across the world.

On this page, each week, we will open the story of the days ahead—and in the feature **Every Day of the War** chart the calendar of the epic. *Begin the journey now. This is the way it was.*

1st: Germany invades Poland. Britain and France mobilize.
2nd: RAF fly to France.
3rd: Hitler leaves for Polish Front. Britain, France, Australia and New Zealand declare war on Germany.
4th: French military operations start. BEF starts crossing Channel. *Athenia* sunk.
5th: Polish Corridor in German hands. Roosevelt declares US neutrality.
6th: Cracow falls, Polish Government leaves Warsaw. South Africa declares war.
7th: First British Atlantic convoys.
8th: First French and German planes lost on W. Front.
9th: Panzers repulsed from Warsaw. Poles counter-attack on Bzura river.
10th: Canada declares war.
11th: Polish Government leaves Brest-Litovsk.
12th: Allied Supreme War Council meets at Abbeville, France. Poles regroup on Bzura.
13th: French War Cabinet formed.
14th: Germans capture Gdynia, Hitler drives through Lodz.
15th: Warsaw surrounded.
16th: Russo-Japanese ceasefire signed, ends Mongolian border war.
17th: USSR invades Poland. Polish Government flees. *Courageous* sunk.
18th: Russians and Germans meet near Brest-Litovsk.
19th: Hitler in Danzig. Bzura battle ends.
20th: RAF shoots down first German plane. Hitler discusses euthanasia in Germany.
21st: Rumanian PM murdered by Iron Guard neo-Nazis.
22nd: Former German Army C-in-C von Fritsch killed by sniper outside Warsaw. Lvov falls.
23rd: German Jews forbidden radio sets.
24th: French Army ordered on to the defensive.
25th: 510 planes drop 486 tons of bombs and 3310 incendiaries on Warsaw.
26th: Warsaw seeks truce. Hitler returns to Berlin.
27th: Warsaw surrenders. Polish Enigma team escapes.
28th: Modlin surrenders.
29th: Russo-German treaty partitions Poland.
30th: Raczkiewicz replaces Moscicki as Polish Head of State.

POLAND: A Gambler's Throw

At 8pm on 31 August 1939 voices and stamping feet roused the night-shift watchman from his vigil at the remote German radio station of Gleiwitz. Eastwards, the long summer's day was just beginning to fade over the first fields across the Polish border.

To the watchman's horror, the door burst open. Several Polish-uniformed soldiers bound and gagged him, then proceeded to invade the recording studio. Gleiwitz, they told the world, was now in Polish hands. Shots were fired. There were cries of 'Long Live Poland'. Then silence.

German police cars, arriving within minutes, found a trail of corpses leading back to the border. All wore **Polish Army** uniforms. Conveniently, a group of foreign journalists was touring nearby. Before night fell, they were wheeled in to view this latest 'Polish violation of German territory'.

First shooting of the war

Next day, Adolf Hitler would cite it as justifying evidence for Germany's invasion of Poland. In fact, the raid on Gleiwitz was made by SS troops. Code-named Operation Canned Goods, the attackers brought their own corpses with them—concentration camp victims dressed in the uniforms that Hitler had instructed his Intelligence chief, Admiral Wilhelm Canaris, to procure.

Though few outside Germany would give much credit to the Nazi version of events at Gleiwitz, the story would help to stiffen the resolve of 1,512,000 German troops already poised to strike across the Polish border. Their zero hour was 4.45am, 1 September.

But it was in the port of **Danzig** that the first serious shooting of the war began. Hitler was determined that this key city of the **Polish Corridor** should be repossessed on the very first day of battle. In the harbour the aged German battleship, *Schleswig-Holstein*, turned her 11in guns on the Polish fortress of **Westerplatte** and began a week's bombardment.

In Poland, as day broke, General Wladyslaw Anders and his men looked up as the clear sky began to throb. They saw squadron after squadron of high-level bombers swooping south, aimed at wrecking the Polish rear. The planes struck at air bases in Warsaw, Lodz, Cracow; hammered nine other bases and 75 emergency airstrips. Stranded on the cratered runways, much of the **Polish Air Force** burnt where it sat.

Now, across the frontier, poured the men and the **panzers**. The speed of their advance was astonishing.

Never in the history of war had such a huge army moved so quickly. But in truth, both Polish and German armies relied overwhelmingly on horse-drawn transport. No fewer than 197,000 horses dragged in the vast amount of munitions needed by the **Wehrmacht**—and it took 135 railway trucks of fodder to fuel this vast horsepower.

But the Poles, right up to the eve of war, were convinced that horsepower would not simply supply the sinews of war but would finish the job. Cavalry, however, was no match for the war's new weapon, the tanks of General Heinz **Guderian.**

In Guderian's postwar account—vigorously denied by the Poles ever since—'the Polish Pomorska Cavalry Brigade, in ignorance of our tanks, charged them with swords and lances and suffered tremendous losses'. True or not, the Poles had certainly trusted in the Allied propaganda, which claimed that many panzers were cardboard or tinplated dummies. And above all they put their faith in the powers of the Polish

weather and countryside to halt the motorized Blitzkreig in its tracks. When the rains of autumn came, the tanks would bog down in the morass of Poland's unmade roads.

But the rains did not come. This was 'Hitler Weather'—baking the roads to parade-ground hardness. In Poland's sprawling, unkempt countryside the swift thrust of the armoured columns cleared paths for the supporting infantry at little cost to German lives. Indeed, in the first five days of war Guderian's all-motorized force of 50,000 men suffered only 150 killed and 700 wounded. To Guderian, mastermind of German tank strategy, the tank was 'the life-saving weapon'.

Against the oncoming hordes, Poland's ageing, autocratic C-in-C now made his move. Marshal Edvard **Smigly-Rydz** was incapable of defeatist thinking. His men shared his confidence. They had seven armies to counter the German attack.

Smigly-Rydz was counting on the promised British and French support for Poland. France, he was confident, would attack Germany's West Wall defences. Hitler's forces would turn round to defend their Fatherland. And then the Poles planned to ride after them and deal the deathblow.

It was a brave illusion. For the Polish Army could only field 225 tanks against 3200 panzers. Five huge German armies closed in, squeezing Poland from three directions—Pomerania in the west, East Prussia in the north and from Silesia and the protected Czech territories in the south. Like the rains, the French support never came. Polish soldiers marched straight ahead into captivity—or, in hurried retreat, tangled with reservists still trying to reach their bases, and with refugees blocking the roads.

Some Polish citizens, however, were welcoming the German advance. These were the German communities who, since borders had been redrawn in 1918, had been cut off from the Reich.

'So it is now our job to free the Polish people from all this wretchedness and . . . make it into one of the happiest nations on earth . . .'

Diary of a German soldier, 12 September 1939

Gen. K. S. Rudnicki

Regimental colour party of Poland's 9th Lancers on parade in 1939.

Many had been trained as fifth columnists to spread rumour and carry out acts of sabotage. They cut rail links, brought down telephone lines. On 3 September, fighting broke out between Polish troops and the local German population of Bydgoszcz (Bromberg)—an important rail centre through which many thousands of retreating Polish troops had to pass. Hundreds of Germans were rounded up and summarily shot. In all, some 7000 Germans are believed to have died in this way during the first few days of the war in Poland.

News, on the 3rd, that Britain had at last entered the war brought a brief moment of joy to the citizens of Warsaw. They crowded on to the streets, crying 'Long Live England and Poland' and 'Long Live King George'. 'We'll soon be in Berlin now!' Outside the British Embassy in the fashionable Street of the New World, crowds surged forward as Poland's Foreign Minister, Jósef **Beck,** joined British Ambassador Sir Howard Kennard on the balcony. Kennard seemed reserved, even gauche. He knew how little Britain could do to help.

That night Hitler boarded his personal train *Amerika* in Berlin. Two powerful steam engines hauled it eastwards to view the prizes of war.

It was a curious train, and a curious journey. Anti-aircraft guns, mounted on armoured wagons, protected the Führer's personal coach with its drawing room, sleeping compartment and private bathroom. Separate wagons housed the operational nerve centre and the adjutants, and secretaries of the Hitler entourage. Behind them trundled Heinrich Himmler's own train, *Heinrich*.

Hitler was depressed by the ragged, squalid, Polish countryside and later confided his 'awful impressions' of Poland. 'To think,' he said, 'for this wretched country millions of Englishmen and Germans were to lay down their lives.' For ten days his staff baked in the scorching sun, while Hitler sallied forth to meet his troops.

It was, indeed, a hazardous tour of inspection, for behind the lines there was no shortage of violent activity. On 4 September Colonel Eduard Wagner, responsible for occupation policy wrote: 'Brutal guerilla war has broken out everywhere, and we are ruthlessly stamping it out.'

The task of the dreaded **Einsatzgrüppen,** the 'special duty' forces that followed in the Army's wake, was broadly defined 'Combating anti-German elements in the rear areas'. On the 7th, Reinhard **Heydrich** was more specific: 'The Polish ruling class is to be put out of harm's way as far as possible.' And the 'lower classes that remain' would be 'kept down in one way or another'. Day by day, the shape of total war was being made plainer.

New-style war

In Warsaw, the Polish General Staff and the Government now frantically prepared to abandon the city. In a general exodus on the 7th they set off to seek safety 125 miles east at Brest Litovsk. With them, in a long column, went foreign embassy staff and anyone who could lay hands on a car or lorry. Mrs Clifford Norton, wife of the British Counsellor, paid £500 for a truck to move the British embassy staff.

By evening, German saboteurs and fifth columnists had seized a Warsaw radio station and broadcast the news that the capital had fallen. For a while, it fooled the world. From Moscow, Russian Foreign Minister Molotov sent 'congratulations and greetings to the German Reich Government'. In fact, 4th Panzer Division had only reached the suburb of Ochota. The real agony of Warsaw was only about to begin.

But first it was the panzers' turn to learn a harsh lesson of the new-style war. Unstoppable in the open Polish plains, they were trapped entering the narrow suburban streets of Warsaw—by

Polish cavalry anti-tank gunners accounted for many of the 217 German tanks lost during the campaign. Their 37mm Bofors gun could only penetrate the 15-30mm armour of the Panzer Mark Is and IIs under 400 yards. Each Polish cavalry regiment had 4 horse-drawn anti-tank guns.

'The gunlayers mastered their nerves and opened fire at point-blank range, three tanks immediately burst into flames and the others disappeared behind cover . . .'

Lt-Col K. S. Rudnicki watching an action, 18 September in the battle for Warsaw

rubble, barricades of tramcars, even burning rags thrown beneath them by intrepid citizens. In three hours 4th Panzer lost 57 of the 120 tanks committed. By 14 September, though they had the city surrounded and sent in a demand for surrender, the Germans received only defiance. Every 30 seconds, Warsaw radio broadcast a snatch of a Chopin polonaise, to prove the city was still in Polish hands.

Bombers now hit Warsaw every hour of the day. Ninety struck the capital on the first day alone. The dead were buried in any available patch of earth. An eyewitness recorded: 'These humble tombs of martyrs were flowered by flickering flames from tiny candles. They were everywhere . . . pitiful graves dug in haste, under the hail of bullets and shells, by nameless passers-by.'

In cellars and shelters foul air and cramped conditions drove people back into the sunlight in any brief lull. Sewage, overflowing into the streets, brought disease. Horses dying in the same streets were picked to the bone where they fell. The wounded lay untreated in fire-gutted hospitals. The city still refused to surrender.

There was one battle which was slightly less than hopeless for Poland. Along the Bzura river Lieutenant General Kutrzeba's Poznan Army, which had been retreating all week from its exposed position in Western Poland, struck the flank of the German forces driving on Warsaw. For a moment, on the 10th, the invaders were checked. The advance stopped while the panzers and **Stukas** were switched to the Bzura. By the 14th, encirclement was threatening Kutrzeba's men as they fought to reach Warsaw; 30,000 did so, helped by the covered approach of the Kaminow Forest. But on the 19th a pocket of 170,000 troops trapped west of the Bzura had to surrender.

The last possible chance of hanging on ended suddenly on the 17th. On this day Hitler's newest ally, Stalin, sent his own massive armies across Poland's eastern borders. A million Soviet soldiers walked in to claim their part of the package deal that Hitler had secretly sold Stalin back in August. The German General Staff was stunned at the news. As the armies of the two super powers met in mid-Poland, sporadic skirmishes broke out between them. Then, for the cameras, came handshakes, binding the uneasy alliance over the corpses of Poland, partitioned for the fourth time in her history.

'Wrath of heaven'

In Warsaw, refugees began to stream out. Tons of leaflets, dropped by the **Luftwaffe,** had given them just 12 hours to surrender. Typically, the local German artillery commander was not informed. Shells met fleeing civilians, who looked, said an eyewitness 'like the flight of some biblical people, driven onwards by the wrath of heaven, and dissolving in the wilderness'. Yet the Polish commander of Warsaw, General Juliusz Rommel, rejected the surrender ultimatum. Without hope, though desperately appealing for the world's promised aid, the citizens went on digging anti-tank ditches, earthworks and escape tunnels.

The end came on the 27th. Within the city there was no water, no electricity, no gas, no telephones. Many quarters were burning uncontrollably. Rommel surrendered. Broadcasting for the last time, Warsaw radio replaced the fragment of Chopin's polonaise with a funeral dirge.

Entering the fallen city a German soldier looked up to the sky to see 'in heavens the clouds as red as blood'.

In Warsaw, they had not yet learnt to run for cover when the planes came over.

War Notes

POLAND

BECK, Józef: Polish Foreign Minister from 1932, b. 1894 Warsaw. Pilsudski's Polish legions 1914–18; Military attaché Paris 1922–3. Reputed to be a devious, ambivalent politician. Signed non-aggression pact with Germany 1934. Negotiated Teschen region as Poland's part of Czechoslovakia in post-Munich annexations, March 1939.

DANZIG: Baltic seaport on River Vistula. Made free city in 1920 with League of Nations high commissioner to give Poland access to sea via Polish Corridor. Danzig's internal administration was German (96% of 404,000 population) but Poland controlled customs office and foreign policy. Europe's main trouble spot from Oct 1938.

EINSATZGRÜPPEN (Action Groups): 1000-strong SS units set up by Heydrich's RSHA (Reich Central Security Office) for use in occupied territory. One grüppe was attached to each invading army. Held lists of up to 60,000 Poles for liquidation.

GUDERIAN, Heinz Wilhelm: German general, b. 1888 Kulm (Chelmno, Poland). Pioneer of modern tank warfare. Ensign in father's 10th Hanoverian Jager Battalion (Bn) 1907–12. Berlin War Academy 1913–14. Signals and staff officer with one month as Bn CO 1914–18. Frontier defence and internal security 1918–21. Major 3rd Motor Transport Bn, Berlin-Lankwitz 1930–1. Insp of Motorized Troops 1931–5. CO new 2nd Panzer Div Oct 1935. Maj Gen Aug 1936. Lt Gen 16th Corps for Austria and Sudetenland occupations Feb-Oct 1938. Promoted to General as Chief of Motorized Troops on Army General Staff Nov 1938. CO 19th Corps Aug 1939.

HEYDRICH, Reinhard Tristran Eugen: Head of Reich Security, b. 1904 Halle, Saxony. Naval cadet on cruiser *Berlin* 1923 and chief signal officer by 1930. His affair with steel magnate's daughter resulted in court martial and his dismissal from the Navy March 1931. With Himmler June 1931 he set up SS Intelligence Service (SD). Married Lina von Ostau Dec 1931. SS Col and Head of SD with monopoly on Nazi Party Intelligence and counter-espionage July 1932. Moved to Berlin, and Head of Security Police Admin (plain clothes police) June 1936 which he combined with the SD to form RSHA (Reich Central Security Office) on 27 Sept 1939, with himself as Chief and SS Lt General.

LUFTWAFFE: German Air Force officially established March 1935 but existed secretly from 1920. Strength on 1 Sept 1939; 4093 front-line aircraft (1176 twin-engine bombers, 335 dive-bombers, 771 single-engine, 408 twin-engine fighters and 552 transports) with 2500/3000 trainers and 1.5 million men (pre-mobilization 373,000), almost a million flak defence. Air Fleets 1 and 4 had 1939 aircraft, including 897 bombers, 200 Me 109s and 335 Stukas, against Poland. Losses were 203 with 572 aircrew. 60% of bomb stocks dropped.

PANZERS (Pz): German translation for armour but applied to German tanks (panzerkampfwagen) 1939-45. There were 3200 in 6 Panzer divisions and 4 light divisions against Poland. Only 98 were 37mm gun Pz IIIs and 211 75mm-gun Pz IVs. Otherwise 1660 were obsolete Pz I (MGs) and 1226 Pz II (20mm). All had good cross-country performance and mechanical reliability.

POLISH AIR FORCE: established 1919. In 1939 it had 15,000 men and 400 planes: types included 120 P23 Karas light bombers, 36 Los medium bombers 30 P7 and 128 P11 Zedenastka biplane fighters. The P11s were split between Warsaw and support of 4 armies. By 3 Sept half the P23s and 46 fighters had been lost for 55 Luftwaffe planes. Ten days later Poland had fewer than 100 planes; the Germans had lost 150. By 17 Sept Polish losses totalled 333, and 116 aircraft were being flown into Rumania.

POLISH ARMY: 370,000 regulars, 2.8 million reserves organized in to 35 infantry divisions, 11 cavalry and 2 motorized brigades. Tanks: 225 medium Vickers-pattern 7TPs and 88 obsolete light. Recce carriers numbered 534 and armoured cars 100. Anti-aircraft units had 414 modern and 94 obsolete guns plus 750 MGs. An infantry division had only 48 field guns (6 heavy), 27 anti-tank guns and 92 anti-tank rifles. Radio equipment was not fully modernized. From 1937 cavalry was reduced by 25% and, though mechanization had begun, only 6 motorized and armoured brigades were planned by 1943 due to Poland's lack of suitable industries.

POLISH CORRIDOR: strip of land, 20–70 miles wide, between Pomerania and E. Prussia giving Poland access to the Baltic and Danzig.

SMIGLY-RYDZ, Edvard: Polish C-in-C, b. 1886 Brzezant (SE Poland). Art student, Cracow. Pilsudski's Polish Legions 1914–18, succeeding Pilsudski as Inspector-General of Polish Army May 1935. As Marshal of Poland 1936–9 he was the most powerful man in the country. Smigly ('hare') was a cover name from Polish Legion days. Escaped to Rumania 17 Sept.

STUKAS: sturzkampfflugzeug, German for dive-bomber but applied only to Junkers 87. First flew Dec 1935. In service April 1937. 952 were made by the end of 1939 with 335 in Luffwaffe on 1 Sept. Weight 4.2 ton (Ju 87B-1 data). Dimensions: 36.4 × 45.2 × 13.1ft. Engine: 1200hp Junkers Jumo 211Da 12-cyl liquid-cooled. Speed: 238mph at 13,140ft. Range: 370 miles. Ceiling: 26,600ft. Guns: 2 × 7.9mm wing MGs, cockpit 7.9mm. Bombload: 1102lb or 551lb + 4 × 110lb. Crew: pilot, gunner/radioman. A slipstream driven siren called 'Trombone of Jericho' was attached to the port wheel for added terror. Stukas flew 6000 sorties in 26 days over Poland for a loss of 31 planes.

WEHRMACHT: (Defence Force). Official name for Army, Navy and Air Force in the Third Reich, by decree of 21 May 1935 replacing Reichswehr. Losses in Poland (to 30 Sept) totalled 10,572 killed, 3400 missing and 30,322 wounded.

WESTERPLATTE: Polish fortress of 14.8 acres at Danzig. Major Koscanski's garrison of 6 officers and 182 men held out against 13 attacks until 7 Sept. The Germans called it 'a little Verdun'. 60 Stukas bombed the fort on 2 Sept.

DECLARATIONS OF WAR

One minute before Neville Chamberlain, Britain's Prime Minister, faced the microphone at the Cabinet Room, 10 Downing Street, London, to tell the world that war was on, he hesitated. The time was 11.13am.

The moment's delay was caused by the arrival of yet another message from plump Swedish businessman Birger Dahlerus, who had carved for himself a niche as unofficial peacemaker extraordinary between Berlin and London. 'As a last resort' ran the message, 'might I suggest that Field Marshal Hermann Göring should fly over to discuss matters?' **Chamberlain** dismissed this flicker of hope, then told his listeners: 'You can imagine what a bitter blow it is to me that all my long struggle to win peace has failed.'

In his vast office on Berlin's Wilhelmplatz, Adolf Hitler 'sat immobile, gazing before him' (his personal interpreter Paul Schmit remembered). Dr Josef Goebbels, head of the largest propaganda ministry ever created, had nothing to say either. He 'stood in a corner by himself, downcast and self-absorbed'. Herman Göring, master of an air force that—as Britain believed—could smash London in nightly 1000 bomber raids,.was appalled by the news. 'If we lose this war, then God have mercy upon us' he said.

Fox Photos

The hours between Hitler's invasion of Poland on 1 September and the final declaration of war are among the most bewildering in British history.

For Hitler, every hour counted. Not until seven hours after the invasion of Poland did the British Cabinet, and in Paris, the French Council of Ministers, sit down to decide what to do.

In Washington the news of the German invasion was treated more urgently. At 2.50am local time Secretary of State Cordell Hunt scrambled into his clothes and reached the empty corridors of the State Department 40 minutes later.

In London Count Edvard Raczynski, the Polish Ambassador, chased round to Downing Street at 10.30 that Friday morning, demanding Britain's promised help. Foreign Secretary Lord **Halifax** was cautious. Maybe the next visitor, Theodor Kordt, Chargé d'Affaires at the London German Embassy would explain. Kordt passed the Pole on the way out, shook hands with Halifax, and politely explained he had no clue as to what was going on in Poland.

If the Poles were dismayed by Britain's lack of purpose, America's Ambassador Joseph Kennedy was doing little to help resolve them. Believing Britain was incapable of waging a successful war against Germany, he spent his time sending defeatist communiqués to President Roosevelt. Meeting King George VI on 9 September, he impressed upon the King that even if Britain won the war, she would be left bankrupt.

The French were dithering as energetically as the British. All over France, men were still scrambling back to their barracks. The French begged time before taking the final, terrible step. Messages flew from London to Paris, and back. Should the ultimatum to Hitler be long or short? Faced with French reluctance to get involved Chamberlain hesitated too. He faced a revolt from his own party if he did not declare war soon. The warmongers in his Tory party were growling in the wings: none louder than Winston Churchill.

By early evening, nothing had been decided. In Berlin it was warm and heady. In the Winter Gardens of the old Reich **Chancellery**, the Nazi leaders gathered spontaneously to celebrate

'You can imagine what a bitter blow it is to me that all my long struggle to win peace has failed'

Neville Chamberlain, BBC broadcast
3 September 1939

events so far. Only the army professionals viewed the scheme with alarm. Colonel Walther Warlimont of the Supreme Command (OKW) Operations Staff looked at the gay throng and decided this was no way to run a war. The place looked like the set for a comic opera. One of his men went up to Göring with 'Directive No. 1 for the Conduct of War', a closely reasoned staff report. Said Göring: 'What am I supposed to do with this bumf?' The only reports anyone wanted tonight were the ones rushed in by shrill messengers telling how far the Blitzkrieg had clawed into Poland. The OKW colonel left early.

At 9.30pm Britain's Ambassador to Berlin, Nevile **Henderson** finally met Foreign Minister Joachim von **Ribbentrop.** Henderson carried the fruits of the day's agonizing in London, though five hours had elapsed between framing the message to him and actually telephoning him the contents. The message was hardly intimidating. In fact it was a 'severe warning'. Ribbentrop listened, then said he would have to show it to Hitler. Another few hours had been won.

Saturday, 2 September dawned. In Poland the Wehrmacht and Luftwaffe were still advancing.

In London and Paris the politicians were still talking. But a mood of tense anger and frustration was gathering over Chamberlain's head.

'Hitler will collapse the day war is declared on Germany' French Commander-in-Chief Maurice Gamelin had declared. 'We shall go through Germany like a knife through butter.' But the butter knives in London and Paris stayed in their sheaths. While Foreign Secretary Lord Halifax was pleading for more time with Raczynski, an astonishing secret conversation was taking place in another Foreign Office room. Fritz Hesse, press advisor to the German Embassy in London, came to bargain with Sir Horace **Wilson.** Acting on the direct instructions of Adolf Hitler, Hesse offered withdrawal of German troops, plus compensation to the Poles, in return for Danzig and a road across the Polish Corridor. Why not, suggested Hesse, fly to Germany, meet Hitler and discuss the whole position 'heart to heart'. Wilson refused.

A restless House of Commons waited for a promised statement from Chancellor of the Exchequer John Simon, timed for 2.45. MPs on both sides of the House were raging now. Enough was enough. Hitler was smashing Poland and it was time he was stopped. Just how he was going to be stopped, no one seemed to know.

Fifteen minutes before Simon was due to rise in the House, the telephone rang again in Downing Street. This time it was the Italians, proposing a five power peace conference. Foreign Secretary Halifax raced round to the House of Commons and

'This night for the first time Polish regular soldiers fired on our territory. Since 5.45am we have been returning the fire, and from now on bombs will be met with bombs'

Hitler to the Reichstag, 1 September 1939

told Simon to stay in his seat. In Whitehall the politicians thrashed out the new idea with Paris.

Locked up in the humid House of Commons, MPs became restless and angry. Several refreshed themselves at the bar. By 7.44pm as Chamberlain finally rose to speak, tension and tempers were at breaking point.

Chamberlain spoke for four bleak minutes. The words were flat, uninspired. There was no declaration of war, no ultimatum. 'If the German Government would be willing to regard the position as the same as it was before the German forces crossed the Polish frontier. That is to say . . .'

The House gasped. Then shouting started. 'Speak for England' shouted Tory MP Leo Amery, as the Labour Party's acting leader Arthur Greenwood stood to reply. He demanded to know 'how long are we prepared to vacillate at a time when Britain, and all that Britain stands for, and human civilization, are at peril?'

'This means war'

But Chamberlain's few flat words had not been only directed at the House. Their text had been telegrammed to Ambassador Henderson, in Berlin, with a covering message: 'You may think it well to pass it immediately to certain quarters.' It was Chamberlain's last desperate effort for peace. Henderson pinned his visiting card on the speech and sent it round to the dinner table of Birger Dahlerus, the friend of Göring and self-appointed peace envoy. Dahlerus scanned it, and decided to finish his dinner anyway.

In Westminster, Chamberlain had a palace revolt on his hands. A group of ministers went on strike. They trooped in to the Chancellor's rooms, sat down by a direct phone link to No. 10, and made it plain they would wait there until war was declared.

By the time the ministers finally got their summons to No. 10 they were 'really scruffy and smelly', one admitted later. There they faced Chamberlain and a hastily summoned Halifax. The two men heard the rebels out. Chamberlain looked ill. Finally, he said: 'Right, gentlemen, this means war.'

In Berlin, Henderson at last got the text of his ultimatum, in telegram 317, initialled by Halifax. 'You should ask an appointment with Minister of Affairs at 9am Sunday morning.' Unless Germany ceased hostilities by 11am, it would be war. Wishing to avoid the unpleasant duty, Ribbentrop tossed the appointment to Hitler's interpreter, Paul Schmidt. 'There's no reason why you shouldn't receive the British Ambassador instead of me,' said Ribbentrop.

In the event, even Schmidt nearly missed the appointment. He woke on Sunday, 3 September to find, to his horror, he had overslept. His taxi hurtled into the Wilhelmplatz in time to see Henderson mounting the steps to the front door. Schmidt just made it to Ribbentrop's desk, via a side door, in time to greet the Ambassador.

At last, the die was cast. In London, Chamberlain faced the microphone to confess the failure of his life-long mission, and to plunge Europe into war.

War Notes

HENDERSON, Sir Nevile Meyrick: British Ambassador to Berlin from 1937, b. 1882. Ambassador to Argentina 1935–7. Well liked by Hitler and friend of Göring, his firm belief in Chamberlain's policy of appeasement led him to be dubbed by the press 'our Nazi British ambassador'.

CHAMBERLAIN, Arthur Neville: British Prime Minister, b. 1869 Birmingham. Educated Mason College, B'ham. Managed estate in Bahamas 1890–7. Successful hardware manufacturer B'ham. As Lord Mayor 1915–16, set up the first municipal bank in England. MP 1918. Postmaster General 1922–3. Minister of Health 1923, 1924–29. Chancellor of Exchequer 1923–4, 1931–7. Succeeded Stanley Baldwin as PM May 1937. Believed in policy of appeasement and conciliation. A signatory of the Munich Agreement Sept 1938.

CHANCELLERY: 400yd yellow stucco and grey stone frontage along Voss Strasse at right angles to Old Chancellery. Enlarged by Albert Speer Aug 1938-Jan 1939, new Chancellery had 400 carpeted marble rooms. A dining room and corridor connected the new and old Chancelleries.

HALIFAX, Edward Frederick Lindley Wood, 1st Earl: British Foreign Secretary, b. 1881. Educated Oxford. MP 1910. Under Sec for Colonies 1921–2. Minister of Agriculture 1924–5. Raised to peerage as Baron Irwin of Kirkby Underdale. Governor-General of India 1926–31, where he tried to quell the riots that had prevailed since 1921 and co-operated with Mahatma Gandhi. Sec of State for War 1935. Lord Privy Seal 1935–7. Leader House of Lords 1935–8. Lord President of Council 1937–8. A leading advocate of appeasement.

RIBBENTROP, Joachim von: German Foreign Minister, b. 1893 at Wesel on the Rhine. Studied in Metz, London and Switzerland. Military missions to US and Turkey 1914–18. Awarded Iron Cross (1st Class) believed by some because of own petition. Member of German delegation to Versailles Peace Conference 1919. Married wealthy champagne producer's daughter and added the noble 'von' to his name through his adoption by a distant titled relative 1926. Joined Nazi Party 1928 to become Colonel of SS May 1932. Disliked inside and outside the Party because of his vanity and self-importance, but his indulgence to the Führer won him Hitler's admiration. Set up Ribbentrop Bureau as rival to Foreign Ministry 1933. Reich Commissioner for Disarmament 1934. Negotiated Anglo-German Naval Treaty June 1935. As Ambassador to Great Britain to encourage Anglo-German understanding Aug 1936, he offended English society by giving Nazi salute at court reception by King George VI. Signed Anti-Comintern Pact with Japan Nov 1936. Reich Minister for Foreign Affairs 1938, signed non-aggression agreement for partition of Poland 23 Aug 1939. Signed a second German-Soviet Treaty to readjust partition 28 Sept 1939.

WILSON, Sir Horace: British civil servant, b. 1882. Chief industrial adviser to government 1930–9. Permanent Sec of Treasury and Head of Civil Service 1939. Much admired by Chamberlain, he became his adviser on foreign policy. Involved in Munich and pre-war negotiations.

U-BOATS STRIKE

Within nine hours of the start of war news broke that an unarmed ocean liner, the Athenia, was sinking in the North Atlantic, victim of a U-boat's torpedo. Few were more appalled than Adolf Hitler to hear so.

At sea, on the wider war's first day, German merchant ships began to scurry towards neutral ports. Throughout the **Royal Navy,** the message 'Winston's back' (at his old World War I post as First Lord of the Admiralty) raised cheers. For Captain James Cook, master of the 13,581 ton British-owned **Athenia,** the day was tense—but until 7.30pm, without much incident.

Departure from Belfast that morning had been emotional. Of a 1103-strong passenger list, three in four were women and children en route to Montreal, away from Europe's spreading war. Also on board were Germans, Poles—and American citizens. It was the American presence on board that would most alarm Hitler.

Stricken liner

By 7.30 dinner was being served. Ireland lay 250 miles behind. Only the constant zigzag of the ship's course reminded anyone of the war.

Beneath the Atlantic swell, nearby, was 26-year-old **U-boat** commander Lieutenant Fritz Julius Lemp. U30, his Type VIIA U-boat, away from her Wilhelmshaven base since 22 August, was coming to the end of two dramatic weeks. Lemp, along with 15 other submarine commanders loose in the North Atlantic, had been keyed up to strike as soon as war began. In the close, throbbing quarters of U30, Lemp's crew waited keenly for their chance. The German Navy's Goliath radio station at Frankfurt-on-Oder, 40 miles east of Berlin, had told them that war had begun. But the U-boats were bound by radio silence, lest their position be identified.

Other rules bound them too. Commodore Karl Dönitz's U-boats were still subject to the London Submarine Agreement of 1936. This banned the sinking of unescorted merchant shipping without warning. Indeed, Hitler's second war directive, that very day, reminded U-boats of just this fact. The last thing Hitler wanted was another **Lusitania** incident.

Now, this September evening, Lemp and his men were the hunters, alert for a quarry. As he watched the zigzag course of the unlit vessel crossing his path Lemp made a fatal decision. Identifying *Athenia* as an armed merchant cruiser he gave the order at 7.43 that let a 1.5 ton projectile rip across the waters.

'The torpedo went right through the ship to the engine room. It completely wrecked the galley,' recorded Captain Cook. Some died at once in the impact. Others were killed by flying fragments as hatches blew off the deck through the air.

As sea poured into the stricken liner, families struggled towards the lifeboats. One mother handed her two-year-old child up to the only remaining place. For the next 12 hours she would be adrift in another boat, not knowing if her child would survive. It did—others were less lucky. One lifeboat dropped 30ft from *Athenia*'s tilting portside. Another slewed into the propeller of a rescuing Norwegian vessel. In all, 112 died.

U30 surfaced half an hour after the torpedo hit to survey her handiwork. Lemp ordered his deck gun crew to shoot away *Athenia's* radio aerials. After two shots, the submarine dived—without giving assistance to passengers required under the London Agreement.

U30 kept radio silence until she got back to base on the 26th. To his surprise, Julius Lemp found no hero's welcome as Dönitz met him on the dockside at Wilhelmshaven. Instead he risked

'We saw the bodies of children on the deck and in the water. Other little ones had lost their parents and ran around screaming. The terror increased as the shells hit the ship . . .'

An *Athenia* survivor

Safely ashore at Galway, Ireland, a survivor from *Athenia*. This boy was one of many survivors picked up by the Norwegian merchantman, *Knut Nelson*.

ILN

court martial. The relevant page was torn out of U30's log and rewritten. In the whole history of the U-boat arm this was the only time this happened.

Churchill's bomb plot?

Rightly terrified about the implications of what had happened, Hitler sent a special order on 4 September that even escorted passenger liners were not to be attacked. Josef Goebbels' propaganda machine acted swiftly. On 5 September the Nazi Party newspaper *Volkischer Beobachter* suggested: 'Maybe Churchill had the bomb planted himself.'

In London, news of *Athenia's* fate confirmed the Admiralty's worst fears. They concluded Germany was committed to unrestricted submarine warfare, as in 1917. Henceforth, all ships on ocean and coastal routes would sail in **convoy.** Whatever the present misplaced confidence in **asdic,** no naval expert in Britain underestimated the power of a larger U-boat force to turn off the tap of Britain's essential wartime supply routes and starve her to death. By the month's end 40 British merchant ships had joined *Athenia*.

In the shadowy warfare of the rival British and German code-breaking organizations, the German Navy's **B-Dienst** was winning. With an English section directed by Wilhelm **Tranow.**

The 36 men and women in the Royal Navy's **Operational Intelligence Centre** (OIC) puzzled over the scant German radio traffic that came their way. Britain's ten **Direction-Finding** stations around the coast were not yet fully operational. For the vital task of air reconnaissance, in stark contrast to the well-served **Kriegsmarine,** OIC sent up a young Canadian pilot and a passport photographer on the first day of the war. In their light Beechcraft plane they prowled up the Dutch coast seeking the German fleet. As two Luftwaffe fighters came in to chase them off, they managed five long-range pictures with a German camera.

If the position of warships and U-boats remained mysterious, at least steps could be taken to keep them out of sensitive waters. During 11-16 September the minelayers *Adventure* and *Plover*, accompanied by six converted train ferries, fenced off the Straits of Dover with 3000 mines.

The Royal Navy embarked on offensive operations, too. The aircraft carriers **Ark Royal, Courageous** and **Hermes** sailed out into the Atlantic, to cover the incoming merchant vessels.

On 14 September they made their first kill—though, for *Ark Royal*, the Navy's only modern carrier, it was a narrow escape. Three torpedoes from U39 passed her astern, then detonated. The five escorting destroyers swung into action, sinking U39 and capturing her crew of 43. She was the first of 781 U-boats to perish. That same afternoon, 200 miles away, two of *Ark Royal's* Skua dive-bombers hurtled down to attack U30—but were brought down in the explosion of their own anti-submarine bombs. Lemp added two

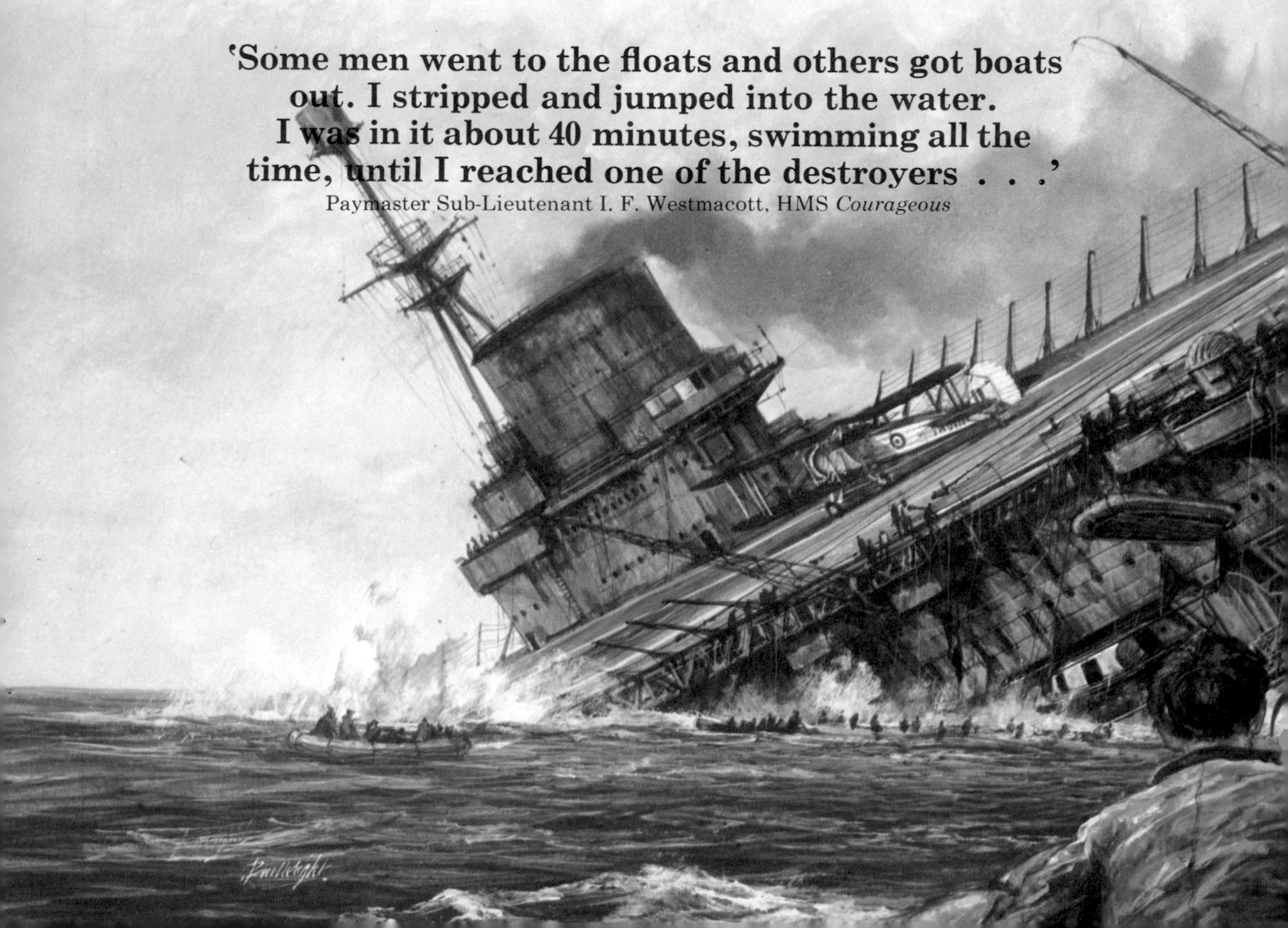

'Some men went to the floats and others got boats out. I stripped and jumped into the water. I was in it about 40 minutes, swimming all the time, until I reached one of the destroyers . . .'
Paymaster Sub-Lieutenant I. F. Westmacott, HMS *Courageous*

captured pilots to the score of U30.

Courageous, meanwhile, ploughed on through the Western Approaches in confidence, her 24 Swordfish biplanes responding to every distress call. When, on the 10th, the first plane failed to return, Lieutenant Charles Lamb, Fleet Air Arm, mildly suggested to his squadron CO that it might be sensible if aircraft guns were loaded. The CO scoffed: 'You've been watching too many films about the last war. What on earth do we want bullets in our guns for?'

A week later eight Swordfish sped away from *Courageous* in response to an SOS from the liner *Kafiristan* which had been stopped by a U-boat. At 5pm, a Swordfish spotted the sub, forced it to dive, and the patrol returned to the carrier. For Lieutenant Lamb it was a memorable flight: his fuel gauge had been reading empty for 10 minutes by the time he touched down on the deck. He made for the wardroom with his flying observer when two torpedoes hurtled into the ship's engine room on the starboard side. Power and lighting failed instantly. As the ship listed over, the 22 aircraft in the hangar tumbled and crashed towards the port bulkhead, increasing the already fatal angle.

It took just 20 minutes for *Courageous* to die, her steam-operated siren sounding hideously to

The 22,500-ton aircraft-carrier HMS *Courageous* sank just before sunset 17 Sept. 23 Swordfish aircraft were also lost, including the one seen on deck. *Courageous* was the Royal Navy's first ship sunk in the war.

the last moment. The order to abandon ship was passed by word of mouth. For many there was no way out. Others plunged 70ft from the flight deck. Lamb saw *Courageous* sink, bows-first. With her went 514 of the 1200 crew—and Captain W. T. Makeig-Jones.

For the U-boat captain, and his entire crew there would be an Iron Cross apiece as well as a visit by Hitler on the 28th. Two of his three torpedoes had found *Courageous* in a perfect beam shot from 3000 yards. Evading 29 **depth-charge** attacks from *Courageous*' guardian destroyers, U29 headed for home.

Grimly, the Royal Navy licked these and other wounds—one of which was cruelly self-inflicted. On 10 September in a dark night and heavy North Sea, the submarine *Triton* twice challenged the sub *Oxley*. Receiving no reply she torpedoed her flotilla-mate; only the captain and one rating survived. It would have made a fine propaganda story for Dr Goebbels. Certainly a better one than the fairy tale claim he flourished as the month ended: the sinking of *Ark Royal* herself.

At 11am on 26 September one of *Ark Royal's* Skuas shot down a shadowing Dornier 18 flying boat over the North Sea—but not before it had radioed in four Junkers 88 bombers. In command of one of these brand-new and very fast aircraft was Lance Corporal Adolf Francke, who loosed off a 1000lb bomb from 1200ft to within 30 yards of *Ark Royal's* port bow. 'All it did was to break some crockery' said the captain.

In the next week, German radio broadcast the news of *Ark Royal's* demise 27 times. Francke won promotion to Lieutenant and an Iron Cross, 1st and 2nd class. The Propaganda Ministry rushed out a boy's book, with artists' impressions, entitled *How I Sank the Ark Royal*. When, inevitably, the lie was revealed, Francke had to endure the mockery of his colleagues. It preyed on his mind. He confided to an American journalist that at one stage he contemplated suicide. The men of *Ark Royal* listened with amusement as the ship's radio brought them the voice of Lord Haw-Haw, Germany's English-speaking propagandist: 'Where is the *Ark Royal*?' demanded the sneering voice.

'We're here, you bastard' roared the crew as one man. And here, until a fateful November day two years later, she would stay.

'The key to German power at sea lies below the surface. Give us submarines and we shall have the teeth to attack'

Gröss-Admiral Erich Raeder, C-in-C German Navy

War Notes

U-BOATS STRIKE

ARK ROYAL: 27,000-ton aircraft carrier laid down Sept 1935 Launched April 1937. Completed Nov 1938. Dimensions: 721.5 × 94.7 × 22.8ft (797ft flight deck). Powered by 3-shaft steam turbines (6 boilers) 102,000 shp. Speed: 30.75 knots. Guns: 8 × twin 4.5in anti-aircraft (AA), 48 × 2pdr AA (6 mounts), 8 × quad .5in MG. Aircraft: 60 (3 lifts). Armour: 4.5in belt, 2.5-3in deck. Crew: 1860 (including airmen).

ASDIC (Allied Submarine Devices Investigation Committee): underwater echo-sounding equipment developed by Allied scientists from 1917. Asdic went to sea 1920. An Underwater Detection Establishment was set up at Portland, Dorset 1927. Four destroyers equipped 1923 and by 1939 most Royal Navy ships operated one of 5 types. In 1936 Admiralty felt the U-boat menace was largely removed by asdic. It could detect a submerged sub at 2500 yards (normal range was 1500 yards) with 3-second 'pings' from a transducer in the ship's keel that scanned 160° ahead in 5° steps. Asdic became distorted at 8 knots, was not reliable over 18 knots and unusable at 24. Asdic operators were known as 'Pingers' and 'lowest of God's creatures'.

ATHENIA: 13,581 ton passenger liner. Launched 1923. Crew: 315. Passengers: 1103. She sank at 10am on 4 Sept 1939 losing 19 crew and 112 passengers, including 50 British, 28 Americans, 7 Poles and 4 Germans.

B-DIENST (Beobachtungs-Dienst): German Naval code-breaking and intelligence service. Founded April 1 1919 in Berlin. The 8-man team (including Tranow) under Lt Martin Braune gave priority to British, French and Italian signals. A Mediterranean surveillance post was created in Black Forest 1925. In 1937 B-Dienst's 14 listening posts were receiving 700 signals a day. Captain Kupfer was CO in 1939.

CONVOY: merchant ships sailing with a warship escort. Convoys are a part of naval history, especially the Royal Navy system 1689–1815. They were not used in WW1 until April 1917, in an attempt to halt the catastrophic losses. Admiralty Plans Division decided in 1938 to use convoys from the outset of the next war.

COURAGEOUS: 22,500 ton aircraft carrier. Laid down March 1915. Launched as battlecruiser Feb 1916, completed Jan 1917. £2 million was spent on conversion 1924–8. Dimensions: 786.2 × 90.5 × 24ft. Powered by 4-shaft steam turbines (18 boilers) 90,000 shp. Speed: 29.5 knots, less by Sept 1939. Guns: 16 × 4.7in anti-aircraft (AA), 24 × 2pdr AA (3 mounts); 8 × ·5in MG (2 quads). Aircraft: 48 max, only 24 in Sept 1939 (2 lifts). Armour: 2–3in belt, 1–1.75in deck. Crew: 1200 including 460 airmen. Sister ship: *Glorious*.

DEPTH-CHARGE: hollow cylinder filled with amatol High Explosive (HE), set off by a hydrostatic pistol to explode underwater. First used 1916, the weapon sank 27 WWI U-boats. In 1939 the Royal Navy had the 410lb Mk7. It sank at 10ft per sec. A hand-turned key opened holes in the charge to explode at any of 6 depths from 100–600ft. Destroyers had stern-throwers and rail chute for 30 depth-charges to be laid in patterns round an asdic-located sub.

DIRECTION-FINDING (DF): 24-hour British intercept service that tracked range, network and volume of enemy radio traffic. Known as 'Y' service. Main naval home stations: Chatham, Scarborough and Flowerdown. Three DF stations in Mediterranean, two in the Far East.

HERMES: 10,850 tons, the first RN purpose-built aircraft carrier. Laid down 1918. Launched Sept 1919 and completed 1923. Tonnage: 12,900. Dimensions: 598 × 70.2 × 18.7ft. Engines: 2-shaft steam turbines (6 boilers) 40,000shp. Speed: 25 knots. Guns: 6 × 5.5in, 3 × 4in anti-aircraft. Aircraft: 15 (2 lifts). Armour: 2–3in belt, 1in deck, 1in gunshields. Crew: 664 excluding airmen. She carried 12 Swordfish transferred from Ark Royal 4 Sept.

KRIEGSMARINE: 'War Marine', German Navy. In the 1935 creation of the Wehrmacht the Reichsmarine was renamed. In Sept 1939 the surface fleet had 2 battlecruisers, 3 pocket battleships, 2 old battleships, 2 heavy and 6 light cruisers, 22 destroyers, 20 torpedo boats, 10 sloops, 48 minesweepers, 40 motor minesweepers and 8 mine layers.

LUSITANIA: 32,500 ton Cunard liner, sunk 10–15 miles off Kinsale, Ireland, on 7 May 1915. Hit starboard amidships by 2 torpedoes when steaming at 18 knots, she took just 15 minutes to sink. Out of 1906 aboard, 1198 lives were lost. Among them were 198 American citizens which helped push the United States into the war.

OPERATIONAL INTELLIGENCE CENTRE (OIC): established by Rear-Admiral James Troup, Dir of Naval Intelligence under Lt-Cdr Norman Denning June 1937. Started with one assistant and a cipher course for Denning. Acquired power to signal ships direct 1938. Italian, Japanese and Spanish intelligence supervised by one officer. Mobilized during Munich crisis. Basement war room with outside teleprinter links and inside pneumatic tubes by Sept 1939. Capt Jock Clayton appointed head March 1939 in event of war. Merchant Shipping and U-boat Tracking Sects set up by July. Mobilized in Aug with Italian and Japanese Sections and German Surface Ship Section. Telephone links with DF stations. Another OIC at Malta.

ROYAL NAVY (RN): world's largest and most far-flung Fleet comprising 12 battleships and 3 battlecruisers, 8 carriers (2 seaplane), 61 cruisers, 2 monitors, 181 destroyers, 46 sloops and corvettes, 7 minelayers, 42 minesweepers, 56 trawler minesweepers, 20 river gunboats, 27 MTBs and 59 subs. Fleet Air Arm had 340 planes. RN manpower 30 June 1939 was 129,000 by 30 Sept 180,000 + 1600 women.

TRANOW, Wilhelm: German cryptographer, b. 1896. Radioman on battleship *Pommern* 1914. Began codebreaking ashore 1916–18 and was recruited to the embryo B-Dienst April 1919. He solved the British Governments Telegraph Code in the 1920s and broke the 4-letter naval code, following British Atlantic convoy exercises 1932. Resisted Führer's order to concentrate on French Navy 1935. Read Convoy OB-4 assembly orders 11 Sept 1939 resulting in the 4060 ton *Aviemore* being sunk by U31 on the 16th, the first of only 4 ships lost in convoy during 1939.

U-BOAT: unterseeboot, German submarine. Kriegsmarine had 56 on 1 Sept 1939: 10 in port and 10 against Poland. 11 Type II boats were in N. Sea mining. 56 U-boats under construction. Type VIIA (U27–36) laid down 1935 and launched June 1936-Feb 1937. Tonnage: 626 surface, 745 submerged. Dimensions: 211.7 × 19.2 × 14.5ft. Engine: 2-shaft diesel and electric 750 shp. Speeds: 16 knots surface, 8 knots submerged. Guns: 88mm deck, 20mm anti-aircraft. Torp tubes: 4 bow, 1 stern (11). Crew: 44. Class: 10 boats.

BRITAIN WAITS

Few doubted that war would come swiftly and terribly to Britain in September 1939. The gloomy theory was: 'The bomber will always get through.' Though barrage balloons **wallowed comfortingly over London like huge, silver, boxing gloves in the sky, most guessed that it would take more than their cables to slice the wings off Göring's Luftwaffe.**

Winston Churchill and his wife were among those who trooped to the shelters as the first air raid **siren** of the war sounded, within moments of Chamberlain's broadcast declaring it. 'My imagination drew pictures of ruin and carnage and vast explosions shaking the ground' he later recalled.

It was feared that when the **bombs** fell, some four million citizens might be wandering the Home Counties, crazed with terror. Throughout the land, 250,000 hospital beds awaited the expected air raid victims. Yet more ominously, swimming baths stood empty, ready for the corpses of the bombed and gassed—for whom thousands of cardboard coffins had been prepared. Outside the premises of veterinary surgeons, the real corpses of cats and dogs piled up on the pavements, painlessly spared the horrors to come.

Between the morning of Friday, 1 September and the evening of Sunday, 3 September, 1,473,391 people had been moved from the city streets to the supposedly safer **'reception areas'** of the countryside. They included the blind, the crippled, young mothers and—above all—the children. The massive exodus began at dawn, as AA patrolmen sped through the streets, changing road-signs.

'It had to happen. My first feeling was one of tremendous relief, that the awful waiting and uncertainty is over . . .'
Housewife on hearing Chamberlain's war broadcast

Sphere

Building an ARP hut in St James's Park.

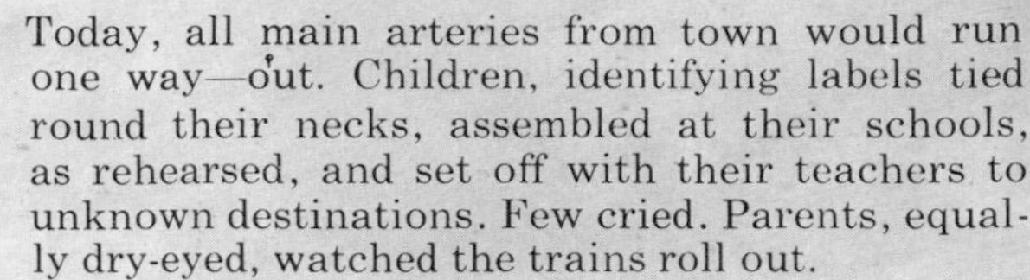

Today, all main arteries from town would run one way—out. Children, identifying labels tied round their necks, assembled at their schools, as rehearsed, and set off with their teachers to unknown destinations. Few cried. Parents, equally dry-eyed, watched the trains roll out.

Evacuation was voluntary: slightly more than half London's schoolchildren stayed behind. In Sheffield, only 15 per cent went; in Manchester and Liverpool more than 60 per cent left.

Disembarked among the strange smells of the countryside—a place which many town children found utterly unfamiliar—the evacuees waited for their 'new' parents to choose them. For many, it was a daunting kind of Dutch auction. The sturdiest and cleanest tended to go first.

The Evacuation opened the nation's eyes to the life of city kids. Almost ten per cent of East End children were found to be verminous. Many would marvel at their first sight of a flush lavatory. Some 'new' parents, creeping into their charges' bedroom the first night were appalled to find the bed empty, the evacuees apparently flown. They discovered them under the bed, their normal resting place at home.

The first night was the worst. The silence and darkness of the countryside was a terror in its own right for a city-bred child. Many, who had lost their parents in the morning, had ended the day seeing their brothers and sisters led off to other homes.

Every day the front page of *The Times* was crammed with small ads, signposted ARP **(Air Raid Precautions),** and offering sanctuary. 'Refined children only', one insisted. 'Doctor in safe area would receive MILD MENTAL case (lady) in perfectly appointed country house' ran another. 'Funk holes' was the unprinted but popular name for these retreats.

Three million evacuated

In all, some two million citizens moved home from the perilous cities that summer and autumn, on top of the official evacuation figures. Many took their work with them. Luxurious seaside hotels were ousted of their regular guests in favour of civil servants, who pushed their paperwork up and down the grand ballroom in considerable comfort.

For those who stayed in London, there was no shortage of activity. Exhorted by such posters as the one plastering the plinth of Nelson's Column —Civil Defence is the Business of the Citizen— Britons had flocked to enlist in the legions of the ARP. By September, close on one and a half million **wardens** were enrolled in this multi-headed monster, scanning the skies for bombs and **gas** attack, and their neighbour's windows at night for breaches of the **blackout** regulations. Since most volunteers were paid £3 a week (and some families managed to enrol five members) the bill was clearly headed for the astronomical.

But at the start of war, no one was counting the cost, not for the ARP, nor for the 200,000 men of the **Auxiliary Fire Service,** nor the 250,000 **Special Constables.** No price was too high in the expected battle for survival.

Gas attack was the most dreaded horror. Memories were fresh of the hideous green clouds of chlorine gas that had drifted across the trenches of World War I. Now every citizen had to carry his **gas mask** in public: from the King down to the man in the Old Bailey dock, who, though having just received a death sentence, was reprimanded for failing to pick up his mask on leaving. In the streets, pillar boxes were capped in yellow, gas-sensitive paint.

As for the awaited bombs, many special measures had been taken. The walls of London's National Gallery were stripped of their treasures, which were despatched to deep slate mines in Blaenau Ffestiniog, North Wales. From cathedrals, medieval stained glass windows were stripped, fragment by fragment. In Canterbury, four feet of earth layered the floor of the nave, to bomb-proof the crypt beneath.

Less thorough arrangements had been made for the ordinary citizen's bomb shelters. Fearing, on psychiatric advice, that people might take to the platforms of London's Underground and refuse to emerge (deep-shelter psychosis was the phrase for it), London Transport banned the use of the tube system for purposes other than transport. Though six million metal **Anderson shelters** had been distributed—and were now neatly garlanded by flowers and vegetables in millions of suburban gardens—they were of no use to inner-city dwellers who lacked any patch of earth on which to erect them.

For most city dwellers, the grimmest reality of war came every night, with the rigidly enforced blackout, designed to make Britain invisible from

'To be inside an Anderson shelter felt rather like being entombed in a small dark bicycle shed, smelling of earth and damp . . .'

Norman Longmate, *How We Lived Then*

Gloria Cigman

Eye Witness

Gloria Cigman was 11 years old when she and her brother were evacuated from London in 1939.

'None of us knew where we were going. We were taken on a 7-hour train journey of which all I remember is a sudden plunging darkness of what I afterwards learnt was the Severn tunnel (7 miles long?) through which we seemed to roar interminably in our entirely unlit carriage. I screamed hysterically all the way through the tunnel, even after the teacher had slapped my face. Abrupt emergence into sharp daylight to see my small brother standing pale and silent by my side, watching me.

'We arrived at Cardiff station and were transferred to waiting coaches. Our train had been filled with children from many different schools. Each coachload went to a different village in South Wales. We were set down at Rudry, a small mining village three miles from Caerphilly. Villagers stood around watching us as we got out of the bus and went into the village school. We were given mugs of tea and buns. What followed was like an auction sale. Villagers came in, usually in couples to choose children. "Mr and Mrs Jones would like a nice little boy." "Which little girl would like to go with Mrs Griffiths?"

'Nobody wanted the awkward combination of a girl of 11 and such a small boy, from whom I had promised my mother under no circumstances to be separated. We were left until the very last. The room was almost empty. I sat on my rucksack and cried. My brother stood beside me, as he had on the train, still pale and silent and small, watching me. Eventually, a young couple, very newly married, took us home with them. They put us in a room with no curtains or floor covering and no furniture except a single bed. Nails were knocked into the back of the door for our coats . . . We had baked beans for tea.'

'The children were treated as first-class passengers and nobody collected tips.'
Herbert Morrison, Leader of LCC, on the evacuees

the air. Even when the Blitz did arrive, the blackout continued to top the list in opinion polls as the most unpopular aspect of the war. Certainly, this September, it cost more lives than were lost on both sides in the fighting on the Western Front.

Nightly, their headlamps reduced to the merest slit, drivers careered about in unlit streets, peering for newly chequered black and white kerbs.

Magistrate courts began to crowd with offenders whose faulty blackout had been seen by the ever-prowling ARP wardens. Other irresponsible citizens landed in the dock, too: among them nine Birmingham youths who had warbled a convincing siren noise for the pleasure of 'sending the buggers to the shelters'.

There was little to do of an evening. Pubs and churches were now the only places of public resort left open: sport, theatre and cinema had been axed at a stroke; the infant TV service (20,000 sets strong) stifled at birth. 'Listening in' to the **wireless** became the major leisure pursuit.

Hard news, via wireless or the press, was in short supply this September. The Poles, it seemed, were advancing. Censorship of the news lay in the firm grip of the Ministry of Information—which, in a few days from the outbreak of war had mushroomed into an organization of 999 employees, devoted to the art of stifling rather than purveying information. Newsmen battled in bewilderment against them. By the month's end, alarm at the censor's powers and the sweeping scope of the **Emergency Powers (Defence) Act** was clamorous. *Picture Post* cheekily printed black squares for the 'pictures we are not allowed to print'.

Among the 'censored' was any news of the British Army's whereabouts. In total secrecy the British Expeditionary Force had begun to cross the Channel on 4 September. They marched from their barracks by night, through the unlit streets, steel-helmeted, rifles slung, gas masks ready on their chest. Their destination, for the most part, was Cherbourg—far west of the expected front line. It was a sombre journey in darkened ships, refreshed only by bully beef, biscuits and tea.

As the news began to come in of Poland's final collapse, Britain tightened her belt one more notch, tuned the wireless to the six o'clock news once again—and waited with bated breath for the action to begin.

War Notes

ARP (Air Raid Precautions): necessary measures for defending civil population against bomb attacks. ARP 1924 sub-committee was formed into a Department of the Home Office May 1935. ARP Act became law 1 Jan 1938, giving full powers to the Home Office and local government. Voluntary recruitment of Wardens rose dramatically during and after Munich. By March 1939 a million wardens had been recruited. There were ARP controllers (mainly local government officials or chief constables) for each of the 250 local authorities. Wardens' reports were passed from their posts to Report Centres which passed them on to Control Centres which informed the ARP controllers.

ANDERSON SHELTER: made of 14 corrugated iron sheets and packed earth, it would give shelter to 4–6 people during an air raid. Designed by Scots engineer Sir William Paterson, it was suggested for use by his friend Sir John Anderson, Minister for Civil Defence, 1938. Available free to families with an annual income below £250.

AUXILIARY FIRE SERVICE (AFS): founded Feb 1937. 36,000 strong with 3000 fire engines in London alone by July 1939. Uniforms were established for the 5000 women in the London brigade April 1939; navy double-breasted jacket with silver buttons, and skiing cap with red AFS badge.

BARRAGE BALLOON: designated LZ (low zone) 62 × 25ft with hydrogen capacity of 19,000 cubic ft. Flown from mobile winch to 5000ft the balloon was hauled at up to 400ft per minute (full development required 11 minutes). The balloons were operable in winds of up to 60mph. A double parachute link was being developed to improve aircraft stopping power of the steel cable. RAF Balloon Command had only 624 of the 1450 required on 3 Sept 1939. London had 450 at a density of 9 per mile. A severe electrical storm on 15 Sept destroyed 78 balloons before they could be hauled down.

BLACKOUT: official requirement for all street lights in built-up areas to be extinguished and all house windows to be curtained. The total darkness deprived enemy aircraft of landmarks at night. First used against Zeppelins 1917. The blackout began on 1 Sept 1939, from sunset to sunrise; sunset being around 7.40pm that month. Householders were asked to check no light was showing from their homes. Motorists had to cover their car lights. Blankets and thick brown paper were recommended for improvized screening. Fines and imprisonment awaited breakers of these regulations.

BOMBS: early in 1939 British air staff estimated that the Luftwaffe could drop 700 tons a day on London for 2 weeks. An estimate of 50 casualties per ton was derived from 1914–18 figures of 2915 casualties caused by 74 tons dropped. In fact, 110 tons had been carried to Britain and early lucky hits secured.

Fox Photos

EMERGENCY POWERS (DEFENCE) ACT: passed within hours on 24 Aug 1939. The Act enabled the government to make almost any regulation it wanted by orders in council. The first 100+ regulations were published on 29 Aug.

EVACUATION: protective measure to transfer children from cities to the relative safety of the countryside. Originally planned for Sept 1938, a dress rehearsal for London children was held on 28 Aug 1939, after an early return to school. In the real thing 376, 652 schoolchildren left London and 757,583 the provincial cities, mainly by rail. Expectant mothers, the blind and crippled also went. Clydeside, Tyneside, Merseyside, the Midlands (Coventry etc), Portsmouth and Southampton were evacuated as well as London. Plymouth, Bristol and Cardiff were not. In Scotland 31,000 mothers left Edinburgh with their children. All Glasgow's 200,000 schoolchildren were moved out to the Lowlands.

GAS: first used by Germans against the Russians at Bolimow (Poland) Jan 1915. First British victims April 1915 when chlorine gas was introduced. 1914–18 British gas casualties totalled 185,706 of which 5899 resulted in death. Gas had most recently been used by the Italian Air Force in Ethiopia 1935–6.

GAS MASK: breathing apparatus which trapped the poisonous elements in charcoal filters as the wearer inhaled. Air was exhaled through an open/close valve in front. 38 million were made by 1939. There was no penalty for not carrying or losing one, but damaging a mask was an offence.

RECEPTION AREA: church halls, schools and other public buildings where evacuated children were gathered together for billeting with local families. Postcards were written to the evacuee's homes to inform parents where their children were staying.

SIREN: device producing penetrating sound, installed at police stations in urban areas, to give warning of air attack. Long wailing sound called for 'alert' and a continuous tone 'all clear.'

SPECIAL CONSTABLES: a reserve police force. Together with the War Reserve, they numbered 250,000.

WARDENS: ordinary ARP personnel, comprising 'responsible and reliable' members of the public. Only 400,000 were paid full time. Their duty was to help the public in every way possible before, during and after an air raid. Each warden was issued with an ARP armlet, identification card, steel helmet, oilskin, torches, whistles, hand rattle, a hand bell, first aid box and a book for recording incidents.

WIRELESS: radio transmitting news and light entertainment. For many families a source of information and enjoyment. Held a place equivalent to television today. 8.9 million licences were issued in 1939.

THE ENIGMA HANDOVER

Anthony Dawson/courtesy Sikorski Museum

The best-kept secret of the war came in a wooden box—which, when opened, revealed something like a small cash register with a typewriter keyboard. If, by September 1939, this machine had not been brought safely to the Western Allies, the Allies might not have won the war.

The Enigma cipher machine, as it was called, remained a secret long after the war. Not until 1974 was the staggering truth about its importance made public in Britain. Even now, some facts are still under lock and key.

When the story did break, historians all over the world settled down to the task of rewriting much of the history of the war from scratch. Churchill had called Enigma 'my most secret source'.

Yet, the machine itself was scarcely a secret. As early as October 1919, Hugo Alexander Koch of Delft, Holland, had patented a design for a secret writing machine. In 1923 he sold his rights in it to a Berlin engineer, Dr Artur Scherbius. Scherbius christened his acquisition Enigma—from the Ancient Greek word for puzzle. But the owner of a device that would one day have 150,000-160,000 copies in service among the forces of the Third Reich alone died bankrupt.

Two other firms bought up his patents, cheaply. Few guessed Enigma had any future. But the device had merits that no sharp-eyed military expert could ignore.

On 9 February 1926 the Reichsmarine (German Navy) took a modified version of Scherbius' Enigma into service. In July 1928 the Army followed suit and in 1934 so did Hitler's new secret air force, the Luftwaffe. Only then was the commercial model withdrawn from the market.

'Playboy who spied for money'

With good reason to keep up to date with her dangerous neighbours' secrets, experts of the German Section of Poland's cipher Bureau, Biuro Szyfrow 4 (BS4), had been reading German radio traffic skilfully—until Enigma arrived. Then they were in the dark.

Their luck changed in 1929. Frantic inquiries being made by a German diplomat at the Railway Parcels Customs Office suggested that the package he was looking for might be of special interest. As a result BS4 was able to study an early military Enigma at leisure over a weekend. Within four and a half months they had beaten the machine.

Without assistance from French Intelligence, however, their task would have taken longer. In October 1932 a German cipher clerk in the War Ministry approached France's Service de Renseignements (Secret Service) with an offer of Enigma's secrets. Captain Gustave Bertrand of Section D checked on the would-be traitor's story and decided to give him a hearing. Code-named Asche, the clerk Hans-Thilo Schmidt, a 'playboy who spied for money', handed over 303 documents for photocopying. Among the most valuable were tables of Army keys used in 1932-3-4, an Enigma instruction manual, and an enciphered message with plain text. Knowing that Poland was leading the way into Enigma research, Bertrand handed the illuminating documents to Colonel Gwido Langer, Head of BS in December 1932.

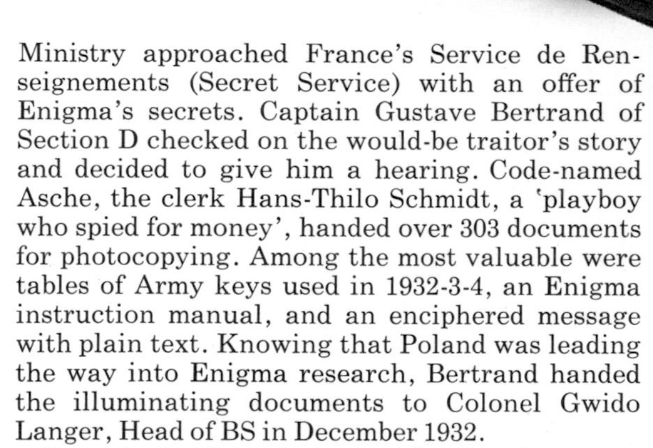

Soon, in the Ava telecommunications factory at 25 Stepinska Street, Warsaw, BS4 was making its own Enigma machines. By September 1939 there would be 15.

Now, if only they knew the frequently changed key settings used by the German operators, listening in to the business of the Third Reich would be straightforward.

But guessing the correct key, from a myriad possible settings, remained the constant problem. To speed the work of trying out various alternative settings in 1937, the Poles wired up six machines to devices of their own: electro-mechanical pieces of wizardry they christened Bombas.

But then, on 15 September 1938, the Bombas

Bundesarchiv

suddenly ceased to yield their treasures. The Poles swiftly found out why. At a stroke, right across the services of the Reich, a new kind of Enigma had been introduced.

Bravely (for no one likes to share hard-won intelligence) the Polish High Command decided: 'In case of a threat of war the Enigma secret must be used as our Polish contribution to the common cause of defence, and divulged to our future allies.'

By July, the Poles were ready to tell all. War looked imminent. Enigma remained obstinately impenetrable. The Poles summoned French and British Intelligence experts to a meeting 16 miles SE of Warsaw, at the underground building in Kabacki Forest.

Official secret

Even today, the full guest list for 25 July 1939 remains an Official Secret. It is known that Bertrand and Commander Denniston were there. But who was 'Professor Sandwich', introduced as a mathematics don from Oxford? Though not officially confirmed, the Professor's identity was Colonel Stewart Menzies, Deputy Head of SIS, immortalized as 'M' by author Ian Fleming later in the James Bond stories.

The Poles astounded their guests by the treasures they were prepared to yield. Colonel Langer presented technical drawings of the Bomba, and announced that British and French representatives could each take one of BS4's replica Enigmas away with them. Now the best brains of two more nations could bend themselves to the task.

The two Enigma machines went by diplomatic bag by sea from Gdynia to France. Bertrand flew home to Paris. Stopping off in Berlin, he enjoyed a four and a half hour break in the capital city.

The British took their Enigma home from Paris in a diplomatic bag. Tom Greene, a British Embassy courier, had charge of it, all the way by boat train from Paris. At Victoria Station he was met by the legendary Menzies himself, resplendent in evening dress for a party later on. It was 16 August. Sixteen days later, Poland was invaded. Enigma was in safe keeping, unless the Germans now discovered the remnants of BS4, along with evidence of its recent activities.

Most secret place in Britain

With its intercept stations overrun and liaison radio link with France broken on 12 September, BS4 destroyed its Bombas. By train, the unit fled east. Under continual air attack it reached Calimanesti, Rumania, in the Carpathian Mountains on the 27th. Colonel Langer had 15 of his men with him—and two surviving Enigma replicas. From here in Rumania, Langer could breathe again, and gladly accepted safe conduct from a French Army captain to Paris.

By 1 October the brave BS4 was back at work—as Equipe Z of Bertrand's Enigma organization, 40 miles NE of Paris at the Chateau de Vignolles.

Britain's Enigma machine had also gone to a country home: it was now lodged in a dull, two-storey, redbrick Victorian country house, 50 miles north of London. Henceforth, Bletchley Park was the most secret place in Britain.

The only picture published of an Enigma machine in use. General Guderian's cipher clerk puzzles over a signal to be enciphered for radio transmission.

FRENCH 'ATTACK'

All Quiet on the Western Front had been the title of the first war's most famous novel. Though silence was rare in no-man's-land between the German and French lines in those days. Three hundred thousand Frenchmen were killed or wounded in ten days during the 1914 'Battle of the Frontiers'. But in September 1939 the same countryside found war even quieter than peace.

Villagers unlucky enough to live between the massive fortifications that both France and Germany had spent millions to raise were speedily evacuated. The French were given half an hour to pack 66lb of luggage apiece. The entire 200,000 population of Strasbourg was removed.

One of the few who refused to budge, from her village of Schoeneck in Lorraine, was a tough-minded French widow of 79 years, Anne Wallian. With the guns of the French **Maginot Line** on one side, and the guns of the **West Wall** (Siegfried Line) on the other, she went on milking her cows. As the days passed calmly, she became something of an embarrassment. The British Tommies, who had promised to come here to hit Germany and protect Poland, were singing lustily about hanging out their washing on the Siegfried Line, but they were singing far off.

Forty years later, the mystery of what happened—or, rather did *not* happen on the Western Front in September 1939—remains keenly argued.

Poland's welfare had been guaranteed by the French and British. General Maurice **Gamelin,** France's 66-year-old Commander-in-Chief designate, and Poland's War Minister General Tadeusz Kasprzychi signed a detailed plan of action. France promised to commit the bulk of her forces to battle from the 15th day after mobilization. The French Air Force, the Armee de l'Air, would wing about 60 Amiot 143 bombers across Germany in a night flight.

Eighteen days into the war, the widow Anne was still milking her cows; and the British Tommies still singing. Meanwhile, Poland was being crucified.

'The Curtiss flown by Sergeant Pechaud, riddled with bullets was forced down in a field . . . a second was shot down by Mölders himself . . .'
Robert Jackson, *Air War Over France*

Unknown to the Poles, French and British military chiefs had met in March and quietly agreed that 'nothing could be done to assist Poland'. On 28 July the British Chiefs of Staff told their government that Poland's fate must depend on Germany's final defeat, not on rash action at the start of the war. It was the supposed power of the Luftwaffe that clinched the decision.

As for the Allied land forces: the British Expeditionary Force had a long road to march to the Western Front. No fighting units were in transit until 22 September, none arrived at the Front until 1 October.

The French army was closer. But it was obvious to one observer, Captain D. Barlone, a World War 1 veteran, commanding a horse transport company, that the troops were not marching to war with much enthusiasm. 'The men of the reserve come in without undue haste' he noted in his diary on 24 August. They told him they were convinced that they would be sent home in two weeks; were annoyed at not being able to complete the harvest; hoped Hitler would soon be assassinated.

The Maginot Line itself was not designed to encourage aggressive attitudes among the French soldiers now gathering along it. This 'Battleship on Land', with its own underground railway links between a chain of fortresses, was supposed to be an impregnable defence. Ominously, when its guns first opened fire on 9 September, it was discovered that many gun barrels and much ammunition was defective.

French soldiers who did venture in front of the Maginot Line found the empty countryside a pleasant enough place to await the order to attack Germany. 'This is the land of milk and honey' Captain Barlone's diary records for the 11th. Their instructions were to live off the land, and they went vigorously to the task of stripping the deserted farms of the Lorraine country.

On 14 September, he notes: 'The news from Warsaw is disastrous; will our intervention be in time?' From Poland, the desperate High Command demanded to know the same thing.

French C-in-C Gamelin, however, with over two million men, 8000 guns, 2500 tanks and 1100 aircraft at his disposal, had assured his British colleagues that he intended only to 'lean' against the Siegfried Line. For the waiting Colonel General Wilhelm Ritter von Leeb—responsible for the defence of the Reich between the North Sea and Switzerland—Gamelin's restraint was as welcome as the fruits of harvest were to Barlone's soldiers.

Von Leeb had 800,000 men mobilizing westwards, but knew that the Siegfried Line was vulnerable. In fact, it was not complete—and two-thirds of the labour force had left on other assignments. He knew that the French could break through, if they put their minds to it. Most dangerous sector of all was the Dutch and Belgian frontiers. Von Leeb's orders were to sit tight, avoid provoking the French—and wait.

Fortunately for Von Leeb, France had no plans to attack Germany via Belgium and Holland—which would have meant the embarrassment of moving troops across two still neutral countries. Instead, Gamelin chose the River Saar, between France and Germany, as the place to lean on the Siegfried Line. It was near the village where Barlone's men were busy eating.

On the night of 7-8 September, the French Fourth Army's 11th Infantry Division crossed the

MacClancy Press

A Luftwaffe pilot prepares for a mission.

Michael Roffe

20 September—the air war over the Western Front begins in earnest. Six Curtiss Hawks of the French Armée de l'Air, providing fighter cover for a Potez 637 reconnaissance plane, were attacked by four Me 109Es led by the future ace Hauptmann Werner Mölders.

Saar, surprised and took a few Germans as prisoners. But most of the surprises were for the French: in the shape of anti-tank ditches, minefields and booby traps. The infantry lacking mine-detectors poked at the mines with poles, or drove cattle over them. Progress was slow.

Captain Tony de Vibraye, in the lead with a squadron of the 3rd Reconnaissance Group, found the infantry gave him 'an impression of great caution . . . Having assembled all their equipment, they show very little offensive spirit . . . or even basic curiosity.' Possibly they felt daunted to be among the first to probe towards the fabled Siegfried Line. All were reservists, snatched unwillingly from their fields. On its way to the front Vibraye's unit had to buy berets from a departmental store, and 'borrow' civilian vans as transport. Typical of the lack of 'offensive spirit' was another squadron of 3rd Reconnaissance's encounter with machine-gun fire, 200 yards short of the village of Mendelsheim.

They were just three miles inside Germany—and withdrew the next day as fresh troops came up. 'During the last war' De Vibraye told his colonel, 'we didn't spend all this time simply *tickling* the enemy . . . All we've been doing for two days is play wargames under their noses.'

On the 12th the French leant just a little harder on the Siegfried Line. About 150,000 French soldiers dominated the first line of its defences at **Saarbrücken,** and the empty town itself. But the Germans had plenty of defences in store for them should the French choose to plunge farther in. As Hitler scoffed to his Intelligence chief, Admiral Wilhelm Canaris, who warned that the enemy was massed at this point in the line: 'I can hardly believe that the French will attack at Saarbrücken, the very point at which our fortifications are strongest.'

He was right. Gamelin, fearing a German counter-attack put his troops on the defensive. The capture of 20-odd villages and 80 square miles of Germany was a sufficient gesture for Poland. For the whole second half of September the French armies melted gently backwards to the safety of no-man's-land in front of their Maginot Line. Only the artillery was busily occupied, hurling a barrage from 155mm and 220mm guns as well as 280mm mortars against the Siegfried Line defences. They fired with great speed and accuracy—but without delayed-action fuses. The shells exploded before penetrating deeply.

A funny kind of war

Barlone's men were able to add new pastimes to their leisure hours: they organized football matches, barn concerts, even horse races.

By the end of the month the French had gone entirely from no-man's-land, leaving only a screen of reconnaissance troops to keep their eyes on the deserted villages, rotting harvests and howling dogs. Apples from ungathered orchards, not bombs, fell from the air along the Western Front.

A 'drôle de guerre'—a funny kind of war—agreed Barlone's contented men.

They, and their leaders, were relieved to be still alive—that, in contrast to the wholesale slaughter of the last war's opening stage, only 98 French officers, 778 NCOs and 1578 soldiers had become casualties so far on the Western Front. The Armée de l'Air had lost 32 aircraft. The dreaded retaliation of the German Army and Luftwaffe had been averted—perhaps for ever, many hoped. After all, the Germans were holding up placards to the French: 'Let us avoid bloodshed', 'We won't shoot first', 'Let us not kill one another on England's orders' they read. To many ordinary French soldiers the placards made sense. Some were more sceptical about the strange quietness on the Western Front this autumn. As General Maxime Weygand, Gamelin's eventual successor, put it: 'We must be in a pretty bad way if we do nothing but try to deceive ourselves.'

No one has recorded what the widow Anne Wallian said when, eventually, a patrol of the 25th Algerian Tirailleurs spirited her to safety, and away from her beloved cows. Certainly little happened to shake her confidence that there would be no war in these parts.

As for Adolf Hitler, he told his astonished generals on 27 September that he would attack France on 12 November.

War Notes

GAMELIN, Maurice Gustave: French Commander-in-Chief, b. 1872 Paris. Educated Stanislas College and St. Cyr Military Academy (top of 1891 class) 1885–93. Lieut, Algerian Tirailleurs, N. Africa 1895–8. War Academy under Foch 1899. On the staff of Marshal Joseph Joffre from 1904, as Lt-Col drafted Joffre's orders for Battle of the Marne 1914. Commanded brigade in Battle of the Somme, and 9th Div 1916–18. Head of Military Mission to Brazil 1919–25. C-in-C Syria, crushing rebellion 1925–7. CO 20th Corps 1929–30. Dep Chief of Gen Staff 1930 and Chief 1931. Vice President of Higher War Council 1935. Chief of Gen Staff of National Defence Jan 1938.

MAGINOT LINE: from Longuyon facing SE Belgium to the Rhine opposite Basle on Swiss border, the Line had 34 forts facing German frontier between Moselle and the Rhine. Named after War Minister, André Maginot it was built 1929–34 at a cost of 5 billion francs, 1940 prices. It consumed 1.5 million cubic metres of concrete with 150,000 tons of armour plate. In Sept 1939 garrison comprised over 200,000 men, including interval troops to hold minefields and pill-boxes. Each fort had twin 135mm howitzers in turrets or casemates behind 11.8in armour, 75mm guns similarly mounted, and 81mm mortars in turrets; a defensive armament.

SAARBRÜCKEN: evacuated (pop 129,000) capital of Saar (land) district returned to Germany by popular vote Jan 1935 from League of Nations' control. Area had important coal mines.

WEST WALL: German fortified line, extending along Dutch frontier and down the Rhine. Called Siegfried Line by Allies. Construction began early 1938, originally to cover the Saar region opposite Maginot Line. The line had over 3000 pillboxes and other positions to a depth of 2 miles. Hitler visited it four times before the war.

OCTOBER 1939

Associated Press

...WARSAW HAS FALLEN. Now, with macabre efficiency, the people of Poland are marshalled to their fate. Humiliated, Britain and France wait. In tones of sweet reason Hitler invites them to face facts, and end the war here and now. The peace bid fails. In France, the Allies dig in for the duration. This is the month too, when the Baltic Germans come home, and, in the dark waters of the North Sea, a courageous U-boat captain waits...

1st: US recognizes Polish Government-in-Exile. Hitler meets Ciano. Conscription for British 20-22-year-olds. First RAF plane over Berlin.
2nd: Poles on Hela peninsula surrender.
3rd: BEF enters front line.
4th: Khrushchev speaks in Lvov.
5th: Hitler attends victory parade in Warsaw. USSR-Latvia mutual assistance pact signed.
6th: Hitler makes peace offer.
7th: German Fleet sortie into North Sea.
8th: Evacuation of Baltic Germans announced.
9th: Hitler issues directive for Western offensive.
10th: USSR-Lithuania sign mutual assistance pact. France rejects Hitler's peace offer.
11th: War Minister Hore-Belisha announces 158,000 British troops have landed in France.
12th: Chamberlain rejects German peace proposals. Hitler orders bomb production to resume. Russo-Finnish talks start.
13th: British steamer *Heronspool* sunk in U-boat gun duel.
14th: *Royal Oak* sunk by U47.
15th: Mayor of Warsaw arrested.
16th: Luftwaffe raid on Firth of Forth, Scotland. U-boats begin magnetic minelaying.
17th: German Army gives up control of Poland.
18th: Four-power Scandinavian conference in Stockholm.
19th: Anglo-French-Turkish mutual assistance treaty.
20th: Neutral ships joining Allied convoys will be sunk, warns Germany.
21st: Hitler speech to senior Nazis and Gauleiters.
22nd: Soviet elections held in Poland.
23rd: Stalin rejects Finnish proposals.
24th: Russo-German trade agreement. Polish gold reaches Paris.
25th: U-boats sent to Mediterranean.
26th: Hans Frank takes over as Governor-General of Poland. Snow on W. Front.
27th: First German plane shot down on British soil.
29th: German Navy can attack passengers ships in convoy.
30th: Battleship *Nelson* hit by U56 dud torpedo.
31st: Molotov accuses Finland of aggression.

OCTOBER 1939

HITLER TALKS PEACE

'I have always been more afraid of a peace offer than an air raid'
Neville Chamberlain, British Prime Minister, 8 October 1939

October 1939 saw a subtle, determined and nearly successful Nazi bid to end the war.

Two highly mysterious gaps remain in the official records available to historians at London's Public Records Office. As a rule, cabinet papers are released 30 years after the event. But on rare occasions, when state security could still be endangered, an even longer ban is imposed.

Whatever was said in the secret councils of government on 3-4 October 1939 must stay under wraps until the year 2015. Not surprisingly, historians have wondered why. What strange, possibly murky secret can cast so long a shadow?

Plainly, a clue lies in the arrival, on 28 September, at London's Croydon airport of Birger Dahlerus, the one-man peace mission.

He went straight to Downing Street. Whatever was said between him and premier Neville Chamberlain remains a secret until 1990.

The British had become resigned to the attentions of the tireless Scandinavian. 'He's like a wasp at a picnic,' said Sir Alexander **Cadogan.** 'One can't beat him off.' In a world without Hot Lines between heads of state, and in which communications between nations were slowed by the crusted rules of diplomatic niceties, Dahlerus had been flitting to and fro all summer bearing messages of peace and goodwill from Germany.

Will those still secret discussions show that Britain came nearer to throwing in the towel than anyone still wants to admit? Why was Chamberlain so afraid of a peace offer?

Hitler must die

Chamberlain's determination to make no more deals with Hitler had become a personal obsession. 'To my mind it is essential to get rid of Hitler,' he later confided to his beloved sister. His proposals are somewhat whimsical: 'He must either die, or go to St Helena, or become a real public works architect, preferably in a "home".'

But like it or not, Hitler had smashed Poland. Maybe, to accept this ugly fact, and rather than risk putting Britain in the role of aggressor by continuing the war, it would be best to make peace on honourable terms, thought Chamberlain. Men like Foreign Secretary Lord Halifax, Sir Alexander Cadogan and his deputy Orme Sargent, were known to be in a mood to make terms. Even Winston Churchill did not reject an armistice out of hand.

On the eve of Dahlerus' arrival Halifax was toying with the idea that Britain could accept peace if only Germany withdrew just partly out of Poland. Chamberlain, waiting in Downing Street for Dahlerus, found himself lonely and at risk. The Great Appeaser was now in the position of favouring war more strongly than Churchill.

But Dahlerus had to be listened to, he came direct from Hermann Göring. And the liveliest rumour in London was that Göring was poised to make a coup against Hitler.

Chamberlain's peace mission to Munich, September 1938 failed. When Hitler offered peace a year later it fell on deaf ears.

Caricatured by a German stamp of the time: Neville Chamberlain.

Dahlerus was not the only broker in the peace business. From Turkey, German Ambassador Franz von **Papen** made it known that he had been given the job of making overtures. He hinted at a new government to be headed by Göring, and Hitler's relegation to the post of figurehead president. Other go-betweens included German 'opposition' leader Carl Goerdeler; Erich Kordt of the German Foreign Ministry, Josef Müller of the Abwehr. Each time the name of Göring cropped up. The story fitted with reports coming in from Britain's secret service agents abroad: Germany seemed to be a hotbed of plots.

Now Dahlerus arrived to spell out his own version—straight from the horse's mouth.

Chamberlain and Halifax knew that Dahlerus was close to Göring. Just how close would only be revealed long afterwards. Beneath the veneer of honest broker from neutral Sweden was a Nazi sympathizer. His wife was German. His fortunes were built on her farms. Göring had smoothed over official German objections to the marriage. In return for this, Dahlerus acted as guardian to Göring's son by his first, Swedish, wife.

Secret meeting

The two men made a good team. The British failed to realize that Göring and Hitler also made a good team: and that the bait of a Göring bid for power was no more than a ploy in a subtle game.

'From my personal knowledge of the man,' warned Colonel Christie, former British Air Attaché in Berlin, 'I am convinced he could never be classified as a moderate in any shape or form and that under no circumstances could his word be relied on.' But Chamberlain and Halifax listened to Dahlerus. He had little concrete to offer—a guarantee of the British Empire in return for a free hand in Eastern Europe for Hitler. But then came the intriguing hint: Göring was waiting in the wings for a takeover.

The still secret meeting seems to have ended inconclusively. Dahlerus sped back to Berlin to find Göring in amiable good spirits and entertaining another entrepreneur in the 'peace feelers' game, as the British were now calling it. This was American oil tycoon, William Rhodes **Davis,** who claimed to have come straight from the President.

With the help of John L. Lewis, leader of the United States Congress of Industrial Organizations, Davis secured an interview with President Franklin D. Roosevelt on 15 September. While agreeing with Davis that 'it would be tragic if the war should spread,' Roosevelt gave few detailed proposals for peace. But by the time he arrived in Berlin, Davis had freely added his own ideas.

He claimed in his meetings with Göring and Hitler that Roosevelt was totally against involvement in the European war and had little sympathy for England: that Roosevelt's prime concern was to break Britain's monopoly of world trade.

Göring's daydream

Between 1-3 October, Davis met Göring several times. What transpired in these meetings has never been fully revealed, but to Dahlerus, Göring enthused over the American 'proposals'. Especially appealing was the idea of a Great Power conference in Washington, in which he, Göring, would represent Germany.

Another concession, Davis suggested, America was prepared to make, was a return to Germany of all her old 1914 frontiers including her colonies.

Armed with details of Hitler's new peace plan—due to be unveiled in a major speech on the 6th—Davis returned to Washington, accompanied by a Nazi agent, travelling on a false passport. In fact, instead of the expected reception, Davis was refused a meeting with Roosevelt. His passport was taken from him and returned with all reference to his German visits removed.

If Davis' mission ends with such mysterious abruptness so, it seems, did Dahlerus' next move. On 3 October, Dahlerus went strolling with Göring in the garden of his palatial home. Göring, in confident mood, daydreamed: 'If there is going to be peace nothing in the world can stop me taking my boat to Sweden this summer.' He instructed Dahlerus to take advance details of Hitler's speech to London.

At the last moment the trip was cancelled. Dahlerus' secret visits 'are causing suspicion in certain quarters' Lord Cadogan telegrammed Britain's embassy in the Hague, through which the Swede made his approaches. If Dahlerus had anything new to say, he could tell his story there.

But it seems that Hitler himself now intervened to halt the mediator's efforts. Britain could wait to hear the Führer's peace offer from his own lips.

When it came, on 6 October, Hitler's speech was as dramatic as Chamberlain feared. Radio sets world-wide were tuned to hear it. On Chamberlain's secretaries' desks were 1900 letters received so far that month all urging him to make peace. The moment for decision had come.

Hitler spoke modestly, reasonably, without histrionics. His programme had three points. Point 1, involved the setting up of an independent Poland guaranteed by Germany and Russia; point 2, provided for the regulation of living space in Eastern Europe according to national rights and point 3, limited arms by defining the role of such weapons as gas and submarines.

Colorific!

To bring about these conditions, Hitler proposed a conference, and challenged the Allies to reject his plan. 'One day the great nations of this continent must come together and hammer out a comprehensive agreement which will give to all a feeling of security and quiet and peace. . .'

Copies of the speech were to be dropped by air over Britain. The effort could have been saved: *The Times* obligingly printed the full text.

World reaction to the speech was prompt, but mixed. Present at the **Reichstag** was American journalist William **Shirer:** 'It sounded, if you overlooked his latest victim, like a decent and reasonable speech.' But the general response was hostile and suspicious. 'I don't believe in Hitler's sincerity,' remarked Senator King, well-known American isolationist. And Senator Gerald Nye crustily added: 'He has lied so often. . .'

Despite this reaction, there was a feeling gaining considerable currency: now Poland was lost, why continue the war? 'It is foolish to fight a war of extermination to avoid a war of extermination,' opined the *New York Daily News.*

Hitler's popularity reached new heights with his visit to Vienna, March 1939. But by October there were plots to kill him.

But the French, with good reason, were opposed to any deal. On 10 October, Premier Edouard **Daladier** rejected the peace proposals—but without consulting his cabinet.

While the British Foreign Office pondered and the French argued, Hitler planned his next move. He instructed his generals to prepare 'Case Yellow'—the attack in the West.

Finally, in the House of Commons on 12 October, Chamberlain gave his answer. It was an uncompromising speech, delivered in strong and resolute terms. There were to be no negotiations. Blaming the German government for standing in the way of a real and lasting peace, he declared: 'The plain truth is that, after our past experience, it is no longer possible to rely upon the unsupported word of the present German government.' Britain looked for action, not words.

Almost immediately Hitler ordered a resumption of bomb production. His heart had not really been in the peace offensive anyway.

Grimly, Göring told his good friend Dahlerus: 'This means war.'

War Notes

PEACE OFFENSIVE

CADOGAN, Alexander George Montagu: Permanent Under-Secretary of State for Foreign Affairs from Jan 1938, b. 1884 youngest son of 5th Earl Cadogan. Educated Eton and Oxford. Ambassador to China 1933-6. Dep Under-Sec of State for Foreign Affairs 1936-7. One of Chamberlain's principal advisers.

DALADIER, Edouard: French Prime Minister, b. 1884 Carpentras, Vaucluse, S. France. Educated Lycée de Lyon. Soldier and NCO 1914-18, served at Verdun. Entered politics 1919. Member of the Chamber of Deputies, a Radical Socialist and friend of fellow statesman Edouard Herriot. French Premier 1933; 1934 for 11 days only; 1938-40. Also Minister of War 1936-40. A signatory of Munich Agreement Sept 1938. Began French rearmament and limited nationalization of industry. Dissolved Communist Party 26 Sept and published *The Defence of France* 1939.

DAVIS, William Rhodes: Texan oil millionaire, b. 1889. Contributed $300,000 to Roosevelt re-election campaign 1936. Major supplier of oil to German Navy before Sept 1939.

PAPEN, Franz von: Ambassador to Turkey April 1939, b. 1879 Werl, Westphalia. Followed military career 1907-13. Military attaché Mexico and Washington DC, expelled for abetting sabotage 1915. Chief of Staff Turkish 4th Army, Palestine 1918. Entered politics, representing Catholic Centre Party in Prussian Landtag (Legislature) from 1921-32. Failing election to Reichstag he acquired joint control of *Germania* Catholic daily newspaper. Attained valuable connections and access to large fortune by his marriage to daughter of Saar industrialist. A member of the monarchist and nationalist Herrenklub he used his social and ecclesiastic links to advantage. Support of Hindenburg in presidential elections 1932 won him Chancellorship 1 June, despite his lack of respect within political circles. His conservative 'Cabinet of Barons' fell through intrigue of Gen Kurt von Schleicher, his successor 3 Dec. In retaliation, believing him tractable, agreed 4 Jan 1933 to recommend Hitler for Chancellor. As Vice-Chancellor, became an unwilling participant in Hitler's bid for power. Called for return to moderation in protest speech at Marburg University 17 June 1934. Escaped assassination in Röhm Purge by Göring's intercession. Sent as Minister to Vienna July (Ambassador 1936) working towards Anschluss. Recalled 10 March 1938.

REICHSTAG: German Parliament. Deprived of all legislative power since Enabling Act of March 1933. Until their last election of March 1938, the 600 deputies met only to hear Hitler's occasional speeches.

SHIRER, William Lawrence: American writer, b. 1904 Chicago. Graduate of Coe College 1925. Foreign correspondent for Chicago *Tribune* 1925-33 and Universal News Service 1935-7. Correspondent for Columbia Broadcasting System based in Berlin since 1937.

ORDERS TO QUIT

Back in March 1939 Hitler visited the Baltic port of Memel, within hours of the German takeover. By October, Germans were leaving the Baltic for a new life.

Without a single day's warning, boats were sent from Germany on 7 October to bring home an entire community: men, women and children, whose ancestors had lived in the Baltic for more than 700 years.

It was from the misty dawn of the twelfth century that the **Teutonic Knights** came riding to these farthest shores of Europe. By October 1939 they were businessmen, dentists, doctors or factory owners. But they had never forgotten that they were still German.

While the Tsar ruled Russia, the Baltic Germans had prospered. Russia had always leant heavily on the tiny European countries—**Estonia, Latvia** and **Lithuania,** where Germans had settled. Though few in number, they had owned over half the land. They were a master race, and knew it.

World War I had changed all that. New governments, inspired by Communist programmes of land reform, ousted the Germans from their wide estates. Undeterred, the Germans had moved to the town; had swiftly come to dominate the top professional jobs—though it was difficult for a German to rise high in the local armies or civil service. Use of German was banned in public places in Latvia. But they still had their own schools, their own German language newspapers and their own **Lutheran** churches.

On the whole, relations with their hosts were good. Many intermarried—a factor that would prove to be a special cause of agony when Hitler's strange call to 'come home' hit them.

They had no inkling of its coming. 'Who would have thought only last August that we would go back to the Reich for ever?' said one, after the dramatic exodus was over. After all, right up to 6 October, the Baltic Germans had been front-line missionaries for Hitler's dearest dreams. In *Mein Kampf*, he had written: 'The new Reich must again set itself on the march along the road of the Teutonic Knights of old, to obtain by the German sword sod for the German plough and daily bread for the nation.'

Hitler had told no one that, this summer, he had secretly signed a deal with Stalin to pull the Knights' descendants out.

It made cold political sense. A pocket of Germans left stranded behind Russia's new frontier could only prove a thorn in the side of both parties. In the crudest possible sense, the two dictators had agreed to settle the question on cash terms. On 17 October, a train would leave Moscow for Berlin, laden with 17½ tons of gold: first price of the assets the Baltic Germans left behind.

First hint of this stunning deal came on 6 October, in a major Hitler speech. For the first time, he explained his plan to bring all Germans living abroad 'home to the Reich'. He wrapped the message cleverly in his general desire for peace. These 'splinters of German nationality' were a danger. For 'the elimination of international disturbance' and a 'far-sighted ordering of the life of Europe' they had to come home. Next day, German envoys at the ports of **Tallinn** and **Riga**

Richard Hook

'Almost every family seems to be divided and tormented as the full significance of Hitler's invitation is appreciated. Some wish to go, others stay, others hesitate'

The Times, 10 October 1939

explained just why the transport ships from Germany had dropped anchor that morning. The Reich wanted to start evacuation immediately.

Despite problems they had had with their German minorities, the local governments knew that if the Germans pulled out, a huge chunk of their economy would go too. But the shadow of Soviet Russia had fallen over their freedom again. Stalin had pressured them to sign treaties of 'mutual' protection.

Church bells rang in the Lutheran centres of the Baltic German community. Many had never seen the homeland. They looked at the boats riding at anchor and began a great, if brief, debate.

It split families, and generations. The young men, on the whole, were in favour of going. 'The general masses, and especially we, the young people, didn't hesitate for a single moment since it was the Führer who called us and there could be no greater happiness for us than to respond unreservedly to this appeal' wrote one **Baltenbriefe** contributor. For the young, the winds of change that had blown out of the new Nazi Germany made exciting sense. Despite 'good relations' with local governments they knew their career prospects were small in the Baltic states: many students who had gone to Germany to study had not bothered to return. For many of the young, the great 'historical mission in the Baltic had come to an end' as one evacuee put it. 'It is no longer a historical mission if one has to fight for one's mere existence, for a barely sufficient loaf of bread. It is no heroic mission if one faces a slow but certain death.'

The Baltenbriefe are suspect documents. No one had prevented the young men from forming their own youth organizations on Nazi models, treading the Baltic countryside in leather trousers and singing the new German songs. But the young felt that they were on the fringe of the new excitements of Germany. Said one: 'We want to get away from the hopelessness of a life in a country where we are stepchildren, where our neighbours consider us a thorn in their side . . . the return to the Reich is the only way out of this aimless existence.'

Some of the elder Baltic Germans heard the call home with dismay. Observers at the time found them 'ridden by fear and doubt'. It was a classic war between generations: the young, with no stake in real property, but high on ideals: their parents with a lifetime of investment in safe jobs and homes. How could one just get on a ship tomorrow and leave a whole life behind?

But many elder Germans had also endorsed the heady new ideas from Germany. In their 'Baltic Fraternity' members sought to preserve the old feudal ties of the Teutonic Order. But high-minded discussion was something quite different from the harsh choice now placed before them.

There was nothing else for it but obey the

For over 700 years Germans had lived in the Baltic states of Latvia, Estonia and Lithuania. On 6 October 1939 Hitler invited them to return 'home' to the Reich. Faced with Russian domination, thousands chose to leave their homes and possessions for a new life. Many resettled in newly conquered Poland.

'From all the Provinces of the Reich, they come down here, one and all, to wage a merciless struggle against the Polish peasantry'
Artur Greiser, 6 October 1939

Führer's command. Rumour had it that anyone who refused to go would be massacred by Soviet troops within a month. Seven hundred years of tenancy ended with an official farewell to the Latvian and Estonian people. 'This last glance will be one of grief and not reproach . . . we shall bid farewell . . . all that has divided us will appear small and unimportant from a distance.'

On 9 October, just two days after the first announcement of the call to return, grey planes landed in Estonia from Berlin: on board was a Special Commission, equipped with files, registers and lists of names. The efficiency was staggering. Arrangements had even been made to X-ray and health-check the Germans destined for return.

Agonized discussion went on in most of the German families that night. Next day, a Sunday, churches were crowded—many worshippers in tears. Confronted with the choice, some wives who had married into German families told their husbands that they would not leave their homeland. Meanwhile, young Baltic Germans were out in the streets, posting slogans that declared: 'We will go wherever the Führer sends us.'

Treasures of a lifetime

Pathetic small-ads crowded the columns of the local newspapers, offering homes, businesses and furniture for sale at knock-down prices. The total assets of the Baltic Germans had been reckoned at 362 million dollars; a sizeable slice of Estonia and Latvia's economy. Their hosts decided that to let such wealth go would be ruinous.

Thus, in Latvia, banks closed to prevent the Germans converting cash into precious metals and stones. Though 6000 cattle were allowed out of Latvia, no motor vehicle or industrial equipment could be shipped. In Estonia the luggage limit was set at 50lb per person.

The Germans watched, numbed, as customs officials unpacked and rejected the treasures of a lifetime. Yet there were few protests. Administering the exodus was almost exclusively the task of the Germans themselves, who mobilized obediently to perform it. To leave was not compulsory—neither in Estonia nor Latvia was pressure put on the Germans to go. Yet, within 28 days, 10,500 sailed away for ever from Estonia alone.

The total transfer of Baltic Germans to the Fatherland was not completed until 25 March 1941. By 10 January 1941, 63,832 had left Latvia.

They went on seven ships that plied the Baltic three or four times each: women and children had the cabins, men slept on straw. There was entertainment on board: few had much stomach for it.

They arrived at Polish ports to a heroes welcome. Rarely had a red carpet been rolled out with more brilliant precision: almost overnight arrangements had been made by the SS, SA and Red Cross to cover every detail of the homecomer's new life.

OCTOBER 1939: Orders to quit

Photographed, X-rayed, health-checked in hospital, comprehensively questioned on their family history and racial purity, the Germans were each given an identity number and a large brown envelope whose contents directed them in detail to new homes, which were ready and waiting. With brutal simplicity room had been made for the Baltic Germans in Poland by emptying Poles out. The modern port of Gdynia was entirely given over to the newcomers and renamed Gotenhafen.

The aged and sick Germans were sent to coastal resort towns. Farmers were given farms; craftsmen given tools. Instant and generous cash advances were made; credit was given to property owners; fodder provided for cattle. Families, groups and communities were placed together.

Merciless struggle

Some puzzled over the magic carpet-style transformation to prosperity. Shown round his new farmhouse, complete with wine cellar, a Baltic German asked where the previous occupants had gone. He got the stock answer: they had 'run away'. Many Baltic Germans believed the Third Reich had paid the Poles the full value of their deserted homes.

Others were given a clearer picture. In one incident, in the Polish town of Posen, the new German proprietor of a barber's shop was busy serving a customer, who sat quietly while the new barber's cut-throat razor flickered over his chin. The job done, the customer stood up and reached not for his money but a gun—and shot the barber dead. It turned out that the customer, who later shot himself, was the previous owner.

It was a strange life. In their new land, the Baltic Germans stood out from the remaining Polish population and the storm troopers from Germany whose task it was to protect the immigrants. To both Poles and homeland Germans the new arrivals looked peculiar. They wear 'high elk-skin boots and fur caps. They are noisy and arrogant in the streets,' noted one observer. Not everyone found a familiar niche in Hitler's new, instant Fatherland. Former bankers turned their talents to running military soup canteens in military towns. Clergymen became cemetery attendants.

Officially, the descendants of the Teutonic Knights had been given a new version of their age-old mission. As the gauleiter Artur Greiser put it: 'In ten years time there will be no patch of lands which will not be German. Every homestead will belong to German colonists. They are already on their way from all the provinces of the Reich: from the Baltic states, from Lithuania, Russia and the Tyrol. They come down here to wage a merciless struggle against the Polish peasantry.'

A year later, an indiscreet lieutenant of Himmler, Dr Coulon (whose task it was to make the Polish miracle work) expressed a more lasting truth. He remarked, in a newspaper interview: 'During the last 1000 years the Eastern territories, though continuously flooded by new waves of German blood, never became native German soil.'

For the Baltic Germans, inheritors of an ancient dream, the new homeland would prove a poor exchange for 700 years of history.

War Notes

BALTIC GERMANS

BALTENBRIEFE: letters written by German evacuees from Latvia and Estonia, published in Nazi Germany as propaganda. Letters were not spontaneous but ordered by Volksdeutsche Mittelstelle in Posen. It arranged competition among resettlers for 'description of resettlement experience', Best ones were promised publication. List of 20 topics given for an outline.

ESTONIA: northernmost and smallest Baltic republic, independent since Feb 1918. Population 1,126,000 (1934); 60% in agriculture. Size: 18,632 sq miles. Capital: Tallinn (Reval). Signed 10-year Mutual-Assistance Treaty with USSR, 28 Sept 1939, giving trade rights and military base for some 25,000 troops.

LITHUANIA: southernmost and largest Baltic state. Independence declared Feb 1918 and recognized 1920. Seized Memel as Baltic trade outlet 1923. Population: 2.4 million (80% Lithuanians). Size: 25,200 sq miles. Agricultural economy. Cereal products: 4 million metric tons. Exports of dairy and meat products, linen, timber. Signed 15-year Treaty of Mutual Assistance with USSR, 10 Oct 1939. Russian land and air bases in exchange for return of Polish-occupied city of Vilna which Lithuanian army entered 16 Oct.

LUTHERAN: a member of the Protestant Lutheran Churches, spread world-wide after the 16th century Reformation in Germany, begun by Martin Luther. Most Latvians of this faith.

RIGA: major Baltic port on Gulf of Riga at mouth of Dvina. Latvia's largest city and capital, 520 miles WNW of Moscow. Population 393,000. Cultural, political and industrial centre.

TALLINN (Reval in German): capital of Estonia. Population 146,388 (1938), major Baltic port linked by rail to Leningrad, 200 miles to the east.

LATVIA: independent from Nov 1918; created from old provinces of Livonia and Courland after collapse of Russia and Germany. Internationally recognized 1921. 18 governments up to 1934. Population: 1,940,000. Size: 24,900 sq miles, 20% forest, 12% marsh. Capital: Riga. Army: 25,200. Main industries: food processing, textile milling, lumber products. Main exports: dairy products, linen. Signed 10-year Mutual Assistance Treaty with USSR, 5 Oct 1939. Russia to have naval bases at Liepaja (Libau) and Ventspils (Windau) plus airfields and coast defences.

TEUTONIC KNIGHTS, Order of: military order founded c. 1190 to defend Christian territories in Holy Land (Palestine). Moved to E. Europe 1211. Crusaded against and exterminated heathen Prussians. By 1283 the order had conquered area forming E. Prussia. Teutonic Order of E. Prussia menaced Christian Poles and pagan Lithuanians, brought about the union of Poland and Lithuania. Battle of Grünwald (1410), near Tannenberg, saw military eclipse of order. Order ceased to exist politically in 1525 when last grand master became Lutheran.

POLAND'S FATE

October was exactly one hour old when the horses began to move across the black cross-roads of Warsaw's Ksiazeca Str and Nowy Swiat. Their riders were the cavalrymen of the Polish 9th Lancers. They walked westwards, towards the German guns.

Warsaw had fallen. The regiment had fought, bloodily, through Poland's forests all September. The Polish **9th Lancers** had won their way to Warsaw only to be told to get out—the city had no food for horses. Helplessly, the Lancers' Colonel **Rudnicki** had watched his horses stand like saddled skeletons as the German bombardment ripped into them. The horse Cenzor, pride of the regiment, winner of the Army's Challenge Cup in **Tarnopol** lay dead, his bowels ripped out. Soon some starving citizen would slice a joint from his loins.

Colonel Rudnicki knew there was nowhere left to go except westwards. The evening before, he had persuaded an old and frightened priest to hide the regimental colours in his church. Then, with his officers, he began some serious drinking.

The end of free Poland had been celebrated elsewhere, and not in wine, but Vodka. In the Kremlin Palace, Stalin flickered his yellowish, basilisk eyes towards Comrade Molotov as the Soviet Foreign Minister weaved once more to his feet to propose a toast to his chief. Glazed with fatigue, his German counterpart, Ribbentrop, reached for his glass. He had been three nights without sleep.

Stalin was in a good mood. All day, a roomful of mapmakers had been busy working and reworking the map of Poland. The dividing line between Russia's and Germany's slice of the corpse had started as a rough line. As the negotiators haggled on, the mapmakers' pencils had to be sharpened even more finely. Stalin signed the finished map.

He had reason to be pleased. For the price of 737 dead Russian soldiers he had acquired 77,000 square miles of Poland, just over half the area of the pre-war Polish state. 'It's all a game to see who can fool whom,' Stalin confided, as Ribbentrop flew wearily back to Berlin. 'I know what Hitler's up to. He thinks he's outsmarted me. But actually it's I who have tricked him.' Some, in Berlin, were inclined to agree when they studied the map more carefully: henceforth Germany would have no common frontier with **Rumania**. Her only link with the Rumanian oilfields and the Black Sea, would be through Russian-controlled territory.

Polish cavalrymen in captivity. Over 700,000 Poles became prisoners of war.

Despite the festivities in Moscow and the cheerful sight of swastikas flying over the Kremlin, Russians and Germans had few warm feelings for each other. On orders from Berlin, there was to be no fraternization at the frontier where the two armies stood face to face. On one thing the new allies were agreed: all possible centres of Polish resistance must be rubbed out.

In a grisly codicil to the Kremlin agreement, the world's two most awesome secret police organizations, the German **Gestapo** and the Russian **NKVD** arranged to co-operate on this vital task.

The Germans, more experienced in these matters, acted swiftly and skilfully. The Blitzkrieg had shuffled the population about. Women and children had fled to the villages, away from bombed cities. Polish men were straggling back home from their army units, in ill-fitting and hastily borrowed civilian clothes. There was no need to worry, said the German authorities. They repaired the railways and announced free rail travel for all. In Warsaw, posters asked all Polish officers to attend at the General Staff building in Pilsudski Square to register themselves.

The Polish officers who had registered went back to the cafés and discussed events with their friends. The cafés of Warsaw had always been close to the pulse of the city's life. Now they were its very heart. At Lourse's and Blikle's the scent of intrigue was as strong as the aroma of black coffee: no Germans ventured here. Rumours spiralled headily in the thick air: the French and British were dropping parachutists in Eastern Prussia; a secret resistance army was being formed right here in Warsaw.

Some, however, like Colonel Rudnicki of the 9th Lancers, who had marched with his cavalry into captivity and then escaped back to Warsaw, wanted only one thing: to get out of Poland before it was too late, and continue the fight from abroad.

His judgement was right. The brief lull ended before the first week of October was out. On 5 October, Hitler flew to Warsaw to review a victory parade. It was not a success.

The stench of corpses hung over the ruins. This time, no cheering crowds lined the roads from the airport. Hitler looked grim. He warned foreign journalists: 'Take a good look around Warsaw. That is how I can deal with any European city, I've got enough ammunition.' He was in no mood

'We will let the small fry off; but the nobility, the papists, and the Jews must all be killed'

SS General Reinhard Heydrich, October 1939

to celebrate even though the attendant Colonel General Gerd von Rundstedt was to describe his visit as 'Affentheater' (monkey theatre).

Swiftly, the Polish officers who had so trustingly registered their names and addresses were snatched away to prisoner-of-war camps. In the food queues, Jews (recognizable by long beards, sidelocks and black coats) were chased off. On 8 October, listening to foreign radio stations became an offence punishable by death.

Synagogues began to burn. The Nazi master plan for Poland had begun.

It was an astonishing programme, unlike anything ever attempted on a nation's population before. On 7 October, Hitler signed a decree appointing Heinrich Himmler 'Reich Commissioner for the Consolidation of the German Population'. His task would include 'eliminating the injurious influence of such non-German segments of the population there as are a danger to the Reich'. The net would be cast widely: Jews, gypsies, teachers, community leaders, priests were to have priority attention. Some 60,000 names of eminent Poles were already in 'Black Books' prepared by Fifth Columnists before the war.

Himmler's SS went to their task with a will. Throughout the Blitzkrieg, each army corps had travelled with a 100-150-strong Einsatzkommando in SS military uniform. Their methods had already shocked many regular army men. Now outraged soldiers sent detailed reports to Berlin narrating the casual slaughter in Jewish cemeteries of children aged six and eight. Hitler's comment was that one could not fight a war with the methods of the Salvation Army.

The SS toured the streets of Poland, leaping from their cars to snatch suspects. Some delivered themselves like lambs to the slaughter: at the ancient **Jagiellonian University** of Cracow the staff obediently attended to hear a lecture by Dr Bruno Muller on 'The Third Reich and the National Socialist view on Education and Science'. The lecture was brief: Dr Muller simply entered the hall and informed his audience that they were all under arrest.

Army protests at SS brutality were of no avail. They succeeded in ousting one particularly vicious operator, SS General Udo von **Woyrsch**, whose independent 'task force' had been responsible for the worst acts of terrorism against Jews during September. Hitler had determined that the Army's day in Poland was drawing to a close. On

Lightning arrests by SS men leaping from cars became common in Warsaw. Suspects were sometimes shot on the spot. A group of Jews (inset) being frisked by the SS.

17 October he told the Army to hand over control of Poland to new, and sinister, civilian governors.

The plans for Poland went beyond the slaughter and arrest of undesirables. Huge movements of population now began, to settle the Polish question for ever. Two new districts of the Third Reich had been decreed on 8 October. These regions, named West Prussia and **Posen** would become a rural paradise, Nazi style. There would be model villages, with sports halls, community centre, bell towers. There would be an accent on folk dancing and music. The original inhabitants would not enjoy these facilities: to make room for new colonists (among them the Germans already trekking west through Poland from the Baltic states on Stalin's slice of the map) they were simply and brutally ousted.

Heydrich was in charge of the removal. Obediently, councils of prominent Jews carried out the task of registering and preparing their own people for transport by cattle truck. They went quietly, already crushed in spirit by long experience of anti-Semitism at the hands of the Poles pre-war. Many hoped there would be safety in the huddled numbers now forced together eastwards.

The Poles went with them, driven into a no-man's-land area in central Poland whose Governor General was appointed on 12 October. There were no plans for model villages in this 'Polish reservation'. As Hitler put it on 17 October: 'The country is to continue under a low standard of living: we want to draw only labour forces from it.'

The man chosen for the task of reducing the heart of Poland to 'a pile of rubble' was Hans **Frank**, Hitler's personal lawyer in earlier days. Frank installed himself in lovely splendour in Wawel Castle, Cracow, and began the rule of an oriental despot. His briefing from Hitler had been simple: 'The ruling class that we have already unearthed in Poland is to be exterminated. We must keep close watch on whatever grows up in its place and dispose of that too after a suitable time has elapsed.'

For some Jews driven from their homes that October, the journey did not end in Frank's terror state. At this stage no clear-cut plan for extermination existed: the message was simply 'get rid of them'. Those who chose to cross the river San into Soviet-held territory, jokingly referred to as 'Paradise' by the German frontier guards, were free to do so (having first yielded up their cash and valuables).

Here, in the Russian zone, October had brought a very different regime. There were slogans everywhere: 'Proletarians of all countries, Unite!' Loudspeakers blared music and speeches from every corner. Soviet soldiers thronged the town streets. The Poles in the eastern sector were, at first, agreeably surprised at their docility. Colonel Rudnicki was one who had found his way to the East, still determinedly planning to escape Poland altogether. In the Russian-controlled city of **Lvov** he found the Russians 'at first sight not formidable, but childish, stupid and clumsy. Even the authorities were ridiculous: they introduced confusion in all spheres of life, and nobody could take them seriously.'

Looking after Russian interests in Lvov was a down-to-earth, colourful character called Nikita **Khrushchev**. He announced elections for 22 October. The Communist candidates emphatically won the day, winning the support of 91 per cent of the electorate. It was true there were no other candidates to vote for.

While, in German-held Poland, the machine-guns chattered at hundreds of impromptu executions, the Russians seemed more concerned to remove crucifixes from public buildings, turn

At the outbreak of war Poland's cavalry numbered some 20,000 men. Spread out along the vast 900-mile front, they could do little against Hitler's panzers. Most cavalrymen carried a lance, sabre, rifle, bayonet, gas-mask, shovel, knapsack and cooking utensils.

churches into social centres and replace the history books in the schools. But, as in German-held Poland, the lull was brief.

Behind the Russian Army came the secret police, the NKVD—every bit as efficient as its German counterparts. Like the SS, it had lists of undesirables marked for arrest. Lists that, if anything, were even more comprehensive in their categories. Postmen, policemen, dustmen—anyone who had served the Polish state in any capacity, however lowly, could be accused as a 'socially unreliable element', tried by a three-man tribunal, and deported to hard labour in Siberia. High on the list were members of the Polish **Communist Party.**

The mass arrests proved more effective than the German mass executions. In German-held Poland, the slaughter of one in five Polish citizens never dimmed the determination to fight back against the oppressors. But in the Soviet 'paradise', two million arrests silenced the voice of protest.

As October's days grew shorter, the hope of those trapped in the Russian sector began to fail. The huge bulk of Russia to the East was alien, godless, enigmatic. However little the Allies had done so far to oust Germany from Poland, they were, at least, at war with Germany. Hitler's headlong, murderous career must surely be destined for swift ruin. Stalin seemed by far the less removable. As the Polish commander-in-chief had put it at the war's outbreak: 'With the Germans we may possibly lose our freedom, but with the Russians we could lose our soul.'

Colonel Rudnicki set his face resolutely eastwards on his lonely mission: but it was westwards that the throng of refugees from Stalin's Paradise marched. 'Don't be in a hurry,' the Russian soldiers told them. 'The Red Army has crossed the Vistula. Soon all of Poland will be under Soviet rule.'

'The weather became foul: it drizzled and was cold; and we were hungry. No food . . . for us or horses: we had to live off the fields, on the cabbages and potatoes we found there'
Colonel K. S. Rudnicki, Polish 9th Lancers

War Notes

COMMUNIST PARTY of Poland: not officially in existence having been dissolved on Stalin's orders in summer 1938 after most leaders were summoned to Moscow and liquidated. Was suspected of Trotskyite leanings and infiltration by Polish Intelligence. Perhaps 25% of membership was Jewish. In Lvov Communist *Czerwony Sztander* (Red Banner) newspaper was one of few tolerated in the Soviet Zone.

FRANK, Hans: Gov-Gen of occupied Poland and close friend of Hitler, b. 1900 Karlsruhe. Served World War 1 1917-18. Joined Freikorps and Nazi Party 1919. SA trooper in 1923 Munich Putsch. Qualified as lawyer in Munich 1926. Defended SA members arrested for street fighting. Head of Nazi Party legal dept 1929. Investigated Hitler's possible Jewish ancestry. Member of Reichstag 1930. Bavarian Minister of Justice 1933. Reich Minister of Justice 1933-5, and without Portfolio 1934. Founder and president of Institute of German Law. Mission to Mussolini Sept 1936.

GESTAPO (Geheime Staatspolizei): State Secret Police. Founded April 1933 when Göring as Prussia's Minister of Interior purged that state's police to make room for Nazis. On 26 April its HQ was set up at 8 Prinz-Albrechtstrasse, Berlin. Himmler established Gestapos in Bavaria and 8 other German states. On 20 April 1934 Göring ceded his Gestapo role to Himmler. Now linked to the SS, the Gestapo became an independent national police force under career policeman Heinrich Müller Feb 1936. In June Heydrich became Chief of Security Police, Gestapo, Criminal Police as well as his own SD. Opponents given a warning, then arrested.

JAGIELLONIAN UNIVERSITY: founded 1364, Poland's oldest university. Under German occupation, almost all its professors were arrested.

KHRUSHCHEV, Nikita Sergeevich: Soviet politician, b. 1894 Kursk Province near the Ukraine. Educated village school. Worked as metalworker in mining town of Stalino (now Donetsk) from 1909. On strike 1912 and reserved occupation 1914-17. Avid reader of *Pravda* from 1915 joined Red Guards and Communist Party 1918. Served in Red Army from Jan 1919 with 9th Rifle Div, defeating Whites and marching to Black Sea by April 1920. Returned to Stalino as deputy director of Ruchenkov mines 1922. Studied at Worker's Faculty. Non-voting delegate 14th Party Congress Dec 1925 making first public speech 1926. Became voting delegate at 15th Party Congress 1927. Dep Chief of Organizational Sect, Ukraine Party Central C'tee, Kiev 1928. Studied metallurgy at Stalin Industrial Academy, Moscow. A Stalinist, he helped purge anti-Stalinists 1929-32. 1st Secretary of Red Presnya District 1931. Elected to Central C'tee at 17th Party Congress 1934. 1st Secretary of Moscow Regional and City C'tees completing Metro 1935 for which he was awarded Order of Lenin. 1st Secretary of Ukrainian Central C'tee early 1938. Purged 86-strong c'tee down to 3. Attended Moscow Central C'tee Plenum Feb 1939 and made full Politbureau member March. Civilian Member of the Kiev Military Council and moved into Poland (Western Ukraine) with military commander Semyon K. Timoshenko Sept 1939.

LVOV: present day name, in Polish Lwow and in German (pre-1918) Lemberg. Population 316,177 (1931) of which about 100,000 were Jews. This industrial and transport centre held out for 10 days against the Germans before the garrison of 8500 surrendered to the Russians.

9th LANCERS: one of Poland's 33 cavalry regiments. CO, Lt.Col. K. S. Rudnicki. Fought its way into Warsaw on 22 Sept with 350 mounted lancers and about 175 dismounted (out of 600) with 6 machine-guns and one anti-tank gun. Defended and lost Dabrowski Fort 25-26 Sept. Awarded 3 Virtuti Military Crosses and 26 Military Crosses at last parade on 29th. A third of the survivors and most NCOs went home to Soviet occupied zone. By 10 Oct men were repatriated, leaving officers in a match factory at Blonie en route for PoW camp in Germany.

NKVD (Narodnyi Kommissariat Vnutrennykh Del): Commissariat of Internal Affairs, formed July 1934 when OGPU (Unified State Political Admin) was renamed. NKVD was far more powerful than the Gestapo because it monopolized all police functions, the concentration camp system, fire brigades, links with foreign Communist Parties, even geological surveys. Its first two chiefs were executed and succeeded by Laventry P. Beria in July 1938, a fellow Georgian of Stalin. In power and efficiency Beria surpassed Himmler. The NKVD rounded up 15,000 Polish officers who were mostly put in 3 camps, Smolensk, Kharkov, Kalinnin.

POSEN: German name for Poznan, province and 3rd city of Poland since 1918. Poznan (175 miles W. of Warsaw) was a major industrial rail centre with a population of 272,000 out of the province's 2.1 million (1931 figures). The birthplace of Hindenberg, ruled by Prussia 1815-1919, Posen was one of the Third Reich's most cherished objectives. It suffered little from bombing and was evacuated by the Polish Poznan Army on 5 Sept, though many refugees left too. Posen became capital of the new German Gau (district) of Wartheland (named after the river by which Poznan stands) under Gauleiter Artur Greiser, 26 Oct 1939.

RUDNICKI, K. S.; Lt-Col and CO 9th Lancers, b. 1897 SE Poland (then Austrian Galicia). Austro-Hungarian Army 1915. Wounded while serving on Italian Front, and promoted Lieutenant 1917. Joined Polish Army 1918. Cavalry captain v Soviets 1918-20. Promoted Major and joined Warsaw Staff College 1928 where he lectured on strategy 1934-8. Escaped from German transit camp with 4 other officers and reached Warsaw on 22 Oct 1939.

RUMANIA: an unstable kingdom coming more and more under German influence despite the Anglo-French Guarantee of her security on 13 April 1939. The fugitive Polish Government was interned under German pressure (though lesser people usually got away). Rumanian oil was vital to Hitler's war economy. An agreement of March 1939 increased oil imports and the passage of German exports farther afield. In 1937 19% of Rumanian exports went to the Reich, 44% in 1940.

TARNOPOL: town of SE Poland with 39,900 people. Agricultural and horse-trading centre on the River Seret, 75 miles ESE of Lvov.

WARSAW: capital of Poland on River Vistula. Population about 1,289,000 (359,287 Jews) in 1939. Some 12% of buildings had been destroyed. On 7 Oct electricity was partly restored. The editors of *Gazeta Wspolna* newssheet were detained on 8th. Nazi daily *New Warsaw Courier* first published on 11 Oct.

WOYRSCH, Obergruppenführer (General) Udo von: commanded an Einsatzgruppe in S. Poland. Col Gen von Rundstedt asked for his immediate removal and that of his unit before 23 Sept. Himmler's orders of 3 Sept for von Woyrsch required 'radical supression of the incipient Polish insurrection in the newly occupied parts of Upper Silesia'. Himmler acquiesced in his sacking but Heydrich was upset.

GATES OF HELL

Some of the most vicious tides in the world rip near Scotland's John O'Groats. The Atlantic Ocean and North Sea meet and struggle here between the rocky walls of the Pentland Firth. But northwards, via these dangerous waters lies a calm anchorage. This is Scapa Flow. Until midnight on 14 October 1939 it was the safest place to keep a fleet.

Winston Churchill had confirmed this view as recently as 16 September. Standing on the after-capstan grating of the old battleship *Iron Duke* he explained to his commanders that exactly 25 years before he had stood on this same ship, in the same harbour, doing the same job as First Lord of the Admiralty. Then he toured the harbour's defences, and was assured they were just as daunting as they had ever been. It remained unbelievable that any U-boat could gain entry to **Scapa Flow**. The hurtling currents would smash a sub like an egg against the rocks, sunken block ships and cables that littered the entrances. The guardians of Scapa Flow looked skywards to the only conceivable threat to the great Fleet. Against the risks of air attack, the rule was that most men should sleep well below decks. That rule was just one factor to magnify the disaster when it struck.

Lulled by the natural security of the surroundings, the Royal Navy had not been in a hurry to complete Scapa's seaward defences pre-war, lest this upset the current mood of appeasement towards Germany, or upset the locals.

On 1 October, Commodore Karl Doenitz, submarine chief in Hitler's navy, invited his favourite U-boat commander to consider a mission so perilous that no criticism would come his way if he turned it down, flat.

Lieutenant Commander Günther **Prien** gathered up the charts, aerial reconnaisance pictures and details of the ugly tides and went back to his depot ship for two days' intensive calculations. When he reported back it was with a route map to the heart of Britain's naval pride. On 8 October **U47** slipped out of Kiel on a journey that, even before the action started, would strain his crew's nerves to the utmost.

By day, U47 rested, submerged. By night she travelled: on the surface and into the teeth of worsening gales. There was plenty of time to brood on the hazards ahead. 'Sir, do you really believe we will get in there?' navigator Spahr asked. 'I'm no prophet,' said Prien. 'And if it goes wrong?' 'Then we just had bad luck, Spahr.'

The last hot meal was eaten at 4pm on the 13th. At 9.31 Prien raised his U-boat to the surface, and from the conning tower took in a view that, despite all his careful study, was totally unexpected.

Autumn nights come early to the Orkneys. In mid-winter, daylight appears for no more than a few brief hours. By 9.31pm in October, quite obviously, there should be total darkness. But not tonight. The whole harbour stood out in an eerie light. Looking up, Prien saw the weird red and green curtains of the aurora borealis in the sky.

Colin Backhouse

'There is a flaw in the defences of Scapa Flow . . .' Did this message, claimed sent by Swiss clockmender Albert Oertel, lead to the sinking of the Royal Oak? Was he a German agent? No one knows.

M.O.D.

The submarine lay on the surface, plain for any watcher to see. A little later, as if to rub the point home, car lights on shore stabbed over the water, gleaming on the conning tower.

For the first time, Prien hesitated. Perhaps the venture could be postponed until tomorrow. Did the Northern Lights show two days running?

The sub eased towards the harbour entrance. There were several channels: Kirk Flow was their chosen route. Prien aimed at its bottleneck passage and drove the 218ft long steel craft ahead. He was draining his batteries now to drive the propellor by electricity instead of noisy diesel. The U-boat slunk onwards low in the water, tanks partially flooded, trying to be invisible.

The first **blockship** loomed: a wrecked, two-masted barque. U47 slid past without problems. But two more wrecks lay ahead, linked to each other and the shore by the deadly steel cables.

Prien gave his orders calmly: stop port engine, starboard slow ahead, rudder hard to port. The sub stayed exactly where it was. There was one card left to play. He ordered air pressure to empty the flooded diving tanks. U47 lifted, and was free.

Quietly, the sub passed into the calm expanse of Scapa Flow, where no U-boat had ever penetrated before. Prien scanned ahead for the awesome sight that should now be awaiting him: the British fleet at anchor.

But this extraordinary night had only begun its list of surprises. The black waters ahead were empty. On his own initiative, the C-in-C Home Fleet Admiral Sir Charles **Forbes** had taken the bulk of his ships, after a North Sea sweep, to anchorage elsewhere, in Loch Ewe on the west side of Scotland.

For a whole hour, Prien roamed the water, in in search of the absent quarry. Then at 3250 yards distance, he saw it. Bulking out of the night were the profiles of two ships, which Prien identified (rightly) as the **Royal Oak** and (wrongly) the *Repulse*. Prien steadied his sub, then ordered a salvo of three electric torpedoes. With a hiss, they sped on their way. It was 1am. Carving through the water, their journey would take just three and a half minutes.

Prien's men watched the darkened, anchored target packed with sleeping men. Her crew slept

Barnaby's

For sinking *Royal Oak* at Scapa Flow, 31-year-old Kapitanleutnant Günther Prien received the Iron Cross (First Class) from Hitler on 18 October. Each member of U47 was awarded the Iron Cross (Second Class).

'The surface of the sea was lit... depth charges exploded behind us. You can imagine how cheerful and happy I felt when a few minutes later a thundering cheer sounded over the sea from my crew.'

Günther Prien, commander U47.

soundly. Many went on sleeping when, at 1.04am, a torpedo struck and exploded, forward.

Now began a chapter of misjudgement and accidents (unravelled later by a grim official inquiry) that explain why the events of the next 25 minutes were so disastrous. Just as those aboard the *Titanic* had heard the iceberg rip out their ship's bowels with the calm of disbelief, so did *Royal Oak's* men hear the first explosion without alarm. 'A compressed air bottle blew up,' ran one rumour. 'A trawler bumped us: no worry,' ran another. No one panicked. No alarms sounded.

Ten calm minutes passed. Then Prien struck again. This time, three torpedoes from U47s bow tubes smashed home—and the last sleepers awoke on *Royal Oak*.

A wall of water shot vertically from the sea to flood over the decks and meet a boiling flash of flame that erupted out of the ship herself. Shock-waves tumbled through the bulkheads, bringing down decks like packs of cards. Men died instantly in their hammocks as the fireflash scarred across them. Others flung themselves into practised—and fatally wrong—evasive action.

Instead of clambering upwards through the rapidly tilting ship they burrowed deeper—believing the onslaught was an air attack, the only hazard they had been trained to guard against. While tons of water poured into the bowels of the ship men struggled downwards to their death.

But even those who did try to fight their way up through the burning, sinking coffin—in the few minutes left her—found their way barred: queues built up at escape hatches that had either been sealed for 'safety' or were now immovable.

One of many heroes in the last minutes of *Royal Oak's* life was Marine corporal H. D. Jordan, who lost his own life through holding open a hatch on his shoulders, to let others escape.

Royal Oak's commander, Captain William Benn, in no doubt that his ship was lost, walked along the now horizontal side into the water and swam away. Rear-Admiral Henry **Blagrove**, visiting the

Over 39,000 officers and men served in German U-boats in World War II. Only 7000 survived the war. The average age of crew members was 18.

ship, was offered the use of a lifebuoy by an escaping steward. He declined it.

Men swimming in the sea reported a massive explosion followed by a great glow. The 15in guns twisted from the force and heat of that explosion. Then the ship went down.

It was about 33 minutes past one o'clock, just 17 minutes after the second torpedo salvo had hit *Royal Oak*.

Among the most tragic victims were men who had escaped the inferno in the ship, but succumbed to the cold and exhaustion in the water. Recalled one survivor: 'There would be a group of three or four men in the water hanging on to some floating debris. They would let go to reach for the lifebelt we had thrown and one would just suddenly sink below the surface of the water and not come up again.'

Nobody came to help

Perhaps most terrifying was the fact that despite the huge explosions, except for some small boats from the depot ship **Pegasus**, nobody came to help.

As for Prien in U47, he did not wait long after the explosion. He knew the dangers of waiting in the anchorage and risking an asdic contact from the searching destroyers.

Prien decided to make his exit by the southern channel round the blockships in Kirk Sound. Two hours after they had entered Scapa Flow, Prien and his crew were out in the North Sea.

That morning while they lay submerged, a bottle of beer was produced for each member of the crew to celebrate. They still had five torpedoes left. 'A pity that only one (ship) was destroyed' Prien wrote.

The crew was flown to Berlin for victory parades, and Prien became a celebrity and a hero throughout Germany. He was also granted an audience with his beloved Führer, who invested him with the Knight's Cross of the Iron Cross.

'I regret to inform'

On the Wednesday following the attack, three senior Royal Navy officers met in a rough corrugated iron shed at Scapa Flow to hold a Board of Inquiry into the loss of *Royal Oak*. Its conclusions were of little use. They laid the blame variously with the Admiralty and the local commanders-in-chief, and on the fact that no single officer was responsible for the defence of the anchorage. They observed with regret that the defences were so slack that a submarine could easily pass below the anti-submarine net in Hoxa Sound at high water, and of the seven entrances to Scapa Flow, it was possible for a submarine to find its way in through no less than five of them.

Churchill announced the loss of *Royal Oak* in the House of Commons on 17 October. He had to admit: 'This entry by a U-boat must be considered as a remarkable exploit of professional skill and daring . . . I deeply regret to inform the House that upwards of 800 officers and men have lost their lives.'

The final loss amounted to 833 men. Only 424 survived the sinking of their ship.

War Notes

GATES OF HELL

BLAGROVE, Henry Evelyn Charles: British admiral, b. 1887. Entered Navy at 15. Commander 1919. Appointed Rear Admiral March 1938. Admiral Superintendent of Chatham dockyard. Died 14 October 1939 in *Royal Oak,* after helping men below decks to escape.

BLOCKSHIPS: vessels deliberately scuttled to form a barrier in shallow water. Usually old ships, cement-filled linked by cables or chains to act as further barrier. An additional blockship for entrance to Scapa Flow used by U47 was to arrive day after *Royal Oak* sinking.

FORBES, Sir Charles Morton: British admiral, b. 1880, son of James Forbes of Ceylon. Entered Navy aged 13, 1894, in cadet ship *Britannia.* Gunnery specialist in WWI, 2nd in command of battleship *Queen Elizabeth* during Dardanelles campaign 1915. Captain of flagship *Iron Duke* at Jutland 1916, where he earned DSO. Director of Naval Ordnance 1925-8. Rear-Admiral 1928. Commanding destroyer flotilla in Mediterranean 1930-1. 3rd Sea Lord 1932-4. Vice Admiral 2nd in command Mediterranean Fleet 1934-6. Admiral 1936 and C-in-C Home Fleet 1938.

PEGASUS: 6900-ton seaplane carrier. Launched 1914. Dimensions: 366 × 50.75 × 17.5ft. Engines: 1-shaft reciprocating, 3000ihp. Speed: 11 knots. Guns: 4 × 12pdr anti-aircraft (4 mounts), 10 seaplanes. Crew: 139. Originally named *Ark Royal,* in 1939 she was being used for experimental work with aircraft landing rafts and catapults.

PRIEN, Günther: U-boat ace, b. 1908 Lübeck. Went to Seaman's College at Finkenwerder near Hamburg at 15 then signed on as deck boy on square rigger. Received Master's ticket 1932, but with no sea work available he joined road building gang. Joined Navy Jan 1933; Kiel U-boat Training School 1935. Watch officer U26, on Spanish Civil War Neutrality Patrol. Commander of U47 since Dec 1938. Led daring attack against battleships in Scapa Flow 14 October 1939.

ROYAL OAK: 29,150-ton R-class battleship. Laid down Jan 1914 and launched Nov 1914. Completed May 1916. Dimensions: 620.5 × 102.5 × 28.5ft. Engines: 4-shaft steam turbines, 40,000shp. Speed: 21.5 knots. Guns: 8 × 15in (4 mounts), 12 × 6in (12 mounts), 8 × 4in anti-aircraft (4 mounts), 4 × 3pdr, 1 × 12pdr field, 5 MG, 10 Lewis, 4 × 21in torp tubes, 1 aircraft. Armour: 4-6in belt, 1-5.5in decks, 4.25-13in turrets. Crew: 1146. Sister ships: *Ramillies, Resolution, Revenge, Royal Sovereign. Royal Oak* sank at 1.30am on 14 Oct 1939 after torpedo attack by U-47.

SCAPA FLOW: almost land-locked basin among Orkney Isles, to north of Scotland. Name *Scapa* is Norse, meaning 'cleft in two', as it splits up the islands. Long used as a safe anchorage for the British fleet, particularly in WWI. Being some 8 miles across, it had ample room for entire fleet, but was not as sheltered as other locations. Well known in Germany as final resting place of Germany's WWI fleet: 74 ships scuttled there in 1919.

U47: 753-ton German Type VIIB submarine. Laid down 1937. Launched Nov 1938. Commissioned Dec 1938. Dimensions: 218 × 20 × 15.5ft. Engines: 2-shaft diesel/electric. Surface performance: 2800shp diesel, 17 knots, 6500 mile range at 12 knots. Submerged performance: 750 shp electric, 8 knots, 80 mile range at 4 knots. Guns: 20mm AA, 5 × 21in torp tubes (4 bow, 1 stern). Crew: 44.

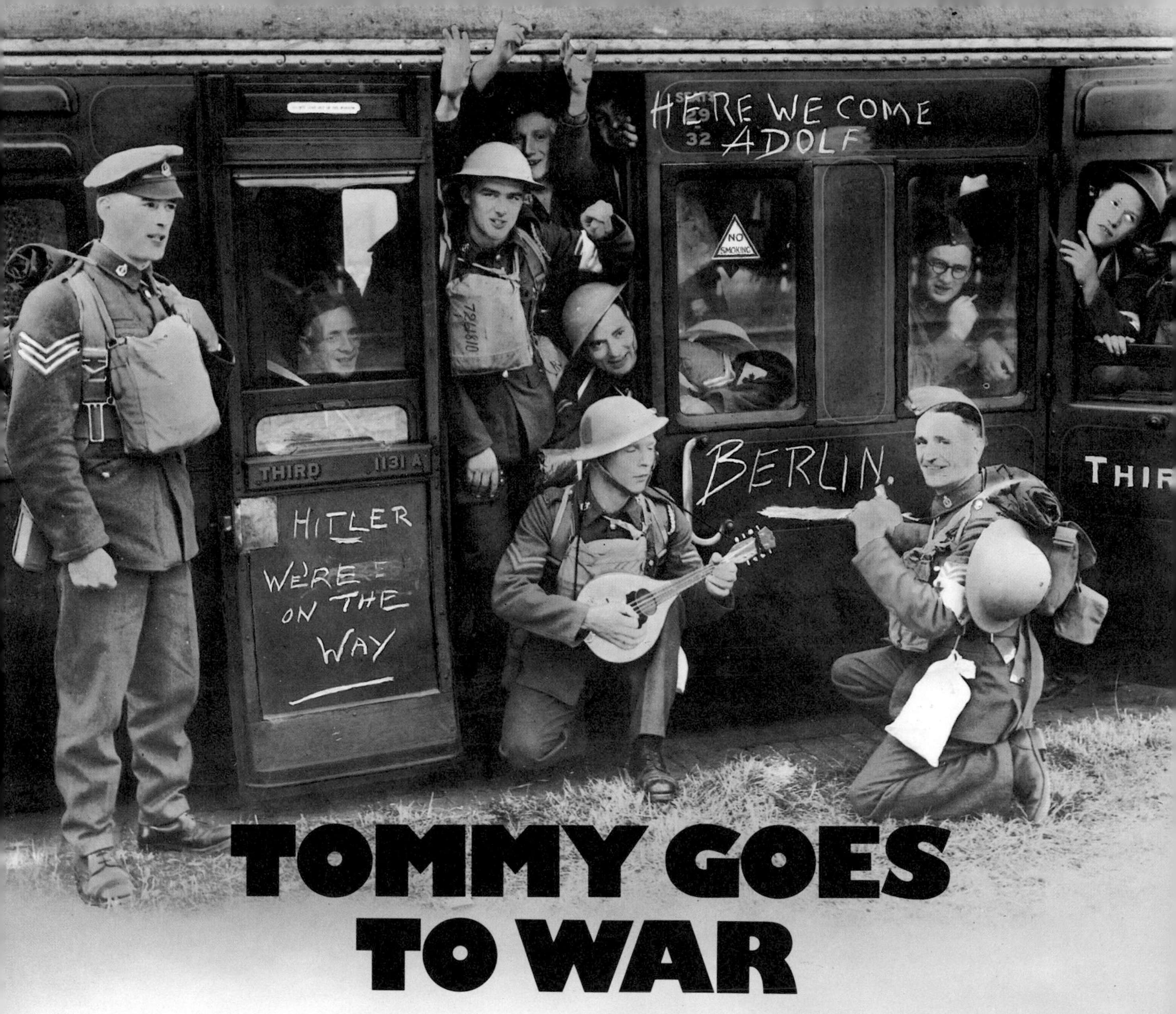

TOMMY GOES TO WAR

Britain's army started World War II with high hopes that this war would be different. 'Tact, commonsense, and understanding' were to motivate the modern NCO.

'Care must be taken' ran the War Office circular of 1 May 1939, 'that the recruit is welcomed, that he is treated as a human being.'

Fine ideals. But what sort of reception did the recruit receive? When 29-year-old Thomas Firbank joined the Brigade of Guards, his first impression was less than reassuring: 'You bloody fool' bawled the sentry, 'wait till they get their hands on you.'

With name, rank and number stamped on a white card, Firbank reported to his barrack hut.

A typical barrack room was long and narrow, with some 25 beds arranged down two sides. Some beds were a mere 3ft long, but all had 'biscuits', three sections of mattress and blankets. Windows were half open, even in winter, and invariably the old coal stove was unlit. As Firbank says 'troops did not in those days feel the cold until after 1600 hours on weekdays, or 1400 hours on Sunday'.

But perhaps his experience was rare. Certainly there was no shortage of good advice on how to receive, equip and train Britain's fighting men. The problem was translating these good intentions into practice. Most of the Army's NCOs were old hands. They had joined up, many of them, during the years of depression. Others were veterans of the first war. They had learnt their job the hard way, so they treated the recruit likewise: it was simply the way things were done.

Square-bashing and marching still formed the basic introduction to military life. As Firbank recalls: 'We were marched everywhere . . . to meals, to the barber's shop (where 24 men could be sheared in 18 minutes), to the Quartermaster's store, to church, to pay.' And always to the sound of the drill sergeant: 'Swing your left arm straight . . . Heels! Heels!'

Boots were a major preoccupation. Often they were too small, or too big, and they needed a lot of getting used to. They were heavy, covered in thick grease and gave you blisters.

Firbank came to admit later: 'I learned that the attention to detail which is essential in the field cannot be picked up in a moment.' The ability to carry out an order promptly saved many lives under fire.

Often it was the civilian misfit who found the

Army tolerable. He was housed, clothed and fed, and his mind kept occupied for him.

Like their fathers before them, recruits were destined for France. An advance party had gone out the day war was declared. But it was on 11 October that War Minister Leslie **Hore-Belisha** informed the House of Commons that the **British Expeditionary Force** (BEF) had taken up positions on the Western Front.

They travelled to France in crowded, blacked-out ships. Disembarking at Cherbourg they found no reception committee, just a few gendarmes, and the odd fisherman. They were not told where they were going: some did not even know where they had landed. Some believed they were in Spain.

There were, in fact, three British armies arriving in France: the **Regulars**, together with their **Army Reserve**; the **Territorials**, and the **Militia**. After the inevitable delays and waiting, they were crammed into trains, shunted around before finally arriving at the 'front'.

To the veterans of the first war—most of the officers—it was all too familiar. They occupied the same countryside they had left in 1918.

For those arriving at the front, life was leisurely and not unpleasant. A fine Indian summer gave to many an almost holiday mood. 'Lovely October afternoon' wrote one soldier in his diary, 'the sky flecked with grey clouds . . . you can imagine yourself on the Sussex Downs or the hills of Surrey.' Billeted in schools, warehouses, private homes and barns, at first there was much to do.

'They're all anxious to know how they'll shape up when the fight comes: the waiting isn't easy. Those who waited to go over the top last time know what it was like.'

A battalion CO, somewhere in France, October 1939

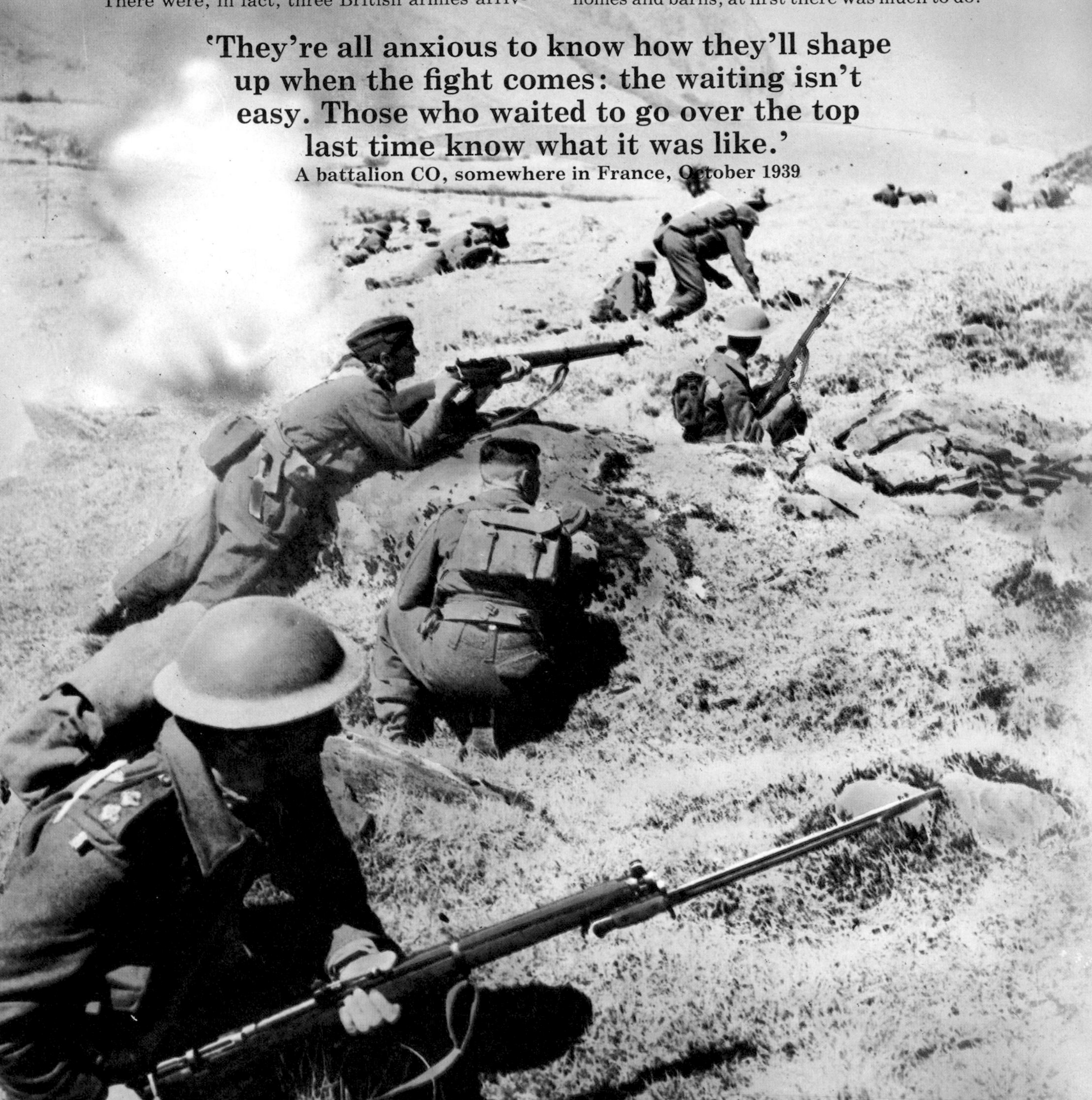

But as summer gave way to the wettest autumn in 48 years, the novelty soon wore off. One lad from Blackburn had to stand duty in the middle of a ploughed field without a greatcoat—because of a shortage of supplies.

Complaints about food—or rather the lack of it—increased. For those fortunate enough to be stationed near an estaminet, there was egg and chips to supplement rations. J. L. Hodson, the war correspondent, was told by a 'fresh faced, brawny' sergeant in his twenties, 'the people living yonder bring us sausages and chips, and they won't let us pay for them'. Others, less fortunate, had to wait 16 hours before being fed.

More disturbing, from the military point of view, was the shortage of weapons. Effective training proved difficult so the Army authorities resorted to digging and parades to keep the men occupied. As a Gordon Highlander recorded 'It's all digging so far and no shooting. Digging and sentry-go and lights in pillboxes.' Reveille was at 6.30am, followed by a shave in cold water, then a breakfast of bacon, bread and tea between 7.30 and 8. The most vivid memory of one infantryman, was wading through 'the stickiest clay you ever dreamed of and you dig till 12 . . . then stew and maybe a drink of tea—and then to dig again till about 4.30 when you pack up for the day, unless you're unlucky and "click" for a fatigue, or some other soldier's delight'.

Female impersonators

Not surprisingly, boredom set in. Some visited the special brothels set up to cater for the troops. Treated with caution by the general staff, arrangements were rudimentary, to say the least. 'Dreary' brothels at Lille, Arras and Lens closed at 9pm for the 'Other Ranks' to allow their officers—queuing outside—the opportunity to enjoy themselves. But the system proved bad for morale.

Other, less dubious, forms of entertainment depended largely on where you were stationed. Sometimes there was a local cinema showing Charlie Chaplin or the Marx Brothers. Or you could catch a 'liberty bus' to the nearest town. Otherwise the BEF made their own entertainments. Female impersonators were popular, so were bawdy songs about the army.

Visits to the front by generals from **General Headquarters** (GHQ) and the C-in-C, Viscount **Gort,** also helped to break the monotony. 'At heart a puritan,' Lord Gort believed his men should live an almost monastic existence. Visiting billets, eating bully-beef sandwiches with them in the rain, Gort managed to inspire loyalty and respect. It was Gort who bullied the BBC into providing a 'Forces Programme'.

In all 152,031 soldiers, together with 23,894 vehicles, 36,000 tons of ammunition, a consignment of poisonous gas—and 60,000 tons of frozen meat—crossed the Channel that first month of war without suffering a single casualty. As one staff officer was heard to say, 'a wonderful show'.

Battle conditions were simulated for the recruit at British Army Battle Schools.

War Notes

BRITISH ARMY

ARMY RESERVE: 150,000 men who had left the Army after a minimum of 7 years service still eligible for refresher training and immediate call up for war.

BRITISH EXPEDITIONARY FORCE (BEF): the 1914-18 BEF had grown from 5 divisions to 60. That of 1939 had 4 divisions—60,000 fighting troops out of 158,000 men (total Army strength 897,000 on 30 Sept). Remainder were needed on the lines of communication across France from Nantes, and Cherbourg via the staging area of Le Mans-Laval to the 45-mile front line around Lille. Gort's command included French 51st Infantry Division. The 25,000 vehicles of 50 types absorbed vast manpower: 720 Military Police on traffic control. The BEF's most crucial weaknesses were in tanks and heavy artillery.

GENERAL HEADQUARTERS (GHQ): the BEF's HQ, first set up at Arras with Gort in the spartan Château Habarcq and his GHQ departments dispersed (for fear of air attack) in villages W. of the town.

GORT, John Standish Surtees Prendergast Vereker, 6th Viscount: British general, b. 1886. Educated Harrow and Sandhurst. Succeeded father as Viscount Gort 1902. Commissioned as 2nd Lt in Grenadier Guards (Gds) 1905. Nicknamed 'Fat Boy'. Captain and ADC to Sir Douglas Haig. Staff officer at an Army HQ 1915-17, MC and DSO. CO 4th Bn Grenadier Gds, Passchendaele and Cambrai, DSO; 3 wounds. CO 1st Bn, won DSO then VC 27 Sept 1918 for leadership in crossing the Canal du Nord. Befriended military thinker Liddell Hart 1919. As Colonel revised Infantry Training Manual 1926. Shanghai Defence Force chief of staff 1927. Learnt to fly. Director of Military Training, India, 1932-6. Major-Gen and Commandant of Staff College 1937. Military Secretary to Hore-Belisha Aug and Chief of the Imperial General Staff Dec above 90 more senior generals. Dubbed 'Tiger' by the Press. Appointed C-in-C of BEF 4 Sept. Crossed to France in destroyer HMS *Skate* on 14th and set up GHQ 21 Sept.

HORE-BELISHA, Isaac Leslie: British politician, b. 1893 London. Educated Clifton College public school and St John's College, Oxford. In Heidelberg at outbreak of war, 1914. Joined Public Schoolboys Battalion Oct 1914. 2nd Lt to Major, Royal Army Service Corps on W. Front and Salonika 1915-18. *Sunday Express* reporter and Liberal MP for Devonport 1923. Parliamentary Secretary to the Board of Trade 1931-2. Secretary to the Treasury 1932-4. Minister of Transport 1934-7. Secretary of State for War and President of Army Council since May 1937.

MILITIA: part-time British local troops from 16th century. Term revived in May 1939 when Military Training Act made 20-year-olds liable for 2 years conscription. First batch of 34,000 called up in July.

REGULAR ARMY: strength stood at 224,000 on 27 April 1939: equivalent to 6 divisions, with 1 armoured division (7th forming) in Middle East. One division and 1 brigade in India, 2 brigades in Malaya. Many colonial garrisons.

TERRITORIAL ARMY (TA): volunteers signed up for 4 years part-time training. Administered by County Territorial Assocs but trained by War Office. Founded 1908 as Territorial Force to rationalize volunteer units. Renamed TA 1922. Given anti-aircraft (AA) home defence responsibility 1935. First AA Division formed Jan 1936. On 27 April 1939 the TA Field Force totalled 325,000 and AA units 96,000. By Sept additional 36,000 Territorials were recruited. Hore-Belisha announced that 12 TA Field divs would be formed.

INSIDE GERMANY

Hitler was unwell and would be retiring from active duties. Göring was under arrest for embezzling the taxes of the German worker. Himmler was in prison too: the Gestapo would be abolished. The Black out was over. Free elections would be held shortly.

Such were the proposals being circulated at a high level inside Germany in October 1939. Those anxious to oust Hitler before he plunged Germany into a ruinous attack on the Allied forces included Admiral Wilhelm **Canaris** and General Franz Halder. Halder, the Army Chief of Staff, took a loaded pistol with him on his frequent visits to Hitler, but he could never nerve himself to shoot.

One reason for the conspirator's hesitation: would the German people accept the argument that the Führer had misled them? Would the Army accept it? Gauging the mood of the nation was a question of key importance this month.

Certainly the British Government was convinced that German morale was low; that, once the blockade of German sea-trade began to bite, the Third Reich would collapse from within. British economists were sure that Germany could last no more than six months without iron ore and oil from abroad. Rumours of severe rationing and food riots were music to Allied ears.

But what was the true picture? Gauging public opinion was no easy matter in the Third Reich, for in one sense there *was* no 'public opinion'—only Dr Goebbels' **Propaganda Ministry.** Goebbels kept his finger on the pulse by means of weekly 'Activity Reports' sent in from 42 Reich Propaganda Offices around the country. First evidence, this October, was that morale was good.

Admittedly, the mass of the German people had hoped Hitler would win his way over Poland by threat and will-power, rather than force. When, on 11 October a wild peace rumour circulated in Berlin—to the effect that the King of England had abdicated and Chamberlain had resigned—cabbage sellers in the markets flung their wares in the air and soldiers returning from the Polish front were joyfully told to 'go home, the war is over'. Goebbels quelled the story with a special broadcast.

The returning soldiers had little reason to doubt

'The average German feels (about the war) like a man with chronic toothache – the sooner it is out the better'

Dr Josef Goebbels, Minister of Propaganda and Public Enlightenment

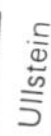

Café scene along Berlin's fashionable Kurfurstendamm: a young Luftwaffe major-general reads the latest war news.

the Führer's masterly ability. Wilhelm Prüller, a typical conscript, came home on 8 October. As his express train roared homewards to Vienna he noted: 'In all the towns of the Reich, the flags of our nation adorn the windows: the visible signs that the war with Poland has been brought to a victorious end. It is a victory of indescribable importance. It is a victory of heroism, a victory of right . . . 82 million Germans have fallen in to report to the Führer.'

The soldiers would, by eyewitness accounts, add to the enthusiasm being drummed up by the massive propaganda machine. For the cinema, Goebbels was already getting together a full feature documentary on the war in Poland. Eventually **Baptism of Fire** would show at 55 cinemas in Berlin alone; mobile film vans would take it to villages of the Reich; airplanes to German embassies as far afield as China and Turkey. A law was passed forbidding any German walking out during the showing of a war documentary.

'We do not read'

There was no shortage of newsreel material about the progress of the German utopia. Travelling through Germany six weeks before the war, British author Sir Evelyn Wrench attended a typical German newsreel show: 'The first picture showed the launching of a steamer, a part of the **Strength Through Joy** movement. The next picture showed the Führer inspecting Germany's new cheap car, the **Volkswagen**, manufactured by mass production and costing about £70. Another film showed a demonstration of thousands of young women, carrying torches and marching.'

But radio was the main medium for keeping the national will intact for Hitler. With 15,309,613 radio sets in operation on 1 July, Germany was second only to the United States as a 'listen-in' nation. The spoken word was seen as a more persuasive tool than written language in the vital propaganda war. 'The radio is the most important and far-reaching instrument for leading the people' Goebbels claimed. As writer Reinhold Schunzel had put it: 'In this land we do not read books. We swim, we wrestle, we lift weights.'

Radio broadcasts were not, in quantity, political. Eighteen out of every 21 hours broadcasting stressed light entertainment and light music. Music, too, announced the day's main broadcasting events: nine news bulletins for which, in factories, work halted on solemn occasions. Top of the listening priorities were the Special Announcements, preceded by fanfares played by a 100-strong band; or sometimes, to heighten the tension still further, the solemn words: 'We shall now have a total air silence.'

Goebbels had a fit of fury when a luckless magazine editor published a picture of the record disc on which the fanfare was enshrined. Anyone else who deglamourized the Third Reich this way would do a stint in a concentration camp, he warned.

The Nazi Party, by owning or closely supervizing more than 3600 newspapers and hundreds of magazines, had become the world's largest publisher. The responsibilities of the news media were simple: 'News policy is a weapon of war,' Goebbels' diary records, 'its purpose is to wage war and not give out information.' The Reich Press Chamber, controlled by Max **Amman,** Hitler's sergeant from the trenches of the first war, kept a close watch on the editors' activities—inflicting fines and closures on any who stepped out of line. Amman had also masterminded the publication of that Nazi bible, *Mein Kampf*, into

11 languages and innumerable editions, so that by 1939 sales exceeded 5.2 million copies.

Even so, irksome feuds and divergencies continued to plague Dr Goebbels—in particular the flourishing and filthy newspaper **Der Stürmer,** owned by gruesome anti-Semite Julius **Streicher.** Salacious scandals, vicious cartoons and maudlin praise for Hitler filled its pages, which Hitler read cover to cover. Goebbels knew that all efforts to present the acceptable face of Nazism to Berlin's foreign newspaper correspondents (by providing them with lavish quarters and entertainment) would fail to impress while *Der Stürmer* continued. Hitler refused to have it banned.

Cocooned in the all-embracing propaganda machine of the Nazi Party, the ordinary man, woman and child in the autumn of 1939 could do little but succumb to the tide of events. The flags waving to welcome the return of soldiers from the Polish front waved also to express a nation's faith in the miraculous leaders who had, so recently, brought full employment back to Germany. Whereas, so few years ago, millions were out of work, the coming of war had created a labour shortage so acute that posters were placed in foreign capitals seeking the return of

Time-Life/Colorific!

At the Volkswagen factory Hitler admires a production model. Thousands paid 5 marks a week for the car, but none were delivered.

War Notes

INSIDE GERMANY

AMMAN, Max: Nazi publisher, b. 1891 Munich. Educated public and business schools. 16th Bavarian Infantry Regt 1914–18. Hitler's company sergeant, and won Iron Cross 2nd Class. An early Hitler follower, became first Nazi Party business manager 1921. Director of its publishing firm Eher Verlag 1922. Retitled Hitler's MS '4½ Years of Struggle against Lies, Stupidity and Cowardice' into *Mein Kampf* and supervised its world-wide publication. Publisher of Nazi daily *Völkischer Beobachter,* weekly *Illustrierter Beobachter* and monthly *Nationalsozialistiche Monatshefte.* Assured Hitler large fees for literary contributions. Made Reich leader of Nazi Press Nov 1933.

BAPTISM OF FIRE: documentary film about Luftwaffe in the Polish campaign. Director Hans Bertram. Made and released because of success of more Army-biased *Feldzug in Polen* (première 8 Feb 1940). Göring in last scene: 'What the Luftwaffe has promised in Poland, it will make good in England and France.'

CANARIS, Wilhelm: German Intelligence (Abwehr) chief, b. 1887 Dortmund. Joined Navy as cadet 1905, interned with crew of scuttled cruiser *Dresden,* Chile 1914 but escaped to Germany in two months via Falmouth and Holland 1915. Naval agent, Spain 1916. Captain of UB-128 in Mediterranean 1917-18. He backed Kapp Putsch 1920. 1st officer in cruiser *Berlin* with Heydrich 1923-4. Secret U-boat construction in Spain. Captain, battleship *Schlesien* 1932-4. Head of Abwehr 1 Jan 1935 changing it to pure espionage. Set up posts in Spain, Shanghai and Holland 1937–8. Became anti-Nazi.

DER STÜRMER (The Stormer): weekly obscene racist newspaper founded and edited (till 1933) by Julius Streicher 1923. Circulation about 500,000.

HITLER YOUTH (Hitler Jugend): boys movement of Nazi Party for 10-18-year-olds. Set up nationally 1933 to absorb all existing youth clubs. Comprised 65% of German youth by 1935. 54,000 marched before Hitler at the Sept Nuremberg rally. On 1 Dec 1936 membership became compulsory. Enrolment only on 20 April (Hitler's birthday). Activities had priority over ordinary education. Million youths taught to shoot, 1938. In 1939 Hitler Youth had 8000 full-time and 765,000 part-time officers and NCOs.

HORST WESSEL: official Nazi Party marching song. Composed 1930 to commemorate the 'martyr' Horst Wessel, a stormtrooper, killed probably by Communists in Berlin and lauded by Goebbels.

I. G. FARBEN: short for Interessen Gemeinschaft Farbenindustrie Aktiengesellschaft (Community of Interests of Dye Industries). A cartel or monopoly controlling 900 chemical factories with 220,000 workers (1938) in the Reich. It had 2000 cartel agreements worldwide, made 43 major products and controlled about 500 firms in 92 countries.

LEAGUE OF GERMAN GIRLS (Bund Deutscher Mädel, BdM): 2 million strong by 1936. Organized like Hitler Youth and also under Reichsjugendführer von Schirach. Split into Jungmädel of 10-14 and older girls, 15-17. Glaube and Schönheit (Faith and Beauty) branch set up 1937 to prepare 17-21-year-olds for marriage. Smallest unit 2-4 girls in a Mädelschaft, 2-4 of which made a Gruppe, 5 Gruppen made a Ring; 5-6 Ringe formed 684 Untergau split into Obergau. BdM had 125,000 leaders trained at 35 provincial schools. Could join Party after 4 years. Uniform: navy blue skirt, white blouse and brown jacket with hair in twin pigtails.

PROPAGANDA MINISTRY: set up 12–13 March 1933. Worked 24 hours a day. Employed 800 civil servants in building on Wilhelmplatz, Berlin. There were 8 divisions by 1937: propaganda, radio, films, theatre, music, art, literature and press (divided into German and foreign press 1938). Propaganda was most important division headed by old Party local newspaper editor and rally organizer Dr Leopold Gutterer since 1937. Ministry spending began at RM14.2 million (about £695,000) and was up to about RM95 million (about £4.6 million) by Sept 1939; 75% of radio listeners' fees came to the Ministry.

STRENGTH THROUGH JOY (Kraft durch Freude, KdF): Nazi organization imitating Italian Fascist Dopolavore. Set up 1933 by Dr Robert Ley's German Labour Front to provide subsidized holidays and cheap culture for German workers so as to demonstrate Nazi Germany's eradication of class. Largely thanks to KdF, tourism in the Reich doubled 1932-8. In 1938 KdF gave 10 million Germans holidays. 180,000 people went on cruises in the 20 Kdf ships.

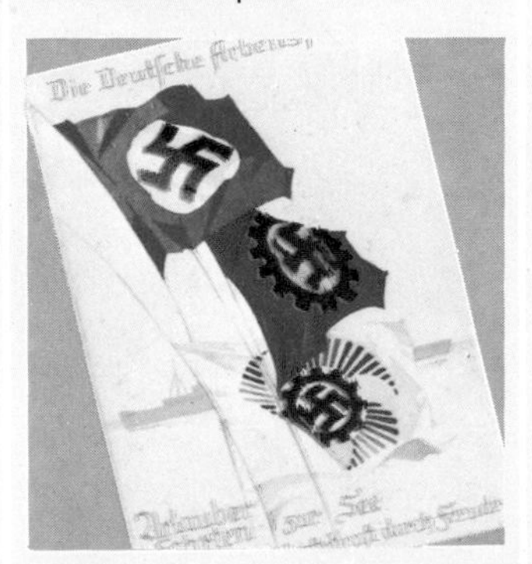

STREICHER, Julius: Nazi politician, b. 1885 Fleinhausen village, Upper Bavaria. Teacher in Nuremberg 1909. Won Iron Cross 1st and 2nd Class and rose to Lieutenant in Bav Army 1914-18. Returned to teach in Nuremberg, set up anti-Semitic political party. Joined Nazi Party 1921. Founded *Der Stürmer* 1923. Took part in Munich Putsch, Gauleiter of Franconia 1925. Ousted Communists in Nuremberg. Dismissed as teacher 1928. Was elected as Nazi delegate for Franconia to Bav Landtag. Elected to Reichstag for Thuringia Jan 1933. Promoted SS-Gruppenführer (Lt Gen) 1934. He urged demolition of Nuremberg synagogue 10 Aug 1939. Unwisely disclosed Hitler's military plans in speech to Franconia Nazis 25 Oct 1939.

VOLKSWAGEN (People's Car): factory foundation stone laid May 1938. Show models were displayed in Munich and Vienna, September. Weekly hire purchase scheme attracted 300,000 buyers by Nov 1940 but war put paid to civil production.

professionally qualified Germans, including Jews.

Some employees became over confident in the new atmosphere of job security. At one **I.G. Farben** factory some workers, aware that the firm had 600 vacancies to fill, felt safe to ease off in productivity. But National Socialist enthusiasm returned after the offenders were turned over to the Gestapo.

'Kids, kitchen and kirk'

Women, by the autumn of 1939, had also returned to their workplace. Early in the war against unemployment they had been firmly sent back home to the three Ks: 'Kids, Kitchen and Kirk' as the Nazi phrase had it. But gaps in the ranks of the work force had now called them back to state service. Three out of every five workers were women—on the farms they worked an average 10¾ hours every day of the year. The women of Germany worked longer hours than their men, and for a fraction of the pay. They also had the problem of bread and flour rationing to cope with: by 25 September all German citizens had been issued with food ration cards. Nazi Germany was a man's world—few women ever reached high professional positions, however hard they worked.

Finally, what of the little National Socialist fledglings growing up in their brave new world of 1939? Three million German mothers had been awarded their official medals for presenting a child to the Reich that summer. These children rated highly in the survival plans of the 1000-year Reich. 'A violently active, dominating, brutal youth—that is what I am after. Youth must be indifferent to pain' declared Hitler. By October 1939 virtually every young male German between ten and 18 was enrolled in the all-marching, all-singing ranks of the **Hitler Youth.** Every tot of ten years had its own dagger, knew all the verses of the **Horst Wessel** song, and played war games with deadly seriousness. On 4 October 1939 even the term youth was redefined when criminal offenders of 16 were made subject to the adult penal code. The Hitler Youth, with its companion troupe, the **League of German Girls** had already, by the start of the war, created a new kind of person—the arrested adolescent who would serve the State with unthinking obedience. 'We are born to die for Germany' was one of the most popular Hitler Youth Slogans. The years to come, would ensure that vow fulfilled.

'The whole function of all education is to create a Nazi'
Dr Rust, German educationalist

MacClancy Press

NOVEMBER 1939

...BEHIND HIS BACK, Hitler's generals are plotting, this month, to rid the world of him. But it takes one lonely craftsman, in Munich, to place the bomb that so narrowly failed to bring the roof down on the Führer. It is the month of missed opportunities. Nowhere more so than in Paris, where the Allies meet to thrash out how to meet the invasion that now looks dangerously near...

1st: Experimental He178 jet displayed to Luftwaffe.
2nd: Soviet Poland incorporated in Belorussia.
3rd: Export of arms embargo lifted by US Senate.
4th: 'Oslo Report' sent to British Embassy in Norway.
5th: German Generals' plot against Hitler aborted.
6th: Air battle over W. Front.
7th: Q. Wilhelmina and K. Leopold issue joint peace appeal.
8th: Munich bomb plot kills 8 after Hitler leaves.
9th: Venlo Incident.
10th: Dutch cancel Army leave.
11th: BEF hold Armistice Day services on WW1 battlefields.
12th: Maurice Chevalier and Gracie Fields star in first ENSA concert in France.
13th: First British destroyer lost: *Blanche* sunk by magnetic mine in Thames Estuary.
14th: Plan D adopted by British and French.
15th: Ribbentrop rejects Dutch-Belgian peace appeal.
16th: British steamer *Arlington Court* torpedoed.
17th: Wilhelmshaven naval base photographed by RAF. Allied Supreme War Council adopts Plan D at 3rd meeting.
18th: Magnetic mines sink 4 merchant ships off British E. Coast.
19th: Jewish quarter of Warsaw barricaded by Germans.
20th: French convoy off Gibraltar repulses U-boats.
21st: New cruiser *Belfast* damaged by magnetic mine in Firth of Forth.
22nd: German magnetic mine dropped on mud flats of Thames Estuary.
23rd: Naval experts defuse magnetic mine at Shoeburyness. Armed merchant cruiser *Rawalpindi* sunk by *Scharnhorst* and *Gneisenau* SE of Iceland.
24th: Former pro-Nazi and Hitler financier F. Thyssen's industries confiscated.
25th: Germans mine inside Swedish territorial waters.
26th: Russians accuse Finns of shelling Mainila.
27th: Nobel Committee cancels 1939 Nobel Peace Prize.
28th: Stewart Menzies appointed British Secret Service chief.
29th: Russia severs diplomatic relations with Finland.
30th: Russia invades Finland.

QUIET ASSASSIN

Georg Elser, a 'loner', a skilled craftsman in wood, described as 'a quiet, shy man' very nearly succeeded on 8 November 1939 in a task that would take the rest of the world five years of unremitting, bloody effort—and the expenditure of millions of lives. By eight minutes only, Elser failed in a brilliantly planned attempt to blow Hitler off the face of the earth.

It was in August 1939 that the 36-year-old cabinet maker from **Württemberg** moved to **Munich,** finding lodgings in this city so long associated with the Nazi party. His choice of a regular eating place was odd for a man who claimed he had seen the inside of Dachau concentration camp as punishment for left wing sympathies. Every night (his landlady later said) he went down to the big Munich Bürgerbräukellar.

Barnaby's

Hitler speaks to the Nazi Old Guard at the Bürgerbräu beer hall unaware of a bomb ticking away in a hollowed-out pillar.

The day came when Elser stayed till the beer cellar's closing time. Then, as the last customers staggered home, he unobtrusively climbed the stairs to the balcony—and hid.

Only much later, in the small hours, did he come down from the gallery. His sensitive hands ran over the object of his interest: one of the gallery's supporting pillars.

Once every year, he knew, Adolf Hitler himself came to stand at this very spot. It was the beer cellar's main claim to fame: back in 1923 the young Hitler had launched himself on the world by striding into the cellar with machine-gun toting cronies, mounted a chair and fired a pistol shot.

Ever after, as his fortunes improved, the anniversary of that day, 8 November, had been a Nazi holiday. On 8 November 1939, Hitler would return to the beer cellar and share his triumph with the usual 3000 capacity crowd of old-timers.

In the dark, stale air of the restaurant, Elser removed his carpenter's tools from his pockets and went to work on the wooden panelling of the pillar.

The first task was to prepare a removable panel that would evade the attention of security checks. On later nights came even more hazardous work: the patient chipping out, fragment by fragment, of the brick and plaster behind.

Gradually, Elser hollowed out the pillar, around its central girder. But despite his skilled carpentry on the panelling, the cavity would sound hollow to any inquisitive rap. Painstakingly he made a steel and cork lining: this would also serve to deaden the ticking of the fuse, and maximize the force of the explosion.

Back in his rooms, he worked on other problems. Again, nothing would be left to chance. The timing device he built from two alarm clocks, fixed to release three firing pins against three percussion caps, which in turn would set off three explosive charges to detonate the main charge.

Hour of Destiny

If Elser's nights were dangerous, so were his days: to acquire explosives he got a job in a stone quarry, and skilfully stole sufficient putty-like explosive to finish the job.

The clocks, in position, began ticking on 5 November, timed to reach their hour of destiny at precisely 9.20pm on the 8th. A lesser man than Elser would have made good his escape on the 5th. But he could leave nothing to chance. He was back on the 7th, to make one last check on the mechanism. A curious chance of fate aided him.

The Bürgerbräu rally was a sentimental reminder of the good old days, a turn-out for the original **Old Guard** of the Party, who predated the state's new security police. At the Bürgerbräu, decreed Hitler, only the Old Guard should have the honour of protecting the Führer: the SS and Gestapo's responsibilities ended at the cellar's doors. The evidence is that the beery veterans skimped on the practical duties of their responsibilities: no checks were made on the building until the day of the big speech.

Like Elser's fuse, the annual rally always ran like clockwork. It was exactly on this feature that Elser's plans depended. The big bang was timed to coincide with the very climax of the Führer's speech.

By six in the evening of the 8th, the beer cellar was crowded. The audience rose as the old **'Blood Standard'** was carried in. It was a good turn-out, which included Heinrich Himmler, Goebbels, Rudolf Hess and Joachim von Ribbentrop.

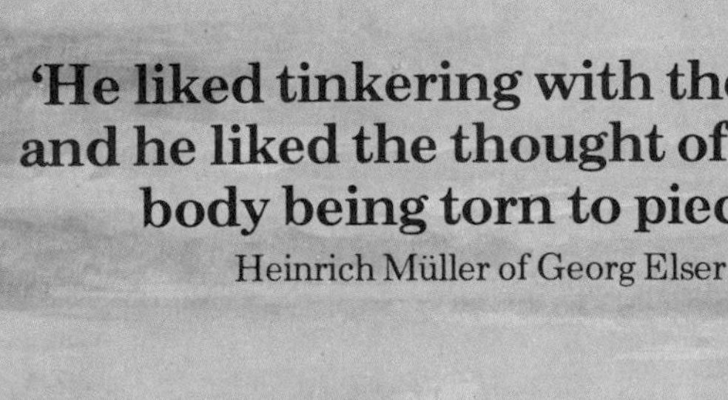

'He liked tinkering with the bomb and he liked the thought of Hitler's body being torn to pieces.'

Heinrich Müller of Georg Elser

The speech began quietly. Hitler seemed tired. Throughout the Reich, Germans listened to it on their radios, or through the loudspeakers hanging on every street corner.

Target for the Führer's wrath tonight was England, and Winston Churchill in particular. 'No matter how long the war will last Germany will never capitulate. England claims to be prepared for a three year war. On the day when England declared war on Germany I gave orders to prepare for a war of five years.'

'There can only be one victor, and that is us,' Hitler went on, his voice rising. For Churchill he had a special message: 'I would tell him: "Sir, get back to your Thames".'

It was fine Hitler oratory: rambling and aggressive. But tonight, there was a difference. As the clocks moved smoothly towards 9pm one of Hitler's aides began checking his watch, then started to pass a succession of notes to the Führer. Julius **Schaub's** mind was not on his Führer's rhetoric: his task tonight was simply to get Hitler on a train to Berlin. And the train left at 9.31.

Just after nine, Hitler wound up his speech, and by 12 minutes past was out of the hall.

Eight minutes later, the bomb exploded. It wrecked the room. The overhanging balcony crashed down, burying dozens of old comrades in rubble. Six Old Guards died instantly, one later in hospital. A waitress was also killed. Sixty people were wounded, 16 of them seriously.

Meanwhile, Johann Georg Elser was still on his way to freedom. He had reached the Swiss border, at Konstanz, too late. As shock waves of the appalling events in Munich spread, the security forces began to jump. Plainly some vast conspiracy must be afoot, involving foreign agents, Communists, old enemies of Hitler. At the frontier the SS pounced on the cabinet maker and turned him over thoroughly. Hidden under his lapel they found a badge of the former **'Red Front'** Communist movement. In his pockets they found pieces of fuse, sketches of grenades, and a postcard of the Bürgerbräukeller's interior. The pathetic amateurishness of his escape attempt served only to convince everyone that the man could not have been acting alone.

'Ordered from above'

Strange stories began to circulate. Could the entire incident have been an elaborate propaganda confection, designed to rally Germany to the Führer after a 'miracle' escape from death? Elser was handed to the Gestapo, and the attentions of its chief, the brutal SS Gruppenführer Heinrich **Müller,** in particular.

Under interrogation, Elser began to talk. His version of what really lay behind his actions puzzled his interrogators—and historians ever since. He claimed he had been offered 40,000 marks (about £1950) to do the job; that the bomb was 'ordered from above'. On one occasion he claimed to have met Himmler and Hitler personally, who commanded him to fake the assassination attempt.

The interrogators pondered: and meanwhile kept Elser alive and well. Hitler remained convinced that Elser had accomplices—the cabinet maker had to be kept in good shape to face a spectacular show-piece trial. In the special concentration camp of **Sachsenhausen,** Elser settled to a strangely privileged existence which would nearly last the war.

'Arrest them immediately'

One who got to know him there was a British secret service agent, Captain Sigismund Payne **Best**. Their imprisonment together was no coincidence. The dust had hardly settled on the Munich explosion before Heinrich Himmler was on the telephone to a German counter-espionage agent, Walther **Schellenberg,** to tell him of the bomb attempt. 'There's no doubt that the British Secret Service is behind it all. The Führer says—and this is an order—when you meet the British agents for your conference tomorrow, you are to arrest them immediately and bring them to Germany.'

Captain Best's ignorance of Georg Elser was not the only gap in his information early that November. Had he known the true state of the spy rings he was responsible for in Holland he would have taken the next boat home: the German **Abwehr** had penetrated deeply into the murky world of espionage on the continent. Best's agents were being collected up so quietly that the Captain failed to notice. The Abwehr hoped to learn a

Time-Life/Colorific

great deal from the industrious British agents.

For Best and **Stevens'** task was to contact the anti-Nazi Germans, who had been making covert advances to Britain all October, rumouring conspiracies and plans to overthrow Hitler. Heydrich gave his rising young Sicherheitsdienst (SD) agent Schellenberg the task of baiting a trail for Best that might lead the Germans to the identity of the 'Generals' who were thought to be involved in an anti-Hitler plot.

So, on 30 October, at a carefully arranged rendezvous on the German-Dutch border, Best and Stevens were privileged to meet two high ranking German soldiers who claimed to be in personal touch with a 'General' involved in the plot against Hitler. One of them, Major Schaemmel, spoke convincingly of the need to stop Hitler before he led Germany into disaster. But before the plotters could mount a coup they needed assurance that the Allies would recognize a German government. The Major said he was prepared to fly to London to discuss these things at first hand. He was, in fact, none other than Walter Schellenberg himself. And his interest in coming to London was to pick British intelligence clean of any names they might have of genuine anti-Nazi conspirators. His companion, introduced as Colonel Martini, was a friend of Heydrich's, Professor Max **de Crinis.**

Caution was in the minds of Best and Stevens on 9 November as they drove to a new rendezvous with the conspirators at the frontier village of **Venlo**. They reached the rendezvous, the redbrick Café Backus at 4pm: their Browning automatics with them, 'just in case'.

Strangely, the straight road leading to the café on German territory was almost deserted. The black and white frontier pole, which on previous rendezvous was firmly in position, now stood raised. Captain Best slowed the car. 'Go on, it's

Associated Press

The wreckage after the blast. 'Six feet of rubble cover the spot where the Führer spoke yesterday evening . . . One dare not think what would have happened if the assassination had succeeded' wrote General Erwin Rommel.

'The Buick was approaching at speed, then braking hard...I heard the sound of the SS car...there were shots and we heard shouting.'
Walther Schellenberg

all right', said the young Dutch agent, Dirk **Klop**, representing Dutch Military Intelligence.

Best looked at the café. Baby-faced Major Schaemmel was sitting on the verandah and, when he raised his arm, Best took it as a sign that the mysterious General they had come to meet was inside. Best drove round the far side of the café and parked. He was just getting free of the steering wheel when the shooting began.

A large open car drove round the corner and halted, bumper to bumper. It was packed with rough, tough customers, clinging to the running boards, perched on the hood and firing sub-machine-guns in the air.

Major Stevens looked at them, then at Best. He said: 'Our number's up, Best.' In charge of the 12 man hit team was Major Alfred **Naujocks**, the dirty-tricks exponent whose exploits at the radio station at Gleiwitz had stage managed Germany's war in the first place.

Though it suited Hitler to have Best and Stevens arrested, and tied into the Elser plot, Walter Schellenberg, like any good professional, resented this spurious device. For years he tried to get Best and Stevens released, in a swap for German prisoners of war. Eventually, in 1943, Himmler told him exasperatedly never to raise the subject again. The three men languishing in the camp at Sachsenhausen were, in fact, for both sides, a painful reminder of two of the biggest secret service disasters in history. The Germans found Elser a painful topic because he represented an assassination bid that was never prevented or explained. For the British, Best and Stevens' short drive into the arms of Major Naujocks shattered the reputations of many in **M16**—more importantly it also made Britain suspicious of any further overture from German resistance movements. Little encouragement was ever again given to plots to destroy Hitler from within.

Best and Stevens survived the war. Elser's immunity ran out in April 1945, on the same day that other brave conspirators perished. Captain Best later told the story of the lone cabinet maker's fate. Elser was taken into the garden of Dachau concentration camp, to which he had been transferred, and shot in the neck, by a fellow prisoner who was then also shot.

War Notes

ABWEHR: intelligence service of German armed forces, so named 1919. Abwehr means 'guard, protection or defence'. Since 1935 headed by Adm Canaris. From June 1938 Abwehr divided into 4 main sections: I (Col Hans Piekenbrock) dealt with espionage for the 3 services; II was for sabotage and uprisings; III counter-espionage; Ausland (Foreign) Branch covered foreign affairs and press of OKW (High Command). In 1939 a Central Group was founded under Col Hans Oster to administer the rest from Abwehr HQ at Tirpitzufer 72-76, Berlin. Abwehr I controlled 'posts' in each of Germany's 21 military districts and Krieg organizations in Spain, Shanghai and Holland. Perhaps 5000 people employed 1939.

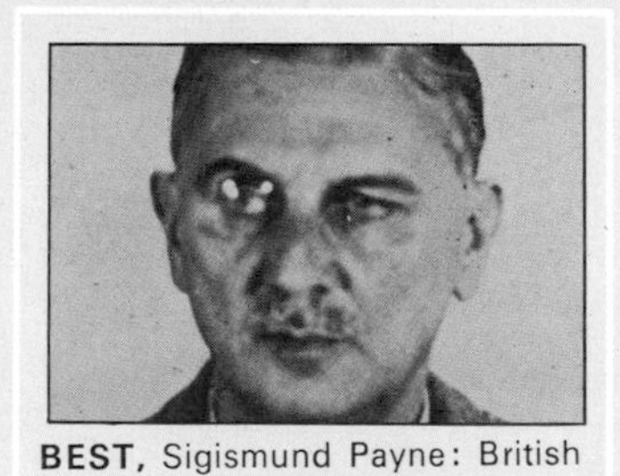
Ullstein

BEST, Sigismund Payne: British Secret Intelligence Service agent. Worked in neutral Holland 1914-18; head of undercover ring known as Z 1939. A good violinist who shared Schellenberg's musical interest. Married to a portrait painter, the daughter of Dutch Gen Van Rees.

BLOOD STANDARD (BLUTFAHNE): Nazi Party's holiest relic allegedly dipped in the blood of the 16 martyrs of the 1923 Munich Putsch. Together with a touch of Hitler's hand it consecrated all other Party flags at Nuremberg Rallies of 1926, (in secret) 1927 (in the open) 1929, 1933 and for the last time 1938.

DE CRINIS, Maximilian: Nazi doctor, born at Graz, Austria. Professor of Berlin University, Director of Charite Hospital's Psychiatric Department and Colonel in German Army Medical Corps, was Schellenberg's best friend. Schellenberg had use of a room at the de Crinis home. While out riding together Schellenberg suggested he go to the Hague as Colonel Martini. As a consultant de Crinis later was to have Hitler and Ribbentrop as patients.

KLOP, Dirk: Dutch Intelligence officer, cover name Coppens. Detailed by Maj-Gen van Orschot, Chief of Military Intelligence, to look after Best and Stevens. Met them at the Hague on 19 Oct. Spoke perfect English. Tried to escape farther into Holland at Venlo when Best and Stevens were captured. Put shots through the German's car windscreen before being sub-machine gunned in the face and arm. His papers gave identity to Germans. Died of wounds in a Dusseldorf Hospital.

M16: alternative name for the British Special or Secret Intelligence Service (SIS). Founded as Secret Service Bureau 1909 for acquiring Intelligence by spying. The bureau's Home Section (M15 from 1916) handled counter-espionage. In 1921 SIS given monopoly of espionage in inter-Service basis under Foreign Office which funded it. The SIS head known as 'C' from the surname of the pre-1914 Foreign Section (Capt Mansfield Cummings). From 1923 'C' was Rear-Admiral Sinclair. SIS expenditure was cut from £240,000 to £90,000 (1919-22). A realistic budget of £500,000 was only finally won by 'C' in Feb 1936 but figure not reached by outbreak of war when more money requested. Had to abandon spying in some Mediterranean countries and rely heavily on French Deuxième Bureau for German Intelligence. Head of Vienna station arrested by Germans March 1938. A year later Czechoslovakia station collapsed. Not able to issue agents with radio until 1939.

Jerry Malone

MÜLLER, Heinrich: Chief of Gestapo, b.1901. Detective in Munich police, acted against Nazis until coming to Himmler's notice. Put in charge of Gestapo June 1936, under Heydrich's control. Not admitted to Nazi Party until 1939. Had idea of using fresh corpses from Dachau with genuine Polish military passbooks for Gleiwitz Incident Aug 1939. A convivial bureaucrat who immensely admired Soviet police work.

MUNICH (**München**): third city of the Reich and capital of Republic of Bavaria. 310 miles SSW of Berlin on R. Isar. Population 840,586.

NAUJOCKS, Alfred Helmut: SS officer b.1911. Worked as welder in late 1920s. Read engineering at Kiel University, and joined Nazi Party. Joined SS 1931 and SD as agent 1934. Ran SD false documents and spy aids section. Summoned by Heydrich on 10 Aug 1939 to run Gleiwitz Incident.

OLD GUARD (Alt Kämpfer): 'old fighters'. Early Nazi Party members honoured for their services. Held civil service and preferential jobs. Those wounded by Communist street fighters got benefits of disabled war veterans.

RED FRONT: Rotfrontkampferbund (Red Front Fighter's Assoc). Communist street army equivalent and foe of the SA. Part trained by Russian instructors. Worst clashes from 1930. Banned by Hitler's Enabling Act of 24 March 1933.

Popperfoto

SACHSENHAUSEN: concentration camp N. of Berlin close to a village of 3397 people. One of first 3 camps set up 1933. Com-

SCHAUB, Julius: Hitler's ADC and chauffeur, a pharmacist and cripple, b.1898. Joined Nazi Party 1923. Imprisoned in Landsberg Castle with Hitler and was one of first SS members.

Keystone

SCHELLENBERG, Walther: SD officer, b.1900 Saarbrücken, 7th child of piano maker. Read medicine and law at Bonn University. Joined SS and then Nazi Party April-May 1933, membership No 3,504,508. Recruited by Heydrich to SD 1935. As a SS-Oberscharführer (master sergeant) went to Italy to arrange security for Mussolini's Berlin visit Sept 1937. Divorced wife March 1939 to further career. Put in charge of RSHA's Group IV E (Gestapo counter-espionage) Sept 1939.

SINCLAIR, Hugh Francis Paget: Head of SIS or 'C', b. 1873. Joined RN 1886 Flag Officer (Rear-Admiral) Submarines 1921-3. Knighted 1935. A dying man by 1939, cancer killed him on 4 Nov. Designated his deputy as successor, Col Stewart Menzies, confirmed by War Cabinet as 'C' 28 Nov.

STEVENS, Richard: SIS officer in charge of Holland spy ring. Served in Indian Army before 1939. His cover was British Legation Passport Officer in the Hague.

VENLO: Dutch frontier town and rail junction of 26,822 (1947) in Limburg Province on R. Maas 15 miles NNE of Roermond, Germany.

WÜRTTEMBERG: self-governing Republic in SW Germany. Area of 7534 sq miles with population of 2,896,920, 30% RCs. Capital Stuttgart (pop 459,538).

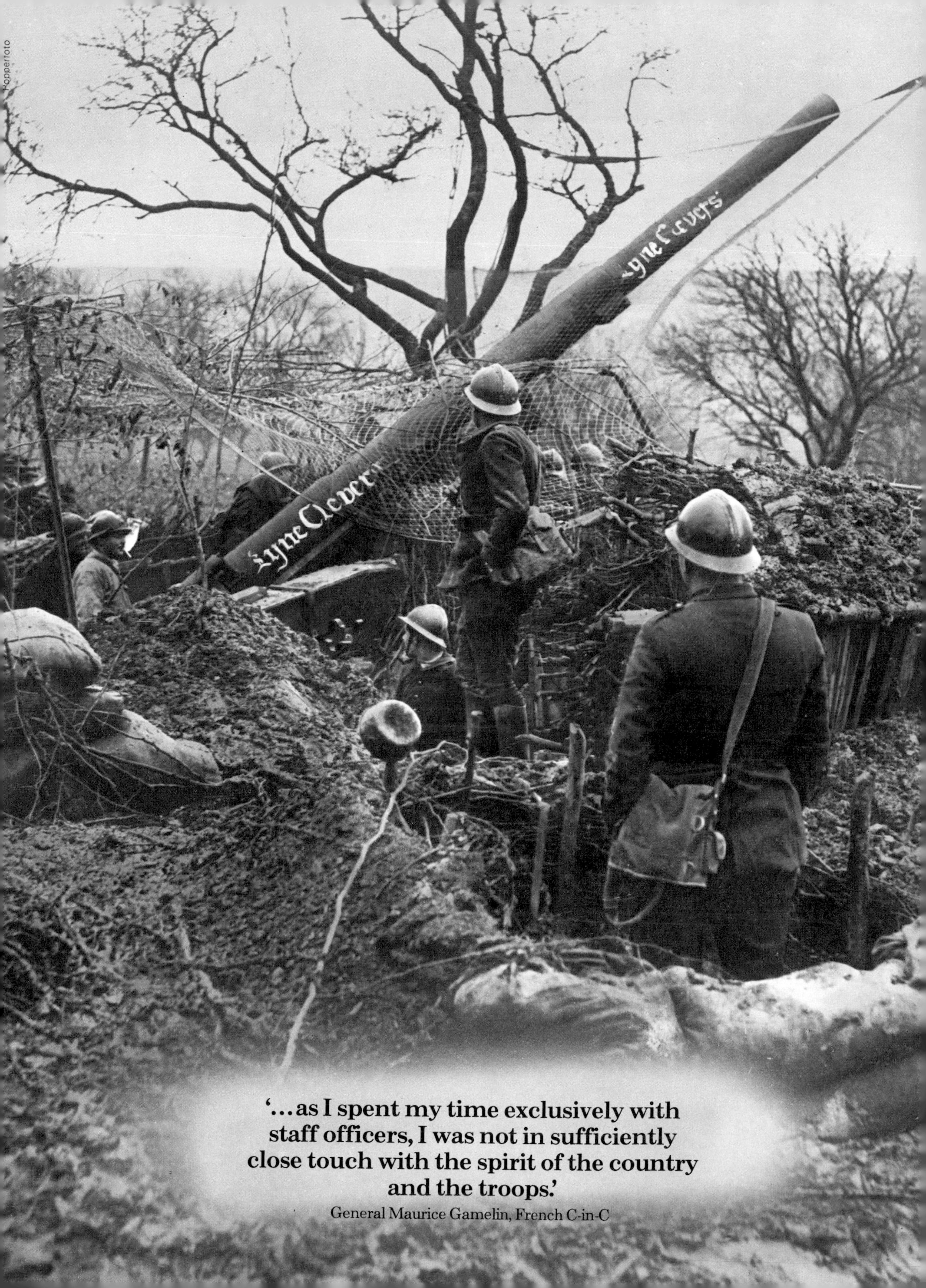

Popperfoto

'…as I spent my time exclusively with staff officers, I was not in sufficiently close touch with the spirit of the country and the troops.'

General Maurice Gamelin, French C-in-C

'A VERY GOOD PLAN...'

Britain's top military commanders filed into the Supreme Headquarters of their French Allies on 9 November with some foreboding. The reasons for the joint meeting were urgent: to agree together how to run a war in which, so far, Hitler had made all the running.

The setting for this key conference was above the gloomy vaults of the dungeons in the Chateau of **Vincennes**, east of Paris.

The French generals seemed more interested in swapping glorious anecdotes of the last war than getting on with the task of fighting this one.

In charge was General Maurice Gamelin, 67, French Commander-in-Chief. 'A nice little man in well cut breeches' was how one British counterpart, General Sir Edmund **Ironside** described him. 'Tiny' Ironside (6ft 4in) was more charitable than others in the British party. RAF Air Marshal **Barratt** summed up Gamelin as 'A button-eyed, button-booted, pot-bellied little grocer.'

'The days pass . . .'

Above ground, the weather had broken. Torrents of rain hammered down on the Western Front while snugly underground, French troops manned the bunkers of the Maginot Line. Question of the day was: what was Hitler going to do next, and what, if anything, could be done about it? On 29 October one member of the visiting British party, Lieutenant-General Henry **Pownall**, BEF Chief of Staff confided to his diary: 'The days pass and still Mr Hitler hasn't shown his hand.' But only four days later Mr Hitler was touring the Front and news reached the Belgium and Dutch parliaments that an attack was imminent.

Top of the agenda at Vincennes was: how best to use the Allies' bombers. And, second, how to make a stand when Hitler struck.

Suppose Hitler struck at **Belgium**. If he did that, Britain would bomb the **Ruhr**—where six in ten German industries were based. To the French, who were wide open to retaliatory German air attack, the scenario was too frightening to think about. Pre-war, France had built up her defences on land, not in the air. It was all right for Britain to concentrate on her RAF: no one was going to walk across the English Channel. But France had good reason to worry about panzers and motorcycle combinations. Her air force was weak. Provoke the Luftwaffe, and French factories might be knocked off the map next day.

If Germany did attack through Belgium, how could the Allies help? Belgium, after all, refused even to discuss with Britain or France how she planned to defend herself. Terrified of provoking Germany, Belgium refused to confer with Allied military leaders.

Between ample, and lengthy meal breaks the British and French generals decided the fate of Europe. Fresh on the table now lay the latest documents from Belgium: a joint appeal from young King **Leopold** of the Belgians and Queen **Wilhelmina** of the Netherlands (**Holland**), on 7 November, for a stop to the war. Both the British and French were aghast. 'I should fancy,' suggested General Pownall in his diary, 'even the King of the Belgians begins to realize now that the policy of the ostrich doesn't pay in the end and that he is likely to get the kick in the backside that is due to him.'

But Pownall was in a minority, and later came round to the agreed plan. Far from making a bold strike, the Allies would 'wait and see'.

Gamelin explained the broad principles behind what he called Plan D: an Allied advance to the River Dyle in Belgium. At a stroke the total front defended in the West would be reduced by 45 or 50 miles, freeing more troops for a central reserve force as well as securing more Belgian territory, especially industrial regions, argued Gamelin. Plan D would deepen the zone of anti-aircraft defences and increase the chances of linking up with several divisions of the Belgian Field Army.

The British listened attentively, but with a kind of gut unease. The French were strong on big project outlines, weak on working out how to accomplish them. 'The French find us rather sticklers for detail,' commented Pownall. 'But even the French admit that if we say we will do a thing it means we will and can. We don't let them down afterwards by saying that we're sorry but we found we couldn't do it after all.'

Britain's Commander-in-Chief Lord Gort, whose men in the British Expeditionary Force were already dug in on the silent Western Front, listened more attentively to the next French speaker, General Alphonse **Georges**, whose task it was to explain the practical details of Plan D's execution.

'No time to make war'

It was well known that Georges, C-in-C NE Front, and Gamelin were rivals. Writer André **Maurois** overheard a British general joke. 'They are so busy making war on each other that they have no time to make war on the Germans.' Even their roles were ill-defined in terms of superiority.

But there was little Gort could do at Vincennes—where the fatal decisions were made which paved the road to Dunkirk—but listen. Britain had contributed a mere five divisions to the Anglo-French Army of 90. Gort saw his role plainly: the question of how to advance on Hitler 'was not for me to comment upon. My responsibilities were confined to ensuring that the orders issued by the

French for the employment of the BEF were capable of being carried out'. 'It never occurred to me,' wrote Sir Edward **Spears**, 'to describe Gort as intelligent above average.' Now, at Vincennes, his straightforward 'Guardsman's feeling for obedience' led directly to the acceptance of France's Plan D.

But perhaps it remains one of the large tragedies of history that General Gort, who saw his job as inspecting what his troops were doing, did not pinpoint to the French the harsh realities of what was going on in the world outside.

'Disgruntled and insubordinate'

Lieutenant-General Alan **Brooke** had already noted, at a parade on 4 November, that the French troops were 'badly turned out and slovenly. The vehicles were dirty, the men unshaven and the horses ungroomed. They had a complete lack of pride in themselves or their unit'. The marching men looked 'disgruntled and insubordinate and when ordered to give the "eyes left" scarcely a man bothered to do so'.

From the grey chateau, the British commanders flew home: some to the tranquil GHQ of the Western Front; others to Downing Street. The message was: the war will go on, but quietly, in full endorsement of Plan D.

Some, in army bases or back home at Whitehall, found the commitment to Plan D frightening. At the BEF HQ in Arras, Lieutenant-General Sir John **Dill** and Alan Brooke heard out their chief, Lord Gort, with pessimism. Wrote Brooke in his diary: 'I only hope to God we do not have to hold the line at Scheldt with such strung out forces. The whole plan of advance was fantastic and could only have resulted in disaster'. General Ironside went to Downing Street to report on events. Premier Chamberlain was in bed with gout: Ironside faced a War Cabinet run, instead, by the Chancellor of the Exchequer, Sir John Simon. 'The cabinet was not as well run as usual,' recalled Ironside. His British political colleagues seemed uneasy that the whole future of the war lay now, apparently, with the French commanders. 'I had to remind them twice that they had a Commander-in-Chief in France and that they had expressly put him under the orders of the French Commander,' said Ironside.

Plan D was made official policy. One critic, Brigadier John **Kennedy**, Director of Plans at the War Office, sent a list of Plan D's 'wait and see' weaknesses to the Head of the British Military Mission at Vincennes, Major-General Sir Richard Howard-Vyse.

General Gamelin saw the report—and blew up. He objected to the criticism: 'It is my plan, it is a very good plan, and I mean to carry it out.'

French troops march. France had an army of over 3,000,000 men by November 1939.

War Notes

BARRATT, Arthur Sheridan: British air marshal, b.1891. Educated Clifton College and RMA Woolwich. Seconded to Royal Flying Corps 1914, won MC with French and Belgian decorations by 1918. CO RAF Advanced Air Striking Force in France.

BELGIUM: constitutional monarchy with 9 self-governing provinces. Area: 11,779 sq miles. Pop: 8,386,533 (31 Dec 1938). Crude steel production: 3104 metric tons. Coal production: 29,844 metric tons. Shipping: 252,191 tons (96 ships). Railways: 2987 miles. Canals: 1000 miles. Private cars: 155,000. Roads: 6574 miles. Unemployment: 57,300. Army: 88,000 + 562,000 on mobilization.

BROOKE, Alan Francis: British general, b. 1883 Bagnères de Bigorre, France. Educated abroad and RMA Woolwich. Joined Royal Artillery (RA) 1902, serving in Ireland. Transferred to India and Royal Horse Artillery 1906. France with Secunderabad Cavalry Brigade 1914. Served on RA staffs at all levels, DSO and bar, Belgian Croix de Guerre. As CO 2nd Corps BEF landed in France 28 Sept 1939.

DILL, John Greer: British general, b. 1881. Educated Cheltenham public school and RMA Sandhurst. 2nd Lieutenant Leinster Regt for Boer War 1901. Captain 1911. Staff College with Ironside 1913. Staff posts in World War I including Brigadier-General GHQ Operations Branch 1918. Colonel DSO with French and Belgian decoration and Chief Instructor Staff College 1920. Dir of Military Ops and Intelligence 1934-6 then Lieutenant-General C-in-C Palestine and Transjordan 1936-7. CO Aldershot Command 1937-9. CO 1st Corps BEF from 4 Sept.

GEORGES, Alphonse Joseph: French general b.1875 son of a gendarme. Enlisted in the infantry 1897 and served in N. Africa. Battalion CO 1914. Staff officer Salonika expedition 1915-18. Colonel and Chief of Operations to Marshal Foch 1918. Head of Economic Service Ruhr 1923. Chief of Staff to Marshal Pétain in Riff War (Morocco) 1925-6. Chef du Cabinet in Maginot Govt 1929. 19th Corps Algeria 1931 and on Higher War Council 1932. Friend of Churchill since 1934.

HOLLAND (Netherlands): constitutional monarchy with 11 provinces. Area: 13,514 sq miles. Pop: 9 million. Coal production: 12.8 million tons. Shipping: 2,254,896 tons (940 ships). Railways: 2105 miles (1938). Canals: Roads: 1250 miles. State spending: 744,830 guilders (about £61.3 million). Defence spending: 134,858 guilders. Armed forces: Army: 40,000 = 270,000 on mobilization. Navy: 72 ships. Air force: 126 planes.

IRONSIDE, William Edmund: British general, b.1880 Aberdeen, son of Army surgeon. Educated St Andrews and Tonbridge School, Kent. Officer cadet RMA Woolwich 1897. Gunner 44th Battery RFA Boer War. Escaped German SW Africa after spy mission as Boer driver. Staff College 1913. Western Front 1914-18. Chief of Staff Allied expedition N. Russia 1918-19. Head of Military Mission to Hungary. CO troops in Constantinople and N. Persia as youngest Maj-Gen 1920. Cmdt Staff College 1922. C-in-C India 1926. GOC Eastern Command 1936. Met Hitler Sept 1937. Gov-Gen of Gibralter Nov 1938–May 1939. Insp-Gen of Overseas Forces July 1939. Appointed CIGS instead of C-in-C BEF as long expected.

The French troops: 'badly turned out and slovenly... men unshaven... horses ungroomed'.
Lt-General Alan Brooke, 8 November 1939

KENNEDY, John Noble: British Army officer, b. 1893 son of a clergyman. Educated Stranraer School and RMA Woolwich 1915. Entered RN 1911, transferred to RA. Served W. Front and Egypt, winning MC 1915-18. S. Russia and Turkey 1919-20. RA England and Egypt as battery CO, staff officer and Staff College Instructor 1922-37. Captain 1927. Brevet Major 1930. Imperial Defence College 1938; Brigadier and Dep Dir of Military Ops 1938.

LEOPOLD: King of the Belgians, b.1901 at Brussels, son of King Albert I (1909-34). Served with 12th Belgian Regt 1914-18. Married Princess Astrid of Sweden 1926. Succeeded to throne 1934. Reaffirmed Belgium's neutrality Oct 1936. Broadcast mediation appeal 23 Aug 1939 in the name of Wilhelmina and Scandinavian monarchy. Took command of Belgian Army 4 Sept partial mobilization and full manning of frontier defences. In his 27 Oct speech said Belgium was 10 times stronger than in 1914.

MAUROIS, André: pen name of French novelist and popular historian, b.1885 Elbeuf, Normandy, Émile Herzog. Son of textile manufacturer influenced by philosophic teacher Alain (Émile Chartier). Liaison officer with British forces 1914-18. Published *Silences du Colonel Bramble* 1918. Biographer of Shelley 1923, Disraeli 1927, Byron 1930, Lyautey 1931, Dickens 1934, Chateaubriand 1938. Elected to Academie Francaise 1938. French official eyewitness at BEF GHQ 1939.

POWNALL, Henry Royds: British general, b.1887. Educated Rugby and RMA Woolwich. Served RA England and India 1906-14. W. Front 1914-18 winning DSO and MC. Brigade Major, School of Artillery 1924-5. Staff College instructor 1926-9. On NW Frontier 1930-1, bar to DSO. Major Military Assistant Sec to C'tee of Imperial Defence 1933-6. Cmdt School of Artillery 1936-8. Dir of Military Operations and Intelligence 1938-9. Spoke fluent French.

RUHR: Germany's major coal-mining and industrial region between border and Hamm, 2000 sq miles and 4 million inhabitants. Continuous built-up area from Duisburg to Dortmund. Occupied by French 1923.

SPEARS, Edward Louis: British MP, b. 1886 son of Charles Spears and French mother. Privately educated. Joined Kildare Militia 1903. Gazetted 8th Hussars and published *Lessons of the Russo-Japanese War* 1906. Transferred to 11th Hussars 1910. As Lieutenant appointed liaison officer to French 5th Army 1914. Wounded 4 times, he won MC and was made Commander, Legion d'Honneur. Head of British Military Mission 1917-20 as honorary Brigadier-General. Retired from Army 1920. National Liberal MP for Loughborough 1922-4. Joined the Conservative Party in 1925. Published *Liaison 1914* and MP for Carlisle 1931. Opposed Appeasement. Published *Prelude to Victory* (*1917*) 1939. Chm of the Anglo-French Parliamentary C'tee.

VINCENNES: castle of a town 4 miles E. of Paris on N. edge of Bois de Vincennes. Built 14th century. Dungeon became state prison in the 17th century.

John Topham Picture Library

WILHELMINA, Helena Pauline Maria, Queen of the Netherlands: b.1880 daughter of King William III and Emma of Weldeck-Pyrmont at the Hague. Reigned with her mother as regent 1890-98; m. Duke Henry of Mecklenburg-Schwerin, daughter Juliana b. 1909. Holland neutral 1914-18. Refused to surrender Kaiser Wilhelm II to Allies 1919. Visited by King Leopold of Belgium 6 Nov 1939 to discuss Low Countries' neutrality.

HITLER'S ARMY

MacClancy Press

Seventy-two hours before Georg Elser's bomb wrecked the Bürgerbräukeller, Hitler inadvertently foiled the attempt on his life planned by his generals.

General Walther von **Brauchitsch**, 58-year-old Commander-in-Chief of the German Army entered the Führer's Chancellery office at midday 5 November in a state of acute nervous tension. Object of the interview was to dissuade Hitler from carrying out Plan Yellow—the attack on Belgium and Northern France—that had been scheduled for 12 November.

Brauchitsch had good reason for wanting the Blitzkrieg stopped. Meteorologists forecast bad weather. The Army was not ready—lacking trained officers, ammunition, powerful tanks and motor transport—and the General Staff from the Army High Command (**OKH**) headquarters at **Zossen** predicted that they would be defeated.

Patiently Hitler heard Brauchitsch out. Poland, Brauchitsch moaned, had shown up many weaknesses in Germany's fighting men. The infantry had shown a reluctance to fight aggressively; officers and NCOs, had on occasion, lost control. In the transfer of units from Poland to the Western Front, continued Brauchitsch, there had been acts of drunkeness and indiscipline. Courts martial had been held. There was even talk of 'mutiny' in some regiments.

Rising to a frenzy of fury, his voice 'hoarse and angry' Hitler demanded to know the names of the units involved. He would fly out to them personally and find out for himself those responsible. 'Not one front-line commander mentioned any lack of fighting spirit' thundered Hitler. 'The spirit of Zossen' was what sapped the Army's willingness to fight. It was the generals who were cowards and who refused to attack in the West.

'Lack of fighting spirit'

Slamming the door behind him, Hitler stormed out of the room. Brauchitsch was left in fear and trembling. It was now 12.30.

Unknown to Hitler, Brauchitsch was at the centre of a plot to kill him. If the Führer refused to stop Plan Yellow, Brauchitsch would back a coup against him.

General Franz von **Halder**, reluctant accomplice in the projected coup, was anxiously pacing his room. Why had Brauchitsch failed to report at the pre-arranged time? At 1pm Hitler was expected to give the order for Plan Yellow. What had happened to delay Brauchitsch's commitment.

The order from Hitler to begin the initial stage of Plan Yellow came at 1.30. Brauchitsch reported to Halder soon after. In a state of panic Halder rushed back to Zossen, arriving at 3pm. Halder took Hitler's outburst against 'the spirit of Zossen'

In a macabre midnight ceremony at Munich's Feldherrnhalle, SS recruits prepare to take their oath of allegiance to the Führer. But it was the ordinary soldier (inset) who did most of the fighting.

to mean that he suspected a plot. Swiftly, he burned the incriminating letters between the generals. The Gestapo might arrive any moment. Clearly, the coup had to be dropped.

For weeks Halder had been the centre of intrigue and conspiracy. Several scenarios had presented themselves as a means of ridding Germany of Adolf Hitler. A series of 'fatal accidents' were to be arranged for Hitler, Göring and Ribbentrop. Another scheme favoured arresting Hitler while reviewing the troops on 7 or 8 November. More bizarre had been the suggestion that a group of Macedonians might be persuaded—with a liberal supply of alcohol and money, together with the promise that they stood a 1 in 10 chance of survival—to perform the task of assassination.

The most practical scheme involved diplomat Erich **Kordt.** He planned on planting explosives, supplied by Major General Hans **Oster** near to Hitler on 11 November. Arguably, Georg Elser's attempt panicked the conspirators into giving up the idea. In any case Oster failed to get the explosives necessary for the incident.

Anxious to save his own skin, yet hedging his bets, Halder instructed Lieutenant Colonel Helmuth **Groscurth** at 5pm on the 5th to inform Admiral Wilhelm Canaris of the events. Perhaps the head of Abwehr could arrange the Führer's assassination? By 8 that evening Canaris was informed. Curtly Canaris told Groscurth, he could do nothing. The initiative must come from Halder.

Disillusionment grew. Army Group Commanders von Leeb, von Bock and von Rundstedt in the West were prepared to argue for a postponement of the offensive on military grounds, nothing more. The invasion was postponed anyway—first till 15 November, then the 19th. Then Hitler changed it to the 22nd. Then again to 3 December. Few now believed it would be launched until spring 1940.

Few, if any, of the men formed in 95 **divisions** on the Western Front would have believed their generals were plotting against the Führer. Though

Taking a break. Some 13 million Germans tasted military life by the end of the war.

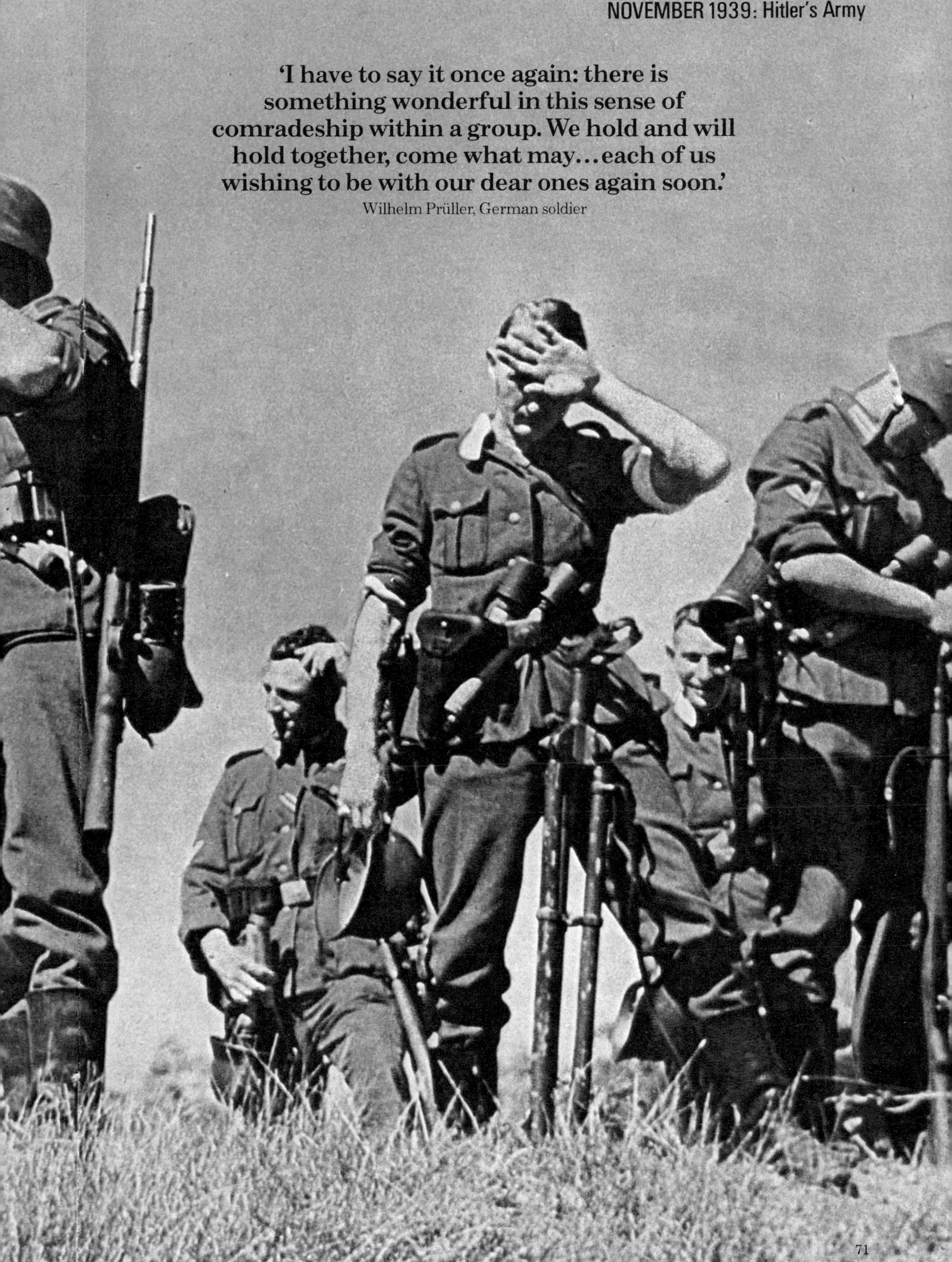

'I have to say it once again: there is something wonderful in this sense of comradeship within a group. We hold and will hold together, come what may... each of us wishing to be with our dear ones again soon.'

Wilhelm Prüller, German soldier

membership of the Nazi Party was small in the armed forces, the average German soldier saw where his duty lay. Germany was at war. Hitler was the leader. It was the duty of the German soldier to fight for Germany under its leader.

Much has been written of the German Army and the campaigns it fought in World War II. But what sort of man was the German soldier? What sort of army did he join? Was the German Landser (pronounced 'lancer') different from the Tommy?

The German Army in November 1939 was a well-trained and highly disciplined fighting force. True, there had been cases of indiscipline and a lack of aggression by some units in Poland. But these had been confined, largely, to older recruits —men who had joined the old pre-Hitler Army. And few had seen war at first hand. They were mostly inexperienced and nervous. But events were to make good Hitler's claim: 'With the German soldier I can do everything if he is well led.' No other army—apart perhaps from the Russian—suffered so much, yet fought so well as the German Army in World War II.

Dressed in his best suit, carrying a small suitcase of personal belongings, the recruit reported to his local barracks. After a medical inspection, he was psychologically screened for the posting best suited to his ability and aptitude. Then came the special oath of allegiance. 'I swear by God this holy oath of obedience to the Führer of Germany and her people, Adolf Hitler the supreme commander of the armed forces, and that as a brave soldier I will be prepared to lay down my life in pursuance of this oath at any time.'

Kitted out in *'feld-granen'* (field-grey but actually green) uniform the recruit began 16 weeks' basic training.

Keeping and cleaning his equipment was high on the list of recruit's priorities. A German infantryman carried some 80lb of equipment: a change of clothing, mess tin, spoon, knife and fork; gas mask, steel helmet (called a 'sweat hat'), 7.9-2mm Kar 98k bolt-action rifle and 'potato masher' grenades.

Ninety per cent of the German Army consisted of infantry-type formations: the glamorous **Panzer truppen,** the motorized and mountain divisions were a small minority. And for the most part, the infantryman marched—the German Army was less motorized than either the British or American

Bundesarchiv

armies. Supplies and munitions were largely transported by horses.

Though discipline was stern, most recruits were well used to obeying orders. Many of them had a long record of service beginning with the Deutsches Jungvolk at the age of 10. From 15 he would have been a member of the Hitler Jugend. Weekend camps and paramilitary training had instilled self-discipline and preparation for Army life.

Morale kept high

Pay was low, the equivalent of £4 a month for a private. But food, though plain, was fairly plentiful. Though civilians were rationed to 2334 calories a day, soldiers received 3720. Mainstay of his diet was a loaf of 'Kommissbrot' baked in the divisional field bakery. Around noon the one hot meal of the day was served from field kitchens. For breakfast and supper he received ersatz tea or coffee, canned goods, sausage, cheese and margarine. In emergencies the Landser could draw on his iron rations of tinned meat, vegetables, biscuits, salt and coffee. Officers and men shared the same food. On active service local produce and plunder supplemented rations.

For acts of heroism and bravery, decorations and badges were awarded liberally. Symbol of bravery since 1813 was the Iron Cross—worn round the neck even in combat. As with his British and American counterpart, the German soldier wore an identification dog-tag around his neck. Made of aluminium the lower half was broken off in the event of death and returned to his file.

Morale was kept high by an efficient postal service and 'home comforts'. Letters and parcels could be sent free of charge. Service, even in remote theatres of war, was swift and efficient. Despite censorship, the German soldier was a prodigious correspondent. Many kept diaries, though to do so was an offence.

'Give Them Sweets'

Teetotal, non-smoking Adolf Hitler made alcohol and cigarettes difficult to obtain. The Führer's solution was 'give them sweets instead'. Lack of sex was another problem. Basically a puritan in matters of sex, Hitler discouraged brothels, but this did not mean they did not exist. To be infected with veneral disease was a court martial offence (for self-mutilation). Consequently a black market in contraceptives blossomed. Even marriage, venerated by the Nazi propaganda machine, was so bound up in red tape that 'war brides' were rare.

But as Hitler himself said: 'Armies for the preservation of peace do not exist; they exist for the triumphant exertion of war!' On the evidence Halder was probably right in thinking that few of the Army's junior officers and men would have backed a coup against Hitler. As events were to prove, the German soldier was to remain loyal to his oath of allegiance through to the bitter end.

A German supply wagon in Poland. Nearly 200,000 horses were needed to keep the invading troops supplied as motorized transport was scarce.

War Notes

HITLER'S ARMY

BRAUCHITSCH, Walther von: German general, b. 1881 Berlin. 2nd Lieutenant 3rd Foot Gds and 3rd Gds Field Artillery 1900–1. Gunner captain and staff officer 1914–18. Major in Truppenamt ('Troops Office') 1922. Colonel 1928. Director of Army Training 1930. Inspector of Artillery 1932 as Major General. As Lt-General CO 1st Div then 1st Corps (Königsberg, E. Prussia) 1935. Clashed with Gauleiter Koch. General of Artillery 1936. C-in-C 4th Army Group (Leipzig) April 1937. C-in-C 4 Feb 1938 as Colonel General after sacking of von Fritsch, a surprise choice. Visited western armies with Halder 1–4 Nov 1939. Hitler did not see him after 23 Nov until 18 Jan 1940.

DIVISIONS: the peacetime Army mustered 52 (730,000 men). Mobilization produced 103 (3,706,104 men), of which 56 infantry, 3 mountain, 4 motorized, 4 light and 6 panzer, 1 cavalry, 1 SS and 15 Replacement Army divisions.

GROSCURTH, Helmuth: Abwehr major in 1938, he became a vital link man for the conspirators when he moved to OKH as Liaison officer in Aug 1939. Lost this post in Feb 1940.

HALDER, Franz: German general b. 1884 Würzburg, Bavaria. Joined 3rd Bav Field Artillery Regt 1902. Munich War Academy 1911. Staff officer 1915–8. Senior Reichswehr quartermaster 1926. Colonel 1931 and Major General 1934. CO 7th Div (Munich) 1935. Lt-General Aug 1936 at OKH. Director of Operations 1937. Chief of Staff 22 Aug 1938 after Beck's resignation. Cancelled coup against Hitler on 28 Sept when Chamberlain Munich visit announced. Hitler called him 'a chronic know-it-all'. Oct 1939 held 2 or 3 Panzer div for coup.

KORDT, Erich: German diplomat, b. 1903. Younger brother of Theodor the London Charge' d'Affaires 1939. Erich joined Foreign Ministry in 1934 and went on Ribbentrop goodwill mission of May 1935. Head of Ministerial Bureau, Foreign Ministry, Berlin from early 1938. With his brother tried to harden Britain's stand during Munich Crisis. Involved in Generals' plot of Sept 1938. Visited London in June 1939 to try and avert Hitler-Stalin pact. Drafted pro-coup memo with Groscurth and von Etzdorf Oct 1939.

OKH: Oberkommando das Heeres, German Army High Command, consisted of Army C-in-C, the General Staff, the Personnel Office and C-in-C of the Replacement Army. Wartime HQ was at Zossen. OKH had lost influence to Oberkommando der Wehrmacht.

OSTER, Hans: German Intelligence officer, b. 1888 Dresden. A cavalryman in 1914-18. Later served in the artillery. Dismissed from Army 1932 due to love affair with senior officer's wife. Joined Abwehr as Colonel and deputy to Major Gen Kurt von Bredow who was murdered in Röhm Purge. Became Canaris' deputy and close friend. In 1939 given charge of Abwehr's Central Group for all admin, personnel and financial matters. A devout Christian who from 1938 was a mainstay of anti-Nazi activity.

PANZERTRUPPEN: wore black uniforms and berets (in imitation of the British Royal Tank Regiment) to emphasize their elite status. First 3 Panzer divisions formed from the infantry 1935, 6 (each 328 tanks and 11,790 men) in invasion of Poland. The 4 light motorized divisions (86 tanks and 11,000 men each) also used were being converted to panzer formations by being given 1 or 2 extra tank battalions of 70–75 vehicles. Panzer division cost about 15 x an infantry one.

ZOSSEN: market gardening town of 5000 people 20 miles S. of Berlin. OKH moved here Aug 1939 into camouflaged complex of bunkers in a forest 3 miles SSE of the town. Codenamed Zeppelin, they were built from 1936. The gas and bomb proof bunkers, (tested 1938–9) each with 3 floors and linked by tunnels, stood in 2 semicircles. The Exchange 500 communications installation, 70ft below ground, linked OKH with all commands as well as the other 2 services.

LAND OF THE FREE

If, in November 1939 you had told young Milburn H. Henke of Hutchinson, Minnesota, that his crystal ball foretold a trip three winters later to Northern Ireland—that, on arrival, bands would play and the Duke of Abercorn would shake his hand—he might well have asked for his money back.

Henke, who in 1942 would be the first GI to land on British soil, had no notion in 1939 that he would be called on to fight in a distant European war. Neither did millions of his fellow citizens. 'The whole of Great Britain—that is England and Scotland and Wales together—is hardly bigger than Minnesota' read a helpful pamphlet later prepared for bemused GIs.

Reluctant Ally

Such basic information was needed. 'All I knew of England was that it's an island off the coast of Europe,' another GI recalled. Nevertheless, this month, the American President took a momentous step towards edging his reluctant nation into war.

A number of sombre opinion polls warned him just how difficult, and politically perilous, this road would prove. In March 1937, 94 per cent of Americans wanted the US to keep out of foreign wars. By 1939 that figure had risen to 99 per cent. There were solid reasons for this sentiment, stretching back to the Pilgrim Fathers.

They had left the Old World and its problems for the New: a world that would be run on Pure and Puritan principles, free from the endless squabbles of Europe's decaying regimes. Later, the War of Independence did nothing to endear Britain to Americans. Young Milburn Henke, like any schoolboy, knew that 4 July was the biggest date in the calendar, and in his schoolbooks the British Redcoats were still 'the baddies'. Nor, with millions of Americans, did Henke trace his family tree back to Britain. Dutch, Polish, German, Irish Americans had no ancestral memories of the distant island that, for the second time this century, had got itself into a war. Some, in particular the Irish Americans, frankly hoped she would lose it—or at least they listened with grim approval when their compatriot, Joseph Kennedy, Ambassador in London, sent home gloomy reports that Britain was 'washed up' and bound to fail.

It had been the fact of World War I that settled the subject for most. Americans had died then to sort out Europe's crisis, and once was enough.

After 1918 a frenzy of scape-goating had risen in the States. Pamphleteers and lobbyists accused the 'blood brotherhood' of international arms manufacturers as the 'merchants of death' who had engineered the war in the first place. Public investigations into the arms business provoked sensational headlines in 1934. Only Allied propaganda had entangled the US in World War I, ran one argument. She should have stayed out.

The hearings over, **Congress** cheered three **neutrality acts** into legislation. On the college campus, students went on anti-war strikes; demanded the banning of Reserve Officer Training Corps. One of the world's finest code-breaking organizations, the **'Black Chamber'** was liquidated on the premiss that 'gentlemen do not read other people's mail'. The code-crackers, out of a job, wrote their memoirs and ran code-puzzle competitions in the papers.

Many other Americans were also out of work. The **Great Depression** was one more reason for America to look inwards and sort out her own problems, rather than bother with anyone else's.

It was against such a setting that Franklin D. **Roosevelt** had come to the White House in 1932. Stockbrokers plunged to their death in Wall Street along with plummeting shares. Overladen jalopies drove south from the dust-bowl farms of the north, seeking illusory fortunes picking fruit in California's orange groves. Banks failed; unemployment soared. Roosevelt, architect of America's **New Deal**, (that legendary 100 days session of Congress in which Roosevelt had pushed through the reforms that would pull America out of the Depression) knew that his voters would tolerate no programme that included the possibility of involvement in Europe's gathering storm.

In 1936 he said: 'I have seen war. I have seen war on land and sea. I have seen blood running from the wounded. I have seen men coughing out their gassed lungs. I have seen the dead in the mud . . .

President Roosevelt may have scored a moral victory with his cash and carry deal, but for drought victims in impoverished Oklahoma and New York socialites the war in Europe remained remote.

MacClancy Press

'I hate war. I have passed unnumbered hours, I shall pass unnumbered hours, thinking and planning how war may be kept from this nation.'

In one of his famous 'fireside chats', on the day war did come, he warned America by radio: 'When peace has been broken anywhere, the peace of all countries everywhere is in danger.'

By now, opinion polls had shown that public awareness of dangers abroad was growing. Ninety-four per cent of Americans disapproved of Hitler's treatment of the Jews. In November 1938, 90 per cent believed Hitler planned to seize more territory in Europe. The most extreme pacifists were silenced: most people now favoured building up a stronger navy, army and air force. But shackles still lay on the arms manufacturers: any sale of arms abroad was banned by law.

When the war began, Roosevelt mounted a campaign to change that law, to open the arsenal of democracy to fighters for democracy in Europe.

It was a hard-fought fight. Powerful members of the Congress banded into a 'Peace Bloc' to keep the arms embargo intact. Though, on paper, Roosevelt was asking only for freedom to sell arms to any belligerent nation, everyone knew that the customers would be Britain and France, since their navies still dominated the ocean. The Peace Bloc saw the move as the first step on a slippery path. Already the US Navy had begun seven neutrality patrols to cover the entire length of the East Coast. Romantic figureheads like aviator Charles **Lindbergh** urged that the arms ban be kept. (Roosevelt never forgave him such speeches; later making him resign his Air Force commission.) North Dakota's senator Gerald **Nye** branded Britain as 'the greatest aggressor in all modern history, and a bad influence on the morals of the world'.

As letters began to pour on to the President's desk, 100 to one against lifting the arms ban,

'This nation will remain neutral, but I cannot ask that every American remain neutral in thought as well. Even a neutral cannot be asked to close...his conscience.'

President Roosevelt

Keystone

Unser
Einiges

Roosevelt mounted his own grass roots campaign to switch public opinion. Cumbersomely named, the Non-Partisan Committee for Peace through Revision of the Neutrality Act began sponsoring radio addresses by prominent Americans. Roosevelt himself lost no opportunity to put the message across. 'Fate seems now to compel us to assume the task of helping to maintain in the Western world a citadel wherein that civilization may be kept alive' he urged Congress on 21 September. 'We cannot be indifferent to the suffering inflicted upon the peoples of the war-torn countries' he told War Relief Agencies on 12 October. 'We have never had the illusion that peace and freedom could be based on weakness' he declared to the Virginia Military Institute on 11 November.

Others used more violent language: Fritz **Kuhn**, German emigré leader of the small but shrill **German-American Bund**, paraded in uniform below entwined Nazi and US flags and denounced Franklin D. Roosevelt as the mouthpiece of 'international Jewish conspiracy'. Isolationist rallies took to the streets under such placards as 'we want work over here, not death over there.'

An outsize picture of George Washington dominates a parade of the German-American Bund, an organization of US Nazis. They got little support from Hitler.

But Roosevelt's quiet and steady persuasion paid off. When **Senate** votes were counted after the final debate, the majority in favour of lifting the arms ban was 63-30. Significantly, most of those in opposition came from America's mid and far West—from those huge prairies Europe seemed too distant to matter. In the lower house, Roosevelt's victory was decisive: a 243-181 vote in favour. Significantly overwhelming support came from the Deep South. For southerners, Germany seemed uncomfortably close—in the shape of the 300,000 German nationals and 1.75 millions of German origin who had settled in Latin America.

Roosevelt signed the new neutrality act on 4 November. Henceforth, in theory, America's arsenal would be open to cash customers abroad.

In France and Britain there was rejoicing. The fine print of the 'cash and carry' deal required purchasers to pay for goods before they left the docks—and to use their own vessels for the job. There was one snag: there were, as yet, few goods on the shop counter. Rifles dating from the nineteenth century were among the first purchases.

But it was the spirit that counted. The rejoicing, and dismay this November signified Roosevelt's success in weaning the US from its ostrich stance on Europe's war. The day appointed for Milburn H. Henke's epic journey to far away Ireland drew just a little closer.

War Notes

BLACK CHAMBER: intelligence organization set up in World War I for 'code and cipher investigation and attack'. Situated in East 38th Street and later East 37th Street, New York, it was finally disbanded in 1929.

CONGRESS: established by the constitution of 1789. Two houses: the House of Representatives and the Senate each with specific but limited powers. Before any law could be enacted it had to be approved by both houses.

GERMAN-AMERICAN BUND: a pro-Nazi organization formed in the US in 1935 by Fritz Kuhn. Its German-style rallies became a focus for US Nazis. Support was very limited and Hitler never gave it his support for fear of arousing US public opinion.

GREAT DEPRESSION: a severe contraction in the economies of Western nations during the 1930s. In 1932 the US economy reached its lowest ebb; contracting by 38% and unemployment was running at 15 million.

Fox Photos

KUHN, Fritz: leader of pro-Nazi German-American Bund, b.1896. Imprisoned in 1940 after being convicted on charges of embezzlement and forgery.

LINDBERGH, Charles Augustus: US aviator, b.1902 Detroit, Michigan. Educated University of Wisconsin. Army flying school Texas 1924-5, became airmail pilot 1926. Folk hero when, in May 1927, he made the first non-stop flight between New York and Paris. Kidnap and murder of his 2-year-old son in 1932 aroused public sympathy. Accepted a German decoration 1938.

NEUTRALITY ACTS: laws passed by Congress originally to keep the US out of any European war. The Act of November 1939 permitted the export of arms to countries at war, on a 'cash and carry' basis.

The Bettman Archive

NEW DEAL: phrase coined by President Roosevelt and applied to a series of sweeping social and economic reforms designed to pull the US out of the Great Depression.

NYE, Gerald P.: senator from North Dakota, b.1892. He argued that US involvement in World War I was result of the weapon industry's desire for profits and that this must not be allowed to happen again.

ROOSEVELT, Franklin Delano: US President, b.1882 Hyde Park, New York. Fifth cousin of Theodore Roosevelt, US President 1901-12. Educated Groton School, Harvard University and Columbia University Law School. Entered New York State senate as a Democrat in 1910. Appointed Assistant Secretary to Navy 1913 by Woodrow Wilson and served in this post throughout World War I earning reputation as an able administrator. Crippled by polio in 1921 but refused to abandon his political and business careers. Elected mayor of New York 1928. In 1932 ran for president against incumbent Herbert Hoover. The only important issue was the Depression. Roosevelt's programme for recovery, the New Deal, combined with Hoover's unpopularity won him a landslide victory. Once elected he set about implementing his New Deal policies. Re-elected 1936 with massive majority.

SENATE: one house of the US Congress, the other being the House of Representatives. Two senators are provided by each state.

NOVEMBER 1939

MINE THAT SAVED BRITAIN

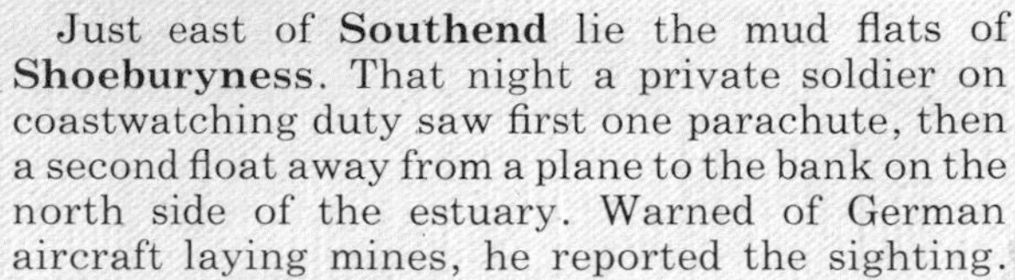

From the North Atlantic a northwesterly wind blew across the coast of Essex. Scurrying clouds blotted out the moon. Rain fell in sheets; 22 November 1939 seemed a typical early winter's night.

Around 10pm a solitary **Heinkel 115** seaplane was seen flying along the northern shore of the Thames estuary. Poor visibility was making navigation hazardous for the pilot. Bringing his plane down lower to get bearings, he focussed on the outlines of Southend Pier—the mile-long structure familiar to London day trippers.

Unknown to the pilot, a machine-gun emplacement and crew were positioned at the end of the pier. Patiently watching and waiting, they had spent many dismal nights doing nothing. Tonight was to be different.

Swooping in low, the Heinkel was greeted by a hail of machine-gun bullets. Startled, the pilot was reminded of the deadly load he was carrying. Fearing a stray bullet blowing up his cargo the pilot ordered the navigator/bomber to jettison it. Arguably, his decision saved Britain the war.

Just east of **Southend** lie the mud flats of **Shoeburyness**. That night a private soldier on coastwatching duty saw first one parachute, then a second float away from a plane to the bank on the north side of the estuary. Warned of German aircraft laying mines, he reported the sighting.

Half an hour after midnight, at his desk at the Admiralty, Winston Churchill, First Lord of the Admiralty, was discussing the incident with First Sea Lord, Admiral Sir Dudley Pound. With them were two of the Royal Navy's most experienced mine experts, Lieutenant Commanders John **Ouvrey** and Roger **Lewis**. Perhaps, as they hoped, the parachutes at Shoeburyness carried German magnetic mines.

For weeks British merchant shipping had been sunk at an alarming rate by the German magnetic mine. Against it there was no known defence. Slowly but surely, Britain's life line at sea was being eroded. And without the raw materials brought world-wide by her merchant fleet, Britain could not continue the war against Germany.

Lewis and Ouvrey left the Admiralty at 1am in a service car for Shoeburyness. Their mission was simple: to recover the mines and reveal their dark secrets.

Driving through the night to Southend they picked up another naval officer and photographer, arriving at Shoeburyness around 4am. In total darkness and pouring rain the four men set out across the mud flats, led by the soldier who had seen the parachutes land.

After ten minutes of heavy going, their guide stopped and pointed to a depression in the sand. Illuminated by a powerful signal-lamp they saw a black cigar-shaped object 6ft long and 2ft in diameter.

Cautiously creeping forward—fearing the mine might explode at the slightest disturbance—Lewis and Ouvrey began their inspection. The object had one end open revealing a large bronze spring. The other end was rounded, with several horn-like projections. These were recognized as devices to prevent the mine rolling on the sea bed. Two circular fittings were screwed in the casing. The object was the answer to their prayer: it was a magnetic mine.

By the light of the signal-lamp Lewis made a rubbing on tracing paper of the mine's fittings. This sketch was to be used to make brass, non-magnetic, spanners. Flash photographs were taken, but with the tide flooding fast, there was little more they could do until low tide; around 1pm. After lashing the mine to stakes driven into the mud to prevent it rolling, they returned.

By lunch time, Chief Petty Officer C. E. Baldwin and Able Seaman Vearncombe arrived from HMS **Vernon**, the Royal Navy's torpedo and mine warfare headquarters. With them they brought a comprehensive toolkit for dismantling mines.

As the tide receded, the second mine was located—300 yards away from the first. Inspection

On 23 November 1939 Lieutenant-Commander John Ouvrey and Chief Petty Officer C. E. Baldwin successfully defused the first magnetic mine to fall into British hands. It had landed on a mudflat at Shoeburyness near Southend.

'Never have I seen anything like the scene on the deck. Men, women and children were hurled to the deck... splinters flew everywhere.'

Survivor of *Simon Bolivar*

showed it to be the same type as the first. But the problem remained: how to defuse a magnetic mine.

The plan of action required courage in large measure. What Ouvrey and Baldwin proposed to do was to walk calmly up to Germany's most secret weapon and disarm it. Lewis and Vearncombe waited behind ready to continue the operation—should the mine detonate and Ouvrey and Baldwin disappear with it. Observing the procedure from a safe distance, Lewis and Vearncombe would know how far they had got, and where they had made their fatal mistake.

First Baldwin bent back a small strip of copper. But tugging too strongly, he pulled half of it off. Together Ouvrey and Baldwin fitted one of the brass spanners. It fitted exactly. Firmly turning the spanner the securing ring gave, the seal of tallow around the fitting broke, and the fitting itself turned. Ouvrey paused and listened. No sound. So far so good. Carefully he removed the fitting. It took three tense minutes to remove the cylinder—containing detonator and several discs of explosives. The mine seemed safe.

Lewis and Vearncombe now came up to help turn the mine over. Together the four men freed the horns, which had embedded firmly in the sand, and eased the mine over. To their surprise a second detonator was revealed. Cautiously, they cut and insulated the electric wires, removed the primers and the hydrostatic arming clock.

Hours of methodical work

With all the external fittings removed, but still packed with 660lb of explosive, a tractor hauled the mine safely away.

It had taken two and a half hours of cold methodical work to render the mine relatively safe. By 4pm it was on its way by road to HMS *Vernon* for complete dismantling, while the second mine was made safe by another party, following the same procedure.

Back at the Admiralty that evening Ouvrey and Lewis addressed a gathering of 100 officers and mine warfare experts on their day's work at Shoeburyness.

The meeting was attended not only by Winston Churchill, but also by Prime Minister Neville Chamberlain. Their presence was evidence of the importance given to the achievement on Shoeburyness sands that bleak November day.

The Royal Navy *had* a minesweeping force, but it was equipped to deal with the threat from the traditional type of mine which exploded on contact with ships. Pre-war Britain had suspected the Germans were developing a magnetic mine and had started building a special type of sweeper to deal with it. But the Royal Navy had to wait till 1940 before HMS **Borde** was ready for service.

In the meantime, merchant ships, six a day on

On 18 November 1939 the liner *Simon Bolivar*, bound for the West Indies from Holland, hit a mine and sank. She was only 18 miles off the English coast and over 100 of her 400 passengers perished.

'Bombers swooped down on us as if from nowhere. I counted nine of them coming from behind a raincloud. They had the sun behind them... This raid was all over in five minutes.'

Crew member of British merchantman

average, were being sunk in the approaches to Britain's ports, despite using only swept channels. Altogether 29,000 tons of shipping were lost in October. By the end of November the figure reached 137,000 tons. Several East Coast harbours were closed and by mid-November 250 ships were cooped up in the Port of London or moored in the Thames estuary unable to approach London to discharge their cargoes.

On 19 November the skipper of a Danish merchantman, the *Canada*, had reported that the sinking of his ship off the British coast had been caused by a magnetic mine. Newspapers of the day suggested that a magnetic device was used to detonate the mine, to scotch the popular belief that a magnetic mine would be attracted to any ship that happened to be near it.

'Secret weapon'

Speculation of this kind was less than useful to Admiralty experts. They needed proof—after all, the mines were wreaking havoc and might be operating with some other mechanism. Perhaps they were triggered by sound waves, or by the increase in water pressure as a ship passed over them. Or maybe they had some, as yet undreamed of, mechanism invented by clever German scientists—the 'secret weapon' that everyone had heard of.

So as Ouvrey and Lewis approached the mine, they were fully aware of its significance—and that the mechanism they had to dismantle might not be magnetic but any one of several unknown possibilities.

Once the recovered mine reached HMS *Vernon*, a team of scientists and electricity experts worked round the clock to dismantle and analyse it. They discovered a 1128lb device containing a 660lb explosive charge. Made of aluminium alloy, it carried a device to release its parachute on splashdown. It also carried a device that detonated the mine if not correctly laid. When the mine landed, either on firm ground or on water, a timing device ran for 30 seconds. If, after this period, the weapon was not covered in 15ft of water, it would explode. Sinking in deep water as intended, a hydrostatic trigger operated and cut off the clock. Fifteen minutes later a second timing device operated the magnetic unit and the mine was live, with the explosive charge ready.

Clearly the Heinkel crew at Southend, in their haste to escape the gunfire, had failed to prepare the mines correctly, and they had not detonated.

Once properly laid, the magnetic mine was designed to lie dormant on the seabed until a ship passed within range. All metal ships carry a magnetic field of their own. Its strength depends on the method of construction, the direction relative to the poles in which the ship was lying while being built, and the latitude of the builder's yard.

The mine was activated by this magnetic field. The firing device consisted basically of a small magnetic needle, held in place by a spring. The ship's magnetism overcame the tension of the spring and forced the needle down, completing a circuit and detonating the mine.

Once scientists had dismantled and analysed the Shoeburyness mine, the job of designing devices to deal with these mines could begin.

Broadly, there were two possibilities. The first choice was to demagnetize individual ships. The most effective method of doing this was to fit the ship with a heavy coil of wire, wound round the hull level with the upper deck. An electric current, passed through this coil as the ship sailed, would produce a magnetic field, and if accurately designed would reduce a ship's magnetic signature to a sufficiently low level that it would not trigger the mine. This process was known as **degaussing.**

But a complete de-gaussing programme required 1500 miles of electrical cable every week, together with large numbers of trained technicians to calculate each ship's requirements. In addition the de-gaussing programme could not remain secret for long.

For small vessels a simpler system was available. The ship could be either 'wiped' or 'flashed'. In 'wiping' an electric cable was drawn upwards on ropes against the ship's side while a current passed through it. In 'flashing' a coil was wrapped round the ship while a current passed through it, rather like a temporary de-gaussing measure. Both processes 'neutralized' the ship's magnetic field, but had to be repeated every few months to be effective.

Wreaking Havoc

The disadvantage of all these measures was that they did nothing to de-activate the mines, which remained live and in position to destroy any unprotected ship sailing over them later.

A device was needed to produce a magnetic field of the kind a ship would generate, exploding the mines at a safe distance.

A most spectacular invention dreamed up to achieve this was a huge coil attached to the underside of a **Wellington** bomber. Inside the bomber a petrol-powered generator produced the current for the coil, and when the aircraft flew low over the magnetic mine, the magnetic field produced detonated the weapon. By the time the force of the explosion reached the aircraft height, the aircraft itself would theoretically have been carried away to safety by its own speed.

More than half the British ships sunk in November 1939 were victims of the magnetic mine. Out of a total of 50 ships, 27 (108,000 tons) were sunk by mines and 23 (66,000 tons) by U-boats and other warships. Each mine weighed 1,128lb, including 660lb of high explosive. It was made of a non-magnetic aluminium alloy.

The coil-equipped Wellington had mixed success. In one incident an aircraft flying at about 30ft exploded a mine, but the force of the explosion blew the escape hatches off the fuselage. The main drawback to this method was that the aircraft could work only over a narrow band, and it was difficult to record its path accurately.

Far more effective were the new surface minesweepers, often converted trawlers. De-gaussed for protection, they carried two lengths of floating electric cable, one 175 yards long, the other 750 yards long, each with an electrode at the end.

A spectacular invention

When a current was passed through them it created a magnetic field around the towed lines. A few seconds in every minutes proved enough, and the impulse was repeated when the end of the line reached the forward point of the cleared area. In a later development, known as the LL (double longtitudinal) minesweeper, two ships steamed together, each carrying its own tows. The impulses of electric current gave a magnetic area between the two pairs of tows of ten acres for each impulse, giving a wide carpet of swept seabed.

Naturally Germany's scientists continued to develop their mines, aiming to outwit British defensive measures. Some extremely ingenious refinements were introduced. They succeeded, for example, in increasing the sensitivity of the setting, so that ships were more likely to detonate the mines. But this also made the mines more sensitive to the magnetic field created by the minesweepers, so that mines could be swept over a larger area. They also introduced a magnetic switch which worked in reverse, so that ships with opposite polarity, such as those built in the southern hemisphere, would detonate the mine.

Ingenious devices

Probably the most ingenious system of all was one which delayed detonation until several ships had passed over the mine. The first few magnetic influences, including, it was hoped, those from any minesweeper, would have no effect. An unsuspecting ship steaming along a swept channel would then be caught.

Ultimately the acoustic mine, detonated by the sound of a ship's engines, was introduced. For a time it baffled mine defence personnel. But they were able to counter it by towing a noise -making machine—a road drill vibrating in a sound box—to detonate the mine at a safe distance from the threatened ship.

But this was the shape of things to come. In November 1939 there was still, around Britain's East Coast, a grim display of ships' masts and superstructures sticking out of the water at low tide to tell its own story of the effectiveness of the magnetic mine.

There was never any complete answer, but in the course of that cold and dangerous day on Shoeburyness sands, the initiative was at last won for the Royal Navy. For Ouvrey and Lewis there was a **DSO** each and **DSM**'s went to their assistants Baldwin and Vearncombe.

War Notes

BORDE: 2014-ton mine destructor. Launched 1921, originally a collier owned by Stephenson Clarkes of Borde Hill, Sussex. Requisitioned Oct 1939 for naval use. Guns: 2 × 12dpr AA, 2 × 2pdr AA, 2 × MG. The first of a small class of mine destructors fitted with large electromagnets.

DEGAUSSING: removal or neutralization of a ship's normal magnetic field by making it the core of an electromagnet of opposite polarity. A bar magnet can be demagnetized by enclosing it in coils carrying current of the correct strength. To demagnetize a ship, it was surrounded by cables carrying current. Magnetism is measured in gauss units—hence removal of field is called 'degaussing'.

DSM: Distinguished Service Medal. British award conferred on officers and men in the Navy for courage in war service. Initiated by King George V in 1914. Medal with blue and white riband.

DSO: Distinguished Service Order. British award conferred on officers of any of the armed forces for distinguished war service. Initiated by Queen Victoria in 1886. Badge consists of gold and white cross with red and blue riband.

HEINKEL 115: twin-engined float seaplane for general purpose marine work. First flew Aug 1937. In service 1939. Dimensions: 56.7 × 3.1ft. Engines: 960hp BMW 132K 9-cylinder radials. Top speed: 186mph at 3280ft; 180 mph cruise at 6560ft. Range: 1550 miles. Ceiling: 16,950ft. Guns: 2 × 7.9mm MG (flexible mounts, 1 nose, 1 dorsal). Bomb-load: 1 × 2000lb bomb or 2 × 1100lb aerial mines. Crew: 3.

LEWIS, Roger Curzon: British mine expert. Naval cadet Sept 1926. Sub-lieutenant March1930, Lieutenant April 1931. Joined *Vernon* Oct 1938. Lieutenant-Commander April 1939.

OUVREY, John Garnault Delahaize: British mine expert, b. Sept 1896, Lymington. Joined Royal Naval College, Osborne in 1909, Dartmouth 1911. Went to sea aboard battleship *Mars* as midshipman 1914. Aboard battlecruiser *Tiger* during Battle of Jutland (31 May 1916). Sub-lieutenant and mining officer light cruiser *Inconstant* during Battle of Heligoland Nov 1917. Lieutenant Sept 1918. Went to *Vernon* 1921. Lieutenant-Commander 1926, specializing in mines and torpedoes. Went to Australia 1928-30 to run torpedo school. Aboard battlecruiser *Repulse* 1930. Returned to *Vernon* 1932 as specialist in sea mines. Worked on development of British magnetic mines.

SHOEBURYNESS: low promontory 4 miles E. of Southend. Pop: 6720 (1931). Marks the end of the northerly shore of the Thames estuary, opposite Sheerness.

SOUTHEND: resort 35 miles from centre of London, south facing on Thames estuary (at this point some 4 miles wide). Pop: 120,115 (1931).

VERNON: shore establishment of Royal Navy at Portsmouth Harbour. In 1939 it was Torpedo School and Experimental Establishment, with 127 officers and 47 civilian scientists and technicians.

Vickers Ltd

WELLINGTON: RAF twin-engine bomber converted to minesweeping with a 45ft diameter concentrically wound aluminium coil. Cover name of DWI meaning First Directional Wireless Installation. First flight on 21 Dec, with Barnes Wallis (Wellington designer) aboard. No 1 General Recce Unit formed 15 Dec and first firing trial with mechanism of Shoeburyness mine 3 Jan 1940. First mine exploded 8 Jan, 24 dealt with by May 1940.

DECEMBER 1939

...FEW COULD HAVE GUESSED, only three months ago, that by December the war would be fought out in places as far apart as the River Plate and the frozen wastes of Finland. The death of the pocket battleship Graf Spee, the first heroic successes of the fighting Finns, cheered the British as they made ready for the war's first Christmas. For Stalin, 60 this month, there was less cause for joy...

1st: Helsinki bombed.
2nd: Finns withdraw to Mannerheim Line. Finland appeals to League of Nations.
3rd: Minefield laid off E. Sweden. Swedish Army reserves called up.
4th: George VI visits W Front. USSR rejects Swedish mediation offer.
5th: Finns bomb Murmansk air base.
6th: Russians complete takeover of 7 Gulf of Finland islands, reach Mannerheim Line.
7th: Allied subs escort 3 N. Atlantic convoys.
8th: Polish squadrons for RAF.
9th: First British soldier killed Cpl Thomas Priday.
10th: First Canadian troop convoy sails for Britain.
11th: USSR ceasefire urged by League of Nations.
12th: Finns get upper hand in L. Ladoga battles.
13th: Battle of the River Plate. Sub *Salmon* damages 2 German cruisers.
14th: USSR expelled from League of Nations.
15th: Chamberlain visits W. Front.
16th: Finns repel Russian attacks on Mannerheim Line.
17th: *Graf Spee* scuttled off Montevideo. RAF Empire air training agreement signed at Ottawa.
18th: Disastrous RAF raid on Wilhelmshaven naval base.
19th: Allied Supreme War Council's 4th meeting, in Paris.
20th: German Infantry Assault and Tank Battle awards instituted.
21st: France publishes 'Yellow Book' on pre-war events.
22nd: Ministry of Economic Warfare announces that 870,000 tons of German goods seized since 3 Sept. Stalin's 60th birthday.
23rd: Finns counter-attack on Karelian Isthmus.
24th: Rail links re-established between two occupied zones of Poland.
25th: Over 30 Finnish towns bombed.
26th: US protest against R. Plate battle infringement of 'Security Zone'.
27th: Viipuri citizens evacuated.
28th: U30 torpedoes battleship *Barham*.
29th: Finnish ski-troops destroy parts of Leningrad-Murmansk railway.
30th: Russian Gen Stern to command N. of L. Ladoga.
31st: Hitler's New Year Proclamation to Nazi Party.

MAN OF HONOUR

To the citizens of Montevideo, capital of Uruguay and busy seaport on the estuary of the River Plate, the departure of a ship from the harbour was an event so commonplace as normally to pass virtually unnoticed. But on the afternoon of Sunday, 17 December 1939, some 750,000 people turned out to watch one particular ship as she prepared to leave: the German pocket battleship Admiral Graf Spee.

Outside the port three British cruisers, HMS **Ajax,** HMS **Achilles** (crewed mainly by the Royal New Zealand Navy) and HMS *Cumberland*, were waiting for her: they were keen to finish off the job begun four days earlier by *Ajax* and *Achilles* in company with HMS **Exeter,** when *Graf Spee*, damaged by shellfire from the British ships, had been forced to take refuge in **Montevideo,** a **neutral port.**

Everyone watching that afternoon knew that the German commander had run out of time. The Uruguayan authorities would not allow him to remain in Montevideo: he seemingly had only two options, to leave harbour and fight it out with the waiting British ships or to hand over his ship and her crew for internment in Uruguay. It seemed that Kapitan zur See Hans **Langsdorff** had chosen the first alternative, for **Admiral Graf Spee** was now apparently making ready for sea. The watching crowds waited for the mighty naval battle that would surely ensue.

Graf Spee's active career had, up to this point, been short but successful. On the outbreak of war she was assigned the role of surface raider, to sink or take as prize merchantmen registered under the flag of Britain or Britain's allies. On 30 September she sighted her first victim.

The **pocket battleship's** reconnaissance aircraft soon confirmed the sighting, SS *Clement*, a 5051-ton British steamer. As the pocket battleship moved to intercept, the merchant ship's crew took to the boats. A German boarding party took the *Clement's* skipper, Captain F. C. P. Harris, and

'My God, it's a pocket battleship!'

Lt-Cdr R E Washbourn, HMS *Achilles*

Since the beginning of the war *Graf Spee* and her sister ship *Deutschland* had been active in the Atlantic. *Graf Spee* destroyed merchantmen *Clement, Newton Beech, Ashlea, Huntsman, Trevanion, Africa Shell, Doric Star, Streonshalh* and *Tairoa*—an impressive total of 50,089 tons.

his chief engineer, Mr Bryant, aboard *Graf Spee* at pistol point.

When Harris arrived at the bridge, Captain Langsdorff saluted him: 'I am sorry, Captain, I will have to sink your ship. It is war . . . I believe you have destroyed your confidential papers? It is the usual thing.'

Graf Spee's men then brought chairs for Harris and Bryant, sat them down, and announced: 'We are going to fire a torpedo.'

At a range of about half a mile, they fired a torpedo from a starboard aft deck tube. It passed 50ft ahead of *Clement*. Langsdorff was not pleased.

A second torpedo missed by 25ft.

'We are going to use the guns,' an officer said. They handed Harris and Bryant cotton wool to plug their ears, and hammered away with the 5.9in guns. Some shots hit. Some fell short. And after 25 rounds the steamer was still afloat.

At last, they opened up with the heavier guns, and *Clement* finally sank.

From then on *Graf Spee* steamed quietly round those springtime southern waters like a marauding highwayman, stopping and sinking British ships where she found them. On 5 October *Newton Beach* went down, 4651 tons; two days later *Ashlea*, 4222 tons. On 10 October she sank the *Huntsman* of 8196 tons, then south to sink three more ships, followed by a brief foray into the Indian Ocean where the tiny tanker *African Shell* went to the bottom off Lourenco Marques. Back into the South Atlantic and by 7 December *Graf Spee* had disposed of nine ships totalling 50,089 tons.

Because Britain relied so heavily on imported goods, secure shipping lanes were vital to her. She had 3000 merchant ships plying the world's trade routes, and could not allow these lines of supply to be disrupted by the activities of a German surface raider like *Graf Spee*.

Faced with these realities, from the moment of the first sinking the Royal Navy spared no efforts to track down and destroy the surface raider responsible. On 2 October, as soon as signals began to arrive reporting the sinking of the *Clement*, senior staff gathered in the Upper War Room at the Admiralty to thrash out a plan. They decided, with French help, to form eight hunting groups, each big enough to tackle an armoured ship of the *Deutschland* class, and spread them out across the Atlantic and Indian Ocean from North America to Ceylon (Sri Lanka).

Some of the groups were comparatively weak.

'To the memory of brave men of the sea from their comrades of the British Merchant Service.'

Wreath to *Graf Spee's* dead from her former prisoners

But, as the Admiralty optimistically promised one group commander: 'A weaker force, if not able to effect immediate destruction may, by resolute attack, be able to cripple an opponent sufficiently to ensure a certain subsequent location and destruction by other forces.'

On 8 December the hunting group Force G, consisting of the cruisers *Ajax*, *Exeter*, *Achilles* and *Cumberland*, deployed in the South Atlantic. Late that afternoon a wireless operator in *Ajax* picked up a signal that a merchantman, *Doric Star*, had been attacked on 2 December by a pocket battleship off St Helena. Early the next morning a second signal arrived. Another ship had been attacked, 170 miles away from *Doric Star*.

Defence of the River Plate

In the chart room of *Ajax*, the group commander, Commodore Henry **Harwood,** sat down with his officers for a conference. Harwood pulled across to him a signal pad and began to score it with straight lines which converged where the sinkings had been reported. Each of the three lines led to a point—and a specified time—where Harwood estimated the raider might show up next to prey on the shipping lines. Rio de Janeiro on 12 December; River Plate on the 13th; Falkland Islands on the 14th.

It was time for Harwood to choose. And his choice was unerring: 'I decided that the Plate, with its larger number of ships and its very valuable grain and meat trade, was the vital area to defend.'

At 1.15pm local time on 3 December, he ordered his ships to concentrate off Montevideo—*Achilles* to come in from Rio, *Exeter* from the Falkland Islands. *Cumberland* was to go to Falklands for a self-refit, but remain ready to sail on half power from two shafts. The three ships came together for the first time at 10am on 10 December, and waited for the pocket battleship to arrive.

Early in the morning of 13 December *Graf Spee's* lookouts sighted the masts of distant ships. Hoping for further prizes, Langsdorff ordered the crew to action stations and proceeded towards the unidentified ships with all speed. It soon became apparent, however, that the ships ahead were no merchantmen. They were identified as British warships, and HMS *Exeter*, a heavy cruiser, was specifically recognized. The other two ships were thought to be destroyers. A pocket battleship should be able to overcome a force of this strength, so Langsdorff held course. Although his orders were to avoid enemy warships whenever possible, Langsdorff argued that a force like this would in all probability be guarding a convoy of merchant ships—a prize too tempting to miss. In the event he was wrong, and he was to pay for his mistake.

As the distance between the opposing forces grew less, the two ships accompanying *Exeter* began to look more and more like light cruisers, and so it proved to be. Now Langsdorff knew exactly what he was up against. Although *Graf Spee's* weapons were significantly more powerful than those of the British ships he could make only 26 knots compared with the British ships 32. If the British cruisers wanted a fight, *Graf Spee* could scarcely avoid it.

At 6.17am, at a range of almost 12 miles, *Graf Spee* opened fire with a full broadside on *Exeter*. Within minutes *Exeter* replied and *Ajax* and *Achilles* joined the action.

It was not an equal fight. In terms of tonnage, the pocket battleship came close to matching any two of the British ships—12,100 tons compared with 8385 tons for *Exeter*, 7030 tons for *Achilles*, and 6985 tons for *Ajax*. And in firepower she outclassed them by a wide margin. Her armament consisted of six 11in guns and eight 5.9in guns. The most powerful cruiser, *Exeter*, packed a punch of only six 8in and four 4in guns. *Ajax* and *Achilles* were equipped with only eight 6in guns apiece—barely more than *Graf Spee's* secondary armament. A broadside from *Graf Spee's* 11in guns weighed 4140lb, compared with *Exeter's* 1600lb, and 900lb for each of the other two cruisers.

Perhaps worst of all, there was a wide discrepancy in their effective ranges—17 miles compared with only about 9 miles—so that *Graf Spee* could hit the British ships while staying out of range of their guns. If Langsdorff had exploited his range advantage he might have picked off the British ships one at a time.

Instead he divided his efforts. *Exeter* suffered the first casualties. An 11in shell landed close to the ship. The splinters killed two men and started a fire. A second shell passed right through the ship, crossing the sick bay on its way, and went out of the other side without exploding.

Exeter retires

In all, shells from *Graf Spee's* powerful 11in guns scored seven hits on the cruiser. The last of them was the worst. It sliced through the ship's side, penetrated four bulkheads, and exploded above the 4in magazine and torpedo gunner's store. The explosion blew a hole in the lower deck 16ft by 14ft. It started fierce fires in the switchboard and forward dynamo rooms, splinters severed many of the ship's electrical cables, and water flooded into the lower steering position.

Almost all of the ship's communication systems were put out of action, and more than 50 men had lost their lives. *Exeter* retired from the action when she could no longer fire her guns.

Harwood, in *Ajax*, could see that *Graf Spee* was well placed to finish off *Exeter*, so he turned *Ajax* and *Achilles* towards the pocket battleship to draw her fire. The ploy succeeded. *Ajax* fired four torpedoes at 7.24am. One missed the pocket battleship by yards but then the light cruiser took a shell hit that put two turrets out of action. With the range closing rapidly to only 8000 yards, the British cruisers scored several hits, but without doing any serious damage, so far as they could see. As Harwood said plaintively: 'We might just as well be bombarding her with a lot of bloody snowballs.'

The funeral of *Graf Spee's* dead. Langsdorff correctly gives the navy salute—the Nazi salute was not to be officially adopted by the navy until 1943.

Harwood's comment, however, was less than accurate. His cruisers may have lacked the firepower to put shells through *Graf Spee's* armoured hide, but they landed at least 17 hits. Damage to the ship's equipment was extensive.

Langsdorff decided not to go on. 'We must run into port,' he told his navigating officer. 'The ship is no longer seaworthy for the North Atlantic.'

So *Graf Spee* turned away, and the British sailors, expecting more punishment from those mighty guns, were astonished to see her steaming off at high speed to the west. *Ajax* and *Achilles* stayed in contact throughout the day, and from time to time each side loosed off a couple of salvos of shellfire.

Shortly after midnight, *Graf Spee* entered Montevideo Roads, and anchored in the temporary haven of a neutral harbour.

Langsdorff knew that he was entitled to stay in Montevideo harbour for 24 hours to make repairs. That privilege was enshrined in international law. If he stayed beyond that period, he could find his ship and crew interned in neutral Uruguay for the rest of the war. Nevertheless he was also entitled to request an extension, and after inspecting the damage to his ship he and the German Ambassador, Dr Otto Langmann, put in an appeal to be allowed to stay for 14 days.

The Uruguayan authorities considered his request, examined the ship, and said he could stay for another 72 hours, until 8pm on Sunday, 17 December.

Langsdorff's other problem was to keep Germany in touch with his situation. Grand Admiral Erich **Raeder** and Hitler discussed the prospects of a breakout through the lurking British fleet.

Finally, Raeder telegrammed instructions to Langsdorff. He should try to break out of Montevideo. If that was impossible, he should scuttle the ship in the Plate estuary. He must at all costs avoid letting the ship be interned by the Uruguayans. They could never guarantee their own neutrality, and the ship might pass into Allied hands.

The British were also busy during that period. Their nearest battleship reinforcements were five days steaming from Montevideo. But there was nothing to stop them mounting a gigantic bluff. And at the suggestion of the Admiralty, the BBC reported that the battlecruiser *Renown* and aircraft carrier *Ark Royal* had left Cape Town on 12 December. This would give them time to assemble off Montevideo. *Renown* was one of the three British ships that could both outrun and outgun *Graf Spee*.

When his own gunnery officer mistakenly reported sighting battleships lying off the Plate estuary, Langsdorff concluded that he would have no chance of a breakout through the mighty fleet the British had now assembled.

So Langsdorff's range of choices was reduced to

Graf Spee **burns after being scuttled.**

War Notes

ACHILLES: British 7030-ton Leander-class light cruiser, sister ship of *Ajax*. Laid down June 1931, launched Sept 1932, completed Oct 1933. Dimensions: 554 × 552 × 16ft. Powered by 4-shaft geared steam turbines totalling 72,000shp giving 32.5 knots. Guns: 8 × 6in (4 turrets), 8 × 4in AA (4 mounts), 8 × 2pdr AA (2 mounts), 12 × 0.5in MG (3 mounts). Torpedo tubes: 8 × 21in (2 mounts). I Seafox floatplane. Armour: 2–4in main belt, 2in deck, 1in turret. Crew: 550 ratings, 36 officers. At the River Plate she was part of the Royal New Zealand Navy with 327 New Zealanders on board. Her commander was Capt Edward Parry. Casualties: 4 killed. Fired 1241 6in shells.

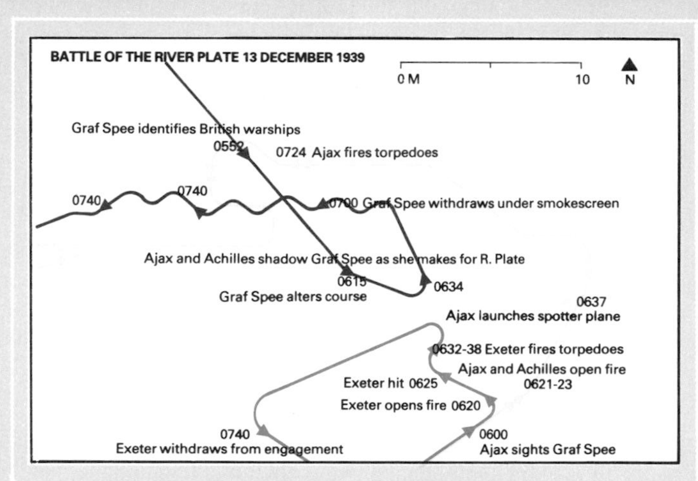

ADMIRAL GRAF SPEE: German 12,100-ton armoured ship (Panzerschiff) or 'pocket battleship'. Laid down Oct 1932, launched June 1934, completed Jan 1936. Dimensions: 617 × 71.2 × 22ft. Powered by eight 9-cyl diesels driving 2 shafts. Max power 56,800 bhp giving 26 knots. Guns: 6 × 11in (2 turrets), 8 × 5.9in (single mounts) 6 × 4.1in anti-aircraft (3 mounts), 8 × 37mm AA (4 mounts), 10 × 20mm AA (single mounts). Torpedo tubes: 8 × 21in (2 mounts). 1 Arado 196 seaplane plus parts for a second. Armour: waterline belt 4in, deck 0.83in, turret 0.5in (rear) to 5.5in (face). Crew: 1124. Named after Vice-Admiral von Spee, victorious German commander at the Battle of Coronel, 1 Nov 1914. Sister ships: *Deutschland* (returned to Germany in Nov 1939 after sinking 2 ships in N. Atlantic) and *Admiral Scheer*. Harwood's squadron thought the *Spee* was the *Scheer* until her name could be read. She fired 414 11in and 457 secondary armament shells.

AJAX: British 6985-ton Leander-class light cruiser. Sister ship of *Achilles*. Laid down Feb 1933, launched March 1934, completed June 1935. Dimensions 554 × 55.7 × 15.5ft. Machinery, weapons, armour and crew as for *Achilles*. She had 2 Seafox floatplanes, one of which was launched under fire for gunnery spotting. At River Plate commanded by Capt Charles Woodhouse. Cmdre Harwood's flagship for the battle. Casualties: 7 killed, 57 wounded. Fired 823 6in shells. She was hit by 2 11in shells.

IWM

EXETER: British 8390-ton York-class cruiser. Laid down Aug 1928, launched July 1929, completed May 1931. Dimensions: 575 × 58 × 17ft. Powered by 4-shaft geared turbines. 80,000shp giving 32 knots. Guns: 6 × 8in (3 turrets), 4 × 4in AA (4 mounts), 2 × 2pdr AA (two mounts). Torpedo tubes: 6 × 21in (2 mounts). 2 Walrus seaplanes. Armour: 2–3in main belt, 2in deck, 1.5–2in turrets. Crew: 574 ratings, 42 officers. Cmdre Harwood's flagship until 28 Oct when she proceeded Falklands for refit, returning to River Plate area 12 Dec. Commanded by Capt Frederick S. Bell. Casualties: 61 killed. Fired over 193 8in shells, scoring 3 hits.

HARWOOD, Henry Harwood: British admiral, b. 1888. Educated HMS *Britannia.* Midshipman 1904 Lieutenant 1908. Torpedo officer in cruiser *Sutlej* and battleship *Royal Sovereign* 1914–18. Commander 1921. Captain 1928. Commanded *Warwick* and 9th Destroyer Division 1929. Imperial Defence College 1931. Flag Captain cruiser *London* 1932–4. RN Staff College 1934–6. Commodore South American Division (hunting group G) aboard *Exeter* 1936–9. Promoted Rear Admiral and awarded KCB after River Plate action.

LANGSDORFF, Hans: Kapitän zur See German Navy, b. 1894. Joined Imperial Navy 1912. Sub-Lieutenant torpedo officer aboard light cruiser *Medusa.* Captain of minesweeper *M36* and later *M76* 1914–18. Lt 1917. Lt-Cdr 1922. Became adjutant to and confidante of Minister of Defence, Kurt von Schleicher, 1932. Joined *Graf Spee* as Staff Officer to C-in-C German Fleet, Adm Carls, 1937. CO *Graf Spee* 1938.

MONTEVIDEO: capital and sea port of Uruguay on N. bank of River Plate and 130 miles E. of Buenos Aires. Population over 750,000. Uruguay's only industrial centre and base for S. Atlantic fishing fleets.

NEUTRAL PORT: the Hague Convention of 1907 permitted a damaged warship of a belligerent nation to enter the port of a neutral nation for 24 hours in order to make herself seaworthy. She was not permitted to re-arm or repair weaponry in such a port. The 24-hour period could be extended by appeal on grounds of severity of damage or 'stress of weather'.

Fox Photos

POCKET BATTLESHIP (Panzerschiff): the Treaty of Versailles 1919 prevented Germany from building warships of more than 10,000 tons, and restricted main guns to 11in or less. The intention was to confine German builders to ships of pre-dreadnought design which were slow (max speed around 18 knots). Germany's brilliant solution was the pocket battleship: weight saved by (a) diesel engines instead of steam turbines, (b) welded hull and (c) reduced armour allowed heavy guns and good speed. Also, 10,000-ton weight restriction was deliberately exceeded by about 15%. The design was perfected before Hitler came to power. Germany had 3 such ships: *Deutschland, Admiral Scheer* and *Admiral Graf Spee.*

RAEDER, Erich: Grand Admiral, C-in-C German Navy, b. 1876. Educated Naval Academy, Kiel. Served in Kaiser Wilhelm II's yacht *Hohenzollern.* Commander 1911. Survived sinking of battle-cruiser *Lützow*, Battle of Jutland 1916. Captain cruiser *Köln* 1918. Vice-Admiral 1925. As Chief of Naval Staff 1928 knew Treaty of Versailles violated by design of pocket battleships. Appointed C-in-C Navy 1935. Grand Admiral 1939. Raeder had planned for war in 1944 with a large German surface fleet to match the RN as in 1914–18. Instead he could use his big ships only as raiders.

one. On Sunday afternoon he transferred the greater part of his crew to another boat, broke out the Nazi ensign from his foremast and mainmast, and *Graf Spee* put out under her own engines from Montevideo. Some minutes later, she ran gently aground in the mud flats, and a specially picked crew set the fuses to explosive charges. *Graf Spee* was about to be scuttled. The crowds watching from the shore were to be denied the great battle they were expecting, but they would soon witness the end of a powerful warship.

At 8.54pm the charges detonated. Flames shot high into the air, competing with the deep red glow of the setting sun. The magazine exploded. Debris flew out in showers, and the great structure of the mainmast crumpled into a useless pile. The ship settled on to the muddy bottom, with the remains of her superstructure poking out above the surface.

For the British, the gain was enormous. They were able to draw in their hunting groups from across the oceans, and put the ships to more vital tasks than scouting the seas for the surface raider. They also sent a radar expert, Mr L. Bainbridge Bell, to examine the wreck of *Graf Spee*. He bravely climbed the rickety and badly listing mast-head, and investigated the gunnery directing radar installation at the top. It was a fine intelligence coup. The British also managed to buy *Graf Spee* through a Uruguayan middle-man for £20,000, ostensibly for scrap. The ship yielded still more secrets, and details of the transaction audits outcome are still locked away in the Admiralty.

Langsdorff and his crew sailed to Buenos Aires to be interned by the Argentinians. Langsdorff wrote his thoughts in a letter to the German Ambassador in Buenos Aires. 'I alone bear the responsibility for scuttling the pocket battleship *Admiral Graf Spee*. I am happy to pay with my life for any possible reflection on the honour of the flag. I shall face my fate with firm faith in the cause and the future of the nation and of my Führer.' Prophetic words, soon to be realized.

'I am happy to pay with my life for any possible reflection on the honour of the flag.'

Captain Hans Langsdorff

The final act

But the letter failed to give any real clue why Langsdorff had chosen to scuttle the ship rather than fight it out in a break for Buenos Aires. Perhaps he felt an explanation unnecessary. Some have accused him of being afraid to take on the powerful ships he thought awaited him, others suggest that his allegiance to the Nazis was suspect and that his heart was not in the war. It is more likely, however, that he simply made a sensible decision based on the information available to him at the time. In doing what he did he saved the lives of his crew.

All the evidence suggests that Langsdorff was a man of honour who was acutely aware of his responsibilities to those subordinate to him. When he captured and sank his first prize, the *Clement*, for example, he was most apologetic to the British captain. 'I am sorry, but war is war,' he had said. And nothing seemed to give him more pride than the fact that in sinking nine ships not a single life had been lost. Then when he handed over his prisoners to the captain of his supply ship, the *Altmark*, he sent one of his own officers with them as escort to protect them.

And when Langsdorff came to his final act, he demonstrated that his loyalty was perhaps to a concept older than the Nazi regime. In a modest hotel room in Buenos Aires he spread out on the floor the flag of the same Imperial Navy he had served all his working life, and put a pistol bullet through his temple.

Captain Langsdorff's crew spent their internment in three places. First they were held at the Naval Arsenal in Buenos Aires; in April 1940 they were transferred to the island of Martin Garcia, north of Buenos Aires in the Plate estuary, and finally they were moved, in 1944, to Sierra de la Ventana, a town in the south of Buenos Aires province. During the period a good many of them managed to escape. By April 1940 as many as 18 officers had made their getaway.

The end of the story came after the war had ended. On 16 February 1946 the British troopship *Highland Monarch* carrying 800 former crew members of *Graf Spee* left Buenos Aires harbour bound for Germany. The cruiser which accompanied *Highland Monarch* on the voyage must have stirred the memories of her German passengers —she was HMS *Ajax*.

FIRST WARTIME CHRISTMAS

Any front-line soldier hoping that Christmas 1939 would offer a sentimental re-run of Christmas in the trenches of 1914–18 was to be disappointed.

There were no games of football between the opposing sides in no-man's-land. No strains of *Stille nacht, heilige nacht* wafted through the frosty air from German trenches.

A bitter, freezing fog rimmed the orchards of the Second Western Front. French soldiers, though in no mood to fight, were in no mood to fraternize either—recent news of attacks on unarmed French fishing boats had soured any lingering mood of goodwill towards Germans.

It was cold, miserably cold. Nature was backing up Man's efforts to make this a bad winter—the coldest in 45 years. 'I don't know how the men keep warm in weather like this,' wrote one observer. 'I suppose they don't . . . everything you touch, metal, stone, sacking is numbing to the fingers.' RAF plane crews had the worst of it; out in all weathers, lacking even canvas hangars.

But, snug in their Maginot and Siegfried Lines, off duty soldiers made the best of it. The Germans unwrapped their small parcels prepared by the Band of German Maidens back home. While, up above, the Feldgrauen kept watch on no-man's-land, German troops below gathered round the accordion and sang: 'My homeland, my homeland, I think of you today. Oh my beloved homeland, where life was glad and gay.'

If their songs did include 'Silent night, holy night' the German press made no mention of the fact. Truly dedicated Nazis, like the members of the SS, had dispensed with Christmas altogether—and celebrated their pagan festival of Yuletide on 21 December. For, among long-term Nazi plans was the abolition of Christianity.

'We do not follow Jesus'

Nativity plays were banned in German schools this Christmas. Though sentimental images in picture magazines showed toddlers gazing at a Christmas star, Santa Claus riding his reindeer and, on one jolly front cover, a helmeted SS trooper with presents and a Christmas tree slung from his rifle—there was no mention of the child born to a Jewish mother 1935 years ago. Today infants of the Third Reich lisped a popular Hitler Jugend song: 'We do not follow Jesus. Horst Wessel is our friend.' Wessel, a brawling young thug who had been beaten to death by communists some years previously, had become top of the Nazi hero list for the young. (Details of his drop-out, garret life-style with a retired prostitute were glossed over.)

Yet, despite the Party line, churches were well attended at Christmas. Back in 1933, Hitler had scored one of his most notable diplomatic triumphs by signing a Concordat with the Roman Catholic Church: support from Catholics (who were a sizeable political force) remained essential. In return for freedom of worship, the Church now exhorted soldiers to be ready to sacrifice their lives in obedience to Hitler.

There was a Christmas message too, from Britain's King George VI. It is still remembered as a moving expression of national unity. The shy king, whose stutter made public speech a painful test of courage, spoke for the country in a way that Chamberlain could never do. 'I believe from my heart,' he said, 'that the cause which binds together my peoples and our gallant and faithful Allies is the cause of Christian civilization. On no other basis can a true civilization be built.'

Every British soldier on the Western Front had a personal Christmas card from his monarch. In addition, as a member of the best provisioned British army in history, he enjoyed a Christmas dinner consisting of hot roast pork, potatoes, green vegetables, plum pudding, beer, coffee, brandy or rum. The RAF waded through cream of tomato soup, fried fillet of sole and lemon, roast turkey, roast pork and apple sauce, roast potatoes, cauliflower, Christmas pudding and brandy sauce.

While the soldiers were eating, or serenading local French cottagers with Christmas carols, German civilians in Berlin were having a less than uproarious time. 'This year it's a bleak Christmas' noted American journalist William Shirer. 'Few presents, spartan food, the menfolk away, the streets blacked out, the shutters and curtains drawn tight.'

The British at home managed rather better. They had endured four months of blackout, evacuation, closed theatres and cinemas. For Christmas, some restrictions were raised and others neatly circumvented. Official dogma was that evacuees should stay away in the country: Britain's railway companies ran carefully timed 'excursion specials', notionally to take townsfolk to the shires, in fact timed to bring evacuees back home to town.

In town, theatres reopened to phenominal business. Thirty London stages supported shows ranging from *Dick Whittington* to *Romeo and Juliet*. In the country at large, 80 touring companies and 30 repertory theatres relit the torch of culture with a flourish. For servicemen in town there were the usual temptations—and opportunities for avoiding them. Lemonade, coffee and

Boris Paschkoff/Time-Life/Colorific!

French General Vieillard toasts Christmas Day with champagne on the Maginot Line. For the children of the unemployed in Britain (inset) conditions were more austere.

First snow on the Western Front. A British Bren gun team in 20° of frost.

cake was available at the 'Me and my Girl' club in darkest Chelsea. The Rev Christopher Cheshire provided his members with a decorous, but brief evening: the club closed at 9.45. Dance halls and pubs were crowded as Britain made the best of the Phoney War's only Christmas: few expected the New Year would prove to be an easy one.

On Christmas Day itself, no guns fired on the Western Front. Adolf Hitler had his vegetarian Christmas dinner at a field aerodrome with men of the Luftwaffe then toured pillboxes on the Siegfried Line, distributing presents. 'He is surrounded completely by our love,' German Army Commander-in-Chief Walther von Brauchitsch reminded his troops. Sentimentality of the season finally reaches even the Führer: he retires, as usual, to his Berghof and Eva Braun snapshots him at a children's party, smiling distantly as Josef Goebbels' and Martin Bormann's infants frolic round him.

Another snapshot survives of him in the twilight of this year: pouring molten lead into water from a spoon. According to this ancient New Year custom, the shape of the future can be guessed from the twisted forms produced. Hitler's expression seems thoughtful.

WINTER WAR

It was Sunday afternoon, a quiet November day. For the handful of duty guards at the border post on the Rajajoki river, snaking across the narrow neck of land that linked southern Finland to the great land mass of the Soviet Union to the southeast, it was mindlessly tedious.

It was a poor apology for a river at this point: more of a stream, just 12ft across. An old stone bridge almost in ruins joined Mainila village on the Russian bank to Jappila, its Finnish counterpart. A log cabin on the Finnish side offered warmth and refuge to the guards waiting to come on duty.

It was a sensitive area, so sensitive that no weapons other than small arms were allowed within sight of the border. Nobody wanted to provoke a Russian reaction.

Without warning the crisp afternoon air was shattered by an artillery shot. Then another shot, from a different gun. And a third. Then more.

The Finnish guard turned out, alerted—and puzzled, because there were no hits on the Finnish side—then relaxed. Probably the Russians were doing some target practice. The patrolman, Jokela, and the other guards logged their observations, and for good measure drew a sketch map. It showed cross bearings locating the firing point just over a mile away on the Russian side of the border. Then they went back and thought no more about it.

In Moscow things were different. Foreign Minister Vyacheslav Molotov summoned the senior Finnish representative, Yrjo Koskinen. Finnish troops had fired across the border at Mainila, the Russians insisted. Four Russian soldiers had been killed, nine others wounded.

'Then we shall go and investigate,' Koskinen replied. 'That is the usual procedure.'

No, they told him. It was too late for that. The damage had been done. They had been warned before about the dangers of concentrating troops on the border. Now they should pull back 15 miles, to avoid a repetition of the incident.

The Finns offered to negotiate a mutual withdrawal. And they would join the Russians in a joint inquiry.

But this was not a matter for negotiation, and on 28 November Molotov formally rejected the Finnish proposals. **Finland's** refusal to withdraw troops was provocative, he told them, so the Soviet Union was renouncing the non-aggression pact between the two countries.

One day later, the Kremlin broke off diplomatic relations with Finland.

On 30 November Soviet tanks and troops poured across the Finnish border, on a front stretching from the Karelian Isthmus in the south to the

Barents Sea in the Arctic circle. Antonov and Tupolov bombers raided Helsinki, the Finnish capital and other towns in the south.

The road that lead to this unequal but heroic war had been long and marked by many complicated turnings.

After her own civil war of 1918–21, Russia had recognized Finnish neutrality and had set up machinery for settling disputes. But in the 1930s both the machinery and the neutrality came under severe pressure. The Soviet Union talked of possible German aggression against Finland. And because Finland was strategically placed between German and Soviet territory, the Soviet Union wanted to support Finland in resisting the Germans. 'Support' began with economic aid. It progressed rapidly in 1938 to include demands for a Soviet airbase in the Gulf of Finland, and Russian offers of help with fortifying and controlling the Aaland Islands in the Gulf.

Finland preferred to hang on to its neutrality and declined all forms of aid.

In April 1939, Germany intervened, also offering the Finns a non-aggression pact.

Finland rejected that too. The only voice of dissent was that of the great Marshal Karl **Mannerheim.** Tall, handsome, aristocratic, and an enemy of the new Bolshevik Russia, 72-year-old Mannerheim was in poor health. But he was still Supreme Commander of Finland's defence forces, and as victor in the civil war still a powerful influence on the Finnish leadership. Mannerheim said it was unrealistic to turn down offers from Russia and Germany in the name of a precarious neutrality Finland had not the strength to protect.

He was right, and in the end Finland was squeezed out. The two great neighbours themselves signed a non-aggression pact. One of its terms specified that Finland was now part of the Soviet sphere of influence.

In October there was more pressure to accept Soviet bases on Finnish soil as the Baltic States were doing. A request came to move the border on the Karelian Isthmus 75 miles back into Finland so that Leningrad would have more territory for defence. Finland refused, and negotiations dragged on. After one meeting at which the two sides could reach no agreement, the Finnish delegation left the Kremlin with a parting remark from Molotov: 'We civilians can see no further in the matter; now it is the turn of the military to have their say.'

It took three weeks of November for the Russians to prepare for war. Their preparations included building some excellent roads up to the border to carry their tanks. Then all that remained was to provoke the conflict. When everything was ready

The Finns were well prepared for the bitterly cold weather. They added petrol to the standard issue gun-oil to stop their weapons freezing up and used an alcohol and glycerine anti-freeze in the machine-gun cooling systems.

Fox Photos

'The enemy does not engage in open battle. Hidden under white robes and thus skilfully camouflaged, they suddenly dart from the woods to fire at our advancing units.'

Soviet newspaper report

Stalin set the Winter War alight from his apartment in the Kremlin with the order: 'Let's get started today.' Then he sent off an official to supervise the bombardment at Mainila.

At first, the civilians took the worst of the attack, as Soviet bombers, from their newly acquired bases in Estonia, flew in under heavy cloud cover, dived low, and released their bombs on Helsinki and other southern towns. In the capital children on their way to the shops were caught unprepared. They had no air raid drill, and they were seized by uncontrolled panic. Those who could packed together a few belongings and fled to the forests, on foot, on bikes, on trams and in trains if they could get a seat. There were squabbles over luggage, fights for the few empty places. The government moved out of the Parliament buildings into new premises in the outer suburbs. The government resigned, and a new determined leader emerged, Risto Ryti. This one-time governor of the Bank of Finland had once declared: 'We will not consent to bargain away our independence.'

The next day the Russian bombers came in again, but the tiny **Finnish Air Force** was ready. Lieutenant Eino Luukkanean shot one of them down, and it crashlanded intact in a snow drift. The Finns found that it had unarmoured wing tanks. Armed with that simple piece of intelligence they were able to shoot down a lot more.

But relief came mainly with the worsening weather. On 2 December a snow storm brought a white-out that ended aerial activity for nearly three weeks.

On the ground, the Russians advanced with a mighty wall of troops. At 8am on 30 November,

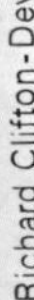
Richard Clifton-Dey

Against tanks, the Finns used **'Molotov cocktails'**—bottles filled with petrol, paraffin and tar ignited by a tube of sulphuric acid in the neck.

they poured an artillery barrage across the frontier, and sent their tanks—BT7-2 lights and T28M mediums, along the narrow icy roads.

In front of them, the Finnish people fled. Lines of pathetic refugees blocked all roads in the frontier districts. Military traffic could hardly move—neither the Russian tanks, nor the Finnish troops trying to get to the front.

Behind the tanks came the infantry, 600,000 Russian soldiers in four great armies. The bulk of this invading force, Seventh and Eighth Armies, moved northwest up the Karelian Isthmus, the obvious route to the capital, Helsinki, and control of the Gulf of Finland. The Fourteenth Army advanced in the north, aiming to take Petsamo and the Fisherman's Peninsula on the Barents Sea. Ninth Army crossed the frontier in the centre of Finland, to cut the country in half and draw Finnish troops away from the more important southern front.

The Russians were led to believe it would be a walkover. Captured plans revealed that the troops had been warned not to violate the Swedish border. They barely crossed the Finnish border before they slowed almost to a halt, confounded by three old enemies—guerilla troops fighting for their homeland; their own incompetence; and that familiar adversary General Winter.

First indications of the part the weather would play in the ground fighting came in the first days of the offensive. The great snowfall blotted out the roads and obliterated targets. Where the tanks wandered on to bogs and lakes not yet frozen they cracked the ice and slithered down into the murky depths. Then as December wore on the temperature went down to a record low of minus 22 degrees F.

'I personally would give up my economy, everything I own, if I didn't have to fight this war . . . they mow us down as with a sickle.'

Russian soldier

The Russians had not come equipped for this kind of weather. Their boots, for example, made from felt, kept out the dry cold but were useless when they got wet in the snow. Their padded jackets could not cope with the frost at night. They had failed to bring food enough for a long campaign, and without it their bodies gave in to the cold. The Finns, as they left their homes to go east, burned their buildings and destroyed every trace of food, so there was nothing for Russians to eat, nowhere they could escape from the cold.

Wax-like stillness

Those killed in the fighting stayed where they died, their features frozen into wax-like stillness that would last through the winter. They froze so quickly you could even see what they were doing when they died. Some were poised to throw a grenade, others held on to the lorries, stumbling forward.

A disillusioned Russian soldier wrote: 'We march already two days without food prepared in the mobile field kitchens. In this severe cold we have many sick and wounded. Our commanders must have difficulty in justifying our being here and finding our way in this strange territory. We are black like chimney sweeps and completely tired out. The soldiers are full of lice. Health is bad. Many soldiers have pneumonia. They promise that the combat will end on Stalin's birthday, but who will believe them?'

Those who stayed to fight had to face a devastating, ghostly enemy in the form of Finnish ski troops. The **Finnish Army** did not amount to much. Often there were only a couple of hundred men to take on an advancing tank regiment. But their fighting technique was right for the conditions. They dug tank traps, and lined the bottom with mines to detonate when the Russians tried to fill them. They laid mines on the paths and roads, in haystacks, beneath any snow banks the Russians might have to cross. *Pravda* paid them an unwitting tribute in its account of the war: 'The Finns were masters of foul play.'

Against Russians who would not leave the security of the roads, the Finns were at home in the forests. They floated silently and ghostlike on their skis, and almost invisible in their white camouflage suits. They emerged from the forests, killed Russian soldiers, and disappeared back into the forests, where the Russians could not follow.

Where they encountered tanks, they learned to ski up alongside them, and knock them out by dropping a Molotov cocktail into the turret. It

was a simple device, just a bottle of petrol and potassium chloride with an ampoule of sulphuric acid to detonate it on impact.

Then they would move off to attack another column. There was no rest for them. They went on for two weeks, snatching a few minutes sleep where they could, often still with their skis on, and going back to fight the moment they woke.

There was no real front line. 'What front?' a young staff officer asked when a reporter questioned him. 'There isn't one. This is the front, here, or half a mile ahead, or half a mile behind.' And the great Marshal Mannerheim himself said: 'The **Mannerheim Line** is the Finnish soldier standing in the snow.'

It had to be. There was nothing in the Mannerheim Line itself to stop an invasion on this scale. In theory it cut the Karelian Isthsmus in two. In reality it amounted to a makeshift line of ditches and trenches, with 66 old fashioned machine-gun nests on a 90-mile front. Boulders—invariably too small—and three stumps formed the anti-tank barrier, all completely ineffective.

Karelian standstill

By 23 December the Finns had fought the Russians to a standstill. They had destroyed 239 tanks on the Karelian Isthmus, and killed Russian troops in hundreds. Now they could even raise the energy for a counter-offensive, on a small scale. They had no hopes of a military victory, but thought they might be able to force the Russians to the conference table to agree a settlement of the conflict.

But the offensive lasted only eight hours. Exhaustion, and lack of experience, meant that the Finns were not nearly as good at organized warfare as they were at guerilla tactics. Their communications broke down. The artillery could not keep up with the ski-troops so it could not operate against the Russian tanks in the early stages. And as they had carried out no organized reconnaissance, they did not know precisely where to attack. The Finns called off the offensive and went back to their own lines. The Russians let them go without interfering.

So, as the year came to an end, an eerie stillness settled over the wintry wastes of the Finnish wilderness.

War Notes

WINTER WAR

FINLAND: Russian province from 1809, republic declared in 1917 and recognized after civil war in 1918. Area: 149,926 square miles (just smaller than Poland), including 12,184 square miles of lakes (60,000). Population 3,696,000. Steel production: 77,000 tons. Shipping: 649,000 tons (837 ships including 227 sailing). Railways: 3700 miles. Private cars: 30,100. National income: 29,999 million markaa (£138.2 million approx). State spending: 8360 million markaa (£38.5 million). Armed forces: 400,000 at full mobilization.

FINNISH AIR FORCE: 145 planes, of which 114 operational on 30 Nov 1939. The C-in-C (since 1932) Maj-Gen J. F. Lundquist had 200 trained airmen. The 2 fighter squadrons had 31 licence-built Dutch Fokker DXXIs and 10 Bristol Bulldog IVA biplanes. 3 recce squadrons flew Fokker CV and CX biplanes in Karelia. A 4th unit had Blackburn Ripon IIF and Junkers K43 floatplanes for lake operations. The 2 bomber squadrons mustered 14 licence-built Bristol Blenheim Is.

FINNISH ARMY: pre-war regulars numbered 33,000 to which territorial mobilization added 94,800 men. Together they formed 9 infantry divisions (6 in Karelia), each of 14,200 men with 11,000 rifles, 250 submachine-guns, 250 automatic rifles, 116 machine-guns, 18 mortars, 18 anti-tank (2 per battalion) and 24 field guns. Units consisted of HQ, 3 infantry regiments (9 battalions), a light brigade, artillery regiment, supply, engineering (2), signals and fortification companies. In addition there were 100,000 reservists and 100,000 Civil Guards. The Army had only 2 months of fuel and arms ammunition and 19-24 days supply of artillery and mortar shells.

MANNERHEIM, Baron Karl Gustaf Emil: Finnish marshal, b. 1867, Louhisaari, Finland, son of Swedish noble. Finnish Military Cadet School until expelled 1882–6. Petersburg Cavalry School 1887. Commissioned 1889. Captain 1903. Explored Asia for 9000 miles on horseback 1906–8 after serving in Russo-Japanese War as colonel. Regimental CO 1909. Major General commanding Guard Lancer Brigade, Warsaw 1914. Fought Austrians in S. Poland winning Cross of St George. Promoted to command Russian 12th Cavalry Corps 1915. Took part in 1916 Brusilov Offensive and was transferred to Rumania for mountain fighting. Lt-General commanding 6th Cavalry Corps June 1917 after witnessing Feb

R.T.H.P.L.

Revolution. Travelled by train from Odessa to Helsinki during Oct Revolution. Organized White Guards and with German help defeated Bolsheviks March-May 1918. Learned Finnish, already spoke German, Swedish and Russian. Became Regent of Finland until defeat in July 1919 Presidential election. Retired from public life except to direct Mannerheim Child Welfare League and Finnish Red Cross. Appointed Head of National Defence Council 1931. Promoted Field Marshal 1933. Visited Germany 1932, London 1934 and 1936, and India 1937. Got modest increase in defence budget and negotiated purchase of foreign arms. Dissuaded from resigning 1937 but resignation accepted in principle few days before Winter War.

MANNERHEIM LINE: Finnish fortifications across the Karelian Isthmus, 12–30 miles behind the frontier. Of the 66 machine-gun concrete bunkers, 44 were of 1920s construction and faultily sited. The 22 newer ones (built 1931–2 by 100,000 unemployed) did not withstand heavy artillery fire. Despite last-minute volunteer labour in 1939, the line had no anti-tank guns and only an average of 3 bunkers per 1000 yards of front. The barbed wire and anti-tank obstacles were too far in front (250 yards).

THE RELUCTANT BOMBERS

On the morning of 18 December 1939 three squadrons of Wellington bombers assembled over Kings Lynn in Norfolk and set course for Germany. Their target—the great naval base at Wilhelmshaven.

Leading the force was Wing Commander Richard Kellet, one of **Bomber Command's** most experienced and able officers. His orders were clear—to bomb any German warship he found in the Schillig Roads, Jade Bay or **Wilhelmshaven,** but at all costs to avoid civilian casualties. As he set out across the North Sea with Nos 9, 37 and 149 Squadrons, Kellet pondered his orders. He knew that effectively they meant that he could only attack warships at sea or moored away from the shore, for to attack a docked ship would risk civilian lives. Moreover to avoid enemy flak he had been instructed to attack from not less than 10,000ft, and this made his task doubly difficult. To hit a target as relatively small as a ship from that height would be an achievement.

There was scarcely a cloud in the sky that December day and visibility was up to 30 miles. Conditions seemed perfect, and the officers of Bomber Command were hoping, at last, for a really damaging strike by the twin-engine **Wellington.** Admittedly earlier operations against German warships had not been greatly successful, but their failure was put down largely to bad luck and bad weather.

If conditions looked right to the **Royal Air Force** (RAF), they looked even better to the Luftwaffe. The force of bombers was detected by Germany's primitive Freya radar installations when still some 75 miles from the target, and squadrons of Messerschmitt 109s (Me109s) and Me110s were immediately ordered to intercept.

The 50 or so German fighters attacked mercilessly in formations of five, each formation concentrating its fire on a single Wellington and attacking from high on the bomber's beam. Unfortunately the Wellington's designers had given little thought to attack from the side, and neither the nose nor the tail guns could traverse far enough for accurate fire at the attacking fighters.

The effect on the British bombers was devas-

At the beginning of the war the RAF had 1911 first line aircraft compared with Germany's 4161. There were five Bomber Groups (numbered 1 to 5) with 39 squadrons in all, and three Fighter Groups (numbered 11 to 13) with 36 squadrons. In addition there were Training, Coastal Command, Maintenance and Balloon Groups.

WITHAMS

'Suddenly we came upon two Wellingtons flying 300 metres below us, on the opposite heading. I attacked the leader from the side and it caught fire. Then I opened fire on the second one ...'

Lieutenant Ullenbeck, Me110 pilot

tating, but they kept formation as well as they could and lumbered on towards the target area. Even when the battered force finally turned for home there was no respite. The Messerschmitts followed them for 80 miles out to sea, attacking all the time.

Of the 22 Wellingtons that reached the target area only seven returned to base. Three more staggered back to Britain but crashed before reaching their home airfields. Damage inflicted on the target was negligible and only two enemy fighters had been shot down.

How could the RAF have mounted such a disastrous attack? After all, they knew perfectly well that enemy fighters would be waiting for them over the skies of northern Germany. At least part of the answer had to do with a misguided but deep-seated belief in the power of the bomber.

Holocaust from the air

The long-range bomber was a relatively new weapon and was regarded with some awe. Nobody really knew what would happen when bombs fell on a major city, but in the back of many minds lurked the memory of **Guernica,** the Spanish town which had been devastated by German bombs in 1937 during that country's bloody civil war.

In September 1939 Britain's air chiefs had expected instant holocaust from the air. Winston Churchill had gloomily predicted that London would be 'reduced to a shambles in half an hour'.

It was the horror of a new sort of war waged from the air against defenceless civilians that caused President Roosevelt, on 1 September 1939, to appeal to all countries engaged in the conflict to limit air warfare. On 2 September the British and French agreed to the President's proposal, and the RAF was restricted to dropping propaganda pamphlets over Germany and attacking the German Fleet. Military targets on land were ruled out only because the danger to civilian life was thought too great. Germany endorsed the appeal on 18 September despite the fact that she was already engaged in an air war against Poland's civilians.

A desire to preserve the lives of civilians was by no means the only reason that Germany, France and Britain readily agreed to the President's proposal. Germany was busy waging war on the eastern front and had no wish to divert valuable aircraft to repel bombing raids from the west. France was weak in the air and she felt that to bomb Germany would only lead to reprisals in which French industry would suffer much greater damage than that inflicted on Germany. And Britain, more than anything else, needed a breathing space to build up her bomber force.

In the autumn of 1939 the RAF was in no condition to fight a major war. Pre-war arguments, along with fanciful notions of what aircraft would contribute to the war, had left gaping holes in the fighter and bomber establishments, and the Munich meeting had revealed that Germany had built a bomber force far greater than Britain's. The Air Ministry had ordered new powerful four-engined bombers but their design and production programmes were beset with problems and they would not be available before 1941.

It was small wonder that Air Vice-Marshal Arthur **Harris,** later the driving force behind the bomber offensive, recalled of that autumn: 'I have in the course of my life rarely been so depressed as when I arrived at Grantham to take over command of No. 4 Group.' He said of the Hampden, one of Bomber Command's standard models: 'It failed to meet the requirements of normal specifications, especially with regard for comfort for the crew. It appeared to have little to recommend it except a very reliable engine and the fact that it had at least materialized in a hurry and was available in some numbers while most of the others were still on paper.' He referred to the Wellingtons, Whitleys, Blenheims and Battles, all deficient in range, armament and bomb load.

To make matters worse, the crews of these obsolescent aircraft were often inexperienced. As Air Commodore John **Slessor,** head of the planning branch of the air staff, observed: 'Crews had little or no experience of really long navigation in bad weather or of training with live bombs. . . Financial limitations conspired with race horses, swanneries and the Society for the Protection of Rural England to put every sort of difficulty in the way of acquiring practice camps and bomb ranges.' He summed up the feeling of the period well: 'One lived in a sort of dream world. . . I suppose subconsciously we all had in the background of our minds the picture of 1914–18.'

It was in this climate that the RAF began the war with operations to drop propaganda pamphlets, and bomb warships. It almost seemed in fact that the most successful achievement in that first autumn of the war was the 'Bombphlet Operation'.

In the early months of the war British bombers dropped propaganda leaflets over German cities. The raids were codenamed *Nickel.* On the night of 3 and 4 September, Whitleys of 51 and 58 Squadrons dropped more than six million leaflets on Bremen, Hamburg and the Ruhr. On 1 October Whitleys of No. 10 Squadron dropped leaflets on Berlin. Later targets included Prague and Vienna.

The pamphlets, which fell as far afield as Berlin, were dropped two or three nights a week by the Whitleys of 4 Group but aircrews bitterly resented the bombphlet missions. They questioned the value of the missions and were angered by the secrecy of their contents and the frivolous security which surrounded them. As Harris wrote: 'Many of these pamphlets were so patently idiotic and childish that it was perhaps just as well to keep them from the knowledge of the British public, even if we did risk crews and aircraft dropping them on the enemy.' In his cogent view: 'The only thing achieved was largely to supply the Continent's requirements of toilet paper for the five long years of the war.'

'Hitler was a corporal'

Unattractive missions, such as the 'Bombphlet Operation', together with the generally depressing start to the war did not deter young recruits flocking from their middle and upper class homes to join the ranks of the junior service.

The combination of a flier's glamour—coupled with the arrival of new technology and the encouragement of initiative and self-reliance within the progressive RAF, all added to the immense appeal the service had for the uppercrust young man of the period. The RAF promised a bright new future, free of the rigid drills and mechanical discipline of the Army regiments and in its upper ranks prided itself on the spirit of independence it encouraged. In reality the message of the 'modern approach' had not reached NCO level and recruits were to suffer a rude awakening once conscripted.

On the first morning after joining up a youthful Nigel Walker, later a squadron leader, recalled being kicked awake by a corporal. 'We were treated more like prisoners carrying out hard labour than recruits to one of the finest services in the world.'

Another recruit reflected 'corporals are by far the most self-opinionated sector of the whole human race. History tells its own story, Napoleon and Hitler were both corporals. Corporals! They have more flash arrogance than field marshals.'

Kitting out was another gruelling procedure unaffected by the new outlook, 'gnarled and elderly men, of indeterminate rank, glare at you

Eye Witness

Christmas Day 1939 was spent by one Squadron-Leader of the RAFVR in a flying boat over the Atlantic. . .

'By dawn we were having breakfast nearly 200 miles at sea—grapefruit, bacon, sausages, eggs, coffee and toast, served piping hot from the galley next door. . . Our boat combed the sea for 550 miles. . .I heard the pilot beside me whistle sharply. 'Blimey!' he said as he lifted the boat from the height of 60 ft at which we were flying. In the nick of time he had avoided the masthead of a ship. . .he was over a convoy.

Wintry sunshine filtered into the flying boat as the crew sat down, two at a time, to a quick Christmas dinner of soup, goose and plum-pudding. There were no submarines about.'

from behind a long counter. Some of them are so shortsighted they wear pebble lenses. But, without the use of a single tape measure, weigh you, and within seconds, reach a final conclusion—garments are hurled at you with the words "this, this, this, two of these, two of these, this, a pair of these; for Christ's sake catch 'em lad! I'm doing this for your benefit, not mine." And "I don't give a damn what size shoes you take. . .we'll soon work your feet into the right shape."

Operations against German warships in the North Sea were to give many of these early recruits their first taste of battle. The warship raids began on the day after war was declared.

On the afternoon of 4 September 15 Blenheims and 14 Wellingtons, known affectionately as 'Wimpeys', set out to attack the light cruiser *Leipzig* at the entrance to Wilhelmshaven, four destroyers in Jade Bay and two warships at the western end of the Kiel Canal. One of the warships turned out to be the pocket battleship *Admiral Scheer*. On deck, young German sailors relaxed. A line of washing hung out to dry.

The bombers that reached the target attacked immediately, dropping bomb after bomb on the

'We had joined the Air Force to fly, and not to parade around like Boy Scouts.'

Richard Hillary, fighter pilot

enemy ships. Fortunately for the German Navy the only damage suffered was a Blenheim crash on *Leipzig* that killed 12 sailors, and three dud bombs striking the *Admiral Scheer*, putting her aircraft catapult out of action. The 500lb bombs had been dropped from too low a height for the fuses to work. The Germans, on the other hand, had shot down seven of the British bombers, five Blenheims and two Wellingtons. Bad navigation prevented several bombers from reaching the target at all, and one of these released its bombs over Esbjerg in Denmark, more than 100 miles away!

Enter the fighters

Partly as a result of this inauspicious start, direct attacks were replaced by armed reconnaissance missions. Up to nine squadrons were to patrol the North Sea with the orders to attack the German fleet wherever found. They were not to seek them out at base or overfly neutral Dutch or Danish territorial waters. But once again poor organization and inexperienced crews forced Bomber Command to change its plans, for late in September five out of a force of 11 Hampdens were wiped out by a formation of Me109s when they attacked two German destroyers.

In spite of these early setbacks, Bomber Command remained stubbornly confident that a force of bombers, given the right conditions, could mount a successful daylight raid against enemy ships in harbour. The idea of the invincible bomber, though a little tarnished, remained.

Another consequence of official enthusiasm for the bomber was a comparative neglect of Fighter Command. The Air Ministry had rejected Sydney Camm's first design for the Hurricane as early as 1933 but Hawker independently continued with the project, giving it the Rolls Royce PU12 aero engine, the famous Merlin. The Ministry insisted that the fighter was impractical, too heavy and at £5000 each, too expensive. Only in 1935, after a successful demonstration did they change their minds and order a prototype equipped with eight machine-guns. The Hurricane entered service in December 1937.

With the battle for the Hurricane won there remained Reginald Mitchell's famous Spitfire, which because of the designer's health was delayed in production. Mitchell, having completed his work died in 1937 and by June the following year the first Spitfires arrived in service.

The truth of the Wilhelmshaven mission was a far cry from the story claimed by politicians and newspapers, or in the Bomber Command documentary film *The Lion has Wings*. The public were told that the entire populations of German cities were fleeing in panic as the bombers came over. They would surely soon demand that their government sue for peace. But those who knew what had really happened were beginning to understand the bomber's limitations and to develop a healthy respect for the fighter. Britain was certainly fortunate to have the Hurricane and the Spitfire.

Public school officer cadets inspect a squadron of Spitfires, winter 1939.

War Notes

BOMBER COMMAND: formed in 1936 when the RAF switched from a geographical to a functional organization. HQ was at High Wycombe, Buckinghamshire. The Air Officer Commanding-in-Chief (AOC-in-C) since 1937 had been Air Chief Marshal Sir Edgar Ludlow-Hewitt. He had 4 Groups Nos 2 (Blenheims), 3 (Wellingtons), 4 (Whitleys) and 5 (Hampdens). All were based in Eastern England. Together they mustered 33 squadrons with 480 aircraft on 3 Sept 1939.

GUERNICA: small Basque town in N. Spain, 15 miles ENE Bilbao. Severely bombed and set fire to 26 April 1937 by 43 German Condor Legion aircraft supporting Nationalist forces in Spanish Civil War. Of 7000 inhabitants a possible 1000 were killed by the 44.6 tons of shrapnel, incendiary and HE bombs dropped. Only 10% of the houses escaped with light damage. Episode made infamous by Pablo Picasso's 1937 painting.

Keystone

HARRIS, Arthur Travers: British air marshal, b. 1892. Father in Indian Civil Service. Educated All Hallows. Worked in Rhodesia from 1908. Served 1st Rhodesian Regt and Royal Flying Corps 1914–18. Specialized in anti-Zeppelin night operations. Awarded AFC 1918. Served and Iraq 1919–24. CO 58 India Squadron and then flying-boat station, England, 1924–31. Air Ministry Operations Intelligence and Head of Plans. Group Captain 1933. Air Commodore 1937. As Air Vice-Marshal, Air Officer Commanding (AOC) Palestine 1938–9. AOC No. 5 Bomber Group 1939.

ROYAL AIR FORCE (RAF): created on 1 April 1918 by the amalgamation of the Royal Flying Corps and Royal Naval Air Service. First airforce in the world to be given equal service status with the army and navy. On 3 Sept 1939 it had 1911 front-line aircraft with 20,033 aircrew and 153,925 ground staff. The Woman's Auxiliary Air Force made the grand total 175,692. Divided into 4 major home commands from 1936, Bomber, Fighter, Coastal and Training. The Chief of Air Staff and thus head of the Service since 1937 was Air Chief Marshal Sir Cyril Newall.

SLESSOR, John Cotesworth: Director of Plans British Air Ministry, b. 1897 Rhanikhet, India, son of Army officer. Educated Haileybury School. Served Royal Flying Corps 1915–18, wounded and won MC. RAF India 1921–3. RAF Staff College 1924–5. CO No. 4 Squadron 1925–8. Air Staff 1928–30. Instructor, Staff College 1931–4. CO No. 3 Indian Wing 1935–7, winning DSO during Waziristan operations 1936–7. Published *Air Power and Armies* 1936. Director of Plans from 1937. ADC to King George VI 1938. Air representative Anglo-French Staff Conversations 1939.

Fox Photos

WELLINGTON: British twin-engine medium bomber. Famous for the geodetic design construction of Barnes Wallis. First flew June 1936. In service Oct 1938. Weight (MkI data): 13.2 tons. Wingspan: 86.1ft. Length: 64.5ft. Engines: Bristol Pegasus XVIII 14-cyl radials, 1000hp each. (MkII Merlin engines). Max speed: 243mph at 15,000 ft. Range: 1800 miles. Ceiling: 21,000ft. Guns: 8 × .303in machine guns, 2 in nose turret, 4 in tail turret, 2 in side mounts. Bombload: 4500lb. RAF had 179 Wellingtons at outbreak of war, but only 6 squadrons were operational. New Zealand had ordered 30 in 1939 and made them over to Bomber Command as No. 75 (NZ) Squadron.

WILHELMSHAVEN: founded as naval base 40 miles NW of Bremen 1869. U-boat port from 1935. Population: 89,727.

A BIRTHDAY IN RUSSIA

The Great Leader of the Toilers of All Peoples, also named this month as The Great Friend of the Finns, celebrated his 60th birthday on 22 December 1939.

Among telegrams received was Adolf Hitler's: 'I beg you to accept on your 60th birthday my sincere wishes. I unite herewith my best wishes for your personal well being and happy future for the nations of our friends the Soviet Union.' In Germany official rejoicing for the Great Russian Führer was in order. It was still a novel idea, after years of criticizing him.

Joseph Vissarionovich Dzhugashvili had come a long way in 60 years. The 5ft 5in cobbler's son from Georgia, whose small frame required specially designed uniforms to enhance his stature (apart from the problem that his left arm was two inches shorter than his right) was now sole master of 170 million souls.

By 1939, of course, no one knew the yellowish complexioned dictator as Dzugashvili. In his time he had used many nicknames—among them Robin Hood ('Koba'). But since 1912 he was 'Man of Steel', in Russian: **Stalin.**

Lenin's troubleshooter in the early days of the revolution had become, by his 60th birthday, the monster that Lenin himself had predicted lay in store for suffering humanity. 'Comrade Stalin is too rude . . . I propose to the comrades to find a way of removing him,' Lenin confided at the end. He would have turned in his grave had he known Stalin was now being lauded in a special 12-page 'Our Own Stalin' birthday edition of **Pravda.** Only one column in all 12 pages carried news about anything but Stalin's personal glory.

But Lenin had no grave to turn in: on Stalin's orders Lenin had been stuffed and put on permanent display in Red Square. Under Stalin, the People's Revolution was back in the business of making gods out of men, just as in Tsarist days.

'Although he performed his task with consummate skill... Stalin never allowed his work to be marred by the slightest hint of vanity, conceit or self-adulation.'

Joseph Stalin, for inclusion in his biography

Columnists of *Pravda* had no easy task in recounting Stalin's birthday. There were no pictures available of the newest 'Hero of Socialist Labour' and member of the **Order of Lenin** (just one more unexpected birthday present today) that showed him mingling with the workers. Stalin, in truth, had not visited a farm since 1929.

While Adolf Hitler might spend Christmas distributing presents on the Western Front, Stalin had not, and would not, mix with the troops.

Nevertheless, the columnists did their best. Ensconced in her former palace at **Tiflis,** 'her who had given the world the Great Leader', Stalin's mother, gave interviews explaining how perfect young Joseph's childhood had been. There was news, too, that 29 annual prizes were now available, worth 100,000 roubles each, for outstanding achievements in the arts and sciences. Plus 4150 Stalin studentships. And a motion picture was going into production in Georgia entitled: *Through historical localities*. It would show every inch of the hallowed ground on which the leader had trod.

All this good news crowded out the unpleasant realities of events in Finland. Just a six-line communiqué reminded readers that all was going well there. Cries and groans from Moscow's overfilled military hospitals suggested otherwise. For three weeks now, the Red Army had been busy cementing the 'firm and indestructible' friendship between the Soviet and Finnish peoples, and trying to ensure that the Soviet pledge of 1 December was carried through. It read: 'We firmly hold that the Finnish people should itself decide its external and internal affairs.' The Finns had proved surprisingly resistant to Stalin's brand of friendship. They were fighting—and winning.

It is difficult to know how much of this bad news filtered to Stalin in his strange, hermit-like seclusion. 'Stalin's most creative hours were the hours of darkness' Alexander **Solzhenitsyn** wrote of him. His ventures into the outside world were rare. Preferring night to day, he spent long hours in his vast office, a supply of well sharpened blue pencils to hand, gutting reports from the outside world. Occasionally, his successor Khruschev recalled, he would indicate his grand plans not on a map but a globe, jabbing his stubby peasant fingers to indicate some other vast arena for action. By December 1939, Stalin's ascendancy and loneliness was complete. A 'birthday gift' from the ailing League of Nations, one week previously, had been Russia's expulsion from that organization. He had taken it with a sneer.

Stalin reviews a pre-war parade in Moscow. Few of those surrounding him were to survive the purges of the late 1930s.

Rule of terror

In the ten years since his 50th birthday he had won his way to a pinnacle of power that rendered world opinion irrelevant.

The decade had been paved with the corpses of his closest associates. In 1929, some brave souls had still dared to heckle their Party Secretary, Stalin, at a **Communist Party** central meeting. It was the last such occasion this happened. Party Congresses, formerly annual, were systematically postponed; became no more than mass rallies packed with docile, cheering delegates. Even so, they did not cheer loudly enough. Of the 1966 delegates to the 17th Congress of 1934, 1108 were later liquidated. Of the 35 members of the original 1919 Politburo, 20 had vanished by 1935. That was but the beginning. Show trials became a feature of Soviet summers between 1936 and 1939.

It became commonplace for new books to appear lauding some hero of the party—while the unfortunate victim was appearing (suitably drugged, brainwashed and threatened) to make abject confession of his crimes. Army leaders were objects of special attention. On 23 March 1937 the American ambassador to Moscow described the last full dress appearance of the Soviet military leaders at a gala dinner. 'Within nine weeks, 11 of the principal officers of the Army and many others were tried by court martial and shot.'

Stalin's aim was simple: to rout out all possible opposition to him that might survive in the ranks of the Red Army or the old **Bolshevik** party. To fulfil it, he had the energetic help of the most terrifying secret police force the world has ever seen: the NKVD. Recently installed as its head was Stalin's devoted fellow Georgian, Laventri

Beria, a man who put Himmler in the shade.

The NKVD came by night, always by surprise. The agents had little knowledge of the charges against their quarry, and cared less. For weeks after an arrest, the victim's families would have no knowledge of the vanished man's whereabouts or reasons for his fall from grace.

When functionaries and officials disappeared, it was often the result of denunciation by some inferior with a grudge, or a shrewd eye on promotion prospects.

While the purges raged, servants of the state lived on their nerves. 'When I reached Moscow I found an atmosphere of terror,' recorded diplomat Krivitsky in 1937.

But the terror embraced every industrial site too. 'When I sink a new oil well, I get skin eruptions', confided an engineer. 'If it is a dry hole,

Sergi Korolkoff drew a series of prints of life in Stalin's 'corrective' labour camps. This illustration is based on them.

they will say I'm a saboteur and send me to Siberia.' Slogans menaced from the walls: 'In every department there is a wrecker.' Shock troops of supposedly dedicated communists, but often common criminals, roamed factories seeking out the myriad spies and capitalist agents supposed to be at large in the land.

A cook was arrested under Paragraph III, 'failure to perform official duties' for neglecting to salt the dinner. But no specific charge was necessary: to be a 'kulak', 'priest', 'German', Pole or Marxist Deviationist was sufficient ground for a six to eight year sentence. The NKVD, under the command of Iron Commissar, Yezhov, could dispatch a citizen for up to five years in a corrective labour camp as a 'dangerous individual'.

The totals of those in detention were mind-bending. At most times in the 1930s up to ten per cent of the population was in detention. In 1938 some 11.5 million people were arrested. To handle this huge state within a state a specially dreadful organization arose within the NKVD, the Gulag camp administration.

Life in the camps was harsh. A survivor of an 18 month spell in Kargapol forced labour camp near Archangel revealed: 'The camp was established in 1937 in the heart of the Archangel forest as part of a timber industry plan. The first prisoners had to build their barracks and clear the camp area working in temperatures of 30–40 degrees below zero. Their daily ration was two portions of soup and a pound of black bread.'

Many of the prisoners hewing wood here were qualified forest engineers who had taken no thought to politics in their lives. But that was precisely the plan behind the whole monstrous exercise. By sheer brutal coercion, the nation was being rebuilt to fit the Communist dream.

Stalin's aim in this decade was straightforward: to drag the peasant millions of Russia off their own smallholdings and force them to build the heavy industry that Russia so lacked. Those who stayed on the land would work the **'collective farms'** so dear to Communist ideology.

The peasants had resisted. Some killed their animals and ate their seed corn in protest. In

'The camp did not allow the prisoners to forget for a single moment that they had no rights at all.'

V. Lashkin in *Novy Mir*

resistance to 'collectivization' Stalin's answer was swift. Those who wished to could starve. He rationed food and starved four million peasants to death to break the peasant's rugged opposition. Writer Ilya **Ehrenberg** watched the results as millions left the doomed land for the new industrial centres. He documented the exodus of thousands of peasants abandoning their village homes and making their way eastwards. Here it was told, there was some means of sustenance, bread, smoked fish and even sugar. These peasants hopelessly believed that a new and wonderful future was to be had by all. But they moved, a voiceless crowd with no flag-waving joy, dead at heart.

Opposition crushed

The work of 'urbanization' crashed on. In the far north, 300,000 inmates of forced labour camps dug out the Baltic Canal. In the goldfields of Lower Kolyman brigades who failed to fulfil their 'norm' 'had to work throughout the night and then continue the following day without rest or food', one conscript told. The speed at which the inexorable 'Five Year Plans' had to be fulfilled ensured that work progressed with near maximum inefficiency and hardship for those involved.

In February 1939 Victor Kravchenko was appointed director of a metals factory in Siberia. He arrived in a town that had swelled from 30,000 to 150,000 in a few years—and one of the world's worst climates. 'Newly built administrative structures and residences for the upper crust of workers, erected mainly by prisoners at terrific speed, were already sagging and cracking. . . The overflow of population, thousands of families, lived in damp dugouts in the ground.'

By 1939 the worst of the purges were over. The job had been done. A huge country had been dragged, forcefully, into the 20th century, her 16 republics welded into a Soviet Union where all opposition to a single man, Stalin, had been stamped out. 'I bow my head beneath the executioners axe which is not the axe of the proletariat,' Bukharin, described by Lenin as 'the party's favourite child,' had written. 'I can feel how powerless I am before this infernal machine.' Bukharin was dead. Yaroslavsky, Kamenev, Rykov, Tomsky, Chubar, Zinoviev were dead. Leaders of the party Central Committees in the Ukraine, Uzbekistan, Tadjikistan, Turkmenistan, Armenia and Georgia were dead. The long arm of Stalin's terror state had reached abroad to slaughter foreign communists, and heads of the party.

Reflecting on the past decade, in the solitude of the Kremlin, Stalin puffed his fat Georgian cigarettes and decided to attend a small party being given in his honour. It was a modest affair, held in a simple suburban cottage. The guests greeted him with the usual watchful devotion. On previous form, most if not all would end up in the concentration camps of the Soviet paradise.

Far away on the Finnish front a Russian officer notes in the journal that will later be found on his frozen corpse: 'We are told that on 22 December, Stalin's birthday, the war will be ended.'

The dying had only just begun.

War Notes

BERIA, Laventri Pavlovich: b. 1899 Georgia. Made himself indispensable as an informer and inquisitor in Transcaucasia. Delivered address to 9th Congress of Georgian Party, 1935, which established him as one of Stalin's official biographers. Stalin transferred him to Moscow to replace Yezhov as head of the NKVD 1938. Began to manipulate Stalin's suspicions of others for own purposes. Became Deputy Chairman of People's Commissars and national co-ordinator of security operations.

BOLSHEVIK: Russian word, meaning 'majority men' applied to left wing members of Russian Social Democratic Labour Party, who seized power in 1917 led by Lenin. Word was coined after a split in the party which took place at end of 2nd Congress in London 1903. Their opponents were Mensheviks—'minority men'.

COLLECTIVE FARMS: system in which all land, machinery and labour are in common ownership. Peasants were forced to give up their small holdings and join large collectives known as Kilkhozy. Stalin wished to eliminate wealthy peasants as a group. By 1936 almost all land had been brought into system but millions of peasants had been deported.

COMMUNIST PARTY: founded in Minsk 1898, as the Russian Social Democratic Labour Party. Main characteristics were established at Brussels-London Congress 1903. Lenin insisted that Party members should be activists, ready to accept leadership decisions without question and to seize power through revolutionary rather than democratic means. Under his leadership, the Bolsheviks seized power in October 1917. Party membership in 1939 was 2,306,973.

EHRENBERG, Ilya Grigorievich: Russian writer, b. 1891. Began literary career at 20. Political exile in France 1909–17. War correspondent 1914–17 before return to Russia. Returned to Paris as *Pravda* correspondent in 1930s.

ORDER OF LENIN: instituted 1930, the highest civilian order of the USSR. Awarded to individuals, institutions and foreign citizens.

Barnaby's

PRAVDA: means truth, is the name of the official newspaper of the Communist Party of Soviet Union. Established and edited by Molotov and Stalin 1912. It replaced Zvedza (Star).

Popperfoto

SOLZHENITSYN, Alexander: Russian writer, b. 1918 Kislovodsk. Graduated in mathematics from University of Rostov-na-Donu. Followed a correspondence course in literature at the Moscow State University.

STALIN, Josef Visarionovich: Russian dictator, b. 1879 Gori, Georgia, as J. V. Dzhugashvili, son of a shoemaker. Educated Tiflis theological seminar 1894–6. Joined Social Democratic Party 1896; sided with Bolsheviks in Party split 1903. Met Lenin at Stockholm 1905. Party Conference, London 1908. Member of Petrograd Central C'tee 1912. Adopted title Stalin (man of steel). Exiled to Siberia for 7th time 1913–17. Freed after Feb Revolution. 12th and most junior commissar after Oct Revolution. Co-founder and editor *Pravda* 1917. Defence of Tsaritsyn (Stalingrad) 1918. Gen Sec of Central C'tee 1922. After Lenin's death (1924) defeated rivals Trotsky, Zinoviev, Bukharin and Kamenev for succession by 1929. Put through collective farm policy and industrialization at cost of millions of lives by 1932. Purged party and a third of Red Army Officer Corps 1934–8. Concluded Non-Aggression Pact with Germany Aug 1939.

JANUARY 1940

Associated Press

...THE RUSSIANS had been promised a four day war in Finland. Now it was January and they were still there. The evacuee children of Britain had been promised safety from air raids. Now it was January and there were still no air raids. Hitler had promised his army an invasion of the West. Now, in January, his most secret plans had been captured. For everyone concerned, it was the worst month so far...

1st: 7400 Canadian volunteers arrive Aldershot barracks.
2nd: Fighting in Karelian Isthmus stopped by snow.
3rd: Finns air-drop 3 million pamphlets over Leningrad.
4th: Göring appointed head of German war economy.
5th: Oliver Stanley replaces Hore-Belisha as Secretary of State for War.
6th: 1st ANZAC contingents sail in convoy to Suez.
7th: Timoshenko to command Red armies in Finland.
8th: Food rationing begins in Britain.
9th: British sub operations in Heligoland Bight temporarily abandoned.
10th: Mechelen Incident.
11th: Russia's 168th Div encircled N. of L. Ladoga.
12th: Russians begin assault on Mannerheim Line.
13th: Belgium and Holland mobilize.
14th: Russians bomb Sweden by mistake.
15th: Air Marshal Barratt to command British Air Forces in France.
16th: French Chamber of Deputies eject 66 Communist members.
17th: Finns recapture Kursu, SW of Salla.
18th: Explosions at Waltham Abbey explosives factory
19th: Heavy fighting continues on Karelian Isthmus, N. of L. Ladoga and the 'Waist' during 81° of frost.
20th: Churchill appeals to neutrals to join Allies to resist Nazis.
21st: Finnish Blenheims bomb Kronstadt naval base.
22nd: Finns announce formation of a Foreign Legion.
23rd: British speed limit reduced to 20mph due to blackout casualities.
24th: Finns repel fierce attacks NE of L. Ladoga.
25th: Top secret Göring-Frank circular obtained and publicized by Poles.
26th: US-Japan Treaty of Navigation and Commerce allowed to lapse.
27th: Churchill broadcasts to Dominions and US.
28th: R. Thames and Southampton Docks frozen.
29th: USSR indicates willingness to negotiate with Finland.
30th: Hitler ridicules Allied leaders in speech at Berlin Sportpalast.
31st: Secret British military mission to Italy.

BRITAIN IN DISARRAY

Canadian soldiers who arrived in Britain this month found Britain surprisingly cold. So did the natives. The New Year brought with it the most savage winter in memory. In Scotland, trains were reported 'lost'. On the beach at Bognor Regis, parents took children to witness a rare sight indeed in British history: a frozen sea.

The weather was not the only thing wrong this month. Unemployment still topped 1,300,000. The blackout still tolled 33 deaths a day. Secret polls and surveys reaching Whitehall were increasingly alarmist. Four million Britons, they revealed, were now ready to have peace at any price. One in six adults were listening to German propagandist Lord Haw Haw, broadcasting out of Hamburg. 'As a radio personality, he's far more dynamic than the majority of the suave young men the BBC puts on the air,' wrote London-based *The New Yorker* correspondent, Mollie **Panter-Downes.**

After four months of enduring the 'Phoney War' Britain was beginning to demand: where are the air raids? What, indeed, is the war about?

With increasing nervousness Britain's top secret Postal Censor staff fingered its way through the nation's mail and reported bad news: boredom, apathy and discontent were spreading fast.

Fair shares for all

So was hunger. Via Harrods and Jackson's of Piccadilly, the rich continued, patriotically, to eat the best delicacies from France (what better way to aid the ally?). The middle classes went raiding working class shops, to strip shelves of the shortening supplies. But there was a majority in favour when, on 8 January, **rationing** finally became part of the British way of life: it should mean fairer shares for all. There was now 4oz of bacon and ham per week; 4 oz of butter, 12oz of sugar—more for marmelade makers.

The poorest now had coupons in their ration books, but no cash for their rations. Their well-to-do neighbours came back to the same corner shops, and a new phrase entered the language: 'under the counter'. The Black Market had begun.

The Black Market would come to mean much more than the slipping of an extra bag of sugar at the week's end to favoured customers. Already, on 6 January, the *Daily Mail* was reporting the theft of another food lorry from a city street. 'There have been so many thefts of food, especially rationed food, recently, that the police are taking special precautions at distribution centres. It is believed the food is sold at big prices in illicit markets.' The era of spivs, racketeers and profiteers started, increasing the man in the street's suspicion that 'they' were making a good thing out of the war.

Even unrationed foods were now in short supply. At midnight on 14 January the government became the nation's only butcher, taking full control of slaughtering and distribution. Weather and mishaps in allocations promptly slashed supplies.

Long years of easy reliance on grain imports from abroad had ended abruptly when U-boats

started to harry Britain's trade routes. Now Britain's hatchlings were going hungry. If they were not fed, fast, there would be no eggs next winter. On 25 January government ministers promised action: 1,270,000 acres of grassland would be ploughed up as soon as the weather broke, to raise home grown fodder.

If the Government was now hurrying to make grand plans, ordinary folk were moving faster. News that refuse collectors in the North London suburb of Tottenham had housed 42 pigs in home-made sties reached national headlines. The pigs were fed from 20 tons of weekly refuse collected on the rounds. Pig farmers 100 miles distant wrote to them, seeking surplus scrap supplies.

January saw the rebirth of inspired British amateurism. Soon, backyard pigs, and refuse sifting, would figure in most homes. But while Madame Clara Novello Davies drummed up support for her campaign to provide a musical instrument for every soldier in the ranks, millions were resentful of the upheavals that the 'Phoney War' had brought.

The evacuation plans of the autumn were now in complete disarray. Nearly half the women and children sent from major towns had now sneaked back home. Many stayed in town after the Christmas reunion with husbands and fathers, preferring the notional risk of air raids to the real miseries of the snowbound countryside.

But while citizens drifted home, the policy of dispersing civil servants to out of town bases continued. A further 2700 entrained for 'the North-West' on 3 January. Those who couldn't face the prospect and resigned found themselves in the 400,000-strong ranks of the professional classes now out of work as a result of the war's disruptions. While manual workers received

Despite 5 months of war, dole queues were a familiar sight, with unemployment over 1.3 million. And rationing was introduced to cope with food shortages in the shops.

'He was standing there as motionless as a statue, cap neb pulled over his eyes, gaze fixed on pavement, hands in pockets, shoulders hunched, the bitter wind blowing. . .'

Walter Greenwood

public assistance, the Ministry of Labour seemed to find it difficult to believe in unemployed white collar workers. Complaining to *The Times* on 27 January, one victim claimed: 'The authority given to the Unemployed Assistance Board to pay meagre allowances is so loosely worded that 75 per cent of those applying do not qualify.' The writer, with an invalid wife to support, spoke from the heart: 'Many have exhausted their small savings and face literal starvation, without food or fuel in the house.'

One focus for this month's mood of frustration was the still expanding army of full-time ARP and Auxiliary Fire Service volunteers. There were close on 300,000 of whom 286,000 were getting £2 or more weekly.

Anyone who imagined that ARP workers spent their days 'playing darts and smoking cigarettes' was wrong, said Admiral Sir Edward Evans, Joint Commissioner for Civil Defence for London. It was true that much time was being spent on assisting imaginary casualties from imaginary fires caused by imaginary raids. The public remained sceptical.

Auxiliary firemen, who had so recently put on their armbands with pride, now removed them in public, shunning ridicule. Nor were they popular in fire stations: the regulars in some instances refused to eat with them. Air raid wardens, however, continued to be the targets of most wrath. By now, the blackout had turned the icy nights of midwinter into a special kind of hell.

On 1 January a chink of light in the gloom was announced: new street lighting would provide the equivalent of 'bright star light'. The statistics of death and destruction on the roads were sombre. Figures released this month revealed the death rate: 4133 in the war's first four months—twice the average for the previous year; twice the deaths caused by enemy action. Thirty thousand had been injured in December alone.

The interfering minister

Pedestrians were taking the brunt of it. And would continue to do so. Pedestrians could see a car before a car could see them, government spokesmen explained. In other words, it was up to them to jump for it. Motoring organizations, opponents of speed restrictions, heartily agreed. At street level the war was still dangerous.

It was also a dangerous occupation for the politicians running it. Headlines of Saturday papers on 6 January revealed that the chief of the little-loved Ministry of Information, Lord **MacMillan,** had resigned. More importantly, so had the Secretary of State for War, Leslie **Hore-Belisha.** Which meant, many suspected, he had been fired. No reasons were given, and in the absence of reasons, rumours flourished. ' 'is nose 'appens to be the wrong shape, that's all' commented a cockney on a bus, a crack at Hore-Belisha's Jewish background. MPs surmised he had been misleading the public about the state of the Army's equipment. The public guessed that he had fallen foul of the Army brass-hats.

The truth was that it was not the shape of Hore-Belisha's nose that was at fault but a habit of sticking it in places that did not concern him. The Army view was that: 'Noble statesmen should not itch, To interfere in matters which, They do not understand.' Hore-Belisha had fought a long hard battle to boost the fortunes of the tank arm rightly realizing its importance in the coming war. That campaign had won him enemies. But the seeds of the War Minister's downfall now had been sown on a visit to the Front in France, back in November.

The Military Attaché who greeted him on arrival was always glad to see Hore-Belisha. He felt it was good for his soul. He loathed Hore-Belisha so much, he explained, that it was a marvellous exercise in self control.

Disliked for his boots

A jammed throttle on the plane bringing him to le Bourget airfield, Paris, had already nearly ended the minister's career. Next, it seemed, Lord Gort, the man Hore-Belisha himself had chosen for the job of C-in-C, seemed to have chosen pneumonia as the weapon with which to rid himself of the visitor. Gort took Hore-Belisha on an extended tour of battlefields, pointing out places of interest. The battlefields were those of the last war, not this. The weather was vile. The curious boots that Hore-Belisha had personally designed—they had no laces but a zip fastener up the back—leaked badly. These boots in themselves were reason to dislike Hore-Belisha, so far as Britain's top soldier, Sir Edmund Ironside, was concerned. 'How can one get on with a Secretary of State who does that sort of thing?' he had said. Ironside was another Hore-Belisha nominee. Now both commanders were against him.

Hore-Belisha endured the tour with good grace. He sat through a dinner at Gort's chateau and listened to further details of World War I campaigns. He sat through a conference of senior staff officers afterwards and heard Gort raise a key issue: should soldiers wear their tin hats on their left shoulder or the right?

Paul Slater

Keystone

The blackout doubled the number of road deaths. So in January 1940 dim street lighting was restored and on 1 February a 20mph speed limit was introduced.

Eventually Hore-Belisha steered attention to the present war, topics possibly more important than the arrangement of tin hats. When reminiscing to Major-General John Kennedy, the War Office Director of Military Operations, more than a year later, he said: 'I remarked to Gort that I did not think very much of the defences.' It was

By the end of January 1940, said Home Secretary Sir John Anderson, Air Raid Precautions (ARP) would have provided bomb shelters for eleven million people.

exactly the kind of remark for which professional soldiers disliked the interfering politician.

Gort explained that if the defences against the might of Germany looked flimsy there were good reasons why. He had 17 designs for pill-boxes, but had not yet been able to get a decision as to which should be adopted. Hore-Belisha's well known enthusiasm for improvisation was aroused. The man who had invented the Belisha beacon (which still stands at British pedestrian crossings as his memorial) now threw caution to the winds.

Back in Paris he told the French C-in-C Gamelin of the pill-box problem in the British sector. Then, in London, sent for engineering experts and summoned the Army Council to discuss the problem.

Ironside was icily dismissive. 'You can't make a Maginot Line with mud,' he told Hore-Belisha. His temper was not improved when the meddlesome War Secretary told him that one of the engineers had just suggested such a proposal: frozen mud.

It was plainly time for Hore-Belisha to be axed. 'All France is in an uproar at your criticism of the defences,' said Ironside.

Visitors from the Dominions had been picking up the story and expanding on it. The Army commanders closed ranks and trooped to see Premier Chamberlain.

Thus Hore-Belisha's career was ended, to be replaced by the little-known Oliver **Stanley.** He refused a proffered alternative post, and went quietly. 'There will be intense relief at his going' Ironside noted in his diary. Chamberlain shared it. Hore-Belisha, the premier wrote to a friend, had a 'self-centredness which makes him careless of other people's feelings'.

The public at large, this dark and rumour-ridden January, did not share the professionals' relief. They had seen the War Secretary as a fighter, a man with a talent for cutting through red tape. As the combined chaos of blackout, food shortages, vile weather and domestic disruption deepened, the public began to look at its war leaders with increasing wonder.

When Winston Churchill rose to speak on 26 January in Manchester, his audience was ready for a rallying call to action. They got it. 'Come then,' he said at the end, in that increasingly familiar growling voice. 'Let us to the task, to the battle and to the toil. . .Fill the armies, rule the air, pour out the munitions, strangle the U-boats, sweep the mines, plough the land, build the ships, guard the streets, succour the wounded, uplift the downcast, and honour the brave.

'Let us go forward together in all parts of the Empire, in all parts of this island. There is not a week, not a day, not an hour to be lost.'

One never heard Chamberlain talking like that, people reflected. Across the dark land, despite the gloom, the people sensed that a wind of change was blowing. It seemed high time.

War Notes

R.T.H.P.L.

DAVIES, Clara Novello: b. 1861, Cardiff, Wales, daughter of musician Jacob Davies. Mother of Ivor Novello. Founder and conductor Royal Welsh Ladies' Choir. Made Royal Command Performance before Queen Victoria 1894; George V and Queen Mary 1928. In WWI founded movement to provide some 50,000 mouth organs and 10,000 tin whistles to the soldiers in France.

HORE-BELISHA, Leslie: resigned as Secretary of State for War 5 Jan 1940. The announcement caused a great deal of speculation with press and public alike when no reason was given for his action. A popular figure with the public, he was responsible for modernizing the Army; bringing better pay and conditions, improving military education and prospects, making it possible for men to rise from the ranks. Gave the War Office a Public Relations department. With his adviser, Captain Basil Liddell Hart, promoted the need for a mechanized and mobile Army.

MACMILLAN, Lord (Hugh Pattison): b. 1873. Resigned as head of Ministry of Information Jan 1940. A distinguished judge with a long public service record, he was appointed Minister of Information in Sept 1939. Its function to sustain civilian morale —handling censorship, news and press relations, domestic and foreign propaganda—proved a dismal failure. Constant blunders by the civil servants and petty squabbles over censorship left the public with no real news at all.

PANTER-DOWNES, Mollie Patricia: London correspondent *The New Yorker*, b. 1906. Private school education. Married Clare Robinson 1927. Wrote *The Shoreless Sea* at 16 (published 1924). Contributed to various English and American publications. Published *Letter from England* 1940.

RATIONING: introduced 8 Jan 1940 to prevent wastage and to ensure equal shares for all. Everyone was issued with 3-monthly ration books containing coupons. Rationing of food was introduced in easy stages, beginning with a weekly ration per person of 4oz bacon and ham, 4oz butter, 12oz

Popperfoto

sugar. Bacon and butter rations were doubled to 8oz 29 Jan. By the end of Jan sugar allocation for bakers, confectioners and ice cream makers was cut by more than half. Saccharin (sugar substitute), however, was not affected and manufacture increased. Meat rationing was introduced in March with a weekly ration of 1s 10d worth for everyone aged over 6, and 11d worth for infants. Tea was rationed to 2oz per week in July, with 2oz cooking fat, 4oz margarine later in the year.

STANLEY, Oliver Frederick George: b. 1896, son of 17th Earl of Derby. Educated Oxford.Served in WWI. MP 1924. Minister of Transport 1933–4; of Labour 1934–5. President Board of Education 1935–7; of Board of Trade 1937–40. Appointed War Secretary 5 Jan 1940.

THE CONCRETE BATTLESHIP

Rumours of a planned German attack through Belgium sent few shivers down French spines this month. France was safe. Along 400 miles of frontier she had built the world's most formidable defence system. This was the fabled Maginot Line. In January 1940 it was home to 1,800,000 soldiers: 200,000 of them living permanently underground.

No visitor to this extraordinary construction failed to come away unimpressed. Between Basle on the Swiss border and Longwy on the edge of Belgium, the Maginot Line formed a concrete crust on the soft earth of France. With good reason, the visitors found that its vaults and fortresses reminded them of life on board ship. The Maginot Line was 'a battleship on land', said Lieutenant-General Alan Brooke, commanding Britain's Expeditionary Force II Corps. 'More like a submarine than any submarine I've ever been in' agreed historian of the line Vivian Rowe.

The ancient enemy

Indeed, the Line was intended to serve France in much the same way that Britain's navy guarded the high seas. The Line's purpose was brutally frank: to set a wall across Europe behind which Frenchmen could live secure, never again threatened by her ancient enemy eastwards.

Young American Clare **Boothe,** whose determination had won her a personal invitation from French C-in-C Gamelin to tour the line, thanked him nicely, but in private put her finger firmly on the flaw. The trouble with the Maginot Line, she felt, was that 'it was not on wheels'.

Time would tell just how right she was. The bitter truth would prove that all that immobile concrete, all that firepower was, quite simply, in the wrong place.

It was in the early 1920s that a World War I veteran, André **Maginot** gazed across the scarred battlefields of France and had his vision.

Maginot now rising in a political career that would take him to the post of War Minister, vowed 'Never again'. He knew that World War I had been fought, mostly, on French soil; that each inch on the eastern frontier was soured and drenched in blood. It would take more than scraps of paper, political wheeling and dealing to guarantee this could never happen again. What was needed was concrete and steel: lots of it. A machine so fixed and impregnable that it would keep the ancient enemy, Germany, at bay for ever.

On 4 January 1930, Maginot's vision of castles underground began to come true. The French National Assembly voted their War Minister Maginot £24 million—a vast sum in those days. Digging began at once.

It took five years. By 1935, the year fixed for French withdrawal from the Rhineland, the most massive man-made defence system since the Great Wall of China lay buried across Europe. The cost had escalated to a stunning £58 million.

Unlike that Great Wall, the Line was strangely invisible. 'A few carefully guarded entrances to curious, squat buildings' noted young Clare Boothe. 'Perhaps if you were very privileged you might have seen the barrels of big guns protruding from domes of steel.'

Yet the menace of what lay hidden beneath those 'squat buildings' on the grassy hilltops could somehow be sensed. Clare Boothe put it poetically: it was as if France 'bristled with a hidden death like a beautiful woman with a hidden disease'. Another woman, Madame Giraud, wife of the Military Governor of nearby Metz, made a personal gesture aimed at softening the grim outlines of concrete and steel. Planting a rose tree on the Line in 1938, she promised: 'Next summer 10,000 roses will bloom.'

But it would take more than that to raise the

Building the Maginot Line. It was to cost £58 million, over twice the estimate.

spirits of the thousands of men who now began a strange life below these hills. Underground lay a whole new world. The men called it 'the hole'.

For hundreds of miles through Europe: there were cinemas, barber shops, electric trains in these mighty fortresses which, in some key regions were only three miles apart. No two were alike. The biggest hid up to 1200 men, equipped to last out three weeks if necessary should Germany attempt attack. They swiftly acquired a nickname, these pallid gunners, secretaries, telephonists, cooks and medical staff—'the shellfish of the forts'.

First obstacle German troops would find if they came West in surprise assault (which, France feared, was the way it would happen), would be a network of **Maisons Fortes.** Something like a suicide squad lived in these reinforced barracks: their job was to give the alert and slow the attack by blowing up road and rail bridges. While they fought and died, ran the plan, men would pour into the massive defences of the Line behind them. Through the late 1930s these men kept their tinder dry, ready for trouble, while farmers grazed their cows around them.

The plan was that survivors from the Maisons Fortes would fall back to the next line of defence: the **Avant-Postes,** blocks of concrete bristling with 47mm or 65mm guns. More men lived in these posts, sleeping by their weapons. Their guns commanded the roads to the Line itself. They too would fall back when the odds went against them; their task, again, only to delay the onslaught.

Next the invader would run into serious trouble; the 'asparagus beds'. A deadly crop of railroad lengths had been buried, upright, up to six rows deep, in concrete. A nice touch was that no two spikes were at the same height. This was the tank smasher. To deter foot soldiers the spikes were draped with barbed wire; behind them lay a reception party for any infantry man still keen to go further—a 20 foot wide hedge of barbed wire laid over a minefield.

Anyone who got this far would find he was in range of what the Line was all about. Out of the next hilltop they would see a gun **turret** rising sleekly from the ground: twinned machine guns and anti-tank guns from the **casemates** would sweep the men pinned on the wire in front.

Only now would the real battle begin. From the

'The greatest and most powerful fortifications that the mind and labour of mankind have ever called into being'

Journalist on the Maginot Line

Eye Witness

Harold Nicolson, MP, was one of countless VIPs taken over the Maginot Line.
'The great shaft of the gun rose like a lift into the air and then stopped suddenly. "Fire!" remarked (he did not shout) the CO, and at that the shell-casings began to revolve accompanied by an intermittent click. Although the shells were packed all around us they did not actually put them into the cases, but we knew each click represented a shell. There was a click every second and it went on for 80 seconds. The Commandant explained to us that they represented a deluge of fire such as no tank or infantry could possibly withstand . . . the gun . . . descended into its recess and the cupola was closed!'

fortresses under the hills, fire would pour. Huge guns buried here could deliver shells of up to 135 mm. Should the invader luckily silence one gun emplacement he would not cheer for long: underground, men would race, by train and bicycle, to the other end of the fort (perhaps two miles distant) and mount other guns to continue the fray.

Behind concrete up to 30 foot thick, these gunners could go on firing for weeks.

That was the theory. But while the Line continued to impress distinguished visitors as autumn dragged into winter ('Fine concrete. They'll never get through this. Fine concrete' muttered one colonel on tour), the men whose task it was to wait for action found the concrete increasingly depressing. 'It was like living permanently in the Bakerloo line' the Reuters correspondent summed up. The light was harsh—though whitewashing the bulbs helped. The air down below, kept permanently at a greater pressure than in the world above—to deter poison gas attack—was

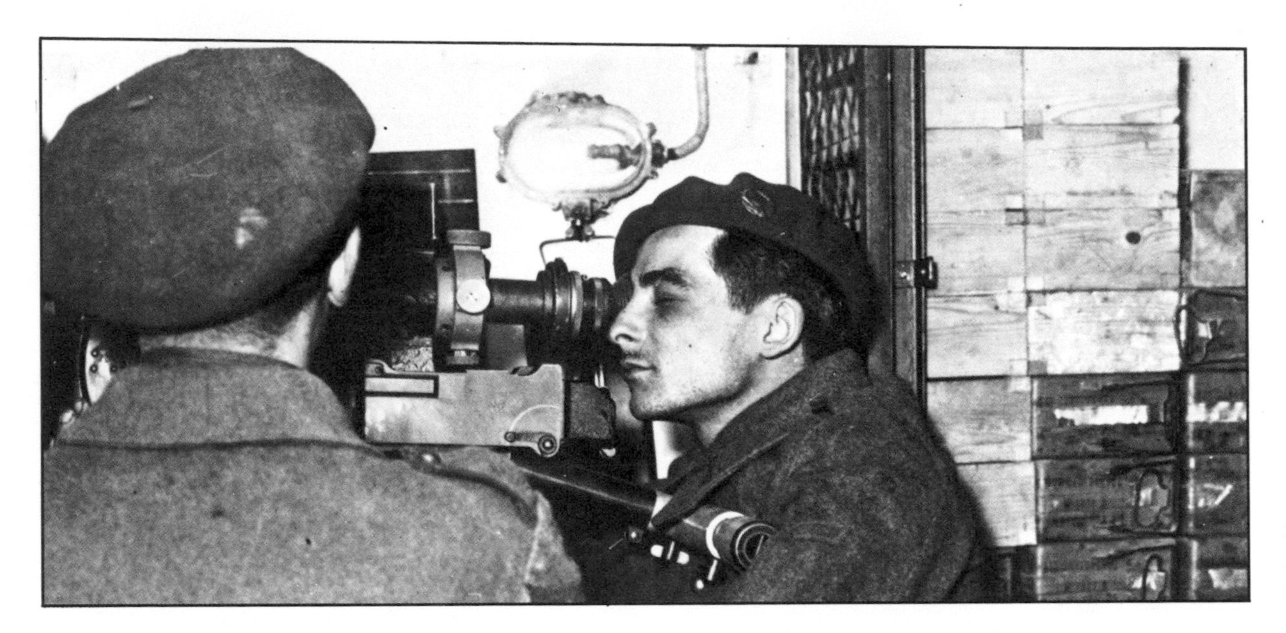

Vögelarchiv

British troops on the Maginot Line (left) were impressed by its weaponry (above) ranging from huge 135mm turret guns down to 7.5mm machine guns.

chill. 'We're no longer fighting the Germans; we're fighting boredom' was how a soldier put it.

Most were local lads: the idea was that they would put more heart into defending their local homelands than recruits from, say, the far Pyrenees. But their morale slumped. A move to raise spirits by extending the licensing hours misfired badly. Soon most major railway stations on the route to the front had to set aside coyly named 'deethylization rooms' where drunken troops on their way to the Line were sobered up.

Patriotic ladies in Paris 'adopted' a poilu (French soldier) and sent him cheering little parcels (carefully checked by censors to root out pornographic literature). But the poilus found that their sexual appetites were strangely depressed anyway: rumour had it that 'they' were putting bromide in the wine.

Top entertainers like Maurice Chevalier were sent from Paris to help jolly things along. But gloom persisted. It was not lifted when, partly to give the men something to do, gun tests were announced. The men watched their 135mm shells bouncing harmlessly across the frozen ground, failing to explode. The fuses were damp: the whole stock had to be replaced.

Up above, the patrols hated their task too. 'Before you, an unknown countryside,' said one patroller. 'The nearest post is several hundred yards away. Your feet are frozen in their stiff boots. Your helmet weighs heavily.' It soon had to be admitted that half an hour was the maximum anyone could spend on the dismal night patrols. After that, soldiers started seeing 'things that weren't there'.

When there was something to see—like a German soldier calmly washing in a river ahead—no one got excited. The Reuters man pointed out one such target and asked a French gunner why he did not shoot. 'They're not dangerous' came the reply. 'Anyway: if we fire, they'll fire back.'

It summed up the war so far. The Reuters man left the Line with the impression that 'France had withdrawn behind the Maginot Line like an aged tortoise into its shell'.

Even so, had the great concrete shell been as secure as it seemed, the boredom of its inhabitants would not have mattered. The truth was that the whole vast enterprise, which had buried so many millions of French francs in its foundations, would prove to have been built on the quicksands of faulty planning. Aged Army chief Pétain had baulked at extending it further south.

The gap in the Line

Much more disastrous, its builders had also halted in the north: the whole frontier with Belgium had been left protected by the scantiest fortifications. For Pétain, the high Ardennes Forest was equal to the best fortifications. Yet, long ago, the great Clausewitz had defined that area as 'the pit of the French stomach'. The classic route for German invaders had been across the plains of Belgium.

There were other reasons for this gap in the Line. To have built it behind Belgium was politically tricky at the time: it would have looked as if France was happy to leave friendly Belgium exposed on 'the wrong side of the Line'. In any case, money had run out.

'We will conquer because we are stronger' ran the government slogan. Since war began, French factories had turned out 30,000 private cars, but not a single tank.

But along the Line, as the patrols stamped their feet on the grassy hills that hid so many guns, so many men, a faint scent of something wrong and rotten seemed to come on the chill January air as the wind blew snatches of accordion music from German encampments to the east. The great battleship on land was beginning to smell like a sunken hulk.

War Notes

AVANT-POSTES: situated up to 2 miles behind Maisons Fortes on the Maginot Line. Armed with naval-type 47mm or 65mm guns, the concrete outposts protected routes leading to the fortresses.

BOOTHE, Clare: American journalist, b. 1903. Married George Tuttle Brokaw; divorced 1929. In 1935 married Henry R. Luce, founder of weekly magazines *Time* (1923), *Life* (1936). Worked on *Vogue* 1930, *Vanity Fair* 1931–4. Permitted to visit Maginot Line by French C-in-C Gamelin. In a letter of thanks, she praised its power and magnificence but commented on the discontent of its garrisons.

CASEMATES: double or single types ran in succession along the Line. Built either in a natural hill or artificial mound, the sides and back walls were 2–3ft thick. Each casemate had two floors: lower contained stores and living quarters for up to 35 men; the upper, protected by 5–12ft of concrete, housed the firing chamber. Armed with 37mm or 47mm anti-tank guns and 2 twin 7.5mm machine-guns, the casemates would give flank fire for the anti-tank and anti-infantry barriers. Single casemates usually had another, connected by an underground passage, close enough to give protective fire in the event of attack. A 10ft deep trench, dug below the firing apertures with barbed wire over 30ft in width surrounding the base, prevented men getting close.

FORTRESSES: situated every 3–5 miles (most parts) of the Line to reinforce the casemates. Made of steel and concrete they varied in size according to location. The largest could house a garrison of 1200 men, contained 15–20 concrete blocks, with guns ranging from 37mm to 135mm mounted in turrets (the only part visible above ground). Each fortress was divided into two parts, connected by deep subterranean galleries, usually $\frac{1}{4}$–$\frac{1}{2}$ mile long but could be as much as $1\frac{1}{4}$ miles, so that if half the fortress was put out of action the other half could fight on.

R.T.H.P.L.

MAGINOT, André: French politician 1877–1932. A former civil servant elected to Chamber of Deputies 1910. Under Secretary of War 1913. Served in WW1 from private to sergeant, receiving crippling wound. Minister of Colonies 1917; of Pensions 1921; of War 1922–4; 1926–9; 1929–30; 1931.

MAISONS FORTES: reinforced barracks situated along the roads and railway lines near the frontier. Permanently occupied by mobile troops who's duty it was to give the alert then blow up the roads and railway lines to delay immediate attack.

TURRET: armoured observation points. Casemate turrets were armed with special heavy automatic rifles and 50mm mortar. Artillery and infantry blocks of the fortresses had either fixed, retractable or rotating turrets. Infantry blocks were armed with 37mm and 47mm anti-tank guns fitted with accurate telescopic sights. Artillery blocks boasted the formidable 75mm guns, as well as 81mm mortars, and 135mm guns.

Looking along the line. It ran for 200 miles from the Belgian to the Swiss border.

Bundesarchiv

THE LOSING OF PLAN YELLOW

The Allies could scarcely have guessed at the start of 1940 that, within a few days, and without any effort on the part of secret agents or decoding machines, they would hold a complete blueprint for Germany's planned invasion of the West.

Perhaps if the information had arrived by a less preposterous route, they would have taken it more seriously.

Few bells rang as New Year came in. Europe realized that a new and terrible enemy had entered the fray: the worst winter of the century gripped the continent. Off Britain's sunny south coast resorts the sea itself froze. In Finland, Russian soldiers dropped by the thousand into the painless death of hypothermia. And in Germany the vile weather caused a parachute major of the Luftwaffe, one Helmut Reinberger to make a mistake that some historians argue changed the course of history.

On 9 January, Major Reinberger was, with reason, a worried man. He had in his yellow pigskin dispatch case the top level, secret, operational plans for Germany's intended airborne invasion of Belgium and Holland. Reinberger's brief was to get the plans to Cologne, for urgent discussion.

The invasion was still, despite many postponements, imminent. Since autumn, Hitler's generals had been waiting for the codeword *Rhine* which would signal attack. Again and again they got only codeword *Elbe* (withhold attack) as bad weather thwarted the Luftwaffe's chances.

Disastrous delays

But now, in early January, time had run out for delaying a winter invasion. Since 27 December, 'A' Day had been targetted for a day between 9 and 14 January, when Hitler hoped for clear weather, frozen ground and good flying. Any more postponements would have to be drastic: the most daring gamble in military history would have to wait until spring, after the thaw.

Major Reinberger knew the urgency. He was not just a courier for the momentous Plan Yellow he was now holding: he had helped draft it. As a Luftwaffe man he knew just how swiftly and invincibly the airborne attack would fall out of the sky between the rivers Meuse and Sambre. But right now Helmut Reinberger was not airborne: he was sitting in a chill railroad carriage that was inching its way through Germany towards Cologne. Like many men before and since he knew how lame it would sound if he got to Cologne too late for the conference and said: 'My train was late.'

The train ground its way into the congested tracks of the Ruhr, halting and hissing steam at every set of points. To Reinberger's dismayed fury it stopped altogether at Munster and tipped him out. The invasion of Western Europe by the world's finest air force was going to be thwarted by the fact that a wretched steam train could not get through to Cologne.

Cold and angry, Reinberger, dispatch case in hand, made his way to the town's Officer's Club, and pushed the door open to a welcome haven of warmth and camaraderie.

An airman's solution

Fate arranged that the man he talked to most tonight was a Luftwaffe colleague, Major Hönmanns, commandant of nearby Loddenheide airfield. Over drinks, the two men got to know each other and swapped stories.

It turned out they had one great thing in common: a passionate desire to get to Cologne. Major Hönmanns' aim was simple: he had a wife in Cologne. Finding that his new friend was anxious to get to the same town, Hönmanns proposed an airman's solution—let's climb in a plane and fly ourselves there.

Reinberger hesitated. There were strict orders against taking secret plans by air. But Hönmanns was impressive: a veteran flyer from the free and easy days of the last war, a man you could trust. Though there were strict orders against, the penalties of failing to get to Cologne at all would be stricter.

Hönmanns led the way to the plane early next morning. It was a fine light aircraft: the Messerschmitt 108 Taifun (Typhoon) courier. Hönmanns explained that the weather would quickly improve. He did not mention that he had only once flown a Typhoon before.

Meanwhile, in Berlin, the Führer had also decided the weather was going to be better. While Reinberger debated his problems in Munster, Hitler had been sending orders. Luftwaffe weather experts told him, that afternoon, that 10–14 days of clear winter weather were due. To Luftwaffe bases and all troop commands the message flickered on to the light bulbs of the Enigma cipher machines. The invasion was set for 15 minutes before dawn on 17 January. Plan Yellow, as Reinberger's documents detailed, would involve the Luftwaffe in four or five days heavy bombing raids on French air bases beforehand. Hitler's generals realized that the hour could finally be near. The 'Great German War of Liberation', as Hitler termed it, was about to begin its second chapter. Two million soldiers were poised to strike westwards across northern France, Belgium and Holland. The details were all in Major Reinberger's case.

The Typhoon climbed into thick cloud. Hönmanns confidently set a compass course. Cologne

The Me108, in which Major Reinberger crashed, first flew in 1935. It was of advanced all-metal, flush-riveted construction used later in the more famous Me109.

was just an hour or two distant.

In Berlin that morning the Belgian Ambassador was pinning a high decoration on the Luftwaffe's second in command, Colonel General Erhard Milch. It was a hopeful gesture of goodwill between two nations. And it would be the last. Up in the clouds, Major Hönmanns made the unpleasant discovery that he had lost his way.

The engine coughed and died

The plane was flying blind, 'as if in a Turkish bath'. Reinberger began to have serious doubts about Hönmanns' ability to get this plane to its destination—or any destination.

Dropping to 600ft, Hönmanns began looking for the River Rhine. Obligingly, a river at last appeared. Reinberger's relief was short-lived. 'That isn't the Rhine,' said Hönmanns. 'It's not wide enough.'

The plane began circling, as Hönmanns pondered and fumbled with the unfamiliar instrument panel. Suddenly the engine coughed and died. The pilot had managed to switch off his fuel supply.

With interest, Reinberger watched frozen ground racing towards them. In yet another demonstration of unusual flying techniques, Hönmanns was now taking the plane towards a gap between two trees: a gap several sizes too narrow for the plane's wingspan. Hurtling through, shedding both wings en route, the fuselage hit the ground and came to rest on a high hedge.

For a man who had just escaped death so narrowly, Reinberger was swift to see the rest of his life was not going to be pleasant. He clambered out with his brief case and told Hönmanns: 'I shall be court-martialled.'

Now, over the fields, came an aging peasant to visit the shaky airmen. They asked him where they were. Then, with sinking hearts, asked him again in French. 'The Maas' said the peasant. 'My God,' said Reinberger, 'we've crashed in Holland or Belgium.'

There was one need now in Reinberger's mind: a box of matches. Neither he nor Hönmanns were smokers. Mystified, the peasant turned over a box, and wondered why Reinberger went behind the hedge and attempted to light a fire.

Now Belgian soldiers were hastening to the scene—and brought their boots down smartly on the flames. It was plain they had made a fine arrest. They marched the disarmed aviators off for Captain Rodrique's inspection at the local control-point, the village of Mechelen-sur-Meuse.

Reinberger looked the picture of misery, slumped in a corner of the guard house. But he was not finished yet. As Rodrique stepped back to let Hönmanns pass on a trip to the lavatory, Reinberger sprang for the papers and stuffed them into the guardroom stove.

Rodrique snatched them out, burning his hand, and once again the flames were stamped out.

When Reinberger next leapt up, in a grab for the Captain's pistol, Rodrique found his temper fraying: 'Sit there and don't move' he ordered, shoving Reinberger into a chair.

Reinberger was finally beaten. He explained he had only wanted to shoot himself.

Was the plan legible?

Just how much of Plan Yellow was still legible would be an agonizing question in Berlin for days to come. First news that his most secret plans had landed in Belgium's lap reached Hitler just before midday. He raved to his operations chief, General Alfred Jodl: 'It's things like this that can lose us the war.' Then he summoned Göring and gave him the biggest dressing down of his life.

Göring later recalled: 'The Führer rebuked me frightfully, as the Commander-in-Chief of the unfortunate courier, for having allowed a major part of our western mobilization and the very fact of such German plans to be betrayed.

It was not the first instance of Luftwaffe's sloppy security: as Hitler reminded Göring, there was the case of the officer who had managed to drop a dispatch case from a moving train.

Whatever other repercussions would come from Reinberger's disastrous trip, security was going to have to be tightened. Hitler would draft a 'Basic Order No. 1' and insist on its display in every military headquarters. Henceforth, no one was to be given any classified information not directly relevant to his job.

But that was closing the stable door after the horse had bolted. It was essential to find out, fast, just how much the Belgians had read from the charred fragments. Headline news in every Belgian newspaper (bar one) next day, announced the German officers had destroyed their documents. That brought no comfort to Berlin: it was exactly the line Belgian Intelligence could be expected to foster. News from General Wenninger, German military attaché in Brussels, was more convincing. He had managed to interview the two airmen in captivity on 12 January. They assured him they had burnt the plans except for a few pieces.

Göring still agonized. He experimented with

stoves and pieces of charred paper. At his wife's suggestion he hired a clairvoyant, and reported to Hitler that psychic intelligence revealed the plans had indeed been destroyed.

In fact, the Belgians were busy reading, with shock and horror, every detail of the planned rape of their country.

It has become one of the war's favourite myths that Hitler cancelled his planned January invasion as a result; that he changed the plans; that, had he invaded in January, Britain and France would have thrashed him; that Helmut Reinberger's trip changed the fate of Europe.

Top-ranking German generals believed so. After the war, General Kurt Student would state that Hitler, after hearing of the disaster 'at first wanted to strike immediately, but fortunately refrained—and decided to drop the original plan entirely'.

The truth is stranger. Hitler stayed cool. At 3.15pm on 11 January, while his High Command was still reeling with the first news of the incident he confirmed his decision to launch the invasion. Weather forecasts of four days' fog between 16 and 19 January caused the next postponement: at 1pm on 13 January Hitler put off the attack

'The information gathered from the German fliers did not, as far as I was concerned, have any influence on our decisions'

General Gamelin, French C-in-C

detailed in Plan Yellow until the 20th.

By now, mid-January, it was plain the Belgians had indeed read Plan Yellow, and passed the bad news to Britain and France. Reports from spies and codebreakers flooded into Berlin. From France news came that Army Group One had been ordered to move up to the Belgian frontier. On 14 January a French cavalry column rode into Luxembourg.

The night before, Berlin's telephone tappers had heard the Belgian military attaché warn Brussels that the invasion would begin next day. On 17 January, Belgium's Foreign Minister, Paul Henri Spaak put the cards plainly on the table. He summoned Germany's Ambassador to Brussels and told him: 'The plane which made an emergency landing on 10 January had put into Belgian hands a document of the most extraordinary and serious nature, which contained clear proof of an intention to attack. It was not just an operations plan, but an attack order worked out in every detail, in which only the time remained to be inserted.'

One of the strangest crossroads in history had been reached. The aggressor's plans had been laid wide open, but he did not change them. The victims, Belgium and Holland, knew now what fate was in store—but they too failed to change their plans. As Churchill recorded in his war history: 'In spite of all the German major's papers no fresh action of any kind was taken by the Allies or the threatened states.' The French C-in-C, Gamelin, agreed: 'The information gathered from the German fliers did not, as far as I was concerned, have any influence on our decisions.'

Hitler's decision to press ahead was well calculated. On 16 January he told Jodl that the entire operation would be put on 'a new basis' to ensure 'secrecy and surprise'. The surprise was a straight double bluff: the plan would not, basically, be changed.

It would, however, be sharpened up. The four day alert detailed in Reinberger's documents would be shortened to 24 hours. The period between a decision to attack and the attack itself would be cut from four days to three.

Plan Yellow ignored

Thus, if the Allies guessed Plan Yellow was still operational, they would be caught short on its new timing. And if they guessed Hitler had scrapped the plan, their surprise would be complete. Hitler explained his 'new basis' on 20 January to key men, including Göring, von Brauchitsch, Halder, Jeschonnek, chief of staff of the Luftwaffe, Keitel and Jodl.

In the Allied camp, experts waited, alert but without alarm. One school of thought believed still that the documents that had crash landed in Belgium were a clever 'plant' designed to focus attention on an attack through that nation. Still fearful that any Belgian military manoeuvres could be taken as an excuse for German aggression Belgium did not mobilize her troops. Quietly, frontier barriers with France were taken down to speed the Allied armies' passage if necessary.

But a whole generation had been bred to believe that if Germany attacked the thrust would come through France. Millions of pounds had been sunk into that frontier's defences. Here, stretching through Europe, was the world's greatest man-made frontier, the Maginot Line. Surely it could not be true that Hitler planned simply to walk round it.

Major Reinberger and Hönmanns settled into captivity. They would end the war as prisoners in Canada. Luftwaffe scapegoats for the debacle began adjusting to demotion: Göring had sacked the two men's commander General Helmut Felmy of Luftflotte 2 and his chief of staff Colonel Josef Kammhuber.

Hitler explained to his generals that bad weather prospects, yet again, had thwarted the invasion: a thaw was expected. The invasion would have to wait until spring.

And, astonishingly, between January and May 1940 the Allies went on waiting, ready for an attack through France: an attack that Plan Yellow plainly showed was never going to happen.

The document Major Reinberger tried to destroy by burning was entitled *General Order of Operations-Air Fleet 2.* It showed exactly what roles various specified units would play in a well planned invasion of Belgium and Holland.

Colin Backhouse

Canadian troops arrrive at a west coast port in Britain. A total of 7400 Canadians arrived in January. At snow-bound Aldershot New Zealanders (inset) are inspected.

THE EMPIRE ARRIVES

On 10 December, five great liners had set out from distant Canada to choruses of 'Roll out the barrel'. On New Year's Eve they arrived at Greenock on the Clyde, and the first of the many volunteers who were to come to Europe disembarked. The Empire was answering the call to aid Britain in her war.

Not many of the 7400 Canadians were singing when they arrived. They had already learnt a few lessons about the strange habits of those tiny islands that had summoned them. The ships had been unheated. For breakfast, British cooks had served curiously shaped fishes that consisted almost entirely of bones. They were, it seemed, known as kippers.

Maybe life would be more reasonable at the famous Aldershot barracks, to which the Canadians went on New Year's Day. They found that at least the barracks had fireplaces, though small ones. They also found that there was no coal. To keep warm, there was combat training. The Canadians looked at the rule book and noted it was based on the 1918 edition.

They wondered what, precisely, their eagerness to enlist had got them into.

Biggest volunteer army ever

No flags now fly in London on Empire Day, 24 May, Queen Victoria's birthday. But in the 1930s the Empire was still an expanding business, and Empire Day an occasion for a half-holiday. This community of nations, colonies and dominions still coloured one quarter of the world's land surface red: included close on 600 million inhabitants. It ranged from Pitcairn Islands (population 50) to the Indian subcontinent (353 million strong).

Whittaker's annual almanack listed the extraordinary way the whole massive enterprise had been got together: 'Jersey, acquired by Duke of Normandy 1066', 'Fiji, cession from natives 1874', 'Cyprus, annexation 1914 . . .'

Though some were already saying the Empire's peak was past, the inter-war years had seen good old-fashioned colonial wars being fought against colourful characters in far away places: the Mad Mullah of Somaliland or the crazy Burmese monk Saya San (who claimed to be able to fly). And memories were still fresh of the greatest exhibition of all: the Great Empire Exhibition at Wembley, 1924. Despite the efforts of the left-wing WGTWs (the Won't Go to Wembley Movement) 27 million people had visited its 220 acres of pavilions.

And now, with a new war begun, this vast Empire came to the aid of a far away country—on a scale that still stuns the mind. The fact remains that the British Empire in World War II raised the biggest volunteer army in history.

It is true that not everyone rushed in without

Australian High Commission

In sunny Melbourne, Australian troops embark for the Suez Canal.

Eye Witness

A special correspondent of the *Manchester Guardian* witnessed the arrival of Canadian troops at a port of disembarkation . . .

'It was a cold grey day. They came in one by one, the transports looking high and heavy beside the rakish warships that escorted them. . . . The sailors on the little warship at the pier cheered them as they passed. We could see what they looked like now as they came alongside singing: thick-set, open-faced boys in the same battle-kit that the British Army wears, but with a maple-leaf badge in their fore-and-aft caps . . . they stood (on the pier) smoked and talked, then on to the troop train that was to take them through a blacked-out Britain.'

heart searching debate. In the **Gold Coast,** a formal debate was held. The Omanhene of Akwapim opened, putting the case for both Great Britain and Germany. Discussion followed. Finally the chief linguist gave judgement for King George VI. There were then three cheers for King George 'for winning the case'. Followed by three hoots for Hitler.

Such votes of confidence heartened King George, who had noted in his diary of September 1939 that Hitler had gone to war 'with the knowledge that the whole might of the British Empire would be against him'. Churchill would pay tribute later in his most famous 1940 speech. 'If the British Empire and its Commonwealth last for a thousand years, men will still say, "this was their finest hour".'

But the question remains: how ready was the Empire to back Britain?

Canada's enthusiasm seemed a curious and dangerous choice to many Americans. As aviator Charles Lindbergh put it: 'Have the Canadians the right to draw this hemisphere into a European war simply because they prefer the Crown of England to American Independence?'

Roosevelt had taken care to pledge Canada's security—it was more than a hint that she should throw in her lot with neutral America. Canadian premier Mackenzie King let a week of war pass before taking the plunge: but this was no sign of hesitation. The days were well spent in freighting war materials in from the States—before the declaration of war that would, under America's neutrality laws, turn off the supply tap to belligerent nations.

King, who had come to power on an isolationist policy himself, knew now that Canada's future could lie only with Britain's. It was fortunate that France was in the war too—else King could have faced trouble from the French-speaking Quebequois community. As it was, though he still kept a signed photograph of Hitler on his desk he had already warned the Führer that, in the event of war, 'there would be a great many Canadians willing to swim over the Atlantic'.

King knew, however, that though many might take that plunge of their own free will, there was no political future for an administration that proposed to force Canadians to the fray. He promised there would be no conscription. Later, when conscription became necessary, he would have a hard time pushing it through.

At the world's opposite corner, **Australia** and **New Zealand's** response had come more swiftly, apparently without a dissenting voice. These nations were still tied tightly, by trade and

'The Princes and the States of India have without exception rallied round the Imperial Throne and the Empire in this hour of trial...'

Maharaja of Bikanir

The Viceroy and Vicereine of India, Lord and Lady Linlithgow, flanked by the Viceroy's Guard, leave their Delhi residence.

sentiment, to what was still known as the Mother Country. On 23 August Robert Menzies, Prime Minister, had pledged: 'Britain has the fullest co-operation in her magnificent efforts to avoid the injustice and insanity of war. If her great efforts fail, we will stand by her side.'

Peace lobby

But, when news of the war's outbreak crackled in over short-wave radio at 8pm, Eastern Australian time, on 3 September there were many who hoped that distant Europe could sort out her problems with the least help possible.

Australia, after a long and lonely inter-war depression, still had 250,000 unemployed—12% of all workers. Peace lobbyists argued that war would once again wreck trade along Australia's lifeline sea routes. President of the Australian Labour Party, Fallon, urged Australians to stay home. 'Every man who leaves Australia to fight in Europe increases our national debt, reduces our capacity to defend Australia against possible foreign aggression and also our capacity to supply Great Britain with materials and goods which she needs and which are essential to her success against the curse of Hitlerism.' Most vocal was the Australian Communist Party, which distributed close on three million pamphlets calling for a speedy peace.

But many were willing to fight. On 24 January a crowd of half a million watched a march past of the 17th Brigade in Sydney. In the first six months of war 22,000 enlisted in the Australian Imperial Force; 11,000 joined the RAAF (and 60,000 more candidates were disappointed).

The first fruits of Australia's and New Zealand's manpower contribution left for Port Said in January, under the command of Major-General Iven Mackay. Tough pioneers from sheep-stations in the burning outback of Australia and youngsters from Sydney's sprawling suburbs, looked at the prospects of Cairo's sleazy attractions with interest. General Archibald Wavell, whose task it was to weld them into Middle East Command, felt it necessary to warn them 'to show the Egyptians that their notions of Australians as rough, wild, undisciplined people given to strong drink are incorrect'. Then he sent them off for tough training in Palestine. Some veteran **ANZACS** had been there before: fighting Turks in World War I. As yet, few could guess how far and fiercely they would have to fight this time.

Radio Times Hulton Picture Library

While Gandhi (left) wanted independence in exchange for India's participation in the war, Jan Smuts of South Africa had no hesitation in declaring war on Germany.

Canada and Australia, both vast and empty lands, contrasted hugely with the other great slices of the Empire map—**India** and **South Africa.** No one bothered to consult the opinions of Canada's Red Indians nor Australian Aboriginals. But elsewhere, the original natives had not been reduced to a silent minority. India's 240 million Hindus and 78 million Muslims were among those whose feelings about a European war would, to say the least, be mixed.

Yet in India, Viceroy Lord Linlithgow wasted no time in consultation. He baldly announced that 'war has broken out between His Majesty and Germany'. To Pandit Nehru, co-leader of the Indian Congress Party with Mahatma Gandhi, the statement was infuriating. 'One man,' said Nehru, 'a foreigner and representative of a hated system, could plunge 400 millions of human beings into war without the slightest reference to them.'

The Congress Party, controlling eight of 11 now self-governing provinces, was some way on the long road to achieving an independent India. Though the Party expressed 'entire disapproval of the ideology and practice of Fascism and Nazism' it was swiftly made plain to the Viceroy that support from India's millions would have to be paid for. On 17 October 1939, Linlithgow offered Dominion status—but when the war was won. It was not enough.

Yet, though a few Indian nationalists were to throw in their lot with Hitler's Germany, even forming a fighting unit for the Reich, and the Japanese, Britain's long hold on the sub-continent would not, as yet, be loosened. In South Africa the situation looked more tricky.

Many here had reason to approve Hitler's view

Central Press

New Zealand troops posted to the Middle East take time off to visit the Pyramids.

on race and destiny. Like him, they saw a future run by a 'pure' white race. Some saw a vision in which Hitler would run a European Empire and South Africa an African Empire. If Britain and France were humbled, South Africa could move north and sweep them from the colonies there. Those Afrikaaners with bitter memories of the Boer War had yet more basic reasons to wish for Britain's final defeat now.

Accident of history

But there was a problem, and its name was **South West Africa.** Until 1915 it had been a German Colony. There could be no doubt that, if Hitler won, he would demand it back.

Premier James Herzog was a known German sympathizer. Britain was resigned to the fact that when war broke out, he would declare neutrality. He had the right to do so. He intended to do so. But an accident of history now thwarted him.

On 6 September, just three days after the war had begun, the South African Senate reached the end of its ten year mandate. The status quo could not be prolonged without approval of Parliament. Parliament met, and the debate about the nation's stance had to be heard.

Jan Smuts, Minister of Justice, rose to challenge his boss. He said: 'When the day of trouble comes. . .faced with the demand for South West Africa at the point of a bayonet, we shall have to say whether we are going to face that issue alone, because our friends would be against us.' Smuts' amendment was carried. Herzog resigned, hoping that new elections would win him support for his stance. He went, as the constitution demanded, to Governor-General Patrick Duncan, seeking a dissolution of parliament. The King's representative's reply stunned him—there was no need for a dissolution if someone else in his party could command a majority.

Smuts became Prime Minister on 5 September and declared war on Germany on the 6th. It was a notable British coup. Once again a major part of the Empire had been won to the cause.

But in Britain, little note was paid to the voices of dissent in the Empire as the New Year got under way. Pictures in every paper and magazine showed the Empire's colourful chiefs from remote Pacific Islands, deepest Africa, dusty Gulf States pledging support. The Sheikh of Bahrein sent a cheque for £30,000.

It was a morale booster of the first order.

If Hitler did not immediately throw in the towel at the news that one quarter of the globe's surface was now against him, the reason might be found in those cold Aldershot barracks where, this January, the newly arrived Canadians were inspecting the equipment now placed at their battalion's disposal. It consisted of one typewriter, three cars, a clutch of Bren guns.

The truth was that Britain had the men, but not the tools for the job. Many of these Canadians would not see action until four years later. They were by no means the only men in Britain who began to wonder just what kind of war the Government thought it was running.

War Notes

ANZACS: term used to describe the combination of Australian and New Zealand troops at Gallipoli, Turkey, 25 April 1915. Annual anniversary celebrated on that date.

R.T.H.P.L.

AUSTRALIA: an island continent between the Indian and Pacific Oceans and SE Asia and a British Dominion of the Commonwealth. Federal capital Canberra. Population reached 6,620,000 in 1939. Premier Robert Menzies.

CANADA: country of N. America north of the US (except Alsaka), consisting of 10 provinces. British Dominion of the Commonwealth. Government independent of Britain. Capital: Ottawa. Population: (1941) 11,506,655.

GOLD COAST: name applied to section of W. African shore line on Gulf of Guinea, off Gold Coast colony.

INDIA: peninsula south of the Himalaya Mountains, south of central rim of Asia. Capital: New Delhi. Population 353 million. Indian National Congress Party formed 1885. Long range goal was self-government. Reforms in 1909 provided for separate Muslim electorate, as requested by Muslim League, formed 1906. During WWI both Congress and League backed war effort and 680,000 Indian troops served in Middle East and France. The 1919 Government of India Act fell short of Nationalist hopes. Under 1920s leadership of Mahatma Gandhi government grew. Both Hindus and Muslims demanded independence. Three conferences held in London 1930–2 lead to 1935 Government of India Act. Provided for enlarged franchise and autonomous provincial governments. Member of the British Commonwealth of Nations. No constitutional reform till 1937 when first elections held.

R.T.H.P.L.

Central Press

NEW ZEALAND: chain of islands in S. Pacific, 1200 miles SE of Australia. Was British Dominion, though had home parliament. Capital: Wellington. Population 1,536,000. PM was Adam Hamilton, of National Party. New Zealand declared war on Germany, 3 Sept 1939.

SOUTH AFRICA: most westernized of African countries, occupies 472,494 sq miles between the Atlantic (W) and the Indian Ocean (E). Pop (1940) 11,138,684 of which 9,054,659 are non-whites (mostly Bantu) of the British Commonwealth of Nations. Administrative capital is Pretoria, legislature at Cape Town; largest city and industrial centre is Johannesburg. Union of S. Africa established in 1910. At the outbreak of war PM General J. B. M. Hertzog refused to join forces with Britain and break off relations with Germany attempting to secure a S. African neutrality. Subsequent to Hertzog's defeat in Parliament by General Smuts, South Africa declared war on 6 Sept 1939. 345,049 men and women enlisted as volunteers—comparing favourably with other Commonwealth countries. S. Africa's greatest contribution to the Allied war effort was industrial. She provisioned thousands of ships in convoy and built up innumerable munition works.

SOUTH WEST AFRICA: Capital: Windhoek. Population 384,627 in 1946. British annexed Walvis Bay in 1878. Area became German colony in 1892. Outbreak of WWI, Union forces occupied Luderitz and Swakopmund. Gen. Louis Botha lead major campaign against Germans, who surrendered at Korab, 9 July 1915. Union troops occupy entire territory. Under Treaty of Versailles declared League of Nations mandate of Union of South Africa 1919.

JANUARY 1940

FINLAND FIGHTS ON

'Inside one of the tanks were the charred remains of its Russian occupants – all in ghastly postures ... we counted more than 40 such tanks'

Newspaper account of Winter War

On New Year's Day the unbelievable happened. A single airplane flew jauntily over the lines of the mighty, invincible Red Army and the soldiers on the ground watched bundles of pamphlets flutter towards the snow.

Finland was coolly inviting the Red Army to surrender: even promising a safe return home for those soldiers who saw sense and gave up. Meanwhile, from the dark woods, this strange and unaccountable enemy was still hurling grenades and artillery fire. Since New Year's Eve, the unthinkable looked more like sense, every passing minute. The Finns really looked like winning.

The dead darkness of midwinter with four short hours of bleak daylight; those silent and sinister forests; the endless snows that could bring Russia's best tanks to a soft and fatal halt and the cold that froze men to death—it was difficult to tell which was now the worst.

Fighting at **Suomussalmi** had reached its peak on the evening before: New Year's Eve. The **Russian Ninth Army** column was strung out over 20 miles on the road to Raate. Already it was beginning to look like a disaster area. Cold gnawed at the Red soldiers from without, hunger from within. Commanders of the 44th Division had lost contact with the 163rd Division further on.

The Finns had already dealt with the Mongols of the 163rd. Five thousand dead had been counted. Countless others would lie beneath the snow until spring. Now the Finns were ready for the 44th.

They came in the darkness, creeping to within a hundred yards of the road and opening up with machine guns, rifles and mortars. Then, like ghosts, came the men on skis, swerving through the forest, hurling grenades as they turned to ski as silently away.

Two days the Russians suffered on the road before urging their commander, A. E. Vinagradov, to let them retreat from this white hell while there was still time. But their general preferred a probable death from a Finnish gun than a certain bullet from a firing squad back home. Next day, on his orders, two companies tried to force a way back to the frontier to get supplies. The hidden guns swept them as they went. Casualties reached 70 per cent. For three days, Vinagradov sent more men after them. Each time, they joined the frozen corpses of those who had gone before.

Now, along the deadly road, the strung out Red division was being prepared for the final kill. On 5 January the Finns began cutting it into slices, punctuating it with barriers of fallen trees and minefields. The Russians were now trapped in isolated segments, unable to move.

There was no path for the tanks off the road, through the deep forest and deeper snows. Be-

The remains of the Soviet 44th Division. The Finns took 40 tanks, 1200 horses, 100 field guns, 278 trucks, hundreds of small arms and 1000 prisoners (inset).

latedly, the Russians began studying newly provided 'How to Ski' manuals, and wrestle with elaborate catches. Stacks of manuals and bundles of skis would be found later at the roadside.

Picking off blundering Russian soldiers in the woods was 'almost too easy' admitted one veteran Finn. 'We only have to follow their footsteps in the snow . . . or wait till they were desperate with the cold and they light a fire.' Faced with such perils out there in the Arctic wilderness, most of the Russians on the road chose to stay where they were, dig in and shoot it out.

Macabre cavalcade

Hopefully, they could hang on until help came. The Finns lacked heavy weaponry to break up the enclaves, nor did they have anti-aircraft guns to turn on the Russian planes that still, occasionally, brought in supplies.

But those planes were getting fewer. The Russians began to eat their horses. Only starvation drove them out of their enclaves to make desperate efforts to meet up with the next isolated group down the road. Few ever got through.

Threading through the forests, the Finns kept coming. Reporter Geoffrey Cox watched them. 'It was dusk. The hour of troop movement. The road was crowded with a macabre cavalcade of war. Coming towards us in one long stream were the men who had fought the battle returning to rest. Moving up with us were the fresh troops. The men from the forest came on skis, on foot, piled four or five on sledges pulled by ponies.

'. . . Their faces were the faces of men who had seen terrible things and looked on death for many days. Many had cheeks and foreheads blackened with fire of machine-guns. Almost all had dark, staring exhausted eyes.'

Applause for gallant Finland reached new heights in the world. But as their leader, Dr Risto Ryti knew well, more than applause was needed. Finland needed men and material without delay, not fine sentiments.

There was no shortage of the latter. King Gustav V of Sweden had sent a New Year's message, wishing success. Unknown to him his country's codebreakers under Dr Arne **Beurling** were doing rather more, passing on decrypts of Russian radio messages to the Finns.

Mussolini wrote Hitler a long letter on 3 January warning that Italy was favourably disposed towards 'brave little Finland'—and that Hitler had backed the wrong horse in her alliance with Russia. Hatred of Communism in Italy was 'absolute, solid as a rock'. In the United States, Roosevelt agreed there was a 'great desire for some action and assistance'—but also fear of 'involvement in European Wars'. In London, Foreign Secretary Lord Halifax told the Finnish Ambassador: 'I wish I had airplanes in my pockets. You would get them all.'

Meanwhile the most concrete contributions to the small nation came, fittingly, from ordinary men and women, not governments. In Belgium, schoolchildren contributed a week's pocket money to the Finnish children's fund. In Sweden, 900,000 workmen put in a voluntary day's work on 6 January, a public holiday, and handed over the proceeds, some £60,000 to the National Fund for Finland.

But if working people were ready to open their purses, the Allied governments seemed less willing. 'Up till now we have given very little reason to show that we attach any real importance to the continued existence of Finland. The war material we have sent . . . is obviously not going to affect the final issue . . . is merely a gesture' admitted Sir Orme Sargent of the Foreign Office. Britain sent just 10 long-nosed Blenheim bombers to Finland this month. French aid to Finland was more generous. Only as the month progressed and the Finns proved how well they could hand out punishment to the Red Army did Allied war

'We cannot say what Finland's fate will be, but nothing could be sadder to the rest of the civilized world than that this splendid northern race should be destroyed and, in the face of incredible odds, should fall into slavery worse than death'

Winston Churchill

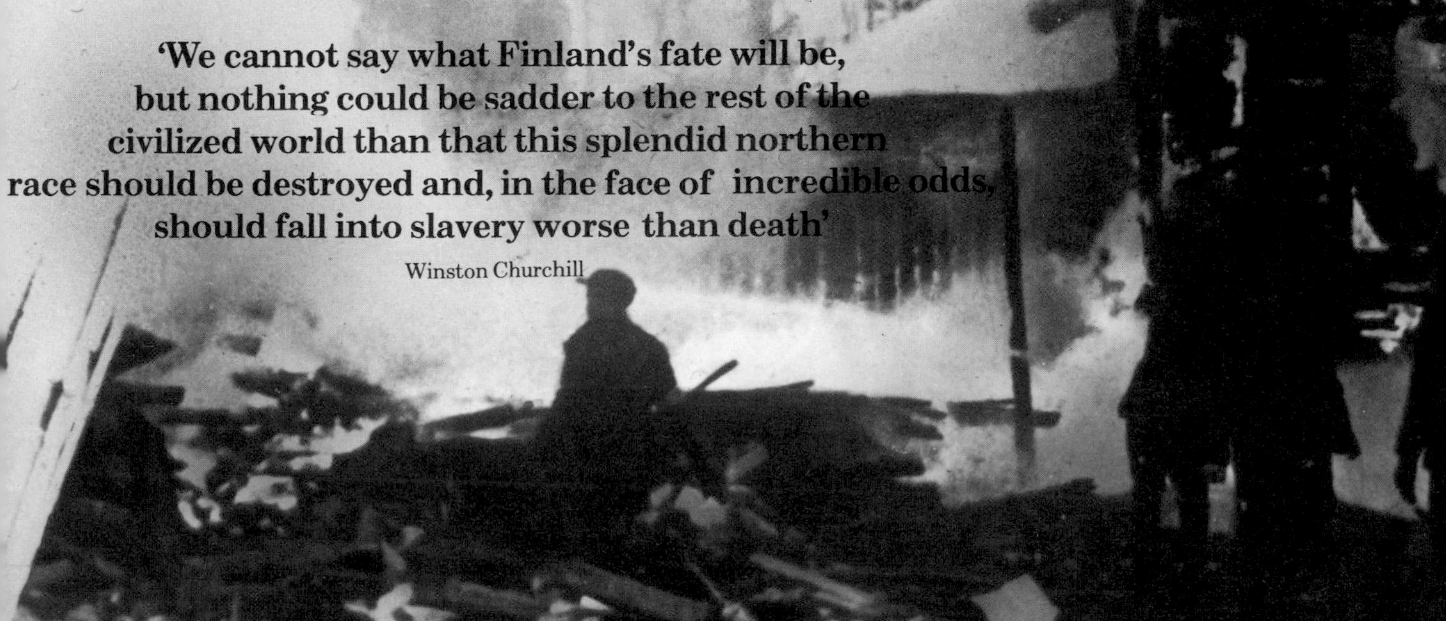

cabinets begin to shift. 'Finnish resistance, if sufficiently supported might result in a defeat of Russia' mused Britain's War Minister, Leslie Hore-Belisha. The War Cabinet agreed in principle to the enlistment of British **volunteers** as well as sending precious equipment that the armed forces could ill afford.

The Finns were not only handing out punishment this month: they showed too that they could take it. On New Year's Eve the second stage of Russia's war had begun. Stalin's aim was to 'demolish the Finnish supply lines to the Front, knock the railroads out of commission, bomb the bridges and strafe the locomotives'. It was also to terrorize the population. Hospitals were frequent targets. Shrapnel bombs, designed especially to maim and kill civilians arrived as the latest expression of the Soviet people's undying friendship for the Finns.

Finland's anti-aircraft guns and air force, outnumbered 10-1, could only take a savage toll of the bombers. In four minutes on 6 January Lieutenant Jorma Sarvanto shot down six Ilyushin DB3s.

By 14 January, 365 towns and villages had been attacked. At **Oulu,** eyewitnesses reported: 'Bombs weighing 500lb crashed among the little wooden houses in which most of the population live . . . soon there were a dozen fires . . . the raiders swooped low. The streets were sprayed with machine-gun bullets. The terror lasted all day.'

Yet casualties were surprisingly low: by the end of January the death toll was only 377. The simple trench shelters, under an 8ft roof of logs, took the onslaught well. The low houses were scattered and thus hard to hit. And by day, women and children hid in the woods to avoid the raids.

Many trekked further. By 8 January there were an estimated 400,000 Finnish evacuees, one in ten of the population. Many found shelter in neighbouring Norway and Sweden.

The women of Finland, indeed, were long used to the horrors and trials of war. While the men fought, the women moved into the jobs they left behind; became postmen, shopkeepers, factory workers. Since Finland's Civil War they had been wearing the grey uniforms of the 100,000-strong Lotta Svard organization, named after a now national folk heroine. Their blue and white swastika badges had been chosen before Adolf Hitler hit on the ancient symbol.

Though the air war failed to crush the Finns it revealed the first stage in Stalin's root-and-branch rethinking of his tactics against the stubborn nation. It was plain that the Finns required all

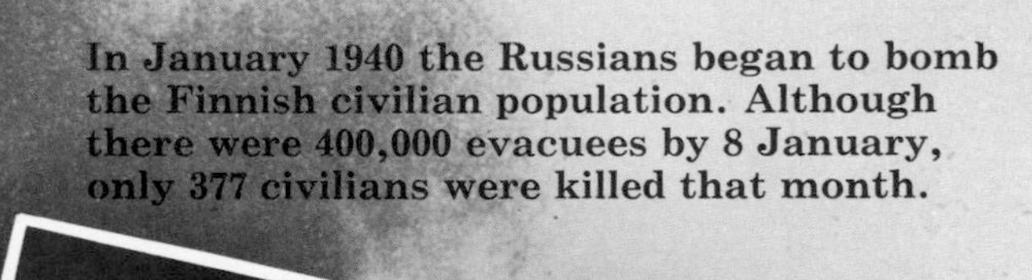

In January 1940 the Russians began to bomb the Finnish civilian population. Although there were 400,000 evacuees by 8 January, only 377 civilians were killed that month.

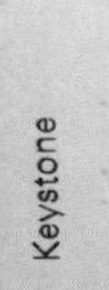

the firepower that mighty Russia could organize.

It was not only at Sumussalmi that things had gone wrong. Five hundred miles north of Helsinki, 250 miles from any other battlefield, a private war had been going on at **Petsamo**—and was not yet over. It was an extraordinary match: locals and employees of the International Nickel Company versus the Soviet **Fourteenth Army.**

From his forester's hut, Major Roinen, Finnish officer in charge, was holding off two Russian divisions with no more than 700 men at his disposal. The temperature plummeted to −41°C. Blizzards raged. Once again, the world began making derisive comments about Stalin's Bolshevik Army.

Criticism came from friend and foe alike. On 20 January Churchill said: 'They (the Finns) have exposed for all the world to see, the military capacity of the Red Army and of the **Red Air Force.** Many illusions about Soviet Russia have been dispelled in those few weeks of fighting in the Arctic circle. Everyone can now see how Communism rots the soul of a nation.'

Russian leaders shot

The German General Staff took an equally bleak view. 'Organization, equipment and means of leadership unsatisfactory . . . Fighting qualities of the troops in heavy fighting, dubious. The Russian 'mass' is no match for an army with modern equipment and superior leadership.'

Stalin had a special solution to problems of poor leadership: it was time to shoot the leaders.

Vinagradov, scapegoat for the debacle on the Raate Road, faced his firing squad after all. So did Commissar Podhomoutov, Commander Sarov and Captain Tsaikowski.

Timoshenko, commander of the Kiev Military District and veteran of the Polish occupation was summoned to Moscow. He was made commander of the entire Finnish campaign and replaced Voroshilov as People's Commissar of Defence.

Suddenly, in the last days of January, a silence returned to the Isthmus on Finland's key line of defence, the 88-mile Mannerheim Line. The weary Finns knew what it meant. The Russians were making ready. Timoshenko had come to his new job with a set of well-laid plans. By the month's end he had brought up 25 divisions. From Helsinki the troop trains once again rolled east to the line.

They were still alone in their epic battle, still confident that the next attack on the Line would be beaten off, as had every attack to date.

But as they went, their leaders in Helsinki were already studying dramatic news from Moscow. 'The Government of the Soviet Union is not opposed in principle to negotiating an agreement with the Ryti-**Tanner** Government' read the letter received on 29 January.

Whatever happened next on the battlefield, January had plainly proved one fact—the Finns had taken on the might of Soviet Russia and there was to be no more pretence that Finland's leaders could be ignored.

On 30 January, the leaders met to draft a reply. February, they knew, would seal the nation's fate, one way or another.

War Notes

FINLAND FIGHTS ON

A. B. Reportagebild

BEURLING, Dr Arne: Swedish cryptographer, b. 1905. Professor of Maths at Upsaala University. Recruited by cryptology chief Yves Gylden among team of 22 before Sept 1939. Based in Swedish Ministry of Defence Gray Building. Paid half-crown a day. Broke Red Army top 5-digit code Nov-Dec, on 5mm squared graph paper. According to David Kahn's *The Codebreakers* (1968) Beurling was thus able to tell the Finns (presumably Mannerheim's HQ around 15 Dec) that Russian 44th Div was advancing from Raate to extricate the 163rd at Suomussalmi.

FOURTEENTH ARMY (RUSSIAN): 8 infantry divisions with tanks and 80 aircraft in direct support. Captured objectives early in Dec but halted at Nautsi on Arctic Highway by weather and 2 Finnish regiments from 18 Jan 1940 to end of war.

NINTH ARMY (RUSSIAN): 5 infantry divisions (44th, 54th, 88th, 122nd and 163rd) with 42 bombers in direct support. Ultimate objective was Oulu on the Gulf of Bothnia to split Finland in half and cut off help from Sweden. 44th Div: motorized formation of 17,000 crack Ukranian troops from Moscow Military District. CO A. E. Vinogradov. Only 1300 men survived, as PoWs. The Finns captured 46 field and 29 AT guns, 43 tanks, 200 lorries, 100 machine-guns, 190 automatic weapons, 6000 rifles, 32 field kitchens and 1170 horses. 163rd Div: a poor-quality formation, mainly composed of Mongol troops. It lost 5000 battle dead and 500 PoWs. The Finns captured 11 tanks, 25 field guns, 150 trucks and 250 horses. Fate of the CO, Selendsov, unknown.

OULU: rail junction and seaport at mouth of R. Oulu on Gulf of Bothnia, 280 miles N of Helsinki. Population 26,446.

PETSAMO: 60 miles NW of Murmansk on Petsamo Fjord border of Norway. Ice-free harbour and fishing centre of 2000 people with important nickel mines including concession owned by British-Canadian Mond company that invested £1.5 m.

RED AIR FORCE: founded 1918. Essentially a tactical air force to support the Red Army and under its command. Against Finland 696 aircarft were split between the 4 invading armies with 200 more in Estonia. By mid-Jan there were 1500 planes despite losses of several hundred to Finnish flak and fighters. The C-in-C (Head of the Chief Directorate of the Air Forces) Yakov Vladimirovich Smushkevich directed air operations from his HQ at Petrozavodsk. He had been C-in-C only since Sept 1939; the purges had eliminated most of the High Command. Air regiments of 60 planes replaced the old air brigades from April 1939; 4–6 regiments were grouped in new air divisions.

SUOMUSSALMI: village of 4000 people 110 miles E of Oulu in N. Central Finland. Built on a peninsula formed by 2 frozen lakes.

TANNER, Vaino: Finnish Foreign Minister, Leader of Social Democratic Party. PM 1926–7. Opposed defence expenditure in 1930s. Minister of Finance 1939. 2nd delegate in Oct-Nov 1939 negotiations with USSR.

VOLUNTEERS: most of the total of 11,500 arrived in Feb and were too late to strike a blow. Among the 8000 Swedes was Flygflottilj 19. This unit of 16 British-built planes arrived on 11 Jan under Maj. Hugo Beckhammer. They operated in the L. Kemi region against Soviet Ninth Army. Despite their airfield being bombed soon after arrival, they shot down a I-15bis Polikarpov biplane fighter on the 12th.

FEBRUARY 1940

Keystone

...GOOD NEWS raises British spirits as reports come in that a daring raid on a prisoner of war ship, the Altmark, *has freed its captives. Good news is needed. The most savage winter in living memory has Europe in its grip. But both sides are planning action–the target is Norway. For the Allies, it will prove an adventure that will unfold into a disaster, and bring down their governments...*

1st: Timoshenko's offensive.
2nd: Balkan Entente Conference at Belgrade.
3rd: 1st German raider (He 111) crashes in England during E. Coast shipping attacks.
4th: Russians bomb 141 Finnish targets.
5th: Dutch C-in-C Gen Reynders resigns over lack of preparedness.
6th: IRA parcel bombs at Euston Station injure 4.
7th: 2 IRA men executed at Winson Green Prison, Birmingham.
8th: Double agent Harry Sawyer arrives US to head German spy network.
9th: German destroyers mine the Wash.
10th: Unarmed Spitfire photographs Wilhelmshaven and Emden.
11th: Russians breakthrough Mannerheim Line. Soviet-German Trade Agreement.
12th: 1st ANZAC troops arrive at Suez. Enigma rotors recovered from U33, sunk in the Clyde.
13th: British aid delegation sees Finnish PM.
14th: *Altmark* enters Norwegian territorial waters.
15th: Finns begin withdrawal to 2nd line defences in Mannerheim Line.
16th: *Altmark* Incident, Norway.
17th: US President sends Sumner Welles to Europe 'fact-finding'.
18th: Japs forced to withdraw after Battle of Nanning.
19th: King Gustav reaffirms Swedish neutrality.
20th: Finns repulse renewed Russian attacks across frozen R. Taipale.
21st: Hitler appoints Falkenhorst to plan Weserübung operation.
22nd: IRA bomb injures 12 in Oxford St.
23rd: *Ajax* and *Exeter* crews on R. Plate victory march through London.
24th: Hitler adopts 'Manstein Plan'.
25th: 1st Canadian Air Force squadron arrives in UK.
26th: *Queen Elizabeth* begins secret maiden voyage.
27th: Finns in Karelian Isthmus begin withdrawal to rear positions.
28th: King and Queen and Churchill visit Clydeside.
29th: Turkish PM denies mobilization reports.

FEBRUARY 1940:

THE WORST OF WINTERS

Of all the events of February 1940, most far reaching was one that people were supposed not to know about—the weather. Their newspapers, firmly pinned down by the iron hand of censorship, could not report on the weather. They could print the rising and setting times for the sun and moon, and high water at London Bridge. But that was all. Weather reports were potentially helpful to the enemy, so they were treated as classified information.

But the people knew. From Scotland to Italy, from France to Rumania, warring or neutral, all countries suffered alike. Europe froze.

England had seen nothing like it for 45 years. Meteorologists at Birmingham recorded 35 degrees of frost. The Thames froze. On the lake in Hyde Park, Londoners skated on the ice.

Even more surprising, on Britain's usually mild southern coasts, the sea froze. From Bognor Regis on the Channel round to Southend on the Thames

'One of the lowest temperatures was recorded at Buxton, where 33 degrees of frost were registered... Among the discomforts were rail and road delays, when drifts formed and had to be cleared away – in some cases cars and lorries remaining buried in the snow for several days.'

Illustrated London News, 10 February 1940

FOX Photos

British soldiers, one with a Bren gun, look out towards the German frontier from their position on the Maginot Line.

Estuary, the older inhabitants muttered sagely that they had never seen the like of it in their lifetimes.

Living conditions, already made difficult by wartime restrictions, became intolerable. The big freeze brought what was left of normal life to a halt. It affected transport and communications and put great pressure on troops. Industry, agriculture and domestic life were all severely disrupted.

Soldiers paraded with shovels to clear 12ft snowdrifts from roads east of London in Kent and Essex. Around Folkestone, villages remained isolated for weeks, and food ran perilously low.

Frozen to death

Trains halted on railway routes to the north. To be 10 or 12 hours late was normal for travellers to Scotland. Bemused railway officials had to report some trains 'lost'. Telephone wires throughout Britain collapsed under the weight of snow.

Water supply was hampered more than usual. When household pipes burst they stayed burst, as many plumbers were engaged in war work so were unavailable to fix them. Pipes burst so frequently that water authorities had to fix standpipes in the streets for householders to use.

Inevitably, there were casualties. A Newcastle family of six were killed when a boiler exploded in their home.

English farmers, attempting to cope with the problems caused by the demands for food and by the wartime restrictions, were now confronted with huge stock losses. Hundreds of sheep perished, frozen to death in the fields. Where the grass was not covered by snow, frost turned it

'I don't know how the men keep warm in weather like this. The answer is, I suppose, they don't... Everything you touch... is numbing to the fingers.'

J. L. Hodson, *Through Night and Day*

yellow and dry, creating a shortage of feed for cows. Winter vegetables—swedes and turnips—were frozen solid and could not be lifted, and kale hung in withered fronds from the plants. This put more pressure on farmers to use the rapidly diminishing stocks of mangels and hay.

Towards the end of February, normally a time to look forward to the prospect of an early spring, the British were altogether fed up. Even Canadian troops in Britain, used to long hard winters, shivered and stamped and cursed the English weather.

Only one thing could be said in favour of the weather—it did make Britain look picturesque. A peculiar weather phenomenon had put warm air in the upper atmosphere and produced rain. On contact with the ground it froze. So did water splashed up from roads by passing cars. The result was a 'silver thaw', clothing trees and hedges in a Christmas card covering of white ice.

British soldiers in France suffered too. The soldiers, sleeping under a single issue blanket kept their overcoats on all night. But they still could not stay in bed beyond about 3am. They simply got up and went walking round the towns to keep circulation going. The incessant shuffling, stamping and arm swinging along the length of the French fortifications, kept away hypothermia,

The winter of 1940 was the most ferocious Europe had seen since 1895. A German soldier (far left) keeps watch on French border positions while French troops continue with manoeuvres.

and gave rise to a new phrase among the troops, the 'Maginot minuet'.

To stave off the cold a French war correspondent recommended that the troops should form up in twos and kick the soles of their partners' feet in turn—right-to-right, left-to-left, change.

One problem was that the men had not got suitable clothing. In one company only 10 per cent of the men had the new battledress which was large enough for sweaters to be worn under its blouse. The others still wore tight fitting tunics. Feet were especially vulnerable. One soldier's feet swelled, so he rubbed them with bacon fat, popped them into sandbags filled with straw, and stood around as if he was on a pair of sandstone pillars.

Still, the troops went on trying to fight the war and do their work. Their dogged attitude was noted by many. Motor cycle despatch riders suffered particularly as they slithered over the ice-covered roads to deliver messages. Often they had to be lifted off their motorbikes, their arms stiff, eyes frozen up, and jaws immobile.

The troops could at least take heart in the knowledge that their leaders were suffering as much as they were. Lord Gort, the Commander-in-Chief, lived a spartan life and seemed immune to discomfort, including cold. Gort's insensitivity amazed visiting Prime Minister Neville Chamberlain. Chamberlain was to regret wearing knickerbockers, boots with the tabs sticking out, and a summer-weight raincoat. Gort took him on a seemingly endless tour of the front line.

Writing to his sister Chamberlain moaned: 'I went over a good part of the line and saw various defence systems of which I understood very little. We finally had a march past on the aerodrome and the icy wind so froze my face that I could hardly move my jaws afterwards . . .'

Throughout Europe there was no escape from the interminable, unbearable winter. In Paris there was a fuel crisis. Because the men were away at the front, the authorities had ordered that rents be waived and so, landlords of apartment blocks refused to light the boilers.

Markets empty

Outside Paris some people enjoyed better fortune. A correspondent to *The Lady* set out the reason for this: 'Thanks to the Kings of France our village need never be cold. We are surrounded by Crown woods, and it is the ancient privilege of the householders, which no revolution has taken from them, to gather dead wood.'

Germany suffered mostly from food shortages. Potato transports foundered in the snow, and their cargoes, scattered wide in innumerable traffic shunts, perished with the frost. The markets were empty of vegetables. Women hung around waiting on the off-chance of a delivery. Then they went home, the day wasted. It was like World War I all over again.

An Englishwoman, married to a German, summed up better than anybody the bleak mood that settled over Europe as the weeks of winter dragged on: 'There was something coldly unreal about those winter months of watching and waiting—watching for the news we hoped would come from America, waiting for the Generals to act. They in their turn, we heard, were waiting for Hitler to attack in the West . . . but the expected attack in the West did not come. We were watching and waiting, they were watching and waiting, even Hitler seemed to be watching and waiting—nothing moved. It was as if the bitter, relentless cold had seeped its way into the very fibre of events.'

Eye Witness

In the winter 1939/40 Second-Lieutenant Evelyn Waugh, the novelist, was posted to Kingsdown, Kent, with the Royal Marines. He describes a typical day:

On Tuesday we spent the morning on the downs, mostly in heavy snow, doing very simple tactical problems which I managed to fail. After luncheon we had another lecture and then marched through a blizzard to see some field latrines. I moved into my hut and enjoyed the privacy, but found it a cold night even with a fur rug and oil stove. The Marines are suffering unendurably. Poor Marine Rose has become quite cheerful at the prospect of so much distress. This morning in deep snow and a keen wind to fresh, easy tactical excercises.

The prospect is extraordinary with white foreground and dingy sea background full of a hundred or more neutral ships awaiting the contraband control. One, an Italian, was wrecked last night.

FEBRUARY 1940:

WILFRED AND WESERÜBUNG

Unannounced and unexpected, a German aircraft landed at Fornebu airport, on the outskirts of Oslo. The moment it rolled to a halt 30 men, in civilian clothes, jumped out. Carrying cameras and notebooks, they scattered across the bleak icy airfield snapping pictures and hurriedly scribbling notes.

Baffled airport officials approached the plane and demanded to see the pilot's papers. He showed them a permit to investigate the *Altmark*. But that was 40 miles away. The pilot waved aside their protests with a meaningless gesture, stalling for time, and before the Norwegians could work out what to do, the industrious observers had hurried back to the plane. The pilot was airborne a minute later, and on his way back to Germany.

With that simple piece of effrontery the Germans pieced together a comprehensive record of the lay-out and facilities of Fornebu airport: vital intelligence for a planned air invasion. But Norwegian airfield authorities had been told that the Germans were planning a commercial airline route between Germany and **Norway**, and failed to see the true significance of the incident.

LUFTHANSA

'It's like an act of fate. I have told my ideas to so many people and nothing ever came of it. And now... we are going to get help.'

Major Vidkun Quisling

Michael Roffe

Norway, innocent, powerless and neutral, at the beginning of the war, occupied the position of a plain but wealthy heiress surrounded by reluctant suitors. None of them really wanted her, yet all were desperate not to see her fall into anybody else's hands. She herself wanted only to preserve her independence.

Winston Churchill was the first to recognize Norway's invaluable assets. The 'zone of destiny', he called that small northern country. Back in September 1939 he had outlined the strategic importance of Norway.

The geographical key to Norway's importance was its neutral territorial waters—the **'Leads'**—running the length of the coastline between the mainland and the string of small offshore islands.

During summer months, German shipping had use of the Gulf of Bothnia, the northern arm of the Baltic, to transport the vast quantities of iron ore, vital to Germany's steel industry: 83 per cent of its 1940 imports were brought from **Sweden's** Gallivare orefields to be turned into steel.

But the plunging temperatures of winter froze the Gulf of Bothnia. With the ore-loading port of Lulea closed, the only alternative was the ocean port of Narvik, north of the Arctic circle. So between October and April, after only a short rail passage across Sweden and Norway, the ore was shipped down the protected coastal waters.

A relatively simple operation, Churchill pointed out, would stop that traffic dead. Starved of its vital raw material in that first winter of war, German industry would have nothing to smelt into steel, no steel to forge into the ships and tanks, aircraft, guns and U-boats that would sustain Hitler's Reich in its war with the Allies. All the Royal Navy had to do, Churchill insisted, was to sow minefields in the Leads.

But the cabinet were not convinced, and months were to pass before they sanctioned mining operations in Norwegian waters.

There was one very powerful reason for Churchill to turn his gaze towards Norway. He knew, from his network of sympathetic German contacts established pre-war, that Germany had interests in nuclear power, promising weapons of a new dimension of devastation. Not more than 25 miles from the German border, at Copenhagen, the Danish scientist Niels **Bohr** had already succeeded in splitting the uranium 235 atom. He could easily be swept into the German ambit.

As for Norway the focus of interest was the

The unscheduled visit to Fornebu airport outside Oslo told the Germans about its layout and anti-aircraft defences. They estimated that at least 1500 men could be airlifted there daily.

Historical Research Unit   Ullstein/Trevor Lawrence

'To writers the word Quisling is a gift from the gods. If they had been ordered to invent a new word for traitor . . . they could hardly have hit upon a more brilliant combination of letters.'

The Times

Norsk Company's factory at Vemork, 80 miles west of Oslo. Here was the world's only source for manufacturing heavy water, the vital ingredient needed to generate an atomic explosion.

Churchill alone knew this. He did not tell Prime Minister Neville Chamberlain, whose misjudgement of German attitudes and events had already been amply demonstrated. Continuing to promote his interests in Norway, Churchill claimed iron ore traffic as his main target.

Norway took on a new strategic significance when Soviet armies invaded Finland at the end of November 1939. Sharing a common border with Finland in the far north, Norway provided the only possible route through which British and French troops could pass if they were to go to Finland's aid. They would have to disembark at Narvik, along with their supplies, and move by train through Sweden to the front. Of course, if Norway could be persuaded to let the Allies take over the ports of Narvik, and Trondheim and Bergen further south, they would automatically cut off Germany's winter iron ore traffic at the same time. What is more, the heavy water plant could be kept from falling into German hands.

Military planning for the expedition commenced. A volunteer battalion of Scots Guards in the Alps were trained for skiing to meet the rigours of Norway's snowy mountains.

After months of hesitation, British and French leaders, meeting at the Supreme War Council of 5 February, confirmed the plan to help Finland—provided Norway and Sweden allowed Allied troops on their soil. But neither would agree, and after the Russo-Finnish armistice of 12 March, the plan was shelved and troops disbanded.

But Churchill would not give up. His new idea for gaining a toe-hold in Norway was simpler. So simple that, with his journalist's flair for dreaming up appropriate codewords for great operations, he chose 'Wilfred'—the youngest of three newspaper cartoon characters, Pip, Squeak and Wilfred.

Under 'Wilfred' Britain would first explain to Norway that her neutrality was too helpful to Germany, and then mine the Leads. If Germany retaliated, the Allies would be ready to step in as protectors of Norway's ports and vital assets.

While the Allies hesitated, Hitler was anxious

to ensure that Norway stayed neutral. But it did not take him long to change his mind. And the impulse came, as it had in the British Government, from the senior men in the navy.

On 10 October, Grand Admiral Erich **Raeder,** Naval Commander-in-Chief, reported to the Führer that the British had designs on Norway and were planning to land an occupying force.

Hitler was not slow to grasp the strategic significance of this intelligence. An occupation by British forces would give the Royal Navy a base from which to prey not only on the ore shipping, but on all Germany's sea-borne movements through the Kattegat and Skagerrak. Also, air bases in Norway would bring Germany's northern cities within range of RAF bombers.

Quisling

If, on the other hand, the Germans themselves were to occupy Norway, they could rapidly develop excellent U-boat bases along the Norwegian coast extending the range of their U-boats out into the Atlantic.

But Hitler was preoccupied with planning an attack in the West, and merely told Raeder he would consider the matter. He was probably unaware that one of his own party officials, Alfred **Rosenberg,** had been busily cultivating a useful Norwegian contact.

Before long this man would be elevated from international respectability to a top place in the annals of villainy: his name would give a new word to the language—Vidkun **Quisling.**

A brilliant soldier—he was awarded the highest marks ever recorded at Oslo's military academy—Quisling dabbled on the fringes of politics. His Nasjonal Samling (National Unity) Party, he swore, would save Norway from anarchy and disintegration and from the threat of Bolsheviks and 'spiritual Jews'. An imaginative invention, for there were only some 1500 Jews in Norway, and Quisling was married to one of them.

As Nazism gathered strength on the other side of the Baltic, Quisling was not alone in his dreams of racial purity. Nazi 'philosopher' Alfred Rosenberg, head of the *Aussenpolitisches Amt*, the department handling propaganda abroad, was of the same mind. Rosenberg's aim was to unite the Scandinavian countries in a great Nordic community, and bring them under the umbrella of German leadership in an alliance of northern peoples. To further this aim, he had revived the **Nordic Society** in Lübeck as a front organization. Quisling joined in 1931.

Quisling and Rosenberg first met in June 1939. Rosenberg instantly recognized Quisling's potential as a leader of the Norwegian arm of Nazism. Quisling promised to change the political situation in Norway to favour Germany, and claimed to have 200,000 supporters. It was an empty boast. In fact he had far fewer supporters and had little prospect of changing Norway's political scene.

What Quisling wanted, however, was Nazi support for the party in Norway. Rosenberg agreed. He arranged for Quisling's supporters to be trained in Germany. In return Quisling would keep the Nazis informed of Allied activities in Norway.

The agreement flourished. Quisling reported to Rosenberg. Rosenberg told Raeder, who also received reports from Abwehr, the intelligence organization under Admiral Canaris.

Rosenberg secured Quisling a series of meetings

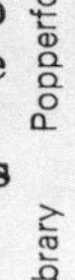

Popperfoto

Radio Times Hulton Picture Library

Each year Germany shipped millions of tons of Swedish iron ore from Narvik in northern Norway, the ships steaming south in the safety of Norway's coastal waters. Churchill was anxious to stop the traffic by mining neutral Norwegian waters.

with Hitler, and on 13 December, the adoring Norwegian first shook hands with his hero.

That same day Hitler ordered General Alfred **Jodl,** his Chief of Operations Staff at OKW (the armed forces supreme command), to start planning for a possible takeover of Norway.

An act of fate

Quisling had his last audience with the Führer on 18 December. While Hitler stressed his preference to see Norway stay neutral, he also made it clear that he would forestall any action by the Allies in Norway that would threaten Germany.

That was enough of an opening for Quisling. 'Herr Reichskanzler, have I correctly understood that you are willing to help us?' Quisling pressed. 'Yes, absolutely, I will' the Führer agreed.

According to Rosenberg, who recorded the exchange in his diary, Quisling was deeply happy. Returning to his hotel by car, Quisling told his escort 'It's like an act of fate. I have told my ideas to so many people and nothing ever came of it. And now . . . at a decisive moment, we are going to get help.'

Before he left Berlin, Quisling discussed details for the German occupation plan with Rosenberg. They arranged that Quisling would engineer a coup, then appeal to Germany for 'help'.

Rosenberg saw Quisling off with a handshake. In his diary he recorded, 'We shook hands, knowing that we should see each other again after the action had been successful, and Quisling could be addressed as Norway's premier.'

Hitler ordered a payment of £10,000 per month into Quisling's funds, to start on 15 March. In return Quisling would supply intelligence reports on Britain's preparations. Beyond that, Hitler left these lesser men to fend for themselves. Quietly he ordered OKW to start 'Study North'—the plan to take Norway. He didn't mind how. It could be a bloodless invasion 'by invitation' or failing that, an invasion by force.

But he kept the planning strictly within the confines of OKW. Even Göring was kept outside the privileged circle. When Göring did eventually learn of the plan, from Hitler's official announcement, he flew into a rage and stopped co-operating with the other services.

Rosenberg also found himself excluded. He would only learn of the plan far later, when the newspapers reported German landings. As for Quisling, nobody told him anything.

The invasion plan

Late in February, alarming intelligence arrived in Berlin. Britain's plans for a Norwegian invasion were at an advanced stage. Hitler, until then coolly indifferent to his own Norwegian plan, became an ardent supporter. When he learned of the Altmark incident, he was convinced. If the British would enter a fjord to attack his ships, they were no respecters of Norway's neutrality. It was time for him to pre-empt the British.

On 21 February General Nikolaus von **Falken-**

War Notes

WILFRED AND WESERÜBUNG

BOHR, Niels Henrik David: Danish physicist, b. 1885. Educated in Copenhagen and studied under Sir Ernest Rutherford at Cambridge, England. Professor in Theoretical Physics, Copenhagen 1916 and head of Institute for Theoretical Physics 1922. His work on atomic energy won him the Nobel Prize in physics 1922.

Popperfoto

Bildarchiv

FALKENHORST, Nikolaus von: German general, b. 1885. Served in German Army 1914–18. CO 21st Corps in Polish campaign 1939, and promoted to General der Infanterie for his efforts. It was his experience as a staff officer during Germany's 1918 seaborne intervention in Finland that led to his being chosen for the Norwegian operation. He submitted his plan for Weserübung within 8 days.

JODL, Alfred: German general, b. 1890 Würzburg, Bavaria. Served as artillery officer then staff officer 1914–18. A brilliant, ambitious man he decided Hitler was the man to follow when introduced to him by Ernest Röhm in 1923. Totally subservient to Hitler, he became his first adviser on strategic and operational problems. Promoted Lt-Colonel and head of the Reichswehr Ministry's Home Defence Department 1935. As Major-General he was appointed Chief of Operations to the newly formed OKW 1938.

LEADS: maze of deep-water passageways between the mainland and belt of islands along the western coast of Norway. Ships were able to navigate the Leads from Narvik, around the southern tip of Norway through the Kattegat to the safety of the Baltic.

NORDIC SOCIETY (Nordische Gesellschaft): formed to encourage amicable relations between Germany and Scandinavia. Inevitably infiltrated by Nazi element, the Society became the 'tool of insidious propaganda and cross espionage'. At the 1939 annual Lübeck congress, Quisling made an impressive speech, establishing himself as a leading expert on the proposed Nordic union.

NORWAY: constitutional monarchy, administratively divided into 20 counties. Comprises an area of 124,556 miles in the W. part of Scandinavian peninsula. Only 1100 miles in length, its extensive coastline, deeply indented with innumerable fjords, extends some 10,000 miles. Population 2,937,000 (1940). Chief industries, fisheries and shipping, agriculture and forestry. In 1939 merchant fleet rated 4th largest in the world with 4308 vessels; whaling fleet was the largest in Antarctic waters. Rapid rivers provide abundant supply of hydroelectric power, also used for logging. Remained neutral in 1914–18.

horst, an expert in mountain warfare, was appointed to develop 'the plan'. Left to his own resources to obtain details about Norway, Falkenhorst performed a simple piece of espionage. In uniform, and wearing his general's insignia, he trudged around the shopping centre of Berlin looking for a bookstall. Out of his own pocket he bought the Baedeker guidebook to Norway. Then, to conceal his real interest, he also bought Baedeker guides for several other countries.

On 26 February Falkenhorst and his small staff were given the official name 'Group 21', and with the support of OKW operations staff they started detailed planning. The operation took the code-name 'Weserübung' (Weser Exercise). It was a less imaginative choice than Churchill's.

By the end of February Hitler was ready, and on the first day of March signed his Directive for Weserübung to complete arrangements. It specified a peaceful occupation of Denmark and Norway 'designed to protect by force of arms the neutrality of the northern countries. If necessary, however, resistance would be 'broken by all means available'.

The size of his forces and thoroughness of German planning was aimed at a complete take-over. Hitler was not worried about a Norwegian invitation. He simply wanted to get there before the British, and there was no time to be lost. 'The most daring and most important undertaking in the history of warfare' must, he decided, be ready by 20 March.

A magazine cover of 1942 shows Quisling inspecting his Nazi-style troops.

War Notes

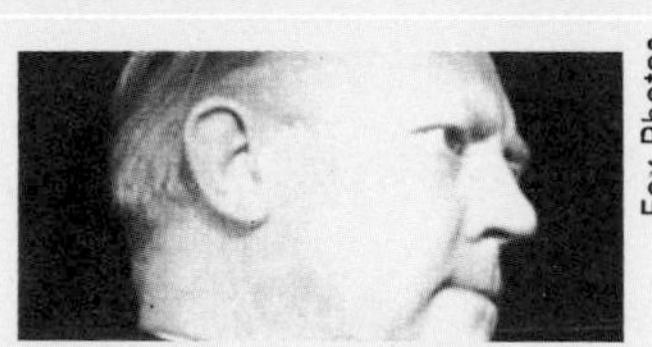

QUISLING, (Lauritz) Vidkun (Abraham): Norwegian politician, b. 1887 Fyresdal, Telemarken. Brilliantly clever schoolboy, he graduated a junior officer from Oslo Military Academy in 1911 with highest marks ever awarded. Captain by 1917, he was appointed military attaché in Petrograd 1918. Worked for explorer and scientist Fridtjof Nansen and League of Nations, responsible for the resettlement of refugees in Transcaucasus. Acted as Britain's representative in Moscow 1927 for which he was later awarded the OBE. Returned to Norway and joined anti-Communist Farmer's Party, becoming Minister of Defence 1931–2. Formed his own Nasjonal Samling Party 1933. It was his collaboration with Hitler that would later lead to his name becoming synonymous with 'traitor'.

RAEDER, Erich: Grand Admiral, b. 1876 Wandsbek, near Hamburg. From 1894 spent 2 years at Kiel Naval Academy and as a young officer cruised to the Orient with flotilla of warships. Served in Emperor William II's yacht *Hohenzollern.* Commander from 1911 and Chief of Staff to Admiral von Hipper during WWI, on mining operations and coastal raids of Britain. Survived *Lützow* sinking in Battle of Jutland. Captain of cruiser *Köln* 1917–18. Vice Admiral 1925. Named Chief of Naval Command and Admiral in 1928, and C-in-C of the Navy 1935. He played a central role in building and directing the new German Navy. Accepted Nazi Party Gold Badge of Honour 1937. Made Grand Admiral 1939.

Keystone

ROSENBERG, Alfred: Nazi philosopher and writer, b. 1893 Reval (Tallinn), Estonia. Studied for engineer's diploma at Riga college of technology. Lived in Paris for a time during WWI. Took up German citizenship and settled in Munich 1920. Impressed by his vast wealth of knowledge, Hitler made him Editor of Party newspaper *Volkischer Beobachter* 1921. Set up German People's Publishing House 1926 issuing monthly magazine *The World Struggle.* Created and lead the Kampfbund for German culture. Entered Reichstag 1930. Became director of new Nazi foreign policy office, controlling a network of foreign branches in 1933. Also administrator of German Academic Service. Regarded as a spiritual leader, he was responsible for training Party members in National Socialist ideology. His *Mythus des XX Jahrhunderts* (The Myth of the 20th Century), subtitled A Valuation of the Spiritual-Intellectual Conflicts of Our Time (finished in 1925 after 8 years work and published 1930), was adopted as the Third Reich official philosophy.

SWEDEN: constitutional monarchy with 25 'governments', comprising an area of 173,345 sq miles in the E. part of the Scandinavian peninsula. Population of 6 million included 5973 German, 2207 American and 1040 British residents. With more than half the country covered in forests lumber, woodworking paper and pulp mills major industries. Central Sweden housed the mining and agricultural industries including her important steel industry. Shipbuilding, shipping and fishing were also major industries. Remained neutral in WWI.

THE ALTMARK

For 299 men of the British merchant navy, February 1940 looked like being the cruellest of months. They had joined the merchant service expecting to sail peacefully from one trading port to another. Instead they were caged like rats in the hold of a prison ship, on their way to a German prison camp.

Packed together in the small dark hold of the oil tanker and supply ship, the **Altmark,** they were rarely allowed on deck. Jailers doled out meagre rations of stew, tea and lumps of black bread. Their only beds were floorboards or carpets, found in the cargo hold. Water was scarce and their latrine was a 40 gallon oil drum, periodically emptied overboard by the prisoners themselves.

To make matters worse the chief jailer was virulently anti-British. Captain Heinrich Dau, the 65-year-old veteran skipper of *Altmark*, had himself been a PoW—of the British in the first war. His dislike of the British was shown in his treatment of the prisoners in his charge.

Altmark had been gathering her harvest of prisoners since 1 October, 1939. On that day the pocket battleship *Graf Spee* acting as a surface raider in the South Atlantic and Indian Ocean, had sunk its first British merchant ship *SS Clement*. It was *Altmark's* task to supply the *Graf Spee* with fuel and to take on loot, including prisoners, from ships eliminated by the *Graf Spee*.

On 22 January, long after *Graf Spee* was scuttled in the River Plate estuary off Montevideo, Dau set course for Germany but by then the Royal Navy were looking for him.

Their search was aided by information supplied by merchant navy officers, who had been handed over to Uruguayan authorities in neutral Montevideo, by Captain Hans Langsdorff, of the *Graf Spee*.

Although the men were able to sight the 12,000-ton tanker with its distinctive single funnel, set well aft, they were unable to establish her name. Her crew regularly painted on false names—one week it became *Sogne*, the next it was *Hangsund*, then *Chirqueue*, and then *Altmark* again.

It was *Altmark* when Dau, enjoying the concealment of murky weather, started the last leg of the voyage home. On board, the prisoners were fully aware of the ship's course. From oddments found in the hold the men had made a simple sextant. Lookouts peered through cracks in the ship's structure and on 11 February they spotted the ice-capped mountains of Iceland.

Three days later they were in Norwegian territorial waters. Rumour had it that a Norwegian pilot had boarded the ship and was guiding her south, inside the three mile limit. Norway was anxious to preserve strict neutrality and so warships were not welcome in her waters.

Norwegian destroyers twice stopped *Altmark*. On the second occasion, Dau was asked by the skipper if there were any prisoners on board. Dau lied, saying there were not. Permission to search the ship was also denied the Norwegian skipper, on the grounds that *Altmark* belonged to the German war fleet and was therefore immune from investigation.

On 15 February *Altmark* entered the **'Bergen Defended Area'.** Below decks the prisoners were beginning to despair. Only 500 miles from Germany, many of them had given up hope of ever being rescued. The continual visits by the Norwegian Navy to *Altmark* only served to increase the sense of frustration among the seamen.

When two Norwegian destroyers and two torpedo boats came alongside and a group of officers boarded the prison ship, the captives shrieked and whistled like wild men to make themselves heard. They banged on plates and the latrine drum, and sounded SOS morse letters on their whistles to attract attention. A Norwegian officer stood not 15 yards from the din, but Dau had ordered the deck winches to run, to prevent the pleas for help from the men below. The prisoners came within an inch of breaking open a hatch, using iron bars, but their captors switched off the lights and forced them back into the hold with blasts of water from hose-pipes.

Incensed by the riot, Dau ordered rations of bread and water and withdrew the prison officer and doctor from their rounds.

'Find the Altmark'

At this stage, *Altmark* was fast becoming the focus of world attention. Newspapers, including those in neutral countries, were telling readers about the German prison ship. Britain's intelligence network in Norway was also following the ship's course. In London, the Admiralty had already despatched a destroyer flotilla to sweep the North Sea in search of German iron-ore shipping. On 16 February, they ordered its commander, Captain Philip **Vian in HMS Cossack,** in company with five other ships of the squadron, to concentrate on finding *Altmark*. Steaming north, then south-east, he found nothing.

The RAF played its part in pursuit of *Altmark*. On the afternoon of 16 February three **Hudsons** from Coastal Command crossed the grey skies over the North Sea and with much difficulty began looking for the elusive *Altmark*. At first, visibility was poor and observation a strain but as the day wore on visibility increased to a clear 40 miles, allowing the pilots' sight of the Norwegian coastline and its dramatic fjords.

At last a smudge of smoke appeared in the distance, and excited, the RAF observers flew in to investigate. The ship they found had the same colours as *Altmark*, but on closer inspection was found to have different markings. Bitterly disappointed, they flew on.

Fifteen seconds later they spotted a second ship. Again it displayed the same colouring as *Altmark*. Cruising at 1000ft they approached the ship, and turned into a dive for a closer look. One after another they swooped down, dipping over the ship's stern so low it seemed to onlookers they would hit the sea.

'As we dived my eyes were riveted on the stern,

On 15 February 1940 a Hudson aircraft of Coastal Command sighted *Graf Spee's* former supply ship *Altmark* in Norwegian waters. The 4th Destroyer Flotilla was alerted.

Popperfoto/Trevor Sutton

Popperfoto

Roy Coombs 79

'It was a filthy place with no fresh air... Conditions were terrible and the Germans made us as miserable as they possibly could with their heartless treatment.'

Frederick Thomas, Altmark prisoner

searching for a name', a Hudson pilot related in the London *Times* a few days later. 'I saw letters about a foot high. Because of the speed at which we were diving the letters seemed to dance in a jumble . . . I could not suppress a whoop of joy when I saw they read *Altmark*. . . . All the crews saw the word *Altmark*. Each man had both thumbs up. For a few moments we went wild as we swept across the decks at funnel height.'

Before long, RAF Coastal Command had details of the ship's position, course and speed. Passing the information straight to the Admiralty, Vian was signalled to 'Intercept at full speed', with the 4th Flotilla Group.

Intrepid was the first of the flotilla on the scene to spy the almost invisible grey *Altmark* against the dark cliffs. *Intrepid* closed in, her crew ready to board but Dau in *Altmark* had forseen the move and angrily bawled to the Norwegian skippers, who buzzed around him on the southward passage: 'The English warships are sailing in Norwegian waters. It is your duty to stop them!'

Obediently the gunboat *Skarv* manoeuvred in front of *Intrepid* and the British destroyer bore away, but there was still no escape for Dau—and he knew it. Even from outside territorial waters the British could shadow him as far as the **Skagerrak** and confront him in the open sea. His only chance was to seek shelter and wait for help to arrive. Abruptly Dau turned *Altmark* into Josingfjord, thrust his ship through the creaking pack-ice and dropped anchor between the towering snow covered cliffs.

Outside the fjord, *Cossack* and the other destroyers prowled like lions around prey.

Vian then ordered *Cossack* into the fjord and through a loudhaler called to the Norwegian *Kvell* gunboat captain to demand the release of the prisoners. The captain replied that Norwegian officers had examined *Altmark* at Bergen and had found no prisoners on board. The *Altmark* also had permission to sail south through Norwegian territorial waters. The demand was rejected.

Vian did not have orders to deal with this situation, so he withdrew and signalled the Admiralty.

Churchill's dilemma

In London, Winston Churchill brooded angrily over the attitude of the neutrals. He had already warned them unless they combined to resist the Germans they had no future. Now it looked as if the Norwegians were positively favouring the enemy. Pacing the floor of the Admiralty War Room, he deliberated what to do. If he acted impetuously and found no proof that British seamen were imprisoned on *Altmark* he could provoke massive retaliation by the Germans. The consequences for the Norwegians were unimaginable, and other neutrals, perhaps led by the United States, might well turn against Britain. On the other hand he knew he could not leave British merchant seamen unaided.

Finally he called Foreign Secretary, Lord Halifax, to clarify the international implications. Churchill then ordered a signal to Vian. 'Unless Norwegian torpedo boat undertakes to convoy *Altmark* to Bergen with a joint Anglo-Norwegian guard on board, and a joint escort, you should board *Altmark*, liberate the prisoners and take possession of the ship pending further instructions. If Norwegian torpedo boat interferes warn her to stand off. If she fires on you do not reply unless attack is serious, in which case defend yourself, using no more force than necessary.'

Action stations

If no prisoners were found on board, Vian was to bring the captain and officers to Britain to establish what had happened to them.

By 10pm that night, Vian was ready. His crew briefed, armed and at action stations. He crashed *Cossack* through the drifting ice and forced his way into the fjord, behind *Altmark*.

First he closed with the Norwegian gunboat *Kvell* and through an officer with a working knowledge of the Norwegian language told the captain that time was short; at daybreak German aircraft would be flying in to attack. It was suggested that the Norwegians submit to the superior force, to which the Norwegian captain agreed and with honour satisfied, allowed *Cossack* to pass into the fjord.

Along the coast lay *Altmark*, her bows rammed into the packed iceflows. On her bridge a search-

During their captivity, *Altmark's* prisoners tried to send an SOS message in a sealed tin, but the attempt was discovered and the offenders confined to the ship's hold until their rescue by HMS *Cossack*.

Ray Coombs

light flashed on, searching to identify the approaching ship, blinding the officers on *Cossack's* bridge. Moving, *Altmark's* propellers churned the icy waters, her huge bulk pulling back to ram *Cossack*. A collision amidships and that bulbous stern would crush the *Cossack* like matchwood.

Rapidly, Vian barked out orders for evasive action. The ship's artificers responded with skill born of months of training. Manipulating the main engine valves, *Cossack* swung out of line with *Altmark's* stern.

On *Cossacks'* deck Lieutenant-Commander Bradwell **Turner,** in command of the boarding party, stood poised, as the destroyer's rails were let down and fenders hung out, to ward off a crunching collision. The manoeuvre brought the *Altmark* into *Cossack's* other quarter and the boarding party ran across the deck to the port side, as a painful grinding sound signalled that the two ships were sliding into contact.

The German armed guard, provided by *Graf Spee*, leapt down on to the ice, blazing away at the men on *Cossack's* deck. Gunners returned the fire, mowing down German sailors, silhouetted against the glittering ice. Six of them died while more men fell wounded.

As the two ships collided, Bradwell brandishing his pistol and shouting to the rest of the boarding party to follow, leapt across to grab the tanker's rail. Instantly the 24-man-detail followed him. German sailors attempted to repel them, but against the trained British sailors, the merchant seamen stood little chance.

After a brief struggle, the Germans gave up the fight and surrendered.

'The Navy's here'

On the bridge of the captured ship, Bradwell Turner thrust the muzzle of his pistol at Captain Dau and, through a German linguist, ordered him to produce the prisoners. Bradwell's men were already searching *Altmark*, opening every hatch and compartment they could find.

'Any Englishmen here?' questioned a voice in the depths of the ship.

'Yes,' a chorus shouted back.

'The Navy's here!'

And with that the prisoners cheered themselves hoarse.

There was little chance of taking *Altmark* as a prize. During the siege she had run firmly aground on the rocky bottom of the fjord, but the prisoners were soon aboard *Cossack*, including one bitter seaman, who tried to obtain a rifle to shoot Captain Dau.

By midnight, *Cossack* was backing out of Josingfjord, and speeding across the North Sea towards **Rosyth.** Behind them lay a frustrated and humiliated German crew, prevented from pursuit by the ice. Ahead, the battleship *Warspite* and the battle cruiser *Hood* and three cruisers, *Edinburgh*, *Norfolk* and *Southampton*, waited to escort them back home.

The *Altmark* rescue impressed the neutrals, especially the Americans, who were quick to appreciate and acknowledge the episode. The only voice of dissent was from Norway. Her government bitterly protested against the 'infringement of neutral waters by British warships'.

In Berlin Dr Josef Goebbels was furious. He laid down strict instructions to all Nazi newspaper editors: 'All propaganda must be focused on this single incident. Tonight the sea must boil.'

Hitler, finally forced into decisive action by the blow to his pride, quietly confirmed the invasion.

In Britain the incident provided a welcome boost to morale, adding a neat postscript to the story of *Graf Spee*. A new battle-cry was added to the senior service—'The Navy's here!'

Eye Witness

Captain Philip Vian of HMS *Cossack* wrote a characteristically self-effacing account of the episode which began his rise to naval fame.

'We had, in fact, no firm information even about the appearance of our quarry . . . a wardroom copy of an *Illustrated London News* . . . showed a picture of two vessels, the caption read: 'German raider *Altmark* examining a neutral merchant ship in the Atlantic.' Which . . . was *Altmark* it did not say, and we assumed it was the four-masted ship in the foreground, rather than the tanker-type further away. So when a four-masted freighter was sighted making south along the coast I thought we had found our intended victim. . . . Salvation was provided by a young officer in *Arethusa*. His keen eyes detected, far away, a shadow passing close to, and interrupting the black-and-white land background, and, significantly, the mast and funnels of a torpedo-boat, which must be a Norwegian escort. . . . *Arethusa* . . . sent the destroyers in. *Altmark* . . . disregarded their signals to stop . . . Norwegian torpedo-boats —there were now seen to be two—ranged along either side, preventing the destroyers from boarding. Abreast Josing Fjord, *Altmark* turned hard to port, increased speed . . . the Norwegians closed in behind her, blocking the channel. At this point Craven, a RNVR officer who spoke German and Swedish, came to the fore. From *Cossack* he hailed *Kjell*, the senior Norwegian, and invited the captain aboard. To the latter I said that British prisoners were . . . on board *Altmark* . . . he stated that the German ship had been examined three times since her entry into Norwegian waters, and that no prisoners had been found . . . his ships had their torpedo-tubes trained on *Cossack*. Deadlock.'

When HMS *Cossack* captured the *Altmark*, 299 British merchant seamen were released. Inset is a directive to the prisoners from *Altmark's* captain, Heinrich Dau.

Keystone/Trevor Lawrence

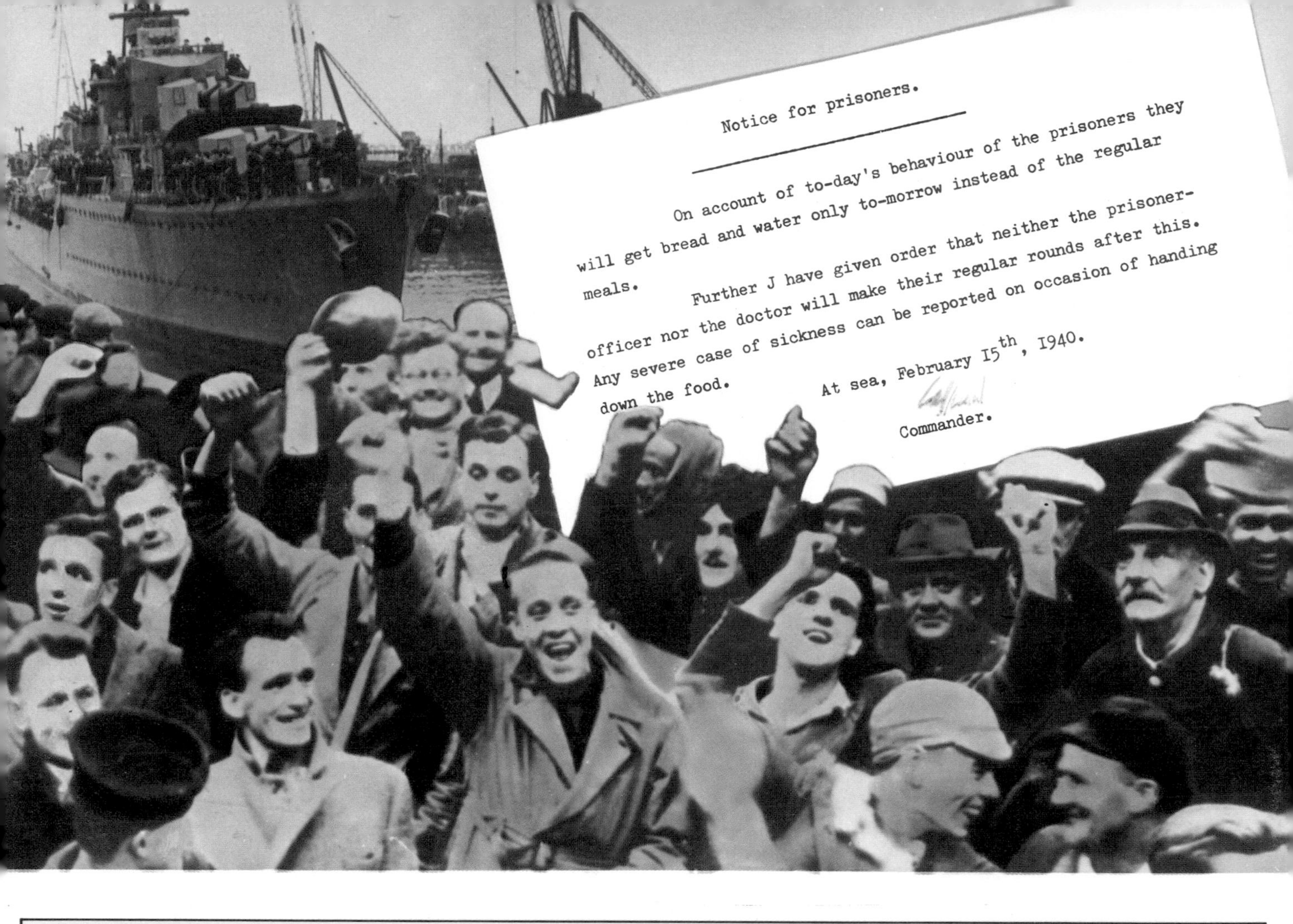

Notice for prisoners.

On account of to-day's behaviour of the prisoners they will get bread and water only to-morrow instead of the regular meals.

Further J have given order that neither the prisoner-officer nor the doctor will make their regular rounds after this. Any severe case of sickness can be reported on occasion of handing down the food.

At sea, February I5th, I940.

Commander.

War Notes

ALTMARK INCIDENT

ALTMARK: 7000-ton German tanker. Completed 1938. Dimensions: 463×68×27ft. Engines: geared steam turbines giving 22 knots. Guns: anti-aircraft and pompoms. Crew: 130. On German auxiliary list, formerly of Hamburg-Amerika Line. Supply ship of *Graf Spee*. Took on supply of diesel oil from Port Arthur, US, 5 Aug 1939. Refuelled *Graf Spee* 1 Sept. Took on 85 British prisoners from *Graf Spee*, captured from SS *Huntsman*, 14 Sept. Renamed *Uckermark* after rescue of British prisoners by *Cossack* in Norwegian fjord, 16 Feb 1940. Destroyed by fire caused by petrol vapour explosion at Yokohama, 30 Nov 1942 with raider *Thor*.

BERGEN DEFENDED AREA: the three mile territorial zone, protected by mines and coastal guns. Bergen, second largest city to Oslo, chief shipping centre with large mercantile fleet.

COSSACK: 1870-ton British destroyer (Tribal class). Launched June 1937. Dimensions: 337.5×36.5×9ft. Engines: 2-shaft geared turbines giving 44,000hp and 36 knots. Guns: 4 twin 4.7in turrets, quadruple 2pdr anti-aircraft guns, 2 quad .5 machine guns, 4×21in torpedo tubes. Crew: 219. Sister ships 16. After *Altmark* incident, laid up for refit for 7 weeks.

HUDSON: converted Lockheed, American built coastal reconnaissance light bomber. 200 ordered, first delivery Feb 1939. First enters RAF service, 244 Squadron, May 1939. Mid-wing monoplane construction, powered by two 1100hp Wright R-1820-G102A, Cyclone single row radials driving 3 blade propellers. Armament: power operated dorsal turret with 2× 0.303in Browning machine guns, non-retractable 0.303in gun in lower rear fuselage. Crew: 4. Bombload: 1600lb. Mk II introduced 1940, strengthened airframe, constant speed propellers, 5-man crew.

ROSYTH: town in Inverkeithing parish in SW Fifeshire, Scotland, on Firth of Forth. Naval base built 1909, one of three area RN headquarters.

SKAGERRAK: area of North Sea between Norway and Denmark, continues SE by Kattegat and Danish Sounds. 150 miles long, 85 miles wide. Shallow Danish seabed deepens to more than 2000ft on Norwegian coast. Battle of Skagerrak, 60 miles west of Jutland 1916.

TURNER, Bradwell Talbot: British naval officer, b. 1907. Educated Christ's Hospital and RN Colleges Osborne and Dartmouth. RN 1921–57. DSO 1940, OBE 1951. Commander of Royal Victoria Order 1955. Naval attache, Oslo, Norway 1954–7. Barrister 1956.

VIAN, Philip: British admiral, b. 1894. Began naval career as cadet at RN College Osborne, 1907. Passed out from Dartmouth, 1911. Served at Battle of Jutland in destroyer, later specialized in gunnery. Spent first two years of WWII as captain of 4th Destroyer Flotilla.

TIMOSHENKO'S STEAMROLLER

The Russian commander, Timoshenko.

... the hurricane of our bombs and shells descended on Summa. After the artillery had shifted its fire ... infantry and tanks simultaneously attacked.'

N.N. Voronov, Soviet marshal of artillery

'We shall fight to the last old man and child. We shall burn out forests and homes, destroy our cities and industries—and what we yield will be cursed by God.' Feeling ran high. Marshal Mannerheim, the Finnish C-in-C, was determined to resist the Russian foe with his last breath.

What had been confidently predicted as a 12-day war of glorious conquest for the Red Army had turned into a 63-day horror of ignominious defeat. Finland had given the Russian bear a bloody nose. Predictably, Stalin was not amused. Nikita Khruschev recalled Stalin's attack on the People's Commissar of Defence, Marshal Klementi Voroshilov: '. . . Stalin jumped up in a rage and started to berate Voroshilov. Voroshilov was also boiling mad. He leapt up, turned red, and hurled Stalin's accusations back into his face: "You have yourself to blame for all this! You're the one who had our best Generals killed." Stalin rebuffed him and Voroshilov picked up a platter with a roast suckling pig on it and smashed it on the table.'

The Russian leaders knew that their offensive would have to bring victory before the spring of 1940. They also knew that the sought-after breakthrough would have to come on the Karelian front. But who could do it? In all previous offensives the Russians had lost hundreds of tanks and thousands of cold, ill-fed, gangrinous men who, for the most part, didn't know what they were doing in the 'strange territory' of northern Finland. The Finns had shot Russian planes out of the skies from antiquated Fokker DXX1s. They had attacked massing tank and infantry regiments in ones and twos with bottles of gasoline and hand grenades. The Russian dead lay like grotesque statues, some in scattered pieces, frozen under the fresh snowfalls of January and February.

A hand pointing through the snow a long way from home—this was the reality of the winter war. Half-trained Russian troops had played at soldiers according to the rules. But the Finns were fighting for their survival.

General Semyon **Timoshenko,** a man after the Soviet leader's heart, now entered to fill the breach. Powerfully built, Timoshenko came from Belorussia and was a strong disciplinarian and a soldier of enterprise.

And he was practical. When asked to undertake the assignment as C-in-C of the Russian army in Finland, he agreed only when promised that any losses of men, however great, would not be his responsibility. Formerly an NCO in the Tsarist Army when Mannerheim was, ironically, a general above him, Timoshenko's exploits in the Civil War were well known: 'Don't ask what the strength of the enemy is, ask where it is; then hunt it down and destroy it', he is reported to have told his subordinates.

Russians confused and depressed

Timoshenko was quick to join the Red Army in 1919. After a succession of increasingly important military posts, culminating with the responsibility of the Polish occupation, he now faced a real challenge.

Timoshenko looked at the balance sheet. First the appalling losses so far. The 104th Division had withdrawn, the 88th had been badly beaten and forced back 55 miles, the 122nd had been knocked back 20 miles—the list was endless, the casualities ridiculously high. And in the bitter weather 10 per cent of the slow-advancing columns of Russians in the northern sector had died of frostbite. Every time they made fireless camp in the gloomy freezing forested areas, without sight of a single Finn, the sentries had their throats cut or simply disappeared. The Finns were everywhere, but they were not seen. The Russians confused and depressed on every front, had been severley beaten by this stage.

Now, the lull in the fighting at the end of January gave Timoshenko time to address himself to the problem. The battle could only be won by more men and firepower in a massive open attack for which the Red Army was trained.

The main weight of Timoshenko's attack was to be hurled against the Finnish troops defending the Mannerheim Line across the Karelian Isthmus—90 miles of land lying between Lake Ladoga in the east and the Gulf of Finland in the west. Deprived of cover, without space to manoeuvre as they had in the north, Finnish guerillas would have a tough time. And the terrain was well known to the Russians. Here they had suffered repulses in December.

Along new roads behind the Finnish frontier, free from the dreaded attacks of the ghostly Finnish skiing snipers, came 25 divisions. Timoshenko amassed huge quantities of men and materials, tanks, including the new **KV-I**—and

Keystone

artillery. A crash course taught troops, fresh from the Caucasus and Siberia, how to destroy a Finnish bunker. They were keen. They learnt new tricks with models, and perfected their technique in small local attacks.

Timoshenko had two armies at his disposal for the Karelian offensive. To the west of the isthmus, General Kiril Meretskov commanded the **7th Army**, experienced in the horrors of the previous month. To the east General Grondhal, once a colonel in the Tsar's army, commanding the 13th Army, fresh and ready for action.

Timoshenko was sure of his ground. Reconnaissance patrols by expert Russian skiers, as well as reports from the few surviving radio-equipped spies dropped behind the Finnish lines, together with pictures from aircraft and balloons, gave Timoshenko the means to produce detailed maps needed for the campaign.

The Finns meanwhile were busily reinforcing their own Mannerheim Line on the isthmus. They were confident. Even as the powerful new Russian offensive trundled to the borders from the east, troop trains left the bombed city of Helsinki and rolled to the border. Men went singing the melancholy peasant songs of their harsh, remote native land. They joked and warmed themselves with schnapps. They sat on their kit bags and coats in temperatures down to −22 degrees, guns at the ready.

Commanding a key section of the line was General T. Laitikainen, who had seen his troops beat back all Russian attacks so far. 'The others will be too, even though the Finns have few men', he told the reporter Geoffrey Cox.

At midday on 1 February, Timoshenko began his offensive. A massive force of 500 bombers headed for the Finnish positions. Bombs rained down on the hapless defenders. Then came a bombardment from 400 guns ranged along the Russian line—as many as seven guns to the mile blazed across the short gap.

Hub to hub, the Russian guns pointed at the Mannerheim Line. Within 24 hours 300,000 shells fell on five miles of the Summa positions alone—the heaviest artillery bombardment since Verdun in World War I. 600,000 troops including Timoshenko's well-seasoned Ukrainian forces were massed for the attack.

Day after day of carnage

Timoshenko sent nine of his 12 rifle divisions into the fray. Wave upon wave of Russians flung themselves against the Finnish line. Each wave crumbled before the accurate fire power of the Finns. One Russian division followed through the carnage of another, day after day. Adding to the horror, came a new Russian weapon, not seen in the fight until then—the flame-thrower.

Five tank brigades trundled over the snow, machines specially built for the job with rollers welded to the front to clear roads through the minefields. They towed sleds with armoured shields and advanced pulling troops over the frozen bodies of the last victims.

The main thrust came at the Summa sector where 500 aircraft and six divisions battered an area 16 miles wide. The idea was to smash this front and get through to Viipuri, the gateway to Helsinki and the Gulf of Finland. But there was to be no easy path into the Finnish lines.

The Russians advanced in an overwhelming mass. In one area, aided by the first wartime use of paratroops, tanks and infantry cleared each tank trap in turn, cut away the barbed wire entanglements and neutralized the machine-gun emplacements. The clumsy monster weight of the tanks crashed into the bunkers blasting their shells through the gun apertures. The Finns were helpless. They had few anti-tank guns.

A *Times* correspondent described the ordeal of the Finns: 'The only thing more persistent than the blizzard of hail and snow is the Russian artillery . . . firing in batteries of three, they alternate between 10 and 20 shots a minute so cleverly that it is impossible to calculate with accuracy how many guns are engaged.'

With amazing tenacity, despite this new-found orchestration of Soviet artillery and infantry, the Finns kept their lines intact. But they were dog-tired. Even after they had knocked out 64 Russian tanks—now smoking relics or jagged snow mounds in front of them—Timoshenko knew that a gradual wearing down would eventually bring about the defeat of the Finns.

Popperfoto

Tired, short in numbers and low on ammunition, the Finns held on. North of Lake Ladoga they sought out pockets of encircled Russians—the mottis. Enclaves of Russians cut off from the front cowered in their snowbound bunkers—brigades, battalions, but mostly engineers and supply troops, some of them numbering over 3,000 men.

On 2 February the 4th Jaeger Battalion fighting in the vicinity of West Lemetti, reinforced by a company from the 37th Infantry, were given orders to break up the Mylly *motti*. Here the Russians had constructed mottis made from timber, dug into the ground, covered with snow, criss-crossing the area.

Colonel Matti Aarnio, the Jaeger commander, together with another Finnish company commander, skied round the Russian lair. They were seen. 'Good,' he said, 'now that we've been spotted in the northeast they'll expect our attack to come from here.'

Armed with hand weapons and attacking by night from each flank, the Finns sneaked into the motti. Some of them dived into snowbanks and emerged with the added protection of heavy snow. 'It makes my hair stand on end' one of the older men outside commented as he peered into the cold midnight air watching the ghostly skiers advance into the centre of the Russian nest.

Outside they waited, everything was quiet. Flashlights signalled, then came the sound of muffled explosions. In the darkness the Russians could not fire their machine-guns, they were bewildered and couldn't identify friend from foe. They screamed trying to frighten the attackers.

The Russians fought back. But they were beaten off by the Finns advancing with Molotov cocktails. Panic stricken, the Russians ran leaving their equipment. They were picked off in the forests. One by one the mottis were knocked out—given time few would survive.

But Timoshenko launched his final offensive on the Mannerheim Line on 6 February. He had the luxury of yet more reserves. The Finns were exhausted. Timoshenko shifted the spearhead of hi attack to Lädhe, two miles east of Summa an launched simultaneous artillery and infantr attacks right along the line of the isthmus. Thi way he preyed remorsely on any reserves tha Finns might have left. More tanks rumble towards the Gulf of Finland and towards Lak Lagoda. If the ice held here, they could outflan the defences.

Inevitably, the line began to break. At Länd

Two Finnish soldiers risk their lives cutting through Russian barbed wire defences. And a Finnish telephonist (inset) deals with a constant stream of messages. Behind him two soldiers take a break from the bitter fighting.

Radio Times Hulton Picture Library

the trenches and machine-gun posts vanished under Timoshenko's barrage. By the 11th, Finnish reserves were down to two divisions. Many of the Finns were so tired by now that even the roar of the tanks couldn't keep them from falling asleep in the trenches. Desperate, the Finns mustered their quartermasters and cooks to man the front line along with inexperienced young recruits and old men from the Home Guard.

On 14 February, 72-year-old Marshal Mannerheim personally inspected the front line. He decided to withdraw the pitiful remnants to the weaker intermediate line built behind the Mannerheim Line. The Finns retreated to the multiple-defence position between two and ten miles back.

Jubilant Russians advanced to empty trenches. One group, climbing to the top of a bunker, planted their red banner. An angry Finn, his face blackened by mortar fire, rushed out and shot down the victors with his sub-machine-gun. The hammer and sickle was pulled down and stamped into the ground.

Summa fell. Not even Moscow could believe it. Chief artillery general, Nikolai **Voronov** had to report to the new People's Commissar for Defence—Timoshenko. 'I gave a detailed report of the course of the battle to the People's Commissar. Nonetheless he asked me three times if the report that the strongpoint had been taken was true. . . . Finally his irritated tone became warm and friendly. The People's Commissar wished the troops a successful completion of this offensive.'

'The machine gunning was worse than the bombs. I saw horrible sights when the tack-tacking of the machine-guns started from the Soviet planes.'

Mrs Chollerton, wife of Daily Telegraph correspondent

On the western flank, the defenders held the coastal batteries of Koivisto Island. Heavy guns pounded the advancing Russians until the shells ran out. On 22 February the Finns spiked their guns and blew up defence installations with their last explosives. The island was left abandoned to the Russians. Their 25-mile retreat across the frozen Viipuri Bay was hidden by a timely blizzard.

Along the intermediate line embattled commander Lieutenant General Harald Ohqvist, took a realistic view. He wanted to withdraw to the rear position. Mannerheim took a hard line. He deposed Ohqvist and looked for a new commander.

To command the Karelian Army he now brought in Lieutenant General Eric **Heinrichs.** Like himself, Mannerheim reckoned that Heinrichs had 'nerves of steel'. But the new commander backed Ohqvist's sensible appeal for permission to withdraw.

Mannerheim's dilemma was cruel. The appearance of a good defence was now more important than defence itself. As the link between government and Army he knew that peace negotiations were in the offing. For any kind of bargaining power, the Army would have to hold as much ground as possible.

Allies asked for help

The first round of peace talks took place on 5 February in Stockholm. The Foreign Minister Vainno Tanner talked with Mrs **Kollontai,** the Soviet Minister to Sweden. But the Russian demands were too great. They wanted **Hanko.**

At the same time, the Finnish cabinet was deep in negotiations with the Allies for arms and men. Promises were given, but time was an expensive premium. The British and the French, when pressed to give details, could not. Sweden would have to get involved if the Allies were to send troops to Finland.

Tanner flew to Sweden and spoke with the Prime Minister, Per Albin **Hansson.** He was flatly refused permission to allow allied troop reinforcements through Sweden.

The Finns were desperate. With Timoshenko's cannon on one side and a resolute neutral on the other, Finland was forced to negotiate. On 23 February the Russians delivered an ultimatum. Two days later on the stroke of the deadline, the beleaguered cabinet responded. Russian terms were accepted in principle but still they played for points.

The debate went on. As night fell on the last day of February the Finnish cabinet split. Mannerheim, fully aware of impending disaster at the depleted front, advised a compromise with the Kremlin. Already he had ordered a retreat to the rear line after Finland's only tank attack turned into a fiasco. It was better to lose something than risk everything. Or was it?

A Finnish woman, terrified by the Russian bombs, is comforted by a nurse. Trains carrying women and children from Viipuri to Helsinki were bombed regularly.

War Notes

TIMOSHENKO'S STEAMROLLER

HANKO: city of 6778 people on 15-mile long peninsula at mouth of Gulf of Finland 50 miles SE of Turku. Sea port and herring fishing centre. Russia wanted a 30-year lease on Hanko as a naval base with 5000-strong garrison.

Popperfoto

HANSSON, Per Albin: Swedish Prime Minister since 1936, b. 1885. Social Democratic Party leader. Friend of Finns but committed to neutrality. Asked by Finnish PM Ryti for 20,000 volunteers on 1 Feb 1940. Publicly rejected this request on 16th. On 20th Finland accepted Swedish mediation in Moscow.

HEINRICHS, Erik: Finnish general, scholar and professional soldier. Major General commanding 3rd Army Corps (7th and 8th Divs) on E. side of Karelian Isthmus from outbreak of war. Promoted Lt-General 19 Feb to command the Karelian Army instead of Lt-Gen Hugo Osterman who pleaded illness.

KOLLONTAI, Aleksandra: Soviet Minister in Stockholm since 1930, b. 1872. Brought Swedish foreign minister letter on 29th not ruling out talks with Finns. Informed by Sweden on 2 Feb that Finland agreed to talks. On 12th gave Sweden USSR's minimum demands—Hanko, all Karelia and area N. of L. Ladoga.

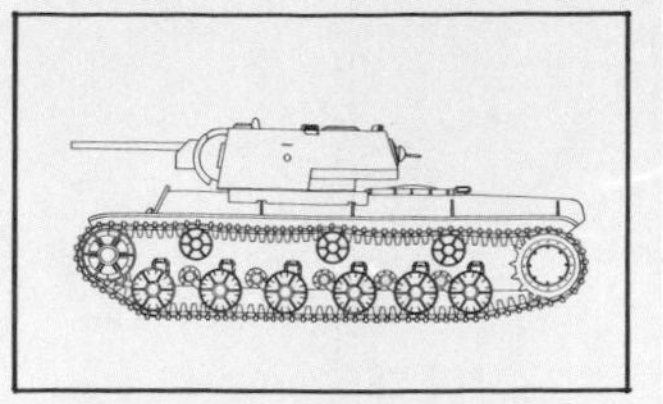

KV-I: Klimenti Voroshilov heavy tank. T35 replacement whose design was influenced by Stalin. Named after People's Commissar of Defence. Prototype Sept 1939, production began Dec 1939. Weight: 42.8 tons. Dimensions: 22.3 × 10.9 × 10.6ft. Engine: 550hp V2k V12 liquid-cooled diesel. Speed: 22mph. Range: 140 miles. Trench crossing: 9.2ft. Fording: 4.75ft. Armour 25–110 mm welded plate. Guns: 76.2mm (111 rounds), 3 × 7.62mm machine-guns (3024 rounds). Crew: commander, gunner, loader, driver and machine-gunner. Twin-turreted pre-prototypes used in Finland before end 1939. KV11s with 122mm or 152mm howitzer, also used against the Mannerheim Line. Its 12-ton turret could only be traversed on level ground and fired at the halt.

7th ARMY (Russian): was in Nov 1939 strongest Soviet army invading Finland (13 infantry divisions and 5 tank brigades). Used only 7 divisions (140,000 men) in Dec offensive. The earlier fighting at Summa raged 17–19 and 23 Dec. Reinforced in Jan by 2 more tank brigades (130 tanks) and 20 artillery regiments (720 guns). The new 13th Army in E. Karelia merely had to tie down the Finns.

TIMOSHENKO, Semyon Konstantinovich: Russian marshal, b. 1895 of peasant parents at village near Odessa. Barrel-maker until conscripted 1915. Cavalry NCO when he escaped court-martial for striking officer by joining Bolsheviks. Befriended Stalin and Zhukov at Siege of Tsaritsyn 1918. Led 4th Cavalry Div in 1920 invasion of Poland. CO 3rd Cavalry Corps between spells of military command training. Asst CO Belorussian Military District (MD) 1933. Went abroad to study foreign armies. Commanded Kiev, N. Caucasus and Kharkov MDs 1935–8, escaping purges. Commanded invasion of E. Poland. Appointed C-in-C against Finland and People's Commissar of Defence 7 Jan 1940. Called up many of the 'purged' officers who were still alive. Appointed Zhukov as Red Army chief of staff.

VORONOV, Nikolai N.: Russian marshal, b. 1899. Joined Red Army 1918. Gunner in Civil War and PoW in Poland 1920–1. Military Attaché in Italy 1932. Lt-General commanding 7th Army's artillery from Nov 1939. Predicted that campaign would take 2–3 months but told to plan for 12 days.

ANOTHER FIGHT GOES ON

In the dark of the early winter evening of 22 February 1940 an unobtrusive man walked along London's Oxford Street carrying a small package. He seemed to be a cultivated man; quiet and respectable, yet with an almost religious dedication to a cause. And a member of the Irish Republican Army (IRA). Nobody stopped him, there seemed no reason to, and nobody noticed when, at a convenient point, he dropped the package into a litter basket.

Minutes later, with the Irishman safely from the scene, the package exploded.

Two shop fronts caved in, scattering broken glass across the street. Twelve people were wounded by cuts and bomb blast; two were detained in hospital for treatment.

The explosion was part of a series of bombing raids. Three weeks earlier two explosions in London and one in Birmingham, aimed at railway targets, had caused serious injuries. A bomb placed in a bicycle basket back in August 1939 had blasted Coventry's shopping centre, Broadgate, killing five shoppers and injuring 60. Compared with the Blitz on London, Coventry and other cities by the Luftwaffe later in 1940, it was no great devastation. But it was a painful reminder of one of Britain's most intractible and lasting problems—Ireland.

The **IRA** had been bombing British targets for years—and were to continue the campaign 40 years later. But in the months after the outbreak of World War II a new and vastly more serious campaign was mounted.

Only a few hours after Britain declared war on Germany three RAF seaplanes patrolling over the Irish Sea hit bad weather. Naturally they sought shelter. Two landed at Skerries, a holiday resort 10 miles north of Dublin, and the third at Dun Laoghaire to the south of Dublin.

Probably it never occurred to the RAF pilots that their action would cause a major diplomatic row. After all, to shelter from a storm was nothing unusual. But Ireland was not at war. And the seaplanes, belonging to a country that was, had technically violated her neutrality.

While the Irish entertained their visitors with customary hospitality, officials from the Department of Defence seriously considered interning the intruders. Alarmed, senior army officers wondered how they would deal with hostile British reaction if the pilots were locked up for the duration of the war. Fortunately, the weather broke. The storm died down and the Irish, diplomatically, helped their guests get airborne.

'A feckless act'

That night, Eamon **de Valera,** Prime Minister of the Irish Free State, broadcast to the nation. Movingly, he informed his countrymen that Ireland would keep out of the war: '. . . with our history and our experience of the last war, and with part of our country still unjustly severed from us we felt that no other policy was possible'.

Irish neutrality was now a fact, to the dismay of the British—and the delight of the Germans.

Britain's fury at the announcement was partly sour grapes. Just a year earlier three harbours in the west of Ireland: Lough Swilly in County Donegal, Queenstown (Cobh) in the south and, most important of all Berehaven in Bantry Bay had been handed back to the Irish.

Irish leader Michael **Collins** had conceded back in 1921: 'Of course you must have the ports, they are necessary for your life'. But in 1938, while the prospect of a submarine war against British shipping grew menacingly real, the British government unaccountably handed the ports back to the Irish. Churchill noted tersely: 'A more feckless act can hardly be imagined.'

But it was Britain's Chiefs of Staff who were responsible. 'The retention or capture of these ports in the face of a hostile attitude on the part of Ireland would at best involve a most formidable military commitment and might, even so, be impossible.'

Churchill had cause to worry about the 'possible succouring of U-boats by Irish malcontents in West of Ireland inlets'. When U47 slipped into Scapa Flow and sank the battleship *Royal Oak*, he became even more determined to get the ports Berehaven and Lough Swilly back for the British Fleet. Angrily he told the Cabinet on 17 October 'The time has come to make it clear to the Irish government that we must have the use of these harbours'. More ominously it seemed, he added

Popperfoto

The IRA 'declared war' on Britain in January 1939. The Oxford Street bomb of 21 February 1940 was preceded by several explosions including one in Coventry (25 August 1939) which killed five people.

Keystone

Keystone

Irish troops on the march. Their uniform was, at first, very like that of the German army. Later it was changed (inset, left) more to resemble British uniform. The picture above shows De Valera reviewing IRA troops in the 1920s—their chief concern was for reunification.

'we intend in any case to use them'.

While the Cabinet deliberated, Churchill cooled down somewhat. He agreed there were other possible fleet anchorages. But he still insisted on securing Berehaven. The place was ideal for British battleships and destroyers. The range of aircraft covering the Atlantic convoys based at Berehaven could be extended by some 400 miles.

Diplomatically Anthony **Eden,** Britain's Dominions Secretary, agreed to put the request to de Valera, and briefed the British diplomatic representative in Dublin, John **Maffey**. Six feet four inches tall and a model English diplomat, Maffey was well liked by the Irish. He had been recalled to the diplomatic service after five years of retirement and was described by one hard-bitten reporter of the *Irish Independent* as 'a miracle of youthful vitality'.

Maffey spent an hour and a half with de Valera. Though persuasive, Maffey failed to break down de Valera's determination to preserve Berehaven —and his country's hard-won independence. Frankly, de Valera told Maffey if he allowed Britain to use the west coast ports his government would fall within 24 hours.

Nominally at least Ireland was still part of the British Commonwealth of Nations. But in 1937 Ireland had passed a bill eliminating from her constitution all references to the British crown. Nevertheless, her Chargé d'Affaires in Berlin was still accredited to George VI. With John Maffey's appointment a problem arose: what was his title to be?

De Valera objected to 'High Commissioner'. It smacked too much of colonial dominance. And Britain would not have 'Ambassador' for this would recognize that Ireland was outside the Commonwealth. In the end Chamberlain suggested Maffey should be known as 'British Representative in Eire'. De Valera pondered this for a few moments, then crossed out the word 'in' and replaced it with 'to'.

Most Irishmen were behind their government's policy of neutrality, though the old links with Britain remained.

The Irish press recognized that a 'certain consideration for Britain' existed. And the apparent bias prompted some newspapers to ask in a typically Irish way: 'Who are we neutral against?'

Yet many British still considered the south of Ireland to be part of their country. They were affronted that Ireland should stay out of the war.

The curious state of affairs that existed between the two countries were again tested on 14 September. Once again a British seaplane sought refuge in Irish waters and again the Irish were careful to let the British pilot go.

These incidents precipitated limited formal agreements between the two countries. British aircraft were permitted to fly over County Donegal (the short route from Northern Ireland to the Atlantic), station a rescue boat at Cobh, and incorporate seven Irish oil tankers into the British merchant fleet. This was as far as the Irish government was prepared to go: Churchill did not get his naval bases in the west.

While the Irish government adopted a policy of committed independence, individual Irishmen took sides. The majority were probably pro-British. Hundreds joined British forces. Some even deserted their own Army to see active service with the British Army. At Liverpool a storehouse of civilian clothes was established so that Irish troops catching the boat home for a few days leave could hang up their uniforms and cross the Irish Sea in government-issue civilian clothes. The streets and bars of Dublin were hardly the place to be seen sporting British uniforms.

Irishmen die for Britain

On the Western Front when the shooting did start a high proportion of Irish names were included among the casualty lists. Why so many Irishmen crossed the Irish Sea to fight—and die—for Britain remains an enigma.

But there were others who were undoubtedly pro-German. More than 400 Germans worked in Ireland, many in important posts in science and the public services. Just a week after the outbreak of war 42 of their most eminent members assembled at Dublin docks to board the *Cumbria* for a safe return home.

Later, the Abwehr—the German military secret service—was to regret that these men had been ordered back home. They could have provided valuable intelligence had they stayed at their posts in Ireland.

For the IRA, dedicated to clearing the British out of Ireland altogether, war on Britain had begun in January '39. Giving her four days to withdraw all British forces from Northern Ireland —predictably ignored—the bombings began.

On 25 August 1939 Coventry was bombed. Police raids on every Irish house in the city

Central Press

brought five suspects to trial. Two of them, Peter Barnes and James McCormack, duly appeared at Birmingham Assizes in December charged with murdering one of the victims. Although neither man was directly responsible foı planting the bomb, both were sentenced to death. The Home Secretary, ignored widespread protests and rejected appeals for clemency. The two men were hanged together on 7 February 1940, behind the grim grey walls of Winson Green prison.

Just two days before Christmas 1939 came the IRA's most sensational coup. The magazine fort in Dublin's Phoenix Park where the Irish Army kept the bulk of its reserve ammunition was raided.

Arriving on bicycle a 'messenger' drew up at the fort. The duty policeman opened the outer gate and the raiders slipped inside. Tying up the guards they loaded ammunition on to a convoy of 13 lorries. The magazine was stripped. More than a million rounds of ammunition was captured, much of it invaluable 0.45 calibre cartridge for the gunmen's favourite weapon, the tommy gun.

Despite this huge haul things began to go wrong. The raiders failed to arrange safe storage for their massive haul. Loyal supporters filled their homes with the stuff, but crates were left piled high on the lorries. Meanwhile police carried out raids over the city. Within a few weeks they recovered all the booty and more besides.

IRA unreliable

De Valera saw the IRA as a serious threat to neutrality: 'No-one can think that this government has any sympathy with it', he said in June 1939. Declaring the organization illegal de Valera had four of its leaders arrested.

Initially impressed by the efforts of the IRA in laying bombs in London and other English cities, the Germans contacted the IRA leaders through their secret service operators in Dublin. The Abwehr went as far as setting up a special Irish desk to cultivate the subversive Irish contacts. After all, the IRA had an elaborate scheme for bringing about 'paralysis of all official activity in England and the greatest possible destruction of British defence installations'.

But the Germans were to find the IRA unreliable, lacking an effective organization. Few of their plans came to anything. But Germany was content with mere Irish neutrality, and did not want to do anything that might push her into the war on the side of the Allies.

To de Valera, American-born and sentenced to death by the British in 1916, the heart of Anglo-Irish conflict remained **partition.** The separation of the six counties of Ulster from the rest of Ireland he found intolerable. Visiting Britons would notice the map on his office wall. It showed the southern counties in black and the northern ones in white. 'Ireland jet-black, Northern Ireland leprous white' he would tell them bitterly. 'All this happens because you maintain the principle of partition in this island'.

The only way the British government could get Ireland into the war on her side was the offer of a united Ireland. In June 1940 when Britain stood alone, the offer was made—and rejected.

War Notes

COLLINS, Michael: Irish leader, 1890–1922. Son of prosperous farmer. Clerk in London 1906–16. Joined Irish Republican Brotherhood 1909. Fought in Easter Rising 1916. Elected Sinn Fein member for West Cork Dec 1918. Organized de Valera's escape from Lincoln jail 1919. Active against British until 1921 treaty. He was one of the signatories. Became chairman of provisional government. Succeeded Arthur Griffith as head of state Aug 1922. Ten days later he was ambushed and killed by republicans who opposed the treaty with Britain.

Keystone

DE VALERA, Eamon: Irish Taoiseach (head of government), b. NY City 1882 to Spanish father and Irish mother. Sent to Ireland as infant after father's death. Educated Blackrock College, Dublin and the Royal University of Ireland. Teacher of mathematics. Joined Irish Volunteers 1913, and in the Easter Rising of 1916 commanded one of the occupied buildings in Dublin. He was the last of the Irish leaders to surrender and was sentenced to death for his part. Sentence commuted to penal servitude because of US birth. Released 1917 and elected president of Sinn Fein. Re-arrested May 1918. Escaped Lincoln jail Feb 1919 and managed to reach US. Returned to Ireland 1921. Opposed treaty with Britain because it recognized Northern Ireland and imposed allegiance to British crown. Sided with republican opposition in civil war after Treaty passed by Dail (Irish parliament). His opposition party, Fianna Fail, entered the Dail in 1927. Leader of Irish Free State from 1932.

Keystone

EDEN, Robert Anthony: Secretary of State for Dominion Affairs, b. 1897. Educated Eton and Christ Church, Oxford. Captain, King's Royal Rifle Corps. Served in France 1915–19. Promoted to Brigade Major at the age of 20 and won MC. Entered parliament 1923 as MP for Warwick and Leamington. Parliamentary Private Secretary to Foreign Secretary 1926–9. Parliamentary Under Secretary at the Foreign Office 1931–3. Lord Privy Seal 1934–5. Foreign Secretary 1935–8. Appointed Dominions Secretary Sept 1939.

IRA (Irish Republican Army): militant republican organization dedicated to the reunification of Ireland and the ending of ties with Britain.

MAFFEY, Sir John Loader: British diplomat, b. 1877. Educated Rugby and Christ Church, Oxford. Indian Civil Service 1900–24. Governor General of the Sudan 1926–33. Permanent Under-Secretary of State for the Colonies 1933–7. British Representative to Ireland 1939.

PARTITION: the separation of Ireland into two parts: six northern counties (Ulster) governed by Britain and the remaining 26 counties governed from Dublin (Irish Free State, later the Republic of Ireland). Following widespread disorder in Ireland during and after WWI (especially the Easter rising of 1916) the Irish Free State was established in 1921 by a treaty signed in London. It was to have the status of a Dominion under the British Crown. Republican elements resisting partition had two main demands: first, the six northern counties must be reunited with the south and governed from Dublin, and second, there must be a complete break with Britain.

MARCH 1940

...WITH a thaw in the weather and the prospect of spring, the final act in the tragic fate of Finland is decided in the wastes of Karelia. In Paris, springtime brings a change of leadership, while in Britain the land girls settle down to the task ahead. Meeting in the Brenner mountain pass Hitler and Mussolini plan what to do next, while far away in China the two year war enters a new and bitter phase...

1st: War Savings Campaign in Britain reaches £100m.
2nd: Finnish fighters foil air raid on Helsinki.
3rd: Russians capture Viipuri railway station.
4th: Finns repel attacks E. and W. of Viipuri.
5th: Germans capture British Maginot Line outpost, 18 casualties.
6th: Finnish peace delegation leaves for Moscow.
7th: Italian ships with German coal cargo detained in N. Sea by British warships.
8th: French arms en route to Finland.
9th: Anglo-Italian agreement releases Italian 'coal ships' in return for use of overland routes.
10th: Ribbentrop has interview with Mussolini.
11th: French gold shipment sails from Toulon for Canada. Meat rationing in Britain.
12th: Russo-Finnish peace treaty. Home Fleet returns to Scapa Flow.
13th: Mannerheim addresses Finnish Army after 11am cease fire.
14th: Finns begin evacuation from ceded territories.
15th: RAF drops leaflets over Warsaw.
16th: Scapa Flow bombed.
17th: 1st British civilian killed by enemy air action.
18th: Hitler and Mussolini meet in Brenner Pass.
19th: RAF bomb Sylt seaplane base, NW Germany.
20th: Daladier resigns.
21st: Reynaud forms new French government.
22nd: 1st RAF encounters with German night fighters.
23rd: British 'Malaya Force' formed to shadow German ships in Dutch E. Indies.
24th: French and German patrols W. Front.
25th: Hitler leaves the Berghof for Berlin.
26th: U21 runs aground on S. coast of Norway.
27th: French/German artillery fire in Saar and Vosges.
28th: Allied Supreme War Council agrees to mine Norwegian waters.
29th: Bloch 174 flown by St Exupery makes 1st recce sortie over W. Germany. Gamelin inspects Canadian troops
30th: Puppet Chinese government formed by Japs.
31st: Temporary French sub base at Harwich active.

Fox Photos

BACK TO THE LAND

The fields that finally shrugged off the long snows of the British winter this March were still a dismal sight: they bore the signs of 20 years' neglect. Britain woke up to this first spring of the war with a jolt of alarm.

The years between the wars had seen Britain's fields go from rack to ruin. The causes were many. Young men once destined to till them lay, by the thousand, beneath the battlefields of World War 1. Young women in the 1930s had fled the low wages of the milking parlours and the henhouses for the bright lights of town—one in three had left. And those bright lights themselves had spread like ribbons through the countryside, swallowing the orchards of Kent and Middlesex. A new term was coined to describe it: conurbation.

Taxation, tithes, sheer apathy had taken their toll too. There were jungles in England again: estates so gone to ruin that a heifer could wander, become entangled and die. Three thousand acres of prime land in Hampshire had been left untended for 20 years. This was a famous case: the McCreagh estate. Ragwort had grown so high here that a man could scarcely push his way through. In the badlands of Suffolk, 40,000 acres had gone back to pheasants and partridges; whole fields of crops left standing for them alone to reap.

Meanwhile, cheap and easy dinners came to the table from abroad. Nine million tons of animal foodstuff, four million tons of bread grains came annually to the docks before the war.

At a stroke, the U-boat threat ended that way of

'I was very doubtful about the wisdom of taking two girls who had no previous experience. My fears were quite groundless...I have nothing but praise for them.'

A Hexham farmer, reported in *Land Girl*

life. Britain's leaders added up the evils of the nation's plight. There were five million mouths more to feed than in 1919. Yet in 1919 there had been two million more acres of arable land in cultivation—and it had been better cultivated.

For many acres, no instant miracles could be worked. 'The land is in ill-health. The blood in its veins is sour' said veteran statesman Lloyd George. Without drainage, these sodden fields could yield nothing. But there *were* places where no man had ploughed before, or rarely, and it was to these that the planners in Whitehall now lifted their eyes this spring. The hills of England, from the South Downs to Long Mountain in Montgomeryshire must now fall to the tractor. So must fenland, parkland, orchards, thickets, railway embankments, golf courses, pastures and paths.

The immediate target of the great Ploughing Campaign was two million acres, with a £2 bonus for every acre—and prosecution for any farmer who failed to meet his quota. As the Ministry of Agriculture put it: it was everyone's job to work 'like blazes'. While townsfolk sheltered in their blacked-out towns by night, farmers should be out in their fields, tractor light ablaze, turning the sod, to ensure the townsman's table would not be empty come autumn.

There was still a problem. Many of the hands now being called to the plough had already been called to the guns.

So it was, this spring, that a new army arrived to make the green land pleasant again, an army that many farmers—and perhaps many more farmers' wives—would greet with suspicion. The suspicion would change to admiration in quick time, and the Women's Land Army join the immortals of British folk lore.

Back to the Land was their official song:
Back to the Land, we must all lend a hand

In 1939 British agriculture was in a bad way —potentially good farmland was badly overgrown and there were still 17 million acres of permanent grassland. The Women's Land Army helped revitalize the industry.

Radio Times Hulton Picture Library

Popperfoto

Fox Photos

The Women's Land Army, first formed in 1917, was revived in June 1939. By March 1940 there were 6000 'land girls' doing all kinds of farm and market garden work.

To the farms and the fields we must go.
There's a job to be done,
Though we can't fire a gun
We can still do our bit with the hoe.

'Backs to the land', joked the dirty minded, would be a fitting motto. The jokes were easy, the reality very different.

Few knew what kind of life they were in for: by definition, these new recruits were strangers to the job. Shop assistants, manicurists, hairdressers, shorthand-typists and ballet dancers answered the call. One in three land girls came from London or the great industrial cities of the north. Their magazine *The Land Girl* spelled out some basic rules of the new life: 'A certain amount of make-up may be used at parties and local village dances, but long nails are quite unsuited to work on a farm, especially when covered with bright crimson nail varnish.'

'I have nothing but praise'

There was no glamour in the uniform. Item one in the kit each girl received on reporting to a training centre was 'a serviceable rainproof mackintosh'; item nine 'a pair of rubber gum boots'. While Waafs and Wrens rubbed smartly tailored shoulders with officers, the land girls' new workmates were the farm labourers of Old England, whose profession was among the least paid and least regarded in the country.

It took four weeks at a training centre to learn the basic skills. Days here began at 6.30am; continued through to 7.15pm. Some, at the end of the course, felt they knew it all—and arrived at their farm posting ready to impart their wisdom. 'After training some girls are inclined to teach the farmer his business,' warned their handbook, 'often with unfortunate results.'

Even with goodwill on both sides, it took a time to break the ice. One land girl recalled the pains the men on her farm took to restrain their language. Finally the stubborness of one cow was too much for 'Old Alec'. 'Cum art road, yer gaupin bugger' he yelled. 'The men turned round in horror. Then seeing that I was laughing and not flat on the floor in a swoon, they joyously received the word back into their vocabularies, their tongues were loosened and the sun shone more brightly.'

Soon, most farmers were won over by the enthusiasm and sheer guts of the new labourers. 'I was very doubtful about the wisdom of taking two girls who had had no previous experience.' reported a Hexham farmer. 'My fears were quite groundless. They have been quick to learn, and have worked at all manner of tasks—not a few of them both dirty and uncongenial. I have nothing but praise for them.'

The land girls ploughed and weeded, spread dung, cleaned ditches. Ploughing, admitted one girl, 'fairly shakes the inside out of you'. Yet even at this, the heaviest work of all, they upset most men's notions of woman's strength and skill: one former hairdresser won a horse-ploughing competition against all comers. Another 19-year-old spoke with pride of her day's work: 'When I saw those furrows stretching behind me, like the wake of a ship only brown instead of white, and knew I had done it all myself, I thought I should fall off the saddle with the thrill.'

Fox Photos

Others found satisfaction in the unending war on the nation's rats—whose population outnumbered the human one in Britain. Armed with long-handled spoons and poison, the girls would 'proudly exhibit to the casual visitor a corn-sack filled with 200 corpses; or hold up a pole with dead rats tied by the tail all along it.'

The earliest risers were the dairymaids—whose task was by no means over when the bucket was full. These girls had also to wash the bottles, fill them, take them on the rounds—and collect the money. 'Is it very hard work?' asked the Queen, at a tea party for 250 land girls this month. 'Well,' replied one girl 'you'd soon get used to it.'

It was, as another put it 'a grand life', though in winter 'it is not good leaving your sense of humour behind.' Though less well paid than the women in the armed services—the wage was but 28 shillings (£1.40) a week—there was a sense of

freedom in this new life, even with only one week's leave a year. There was also the satisfaction of helping to win the war. 'I just couldn't bear to see other girls in all sorts of uniform and feel I was doing nothing but sell shoes in a lovely shop,' explained one recruit.

'The Queen was much impressed' wrote her Lady in Waiting to the woman who had brought this new army into being, Lady Denman. In her own stately home in Sussex, Lady Denman now housed 38 administrative staff (her husband amicably moved out) and in March 1940 commanded 6000 landgirls across the nation. What had begun as 'a bit of a joke'—as one farmer put it—had become a force to be reckoned with. 'I know that by the time they had finished' the farmer admitted 'all of us had a hearty respect for their courage and ability to work. We parted the best of friends.'

MEETING IN THE

MOUNTAINS

It was snowing in the Brenner pass as the two trains steamed into the little station of Brennero just below the tree line on Italy's northern frontier. One train had come from the north, the other from the south. Hitler and Mussolini had come to talk about war.

The **Brenner** was an appropriate place for the encounter. Two thousand years before, Roman soldiers had tramped this way, going north to build the Empire. Later, Germanic hordes had travelled the same route south to sack that Empire. Now, on 18 March 1940, today's leaders of Germany and Italy were to meet.

Hitler was here to nudge, cajole and harangue the senior dictator of Europe into the war. It was a good sign that **Mussolini** was wearing his Fascist Militia black uniform. Germany had been keeping up the pressure for weeks now. Since 22 February Italy had been receiving precious raw materials. Today's meeting had been brought forward by getting **Ribbentrop** to telephone Mussolini only five days back. Mussolini had then raged: 'These Germans are unbearable: they don't give us time to breathe or think.' But, in truth, he was looking forward to this meeting with both eagerness and alarm. He wanted to be in on the winning side, as soon as the time was right. But he wanted to fight his own war, not Hitler's, and win his own share of the spoils: a place in the Mediterranean sun and a window on the Atlantic. It would mark the high point of the new Roman Empire he had built south of the Alps.

What an Empire it was already. The trains ran on time. 'Mussolini is always right' ran the slogans. Benito Mussolini, blacksmith's son, had come a long way since being expelled from school for stabbing a playmate in the bottom with a penknife. 'Your soul is black as hell' a school master told him then.

The **Axis** dictators had not met since their encounter in Munich in 1938, when Chamberlain had signed away Czechoslovakia. The two years that had elapsed since then had done nothing for Mussolini's health. American envoy Sumner **Welles** had recently noted how quickly the Italian dictator had declined. He now seemed 15 years older than his 56 years. 'He moved with elephantine motion, every step appeared an effort. He was heavy for his height, and his face in repose fell in rolls of flesh. His close-cropped hair was snow-white.'

It had been a long road since 1927, when an obscure German party leader, Adolf Hitler, had written to his hero Mussolini to seek a signed photograph. In the years betweeen, Hitler had passed from admiration to imitation; finally overtaken the southern dictator.

Mussolini had not replied to Hitler's fan letter. At a meeting seven years later in 1934, Hitler's now rapidly rising star still failed to impress the **Fascist** dictator. He referred to Hitler (who had come to Venice in a grubby raincoat) as 'that buffoon' and disliked in particular the fact that 'instead of speaking to me about current problems, he recited *Mein Kampf* to me—that boring book'. Fifteen days after the meeting he revised his view when news of the bloody purge of the SA came in. 'He is a cruel and ferocious character and calls to mind legendary figures of the past, like Attila' commented Mussolini. 'Those men he killed were his closest collaborators who hoisted him into power.'

As for Hitler in 1934, he had found Mussolini and Venice 'bewitching'; the cheering crowds a stunning experience. 'The people stand bowed in humility before him, as before a Pope, and he

Mussolini was always an expert performer at Fascist rallies, but at Brenner (top) Hitler wanted action, not words. Would Italy join the war on Germany's side?

strikes a Caesarian pose. . . but all this disappears in a personal conversation, when he becomes human and agreeable.' From here on, Hitler would see to it that his own dictatorship had the style, the stress on costumes, parades, crowd-pulling speeches so well used in Fascist Italy.

If Hitler found the new Italy attractive, the reason lay in part because its style was more German than Italian. By nature peace-loving and with few military ambitions, Italians seemed unlikely enthusiasts for the flag-waving and cheerleading that echoed round Mussolini's instant Empire. Yet, in Italy, it seemed, a new way of life had been invented.

Over the chaos and poverty of post-World War 1 Italy, Mussolini had stamped a fascist order that by the early 30s had won the admiration of many. Winston Churchill praised him in 1933 as a great law-giver and champion against socialism.

Fascism, nowadays, has become an unspecific term of abuse. But behind the bundle of **fasces** that was Mussolini's symbol lay a precise system of power.

Under Mussolini's brand of fascism the state was run, not through the ballot box and elected members of parliament but by 22 corporations that supposedly represented all parts of the nation's workforce and economic interests.

Though these new corporations had unfamiliar names, they seemed closer to the man in the street, or on the farm, than the former **Risorgimento** democracy. Everyone now belonged to some organization or another. And those organizations, grouped in a National Council of Corporations, now ran the economic life of Italy directly. 'Social peace' was the declared aim of the regime at home, as Mussolini had declared on 10 November 1934. He said too: 'Why are there strikes in America? They are not necessary. Here in Italy we have done away with strikes and lockouts: we do not waste time in brawls.'

In place of strife, work was now everyone's 'social duty'. As the Labour Charter of 21 April 1927 put it: 'It is protected by the state. All production forms a single whole from the national point of view. . .a single aim in wellbeing of citizens and development of national power.' The Corporate State sounded good to many.

But national power was the second leg of Fascism. Part of the dream was a self-sufficient Italy. A 'Battle of Wheat' was declared, aimed at weaning Italian farmers from traditional crops

'Only 5 ft 7 in tall, he tries to carry himself so that he looks taller. He rolls his eyes while talking so that the whites show and his eyes pop with emotion.'

Current Biography

like vegetables and fruit and persuading them to raise cereals and industrial crops like sugar beet.

Huge projects were mounted but they did little to change the basic face of Italy: it remained a land of small farmers scratching a living off small parcels of land, often doing a second industrial job on the side. But this was the way of life many wanted. The number of landowners doubled from 1,109,000 to 2,073,000 in the 25 years after 1911.

If enthusiasm failed, there were always the stunts of Fascism for encouragement: parades, adventures into foreign wars, the monumental architecture of new state buildings and (for real backsliders) an increasing state security police.

'What is the aim?'

Though it would prove a pale shadow of Hitler's police state, Mussolini's Italian security forces were well equipped to deal with critics. He had announced his requirements to keep public peace in Rome on 26 May 1927. In this one city it would take 60,000 carabinieri, 15,000 policemen and 5000 guards. Elsewhere were 10,000 militia guarding railroads, ports, roads and postal services; 3600 militia armed the frontiers, 40,000 were on duty behind them and 260,000 more in reserve.

Not surprisingly, key men in the opposition to Fascism, along with many intelligentsia and the whole Communist Party had gone 'underground'.

For a time, the stunts and drama of the regime looked like winning. But projects like draining and settling the **Pontine Marshes** were not much more than cosmetic. In reality the nation was bursting at the seams: overpopulation (encouraged by Mussolini's campaign for bigger families, and restrictions on emigration) had acquired a population of 43 million for Italy in 1936.

As a worldwide depression took hold of Italy's economy between the wars, unemployment soared. Mussolini had taken the classic way out of this mess: he pledged his nation to expansive adventures abroad. In that same speech of 1934 when he had pledged social peace, Mussolini had also declared: 'What is the aim? In relation to the outside world, to increase constantly the global power of the nation.'

On 3 October 1935 Italy went to war in **Abyssinia.** It got rid of many left wing troublemakers, sent off as volunteers. It rallied the nation. It boosted industry, as wars do when there are arms to make. It also set Mussolini on a path of aggression that first looked like, then became, inextricably linked to, the march of the new dictator, Hitler.

From now on, the parades and military bands would celebrate a nation not bent on sorting out its own real problems but a nation that would drown criticism in a call to conquest abroad.

Despite his earlier misgivings, Mussolini was now under Hitler's spell. He trusted him and would have been shocked to know that the Führer had cooked the books for the meeting, by bringing along figures that exaggerated Germany's military strength. For Hitler's part, though he was now confident of manipulating Mussolini to his own ends, something like affection remained for the Italian. He would later call him 'my best, possibly only friend'.

Curiously, on a personal level, the two men had much in common. Both were vegetarians—Mussolini in a now long lost battle to keep slim; Hitler after a personal disaster in 1931, when his beloved niece, Geli Raubal had committed suicide. Neither man touched spirits or smoked (Hitler banned smoking in his presence). Both men, despite the pomp of their public lives, preferred simplicity and near solitude at home: Mussolini's retreat was the comfortably large Villa Torlonia and its 20-acre garden; Hitler's was his mountain eyrie at Berchtesgaden.

The modest life style of the dictators, however, did not exclude feminine company. But while Hitler's faithful mistress Eva Braun lived secluded from the limelight, the Italian's flamboyant sexual habits were legendary. There was never a shortage of infatuated ladies ready to lie down on the marble floor of Mussolini's office. He was a callous lover, holding women in low esteem apart from his wife

Radio Times Hulton Picture Library

Mussolini, a strict vegetarian and non-smoker, announces the winners of the 'Battle of Wheat'. He rode regularly (inset) to keep fit, and is seen (right) with his son Romano.

Rachele, their daughters, and his long term mistress Clara Petacci.

Neither man, indeed, regarded close personal relationships as essential. In that fact, perhaps, lies the ultimate clue to their characters. Both made their greatest rapport with crowds, not individuals. For Mussolini, public adoration was essential. His skill in twisting a crowd round his finger excelled Hitler's. But both were formidable performers, with a keen eye to their public image. Mussolini personally vetted all photographs released to the press; Hitler took care to see no camera caught him wearing his habitual spectacles.

Such men rarely make good conversationalists, it being their nature to talk at, rather than with, their audience. In the train on the Brenner Pass there was no question of which dictator was going to do the talking today. Today was Hitler's.

No doubt he reminded Mussolini of the terms of the **Pact of Steel** which had been signed in Berlin on 22 May the previous year. This treaty, drafted by the Germans, sought to ensure Italy's support in the event of a war. Mussolini, always ready to make a grand, impulsive gesture, had ratified the treaty negotiated by his son-in-law Count **Ciano** scarcely considering its contents.

Hitler laid out two options for the Italian. Mussolini could stay neutral while Hitler dealt with Britain and France without his help. Hitler had enough divisions to do so (he produced the phoney figures) and he *would* do so, by the summer. If Italy stayed out, she could look forward to being a second-rate Mediterranean power for ever. If she came in now she could share the spoils.

It looked like a generous offer, especially if, as Hitler said, the Italian's help was not strictly necessary. (The way Hitler put it was that Italy's efforts might supply the last ounce of strength to tip the balance.) Mussolini considered, as the monologue went on. His Empire, especially after its expensive venture into the Spanish Civil War, was in need of new finances. It was time for another Roman triumph. It was good news too, that Hitler's confidence in German firepower was so high: Mussolini had good reason to be pessimistic about his fellow Italians' appetite for war. 'The Italian race is a race of sheep' he had had occasion to rage recently.

Only a few months ago, the sheep would have bleated loudly at the prospect of marching to war at Germany's side. Hitler's pact with Stalin had roused one frenzy of opposition in Italy; Stalin's blitz on Finland had roused another. Mussolini had, back in January, sent Hitler a long lecture on the topic, pointing out that Russia and Bolshevism remained the true enemy.

But now the sheep might be persuaded more easily. Britain's blockade of the seas had made her highly unpopular with Italians. The idea of adding to the glories of Italy by taking a few lucrative slices off British hands in North Africa was attractive, to say the least.

As the trains rolled back to their respective homelands past the platform's potted plants there were crowds to line Mussolini's track chanting *Duce, Duce*—and with orders to drown out rival chants of *Pace, Pace*. From now on, Italy was on the war road.

In 1937 two large Fascist youth movements, one for 6–18 year olds and one for 18–21 year olds, merged under party control. Total membership in June 1939 was 6,700,000.

'Italians have been given a new life,
Mussolini gave them their new life,
For tomorrow's war.'

Chorus of schoolboys' song

War Notes

ABYSSINIA (Ethiopia): from 1932 Mussolini planned war on Abyssinia, to avenge a humiliating Italian defeat at Adowa in 1896 and to create an E. African empire. Abyssinia lay between Italian Eritrea, on the Red Sea coast and Italian Somaliland on the Indian Ocean. Italians invaded 3 Oct 1935; Adowa occupied 6 Oct 1935, and finally, May 1936, the capital, Addis Ababa fell.

AXIS: Mussolini's term for Italy and Germany after their agreement on 21 Oct 1936. It came to include Japan after 25 Nov 1936 when she and Germany signed the Anti-Comintern (Soviet) Pact.

BRENNER: lowest of main Alpine passes at 4495ft. Divides Otzal mountains of Central Alps and the Zillertals of Eastern Alps. Strategically connects Innsbruck, Austria with Bolzano, Italy.

Popperfoto

CIANO (di Cortellazzo), Count Galeazzo: Italian politician, b. 1903 son of admiral. Educated Rome University. Participated in Fascist March on Rome 1922. Joined Italian Foreign Office 1925, serving at Rio de Janeiro, Peking and Vatican City. Representative to China. Married Mussolini's daughter Edda 1930. Chief of Italian Press Office 1933. Minister for Press and Propaganda 1935. Took charge of bombing campaign in Abyssinia 1935–6. Foreign Minister from 1936. Negotiated 'Pact of Steel'. Increasingly disliked Germans, particularly Ribbentrop.

CORPORATE STATE: Mussolini believed creation of 'corporate state' greatest achievement of Fascism. It was to be an alternative economic system to both Communism and Capitalism. Industry strictly supervised by the National Council of Corporations but private enterprise remained, reserving the right to intervene when the Council appeared inadequate. Banking system remodelled and ailing industries given aid. But those industries 'unfit to survive' were to be liquidated. The council had 170 members drawn from 22 corporations, each with a membership of 800 firms. From 19 Jan 1939 council members sat with Fascist Grand Council representatives in Chamber of Fasces and Corporations that replaced Chamber of Deputies (lower house).

FASCES: Roman bundle of bound rods with or without protruding axe, symbolizing authority. Word from which fascist derived.

FASCIST PARTY: founded and named in Milan by Mussolini 23 March 1919. Within 3 years his oratory, energy and opportunism made the Fascist strongarm squadristi the dominant political party (700,000 members) in a poor and economically stricken country. By 1933 membership 3 million. Party membership was a passport to food and employment. Its youth movement numbered 2 million, trade unions 3.8 million and recreational organization Dopolavore 1.8 million. Catholic Church reconciled to Fascism 1929. Members wore black shirts.

Radio Times

MUSSOLINI, Benito Amilcare Andrea: Italian dictator, b. 1883. Educated School of Silesian Friars, Faenza and Normal School of Forlimpopoli. Taught in elementary school 1902 to avoid military service—attended some lectures at university and befriended expatriate Italian socialists. Expelled from Switzerland for passport offence 1904. Taught again 1907–8. Worked on newspaper *Il Popolo* and, in 1910, became secretary of Forli socialist party, editing the radical paper *La Lotta di Classa* (The Class Struggle). Imprisoned for 5 months for organizing armed uprising again Italo-Turkish War. Director of Socialist Party 1912. At first resisted Italy's entry into WW1, but in Nov 1914 resigned editorship of socialist paper *Avant* and urged Italy to join with Allies in new paper *Popolo d'Italia*. Italy declared war 24 May 1915, and Mussolini served 15 months in the elite bersaglier; before being wounded by bomb splinters. Felt Italy cheated by terms of armistice. Formed Fasci Italiani di Combattimento. Fascist March on Rome Oct 1922 led to Mussolini forming cabinet March 1923. Reorganized economy to form 'corporate state', March 1923. Dealt with Mafia group, known as 'Black Hand', by incorporating it with his own 'Black Shirt' militia. Amended election law to win massive majority April 1924. 3 unsuccessful assassination attempts on his life by 1926. Eliminated remaining legal opposition by 1927. Announced 60-year plan—'by which time Italy will have world supremacy. . . our future lies in Africa and Asia,' 1934. Proclaimed K. Victor Emmanuel III of Italy an Emperor after the conquest of Ethiopia. Sent 50,000 troops and double Germany's monetary aid to Franco in the Spanish Civil War. Over 4000 Italians died, more than in Ethiopia, and Mussolini's popularity waned. Visited Germany in Sept 1937 and became intoxicated with Nazi ceremonial. Anti-Semitism became official Fascist policy in autumn 1938 after Hitler paid a second visit to Italy. Did not expect WW2 until 1942 or 1943 when the Pact of Steel was signed.

PACT OF STEEL: A 10-year formal military alliance between Germany and Italy. Among Hitler's objectives since his visit to Rome in May 1938. After year's talks, was signed in Berlin 22 May 1939. Pact declared that Germany and Italy were 'determined to act side by side and with united forces' for their own security and for maintenance of peace'. Neither party was to conclude a peace or an armistice without the agreement of the other. A secret protocol laid down that the two Foreign Ministers were to set up joint standing commissions on military affairs and the organization of war economies. Italy wanted substantial material aid from Germany.

PONTINE MARSHES: malarial swamp in central Italy, extending for about 300 square miles from Terracina to near Velletri. Notoriously unhealthy since ancient times. Julius Caesar had planned to clear it. Drainage and settlement from 1928 with 4 new towns built 1932–9.

RIBBENTROP, Joachim von: on 1 March US envoy Welles meets Ribbentrop, who though a fluent English language speaker refused to speak English. Through interpreter told Welles that France and Britain had 'brutally rejected attempt of the Führer to spare Europe an armed conflict'. 11 March, visits Pope Pius XII in Vatican. Pope banned swastika from cars collecting Ribbentrop and prohibited photos taken. After 65 minute audience with Pope emerged looking harrassed. Announced coal agreement with Italy, following Brenner talks with Ciano and Mussolini.

RISORGIMENTO: 19th century movement for re-unification of Italy. Greatest leaders were Giuseppe Mazzini, Giuseppe Garibaldi and Count Cavour. Unity of Italy, except for disputed borders, finally achieved in 1870 when French troops withdrew from Rome following Napoleon III's fall.

Keystone

WELLES, Sumner: US diplomat, b. 1892. Under Sec of State (Foreign Affairs) from 1937. Delegate to meeting of Foreign Ministers of American Republics 1939. Visited Europe as personal envoy of President Roosevelt Feb and March 1940. Conferred with Daladier, Hitler, Mussolini, Chamberlain and Pope Pius XII.

Central Press

WAR IN CHINA

From the plane, this town on the rock looks like a dog's head, its muzzle lying where the two great rivers meet. It is rare to have so good a view: between October and April you can count on the town being shrouded in fog. Today the pilot can plainly see his target.

Today the bombs fall into the poorest part of the town. Up the sandstone cliffs that rise from the river the shacks are perched like swallows nests, one on top of another, some braced by poles to keep them in position. As usual, the bombs light fires that burn upwards like torches through the layers of homes.

The pilot had never been there—except this way. They said it was a stinking town, rat-infested, lice-ridden, open sewered. Down there now, they would be running up and down the narrow stairways carved in the rock. And next day they would start rebuilding their shacks. It was routine. The raid was daily routine. The pilot turned for home without emotion. The survivors clambered out of the fetid wet tunnels dug into the rock at river level and inspected the damage. Today's 'ching-pao' was over. Tomorrow the performance would start again.

For the 500,000 souls still clinging to this rock, 1400 miles up the Yangtse river, this was no phoney war. They had been at it two years and more. Ever since that July day, near **Peking** when a Japanese soldier had gone behind a bush to relieve himself. His companions, thinking the Chinese had grabbed him, had begun to turn the town over and the shooting had started. So far two million Chinese had died.

Not all died by shooting. At **Nanking** 46,000 civilians had been done to death by a variety of means. Continued rape was one. So was the Imperial Japanese Army's practice of using live prisoners for bayonet training.

In Whitehall, London, news of this distant turmoil nudged its way briefly into the attention of Britain's leaders. It seemed that the governor of Singapore was worried. The Japanese were swarming through China. Suppose they kept coming south, to grab Malaya, British-owned and source of more than one third of the world's rubber, more than half its tin. Would the Navy get there in time to help? Should the rubber plantation workers and tin miners leave their jobs and train as soldiers? Could Britain now send airplanes and soldiers from home?

It was difficult to take it seriously. Japan couldn't possibly be dreaming of adventures against Britain's Empire bases in Asia—not with one war in hand already. As for airplanes: they were needed in Europe.

But as time would tell, it would have been better if Britain's Foreign Office had paid more attention to the events in China. 'There are always wars in China' goes the tired saying. But this one was different. This one was educating 600,000 Japanese soldiers into that blend of medieval savagery and modern technology which would shortly slice through the Far East as swiftly as a samurai sword. They would come, battle hardened by the war in China, trained to take mountains and jungle in their small stride, capable of living, like peasants, off a handful of rice brewed up in their kidney-shaped mess tins. But capable, too, of flying far and fast in some of the world's best airplanes: a samurai sword in every cockpit.

For Generalissimo **Chiang Kai-shek,** the town on a rock was the latest perch for a government that had been shifting ever deeper into China for some time. The Japanese had taken Nanking, then **Hankow.** Each time, the Nationalist leader had been a long step up the Yangtse ahead. He put a brave face on it. 'We hope to lure the enemy further inland' he said.

The latest retreat, to a once sleepy provincial capital called **Chungking** had been the most spectacular. To this ancient town, whose first walls had been laid in 260 BC Chiang's men had

A bombing raid on Chungking. Far inland on the Yangtze, it had been Chiang's capital since October 1938, the month the important southern seaport of Canton (far left) fell to the Japanese.

Central Press

Eye Witness

On 14 June 1935 the Red Army crossed the Great Snow Mountain. Many soldiers died of exposure on this section of the Long March. Colonel Chang Kuo-hua, already suffering from vomiting and diarrhoea, described the climb to the 16,000ft summit.

'Though this section was not long, every step demanded the strength of my whole body. I purged less frequently, but I felt awfully weak, as if I had not eaten for a long, long time. The air suddenly became thinner when we were some 200m from the summit. Breathing became more difficult. With head spinning and eyes blurred, I could hardly stand, let alone go forward. "Now I am done for," I said to myself, but immediately thought: "Am I going to be defeated when the summit is in sight? I must not fall, for that would be the end of everything." '

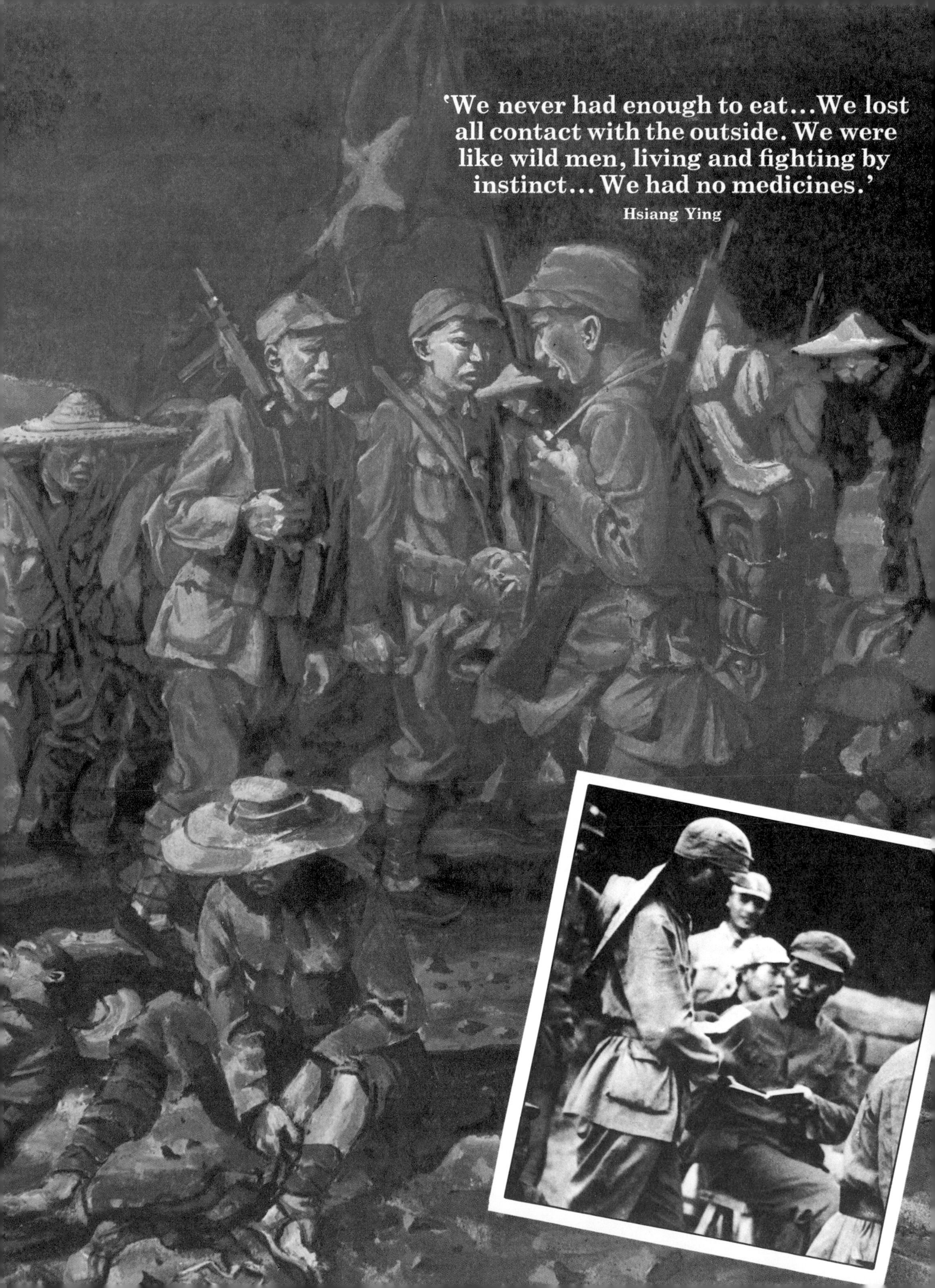

'We never had enough to eat...We lost all contact with the outside. We were like wild men, living and fighting by instinct... We had no medicines.'

Hsiang Ying

brought the salvage of their battered country. They took the precious metal of manhole covers on their backs. They floated 8000 tons of a textile mill's machinery through the gorges of the Yangtse on 310 frail sampans. And when 100 sank they recovered all but 20. Crammed on the rock at Chungking, two million people at one time breathed defiance at the invader's air raids. In his beautiful villa across the brown waters of the Yangtse, and with his beautiful third wife, Madame Chiang, the Generalissimo entertained foreign statesmen (among them India's Nehru), listened to the air raids, and imagined he was winning the war.

On 30 March, news came that back down the river at Nanking, deep in Japanese-held territory—someone had hoisted the same flag which Chiang's government flew and proclaimed a rival regime, with Japanese backing.

Chiang knew all about the wrongdoer. His name was **Wang Ching-wei.** Chiang had lately employed an Inspector Clouseau-type policeman to hunt Wang down. The man had tracked dismally after the dissident Wang through China. When he did fire his assassin's pistol he missed, and killed a bystander. Wang had been one of many thorns in Chiang's side since 1925.

In that year the great Chinese revolutionary Sun Yat-sen had died—the man who had smashed the hated Manchu dynasty in China in 1911. Chiang took over the mantle of leadership in Sun Yat-sen's **Kuomintang** Party, and the 'blue-sky, white-sun, red-earth' flag that Sun himself had designed.

Wang's new bid for power was not too surprising. He had grudged Chiang's grip on the party from the start. Indeed, until this alarming deal he had done with the Japanese, Wang had seemed something of a lightweight problem compared with the mayhem with which Chiang had been contending so long.

Warlords ruled with ferocity

The truth was that since 1911, when the Manchus were ousted, China had been in chaos. Rival warlords then ruled the vast land with colourful, sometimes eccentric ferocity. One of them, the 'Christian General' Feng Yu-hsiang, spread his faith by the speedy means of baptizing his troops with a hose.

Where the warlords rule did not run, that of foreigners did. Korea and Formosa (now Taiwan) had been in Japanese hands since the first China-Japan war of 1894–5. The Japanese, along with British, French, Americans and Germans freely occupied 'concession' areas elsewhere, in which Chinese lived under alien laws. In the teeming underworld of great cities like **Shanghai,** real power lay with the private armies and mobsters of the Red Society and the Green Society, their fortunes based on drugs, sex and gambling.

Radio Times Hulton Picture Library

'If they drive me back to Tibet, in five years I shall be back and conquer all China again.'

General Chiang Kai-shek

Japanese action began in 1931 with the occupation of Manchuria. Chinese troops (left) defend Jehol, Manchuria, 1933. Japanese (above) take Shanghai 1937.

Sun Yat-sen and his protégé Chiang were not the only revolutionaries trying to clean up this cauldron. In 1911, when the Manchus went, an 18-year-old student called **Mao Tse-tung** was also beginning to think seriously about how his country could be purged. Among his favourite reading at the time was a thrilling saga of guerilla warfare called *The Water Margin*. In 1920 he joined the Communist Party.

The lamp of revolution was burning brightly in Moscow in those days. Chiang (six years Mao's senior) had gone to study there in 1924.

For a time, Communists and non-Communists mixed freely in the ranks of Sun Yat-sen's nationalist regime. Fresh from his Moscow training, Chiang led Nationalist soldiers northwards against the warlords, and captured Shanghai in 1927, with the aid of a worker's rising fomented by Communists in the town. The foreigners, who had for so long grown fat from their concessions in the vast port, squealed to Washington and London for help. Foreign battleships began to gather in the Yangtse. For Chiang Kai-shek, whose friends in town were solid capitalists themselves, it seemed that things had been taken far enough.

But it was not far enough for the Communists. By now they had their sights on real reforms; were organizing peasants into revolutionary groups. Chiang decided to take the initiative against the comrades. On 12 April 1927, sirens sounded in Shanghai harbour, and Chiang's men moved through the city at dawn, to massacre key Communists in their beds.

For this death toll of 300 by nightfall, Chiang was sacked by his own outraged party. Nothing daunted, he took his troops to Nanking and set up a rival government. His disfavour did not last long. The rest of the Nationalist Party discovered there was a Communist plot to take over the whole Nationalist movement. The massacres began again with enthusiasm.

By 1928 the Communists looked in a poor way, skulking in the mountains of south east China, no more than 10,000 strong. Chiang meanwhile took his armies into Peking, and made ready for the kill. Even when Japan invaded **Manchuria** in 1931, Chiang turned the problem over to the League of Nations to settle: the Communists remained his first target.

Shadow combat of the guerilla

It should have been easy. But the truth was that time in the mountains had taught the Communists —among them political commissar Mao Tse-tung —a new kind of warfare. If the Japanese in China had learned one style of combat that would amaze the world later, the Communists had learned another. Fifty years later it is still changing maps.

His first Marxist text-books had taught Mao that revolution was a town-based phenomenon. China, he now saw, needed a different theory: here the fight must be based on the countryside, in the hearts and minds of the peasants. Here too, victory must come not in set battles, but the elusive, shadow combat of the guerilla, moving 'like fish through water'.

Such wars could not be won in a day. Mao would sum up his theories in a major book, *On Protracted War*, which he wrote in eight days in 1938, stopping only when a fire burned a hole in his shoe.

Key concepts in the new technique were: 'When the enemy advances we retreat. When the enemy halts we harry. When the enemy retreats we pursue. When the enemy tires we attack.' Just as

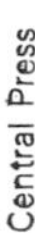

important was the task of educating and winning the sympathy of the local population. Guerilla warfare must fail, wrote Mao 'if its political objectives do not coincide with the aspirations of the people'. At the least, this meant a new code of courtesy. Mao's troops had to remember 'three rules and eight remarks' when dealing with the locals. The remarks included: 'Talk to people politely. Don't damage crops. Don't flirt with women.'

It all added up to a marked contrast to the way the armies of the warlords and the Japanese invaders treated people. These Communists, whose officers practiced the 'four togethernesses' of living, working, studying and eating with their men, who shared a simple red star as insignia—in place of traditional ranks—were making a strong impression on ordinary folk. In time they were able to establish with the peasantry a trust and co-operation unheard of in Chinese history.

Chiang Kai-shek was not slow to realize the danger. 'The Japanese are a disease of the skin' he said. 'The Communists are an illness of the blood.'

By 1934 he had the disease ringed in with a perimeter of concrete and steel. Supplies to the Communists were shut off. In the hills of **Kiangsi** it is likely that some million Communist soldiers and civilians perished.

Keystone

Japanese troops advance through a heavily shelled part of Shanghai in November 1937.

The Communists realized that one more winter in these mountains would be their last. In October some 100,000 men and 35 women made a desperate assault on Chiang's perimeter, broke through, and set off in a huge marching column, aimed at the heart of China. Chiang took pleasure in hovering above them as they went: he spent hours in the air in his private plane, watching the extraordinary, suicidal trek to nowhere.

Epic journey through China

Today, that trek has become known simply as the Long March—a 6000 mile, year-long epic journey through China, aimed at a reunion with a remote Chinese Soviet in the mountains of Shensi.

Winter brought ambush by Nationalist troops and hunger scourged the marchers. Of the 100,000 who set off, only one in ten made it to the end. When they got there, Chiang was ready to organize another expedition to finish them off completely.

The man he chose for the task was Marshal **Chang Hsueh-liang,** who had been forced, with his army, out of Manchuria when the Japanese took it in 1931. Chang, however, had other ideas, and expressed them forcibly. Why were Chinese slaughtering Chinese, when the real enemy was still Japan? Chiang Kai-shek set off in a fine fury to order his marshal to attack—and was promptly arrested by the Manchurian.

The choice put to the outraged Generalissimo was stark: either join with the Communists and attack the Japanese, or be ousted and see China finally ruined in a civil war to end all wars. The deal was made. Henceforth Chiang and Mao were, temporarily, on the same side once more.

Thus, when Japan swept into attack again in 1937, she faced a land newly united, but as vast as ever: a land that could soak up punishment with inexhaustible patience. By March 1940 the bombers might be able to reach Chungking, on its perch far up the Yangtse, but no Japanese soldier could get there on foot. They had long ago given up trying. Since the end of 1938 all China's seaboard and most of her industrial centres were in the invader's hands. But to enjoy these riches a million troops were being tied down in attempts to 'pacify' the countryside.

The new puppet government mounted in Nanking that month, under Wang Ching-wei, has been branded by many historians as a simple, sordid piece of treachery on Wang's part. But, like some Japanese, he saw the war as a deadly stalemate—and could foresee China's eventual ruin from it. He had long been a staunch anti-Communist: and knew well that while Chiang Kai-shek brooded far away in Chungking it was Mao's Communists who were getting the reputation for chasing Japanese. Rather than see China go Communist, or be crushed by Japan, reasoned Wang, let us set up a 'genuine Sino-Japanese co-operation'.

The Japanese promised him that, two years after the war was over, they would pull out of China. He ran up his flag. The Japanese began to tout recognition abroad for their brand new government. No one yet dreamed of the words 'Pearl Harbor'.

War Notes

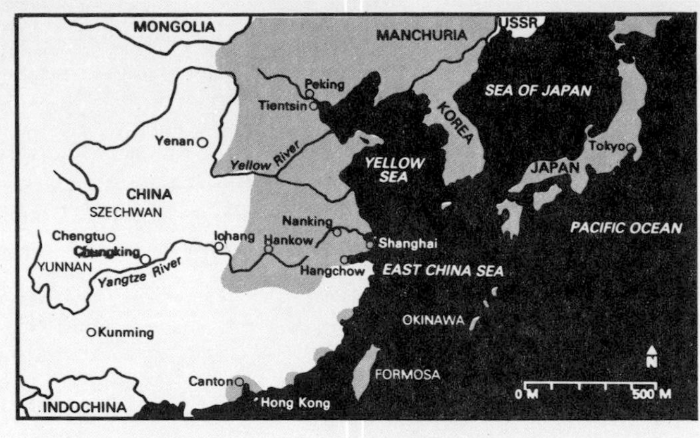

CHANG HSUEH-LIANG: ruler of Manchuria, b. 1898. Took over Manchuria when father, Chang Tsolin, assassinated 1928. Leading role in resistance to Japan. Known as The Young Marshal. Kidnapped Chiang Kai-shek at Sian 1936. After Chiang's release kept under house arrest till 1961.

Keystore

CHIANG KAI-SHEK: Chinese Head of State and leader of Kuomintang (KMT), b. 1887 Fenghua, Chekiang Province. At 18 joined Provincial Army. Entered Paoting Military Academy 1906. Among 40 students sent to Japanese Military College, Tokyo 1907. Met Sun-Yat-sen and others planning overthrow of Manchu regime. Took part in revolution, and after fall of Sun, took refuge with him in Hong Kong. Spent some time in Shanghai, re-emerging when Sun's govt re-established in Canton 1923. Sent by Sun to Moscow to study Soviet system. Returned 1924, and with Russian adviser, Borodin, set up Whampoa Military Academy for officers. President of School. When Sun died 1925, as KMT's leading soldier, took over leadership. Differences with Communists apparent from 1926. Married Soong Mei-ling, sister of Madame Sun 1927. Became member of Methodist Church 1930. After Sian Incident increased Army to 1.7 million and appointed US Capt Claire Chennault to head air force of 200 planes. Got £250 million arms credits from USSR 1938–9. Ordered 'scorched earth' policy against Japan.

CHUNGKING: lies on Yangtse River in SW Szechwan Province at mouth of R. Kialing, 450 miles WSW of Hankow. Wartime capital of China 1938. Leading commercial centre in SW. First bombed by Japanese 3 May 1939, 5000 casualties. Adequate dugouts and shelters by spring 1940.

HANKOW: capital of Chekiang Province, 100 miles SW of Shanghai. Commercial and cultural centre. Occupied by Japanese Oct 1938.

KIANGSI: province of S. central China. Capital: Nanchang. One of China's leading rice-producing areas. Traditionally main N-S corridor for migration and communication. After Communists split with Kuomintang most of Kiangsi came under their control 1927–34. Largely free of Japanese March 1940.

KUOMINTANG (KMT): Chinese Nationalist Party. Founded by Sun Yat-sen 1895. After 1911 Revolution, Sun became president but forced out by more powerful Yuan Shih-k'ai. Sun established a secure base for KMT in Canton Kwangtung province 1923. Intention was to unify China. Power passed to Chiang Kai-shek on death of Sun 1925. Northern Expedition superficially unified China 1928. Chiang began a New Life Movement in the KMT (1935) that reverted to Confucian ideals of an ordered moral state rather than Sun's original Three People's Principles which stipulated social and political reforms.

MANCHURIA: vast area of 585,000 square miles known to Chinese as 'the NE'. Population 43 million 1940. Fertile agricultural land. Capital: Mukden. Modern development largely as a result of railway built by Russians after acquisition of Kwantung Lease 1898. Following Russo-Japanese War 1904–5 Manchuria came into Japanese sphere of influence and was annexed by Japan 1931, with P'u Y'i, last Emperor of China as nominal head of state 1932. Region's economy expanded rapidly with Japanese aid and was a major asset for Japan during WW 2.

MAO TSE-TUNG: Leader of Chinese Communist Party (CCP) b. 1893 Hunan Province. After brief service as soldier in 1911 Revolution became involved in revolutionary activities. Librarian in Peking 1918. Met Li-Ta-chao, early Chinese Marxist and represented Hunan at foundation of CCP 1921. Involved as labour organizer, co-ordinator of CCP and KMT. Interested in and wrote about Hunan peasants' movement. Out of step with city emphasis of CCP but after 1927 able to pursue independent line. Broke with Stalin after Comintern directives led to massacre by KMT forces. Set up base with small group of followers on borders of Hunan and Kiangsi. Expanded as Kiangsi Soviet 1930. Won undisputed leadership after Kiangsi Soviet abandoned. After Long March Mao turned party into peasant-based, highly disciplined organization. Used with KMT forces against Japanese. New alliance between KMT and CCP in face of Japanese aggression Sept 1937. Chou En-Lai led delegation in Chungking. Lasted until Mao decided to fight Chiang rather than Japanese 1940. Expanded Red 4th and 8th Route Armies from 65,000 (1937) to 500,000 (1940). These forces only waged guerilla warfare against the Japanese with one exception. On 25 Sept 1937 the Communist 115th Div (Gen Nich Jung-chen) of 8th Route Army ambushed and defeated the Japanese 5th Div (Gen Seishiro Itagaki) in the Battle of P'ingh-sinkuan (N. Shansi).

NANKING: Chinese city in S. Kiangsu Province on right bank of Yangtse river, 170 miles WNW of Shanghai. Capital of China 1928–37. Capital moved to Chungking before Nanking fell to Japanese Dec 1937: 1/3 of city burnt, over 5000 women raped.

PEKING: China's capital at most periods. Population 1,560,000 in 1936. 70 miles NW of Yellow Sea port, Tientsin and 40 miles within Great Wall. Capital until transfer of Nationalist government to Nanking 1928. Incident on Marco Polo Bridge, at Wanping, 7 July 1937 (known to Chinese as Double 7th) marked beginning of Sino-Japanese conflict. Occupied by Japanese 29 July 1937.

SHANGHAI: port on R. Whanpoo, tributary of Yangtse, 170 miles ESE of Nanking. Largest city in Asia. Divided into garrisoned foreign concessions belonging to British, US and French. Sino-Japanese battle took place there 1932 over trade boycott. City occupied by Japanese Nov 1937 after 3-months fighting costing them some 60,000 men. The battle ruined Chiang's best German-trained troops and cost 300,000 lives.

Keystone

WANG CHING-WEI: Chinese politician, b. 1884. Gained fame as revolutionary with attempt to assassinate the Manchu Prince Regent 1911. Avoided execution because of beautiful calligraphy! Was closely associated with Sun-Yat-sen 1911–21. Rival of Chiang Kai-shek for leadership after Sun's death, but forced into exile. Visited Europe 1932 and set up Nanking pro-peace club 1935. At outbreak of Sino-Japanese War token unity in KMT but not given personal power 1937. Abandoned KMT govt in Dec 1938 after failure to persuade Chiang to make peace. Fled to Hanoi, set up 'Orthodox Chinese Nationalist Party' July 1939.

MARCH 1940:

SPRING IN PARIS

Springtime in Paris usually lifts the heart. But this March the mood was one of political in-fighting. A taxi driver summed it up. He said: 'Russia has a Man. Germany has a Man. If only we had a Man, we could lick all of them.'

The man at the helm in France was Prime Minister Edouard Daladier. As a war leader 'the bull of Vaucluse' had little to recommend him. His horns were more like 'the soft feelers of a snail than the harder, bovine variety' commented Britain's Sir Edward Spears. For Daladier had been a man of Munich, an appeaser second only to Chamberlain.

Foreigners found their first sight of Daladier memorable. He was, said the highly civilized Harold **Nicolson**, 'a drunken peasant. His face must once have had sharp outlines but now is blurred by the puffiness of drink. He looks extremely exhausted and has the eyes of a man who has had a bad night. He has a weak, sly smile.' An American journalist was even less complimentary. Daladier, he reported, is 'a dirty man with a cigarette stuck to his lower lip, stinking of absinthe, talking with a rough Marseilles accent'.

The French had grown more used to him. It was the 55-year-old widower's third time at the political helm. That was the style of the **Third Republic,** where ministers shuffled their portfolios between each other and jockeyed for position in the corridors of power—corridors that 'rustled with intrigue', said soldier Charles de Gaulle.

And it now looked as if Daladier's well-known talent for balancing on political tightropes was deserting him too. With good reason, his enemies were now out to plunge the sword between the ribs of the 'bull of Vaucluse'.

The reason was Finland. The French had watched with mounting shame at their own inactivity, the David and Goliath contest that had been waged in the north. Nothing had been done to aid Poland. Now next to nothing was being done to help Finland. 'It is a heavy moral defeat for the Allies,' noted serving soldier Major Barlone in his diary. 'I realize this when I talk to men who are bewildered by the inactivity of the Allies. . . we are disheartened.'

By early March, Daladier saw, too late, that some action to aid Finland was essential. The trouble was that talk of opening a 'Scandinavian Front' fell on deaf ears in Britain. To attack Russia would have been 'the maddest military adventure upon which this country has ever

March 1940 saw the downfall of France's Prime Minister, Edouard Daladier. But he compelled his successor, Paul Reynaud, to keep him as Minister of Defence.

Popperfoto

'The Bull of Vaucluse had received something more than darts this time, the toreador had placed the sword firmly between his ribs.'

Elie Bois, *Truth on the Tragedy of France*

embarked', Colonel Josiah Wedgwood remarked in the Commons. Daladier's own military advisers felt much the same. But he persisted. On 11 March he told Britain's Foreign Secretary, Lord Halifax, that he would resign if Britain did not agree to an expedition.

The gesture was too late. Next day the Finns signed an armistice. And, immediately, the nation's sense of shame and guilt found a target: Daladier.

In the **Senate** it was now time for fine words and sentiments. 'You had in Finland an almost miraculous opportunity to vanquish the Soviet Union' railed one orator at Daladier. 'You let it slip by. France weeps over it! Her heart bleeds!' 'Tres bien' interjected Pierre Laval, who had already set his sights on ousting Daladier's 'dunghill' government.

'I defy you to explain'

Laval, one of the stealthiest plotters in the corridors of power, had the house on his side tonight. He attacked Daladier for declaring war without 'sufficient military and diplomatic preparation'. He lashed him for the feebleness of the aid to Finland. He made mincemeat of Daladier's excuse that no official request for aid had been made by the Finns. He sat down to applause.

Daladier's defence lacked conviction. He looked old, tired and discouraged and had been drugged with painkillers since falling from his horse on the frost-hard ground in January. Once again, he laid the blame on Britain, for opposing a war on the Russians; on Norway and Sweden, for refusing to allow transit of men and materials across their lands to Finland. He ended with a bid to take the debate out of the grimy machinations of party politics. 'The worst thing in wartime is the intrigues in the corridors of Parliament' he declared. 'Today there are no longer Parties, there is nothing but the French.'

Laval was having none of it. He demanded a vote. It was held in two parts: first a vote in homage to the heroism of the Finns—carried unanimously. Then came a vote of confidence in the government's conduct of the war so far. The tally ran: 236 for, none against, 60 abstentions. A vote against the government would have provided political ammunition to the nation's enemies: but the abstentions were clear evidence that Daladier's grip was loosening.

Worse was to come on 19 March, when the debate was rerun in the lower house. Here the onslaught was led by Pierre **Flandin.** The government should have sent a force to Finland 'the moment war broke out there'. He chided Daladier: 'I defy you to explain why you make war against Germany and not also against Soviet Russia.' This time it took until 4am before the attacks were finished and votes counted. There were 300 abstentions in this part of the **National Assembly.**

Theoretically he could have carried on. The left wing howled for his resignation. President Albert **Lebrun** pressed him to decide. 'The country is waiting! We are at war. It must be either yes or no. Is it yes?'

Daladier had had enough. 'It is no' he said.

His successor, Minister of Finance Paul **Reynaud** looked, to many, a more likely candidate for the job. The 62-year-old lawyer from the far south with a reputation for brilliance in debate had been aiming at high office for a long time: 60 years, according to Laval. Like Daladier, he was an old hand at the games of French political intrigue—he had been a Minister seven times. Long considered a financial expert, his devaluation of the franc and tax measures had assisted France's belated re-armament.

The man who now took on the task of trying to cobble together the Third Republic's 109th government had a reputation as a 'hard' man: a 'fighting cock', his friend, author André Maurois, called him. And the only politician to back de Gaulle's ideas for a mechanized professional French Army had been Reynaud.

His enemies called him Mickey Mouse. Despite the stacked shoes he wore to enhance his height, and the cult of fitness he took care to publicize (he cycled, boxed and did gymnastics), he did not appear a heavyweight. His efforts now to choose a team showed that he, too, lacked weight politically.

Without the backing of a solid political party, and few political friends, Reynaud had a cabinet that liked neither him nor each other.

One thing could be said of this cabinet—it was a big one: Reynaud feared to leave out any figures that could turn on him if snubbed. The satirical magazine *Le Canard Enchainé* joked: for his first cabinet meeting he's hiring the Winter Stadium.

A depressing sight

Some of the appointees were plainly going to be disasters. There was Paul Baudouin, the new Secretary of the War Cabinet, a fervent admirer of Mussolini and pre-war advocate of peace with Nazi Germany. Later there were extreme right-wingers, like Louis Marin and Ybarnegary—men whose views violently opposed Reynaud's. In the attempt to perform his balancing act, Reynaud was obliged to leave out socialist Leon **Blum.**

The balancing act failed.

In his memoirs Reynaud lamented: 'I was in a difficult position. I had not been able to achieve national unity.' The hodge-podge bunch of ministers he presented to the **Chamber of Deputies** on Good Friday, 22 March 1939, made a depressing sight to de Gaulle, who was there to watch, from the galleries of the Palais Bourbon.

De Gaulle had been summoned by Reynaud to write a brief statement setting out the new government's aims for France. It was a crisp statement, well drafted. 'France is engaged in a total war. To win is to save everything. To succumb is to lose

Radio Times Hulton Picture Library

Posters announcing the mobilization of forces decorate the streets as Reynaud's cabinet poses for the camera. The three figures at the front are, from the left, Daladier, Reynaud and Camille Chautemps, Vice-President of the Council.

Roger Viollet

everything. The government which presents itself to you has no other reason for existing than this: to arouse, to bring together, to direct all French energies in order to combat and conquer; to crush treason from whatever quarter it may come.'

Reynaud read it out in a flat, lifeless drone. Then the house got down to the serious business: bickering about who had been ousted in the race for plum ministerial jobs. De Gaulle watched, aghast. 'It was horrible' he recorded. 'The danger for the country, the need for national effort, the collaboration of the Free World were invoked only to decorate the pretensions and the rancour.' In the first vote of the new parliament, Reynaud survived with a majority of one. 'You'll have to resign' jeered Albert **Chichery,** Radical-Socialist leader. 'I would have too,' said Reynaud later, 'if there had been anyone beside him to take over.'

But the biggest obstacle to bringing urgency into the conduct of the war was the man who had just been ousted from the hot seat: Daladier. He had been premier, Minister of Foreign Affairs and Minister of Defence at the same time: now he insisted on clinging to this last post. The price was his support for Reynaud. It was a bitter pill to swallow. With Daladier still running the Army, Reynaud would have no chance of sacking the French C-in-C, Gamelin, or of promoting de Gaulle to secretary of the War Cabinet.

Political opponents, Reynaud and Daladier also had a lively personal loathing for each other: this too would minimize their chances of being able to work together. Behind their mutual hatred lay a typical French scandal: both had formidable mistresses.

'The people deserve better'

All France knew the story. Daladier's was the Marquise de Crussol. Petite, with light curly hair, she had the maiden name of Bezier—a household name in France for a sardine canning firm. Hence derived her nickname: 'La sardine qui s'est crue sole'—the sardine who thought she was a sole. Reynaud's lady had a nickname too: 'La porte à côté'—the side door. Besides being a play on her real name, Countess Hélène de Portes, it sneered deftly at her as a social climber, and more than hinted at her role: she was indeed the 'side door' to the premier.

André Maurois once asked Reynaud why he had made a particularly disastrous political appointment. 'It was not my choice, it was her's' Reynaud confessed. 'That's no excuse' said his friend. 'Ah,' sighed Reynaud 'you don't know what a man who has been hard at work all day will put up with to ensure an evening's peace.' The Countess, described by Sir Edward Spears as 'devoid of charm'—though he granted she had good feet and ankles—behaved like a director of the Cabinet. She plagued the life out of Reynaud, telephoning him at work, sitting in on his top level discussions with foreign heads of state, even, on occasion, taking over his desk to queen it at gatherings of generals, deputies and officials. From the gossip factory of her drawing room she had long waged war on 'the sardine', her pet hate, by spreading rumour of Daladier's incompetence.

She made Reynaud feel 'tall and grand and powerful', guessed diarist Harold Nicholson. As France drifted sleazily under the threat of a German spring offensive her presence at the seat of power summed up, for many, how shoddy a regime it was. 'The people of France,' wrote US Ambassador William Bullitt to Roosevelt, 'deserve better at the moment than to be ruled by a Prime Minister's mistress.'

Major Barlone summed up the dismal scene. 'People see a schemer and a thief in every politician' he wrote. 'Our enemies do not waste their time over parliamentary manoeuvres. Spring is now here, the time of trial is probably at hand, and look what a government we have.'

Radio Times Hulton Picture Library

War Notes

FRANCE

Fox Photos

BLUM, Léon: French writer and politician, b. 1872 son of rich Jewish family. Journalist who became a socialist and co-founded the *L'Humanité* daily. Elected deputy from Seine 1919. Leader of Socialist Party from 1925. Deputy from Narbonne 1928. Prime Minister of Popular Front government 1936–7. Introduced social reforms including paid holidays and 40-hour week; began re-armament. Minister of State and Vice-President under Chautemps 1937. PM March-April 1938 but again fell due to financial crises.

Popperfoto

CHAMBER OF DEPUTIES: lower house of French national assembly. Each arrondissement (district) provided one deputy elected for 4 years. To be elected on first ballot a candidate had to have (a) an absolute majority and (b) at least a quarter of the votes of all eligible electors. Failing this, a second vote was held a week later when a simple majority would suffice.

CHICHERY, Albert: French industrialist and politician, b. 1888. Founded and developed a successful bicycle factory. He was a deputy from 1932 and became president of the Radical-Socialist group in parliament 1938. Minister of Trade 1939.

FLANDIN, Pierre Etienne: French politician, b. 1889, Paris. Educated University of Paris. Delegate to peace conference 1919. Under-Secretary of State for Air 1920. Minister of Trade 1924 and 1929–30. Became Vice-President of Chamber of Deputies in 1928. Then came a succession of ministerial posts: Finance under Laval 1931–2, Public Works 1934; PM Nov 1934–June 1935, Minister of State under Laval 1935–6, Foreign Affairs 1936. French delegate to League of Nations 1930–1. Supported Daladier at Munich.

LEBRUN, Albert: French President, b. 1871 in the Moselle Valley region. Educated Lycée of Nancy, Ecole Polytechnique and Ecole Supérieure des Mines. Worked as an engineer until 1900 when he was elected deputy for Briey. Secretary of Assembly 1903–4. Vice-President of Chamber of Deputies 1913. Ministerial posts: Colonies 1911–14, and Liberated Regions 1917–19. Elected to Senate 1920. President of Senate 1931–2. President of France 1932.

NATIONAL ASSEMBLY French parliament, consisting of two houses—the Senate and the Chamber of Deputies. Laws must be approved by a majority in both houses before they can be enacted. Though theoretically of equal importance, defeat in the Chamber of Deputies is, in practice, more serious than defeat in the Senate.

Fox Photos

REYNAUD, Paul: French politician, b. 1878 Barcelonnette in the Alps son of farmer. Educated University of Paris. Began career as lawyer 1911. Deputy for Basses Alpes 1919 and for second division of Paris 1928. Ministerial posts: Finance 1930 and Nov 1938, Colonies 1931, Justice 1932 and 1938, PM and Foreign Affairs March 1940.

SENATE: upper house of the French national assembly. The 300 senators were elected for a 9-year term. Every 3 years 100 senators were due for re-election.

THIRD REPUBLIC: proclaimed 4 Sept 1870 by Jules Favre and Leon Gambetta following surrender of Emperor Napoleon III at Sedan. In its 70-year lifetime there were no fewer than 109 governments: few of them lasted longer than 2 years and six could not even survive 10 days.

THE END OF THE ROPE

It was going badly now. The best soldiers were dead. Now half-trained schoolboys and old men were filling the gaps in the Finnish line. And the Russians were still coming.

Even Finland's most faithful ally, the bitter winter, had gone to Russia's aid. Unbroken ice now spanned the sea in front of Viipuri. The Russians could simply walk to battle.

There must by now be more than a million of them, reckoned Mannerheim, the wearied Finnish C-in-C. It was horrifying to watch the almost casual fatalism with which they threw their lives away. A whole regiment was torn to pieces as it marched across the Gulf of Finland in closed formation against the Finnish mainland. The bodies piled up below the guns on the beach: but the rest kept on advancing, over the ice, on foot, in motor sleighs, even cars. It took all the night of 4 March, fighting hand to hand, to throw them back on the ice. Next day another whole division arrived, plus 100 tanks. This time the Russians had their bridgehead on the west side of Viipuri Bay.

The ever fewer defenders at the front guessed the end could not be far off. Some were crazed by the battle. In one command dugout, men had to hold down two soldiers who were screaming and babbling as artillery shells rained on the roof. Dead bodies were piled in layers on bunk beds. Suddenly a platoon leader forced his way into the charnel house, eyes bloodshot: 'My wife is coming here with more machine guns. We're going to kill them all. Even the last one.' Then he ran out, screaming, weaponless towards the guns.

A flurry of offers

In Helsinki, a letter to Moscow, accepting Russia's peace terms in principle, was already drawn up by 29 February. But news that the Finns were on the eve of giving in brought a flurry of offers from London and Paris. The French were talking of 50,000 men and 100 bombers by the end of March. The British cabinet shocked by this rash offer, made without consulting them, nevertheless began to sniff round the edges of the old problem: getting supplies through neutral Sweden and Norway.

On 1 March the Finnish Government felt heartened enough to scrap its letter to Moscow and redraft it. It read: 'The Finnish Government is anxious to bring about a cessation of hostilities and the conclusion of peace, but since the new frontier contemplated in the proposal is vague we request exact specifications and information on

'We've had a lot of bombs fall in Hanko...but the worst bomb of all has been this peace.'

Hanko factory worker

Citizens of Helsinki read the Government announcement of peace (above) while three Russian soldiers approach wire defences at the naval port of Hanko, reluctantly ceded by Finland to the Soviet Union.

what compensation Finland would get.'

It postponed the day of reckoning. Russians and Finns would go on dying for a few days yet while the western Allies wobbled on the edge.

The risks remained appalling. Aid from the West would pitch the entire Scandinavian peninsula into war. If Germany joined in the Allies would be fighting on a front that would run from the Arctic to the Mediterranean.

In Berlin, Hitler took time to explain to Swedish explorer Sven Hedin, his guest, that Germany most certainly would join in. 'One thing you in Sweden must be quite clear about,' he warned. 'And that is that the moment British or French troops set foot on Swedish soil, Germany will instantly intervene.'

Sweden needed no convincing. Her foreign minister Christian Günther warned that any effort by the Allies to force their way through to Finland, up the Narvik railway, would result in every inch of track being torn out of the ground to stop them.

Russia reacted bleakly to Finland's delaying letter. The message came back: accept them or we'll make the terms tougher.

Now the Swedes began to put pressure on Finland to give in. The Finns would forfeit all support from Sweden if they carried on the fight for Viipuri and Sortavala, claimed Günther. 'We cannot go to war for Viipuri and Sortavala . . . nor are these cities vital to Finland: their loss would not mean the destruction of Finland.'

Meanwhile the slaughter on the ice continued. News from Mannerheim, now feverish with influenza, was grim. 'The last minutes are at hand' he warned on 5 March. Harsh though the peace terms were, a massive breakthrough by Soviet tanks might endanger any kind of peace at all; see Finland swallowed wholesale. It was plain now, that the Allied help could never come in time. The end came when the men in Helsinki totted up just how small and late that help would be: the promises of 100,000 men meant nothing. The total of Allied troops that could get there by mid-April would be 6000. Tanner told his cabinet colleagues: 'We have reached the end of the rope.'

On 5 March the Finns told Moscow they were sending a delegation to talk peace, and requested an immediate armistice. The request was refused. Russia wanted Finland to negotiate under duress. It was the first harsh pointer to just how grim the negotiations would be.

The delegation, consisting of Prime Minister Ryti, Dr Juho Paasikivi, Major General Rudolf Walden and the MP Vaino Voionmaa arrived at their lodgings in Moscow still hopeful that there were to be genuine talks, bargains to be made,

Keystone

A flag in Helsinki flies at half mast to honour Finland's 25,000 dead.

concessions to be won. 'The terms are a starting point for discussion,' President **Kallio** had said hopefully. 'We are not obliged to consent to everything.'

Next morning they discovered how wrong they were.

They confronted a stone-faced **Molotov,** Andrei Zhdanov and General Aleksander Vasilevski, whose job it was to spell out that Finland had one option: accept the terms lock, stock and barrel—and immediately.

The delegation looked at the map produced for them. It was small scale, out of date, and the lines drawn across it, indicating Finland's new frontiers, had been drawn with a ruler and heavy hand. Passikivi studied it, aghast. The frontier marched through villages and towns, cutting communities in half, villagers from their land. 'That line represents an area at least half a mile wide. Can we not define it more exactly or we shall have endless difficulties,' the Finn asked. Molotov shrugged. 'It is the way we settled Poland with the Germans. It worked all right there. It can work again here.'

The truth was that Finland was being confined to the frontiers laid down by Peter the Great more than two centuries before. She would lose some 100,000 square miles, among them the richest industrial and agricultural regions of the nation. Forty thousand farms would be swallowed. Some 500,000 Finns would face the choice of staying on under the new, alien masters—or getting out. The wood and paper industries, flour mills, iron smelting works would be among the Russian prizes. So, for a 30-year term, would be an entire seaport, Hanko. The Finnish delegates pointed out that when Peter the Great had grabbed his stake in Finland, he had at least paid compensation. Molotov cracked a heavy joke: 'So write a letter to Peter the Great. If he orders us to, we'll pay you compensation.'

An agonizing dilemma

Contact with the rest of the government in Helsinki was difficult: telegrams took up to 12 hours to get through. Back in Helsinki however there was more news of the Allies' latest plans to help. If Finland put in a formal request, Britain would send 50 bombers, eight within four days. Britain would also make one more effort to win Swedish permission to allow the supplies through.

The delegation's dilemma was now agonizing. Should they play the card that unless some concessions were made in Moscow, they would fight on? That would certainly provoke the Russians into tearing up their crude map—and into demanding still more. And what if Sweden refused to allow supplies through?

News reached Moscow on the 11th to the effect that Sweden was still categorically refusing to assist: Helsinki told the delegates to act on their own and get the best deal they could. On the evening of 12 March, with heavy hearts, they signed the **Treaty of Moscow.**

To Finnish soldiers and civilians the news that the war was over came as a total, stunning shock. Censorship had hidden the news that their government was even contemplating giving in. The news broke raggedly. The morning papers of the 13th carried no mention of it. But one by one across the land, flags began to descend to half mast. Red-eyed men and women began to bunch in the streets.

For the men still fighting, the impact of the news was devastating. At Kuhmo, when one company was told, in the small hours, to lay down their arms at 11am, they hurled themselves at the Russian lines as dawn broke, fighting on in desperate rage until almost all were dead. That final, tragic battle was the last thing the tired and hungry Russians of 54th Division had expected. At first they had rushed out to embrace the Finns, had started playing accordions and dancing.

At Taipale, Finnish soldiers along the lakeside heard the news of the war's end and cheered. They had held their positions since the first day of the war, 105 days back. No wonder they believed Finland had won. In front of Viipuri, on the war's most desperate front, the news never got through—until, at 11am, the Russian guns stopped firing. The defenders imagined the silence heralded a new attack and grimly distributed their reserve am-

Fox Photos

munition. Then, to their disbelief, they heard that it was all over.

At noon, the radio brought Tanner's voice, speaking first in Finnish, then Swedish, to give the country its first definite news that all was over. He went through the whole, epic story. 'Peace has been restored,' he said, 'But what kind of peace? Henceforth our country will continue to live as a mutilated nation.'

Foreign correspondent Geoffrey Cox asked the secretary in the press room what she thought of the news. She gave a half smile. 'I live in Viipuri,' she said. 'Last week I saw on a newsreel my flat smashed to pieces by a bomb. But I don't mind that so much as stopping the fight now when we have suffered so much.'

Cox ventured into the streets, with other foreign journalists, all distinguished by their armbands. Their opinion-finding trip met with stony, angry stares. Cox found a group gathered round a car, its radio going. It was a clear, sunny morning. The Finns 'stared at us with our yellow Press armbands, angrily. A strong race, they resented anyone seeing them in this hour of sorrow. They resented the outside world which had given them so many words of sympathy, so little real help,' reported Cox.

Abroad, the correspondents' newspapers began framing their headlines. The scapegoat for the failure to bring help would be Sweden. In France the headlines ran: 'The Cowardice of Sweden', the 'Contemptible Betrayal by Sweden', 'Sweden in the Pillory'. The London *Times* of 14 March would play down the fact that Finland had been left in the lurch. Hard though the peace treaty was, 'It is less severe than the territorial clauses of other similar treaties of recent times.'

But the next few days would show how severe the clauses were.

In an extraordinary, stoic drama, the men and women of Finland voted with their feet, and began to trek west from the lands that Molotov's pencil had now denied them. In a remote fishing village called Lappviki, a housewife combined the task of packing up to leave with baking one last batch of loaves in the oven. 'It is such a good oven' she explained. 'I don't think I'll ever have such a good one again.'

A family in Hanko pack up to leave before the Russians arrive to occupy the town.

An already war-ravaged country had now to cope with the movement cf some half million people. They brought with them what they could, walking patiently behind carts that bore pathetic stacks of furniture, the very young and the very old perched on top. When the cattle died on the long trek, not even the carcasses were left for the hated invader. On a sledge, a woman of 30, with three young children had placed the coffin of her husband.

Deadline for evacuation

The city of Viipuri was emptied to a man. From Helsinki trains were crowded as civilians went back to their home town for the last time, to collect what belongings they could. Many were too late. The Russians were prompt to move in, looting as they went. In the seaport of Hanko the Russians had set a ten-day deadline for evacuation. Its citizens did their best to take everything movable: the furniture from the casino, piles of hay and straw. Every truck and train that Finland could mobilize went into service. 'Nothing that I had experienced during the fighting moved me as deeply as the scenes along the roads' wrote one eyewitness. 'Their faces were brave, the faces of people who would rather starve than live under the rule of foreigners.'

In a way, the task in hand helped to postpone the grief of defeat. In a mood of national unity, those with estates in the west voluntarily gave up lands to the arrivals from the east. In the fishing villages of the Gulf of Bothnia men from the lost coast of Karelia began to spread their nets anew. In Helsinki, the lights began to come on again. Trams ran in the streets. 'We had virtually forgotten what it was like to be at peace,' said one tired soldier. 'To enjoy regular meals undisturbed, to have eight hours continuous sleep.'

Tough and resilient as ever, the Finns began to shape their future: to clear forests, build farms, repair the £5 million worth of damage done by Soviet bombers in the homeland left to them. The Finns had fought a lone and honourable fight. Foreign **aid** and **volunteers** had counted for little save moral encouragement. They had no need to reproach themselves or their leaders in defeat. That was a privilege few other European governments were to share.

Victory in defeat

In Moscow there was recognition that Finland would be too costly to take over and run as a puppet state; it would simply add to the already vast number of **casualties.** 'All of us—and Stalin first and foremost—sensed in our victory a defeat by the Finns' said Khruschev. 'It was a dangerous defeat because it encouraged our enemies' conviction that the Soviet Union was a colossus with feet of clay.

By a hair's breadth, this remote winter war escaped being turned into part of the global conflict. Now that conflict would begin to rage on other fronts. But Finland's example of courage and determination against vast odds would shine out as a beacon among the other small nations soon to be engulfed.

War Notes

AID: before fighting ended the following aid reached Finland, though invariably not the front line. *France:* 48 fairly modern field guns, 136 antique cannon. *Sweden:* another 16 planes, 33 more field guns, 85 AA guns, 18 AT guns, 100 MGs, 77,000 rifles. *Hungary:* 40 AA guns, 30 AT rifles, 300,000 grenades. *Italy:* 60 AA and 12 AT guns, 100 mortars, 28 flamethrowers, 20 tractors, 6000 pistols, 35 torpedoes and 150 mines. *Belgium:* 700 rifles, 7456 pistols and 12 million rounds. *Britain:* 12 Hurricanes, 17 Lysanders, 12 6in coast guns, 24 4.5in howitzers, 42 AA guns, 40,000 grenades, 30 million small arms bullets, 300 field kitchens, 5000 tents and 50,000 khaki uniforms (used on home front). *US:* 5 Brewster Buffalo fighters surplus to USN needs. *Denmark:* 178 20mm AA guns. *Germany:* 30 20mm flak guns. *Norway:* 12 field guns.

CASUALTIES: *Finland* 24,923 killed, 43,557 wounded. Some 700 civilians were killed and 1400 wounded by 7500 tons of bombs. 3 tanks and 61 aircraft lost. *USSR* approx 200,000 killed—'as many as a million killed' claimed Khruschev. 48,745 killed and 158,863 wounded, Molotov to Supreme Soviet 29 March 1940. 1600 tanks, 750–900 aircraft (Finnish Air Force claimed 725, and AA guns 314). The Finns captured over 300 guns and tons of other weapons and equipment.

Popperfoto

KALLIO, Kyosti: Finnish president. Member of Agrarian Party and Speaker of Parliament. Met other Scandinavian heads of state Oct 1939. Told of peace contacts 8 Feb 1940. He reluctantly backed concessions on 12th but spoke for continuing war on 25th. Finally signed peace authorization on 10 March: 'Let the hand wither that is forced to sign such a paper'. Arm paralyzed Aug 1940 and died in Dec 1940.

MOLOTOV, Vyacheslav Mihailovich: Soviet foreign minister, b. 1892 at Kukarka (Sovietsk). Son of shop assistant and nephew of famous composer Scriabin. Educated Kazan High School. Took name Molotov ('hammer') on joining Bolsheviks 1906. With Stalin founded *Pravda* 1911. Twice exiled, he escaped from Siberia. Member of Petrograd Soviet 1917; Central C'tee of Communist Party 1921. Crushed Zinoviev factions in Leningrad 1926. Politbureau member 1921. Chairman of Council of People's Commissars from 1931. Replaced Jewish Litvinov as People's Commissar for Foreign Affairs April 1939. Signed Non-Agression Pact with Ribbentrop. Led pre-Winter War negotiations of Oct-Nov 1939.

Popperfoto

TREATY OF MOSCOW: purpose was 'to create lasting peaceful relations' and ensure 'security of the cities of Leningrad, Murmansk and the Murmansk railway'. Finland ceded all Karelia, the Kuusamo-Salla area and her part of Fisherman's Peninsula. She gave a 30-year lease on the Hanko peninsula. Petsamo was returned to her. Trade agreement with USSR and transit railway to be built across Finland to Sweden. Approved by Finnish Parliament on 15 March and ratified in Moscow on 20th.

VOLUNTEERS: 8000 Swedes joined Volunteer Corps with 725 Norwegians. They were trained at Tornio and Kemi and took over Salla front 22 Feb. A Danish battalion of 800 ready for action when peace came, as were 450 Hungarians. The Finnish-American Legion of 350 just saw action on 12 March; 140 British volunteers arrived before the peace. Their CO Col Kermit Roosevelt (cousin of US president) remained in England. Italy sent 150 men of which a fighter pilot was killed.

APRIL 1940

Keystone

...It was going to be a thumping victory. After long months of lethargy, the Allies decide on action. Target for the fight is Norway. But unknown to the Allies, Hitler too has designs on Scandinavia. On the high seas the rival navies thrash it out. But things go wrong... Denmark is swallowed up in four hours, the Germans fly into Oslo and at Narvik the Allies arrive too late...

1st: France authorizes construction of 53 warships.
2nd: German aircraft mount raid on Scapa Flow.
3rd: First Spitfire lost on home defence duties.
4th: RAF bomb German destroyers off Wilhelmshaven.
5th: First captured German merchant ship arrives London.
6th: RAF Bomber Command ends leaflet raids on Germany.
7th: British Home Fleet leaves Scapa Flow for Norway.
8th: *Glowworm* rams German cruiser *Hipper* and sinks.
9th: Germans invade Denmark and Norway. Landings at Oslo, Kristiansand, Stavanger, Bergen, Trondheim and Narvik.
10th: First Narvik sea battle. Hitler radios Dietl to hold Narvik at all costs.
11th: Sub *Spearfish* cripples pocket-battleship *Lutzow*.
12th: Danish Faeroe Islands accept British protection.
13th: Second Narvik sea battle.
14th: British troops begin landing near Narvik and at Namsos.
15th: Quisling Government resigns. Bletchley Park breaks a current Enigma cipher.
16th: U1 sunk by British submarine *Porpoise*.
17th: Hitler orders troops at Narvik to hold out as long as possible.
18th: British abandon direct assault on Trondheim.
19th: French land at Namsos.
20th: Namsos devastated by bombing.
21st: RAF bomb Aalborg and Stavanger airfields.
22nd: French recce aircraft reach Prague.
23rd: German bombers raid Scapa Flow. 2nd British war budget raises income tax to 7s 6d in £.
24th: *Warspite* and 3 cruisers bombard Narvik.
25th: Luftwaffe sinks 3 British trawlers off Aandalsnes.
26th: Allies halt German advance on Trondheim.
27th: Ribbentrop claims British planned to invade Norway.
28th: *Queen Mary* arrives Cape Town after 12-day record trip from New York.
29th: Hitler orders Luftwaffe to make ready for Plan Yellow on 5 May.
30th: Allies begin evacuation of Central Norway.

STATION X

Early one morning in mid-April 1940 Wing Commander Frederick Winterbotham, Head of the Secret Intelligence Service (SIS) Air Section, walked into the office of the Director of Air Intelligence clutching four small slips of paper.

To **Winterbotham** and his colleagues they were 'like the magic in a pot of gold at the end of the rainbow'. It had taken months of effort, and the concentrated best of the finest intellects in the land. But now they had successfully decoded a handful of radio messages passed between Luftwaffe units in the week-old Norwegian campaign.

Air Commodore Charles Medhurst, Director of Air Intelligence, barely looked up from his desk at Winterbotham. Four scraps of paper on Luftwaffe administrative orders held little interest to him. 'You will have to do better than that,' he muttered, handing them back.

Medhurst's rebuff was a lesson for the brilliant men who ran the **Government Code and Cypher School** (GCCS) at **Bletchley Park;** in intelligence work, genius is not enough. It needs the backing of a huge, systematic, and well-run organization to collect and distribute the information in the right form, to the right people in the shortest time.

Since August 1939 when they first acquired a copy of the Enigma coding machine from Poland, a handful of British scientists had been working to unlock its secrets. As early as April 1937 GCCS had broken a commercial-type Enigma cipher used by Axis and Nationalist forces in the Spanish Civil War but the new military Enigma codes for Hitler's armed forces left it baffled until the windfall from Poland. Even so the Bletchley cryptographers had solved 50 Enigma settings by hand in the first three months of 1940. But the intelligence was too late.

Normal decoding methods proved useless. It would take years to uncover the permutations Enigma could produce.

First they had to recruit the men to do it. Discreetly (you could hardly advertise) senior staff from the Government Code and Cypher School scouted the universities for suitable recruits. Cambridge proved the most fruitful, and soon brilliant mathematics dons brought their incisive minds and colourful eccentricities to Bletchley.

Alan **Turing** was a key figure. A fellow of King's College, he was already famous for a paper on 'computable numbers' presented to the London Mathematical Society in 1937, and now considered a starting point for the computer age. Turing pedalled round on an unreliable bike, wore a gas mask to ward off hay fever, and kept his tea mug

Ray Dunns/M.C.

Bletchley Park, here in the fateful spring of 1940 top brains worked to uncover the secrets of German strategy. Inset. The Enigma enciphering machine—rotors clean.

chained to a radiator for fear someone would steal it. He also buried all his cash in Bletchley woods when war started, then forgot where he had put it. But he was a master mathematician as well as a mechanical genius—the ideal combination for dealing with Enigma.

Gordon **Welchmann,** Dean of Sidney Sussex College, reported to Bletchley as arranged on the day Britain declared war.

Absent-minded geniuses abounded. Dillwyn **Knox,** GCCS's senior cryptographer, habitually greeted long established assistants as if they were newcomers. 'Josh Cooper', a mathematician who sat on the interrogatory panel for captured Luftwaffe aircrew, was—it was claimed—once seen carrying his hat in his hand and his briefcase on his head.

There were international chess players, crossword puzzle experts, amateur musicians, German linguists, professors of classics and of philosophy, lawyers and writers. Backing them up were the hundreds of WRNS and WAAF girls—clerks, typists, administrators, and girls who ran the machines themselves, and throughout the country the men and women of **Y Service**, radio operators who intercepted the messages and fed them to Bletchley to be deciphered. An informed estimate has put the number working in Bletchley and its outstations at 7500 of which 1500 were actually involved in codebreaking.

Cryptologists had long sought a method of sending secret messages that would remain secure even if—as was nearly inevitable—the equipment involved fell into enemy hands. But until Enigma, although ciphers of great elegance had been devised, the codebreaker had many ways to penetrate them.

In every language, some letters occur more frequently than others. If the cipher substitutes z for e, then the true identity of z is easy to find.

In brief, Enigma aimed to baffle codebreakers by yielding no tell-tale repetitions. On a machine with

three rotors, the same group of letters would not appear until 16,900 possible positions for the rotors had been exhausted. Capturing the machine itself would, its owners hoped, be of no value to the enemy. The secret lay in the setting of the rotors at a pre-determined position: this was the key to the cipher, and could be changed frequently.

To encode a message, the cipher clerk checked which three letters should appear in the windows of the machine that day. **Having set the rotors** to show the right letters he simply typed the plaintext while a colleague copied down the illuminated ciphertext in five-letter groups for radio transmission in morse code. The recipient, who also knew the correct rotor setting, simply reversed the process on his own machine, yielding the original plaintext. It was fast, asked no great intellectual effort from the operator, and it was wrongly believed impregnable.

But guessing the right key, from a myriad of possible settings, remained the constant problem. To speed the work of trying out various alternative settings, the Poles had wired up six machines to devices of their own—electro-mechanical pieces of wizardry they christened Bombas. Racing through alternative rotor settings faster than any human brain, the Bombas could unravel Enigma.

The entire pre-war Polish team was working at the Chateau de Vignolles 40 miles NE of Paris as Major Gustave **Bertrand's** Equipe Z. Altogether Bertrand had 70 men. Captain Kenneth Macfarlan was the liaison officer for the BEF and there was a direct teleprinter link with Britain.

Equipe Z made the first wartime Enigma breakthrough. In the second half of December 1939 the Poles managed to read the German Army key for 28 October. They did so with computing sheets of punch hole paper that Alan Turing brought over. Then in February the Enigma rotors came from U33, sunk by the minesweeper *Gleaner* in the Clyde. Soon Bletchley made its own break and took over the Allied codebreaking effort to such an extent that it read 83 per cent of the keys broken up to the fall of France.

A new British **Bombe** was crucial to the Bletchley operation and gave it primacy in the Allied effort. Based on a combination of two ideas, one from Welchman, the other from Turing, the bombe, 'bronze Goddess' Winterbotham called it, stood in a 10ft high shining copper cabinet, consisting of ten sets of three rotors, each set the equivalent of the standard Enigma machine.

Tended by one of the young Wrens, and sounding in operation like a set of busy knitting needles, the Bombe wheels whirred and clicked until they found one of the letters from the 'menu', and connected it with its coded equivalent.

When the letters from the menu coincided with letters in the code, the machine threw a switch. And when it had all the programmed letters, it would stop. Silent young women, patiently enduring the drudgery of watching their machines through eight-hour shifts, thought it a personal triumph if their Bombe produced a 'stop'. Shouts of 'red stop' or 'green stop' (the colour codes signified the importance of the original intercept source) would lead to a flurry of activity. One Wren habitually marked the inside band of her hat—gun fighter style—when she notched up a success.

Then the details went out to the men and women in the sprawl of Nissen huts in the grounds of Bletchley Park. First the cryptanalysts took it. Hut 6 deciphered German Army and Luftwaffe signals. Hut 8 concentrated on German naval traffic, notably the U-boat signals. It was Welchman who insisted that Hut 6 work round the clock in three watches when Bletchley first broke a current Enigma code on 15 April.

Inside each Nissen hut analysts would work round the clock; endless head-scratching, pen-work and an 8-hour shift system.

Ray Dunns/M.C.

Round the clock

Here the Wrens operating the many replica Enigma machines, now built, set their keys to the broken code and produced the clear German plaintext from the jumbled letters of the German morse signals. Then it went to other nearby huts, for outward processing—Hut 3 for the Army and Air Force material, Hut 4 for the Navy traffic.

The Directors of Air and Military Intelligence duly supplied Winterbotham with four handpicked non-flying RAF officers who spoke fluent German as did two Army officers and a sergeant. To these Winterbotham added one of his own MI6 Intelligence officers armed with all available and relevant German military literature. He appointed Squadron Leader Humphreys, a pre-war British travelling salesman in Germany, to head the team. They were to help the translators get their numbers and types of unit right. Within a short time Hut 3 had 60 inmates. They began operating

10-man watches round the clock.

Sitting at tables grouped in a horseshoe shape, with the head of their watch at the centre, ten men —all of them fluent linguists, would pore over the messages, translating them into English, analysing their significance, and adding material to dog-eared index cards in the banks of shabby filing cabinets.

The intelligence produced at Bletchley Park was so special it received a special name. Needing a term to cover a new grade of intelligence, more secret than '*Secret*', '*Most secret*', or the American equivalent '*Top secret*', Winterbotham invented the name *Ultra*. That was in the future. The first decrypts had gone to the Air Ministry and War Office quaintly labelled 'from agent Boniface'.

After that, there remained only the question of distribution—itself a nightmare problem. Security-conscious intelligence chiefs had to assess who should receive the signals. A single leak would tell the Germans that their signals were being read, and destroy the whole operation.

'It is most galling'

As a starting point they worked on 'need to know' principle, which restricted the material to the fewest possible recipients. Teleprinter lines to London conveyed Bletchley's material to the offices of the Chiefs of Staff, the intelligence directors for the three services, the air commands, the C-in-C Home Fleet and other senior admirals who received it in their special flag officers' Hydro cipher. But for the moment such intelligence did not match the success of the German Navy's B-Dienst code-breakers who were reading 30 per cent of intercepted Royal Navy signals. The C-in-C Home Fleet Admiral Sir Charles Forbes commented bleakly on the Norwegian campaign: 'It is most galling that the enemy should know just where our ships . . . always are. Whereas we generally find where his major forces are when they sink one or more of our ships.'

Winterbotham made one more pioneering safeguard. Going to see his chief Colonel Stuart **Menzies** he asked for permission to form Special Liaison Units (SLUs). This was Winterbotham's description for a small team of cipher and radio personnel. Suitably indoctrinated officers and NCOs were to be stationed at all major operational HQs to receive, assess and make secure all incoming signals from Bletchley. By May 1940 the first SLUs were stationed at BEF GHQ and the HQ of the Advanced Air Striking Force. From the radio huts of Whaddon Hall, the Secret Service's own transmitting station, came the Bletchley signals that the SLUs decoded on one-time message pads.

Overall it amounted to a new and vast empire, growing all the time, with none of its parts knowing what the others were doing. And until the Phoney War ended all this organization could not be fully tested by the needs of commanders in battle. Station X, as Bletchley Park was officially known, kept its secrets intact for nearly 30 years. Not until 1974 did a British government admit the existence of Ultra and the organization that cracked the German wartime signals codes.

War Notes

BERTRAND, Gustave: French Intelligence officer, b. 1897. Volunteer 1914. School of Engineers for a year. Cipher officer on staffs of Allied troops, Constantinople 1919-21 and Army of Rhine 1923. General Staff, Ministry of War 1929-30. Head of Section D (Cipher) French Secret Service 1930-9 meeting German traitor 19 times and carrying out 23 liaison missions. Head of Section d'Examen, 5th Bureau of General Staff Sept 1939.

BLETCHLEY PARK: wartime base of GCCS also known as War Station Room 47 of Foreign Office, Station X and BP. Practice occupation during Munich Crisis Sept 1938.

BOMBE: British high-speed electro-mechanical machine that did the same job as the pre-war Polish Bombas. Built by British Tabulating Company, Letchworth, Herts. First one delivered to GCCS by end of May 1940.

DENNISTON, Alistair: Head of GCCS. Taught German at RN Osborne College. Member of Room 40 Admiralty cryptanalytic bureau 1914-18. Joined GCCS 1918, Head by 1937. Recruited graduates Aug 1938 and about 12 more Aug-Sept 1939.

Courtesy Mrs. M. Finch

GOVERNMENT CODE AND CYPHER SCHOOL (GCCS): founded 1919 to devise codes and ciphers and to break those of foreign powers. Foreign Office controlled and funded it from 1922 while the Head of SIS became Director of GCCS 1923. London HQ was 54 Broadway, opposite St James's Park underground. Nicknamed the 'Golf, Chess and Cheese Society' after move to Bletchley.

KNOX, Alfred Dilwyn: British cryptographer, b. 1883 son of Bishop of Manchester. Educated Eton and King's Cambridge. Member of Room 40 Admiralty cryptanalysis bureau 1914-18. GCCS cryptographer from 1919.

MENZIES, Stewart: Head of the British Secret Intelligence Service (SIS), b. 1890 son of Lady Holford. Educated Eton. Served Grenadier Guards and Life Gds 1909-15. Won DSO (1st Ypres) and MC in WWI serving on Haig's staff as a Captain. Joined SIS Dec 1915 working in Spain 1916. Became Deputy Head to Adm Sinclair and took over on his death Nov 1939.

TURING, Alan Mathison: British mathematician, b. 1912 son of India railway chief engineer. Educated Sherborne and King's, Cambridge. Worked under Einstein at Princeton. Recruited as assistant to Knox early 1939.

Courtesy F. W. Winterbotham

WINTERBOTHAM, Frederick William: British Intelligence officer, b. 1897. Educated Charterhouse and Christ Church, Oxford. Served R. Gloucestershire Hussars 1915. Transferred to Royal Flying Corps 1916, shot down by 'Richthofen Circus'. PoW in Germany 1917-19. Read Law at Christ Church, Oxford. Pedigree stock breeder. Studied Farming Africa, Canada and Australia 1920-9. Rejoined RAF as Head of SIS Air Section 1930. Visited Germany 5 times 1934-8 as supposedly sympathetic Air Ministry member. Met Hitler, Hess, Rosenberg etc. Organized clandestine high-altitude photo-recce flights over Axis territory from mid-1938. Helped form RAF PR Flight Sept 1939.

Y SERVICE: British armed forces intercept service to monitor range, network and volume of enemy radio traffic. Essential to Bletchley's success, ie providing the unbroken German signals. Used American RCA AR88 communications receivers able to cut out jamming. Intercepted messages sent over landlines or by dispatch rider to Bletchley. From the Chatham Station at this period the prefix of a signal would be sent to Bletchley by teleprinter and the rest by messenger.

DENMARK: THE SILENT TAKEOVER

In the dawn of 9 April 1940 in Copenhagen, a few early morning workers, still half-asleep, were the first bewildered witnesses of the German invasion of their country.

Danish truckdrivers, ferrying fresh fish across the border to market in Hamburg, had seen nothing like it before. German soldiers—thousands of them—were marching in columns miles long towards the Danish border.

In Copenhagen, stevedores obligingly tied German coal barges to bollards on Langalinie Pier with lines thrown down to them by the German crewmen. Coal was welcome to a city still in the grip of a harsh Baltic winter. A few yards away, silent at their berths, lay the ships of the Royal **Danish Navy.**

In a street in Copenhagen a group of cleaning ladies on their way to work listened, puzzled, to the clanging of trams—unusual so early in the day. The trams had been commandeered. Behind them came the sound of marching feet.

Soon German troops were pouring across the border, welcomed by Danish Nazi sympathizers who threw flowers, gave the Nazi salute, and stood at the crossroads to guide the invaders to the key points.

Out of the barges at Langalinie Pier came not coal but the 2000 German soldiers who had been stowed neatly, if uncomfortably, in the blackened holds, along with their vehicles, guns and ammunition. Fanning out from the pier these troops rapidly overwhelmed sporadic opposition and took the city's vantage points. At the Citadel they forced an unguarded gate, disarmed two sentries, and captured the 70-man garrison without firing a shot.

At both ends of the two-mile British-built Storstombro bridge parachutists arrived. They rushed the guard posts, shouting and firing their pistols in the air. The stunned Danes surrendered immediately.

At 6am those still asleep in the capital were awakened by the sound of German bombers droning overhead. No bombs fell but the threat was menacingly clear.

Outside Amalienborg Palace soldiers dressed in uniforms of the Napoleonic period put up a fight but were quickly overpowered. By eight that morning, when most Danes were having breakfast, it was all over. **Denmark** was in German hands. A near-bloodless invasion had turned the country into Germany's first 'model protectorate'—or so it was intended.

The invasion of Denmark was part of Hitler's Scandinavian assault plan code named Weserübung. Masterminded by Lieutenant General Nikolaus von Falkenhorst, the whole scheme was extraordinarily well executed, precise and almost

clinically painless. Overrun within four hours, the Danes were rendered reluctant subjects of a military occupation that lasted five years.

Stuck out like a thumb on Germany's northern flank, the Jutland peninsula shared a 40-mile border with the mighty military power to the south. To the north of the peninsula the airfields at **Aalborg** were a precious vantage point. Denmark's biggest island, **Zealand,** was strategically placed astride the approaches to Germany's Baltic ports; little Denmark was inevitably and easily encompassed in Falkenhorst's designs.

Of all the neutrals, Denmark occupied the least enviable position in 1940. Apart from its geographical helplessness it was also enmeshed in the German web because of a trade agreement that fed the Reich on its own terms.

By far the most enfeebling factor on the Danish side, however, was the country's impoverished defences. Denmark was effectively without defence and relied for protection on neutrality alone. In World War I this had served her well. She had remained unmolested in return for allowing Germany to mine the Great Belt, one of the two entrances to the Baltic, protecting the German naval base of Kiel.

As Germany's power grew, pre-war, neutrality looked like the best bet once again for Denmark. She had staked everything on it: in 1929 she had cut her defence budget to four million pounds, axed two thirds of the Army and a third of the Navy.

George Smith

German infantry disembark from coal barges at Langalinie Pier, Copenhagen. Another 1400 were landed at other Danish ports on 9 April.

'The Danish Government, under protest have decided to preserve the interests of the country'.

Thorvald Stauning, Danish PM, 10 April

Successive governments had further reduced equipment spending and call up.

When war broke out in 1939 Denmark countered with a final demonstration of fervent neutrality—she announced yet another reduction, by a full half, of her ground forces. In April 1940 the **Danish Army** had only 1600 officers and NCOs. The other ranks comprised ill-trained recruits dispersed in unconnected units across the countryside. The **Danish Air Force** had just 100 planes, the Navy's air arm another 40. There were practically no anti-aircraft guns.

As one commentator put it: Denmark earned 'the dubious distinction of being the only country in Europe to weaken its defences at a time when the danger to the country was growing'.

The night before the invasion a Danish agent in Germany fed Copenhagen a report that the **German invasion forces** would cross the border at 4pm that afternoon, or perhaps the following morning—he was not sure. It was not the first such warning. The afternoon passed calmly.

'No warlike intentions'

King **Christian X** heard the report that night during a banquet at the Amalienborg Palace. 'I don't believe that,' he retorted. Later—on the advice of his Foreign Minister Dr Peter **Munch**—the King went on to a performance of 'The Merry Wives of Windsor' at the Theatre Royal in Copenhagen and laughed as Shakespeare would have wished. It was, after all, only a year before that the Danes had signed a non-aggression pact with Germany.

Munch, himself, however, was concerned and summoned Count Cecil von Renthe-Fink, the German Ambassador. He duly arrived and Munch put the rumours to him and asked for an assurance. Replied Renthe-Fink sincerely and without hesitation: 'Hitler has no warlike intentions towards Denmark!' He also warned that should Denmark mobilize it might provoke German retaliation.

The Germans were determined to deal swiftly and efficiently with Denmark. Hitler insisted on surprise. The operation should involve the smallest number of troops to minimize world indignation.

Falkenhorst's planning went perfectly. Posing as a businessman, the German officer whose job it was to take Copenhagen, had trudged around the port area picking a suitable landing site for his battalion's troopship, the minelayer *Hanestadt Danzig*. Obligingly, a Danish Army sergeant showed him around the Citadel overlooking the harbour, pointing out to him the headquarters of the Danish General Staff. With his targets clear, he returned home.

On 7 April Lieutenant General Kurt Himer, Chief of Staff for the Danish invasion, took a train to Copenhagen wearing civilian clothes. He reported to HQ in Hamburg that the harbour was ice-free and the Danes had so far done nothing to strengthen their defences.

There remained only the diplomatic niceties. At 11pm on 8 April General Himer left his hotel and called on Renthe-Fink. There he passed on the text of an ultimatum that Renthe-Fink was to deliver to the Danish government at 4.15am the next morning. Renthe-Fink was devastated. So much for the assurance he had just given to Dr Munch! At the appointed hour he handed over the note and broke down in tears, declaring Hitler 'a man without honour'.

By 4.15am invasion was already under way. Forgetting that Denmark had no 'summer time'—Danish clocks were an hour behind Germany's—the invaders had given no time to answer the ultimatum.

Munch, desperate, phoned the castle but he was unable to contact the King who along with the court was occupied with the pitiful fight outside. Terrified that German aircraft would soon bomb the city and realizing that precious minutes were wasting as he read the long-winded German document, Munch took a taxi and hurried to raise the court, leaving his officials to contact as many members of government as they could.

The senior Army and Navy officers, General Prior and Admiral Rechnitzer, met at the Ministry of Defence shortly before 5am. At this point General Prior, who had slipped out of his Citadel headquarters shortly before the German troops stormed in, telephoned the Vaerlose air base and ordered the planes into the air. A solitary fighter went up only to be shot down in minutes.

Prior and Rechnitzer then hurried to join the others at Amalienborg where the politicians were in a state of agitation. The German Ambassador was on the telephone as they arrived and demanding a reply to the ultimatum. 'We cannot give one' the ministers replied, pleading for time until the King arrived to make a decision. They were completely incapable of instigating a course of action. A shot rang out nearby and the frightened assembly came close to panic.

Decision taken to capitulate

There was another telephone call, this time to Admiral Rechnitzer from his naval staff. They wanted to know if they should fire on the Germans as they were landing. 'No' Rechnitzer told them. General Prior, anxious to resist the invasion, was furious. He objected vehemently to the Admiral capitulating before the King had come to a decision.

Rechnitzer expected the King would not want to fight. Rumour had it that only the previous night the Admiral had sent several key coastal defence personnel on generous leave.

The King arrived, pale and near to fainting accompanied by Crown Prince Frederick.

'Have the troops fought for long enough?' the King asked. 'The troops have not fought at all,' replied General Prior. 'Take the Government to Hosraeltelejren military base and make a stand from there' he pleaded. But the King refused to leave his capital and, supported by his ministers, Prior found himself alone—and alone, it seemed, in

Top: Danish soldiers on a field exercise manning an anti-tank gun. Middle left. Danish policeman looks on as German troops march in. Bottom: German motorcyclists.

wishing to defend his country.

Shortly before 6am the King decided to capitulate. Twenty minutes later the Germans accepted the surrender. The cease-fire was transmitted to the Danish troops by the Germans on a radio transmitter brought with them for the purpose. A few units, out of touch with Jutland headquarters, did not hear the broadcast, but by 8am the fighting in Denmark was over. In less than four hours the German takeover was complete. Thirteen Danes lay dead and 23 wounded. The Germans suffered 20 dead and 45 wounded.

News of the takeover came as a bombshell. Only the night before Danes had gone to bed in an independent Denmark. This morning they went to work with German troops patrolling the streets. No radio had announced the change, no newspapers reported the event. Few people had heard a shot fired.

Their armed forces had done little to protect them. In the streets of Copenhagen civilians spat on Danish soldiers.

Their attitude found an echo in the United States where isolationists were looking nervously across the Atlantic at Europe's neutral countries. Cadets from the training ship *Denmark* suffered insults and abuse when they went on shore leave in American ports. A boxing commentator observed of one ring fighter: 'He lay down without fighting, like a Dane.'

Others were less harsh. General Prior was fully aware of what his soldiers were suffering. Broadcasting his thanks for their attitude and conduct, he told his forces: 'You can look anyone in the face, with your head erect, knowing that you have done your duty.'

In London, *The Times* took a sympathetic view: 'Denmark with an Army and Navy that amounted to little more than police forces and patrol vessels, could do nothing in reply.'

Back in February, Churchill, who had consistently warned the neutrals against hoping to avoid involvement in the war, had told a group of Scandinavian reporters: 'I could not reproach Denmark if she surrendered to Nazi attack. The other two Scandinavian countries . . . have at least a ditch over which they can feed the tiger, but Denmark is so terribly near Germany that it would be impossible to bring help. Personally, I would in any case not undertake to guarantee Denmark.'

Radio Times Hulton Picture Library Keystone

A 20mm flak gun covers advance of German transport. Inset: soldier to soldier, Danish General Jacobson receives German salute.

Now, the Danes were forced to accept the occupation. All that remained was to agree terms with the Germans and to surrender military installations. Denmark was forced to break off diplomatic relations with all Allied countries and hand over control of the press, radio, and all external communications to German officials. The last, at least, was a pointless demand: the Germans had seized all radio and telephone facilities on the day they invaded. In return the new masters promised to respect Danish neutrality and not to interfere with the country's internal affairs. The Danes could also keep their Army and Navy 'on active duty status'.

On the afternoon of the capitulation, the government issued a statement signed by King Christian and the Prime Minister. It instructed the people to obey orders and to act correctly towards the Germans. The government assured its disgruntled people 'we have saved the country from an even worse fate. It will be our continued endeavour to protect our country and her people from the disasters of war and we shall rely on the people's co-operation.'

The King added his own personal message: 'I count on you all . . . to show an absolutely correct and dignified demeanour, as any unconsidered attitude or utterance may have the most serious consequences. God keep you all! God keep Denmark!'

'It is magnificent work'

But the Germans barely trusted the King. Later that day the commander of the occupying force, General Himer and his reluctant vassal, Renthe-Fink, went to see him. Himer was partly concerned to make sure that the King was not planning to leave Denmark. He reported: 'The 70-year-old King appeared inwardly shattered, although he preserved outward appearances perfectly and maintained absolute dignity during his audience. His whole body trembled. He declared that his government would do everything possible to keep peace and order in the country and to eliminate any friction. He wishes to spare his country further misfortune and misery.'

As the audience ended the King evidently relaxed and confided to Himer: 'General, may I, as an old soldier, tell you something? As soldier to soldier? You Germans have done the incredible again. One must admit that it is magnificent work.'

In the ensuing years of the occupation, the King, when riding on horseback through the streets of the capital, never once returned a German salute.

Henrick Kauffmann, the Danish Ambassador in Washington declared on 9 April that free Denmark continued to exist and that he was her representative. With his persuasion, 90 per cent of the Danish shipping outside Danish ports on this day—over a million tons in all—took the Allied side, along with 5000 sailors who formed the kernel of a patriotic combatant movement.

That evening in Berlin Hitler received a note from Falkenhorst, 'Denmark and Norway occupied . . . as instructed'. The delighted Führer himself drafted the press releases to the German newspapers.

War Notes

AALBORG: N. Jutland industrial city (chiefly cement, textiles and machinery) situated on the south of Lim Fjord; population in 1940 48,000. Aalborg was strategically important with a port opening to the Kattegat, a naval school, and 2 airfields at the commanding height of 1900ft.

Radio Times Hulton Picture Library

CHRISTIAN X: King of Denmark, b. 1870, son of Frederick VIII, succeeding to the throne 1912 and that of Iceland 1918. On 9 April 1940 Christian X capitulated to the Germans at Amalienborg Palace. Stoically anti-German, he remained coldly formal to their approaches in the five years of the occupation.

DANISH ARMY, NAVY AND AIR FORCES: the 15,450-strong Army under Chief of Staff General Prior included 1600 officers and NCOs, in Zealand there were 3311 trained soldiers and 3000 recruits. The Army Air Force comprised 100 planes—Bristol Bulldogs, Gloster Gauntlets and Fokker D.21s. The Danish Navy had 2 old armoured ships, 9 patrol boats and 9 submarines and 40 aircraft.

DENMARK: situated on Germany's NW flank, SSW of the Scandinavian Baltic peninsula, land area of 16,576 square miles with a population of 3.8 million.

GERMAN INVASION FORCES: the 31st Corps comprising 170th and 198th Infantry Divisions (about 35,000 men) was the main force under Lt-Gen Kurt Himer. The 4th Company of 1st Parachute Regt was split; 60 men under Capt Gerlicke taking Storstombro bridge and 30 men taking the 2 airfields at Aalborg. The 305th Battalion backed up the spearhead paratroopers at the bridge. Naval forces comprised the old battleship *Schleswig-Holstein*, experimental vessels *Claus von Bevern, Nautilus, Pelikan*, 2 transports, 2 tugs and 6 trawlers—sent to Nyborg and Korsor; to Esbjerg and Nordby went the command vessel *Königen Luise*, 4 MS (minesweepers), 12th MS Flotilla with 8 large trawlers and the 2nd MMS with 8 ships. The German minelayer *Hansestadt Danzig* and the ice-breaker *Stettin* went to Copenhagen escorted by 13th Patrol Boat Flotilla. To Middelfart and Belt Bridge went the steamer *Rugard* and 5 MS, 2 patrol vessels, the submarine-chaser UJ172 and 2 naval tugs. Backing up those squadrons was the old battleship *Schlesien*, air support came from Fliegerkorps X which put most of its aircraft over Denmark on 9 April.

MUNCH, Dr Peter: Danish Foreign Minister during the war, a strong influence on the King and cabinet. On 9 April 1940, the day of the invasion, Munch seized upon the German's assurances of Danish political independence to put a policy of negotiation into effect.

ZEALAND: largest Danish island between the Kattegat and the Baltic Sea; 80 miles long, it is separated from Sweden by the Oresund. The capital of Denmark, Copenhagen lies on the E side of the island.

The German invasion of Norway and Denmark involved 11 seaborne forces and the first strategic use of paratroops.

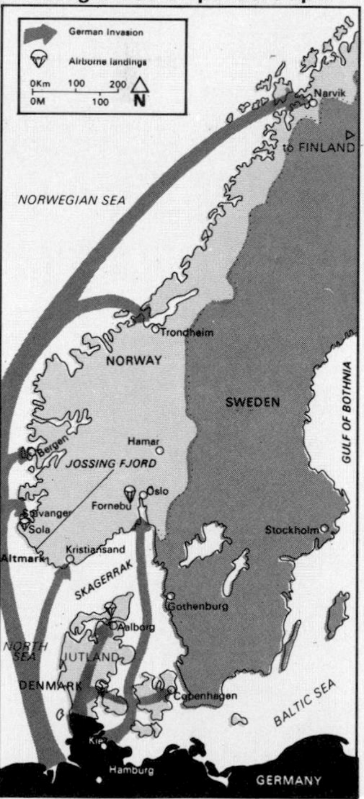

INVASION NORWAY

Captain Wielding Olsen, skipper of the Norwegian whaling boat Pol III was on patrol in the mouth of Oslofjord. There was only a single gun to back up any orders he might give to hostile shipping intercepted in the mouth of the fjord. Nevertheless, when he saw the shapes of three major warships and their escorts looming above him in the darkness, he did not hesitate to challenge.

Ignoring Olsen's challenge the warships sailed on northwards. After warning the coastal defences, the Norwegian skipper ordered full speed ahead, and swung the wheel hard over to ram the nearest ship—the 1290-ton torpedo boat *Albatros* —with his 214-ton craft.

Opening fire, *Albatros* scored a direct hit. *Pol III* burst into flames, and Captain Olsen was blown overboard, his legs shot away.

It was 11.06pm on the night of 8 April, and Olsen was the first casualty in the stealthy German invasion of Norway.

The plan was for a double strike—by sea and by air. For Hitler, it very nearly turned into a disaster.

Coastwatchers at two small lookout forts on the islands of Rauöy and Bolaerne tracked the steady passage of the warships northwards. They had no authority to lay minefields—all they could do to impede the German advance on Oslo was pass warnings up the fjord. To defend the coast against German shore patrols they used rifles.

Alerted by the monitoring lookouts, a second patrol boat, *Olav Tryggvason*, moved to intercept. Her four 4.7in guns opened fire instantly, sinking a torpedo boat and damaging *Albatros* for the second time. *Albatros* limped away. Nearby ships in the German fleet blew the patrol boat to pieces.

The biggest obstacle for the Germans lay ahead at Oscarsborg. Here two fortresses guarded the 600-yard narrows. If a hostile force gained passage beyond that point the way to Oslo would be open.

Although its guns dated from 1892, built by the Krupp armaments company, Oscarsborg was

'None of us dreamed that German warships were in the inner harbour and that Oslo was already doomed.'
Special Correspondent, 16 April

reputed one of the strongest forts in Europe.

Its 65-year-old commandant, Colonel Birger Eriksen gave orders to open fire on the approaching ships as soon as they came into his arc. There would be no time for formal identification of the oncoming vessels—his searchlights were out of action. His first strike would have to be decisive since the heaviest guns would only have one shot each because of their ponderous re-loading drill. Also only two or three were manned.

It was a matter of regret that the planned minefield across the fjord had not been laid. However, in a shooting match between a ship and his fortress Eriksen had good reason to feel confident.

Shortly after 5am a searchlight beam from a mainland observation post picked out an ensign. It belonged to Germany's newest heavy cruiser, the **Blücher**, with 2000 men crammed into her confined quarters. Behind her steamed the cruisers **Lützow** and **Emden**, with their escorts.

Eriksen gave the order. The two big guns fired at almost point-blank range. One shell struck *Blücher's* bridge and knocked out her central gunnery control. The other hit the aircraft hangar and flared the petrol store. *Blücher* passed out of gunfire range, and as her crew struggled to keep the steering under control, they watched as Oscarborg's guns turned to the following ships.

Worse trouble lay ahead of the damaged heavy cruiser. As she drifted slowly north of the main fortress Eriksen loosed two torpedoes. One hit the engine room, the other *Blücher's* own torpedo magazine.

Two violent explosions shook her. As she keeled over, the crew began jumping overboard, intent on swimming the 1500 yards ashore through ice-cold water and flaming fuel oil.

Blücher sank half a mile farther up the fjord, and 1000 men lost their lives. Among them were members of the Gestapo unit whose job was to capture the King and Government. A mighty underwater explosion, followed by a column of blazing oil, signalled the end of the cruiser's career.

Repulsed, the rest of the battered squadron began to land their men on the mainland shore. Ahead of the troops was a 50-mile march to take Oslo. The pocket battleship *Lützow*, was hit by several shells fired from small posts on the fjord.

Spirited action by a handful of coastal defence men had sent the bulk of Hitler's seaborne force scuttling away down the fjord.

The Weserübung planners had detailed the 1st Battalion of 1st Parachute Regiment to take key points in Norway and Denmark. But the force was unrealistically stretched. Three of the battalion's four companies were to capture Norway's main southern airfields; one would jump at Sola airfield near **Stavanger**, the other two at Fornebu airfield, Oslo.

The two companies aiming for Fornebu flew in **Ju52s** of 2nd Group, 1st Special Duty Wing. They

The German convoys arrive at the Oslo quayside. In the port the invader is already in control. German cyclists from the 196th Infantry Division wait to move off.

Radio Times Hulton Picture Library

Vogelarchiv

started for Norway in bad weather, and when two of the aircraft got lost, the Group Commander ordered the others to turn back and land at newly captured Aalborg in Denmark.

An infantry force was following up, flown by 2nd Special Duty Wing. An operational order signed by Field Marshal Göring stipulated that they were not to land until the parachute troops had secured the airfield. Since the paratroopers were in Denmark, there seemed no alternative but to call off the airborne infantry attack.

In the event, a series of misunderstandings and communications failures worked in Germany's favour. First the pilot of the leading troop transport ignored the recall order. As he made his approach run over Fornebu, the weather cleared and he could see no anti-aircraft fire. The order, he decided, was either a mistake or a fake; so he started to land. Then machine-gun fire ripped into his plane and he died instantly. His co-pilot turned the power on and took the plane up again.

The initiative then lay with a flight of eight **Me110s**. Their orders were to strafe the defences as protection for the parachute troops. But they waited too long, ran out of fuel, and had to put down on the airfield. As a defence measure the Me110 flight commander, Lieutenant Hansen, ordered his pilots to turn towards the centre of the airfield. Their rear gunners swivelled the MG15 machine guns round so that they pointed threateningly above each aircraft tail. In the face of that the Norwegians defending the perimeter gave up the struggle.

Oslo taken by sheer bluff

That left the airport open for the transport wing. During the morning the parachute troops tried again, successfully, and by midday on 9 April most of 324th Infantry Regiment had put down. Its six companies formed up behind the regimental band, and marched off in perfect order, and by a combination of effrontery and psychology captured Oslo.

By the time the German troops arrived at 3.30 that afternoon, the Norwegian government had spent 12 hours trying to deal with the invasion. Karl **Hambro**, the President of the Norwegian Parliament, had been occupied for much of 8 April discussing the British minelaying in northern waters, which amounted to breach of Norwegian neutrality, and reports of German invasion preparations. A Polish submarine had sunk the trans-

port ship *Rio de Janeiro* that day. German soldiers rescued from the transport ship proudly announced that they were on their way to help the Norwegians defend their country against British and French aggression.

Hambro went to bed at 11pm, only to be woken two hours later with the first tentative reports of air raid alarms. Later aides reported the fighting at Oscarsborg, and also reported warships moving on Trondheim.

'We were totally unprepared'

Quick to summarize the situation, Hambro wrote later: 'Without warning or ultimatum Germans had started surprise attack on every strategically important point of Norway. Our Army was not mobilized. We were totally unprepared. If the King, Royal Family, and Government and Parliament were taken by surprise, Norway would be at Germany's mercy and cease to be an independant state. We must move out of Oslo.'

After dressing hurriedly, Hambro and his wife left home in a taxi and he attended a cabinet meeting at the Foreign Ministry at 5am.

The first official communication of German intentions came through about 4.15am on 9 April. Lieutenant Colonel Pohlmann, a general staff officer, had sat through dinner at the German legation on the evening of 8 April with a sealed letter in his pocket from Foreign Minister Joachim von Ribbentrop. At 11pm, as instructed, he handed it to the German Minister, Dr Brauer, who broke the seals. Brauer presented the German surrender ultimatum to the Norwegians in the early hours of 9 April. They rejected it. 'We will not submit voluntarily, the struggle is under way.'

Now at the early morning cabinet meeting, Hambro proposed that King **Haakon VII** and Royal Family, together with all members of the Storting (Parliament), the Chief of Staff, and senior civil servants, should leave the capital, for the provincial capital of Hamar, 70 miles north of Oslo, not far from the Swedish border.

They also decided to order mobilization—but by post. Fortunately the Foreign Minister, Dr Koht, interviewed by radio on the platform at Oslo's railway station, let slip the word 'mobilization', and Norway's young men began a mass hike to the north to join their country's new guerilla forces.

At 7am a special train pulled out of Oslo bearing most of the 150 Storting members, summoned by telephone and messenger. Hambro himself had

Oslo's shield against invasion, Norwegians man the 4.7in battery at Oscarsborg. Inset: a sole 20mm flak gun guards the German troopship from air attack.

Vögelarchiv

Vogelarchiv

already sped north in his taxi to make accommodation arrangements. He dropped his wife off at her brother's house 25 miles south of Hamar, went on, knocked on the Hamar police chief's front door, and announced that the King and Parliament were about to arrive. Nobody in Hamar yet had the slightest idea what had happened.

Even so, when the train arrived—late because the party twice had to stop to shelter from German bombing—he had fixed up lodgings and breakfast for the members, and a manor house for meetings.

The first meeting of the fugitive Storting that morning discussed the ultimatum. The German note sought to explain that the British and French were about to occupy Narvik and other northern ports, and that Germany could not allow the Allies to turn Scandinavia into a theatre of war. It called on Norway to raise no resistance, to establish collaboration between German and Norwegian armed forces, and to hand over military establishments and lines of communication. Otherwise—invasion.

This had already been rejected by the Government. Hastily the Storting approved the decision. But that was just the emotional reaction of a government on the run, and within two hours they had changed their minds. Uncertain of the wisdom of plunging the unprepared country into indefinite oppression, they agreed that the government should negotiate terms with the Germans.

Before the meeting ended, news arrived that German troops were advancing in buses and were only ten miles from Hamar. The meeting adjourned and at ten minutes' notice the entire parliament took off once more. The destination was Elverum, a village and rail centre 20 miles to the east and only 50 miles from the Swedish border. There they planned to continue their discussion in the local secondary school.

At the same time Colonel Otto **Ruge** of the Norwegian Army collected together two battalions of local territorial recruits, many of whom had not yet learned to fire a machine-gun, and went out to face the advancing Germans.

The Germans were commanded by the Air Attaché, Spiller, who had made it his own private crusade to capture the King. But the Norwegian recruits laid a perfect ambush in which Spiller was fatally wounded and the German party retreated back to Oslo. Ruge earned promotion to Commander-in-Chief within 24 hours but the Norwegians failed to follow up their success.

The flight to the north saved the King and kept

Watched by a dazed population, the German 324th Regiment enters Oslo.

the Parliament in being. It enabled the Royal Family—Crown Princess Märtha, and her three children, together with Hambro—to cross into Sweden. It also left time for court officials to arrange for importing government records to be moved from Oslo, along with the country's gold reserves, amounting to 20 truckloads.

However, it left a power vacuum at the nerve centre of the country's communications which one man—Vidkun Quisling—was just waiting to fill. Quisling spent the critical day of 9 April visiting key points in central Oslo. As a former defence minister he had a modest influence, but remained a private citizen—until early evening.

Then Quisling acted. Ribbentrop's representative had already said there was no place for him in German plans. But two of Hitler's men in Norway, Hagelin and Scheidt, told Quisling that Hitler would look favourably on any government he formed.

Led on by his supporters, Quisling bluffed his way past the German guards, outfaced the Director of Broadcasting, and at 7.32pm went on the air to broadcast to the Norwegian people.

Quisling assumes control

He told them that England had violated Norway's neutrality by laying mines, and that the government had fled.

'Under these circumstances it is the duty and right of the Nasjonal Samling movement to assume the powers of government, in order to vindicate the vital interests of the Norwegian people and the safety and independence of Norway.

'The **Nygaardsvold** Government had withdrawn. The national government has assumed power, with Vidkun Quisling as its head . . .'

When his secretary congratulated him on becoming prime minister, Quisling was far from confident. 'It is not a position to aspire to. Let's hope the Germans and our people understand our objectives. I shall be called the big traitor.'

With that perfectly accurate prediction to launch his career, Quisling spent the next hours working hard to preserve Norway's delicate equilibrium. Fighting off a high fever, he stayed at work until 2am on 10 April and was at his temporary desk in the Hotel Continental again at 6am, drafting documents and contacting Norway's public figures.

His aim was to reduce German interference to a minimum, and to persuade the King to return to the capital. One of his messages read: 'The Quisling Government requests the King and the Royal House to return to Oslo. Quisling himself will adopt a loyal attitude towards His Majesty and suggests that an arrangement should be made in Norway similar to the one prevailing in Denmark.'

But the King refused to deal with Quisling, and threatened to abdicate if the government accepted the new Prime Minister. And most of Quisling's own nominated cabinet refused to serve with him. Within six days he was forced to resign, and Hitler installed his own Reichskommissar in Oslo.

Captured by military bluff and daring, abandoned by its government, Oslo had fallen under German domination.

War Notes

BLÜCHER: German 17,250-ton heavy cruiser. Launched June 1937. Dimensions: 675.75 × 70 × 25.25ft. Powered by 2 shaft-geared turbines giving 32.5 knots and 132,000shp. Range: 6800 miles at 19 knots. Guns: 8 × 8in (twin turrets), 12 × 4.1in AA (6 twin mounts), 12 × 37mm AA (twin mounts), 4 × 20mm AA. Torpedo tubes: 12 × 21in (4 mounts). Aircraft: 3 and catapult. Armour: main belt 2.75–3.25in, deck 1.25–2in, turrets 3.75in. Crew: 1600 + about 400 troops of 163rd Infantry Div. Sister ship: *Admiral Hipper*. Rear Admiral Oskar Kummetz, CO of Group 5, survived *Blücher's* sinking.

EMDEN: German 6990-ton light cruiser, first warship built in Germany after 1918. Launched Jan 1925. Dimensions: 508.5 × 47 × 21.75ft. Powered by 2 shaft-geared turbines giving 46,500shp and 29 knots. Range: 5300 miles at 18 knots. Guns: 8 × 5.9in, 3 × 3.5in AA, 4 × 37mm AA. Torpedo tubes: 4 × 21in (twin mounts). Mines: 120. Armour: main belt 2in, deck 0.75in, gunshields 0.5–0.75in. Crew: 630.

Fox Photos;

HAAKON VII: King of Norway, b. 1872, 2nd son of Frederick VIII of Denmark. Married Maud (d. 1938) daughter of K. Edward VII of England 1896. Became King in 1905 on separation of Norway from Sweden. Crowned at Trondheim 1906.

HAMBRO, Karl Joachim: Norwegian politician, b. 1885 Bergen. Member of Norwegian Storting from 1919. Became President 1926. Norwegian delegate to League of Nations 1926 and President of League Assembly at Geneva 1939.

JU52 (Junkers 52/3m): German tri-engined bomber, transport and trainer. Developed from single-engine Ju52, designed by Ernst Zindel 1928. First flew April 1931, in service Lufthansa 1932, Luftwaffe 1934. By 1939 1600 built. Used for largest airborne operation yet in Norway and Denmark. First wave carried 6 infantry battalions or equivalent, 6 airfield maintenance companies, and over 37,000 gallons of fuel. Total force of 573 commanded by Lt Col Carl-August Baron von Galblenz. Most returned to German bases after 8-10 days. Losses during Operation Weserübung were over 150 compared with 12 in Poland. Flew most of the 3018 transport sorties during campaign that lifted 29,280 men, 259,300 gallons of fuel and 2376 tons of equipment.

LÜTZOW: German 15,900-ton pocket battleship. Launched May 1931, originally called *Deutschland*, renamed *Lützow* Nov 1939 (Hitler not wanting a *Deutschland* to be sunk). *Deutschland* had sunk 2 ships (1 Norwegian) in N. Atlantic commerce raid, Sept-Nov 1939. Missed by HM Submarine *Trident* with 10 torpedoes off Skagen at 7.06pm on 8 April. Hit 3 times by Oscarsborg's guns and bow turret put out of action. On return from Oslo operation torpedoed by sub *Spearfish*, 11 April. Propellers blown off and steering wrecked, towed into Kiel for refit.

ME110 (Messerschmitt 110): Me110s of 1 Staffel, I Gruppe, ZG 76 were group who landed in Oslo. Altogether 70 of the Luftwaffe's 300+ Me110s were assigned to Norway and Denmark, 25 lost in April.

NYGAARDSVOLD, Johann: Norwegian statesman, b. 1879. Was member of Storting from 1916. Labour Party Leader from 1932 and became president of Storting 1934. PM and Minister of Public Works 1935-40.

Keystone

RUGE, Otto: Norwegian soldier, b. 1882. Colonel and Inspector General of Infantry. Became C-in-C of Army, promoted to Major-General on 11 April 1940.

STAVANGER: Norwegian city in SW Norway on south shore of Bokn Fjord, 100 miles S. of Bergen. Population 50,320.

THE GRAVEYARD FJORD

On 5 April 1940 Captain Bernard Warburton-Lee, commanding Britain's 2nd Destroyer Flotilla, wrote to his wife: 'The war is going to start properly soon, and I am going to start it!' He did, and earned the first Victoria Cross of the war posthumously.

Showing single-minded ruthlessness, a massive German force set out on the morning of 7 April. Compact groups of ships, their holds crammed with troops and equipment, sped northwards. Their destination was the barely defended ports of Norway and Denmark.

Northwards too, went Captain **Warburton-Lee** and five minelaying destroyers of Britain's Home Fleet. Enemy ships off Trondheim were steaming west for the Atlantic, claimed an RAF report. Warburton-Lee was redirected. Vice-Admiral Jock **Whitworth** commanding the Battlecruiser Squadron in the North Sea withdrew his destroyers patrolling the entrance to Vestfjord—the approach to Narvik. Now, the destroyers were to join the rest of the fleet out at sea.

With the British conveniently re-directed, 10 German destroyers commanded by Commodore Friedrich **Bonte**, slipped into Vestfjord with 2000 mountain troops bound for Narvik.

The only ships that could stop them now were two Norwegian coastal defence vessels. The first boat, *Eidsvold*, challenged Bonte. Norwegian Captain Willoch refused the German summons to surrender, and turned the German boarding party off his ship. Promptly, the German destroyer *Heidkamp* sunk *Eidsvold* with two torpedoes. All but eight of the crew were killed.

Surrender without a fight

Bonte's destroyers continued on course. A second Norwegian patrol boat, *Norge*, was not even offered a formal surrender. The German destroyer *Arnim* launched seven torpedoes and *Norge* exploded, leaving no survivors.

In foul weather, and against paltry opposition, the miserable and seasick German troops landed safely in Narvik.

At the eastern end of Ofotfjord, spreading like the fingers of an open hand, are three smaller fjords, Herjungsfjord, Ballangensfjord and Rombaksfjord. At the centre of the system of channels, nestling on the neck of a gently sloping promontory, lies Narvik.

In the early morning of 9 April a thick mist enveloped the harbour. The **Norwegian 6th Division** garrison, led by a supporter of Vidkun Quisling, surrendered without a fight.

By 4.45am, Sir Charles Forbes, C-in-C Home Fleet, knew the Germans were approaching Oslo, Bergen, Stavanger and Trondheim. Rightly, he concluded the Germans were invading Norway. Logic also led him to believe that they were aiming for Narvik, to secure the iron ore. Four hours later, at 8.45am, the Admiralty instructed him: 'Narvik must be watched to prevent enemy forces landing.'

By this time Warburton-Lee had led his nine destroyers back to the entrance of the Westfjord and established a patrol across it. At 9.31amForbes signalled: 'Send some destroyers up to Narvik to make certain no enemy troops land there. Norway is at war with Germany.' But then, contrary orders were received 25 minutes later from Admiral Whitworth: 'Come back'. Ignoring Whitworth's order, Warburton-Lee continued as planned.

With Narvik safely in German hands, Commodore Bonte saw no further business there.

A dawn attack is planned

Confident and secure, Bonte went to bed. True, five British destroyers had been seen out in the Westfjord, but they were steering southwest, away from the entrance to Ofotfjord. But he took the precaution of stationing U51 at the entrance of Ofotfjord.

On his own initiative, Warburton-Lee headed for the pilot station at Tranöy. There, by means of hand signals, drawings in the snow and a baffling combination of English and demotic German, he learnt that four or five, perhaps six German destroyers had gone up into Ofotfjord. He settled for six. A small boy had told him: 'There were lots of them and they were much bigger than yours.' But this wisdom was ignored.

'Intend attacking at dawn high water' signalled Warburton-Lee to Whitworth, Forbes and the Admiralty. The phrasing was precise. In naval terms a message prefixed with the word 'intend' means that the sender plans to carry out the action unless his superiors specifically tell him not to.

At 9pm that evening, First Sea Lord Sir Dudley Pound and Churchill, fired with enthusiasm for the captain's spirited aggression, replied: 'Attack at dawn with all good luck.' They also instructed him to keep a patrol off the entrance to the Ofotfjord to make sure that the German ships did not leave during the night. Ignoring this, Warburton-Lee steamed southwest thereby confusing U51.

Later, the Admiralty became less confident. Perhaps the attack might be too dangerous? Warburton-Lee was signalled: 'Norwegian coast defence ships *Eidsvold* and *Norge* may be in German hands. You alone can judge whether in these circumstances attack should be made. We shall support whatever decision you take.'

In the eerie silence of dawn on 10 April, Warburton-Lee led his destroyers, (*Hardy*, *Hunter*, *Havock*, *Hotspur* and *Hostile*) blanketed by snow and fog, into Ofotfjord.

Hardy was the first to attack. Seven torpedoes splashed into the water from her deck tubes.

German warships off Westfjord fight heavy seas. Left: German destroyers berth or sink after the 10 April Narvik battle.

Ullstein

Heidkamp was hit in her magazine '. . . it was just as if some huge hand had torn the German ship in half. It just split in two . . . ' a sailor aboard *Hardy* recalled. In the explosion Bonte and most of his crewmen died where they slept.

The torpedoes were then released in a crashing series, two of them sinking the destroyer *Schmitt*.

Behind *Hardy* followed *Hunter* and *Havoc*, between them they torpedoed the destroyer *Lüdemann*; putting a gun out of action and starting a fire aft that the crew could only deal with by flooding the magazine. The *Künne* lay protected behind the refuelling tanker but the impact of the explosions put her guns out of action.

Finally *Hunter* and *Havock* turned on the destroyer *Roeder*. Her crew was saved by her captain running the vessel aground in flames.

Warburton-Lee pondered briefly the second part of his orders—to occupy the town. He decided that his sailors were too few to handle the German battalions in Narvik and ordered his flotilla to withdraw.

In an hour of almost unopposed assault, the British sank two German destroyers and wrecked three more. With some satisfaction 2nd Flotilla made their way out of the harbour at a steady 15 knots.

Then their luck ran out.

Warned of six destroyers, Warburton-Lee expected one more would be waiting for him. Now, out of Herjangsfjord to the north came three more destroyers, *Koellner*, *Zenker* and *Giese*, falling into place in the wake of the British ships.

Increasing his speed to 30 knots, Warburton-Lee tried to outrun them to the open sea. Suddenly, looming large from Ballangerfjord came *Thiele* and *Arnim* blocking the way forward.

The German destroyers, each stronger and bigger than the British, were ready for action.

Bracketed between the guns of two hostile ships the British were doomed. *Hardy* was the first to be hit. A salvo smashed the bridge and Warburton-Lee was wounded along with several of his officers. The steering broke down and within minutes *Hardy* was aground on rocks just 300 yards from the shore. With the ship sinking, Warburton-Lee gave his last order: 'Abandon ship. Every man for himself. And good luck.'

A swim in freezing water

Men leapt overboard into the freezing water. Lieutenant G. R. Heppell, *Hardy's* torpedo officer, swam several times from ship to shore and back helping non-swimmers. On shore, those able fought through six feet of snow to the nearest home where Norwegians tore up sheets and clothing to dress their wounds. Eighty survivors found shelter in that five-roomed house.

Of *Hardy's* crew, 170 men survived. Warburton-Lee was not among them. Lieutenant Heppell towed him ashore on a float and there he died. Norwegians buried him at the edge of the fjord.

Hunter and *Hotspur*, next in line, continued the fight. Shellfire from the German destroyers cut the steering gear on *Hunter* and threw her out of control. *Hotspur* swung into her at 30 knots. As *Hunter* sank, *Hotspur's* captain was forced to run back from her to extricate from the wreckage.

The two last 2nd Flotilla ships steered westwards past the tangle of drifting metal to attack the German destroyers, *Thiele* and *Arnim*, as they passed eastwards. Turning to chase the five German destroyers, they laid a smokescreen to hide the remnants of the still-blazing British ships.

The German ships, low on fuel, and with *Thiele* and *Arnim* both wounded, did not stay. They backed off towards the wreckage at Narvik. The three surviving British ships, one of them badly damaged, limped away to the open sea.

As they moved out of the fjord, Commander Wright, *Hostile's* captain sighted a German merchant ship through the mist. A shot was fired

across her bows, then a second in earnest. The gun had scarcely fired when the crew of the merchantman hastily abandoned ship. The ship, the 8460-ton *Raunfels*, was a supply ship bound for Narvik with ammunition. It took just two high explosive shells to sink her and deprive the German invasion troops of reserve ammunition and heavy weapons. The column of flame and smoke rising from her exploding cargo signalled the end of the abrupt and messy first battle at Narvik.

By 13 April the Admiralty ordered Whitworth to take a battleship with a strong destroyer escort into Ofotfjord and annihilate the remaining German force.

Scout plane plays key role

Transferring his flag to the battleship **Warspite,** Whitworth passed the Tranöy pilot station at 11am on 13 April, intent on an afternoon attack.

Monitored by Germany's naval intelligence organization, B-Dienst, news of *Warspite's* progress was relayed to Captain Erich Bey, the new German naval commander at Narvik. But before he could deploy his ships in the outer fjords, *Warspite* was steaming into the narrower waters, with a nine-destroyer escort.

Catapulted from the deck of *Warspite*, a Swordfish scout plane flew overhead. It was to play a key role in the battle. With a 305lb bomb it hit and sank the waiting U64 in Herjangsfjord. It also alerted *Warspite* to the German destroyer *Koellner* heading for Bjerkvik bay. *Koellner* was promptly sunk by torpedoes from *Bedouin* and *Eskimo* and a shell from one of *Warspite's* 15in guns.

Künne fled into Herjansfjord, her captain running her aground so that the crew might escape to shore. Floundering on the rocks she was finished off with a torpedo from *Eskimo*.

Into Rombaksfjord went *Zenker* and *Arnim*. Both were scuttled. Their crews escaped to the mountains to join German land forces. In a desperate rearguard action, the last German destroyers, *Thiele* and *Lüdemann*, lay waiting in Rombaksfjord, their torpedo tubes trained on the 500-yard narrows at the entrance. *Eskimo*, *Bedouin*, *Forester*, *Hero* and *Icarus* soon appeared in pursuit.

Eskimo had her bows blown off by the first torpedo. The other ships, manoeuvred out of the line of fire, blasted the enemy destroyers. *Thiele's* wounded captain ordered his ship to be run aground and the crew abandon her. The captain of the *Lüdemann* scuttled his ship against any attempts of the British to salvage her.

In Narvik harbour itself, *Giese* and *Roeder* turned their guns on the approaching *Warspite*. A thundering salvo reduced *Giese* to a drifting wreck and severely disabled *Roeder*. With the *Cossack* joining battle, *Roeder* was blown up and sank.

Of the German Narvik fleet, only U51 escaped—submerged—to the open sea. For the British it was a resounding victory.

Doug Harker

The British destroyers *Hunter* and *Hotspur* collide in First Battle of Narvik; 108 died in the already crippled *Hunter*.

Still smiling survivors from HMS *Hardy* return home wearing borrowed Norwegian clothes. Churchill was to address them.

Like Warburton-Lee, Whitworth had orders to put ashore—if he thought he could hold the town. But, he decided, his few hundred sailors were no match for 2000 German troops. In fact, the German troops under the command of General Edouard **Dietl,** were terrified by the devastating assault, and completely demoralized. Whitworth knew he could only exploit the position with the arrival of the Scots Guards on board the cruiser *Southampton* scheduled for 14 April, the next day.

Whitworth radioed Admiral of the Fleet **Lord Cork and Orrery** informing him that if *Southampton* could be diverted at once to Narvik, the town could almost certainly be taken with little or no opposition. Unfortunately, bad radio communications prevented the message getting through. The cruiser landed her troops as planned, 35 miles from Narvik, at Harstad and near Salangen on the following day.

Hitler's nerve wavers

Whitworth now felt he had no choice. Stopping only to pick up the survivors of the first battle, he led his destroyers out of the fjord.

Syndication International

Hitler had decided to evacuate Narvik. He dictated to General Keitel, Head of OKW, accordingly. The message did not go far. At OKW offices in Bendlerstrasse on 15 April Jodl's army staff officer, Colonel Bernhard von Lossberg, rebelled at sending it out. If Dietl was to evacuate there was no point in the whole Norwegian campaign. Von Lossberg begged the Army C-in-C, Brauchitsch, to intervene. Brauchitsch refused but did sign another message drawn up by von Lossberg ending, 'I am sure you will defend your position, which is so vital to Germany, to the last man.' Von Lossberg handed the new signal to Jodl and tore up Keitel's handwritten Führer Order. Over the next few days Jodl so stiffened Hitler's resolve that Dietl was ordered to stand fast on the 17th.

Commanders met for first time

On 16 April the last of Major-General Pierse **Mackesy's** Rupertforce disembarked. Apart from one company, the bulk of the 24th Guards Brigade under Mackesy's command landed at Harstad. Originally destined to help the Finns fight the Russians, these men had already been disembarked and re-embarked several times, as Whitehall dithered. Only the day before, the two commanders of the Narvik operation, Mackesy and Cork, met for the first time. It soon became clear that they didn't see eye to eye.

Two days after the meeting, things started to move. On 17 April the War Office and the Admiralty ordered an immediate assault on Narvik. Cork was delighted and set about planning the attack: a naval bombardment from *Warspite* would be followed by troop landings close to the town. As *Warspite* was due to sail for Trondheim in a few days, Cork felt it best to use her while they could. But Mackesy would have none of it. His doubts were extensive: Where were the French reinforcements? How could we land our troops with no available site and no proper craft? And how can we morally justify bombarding a town of 5000 innocent civilians?

The weather cut short further discussion. On 19 April heavy seas and blinding snow made troop movements impossible for a week. Meanwhile, General Dietl continued to consolidate his position, arming the surviving 2600 German sailors.

On 24 April an abortive attempt was made to bombard the immediate vicinity of Narvik. Cork was now the supreme commander of the combined operation (the War Office had conceded the necessity of breaking the leadership deadlock) and brought *Warspite*, with the cruisers *Effingham* and *Enterprise* to positions along the shores of Ofotfjord. Bad weather made the gunfire ineffective and little damage was done.

In the next few days British troops moved to positions either side of Narvik. Still 20 miles from the town, they advanced slowly in appalling conditions. Luckily, they met no resistance from German troops. One battalion reached a point only 10 miles from Narvik, struggling through heavy snow.

'Boldness is required'

With two battalions on the seaward, north side of the fjord and one, the closest, on the southern side, the British waited for better weather. In Narvik, General Dietl's troops were successfully reinforced and supplied from the air.

Cork was disappointed with General Mackesy. The action had been increasingly slowed down by doubts and indecision on the Army chief's part. When the long-awaited French eventually arrived, under General Emile **Béthouart**, Cork was reassured. Both he and Béthouart wanted a direct attack on Narvik, with troops landing near the town, but again Mackesy vetoed the plan.

While Lieutenant General Nikolas von Falkenhorst, the German C-in-C Norway, had complete confidence in Dietl, Mackesy's superiors in London were beginning to question the lack of Allied aggressiveness. General Sir Edmund Ironside noted that 'boldness is required' but confided in his diary 'I think that Mackesy is not doing very much in the way of pushing'.

On 27 April the Allies decided to pull out the forces in southern Norway, in favour of concentrating them on Narvik in the north. Mackesy could expect further reinforcements. Obviously, the Germans would now push northwards.

Aandalsnes was evacuated on 1 May and Namsos on 3 May—on 6 May two battalions of the French legion arrived in the Narvik sector. Then, three days later, came a brigade of Polish troops.

With the Allied force expanded now to 25,000 men a new commander—Lieutenant-General Claude Auchinleck—was appointed to take over from Mackesy. He arrived at Harstad on 13 May. But by then the war in the West had begun.

War Notes

BÉTHOUART, Emile: French general, b. 1889. Graduated St Cyr 1909. Served 1914-18. Training instructor with Finnish Army 1919-20. Took mountain warfare course in Norway during 1930s. CO 5th Demi-brigade Chasseurs Alpins serving at Namsos, then Narvik. After assault at Bjerkvik, given command on 13 May of all Allied land forces at Narvik.

BONTE, Friedrich: Senior Officer, German Narvik Destroyer Force. Led minelaying sorties off E. Coast of England Oct 1939-Feb 1940. Killed along with 80 crew aboard *Wilhelm Heidkamp* when HMS *Hardy*'s 2nd torpedo hit.

CORK AND ORRERY, 12th Earl of, (William Henry Dudley Boyle): British admiral, b. 1873. Served 1914-18. C-in-C Home Fleet 1933-5. Recalled to Admiralty Sept 1939 at request of Churchill. Appointed overall commander at Narvik 21 April. Moved HQ ashore on 16 May, then working with Gen Btéhouart conducted naval landings at Bjerkvik and Narvik.

DIETL, Edouard: German general, b. 1890, Bavaria. Served 1914-18 and with Reichswehr. Personal friend of Hitler. Attended winter warfare course in Norway before 1939. 3rd Mountain Division formed under his command Graz, 1938, incorporating elements of Austrian Army. Led division in Polish campaign and its 138th Regt in Narvik landing.

Bildarchiv Preussischer Kulturbesitz

MACKESY, Pierse Joseph: British general, b. 1883. Served 1914-18. Military mission to S. Russia 1919-20. CO infantry brigade Palestine 1937. Received orders at Scapa Flow on 11 April for expedition to Narvik. As CO 49th Div, landed at Harstad 14-15 April. Proposed landings at Bjerkvik but his plans to delay the Germans in the S. carried out by Gen Auchinleck who took command on 13 May.

NORWEGIAN 6th DIVISION: responsible for Narvik's defence. Concentrated at Narvik but only 400 men available when Germans landed. Some were captured, others withdrew towards Sweden. Fought alongside British and French to recapture Narvik.

WARBURTON-LEE, Bernard Armitage Warburton: British sailor, b. 1895 Isycoed, Flintshire. Educated Dartmouth and Osborne, then training cruiser *Cornwall,* passing out top of form 1912. 1st Lieutenant *Mischief* and *Wrestler* 1917, command of destroyers *Tuscan* 1924, *Stirling* 1926, *Walpole* 1928, *Vanessa* 1930, *Witch* 1934. In command of C-in-C Mediterranean's despatch vessel *Bryony* for 18 months between 1933-4. Promoted Commander 1930 and Capt June 1936. In command of cruiser *Hawkins* and Flag Captain to Vice-Adm Max Horton, commanding Reserve Fleet until July 1939. Took command of *Hardy* and 2nd Flotilla in Mediterranean. Ordered Home Waters Sept 1939. Awarded 1st VC (to be recognized and gazetted) of WW2.

Fox Photos

WARSPITE: Q. Elizabeth-class battleship, 36,450 tons. Laid down Oct 1912, launched Nov 1913. Dimensions: 639.75 × 104 × 33.8ft. Powered by 4-shaft turbines giving 72,000shp and 22.5 knots. Guns: 8 × 15in in twin turrets, 8 × 6in mounted in ship's sides, 4 × twin 4in AA, 4 × 8-barrel 2 pdr and 4 quad ·5in AA. Aircraft: up to 3 Swordfish floatplanes or Walrus amphibious flying boats. Armour: 4-13in belt, 2-5in deck, 4.2-13in turret. Crew: 1124. Refitted and modernized 1934-7. Served as flagship Mediterranean Fleet Jan 1938-Oct 1939.

WHITWORTH, William Jock: British admiral, b. 1884. Vice-Admiral commanding Battle Cruiser Squadron 1939. CO at 2nd Battle of Narvik, in *Warspite.*

FIASCO AT TRONDHEIM

British troops in an Arethusa-class cruiser bound for Aandalsnes, Norway.

It was going to be a thumping victory. While the Germans were struggling up Norway along a single road and railway, the Royal Navy would steam into Trondheim, kick out the Germans already there and start to roll Hitler back whence he had come.

In the holds of four Royal Navy cruisers sailing towards the Norwegian coast on 17 April the men of the **148th Infantry Brigade** were shaping up for what had to be the first serious clash on land between German and British troops. Nine months earlier, these young men from the Midlands had been farmers, bank clerks, estate agents. They were going in without anti-aircraft guns, fighter cover or field artillery.

In the holds too was their equipment—somewhere. The loading had been a shambles. 'What I saw appalled me' a colonel who had peered into the hold at the dockside reported. Cranes were simply pouring new supplies at random into the hold as they came to hand. Food and ammunition mixed with bundles of supplies for the Norwegians. It would turn out that, in the rush, the radio transmitter and the mortars had been left behind.

Commanding Officer of the troops embarked was Lieutenant-Colonel Simpson. He had been summoned to catch a night train to take on the task. Then given 700 sailors and marines most of whom had never fired a rifle in their lives. One of the chores on the journey would be to show them how.

Brigadier Harold **Morgan** was in charge of the infantry. Before the ships had left he was already on his fourth set of orders. The latest came after he had set sail, switching his destination from **Namsos,** 100 miles to the north of **Trondheim** to **Aandalsnes,** 120 miles to the south. He had on board mailbags from the War Office crammed with hundreds of maps. None of them showed the position of Aandalsnes.

It was called Sickleforce, this expedition. Their spirits were high. 'Allies Sea Power Will Save Norway' the *Sunday Times* had trumpeted on 14 April. 'A brilliant piece of combined staff work' complimented the French *Le Temps*. Chamberlain was 'ten times more confident of victory' than he had been at the start of the war, he told the world on the 14th.

Sickleforce steamed into port at Aandalsnes on 18 April, the untried soldiers clutching their rifles nervously. On the quay was a two-man welcoming party: the British consul and an officer of the Royal Marines. It seemed an anti-climax. They began to unload the chaos of stores from the hold. It was cold here. The mountains of Norway looked grimly forbidding. The men of Sickleforce stared bemusedly at the reindeer saddles that had been dropped into the holds. There were no reindeer. There were no skis either.

Far to the north at Namsos the other wing of the invasion codenamed Mauriceforce was landing on equally peaceful dockland. There were 6000 men in Mauriceforce, among them the British **146th**

Infantry Brigade and the crack mountain troops of the French 5th Demi-brigade of **Chasseurs Alpins**.

There was to have been a third force: Hammer, aimed direct at Trondheim itself. At the last moment, Hammer had been cancelled—it had seemed too risky a bet, this direct landing into the teeth of the Germans known to be in Trondheim. The heart had been taken out of the original plan. But no one had changed the plan.

Brigadier Morgan began urging his men north. Their task was to strike towards Trondheim and to relieve Norwegian forces under General Otto Ruge, holding out north of Oslo.

The route lay up a narrow ravine, towards a railhead at **Dombaas.** Reconnaissance groups established that the only Germans in the area were the remnants of a 200-strong paratroop force holed up in a farmhouse a few miles beyond Dombaas.

Encouraged, the main force pushed ahead. Their only real obstacle so far was the terrain of the steep sided valley. They were able to use the trains. By the afternoon of 20 April they reached **Lillehammer,** and welcoming cups of coffee from Norwegian girls for the weary Sherwood Foresters.

Lillehammer was the Norwegian Army chief Major-General Otto Ruge's HQ. Brigadier Morgan went to meet him after midnight, in his blacked out farmhouse. 'We found a friendly man who spoke good English . . . it was bitter to see his disappointment when we had to confess how pathetically small our help was to be.'

Relief for tired troops

Ruge was not enthusiastic about the British plans to go north and recapture Trondheim. His own exhausted troops must be relieved first. Morgan, somewhat reluctantly, agreed.

The Germans struck on the morning of 21 April, as Morgan's men moved to Lake Mjosa, south-east of Lillehammer, to relieve Ruge's tired troops.

As a preliminary, German aircraft flew low over the British and Norwegian positions, raking the unfortunate soldiers with machine-gun fire. The

German infantry trying to open the Oslo-Bergen line, deploy against ambush.

Vögelarchiv

'Mein Führer, I have been there. A campaign there is like a Polar expedition.'
General Alfred Jodl, 14 April

Luftwaffe was able to operate more or less as it liked, for the British had no air support and, unbelievably, no anti-aircraft guns.

Incessant attack from the air

Staff officer Dudley **Clarke** described the scene, 'The aircraft were attacking almost incessantly... Along one side of the road there ran a decent brick wall, and against it half a dozen stunned-looking stragglers were crouching. I ran to join them for a minute as two airplanes came along machine-gunning, and at the same time an open flat-topped truck pulled in for cover with several khaki figures stretched out on bloodstained boards. I experienced an unexpected pang at the sight of blood soaking out of painfully new battledress.'

That afternoon the German infantry started to advance. The Allies had little option but to retreat, and it was soon decided that Lillehammer would be evacuated in favour of a new position at Faaberg, five miles to the north. The retreat was not orderly to Colonel Clarke's eyes: 'Bewildered stragglers were coming in now from right and left while private cars drove past with their owners at the wheel. Norwegian women as well as men, carrying British wounded to the civilian doctors.'

Next day the Germans attacked again. In what was to become a familiar pattern, the assault began with aircraft bombing and strafing, followed by a bombardment from mountain howitzers and heavy mortars. The British were virtually powerless to reply: they had no artillery and it was soon discovered that the only ammunition for their 3in mortars consisted of smoke bombs.

Now the Germans were ready to move. As tanks spearheaded the advance along the road, well-trained mountain troops equipped with skis began to move forward along the sides of the valley to outflank the British position. Once again there was little the defenders could do: they had no armoured vehicles, let alone tanks, and no anti-tank guns (though a few did arrive along the narrow supply line in time for later action). The German ski-troops were highly mobile, but the British had to use the road if they wanted to move quickly.

Lack of transport

By 4pm Brigadier Morgan was forced to order a hasty retreat to avoid total defeat. Now a new problem arose: there was no transport. The only lorries at Faaberg were loaded with valuable stores, including the troops' rations for the next few days. Morgan had no choice but to offload and abandon the stores in order to use the lorries.

As the tired and battered soldiers moved back first to Oier and then to Tretten they were again attacked from the air. Two companies of Sherwood Foresters never even received the order to pull back; most were killed or captured.

In the next few days the British and Norwegian

troops moved steadily back along the narrow valley towards the railway junction at Dombaas. During the day they would take up defensive positions to resist the advancing Germans while at night they retreated to the next village. Fortunately for them the Germans had orders not to proceed after nightfall, so there was a brief respite for the defenders between each action. At Tretten, Kvam, Kjörem and Otta the British and Norwegians put up surprisingly stiff resistance despite lack of air cover, artillery and armour, all aggravated by countless supply problems.

Worst of all was the Luftwaffe's air supremacy. Every day planes bombed and strafed not only the troops but also the long, slender supply line back to Aandalsnes. Aandalsnes was under almost constant bombardment which made it practically impossible to unload equipment from supply ships.

In one particularly heavy raid 300,000 rounds of rifle ammunition, 3000 rounds of 40mm Bofors ammunition and 800 3in mortar bombs were destroyed. Even basic supplies were becoming scarce: 'In the next few days there were going to be many to whom one precious can (of petrol) would mean the difference between England and a German prison camp, while many a brand new Army car, with no other fault but an empty tank has to be rolled down the mountain side to keep a roadway clear' wrote one observer.

As Major-General Bernard **Paget** remarked

A handful of tanks, used from 16 April, greatly aided the German drive on Trondheim. Inset: German mountain troops were expert skiers.

before embarking to take command of Sickleforce, 'The possibility of maintaining any force through the single port of Aandalsnes depends primarily upon whether or not local air superiority can be established and maintained.'

Disastrous setback for RAF

On the very day he arrived in Norway, as the King's Own Yorkshire Light Infantry held the Germans at Kvam, the RAF suffered a disastrous setback in the only serious attempt to oppose the Germans in the air: 13 out of 18 newly arrived Gloster Gladiator biplanes were bombed to destruction on the frozen Lake Lesjaskog between Aandalsnes and Dombaas. Local opinion was agreed that the ice would remain firm for another two weeks, so the RAF had taken the opportunity to bring in fighters to help the hard-pressed troops. But now any possibility of air support was dashed.

After Sickleforce gave up all hope of a northward strike to Trondheim, only Mauriceforce from Namsos, commanded by Major-General Sir Adrian **Carton de Wiart**, was still fighting towards Trondheim.

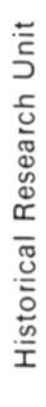

His arrival at Namsos was announced by a hail of machine-gun bullets—an enemy fighter attacked his flying boat just after it landed. His ADC was injured and had to return in the same plane to spend several weeks in a British hospital. The Royal Marines had already made an uneventful preliminary landing and soon the main body of troops arrived. These were the **146th Infantry Brigade** under Brigadier C. G. Phillips. Later to arrive were a demi-brigade of the French Chasseurs Alpins under General Audet.

Of the Chasseurs Alpins, Carton de Wiart wrote '. . . they were a fine body of troops and would have been ideal for the job in hand, but ironically they lacked one or two essentials which made them completely useless to us'. One of the essentials they lacked was a vital strap for their skis. It made them virtually immobile.

Evacuation was inevitable

British troops advancing south according to plan, got as far as Verdal, on Trondheimsfjord, but were now beginning to pull back ten miles or so to Vist. At 6am on 21 April just after the 1st Battalion, the King's Own Yorkshire Light Infantry received orders to withdraw they were attacked by a battalion of the German 130th Regiment, veterans of the Polish campaign.

In the next two days the British and Norwegian troops were pressed back to the village of Steinkjer where the Germans seemed content to halt their advance. Carton de Wiart said of this action: 'The troops at Verdal had a particularly bad time. The road ran through the town on the shore of the fjord in full view of the ships, and the troops had to take the snow-covered hills, ploughing through unknown country in 18 inches of snow, only to be attacked by German ski troops. There is no doubt that not many of them would have survived had it not been for the handling of the situation by Brigadier Phillips.' Evacuation seemed inevitable.

On the morning of 26 April, the Cabinet in London decided that the troops would have to be pulled out of Aandalsnes and Namsos if disaster was to be avoided.

During the evening of 30 April the last 2600 troops of Sickleforce climbed aboard a train waiting for them in a tunnel at Dombaas. The train began the 60-mile journey to Aandalsnes at 11pm, and by 1am next day was within 36 miles of the port. Suddenly the train came to a shuddering halt —the locomotive had been derailed by a bomb crater. The battle-weary troops had no alternative but to set out on foot to the tunnel at Verma, 19 miles from Aandalsnes, where they spent a depressing day waiting for the cover of darkness. 'It was scarcely possible to move without walking on prostrate men' said General Paget.

At last, at 8.30pm on 1 May, the train set out from Verma tunnel and the exhausted troops were able to board transports for home. That same night the Chasseurs Alpins were taken off from Namsos, and the following night Carton de Wiart's troops were evacuated by the Royal Navy.

So Allied operations in central Norway came to an end: they had achieved little and cost much. Altogether 1559 men had lost their lives.

War Notes

AANDALSNES: coastal village 195 miles NW of Oslo and 100 miles SW of Trondheim. Population 1500. Small stone jetty and wooden quay equipped with 5-ton travelling crane. Rail link to Oslo via Dombaas. 40 miles from open sea.

CARTON DE WIART, Adrian: British soldier, b. 1880 Brussels to Belgian father and British mother. Educated Edgbaston and Balliol College, Oxford. Served S. Africa 1901, Somaliland 1914-15 (won DSO), W. Front 1915-18 (won VC CMG and CB). Won VC for rallying troops when British line was wavering. Rose from Captain to Brigadier-General, losing a hand and an eye in the process. Ran British Military Mission to Poland 1918-24. Retired from Army 1924. Lived in Poland to hunt and shoot. Head of British Military Mission to Poland July-Sept 1939. Travelled to England to command Central Norwegian Expeditionary Force. With local rank of Lt-General he was the senior British officer.

Historical Research Unit

CHASSEURS ALPINS: French troops specially trained for mountain warfare. 5th Demi-Brigade arrived Namsos 19 April 1940 under Gen Bethouart and divisional commander Gen Audet. Consisted of 13th, 53rd and 67th battalions with AA and AT guns.

CLARKE, Dudley Wrangel: British soldier, b. 1899. Educated Charterhouse and RMA Woolwich. Served Royal Artillery 1916-36 and with RFC and RAF in 1914-18 war. General Staff 1936. Served Middle East 1939-40.

DOMBAAS: town 55 miles inland from Aandalsnes. Junction of Oslo-Trondheim railway and Aandalsnes branch line.

15th INFANTRY BRIGADE: Arrived Aandalsnes 24 April 1940. 1st Bn Green Howards, 1st Bn King's Own Yorkshire Light Infantry and 1st Bn the York & Lancaster Regt under Brig H. E. F. Smyth.

146th INFANTRY BRIGADE: arrived Namsos 16 April 1940. 1st/4th Royal Lincolnshire Regt, 1st/4th King's Own Yorkshire Light Infantry and the Hallamshire Battalion, York and Lancaster Regt. A Section of 55th Field Company, Royal Engineers. Commanded by Brig C. G. Phillips under Lt-Gen Carton de Wiart.

148th INFANTRY BRIGADE: arrived Aandalsnes 18 April 1940. Only 2 battalions: 1st/5th Royal Leicestershire Regt, 1st/8th Sherwood Foresters plus 168th Light AA Battery. Commanded by Brig H. de R. Morgan.

LILLEHAMMER: Norwegian town, population about 10,000, 80 miles N. of Oslo.

MORGAN, Harold de Reimer: British soldier, b. 1888. Educated Harrow and Worcester College, Oxford. CO Oxford University OTC 1919-22. CO 2nd/5th Fusiliers 1936-9 and 148th Brigade 1940. Directed operations at Aandalsnes until Maj-Gen Paget arrived 25 April.

NAMSOS: Norwegian coastal town, 80 miles N. of Trondheim, 320 miles SW of Narvik. Population 3800. Two wooden wharves and a quay served by railway. Good anchorage 20 miles from open sea. Site of British landings 16 April 1940.

PAGET, Bernard Charles Tolver: British general, b. 1887. Educated Shrewsbury and Sandhurst. Served W. Front 1914-18 winning DSO and MC. Promoted Colonel 1929. Served War Office 1934-6, Quetta Brigade, Baluchistan 1936-7. Promoted Major-General 1937. Commandant Staff College, Camberley 1938-9. Appointed to command Sickleforce 20 April after original choice, Maj-Gen F. E. Hotblack, suffered a fatal stroke on 17 April and his replacement, acting Maj-Gen H. P. M. Berney-Ficklin, was injured in an air crash.

TRONDHEIM: city 400 miles S. of Narvik, 380 miles N. of Oslo. Population 56,000, large port, good anchorage 40 miles from open sea. Rail link E. to Sweden and S. through Dombaas, to Oslo.

MAY 1940

...'GOOD then we can begin' says Adolf Hitler on the eve of the greatest feat of arms in history. With fine weather forecast Hitler orders his panzers into Holland, Belgium, Luxembourg and France. At last the waiting is over...but the Allies are caught unprepared and indecisive. How was it possible for this Blitzkrieg to overrun the world's greatest powers in six short weeks? Even Hitler is staggered...

1st: Hess presents 'golden banner' to Krupp arms factory at Essen.

2nd: Allies leave Namsos.

3rd: Stukas attack Namsos, sink Allied destroyers *Afridi* and *Bison*. French army commander orders removal of unsanctioned anti-tank obstacles in Ardennes.

4th: Papal Nuncio warns King Leopold that German attack imminent. RN sub *Seal* captured by seaplane.

5th: Abwehr Captain Goertz parachutes in near Dublin, to contact IRA.

6th: Ironside welcomes troops back from Norway in Scotland. Spitfire photographs panzers in Ardennes.

7th: House of Commons Norway debate begins. French pilot reports panzers heading for Ardennes.

8th: Norway Debate vote.

9th: Hitler orders attack for dawn on next day. French Cabinet crisis over Gamelin. E-boats attack RN destroyers in Skagerrak; Mountbatten's *Kelly* hit and towed to Newcastle. Luftwaffe mines Dutch and Belgian ports. French Intelligence reports 'no abnormal German movements'.

10th: Germany invades Holland, Belgium, Luxembourg without warning. Germans bomb Freiburg accidentally and blame French. Allied mining of the Rhine begins. Chamberlain resigns. Churchill to form coalition government. British troops land in Iceland.

11th: Attack on Eben Emael ends. Belgians fall back towards R. Dyle.

12th: First panzers enter France and reach R. Meuse. French 7th Army forced to retreat to Antwerp. Interning of enemy aliens in Britain.

13th: Germans cross Meuse around Sedan. French retreat after all-day tank battle in Belgium.

14th: Panzers advance beyond the Meuse. British cease to read Enigma traffic in Norway. Rotterdam bombed. Gen Winkelman broadcasts Dutch ceasefire.

15th: French 9th Army in full retreat from Meuse. German 6th Army attack on Anglo-French front in Belgium is repulsed. RAF Bomber Command begins air attacks on Germany.

'The battle which is beginning today will decide the fate of the German nation for the next thousand years . . . Do your duty.'

Adolf Hitler, Order of Day 10 May

'GOOD, THEN WE CAN BEGIN'

The ninth of May, 1940, eve of the German invasion of the West, was also the day the chief weather forecaster of the Luftwaffe won his gold watch. It was deserved. For the first week of May, the responsibility of launching three million men into battle had largely been his.

Day after day had come up foggy, as he had warned. Göring, whose planes needed the clear start, had taken the postponements calmly. Not so, Hitler. He knew the great secret was already beginning to leak like a sieve. Even the French must soon tumble to the fact that Plan Yellow was poised for fulfillment. The Dutch certainly knew. On the 8th they had started to evacuate cities and, worse, to strengthen guards on the frontier bridges. And it seemed that someone in the Vatican had tipped off the Belgians. Without the element of surprise, it could turn into the same ghastly slogging match the last war had been.

This morning, Thursday, Hitler rose early. As usual, he shaved alone. He could not tolerate a barber hovering round his neck with a cut-throat razor. His naval adjutant, Karl-Jesco von Puttkamer, was up too, telephoning the Front for news of the weather. Then he hastened to his boss. This time there was good news. At Aachen the sun was already burning up the morning mist and prospects looked even better for tomorrow. 'Good,' said Hitler. 'Then we can begin.'

Prepare for a long journey

The girls—the faithful secretaries—were among the first to sense the lifting of the Führer's mood. He told them to pack, for a long journey. Excited, they crowded round Julius Schauber, Hitler's factotum. How long were they going to be away, they demanded. 'A week?' he said. 'Two weeks? A month maybe. Years.' The truth was that he knew no more than they. It was a game that would be played out all day, this mystery trip. Even 'the Boss,' in high spirits, would join in the teasing.

All along the Allied frontier the brilliant spring sunlight warmed even the chill concrete of the Maginot Line. This weekend was Whitsun—many had leave to look forward to.

In Paris this morning, Prime Minister Paul Reynaud had risen, still feeling fragile from last weekend's bout of influenza. Nevertheless, today was the day he had determined for a showdown. He was going to face his cabinet and lay it on the line. Either the ineffectual Gamelin, Commander-in-Chief, retired or he, Reynaud, would resign. After the fiasco in Norway it was obvious that, with Gamelin in charge, the war was as good as lost. 'In charge' was a joke too. Only last month the President of the State Army Committee had complained to the Senate: 'We do not know who is the actual commander at the front.'

There were no fewer than three HQs in France now. Gamelin was in his cellar at Vincennes—that 'submarine without a periscope'. Then there was General Alphonse Georges, the C-in-C NE front, 35 miles up the road at Ferté-sous-Joaurre, and a Grand Quarter General (GQG) halfway between. Apparently when Gamelin wanted to talk to Georges (which wasn't often, since they loathed each other) he had to drive over by car.

On the eve of the battle Hitler confers with Colonel General von Rundstedt.

There was worse. Reynaud had heard that not a single new plane was in production in the factories. Worse still, photo-reconnaissance aircraft had not bothered to get off the ground because of 'bad weather'. When the tank corps did bestir itself to run an exercise it usually ended with the tanks littered about the countryside, out of petrol.

Back in Berlin the keyboard operators on the Enigma machines were getting on with it, at last. Even these methodical men could feel the blood racing now. This was *the* message: 'The Führer and Supreme Commander has decided: Zero day . . . 10 May. Zero hour . . . 05.45. The code names 'Danzig' or 'Augsberg' will be given to the various sections of the Wehrmacht before 21.30 hours on 9 May. Message signed: Keitel.'

Unobtrusively, Abwehr Colonel Hans Oster slipped away from the sudden bustle in Berlin's corridors of power and telephoned a friend. It was an unusual friend for an Abwehr colonel to have—none other than the Dutch military attaché in Berlin, Colonel G. J. Sas. They had had many quiet meetings, under cover of the blackout, at Oster's secluded suburban home.

The story of a journey to Oslo did not fool Oster. He knew today's dramas heralded one thing—the invasion. He warned Sas. The two men arranged to dine together that night. Hans Oster's attitude to Hitler and his plans was simple. 'It is my purpose and my duty to free Germany and the world from this plague', was the way he put it.

By noon, the coded message from Colonel General Wilhelm Keitel was circulating among those entitled to read it in the armies of the Wehrmacht—armies that stretched from the German Ocean to the Swiss frontier.

They totalled 2,760,000 troops in three massive groups. At the top of the map, from the sea down to Aachen was **Army Group B.** General Colonel Fedor von Bock, tough-minded and vain, was in charge here. South of him, in the central section from Aachen to Trier was **Army Group A.** This was Colonel General Karl von Rundstedt's sector. The senior German soldier, his task for tomorrow would be the decisive one. Southwards again, strung along the West Wall sectors facing the Maginot Line, was **Army Group C,** under Colonel General Wilhelm von Leeb.

None of them, come the morning, would be doing what the Allies expected them to do. A few months ago it was not routine for them either.

The invasion plan had changed dramatically from the one that had been on the shelf when the war began. That plan could have been framed in the 1930s by the old war-horses of the High Command. It was little more than a re-run of the 1914 **Schlieffen Plan,** an invasion through the Low Countries, risking a bog-down in the same war-torn fields of World War 1.

It had never fitted with Hitler's dreams since that day in 1933 when, newly in power, he had seen a demonstration of panzers laid on by that resourceful soldier Heinz Guderian. 'This is what I need!' Hitler had said, admiringly, as he watched the tanks on their swift manoeuvres. 'This is what I must have!'

The panzers were too good to waste on the wet lands of Holland and Belgium. Further south lay the concrete hulk of the Maginot. But in between lay a gap, some 35 miles long. It was to this gap that Hitler's attention returned, increasingly, in the autumn of 1939, as foul weather persistently postponed the invasion. The name of the gap was the **Ardennes Forest.**

Today, 9 May 1940, it was looking at its best. Wild raspberry canes were pushing into the spring sunlight beneath the fine canopy of beech, birch and fir. But in winter this vast region of wooded hills, narrow gorges, waterlogged valleys was a sombre place.

In the 1930s it was an article of faith that no one could drive tanks through country like this.

The few thousand Belgian *Chasseurs Ardennes*, whose task it was to cycle the forest paths on leisurely patrol believed it. The guardians of the Ardennes town of **Sedan**, who had lately lifted many of their mines to store them out of the damp, believed it too. In the French lines behind the Belgian frontier, where Major Barlone was now settling to his lunch, everyone believed it. Jokes crossed the table as two officers bolted their food in order to take off on Whitsun leave.

War Notes

ARDENNES FOREST: plateau forming W. part of the Rhine basin. Lies between the Meuse to W, the Moselle and Rhine to E. Extends over parts of France, Luxembourg and Belgium. Highest point 2277ft at Boltrange, Belgium.

ARMY GROUP A: comprised 2nd Army (Gen Baron Maximilian von Weichs) 4th Army (Col Gen Hans von Kluge), 12th Army (Col Gen Siegmund List) and 16th Army (Gen Ernst Busch). A total of 44 divs: 7 panzer and 3 motorized.

ARMY GROUP B: comprised 6th Army (Col Gen Walther von Reichenau) and 18th Army (Gen Georg von Küchler). Total of 28 divisions, including 3 panzer and 2 motorized.

ARMY GROUP C: comprised 1st Army (Col Gen Erwin von Witzleben) and 7th Army (Gen Friedrich Dollmann). Total of 17 infantry divisions.

LUFTWAFFE: the German air force under Field Marshal Goring deployed 2 air fleets or Luftflotten, the 2nd (Col Gen Albert Kesselring) and the 3rd (Col Gen Hugo Sperrle). Each air fleet had 4 subordinate corps, including 2 of bombers and one of fighters. The combined strength of the 2 air fleets was 75% of the entire Luftwaffe. The breakdown was 1300 (95) level and 380 (9) dive-bombers, 860 (6) Me 109 single-engine and 350 (1) Me 110 twin-engine fighters, 640 (26) recce planes, 475 (157) Ju52 transports and 45 gliders. Figures in brackets are the losses on 10 May which with 10 unspecified types totalled 304 planes and another 51 damaged. Aircrew losses came to 267 killed, 133 wounded and 340 missing. Other personnel casualties 326.

MANSTEIN, Fritz Erich von: German soldier, b. 1887. Adopted son of Gen Georg Albrecht von Manstein, surname originally Lewinski. Joined 3rd Guards Reg 1906. Rank of Oberleutnant 1914-18—saw some action but mostly with General Staff. Major 1927, Lt-Colonel 1931, battalion CO 1932, Colonel 1933. Head of General Staff Operations Department 1935. Major General and Deputy Chief of General Staff 1937. CO 18th Div 1938. Chief of Staff to Army Group A Oct 1939. Promoted Lt-General to command 38th Infantry Corps (26th and 34th Divs) Feb 1940.

SCHLIEFFEN PLAN: Germany's pre-WW1 plan to overrun France. Named after Field Marshal Count Alfred von Schlieffen (Chief of Staff 1891-1905), it involved holding the more mountainous southern section of the front with relatively few men while driving powerful armies across in the north through Belgium to outflank the main French forces. By the time WW1 came, however, Schlieffen's successors had weakened it by increasing strength in south at expense of all-important northern armies.

SEDAN: a town in the Ardennes department of NE France. Population about 15,000. The French assumed that the Germans would attack through Belgium, so the frontier near Sedan was only weakly defended. The section from Sedan to Longwy, 40 miles to the SE was the responsibility of French 2nd Army (part of 1st Army Group) under General Charles Huntziger. Scene of defeat and surrender of Emperor Napoleon III, 1870.

German motor-cyclist reconnaissance troops await the order to advance. Each infantry division had 16 motorbike combinations.

However, the three armies, their supporting air fleet, three panzer corps and their seven panzer divisions now assembled on the German edge of the Ardennes believed otherwise.

It had been in October that Hitler had first demanded that his generals rethink the old invasion plan, had first mentioned panzers, the Ardennes and Sedan in one breath. Most of his High Command had been pessimistic.

But there was one eager disciple. Major General Erich von **Manstein,** young chief of staff to von Rundstedt of Army Group A was, like his boss, a tank enthusiast.

Wisely, he spoke to Heinz Guderian, the panzer expert. Guderian was one of the men who had been in the forest during World War I. He knew that, once past the steep foothills the Ardennes opened into a fine rolling plateau, much of it open ground. It was a simple fact to which the western Allies and neutrals remained perversely blind (even though, when running a tank exercise there, the 'German' side had been the decisive victor).

Manstein and Hitler worked on their ideas separately. Then, on 17 February 1940, Manstein finally caught Hitler's ear over a working lunch, and poured out the details of a strike through the forest. Hitler had listened, entranced.

Next day he had summoned Brauchitsch and Halder—and produced the plan as his own. He would only credit Manstein thus: 'Among all the generals I talked to about the new plan, Manstein was the only one who agreed with me.'

By 24 February the new battle directive was ready from Hitler's pen. And it did go beyond Manstein's most dramatic proposals. The main thrust of the invasion,entrusted to Army Group A under von Rundstedt, would now go through the great forest. Von Bock's Army Group B, in the north, would open with an airborne attack on Holland and Belgium. The Allies would stream north to take on the attack from Group B. Then the panzers would come out of the woods in a curving swathe to trap them. 'Sichelsnitt' (sweep of the scythe) was the new operation's code name. It has been called the most inspired blueprint for victory ever conceived.

It was essential to fool Gamelin that the real attack would still come across the Maginot Line. It had not been too difficult. By the afternoon of 9 May, Gamelin was stuffed with false intelligence figures, some of which he put no faith in himself.

However, by this Thursday afternoon, Gamelin's interest in the entire proceedings of warfare looked like being over. Prime Minister Paul Reynaud's demolition job in a two-hour cabinet meeting had been thorough. But it had made no dent on war minister Daladier. Reynaud had thrown down his trump—he resigned. Gamelin, shattered at this crushing vote of no confidence resigned too. It seemed that France now had no premier and no war leader. It seemed that similarly tense scenes in Whitehall and Downing Street had cut the ground from under Chamberlain's feet.

As Hitler's train *Amerika* steamed northwards, the Allies were reaching for their own throats.

On the train, the mystery tour was still bemusing the secretaries. There had been a car drive first, towards Staaken airfield, but the convoy had gone on to the little resort of Finkenkrug, where *Amerika* had been waiting. It left at 4.38pm, towards Hagenow. Then it pulled into a siding at Hagenow, where it stayed until after dusk. The joke of the Norway trip continued. 'Have you brought your sea-sick tablets?' quipped Schaub. Still light-hearted, the Führer promised them sealskin souvenirs. 'If you behave yourselves.'

The invasion was on

After nightfall, however, the train moved off again—and this time, westwards. Hanover was the next stop. It was 9pm as the technicians fixed up telephone lines to the train. Hitler took the phone. Promptly, as Keitel's first message of the day had forecast, the codeword went out. It was

'Send me some chaps who don't bolt – I mean, who will get killed where they stand.'

French General Henri Giraud, May 1940

'Danzig' signalling that the invasion was on.

In Berlin, Colonel Oster and the Dutch attaché Sas had been eating their dinner in gloom. It was something of a funeral meal. At 9.30 they were back at the Wehrmacht HQ, Sas lurking in the shadows. Oster came back after 20 minutes. 'My dear friend,' he said. 'It's for real now. There are no counter-orders. The swine has gone to the Western Front.' The two men shook hands. 'Hopefully we'll meet again after the war' said Oster. Countless others would be using the same words in a few hours time.

Sas raced for a telephone and asked for the War Ministry in The Hague. It was a risky call. Fortunately the man who answered was an aquaintance, Post Witerweer. 'Post,' said Sas urgently. 'You know my voice, don't you. It's Sas in Berlin. I have just one thing to say to you. Early tomorrow at the break of day: be tough.'

That should have been the end of it. But, amazingly, the phone rang back—on an open line from Holland. It was the Head of the Information Service making a heavy attempt at a coded conversation, checking up on Sas. 'I have had such bad reports from you on the operation of your wife. Rotten news. Have you seen all the doctors now?' Sas, furious, got rid of him. 'I don't know why you're bothering me. I told you. The operation: there's nothing more to be done. I have seen all the doctors. It will take place tomorrow at dawn.'

Sas looked out at the darkened city. His career as military attaché in Berlin was over.

In the train, Hitler too was gazing from the window. He was silent now, scanning the darkness for traces of fog as the night grew cool. At 4.25 in the morning of 10 May the train halted again, at Euskirchen. The station name had been removed. They were far in the west now, just 30 miles from the Allied lines. The next part of the journey would be by car again, climbing through small country lanes into the villages of the Eifel. The route had been mapped out with yellow military signposts for the dark convoy of Mercedes limousines.

Dawn was breaking in these fresh spring woods, clear and windless. When the cars halted, it was in front of the new HQ, Münstereifel, a converted anti-aircraft post. For the girls and the rest of the staff, the village below had been evacuated.

There was birdsong. It was, as the **Luftwaffe** weatherman had forecast, going to be a glorious day. The adjutant raised his wrist, then, turning to Hitler, tapped his watch. It read 5.35.

From nearby came the sound of guns, drowning the birds. And then, wave on wave, the planes!

As dawn breaks on 10 May, 2,760,000 German troops swarm into Holland, Belgium and France. Facing them are 3,740,000 Allied troops. The Allies had more and better tanks than the Germans: 3600 against 2574.

DAWN ON BELGIUM

Dressing up German soldiers in Dutch uniforms was Hitler's personal master-touch for the attack on Holland. For Belgium, too, he had arranged an opening gambit in the dawn on 10 May. It hit the defenders of a place called Eben Emael like a thunderbolt.

Pre-war Belgium, like France, had put her trust in defence and had not built up military forces that might provoke her dangerous eastern neighbour, Germany. God had given her the Ardennes Forest and the Dutch frontier, hard work had raised a chain of fortresses—none better placed or better armed than the fortress of **Eben Emael.** It was believed that both forest and fortress were proof against attack. The morning of 10 May would show otherwise.

Three miles south of Maastricht near the Dutch and Belgian frontier, the fortress of Eben Emael glowered from its hill top over the **Albert Canal** There was a sheer drop to the northeast. There was a sheer drop to the northwest. To the south, the land was laced with anti-tank ditches. The firepower from the hill top was formidable—rotating cupolas carried 75mm and 120mm guns.

Beneath the hill 1200 men could live, if necessary cut off from the world. Nearly five miles of tunnel connected the blockhouses, underground barracks, generators, washrooms, hospital and ammunition stores . . . .

There were three good reasons why Eben Emael had to be wiped out, and, in one decisive stroke. First, if the Belgians held out here, the French might come up to join them—and dangerously delay the 'sweep of the scythe' from the south, on which the invasion hinged. Second, with Eben Emael's guns blazing, German tanks would get no further than the wrong side of the Albert Canal—the defenders would have plenty of time to blow the bridges. Third, an attack on Eben Emael could fool the Allies that the main thrust was coming here—while the real onslaught continued to pour through the forest tracks of the Ardennes.

At 5.20am on 10 May 1940, nine DFS 230 'attack gliders' came in to land on the top of the Belgian fortress of Eben Emael. Towed from Cologne by Junkers 52s, they carried 55 German paratroopers whose first task was to destroy the fort's guns.

But how could the attack be mounted? The concrete of Eben Emael would shrug off bombs. Its guns would smash any frontal attack. Its cliffs would take care of anyone attempting to scale them. German munition experts had lately developed an explosive that would blow a hole through any concrete and steel fortification known to man—and certainly cause havoc in Belgium's star fortress—the problem was that this charge could not be dropped from the sky. Each one had to be placed carefully in position, fused and detonated by two men. This weapon, the **'hollow charge'**, was one of the best guarded secrets in Germany—and Hitler felt he had found the way to use it against Eben Emael.

It had been on 27 October 1939 that Hitler had unrolled the map for his airborne forces commander Major General Kurt Student and said: 'I have a job for you. I want to know if you can do it. The Belgians have a fort here. Do you know it?'

'Yes, my Fuhrer,' said Student. 'I know it well. It is a tremendous fortification.'

'The top is like a large grassy field,' said Hitler. He continued: 'I have read something of your work with gliders, General Student. I know you have personally flown the attack glider in tests . . . I think some of your attack gliders could land on the top of Fort Eben Emael and your men could storm these works. Is that possible?'

Student wanted a day to think about it. When

he came back it was with only one condition. The attack would have to be made in daylight, or at least the first light of dawn.

'Good. It will be done your way,' said Hitler.

His generals had pressed for a night attack, to launch the invasion of the West. But from now on the timing of the entire onslaught would be geared to the needs of the 85 men who were destined to land on the daunting 'grassy field' of Eben Emael.

In the days when the victors of World War 1 had kept tight rein on Germany's strength in the air, none had objected to the development of German gliders. There had seemed no threat in these graceful, sporting devices. No one had minded when German aviators of the 1930s carried home cups for their skills in soaring and aerobatics. No one objected to the Germans improving gliders as a means of studying the weather. And almost no one would care that General Student was secretly developing a **DFS 230** 'Attack Glider', or that famous soaring champion Hanna Reitsch was test-flying the experimental model, or that Hitler consulted regularly on its progress.

Assault Force Granite had had its final orders for the attack on Eben Emael on 3 November. The 500 paratroopers not destined for the attack on Holland were all involved. They trained with the threat of a death penalty over them if they revealed the secret to anyone. The new explosive worked well when tested on fortifications in Czechoslovakia's Sudetenland.

At 4.30am German time, 3.30am Belgian time, on 10 May—with 500 of the fort's 1200 defenders in their beds at their billets in the nearby village of Woncke—the 44 Junker 52s of the Koch Storm Detachment took off from two airfields in Cologne. Eleven of them towed the gliders destined for the top of the fort. The rest were packed with the paratroopers whose target would be the bridges below.

The timing had been calculated to the minute. The gliders would be released at 5850ft and float silently to land at 5.25am. Five minutes later the invasion itself would roll over the frontier.

It was 5.05am when the watchers from the fort first glimpsed the strange craft swooping toward them. There had been no warning of attack. No guard between here and the frontier had seen the silent wings coming in over the lark song of dawn. The guards on the fort stared. One gabbled into the phone to his comrades below: 'There are airplanes overhead! Their engines have stopped! They're standing almost motionless in the air!'

Not a shot was fired until 5.20—by then nine of the 11 gliders were coming in to land (two were off target). Battle was now joined. There were 55 men against 700. And among the Germans missing was their CO First Lieutenant Rudolf **Witzig** (his tow rope had broken and he would not arrive for three hours).

The attackers jumped out, hurtled across the expanse of the hill top. There were few wire entanglements, no mines to delay them.

First targets were the gun casements facing north towards the vital bridges. Time was lost blowing up gun emplacements that showed up well on reconnaissance maps—but now proved to be dummies. Then the paratroops began placing their hollow charges on the real steel domes as the Belgians below struggled frantically into position.

The massive explosions began to echo through the tunnels, filling liftshafts with evil smoke. German flamethrowers ripped their deadly path through gun apertures. At one point, when a massive hollow charge failed to damage a dome, explosive charges were stuffed down the very throats of the fort's guns. To deal with gun emplacements on the sheer cliffs, the commandos let charges down on lines.

Down below, rumour had it that thousands of Germans were swarming over the fort. It was a rumour that flourished above ground too. The Junkers 52s had flown back to Cologne to pick up their second cargo. The paratroopers that next pitched out of the skies 25 miles to the west of the canal, were even more of a surprise—and a surprise of a different kind—than the first arrivals. They exploded on landing!

Close inspection would have revealed them as straw and explosive dummies, and the sound of battle to be no more than the charges detonating. But few locals stayed to watch. The word was soon about that Germany was invading in strength, north of the Ardennes.

With Eben Emael in the final throes of takeover, a second and equally important battle was underway. Hitler needed to gain the bridges on the canal. Suddenly awoken by this shock aggression, the Belgian troops managed to get to the bridge at Kanne and blow it before the Germans got there. The German's advanced forces won the bridges instead at Vroenhoven and Veldewezelt. The way was opened for 4th Panzer Division to lead Colonel General Walther Reichenau's Sixth Army into Belgium—and overhead an air armada followed.

There was a wall of black crosses in the sky above the German frontier—the Luftwaffe were patrolling against any bold reconnaissance plane that at this final hour might choose to see what was going on behind the forest. It would have been a heart-stopping sight.

From the air it looked like a 100-mile traffic jam, rolling back through the valleys, its tail still on the east bank of the Rhine as the sun rose. On the ground, Colonel General Ewald von **Kleist's** Panzergruppe could be seen to be in no kind of jam at all. Fifteen hundred tanks were on the move. Some had been rolling much of the night, unlit, the drivers straining to pick out the route ahead.

There was no time wasted on mechanical failures. Casualties were simply shoved off the road. At the far end of the column the infantry, still two day's march from the frontier, were listening to the announcements of today's sporting events while, at the front, General Heinz Guderian's 1st Panzer Division rolled up to the Luxembourg frontier.

They were not the first Germans to cross it recently. Strangely enough, in the last few days a number of 'tourists' had come from Germany, by bicycle and motor cycle to enjoy the Luxembourg spring. Now, with the dawn, these **Abwehr** agents had risen to cut key communications.

For the final assault on Eben Emael German sappers (inset) came in rubber dinghies. After the battle, war weary German troops relax with Belgian prisoners outside the bullet scarred fortress.

War Notes

BELGIUM

ABWEHR: a special commando division of this German intelligence organization called the Brandenburgers shared their duties on the morning of 10 May with the Battalion for Special Tasks. This detachment attempted to secure all the bridges on the Maas canal east of Eben Emael. One group disguised as German deserters in civilian clothing were escorted by bogus Dutch Military Policemen over the Heumann lockbridge and took it by surprise.

ALBERT CANAL: completed in June 1939, a 79-mile canal running between Antwerp and Liège. Constituted a good defensive line compared with the weakly held frontier facing Holland. There are 3 principal bridges on the canal—at Vroedhaven, Veldwezelt and Kanne. These were prime targets for the German invasion forces and the Allied defence. At Fort Eben Emael the canal acted almost as a moat making advances from the east particularly difficult.

DFS 230: German assault glider. This was the major contribution of the German Research Institute for Gliding to Germany's WW2 armoury. The 4630lb glider had a rectangular-section, fabric-covered steel-tube 36ft fuselage with a tapering 72ft wingspan covered in plywood and fabric strengthened in metal struts. It could carry a maximum 600lb of freight at up to 180mph as well as pilot and 9 troops with equipment. After first deliveries in Oct 1939 its operational debut was at Eben Emael on the morning of 10 May 1940.

EBEN EMAEL: Belgian fortress completed in 1935 as the northernmost fortress of Liège. Regarded as impregnable, the fortress measured 975yd N-S and 758yd W-E. The outer area comprised reinforced concrete walls surrounded by barbed wire, interspersed triangular steel anti-tank obstacles, and minefields. Inside, the fortifications were built on 3 levels holding a complex of artillery (2 × 120mm, 13 × 75mm guns, 3 × 45mm anti-tank guns) and infantry installations.

HOLLOW CHARGE: of the 2.5 tons of explosives used on the fortress at Eben Emael, most were the new hollow charges, tested at Gleiwitz in Poland. Charges of 27.5lb were capable of penetrating steel armour 5-6in thick. The larger 115lb charges carried in two parts in the shape of hemispheres could penetrate installations 10in thick. Even where thicker armour was employed, troops within exploded casements could be incapacitated by the splinters caused by these charges. The hollow charges were placed on 7 cupolas at Eben Emael and 5 were totally successful. The Germans kept this weapon secret. A 1941 US magazine cited a Dutch captain's story that pre-war saboteurs planted the explosives.

LUXEMBOURG: Grand Duchy, population under 300,000 in 1940, situated SE of Brussels with an area of 999 sq miles. Previously under German occupation 1914-18 it was again taken by Kleist on 10 May 1940. The 'army' of 400 infantrymen and 12 cavalrymen offered little resistance. To aid the army, the nominally neutral citizens mounted 'passive defence'—erecting barbed wire barricades on frontier roads, closing bridges along their river border with Germany. Grand Duke Jean and family escaped.

WITZIG, First Lieutenant Rudolf: b. 1916 Westphalia. Joined the Luftwaffe as a professional officer in 1935. Promoted in 1939 to 1st Lieutenant and CO of the engineer detachment of the Parachute Infantry Battalion in which role he led the attack on Eben Emael. He missed the first 3 hours of the attack as the tow rope on his glider broke. Sergeant Major Wenzel took charge in his absence. Awarded one of the 9 Knight's Crosses won by the attackers who were decorated by Hitler.

Luxembourg did not put up an epic resistance. It needed only a few planks to repair an attempt to blow up a frontier bridge at Sauer. The Germans brought specially designed wooden ramps with which to bridge the tank obstacles on the way. At the cost of six gendarmes and one soldier wounded, the conquest of Luxembourg was over by 9am—by which hour Guderian was across the other side of the country and ready for Belgium. En route, many farmers continued to work their fields as the tanks thundered past.

By now the news of the invasion was being digested in Brussels, Paris and London. In Belgium's capital, the population had woken to air raid sirens at 5.17am. The bombs began to fall a few minutes later.

Belgium's Foreign Minister Paul Spaak opened the sealed orders he had been given for just such an occasion. They instructed him to call on France and Britain for aid. He did so. Belgium's neutrality was over.

The news of the invasion reached Winston

Churchill by 6am, over a breakfast of eggs and bacon and the first cigar of the day. He took it calmly. At the first Cabinet meeting of the day he would astound those anxious to discuss events on the Continent. He had a report to make on a new kind of anti-aircraft fuse—and insisted on making it. 'We are impossible' grumbled General Sir Edmund Ironside at the War Office.

But Churchill's logic was simple. Next day he would see no reason for a Cabinet meeting at all. 'I do not think there is any necessity,' he explained 'as the armies and other services are fighting in accordance with prearranged plans.'

Those plans rested in Paris on the morning of the 10th. They were the same plans that had been drawn up, signed and settled the previous autumn. Now, as the sun came up over Europe, with the world's most powerful force poised for attack the western Allies went into action to save Belgium.

'It was wonderful,' Hitler would say that day. 'When the news came through that the enemy were moving forward along the whole front I could have wept for joy: they had fallen into the trap.'

The battle at Eben Emael ended at about noon on 11 May. The Belgians stayed below—much encouraged to do so by the 220lb charges that the paratroops spent the afternoon of the 10th dropping down the ascent shafts. Nevertheless, for the Germans the night of 10-11 May was an anxious one, as they waited a counter-attack. The sight of the first rubber dinghy floating across the ditch below the fort, at 7am on 11 May, was a welcome sight. The 51st Engineer Battalion was coming to the paratroops' support.

The last guns ceased to fire from Eben Emael. Battered, blinking in the sunlight, the Belgians came up from below. Astonishingly, the fortress had fallen at a cost of only 23 Belgian lives. And of the 85 paratroops who had flown in to take it, no more than six had perished.

It was a victory for speed and daring over a nation ill prepared for Hitler's new war. In the weeks to come the same lesson would be learned throughout the rest of Belgium.

A dead horse with its cart still tethered lies on the roadside, the victim of an air attack (inset). A creeping barrage preludes an attack by German infantrymen, below.

INTO THE TRAP

'I could have wept for joy; they'd fallen into the trap . . . There, I knew just what I was doing.'

Adolf Hitler, 10 May

General Gamelin paced his chateau headquarters, alternately smiling broadly then humming. The long and glorious career that had ended the previous night with his resignation was now in full flight again. He was back in the job of Commander-in-Chief, with a conciliatory note from premier Reynaud in his pocket. 'Mon General,' it began, 'the battle is engaged. Only one thing matters; to win it.'

Gamelin telephoned General Georges, C-in-C of the NE Front to tell him that, at last, the Belgians had asked for help. It was 6.30am on the morning of the 10th. The war was one hour old. 'Well, General, is it the Dyle Operation?' asked Georges. 'Since the Belgians are calling on us, do you see what else we can do?' 'Obviously not.' agreed Georges.

The Dyle Operation, Plan D, sent the first of the Allies' three army groups into action, hastening eastwards into Belgium to what premier Reynaud described as 'the age-old battlefield of the Flanders plain', in his morning broadcast to the French nation. 'Confronting us, rushing at us, is the age-old invader.'

It would be some time before the truth dawned that the age-old invader was up to something entirely different.

It was the best of the **French armies,** the Seventh and the First, that raced into the Belgian plains north of Namur. But the staff officers, first to arrive at the River Dyle that morning, did not like what they found. Neutral Belgium had not dared share its defence plans with the Allies for fear of provoking Germany. But the Allies had presumed the Belgians had done *something* useful to defend the Dyle. Now all they found was an empty plain, its only protection a series of trestles connected by coils of barbed wire and some anti-tank minefields—on the wrong side of the river.

The decline in good relations between the Allies and the Belgians began. It would dive even lower when Belgian troops opened fire on Major-General Bernard Montgomery's men next day, believing them to be German parachutists, and when King Leopold complained to Churchill's representative, Sir Roger Keyes, that British soldiers were cluttering the roads of Brussels.

At least the advance to the Dyle went with the smooth efficiency its planners had hoped for. It was strangely tranquil. 'It was hard to believe,' wrote Lieutenant-General Alan Brooke later, 'on a glorious spring day, with all nature looking its best, that we were taking the first steps towards one of the greatest battles of history.' Some, already, found the tranquillity eerie. Could the Luftwaffe deliberately be leaving them alone as they marched northeast to the expected invasion?

South of the crack French armies, the Second and Ninth Armies were taking up their positions. General André **Corap's** Ninth Army's task was to hold the twisting frontier along the River Meuse. He had only 9½ divisions for the task, and only two were classified as regular. The rest were 'crocos'—recruits from Brittany, Normandy and the Loire, aged 40 years and more. It had been this army that had so appalled Alan Brooke—'Seldom have I seen anything more slovenly and badly turned out. Men unshaven, horses ungroomed . . . ' One of their own commanders had described them as 'flabby and heavy'. General Charles **Huntziger's** Second Army, on Corap's right, was no more impressive. Most of the men were untrained reservists.

But, according to Plan D, these men would see little of the action. Between them and the enemy lay the impenetrable Ardennes.

It was through the grassy tracks of the Ardennes that the Belgian Chasseurs were already retreating, detonating bridges as they went, but retreating as their orders demanded.

Now the cavalry of the Ninth trotted into the Ardennes. There had been a rapturous reception when they first crossed the Belgian border, 'French flags and garlands were hung from all the windows', a French lieutenant remembered.

Closer to the frontier the mood changed. Empty streets and shuttered houses marked the route through the villages. The men stopped singing.

The first to die was a cavalryman of Huntziger's Second Army, out on reconnaissance. At 9am, riding across a field of clover near Arlon, he came upon an amazing sight—Guderian's 10th Panzer Division. 'They look at us in astonishment,' a German rifleman remembered. 'We ourselves don't exactly look at them cheerfully. Are we to shoot? Major Föst gives the order to fire . . . one of the French somersaults in the clover, the first dead man, who looks completely white. Dead! Something cold grips us round the heart. We will have to get used to that yet.'

The three German armoured columns now churning, nose to tail, towards the Meuse and Sedan added up to the greatest concentration of armour yet seen. General Heinz Guderian's three panzer divisions were aimed at Sedan itself. Close behind on the right came General Georg-Hans Reinhardt's pair of panzer divisions pointing at Mézières, west of Sedan. On their right was General Hermann Hoth's similar force and motorized division making for Dinant on the Meuse in Belgium. Between them they had 2445 tanks. Behind them they had three motorized infantry divisions with another 37 on foot.

So far, the generals had to admit, Hitler had been proved right. The forest roads were passable—but they scanned the skies with foreboding. Allied air attack could wreak havoc on their dense vehicle columns. Anti-tank guns hidden in the wooded hills ahead could do the same. And when they finally got to the Meuse, they feared massive French resistance.

At their joint HQ, the Allied air chiefs, General François d'**Astier** and Air Marshal Arthur Barratt, waited out the first morning of the attack, hoping in vain for permission to strike at the panzers rolling through the Ardennes. Photo-recce Spitfires had brought back pictures as early as 6-7 May. But Gamelin would have none of it. There were Belgian villagers in the Ardennes. People could get hurt. Gamelin—who had happily said in 1938 'We have no planes? Then we will make war without them'—still believed the war could be kept on the ground. In any case, whatever was coming out of the woods in the Ardennes held little which was of interest to him at this stage.

'I was above all preoccupied with Holland' he admitted in his memoirs later. His colleague, Georges, shared the C-in-C's talent for obstinacy. Reports from General d'Astier rained in on him. There is 'a strong concentration of German motorized vehicles' he was told on the 11th. 'The enemy is carrying out a very serious movement towards the Meuse.' On the night of the 12th, news arrived that the Germans were driving through the Ardennes 'with their headlights full on'. Georges ignored it. The Ardennes did not figure in Plan D.

Monitoring the unhindered progress of the panzers, back in OKW Operations Department, Colonel Bernhard von Lossberg was one among many who could scarcely believe in the good luck so far. 'It looks as though our enemy is doing exactly what we hoped he would do!' he commented. 'They have poured into Belgium and are falling into the trap' agreed Colonel Adolf **Heusinger.** There was more good luck to come.

By the afternoon of the 12th, all three German armoured columns had reached the Meuse, and were spread out on an 80-mile front from Dinant to Sedan. They had covered 75 miles in three days, 24 hours ahead of schedule. The French cavalry had retreated behind the Meuse and had blown up all bridges across it except at Mézières.

In Sedan, the French troops looked round them at the narrow streets. To their horror they found that Sedan lacked any defences at all. 'This town appears to have been abandoned,' admitted Gamelin, 'though it should have been defended at all costs.'

The French knew, too, that the formidable looking defences down on the Meuse nearby were not complete. So did the Germans.

To Colonel Günther Blumentritt it was the second miracle of the invasion. In the exalted company of Colonel-Generals Ewald von Kleist and Rundstedt he drove to look at the river. 'Here and there a few French machine-guns were firing from small, ludicrous, concrete emplacements . . . the dreaded Meuse position was almost non-existent, and only weakly defended. Then the panzer-race across the river began.'

Kleist chose a stretch of the river $1\frac{1}{2}$ miles long, just west of Sedan, for the crossing at 4pm on 13 May.

By now the French knew plainly what they were in for. Since early morning, the officers at GQG had been looking gloomily at a map on which Captain André Beaufre had marked the line of Germany's main attack with a wax crayon.

The appalling truth was that the Allies—who had started two days earlier with more men in uniform than Germany, more guns and only slightly fewer tanks—had been manoeuvred into a position in which the best of Germany's forces were lined up against the worst of the Allied defenders.

Tanks of Guderian's 19th Panzer Corps roll over the vital bridge at Sedan. The way is now open for the infantry to strike into the heartland of France. With the capture of Sedan thousands of French prisoners (inset) are taken.

'We are not fighting for this land we are swamping it.'

Sapper Lt. Karl Mende

Under the bombardment that von Kleist unleashed at 11am on the morning of 13 May, as preface to his river crossing, those defenders—the 'crocos' of Corap's 61st Infantry and 102nd Garrison Divisions, and Huntziger's 55th and 71st Infantry—now went to pieces. On the eve of battle their corps commander had summed them up as 'a sector incompletely organized. Troops insufficient in number, very badly armed against tanks and planes, of rudimentary training and uncertain toughness.'

No one had told those men about the 100 Stukas that came plummetting, screaming, out of the sky. 'The French are not used to this form of attack' wrote observer Jacques Benoist-Méchin. 'The Stukas made a diabolical noise as they dived . . . the soldier had the impression the plane was about to land on *him*.'

Paralyzed, the French stopped firing and kept their heads down. The air and artillery bombardment lasted five hours, then at 4pm, the first inflatable dinghies began to come across the river.

By the end of the afternoon enough men were across to hold a bridgehead round Sedan, four miles wide and four miles deep. But they were only men. The task of building pontoon bridges and getting the panzers across was still to come. The French, in Sedan, in theory still held the upper hand; could have struck back.

But at 6pm the cry went up 'enemy tanks', and total rout ensued. General Lafontaine's 55th Infantry suddenly ceased to exist. The division's Parisian soldiers threw down their rifles and followed their officers in a dash down the road to get out of the hell. It was a 'phenomenon of collective panic' said one French chronicler. There *were* tanks on the road—French, coming up in support!

As dusk turned into night in France, the full horror of what was happening down on the Meuse finally sank into the minds of the nation's high command. The breakthrough was not confined to

Sedan. The Germans were coming across at two other points, north and south of Houx. In the south, Major General Erwin Rommel's men were building a pontoon bridge at Bouvignes.

France's General Georges was giving the Ardennes front his whole attention now. He summoned Captain Beaufre to his HQ in the small hours of 14 May. 'All was dark,' recalled Beaufre 'except this room which was barely lit . . . The atmosphere was that of a family in which there has just been a death. Georges got up quickly and came to Doumenc. He was terribly pale. "Our front has been broken at Sedan! There has been a collapse." He flung himself into a chair and burst into tears. He was the first man I had seen weep in this campaign. Alas, there were to be others.'

When day broke on 14 May the Germans were not only in control of the Meuse, but ready to push north, to the Channel. The sweep of the scythe, designed to cut up and cut off the troops in the north, began to swish through another sunny, spring day. Rommel's men had a fine view from their tanks of the total confusion their attack through the Ardennes had created. 'On the way,' wrote Rommel, 'the panzer division passed numerous guns and vehicles belonging to a French unit whose men threw themselves flat at our approach.

'The people in the houses were rudely awakened by the din of our tanks, the clatter and roar of trucks and engines. Troops lay bivouacked by the road . . . civilians and French troops, their faces distorted with terror, lay huddled in the ditches alongside hedges and in every hollow beside the road.'

As the motorized Blitzkrieg thrusts deeper into France, anti-aircraft guns at the ready, Erwin Rommel, a new panzer leader, scans the battle.

Terrified by the screaming Stuka raids on towns and villages, millions of refugees took to the road.

Refugees now began to flood through Western Europe. First came the cars, some chauffeur driven, then flocks of young boys and old men on bicycles. Then the pathetic handcarts, the distraught families. Their flight south out of Belgium and Holland took them into the most dangerous place imaginable—the roads. Had they stayed in their farms and cottages the Blitzkrieg would have rolled past them. As it was, their columns were easy targets for the howling Stukas; fine obstacles for the Allied troops struggling to get to the Front. At the height of the exodus there were 10 million French, Dutch and Belgian civilians on the roads.

Arrival of the refugees in Paris brought home to the citizens, still sipping their aperitifs in the open-air cafés, that things could be going less well than their newspapers claimed. Shocked, Parisians watched a train draw into the Gare de l'Est. 'It came slowly to a halt along the platform. People were amazed to see no one get out. Exhausted from their sudden uprooting, from the danger and the journey, the poor devils only gradually recovered from their torpor . . . the children's drawn faces made them look like old men and women.'

By the 14th, the same state of shock could be read in the eyes of the nation's leaders. Georges seemed to have lost any sense of direction. When Huntziger asked him whether the armies should now cover the Maginot Line or Paris he replied 'Do as you think best'. When pressed to ask for British bombers to blast the German positions on the Meuse, he refused. That day 100 French and 67 British planes went down in flames trying to do the job.

In the afternoon, the enormity of what was going on finally got home to Reynaud in Paris. He telephoned his old enemy, Daladier, the War Minister, demanding to know what counter-measures Gamelin was going to produce. 'He has none' said Daladier. Reynaud reeled. It looked as if the elderly Gamelin had turned out to be exactly the disaster he had feared. Urgently, he picked up the phone and demanded a line to London.

Churchill, in London, was getting to grips with his new job as Prime Minister. Juggling the 60 portfolios involved in the British Government had been a full time task. And on top of this paperwork came the flood of dramatic news from Belgium, France and Holland. There still seemed no option but to leave events to the professionals.

Even when Reynaud came on the line in person, on the dawn of the 15th, Churchill found it hard to believe things could be as bad as the French premier claimed. 'We are beaten' said Reynaud flatly. 'We have lost the battle. The front is broken near Sedan. The tanks are pouring through.'

'The French Army is finished'

'Surely it can't have happened so soon?' said Winston. Reynaud must be panicking. After five or six days an armoured invasion would have to halt for supplies, Churchill explained. That would be the time to counter-attack. That was how it had been in 1918. Winston had 'learned all this at the time from the lips of Marshal Foch himself'.

Later, he admitted how out of touch he had become with technological progress. These tanks were different. They kept on coming, refuelling from simple jerrycans, while the French tanks ground to a halt awaiting their special tankers for new supplies.

Jubilant, Rommel was now hurtling along, at the head of his division. He was through the Maginot Line. 'Driving deep into enemy territory. It was not just a beautiful dream. It was reality.' The tanks blazed on, day and night, firing as they went. 'We'll do it like the navy' ordered Rommel. 'Fire salvoes to port and starboard.' Columns of French troops, seeing the juggernauts roaring down the road towards them, stood in bemused terror, as Rommel yelled at them to throw down their arms as he rushed by. Most did.

Gamelin phoned Daladier. A column of tanks had broken through towards Laon. Paris was wide open to attack. 'You must counter-attack at once,' roared Daladier. 'What with?' asked Gamelin bleakly. 'I don't have any reserves.' 'Then the French Army is finished?' asked Daladier. 'It's finished.' said his Commander-in-Chief.

The news had also arrived, that black 15 May, that Holland had gone under. The Seventh Army, the best and most mobile, had been wasted in the north. No one dared to speak to Gamelin now, as he paced his HQ at Vincennes.

War Notes

FRANCE

ASTIER de la VIGERIE, Baron Francois Pierre Raoul d': French airforce officer, b. 1886. Educated St Cyr military academy. By 1935 head of Fighter Command. In 1937 CO 4th Air District and in 1939 became director of training and airforce representative at the Centre of Defence Studies. After war was declared he took charge of the airforce on the NE front.

CORAP, André Georges: French general, b. 1878. Educated St Cyr military academy. Joined Algerian Infantry and served at Touat and Gourara in N. Africa. With Algerian Division in Morocco 1907-10. Promoted Captain 1910, took part in march on Fez 1911 and Marrakesh 1912. Served as staff officer with 2nd Army and later 38th Division, 1914-18, under Marshals Foch and Pétain (who had taught him at military school). Staff officer to generals Buat and Debeney 1919-24. Promoted to full Colonel and returned to Morocco to command 3rd Brigade of Moroccan Div, capturing Abd-el-Krim to end the Riff War 1926. Promoted Brigadier 1929, stationed at Toulon. In 1934 took command of Algerian Div with rank of Major-General. C-in-C Morocco 1935, promoted Lt-General. Recalled to France 1936, given command of 2nd Military District. General Jan 1940 in command of 9th Army.

FRENCH ARMIES: 1st (Gen Georges Blanchard) consisted of 4 infantry divisions, 2 light mechanized divs and 2 motorized infantry divs. Along with 2nd and 9th Armies, it was part of the 1st Army Group under Gen Gaston Billotte which extended from Maulde in Belgium to the western end of the Maginot Line. 2nd (Gen Huntziger) comprised 5 infantry divs and 2 cavalry divs. 7th (Gen Giraud) comprised 4 infantry divs, 1 light mechanized div and 2 motorized infantry divs. The 7th were the elite of the French Army and were deployed between Dunkirk and Bailleul in the N. 9th (Gen Corap) comprised 5 infantry divs, 1 motorized infantry div and 2 cavalry divs.

HEUSINGER, Adolf Ernst: German soldier, b. 1897 son of a headmaster. Educated at secondary schools of Holzminden and Helmstedt. Joined 96th Infantry Div as 2nd Lieutenant (1915) and saw action in France. Captured by British 1918. Released 1919. 1st Lieutenant 1925, served Ministry of Reichswehr. Captain 1932, attached to General Staff. Served as major in Army High Command (OKH) from 1936. Lt-Colonel 1938, Colonel, 1940.

HUNTZIGER, Charles Léon Clement: French general, b. 1880. Educated St Cyr and l'Ecole Superieure de Guerre. From 1900 served in Madagascar, Senegal and the Sudan with 2nd Colonial Infantry. Served in Europe 1914-18. Gallantly resisted superior German forces near Mantez, Dec 1914. Won Croix de Guerre. Major 1916. Served Ministry of War 1922-4 as Lt-Colonel. In 1924 took command of army of occupation in China. Promoted Brigadier 1928. CO French troops in Near East 1934 with rank of Major-General. In 1940, with rank of full general, commanded the French 2nd Army. Described as 'lean, unsmiling and poker-faced', he was not well disposed towards the British, having come into conflict with them several times during his service in the colonies. But he liked the Germans less. Tried to raise his army's morale with a fortnightly newsletter.

At seven in the evening Reynaud 'phoned Churchill again. 'The route to Paris is open. Please send all the troops and planes you can.' Churchill could make no sense of it. He had spoken with Georges, his old friend, earlier, and had been assured that the breach at Sedan was 'being plugged'. The request for planes was a tricky one. There was no point in hurling vital machines into the French bonfire—they could be needed soon enough to defend Britain herself. Plainly the French were going to pieces—the only troops who seemed to be holding their ground were the BEF on the Louvain-Wavre line. Churchill told Reynaud he would visit Paris next day to find out what was going on.

The next day was worse.

Refugees poured southwards

Before the day was over, German armoured units would smash through the frontier at Maubeuge, Rommel's 7th Panzers would reach Avesnes, Reinhardt's armoured corps would reach the Oise. 'Hopeless, gaunt, dazed with fatigue' the French Ninth Army was disintegrating, straggling back towards Paris. A *New York Times* correspondent found remnants of it, 'as they sat on their horse-drawn carts in their dirty uniforms: they did not look like soldiers but like gypsies'. Shattered, soldiers flinched at the sight of an airplane. Few had kept their rifles.

The floodgates had opened for the refugees again. Belgium was emptying southwards. In Paris waves of panic swept the city. Taxis and buses became thin on the ground as Parisians began to pack up and leave. There was a run on walking shoes in the Galeries Lafayette. Hélène de Portes was just one of the people packing.

Gamelin had completely given up now. In the small hours of the morning of 16 May he had warned Reynaud that he couldn't guarantee Paris after nightfall; advised the Government to get ready to flee Paris.

Reynaud said nothing to raise anyone's spirits when he addressed a near hysterical Chamber of Deputies in the afternoon. He hinted that Gamelin faced the sack. 'Wishful thinking I call it' said Britain's *Manchester Guardian* correspondent.

Winston Churchill arrived at this dismal scene at 5.30pm. 'From the moment we got out of the Flamingo,' he remembered, 'it was obvious that the situation was incomparably worse than we had imagined.' At the Quai d'Orsay he joined Reynaud, Daladier and Gamelin round a map pinned onto a student's easel. Through the window, Churchill could see the bonfires in the gardens of the Quai d'Orsay, fed by aged employees bringing wheel-barrow-loads of government archives to the flames.

When Gamelin had finished his lecture, there was a silence. Churchill broke it. 'I then asked: "Where is the strategic reserve?" and, breaking into French, which I used indifferently (in every sense): "Ou est la masse de manoeuver?" '

Gamelin turned to him, shook his head and shrugged. 'Aucune' he said. 'No strategic reserve?' repeated Churchill.

There was another silence. Then from the gardens a dull thud. The French were throwing bundles of documents from the upper windows now. Churchill lit a cigar. He looked, to Baudouin, like a smoke-crowned volcano.

FALL OF HOLLAND

There were two views of how things would go if Hitler invaded Holland—the Dutch view, and Hitler's. Neither was to prove correct.

It would take but the press of a button, the Dutch believed, to transform their low and level land into a defender's paradise—'Fortress Holland' was the catchphrase. The dykes would open, the tulip fields be drowned by exactly calculated floods. North of the great rivers of the Maas (Meuse) and Waal, on the safe side of dynamited bridges, even the poorly equipped army could halt the **German forces.** Water was Holland's secret weapon. What matter if the **Dutch forces** had no tanks, a scant 104 airplanes, and only notional anti-aircraft artillery?

In Hitler's view, the conquest of Holland would take only one day. By the end of that day he hoped to have the Dutch Royal Family, the top civil and military leaders captive and a signed capitulation on the table.

Some people had been inclined to take the curious message from Colonel G. Sas in Berlin

> 'The paratroopers are so valuable for me that I am only going to use them if it's worthwhile. I am not going to reveal the secret of the new weapon prematurely.'
>
> Adolf Hitler

lightly, but not Prince **Bernhard** of the Netherlands. It was his decision that the Royal Family should spend the night of 9 May in the air raid shelters. It was plain that the invasion was imminent. Army leave had been cancelled since 7 May. Soldiers poured into the central 'Fortress' area, ready for the fray.

All speculation ended at 3am on 10 May, with the arrival of a crisply worded memorandum from Berlin. 'To forestall a projected Anglo-French action' it read, Germany would have to invade Holland. The roar of close on 1000 aircraft filled the sky shortly afterwards.

A new chapter in the history of warfare began that dawn over Holland. For the first time, success in battle would depend entirely on an airborne invasion. The Dutch had put their faith in Holland's oldest defences—the rivers and dykes. The Germans put theirs in the 4000 untested paratroopers of 7th Airborne Division. 'It was imperative that we should succeed,' said their commander, Major General Kurt **Student.** 'A failure by us would have led to the failure of the entire offensive.'

Nothing had prepared the Dutch for such a sight. One witness was Miss Rona Riccardo, an acrobatic dancer from England, engaged to a Dutch pilot. 'We saw the parachute troops drop. Some had boats, some bicycles. All had guns. We saw some racing along over the Maas bridge on their cycles. They were in Dutch uniforms, but you could tell they were foreigners because they stopped at every street corner and looked at the names of the road.'

The Dutch uniforms, a personal touch from Hitler, proved to be a master-stroke. Just before the invasion a large theft of Dutch uniforms was organized for this purpose. From now on, rumours would fly round Europe that the Nazis arrived in disguise—dressed as travelling salesmen, policemen, nuns, priests.

Planes blocked runways

The many parachutists who landed off target of the three airports round The Hague were glad enough of their uniforms as they hastened to the noise of battle.

The bombers had struck first at these airports. Then, the plan was, the paratroops would wipe out the remaining defenders. And then the planes would land to disgorge the troops.

One fact was missing from the scenario. The detailed maps on board the Junker 52s that descended to the airstrips of Valkenburg, Ypenburg and Ockenburg did not show that Valkenburg's runways were still under construction. The pilots discovered this as their planes sank into soft earth—safely enough, but with no chance of lifting off to fetch the second wave. They ran into trouble at the other two airports as well. The Dutch fought back—smashing enough planes to block the runways and prevent further landings.

The smoke now rising from Holland's airfields in the early morning sun suggested that, so far, the score was one-all.

But elsewhere, the invasion was going like a dream. At Rotterdam, the Gt Willems bridge spans the River Maas. It was high on the list for dynamiting if necessary. But none of its defenders guessed the battle would begin with the arrival of six Heinkel 59 bi-planes from the east, another six from the west, each equipped with floats that landed them on the water with a splash that frightened not only the nesting wildfowl. In these aircraft at take-off were 120 men, but only 70 hit the water. The rest floated down on parachutes as the planes in the river opened their hatches to let loose inflatable dinghies, into which men climbed to paddle to the shore. Workers crossing the bridge to the factories thought the seaplanes were English. The invaders were helped up the bank.

Home-grown traitors

The Dutch stared. They were staring still as German reinforcements arrived—by tram. This kind of warfare was not in any textbook.

It was from such surprises that the great Fifth Column myth began. Surely, people in free Europe would argue, no one can conduct such warfare

78,000 people were made homeless and 980 died in the fire that engulfed Rotterdam on 14 May after an air raid by 43 Heinkel bombers. The message to turn back had not been received.

without help from a hidden army of home-grown traitors.

There *were* Dutch traitors. It took only three Dutch Nazis, dressed as policemen, to march a bunch of 'captured' German prisoners of war onto the railway bridge at Gennep. Then captors and prisoners shot it out with the Dutch guards. In minutes, a German armoured train rolled into Holland over the bridge.

The bridges were a priority target in the invasion plan. The airborne troops would not have long to enjoy the advantage of surprise. While the paratroops fought for the airfields, and the Dutch Navy shelled them at the Willems Bridge from 100 yards, General Georg von **Küchler's** Eighteenth Army poured west across the captured bridges.

At The Hague, the German General Count von Sponeck's plans to press into the capital, seize the Royal Family and the war ministry were in trouble before the morning was out. Worse, the plans were even now being removed from a briefcase found aboard the shot-down plane in which General von Sponeck's staff now lay dead. The news stiffened the mood of the Dutch defenders. By nightfall, their infantry and artillery had recaptured the three airfields and rounded up 1200 paratroopers ready for dispatch to England as PoWs. It was heartening. So was the news that the Allies were coming to the rescue—General Henri Giraud's French Seventh Army was marching towards Breda and Tilburg, to defend the mouth of the Scheldt.

Meanwhile, in the thick of war, the Dutch civilians got on with everyday life. A *Times* reporter wrote of Rotterdam's first day of the war: 'People sit quietly outside the cafés enjoying their drinks, while a quarter of a mile away the machine-guns hammer away at intervals.' Even the German paratroops had come equipped with Dutch guilders with which to buy refreshments and souvenirs.

The air of unreality carried into the second day of the war, first day of the Whitsun weekend.

Rotterdam was a fiery nightmare

Von Küchler's army sped on through Holland. Giraud's French army did not. The tanks were the problem—they were due to be freighted in by train. Lacking armour, anti-aircraft and anti-tank guns, Giraud ran full tilt into 9th Panzer Division and a hail of Luftwaffe bombs. The plan of linking up with the Dutch was abandoned. The Dutch too were falling back into Fortress Holland. But the Germans chased through one of the main lines of defence of the fortress—the Grebbe-Peel line. As a German 'tourist' had noted previously, the guns here faced only one way—once across, the Germans were home and dry.

Rotterdam, encircled from the south, was becoming a fiery nightmare with three air forces battling it out overhead. But the bridges to it were still being held by the Dutch Marines. To the north at the port of Ijmuiden, the first ships of the Royal Navy were arriving. They had a twin task to perform—the evacuation of the Dutch Royal Family, and of a vital cargo—the nation's bullion. In the end, this weekend, both cargoes went out together.

Fifth columnists were swarming everywhere now. One gang had the palace in The Hague under siege and were taking pot shots at anything that moved through the gates. Prince Bernhard grabbed a hunting rifle with a telescopic lens and fired back. A sniper tumbled. Encouraged, the Prince took aim at passing aircraft.

It took until Sunday afternoon, the 13th, to make the break out of the palace for the coast. By then it looked as if the fall of Fortress Holland could be imminent. Even so, Queen Wilhelmina insisted on staying. A tough, dumpy little figure in the Queen Victoria mould, Wilhelmina was German-born, but ready now to die fighting Germans.

She gave Prince Bernhard her ultimatum. He must leave with his wife Princess Juliana and their children. And if anything happened to her daughter Juliana, she would shoot herself. A steel-plated bank van slipped into the palace grounds. The Prince, Crown Princess and the children climbed in. Bernhard had not packed for the trip to England. 'I remember being a trifle worried

about having dinner at Buckingham Palace in a dirty shirt with no cufflinks' he recalled later. But he still expected to be back in Holland in a day. The children, Beatrix and Irene, perched themselves on the big boxes in the back of the van.

The crates were stacked with gold. Twelve lorries that went down the road along with the van were similarly packed. In a cardboard box, done up with string, on the passenger seat of the van lay the nation's Crown Jewels—'Worth more than £1.5 million' recalled Bernhard.

The convoy, strung out, took the back roads. It had no escort, to avoid German attention. Even so the normally short journey to Ijmuiden took three hours. German bullets spattered off the armour of the van. The roads were clogged with refugees.

At the port, the scene was ugly. The air was thick with snarling dog-fights. Refugees were brawling over small boats. Captain George Creasy of HMS *Codrington*, who had made a high speed dash from Scapa Flow to pick up the Royal party, was already an angry man, and had sacked the Dutch pilot detailed to bring him to anchor. Not until just before midnight did the Royal Family manage to get alongside *Codrington* on a ferry-boat—even then they were under intense air attack from German planes. The destroyer took the family aboard and made off for the open sea. They left with a bang—a German plane dropped a magnetic mine less than 100 yards away.

It took longer to get out the gold. The state bank had managed to hire two ships, the *Iris* and *Titus* from the Royal Netherlands Steamship Company for the emptying of its vaults. There had been some haggling over the going rate for the task. The bank offered 415,000 guilders to save Holland's 166 million guilders from German hands. The company wanted 500,000 for the trip. Now, as Sunday night ticked away at Ijmuiden, the crew of *Iris* were getting restive. Their wives and families were on shore. Bombs were tumbling out of the sky. Mines were sprinkling into the sea ahead. To stay here in harbour, with no explanation except to await orders was intolerable.

But their captain was the stocky, unshakable Klaas de Jong. He told his men that Holland needed this ship. To back up his words he made every man sign a paper pledging loyalty to Holland. Neither de Jong, nor the men on board, knew what cargo awaited loading. Finally, late at night, the cargo arrived. De Jong guessed what was in the boxes being so heavily manoeuvred down the sloping planks to the ships' three hatches. Confirmation came when a bank official asked him to sign on the dotted line for his cargo. The manifest listed it as 87 million guilders worth. Siren blasting, *Iris* took off across the North Sea for Tilbury in the Thames Estuary.

By Monday, Hitler was in an irritable mood. Holland had not fallen in the allotted day. Instead the Royal Family and Government had gone. Even indomitable Queen Wilhelmina had seen reason, rung up King George VI of England late at night and asked him to send a ship. The gold had gone.

And the German attack was still pinned at Rotterdam by Dutch defenders holding the north end of key bridges against the panzers now queued up to finish the job.

There was no room in the invasion schedule for such a delay. Hitler needed the armies still tied up in Holland, to finish the job in Belgium. Accordingly, on 14 May, he issued Directive No. 11: 'The power of resistance of the Dutch Army has proved to be stronger than anticipated. Political as well as military considerations require that this resistance be broken speedily,' it stated.

The solution would be brutal. If Holland did not give in, immediately, Rotterdam would be bombed first, Antwerp next.

Diaries of Rotterdam citizens tell the tragic story of the day. Its tragedy was that Dutch surrender terms were nearly ready when the first wave of bombers went in.

'Which Rotterdamer cannot remember that day? It was a beautiful spring day. People had spent the Whit Sunday and Monday at home and wanted to get out. . . . Everyone gravitated to the centre of Rotterdam, the Coolsingel . . . it was almost as if people sensed that something was about to happen.'

As the hour of the ultimatum neared, a Dutch delegation met the local German Commander, General Rudolf Schmidt, in an ice-cream parlour on a main street. There had been air raid warnings throughout the morning. Among the ice-cream, the Dutch won the German's agreement that, if the terms of surrender could be agreed before the deadline for the bombing raid, red Very lights would be sent up to tell the bombers to fly on.

As the hour approached, negotiations were on the brink of completion. From an island on the Maas, the Very lights went up. Their light was lost in the haze of fires already burning. The pilots of the 57 Heinkel 111 bombers already droning

A curious Dutch schoolboy looks on as a German tank commander chats to infantrymen on the way to the front. The speed of the advance left most of Holland unscathed.

towards the city never saw them.

The raid was particularly well planned. High explosive bombs, falling in a triangle on the old city and its port, turned narrow streets and warehouses stuffed with oil and margarine into candles from hell. 'With every bomb attack, we threw ourselves against the wall, which shook violently and was like clutching at a straw' wrote one citizen. A 20-year-old student recorded: 'We see nothing more because we dare not come out of the cellar. We hear only the frightening drone of the endlessly returning aeroplanes and the shrieking and explosions of the bombs all around us.'

No fewer than 25,000 houses were burnt out, 78,000 made homeless and 900 killed in this afternoon's work. It could have been worse. The tail-enders of the bombing raid finally saw the red lights of surrender coming up from the river—and flew on.

For pilots doing their job, it had been a fine raid. 'The approach is like a manoeuvre, quiet and secure,' recorded one German observer. 'The planes are searching systematically for their targets. Soon the centre of Rotterdam is burning in many places. Within a few minutes the centre is enveloped in dense black and sulphur-yellow clouds. The bombers are flying quite low over the city. A splendid picture of invincible strength.'

Defenceless citizens slaughtered

Smoothly, the German war machine adapted to the task of slaughtering defenceless citizens on their own doorstep. No anti-aircraft gun fired at these bombers. No Allied plane flew in Rotterdam's defence. The Dutch Air Force had long been shot out of the sky.

In the early evening of 14 May, General Henri **Winkelman** of Holland surrendered. This was not the entire nation nor even all the armed forces —those in Zeeland had orders to fight on. The Dutch Government was now safely abroad, with much of the nation's gold. Two hundred bound steel boxes had been sunk in the desperate attempts to get them out. The Germans salvaged them, melted the gold down and restamped it.

Surprisingly, though 78,000 homes burnt out in Rotterdam alone, the total number of Dutch deaths during the whole invasion were 2500 civilians, 2500 soldiers. Dutch soldiers went into captivity, but on Hitler's orders were speedily released in a bid to win popularity for the new masters of the Netherlands.

In Holland there would be criticism, for a while, of the escape by the Royal Family and the Government. Stirring speeches by their dauntless Queen transmitted by Britain's BBC would swiftly dispel the notion that the nation's leaders had taken an easy way out. Her message from abroad was—fight on.

Queen Wilhelmina arrived at Liverpool Street Station, London, and went straight to Buckingham Palace. Prince Bernhard kept his promise to return to Holland immediately. It was not a useful trip. Incognito, he travelled the south of Holland by car, found it swarming with Germans and returned to London. There he faced up to the fact that he was going to be a guest for some time.

War Notes

HOLLAND

BERNHARD, Prince of the Netherlands: b. 1911. German prince of Lippe-Biesterfeld. Grew up in Germany during Hitler's rise to power. Opposed Nazis and spent period in Paris in voluntary exile. Married Crown Princess Juliana of Netherlands 1937 and renounced German citizenship.

DUTCH ARMED FORCES: the Home Forces consisted of a permanent corps of 1430 officers and 6477 other ranks. Annual conscript levy produced a further 32,000 men serving for 11 months. On mobilization including reserves the total strength was 270,000 (11 divisions). The Navy consisted of 12 protected and 60 unprotected vessels. Most ships escaped and continued to fight in the Far East and with British Fleet. The Royal Marine Corps consisted of 1500 men. Known as the 'Black Devils' they tenaciously defended Rotterdam. The Army Air Force had 126 planes and 600 men in 2 air regiments. Fokker CX biplanes and DXXI monoplanes, Fokker TV bombers. None airworthy by noon 14 May. Many airmen escaped to England via France, joining RAF Coastal Command. Total casualties 2890 killed, 6889 wounded.

GERMAN FORCES: von Küchler's 18th Army launched the main ground invasion. Its 1st Cavalry Div advanced 110 miles across NE Holland in 2 days. 9th Panzer Div (Gen Hubicki) was in the lead after the Dutch frontier defences were breached. Its tanks reached Moerdijk bridge on evening of 12 May as planned, to link up with 7th Air Div. The 10,000-strong 22nd Airborne Div in the Hague lost 40% of its officers and 28% of its men fighting 3 Dutch divisions of 1st Corps. Kesselring's Luftflotte 2 provided the air support. Of 162 crashed Ju 52s recorded, 53 were repaired and 47 cannibalized.

KÜCHLER, Georg von: German general, b. 1881 Prussian nobleman who joined German Army 1901. Served in WW1 as a General Staff Officer with artillery. Freecorps officer in Baltic States 1918-20. Risen to rank of Lt-General 1936. Took command of 1st Corps, Königsberg 1937. Retired in 1938 generals' purge. Commanded German force which occupied Memel when taken from Lithuania 1939. Commanded 3rd Army of Gen von Bock's Army Group North in Sept 1939. Opposed SS and Nazi Party in occupied Poland. In May 1940 served under Bock as commander of 18th Army which broke Dutch defences at Yssel and Grebbe line.

STUDENT, Kurt: German general, b. 1890. Educated at Potsdam Cadet School 1901-6. Pilot in Imperial German Air Service from 1913. Fighter squadron CO 1916. Sole member of Aviation Section of Reichwehr 1919-28 during which time secretly trained 300 German pilots in Russia and ran glider courses. Returned to infantry 1929, CO 2nd Infantry Regt 1931. Promoted as Lt Col and transferred to Air Ministry 1933 where was one of leading personalities in creation of Luftwaffe. Commander of Experimental Staff, Rechlin 1936. Promoted Major-General 1938. Appt to command 2 paratroop battalion that formed basis of 7th Air Div. Cut para training from 3 months to 6 weeks. Never jumped himself for lack of time. Invasion of Holland commanded 22nd Airborne Division as well. In confusion of Rotterdam 14 May when surrender negotiated was caught in machine-gun cross-fire and wounded by SS Leibstandarte bullet.

WINKELMAN, Henri: Dutch C-in-C, b. 1876. Recalled from retirement Feb 1940 after resignation of Gen Reynders. Planned to make defensive stand in central bastion of Fortress Holland.

MAY 1940

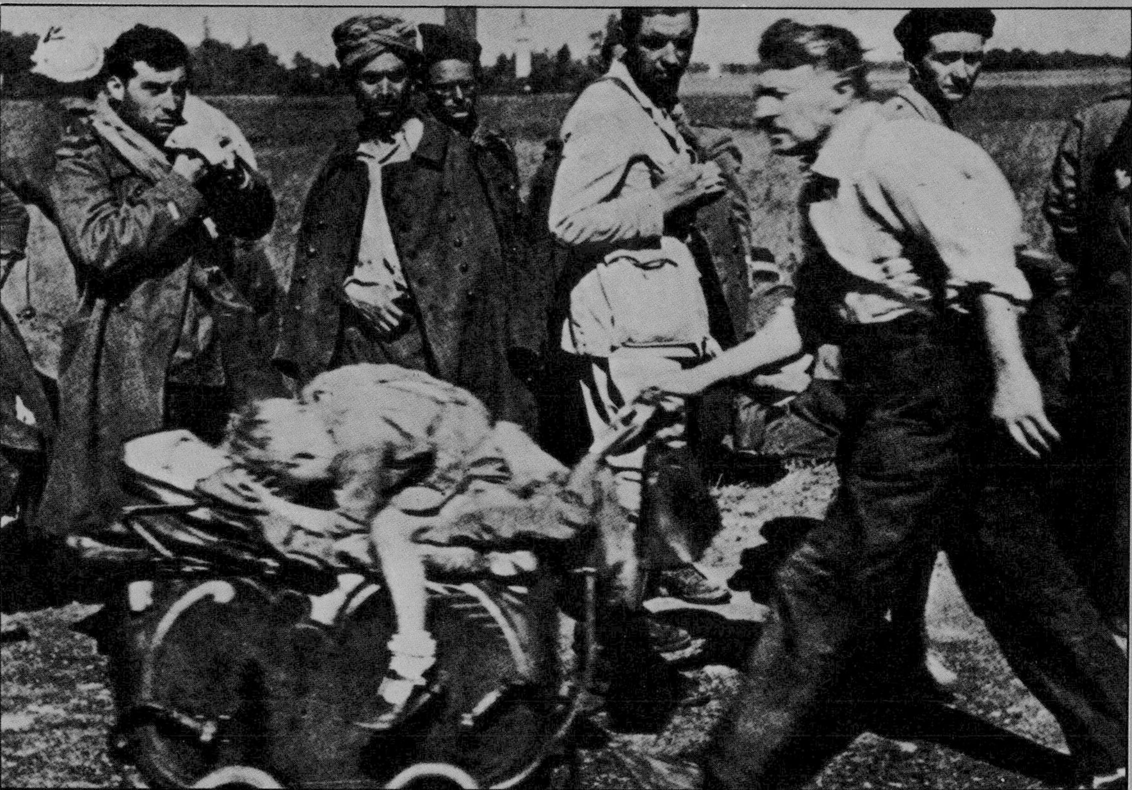

...ON THE DAY Hitler's panzers tear into France and Belgium, Winston Churchill takes over in Britain. Nothing goes right for the Allies. Belgium falls, the French give way to panic and despair and the BEF are forced back to the sea. Then at Dunkirk Hitler calls his panzers to a halt. On the beaches of Dunkirk the remnants of Britain's Army is brought safely home to fight another day...

16th: Panzers 55 miles W of Sedan. Allies begin withdrawal to Scheldt from Dyle. RAF in France moves to bases E of Paris. Churchill flies there.

17th: German 6th Army enters Brussels, Belgian government leaves for Ostend. De Gaulle counterattacks. Hitler orders infantry to catch up with panzers.

18th: Antwerp falls. Panzers reach Somme. French Cabinet reshuffle.

19th: Weygand replaces Gamelin. De Gaulle's 2nd attack. BEF plans retreat to sea.

20th: Panzers reach Channel. US London Embassy cipher clerk arrested for passing secrets to Axis. Hitler and High Command confer on how best to conduct phase 2 of French campaign.

21st: BEF counter-attack at Arras. Weygand flies to Ypres conference.

22nd: British break Lufwaffe Red Enigma key for good. British Parliament passes Emergency Powers Defence Act. Luftwaffe stops French counter-attack on Cambrai.

23rd: Boulogne evacuated. BEF on half rations. Sir Oswald Mosley arrested.

24th: Hitler confirms panzer halt order. Bletchley first sends BEF Enigma decrypts. Calais battle begins. First civilian casualties in air raid on England. Allies decide to evacuate Norway.

25th: Gort decides to retreat on Dunkirk.

26th: Dunkirk evacuation begins. Calais falls.

27th: 7669 troops evacuated. SS shoot 90 British PoWs near Dunkirk. Allies attack German Abbeville bridgehead S of Somme.

28th: 17,804 evacuated. Belgian Army surrenders. 2nd SS massacre of British PoWs. Allies capture Narvik.

29th: 47,310 evacuated. Three destroyers and 15 other ships sunk. Seyss-Inquart becomes Holland Reichskommissar.

30th: 53,823 evacuated. Mussolini tells Hitler that Italy will enter war.

31st: 68,014 evacuated. French 1st Army surrenders at Lille. Japanese Army in China announces that Chungking will be bombed daily.

CHURCHILL TAKES OVER

"Don't Shoot the Pianist He's Doing His Best!"

On Tuesday, 7 May, Neville Chamberlain hurried to a House of Commons 'filled with members in a high state of irritation and distress'. Today's debate was to be on the Whitsun recess. In reality, it became a censure on the Government's performance. Three days later, Chamberlain was to resign as Britain's Prime Minister.

The House was packed. Ambassadors from overseas settled down in the Distinguished Strangers' Gallery to see whether Chamberlain's government would survive. In the chamber itself, too small to provide seats for all its members, MPs sat, uncomfortably, on steps and in the aisles.

The atmosphere was electric. Some members, had already made up their minds to press for a change of government. Small pressure groups were forming round leading government critics, many of them within the ruling Conservative Party.

The focus of the hostility was the Prime Minister, Neville Chamberlain — the man who still believed the war should be of a limited duration. Leo Amery, leading a group of critics that had included Winston **Churchill** and Anthony

Eden, until they joined the government, thought Chamberlain was 'temperamentally unfitted to the task'.

Only that morning Sir Stafford **Cripps**, writing anonymously in the *Daily Mail*, called for an all-party government with a small inner war cabinet under Lord Halifax as Prime Minister.

Chamberlain faces his critics

But Chamberlain, who had no notion of how widespread opposition to his running of the war had become, went to the House on the afternoon of the 7th full of confidence. He had the support of a big majority in the House, and unless a large group of his own party deserted him, he could not be deposed. An unlikely event, anyway, as there was no apparent successor.

Lord Halifax, the leading contender, was a tired man; Lloyd George, the World War 1 leader, was a possible candidate, but too old to be convincing. And Winston Churchill was widely dismissed on a number of grounds.

A leading Chamberlain supporter, Sir John Simon, said that it would be 'an odd result if Churchill . . . who is more directly responsible for recent decisions on tactics and strategy in Norway than any of his colleagues, should be elevated into the PM's place'.

Colonel Hastings Ismay, secretary of the Military Co-ordination Committee on which Churchill was a powerful figure, indicated the personal dislike many leading politicians felt for him.

Churchill, impulsive, acting on hunches, without making sufficient sober calculations and preparations, would be a dangerous man to have at the helm, many felt.

Sir John **Colville** reflected the views of Whitehall's civil servants — 'In May 1940 the mere thought of Churchill as Prime Minister sent a cold chill down the spines of the staff working at 10 Downing Street . . . Churchill's impetuosity had, we thought, contributed to the Norwegian fiasco.'

At the beginning of May 1940 there was no clear way forward — only a conviction, summarized by Leo Amery, that anything would be better than the existing position.

When he entered the chamber on the afternoon of the 7th, Chamberlain was prepared to ride out the storm. Chamberlain momentarily was thrown off balance by the chorus of hissing, boos, and shouts of 'missed the bus' that greeted his entry into the Commons. Recovering quickly, he took his seat near the despatch box and, in due course, rose to speak.

It was an unimpressive performance. The 'yes-men' cheered in the right places. Opponents cheered too, but with heavy irony.

Throughout the debate Labour members kept up a hostile barrage of jeers and interruptions. Clement Attlee, the first speaker for the opposition, produced an incisive antidote to their emotional heckling. He advanced cold reasoned arguments on the government's record of failures, and urged Tories to vote for a new leader.

But Attlee's efforts were not enough. Chamberlain would resign only if a large number of his own party were against him. And before long, it became obvious that some of them were.

First to speak was Sir Roger Keyes, member for Portsmouth. Hero of the Zeebrugge raid in World War 1, Keyes, a slight figure, made maximum impact by turning up in the full uniform of Admiral of the Fleet with three rows of medals. 'Questionable taste,' muttered Leo Amery.

Keyes' speech was a powerful, blistering attack on the government. Harold **Macmillan** had drafted it for him, but it still represented Keyes' own views.

The House listened in breathless silence to the words of the respected fighting admiral. He denounced the government for not ordering a major naval attack on Trondheim, which the naval staff had told him would not be necessary because of the success of the military. But the military attack had failed, and that was the fault of the government, not the servicemen.

Keyes sat down to thunderous applause. Harold Nicolson thought his attack 'by far the most dramatic speech I have ever heard'.

The Speaker, with unparliamentary partiality, had delayed the debate until dinner, when the House was almost empty. He knew that Amery was out to make trouble. And because of this timing, Amery nearly called off his own speech, to save the attack for another day.

It was the leading Liberal critic, Clement **Davies**, who changed the course of the debate. Sensing that Amery might go ahead with his attack if enough members were prepared to hear him, he hurried through the corridors of the Palace of Westminster drumming up an audience for Amery's speech. Sensing the tension, members returned to the chamber.

Lord Halifax, Chamberlain's Foreign Secretary, was the King's favourite for PM . . . not Winston Churchill.

'I felt as if I were walking with destiny...all my past life had been but a preparation for this hour...'

Winston Churchill on the events of 10 May

Amery started his speech in mild mood. But once he saw that he had 'the makings of a house', he went straight into the attack. The small, squat figure smashed into the government with point after telling point, like 'volleys fired into sandbags' as one MP saw it. He attacked the government's deficiencies in foresight, clear decision and swift action, and, again, their handling of the campaign in Norway. 'We are fighting for our life, for our liberty, for our all; we cannot go on being led as we are.'

Amery finished resounding by quoting Oliver Cromwell's words dismissing the Long Parliament: 'You have sat too long here for any good you have been doing. Depart I say, and let us have done with you. In the name of God, go!'

Chamberlain heard nothing of Amery's speech, but he did hear the buzz in the corridors and smoking room after it. He was devastated by the attack.

The last throes

The next day, 8 May, was critical. The Parliamentary Labour Party's executive sat down at 10.30am to decide whether to force a vote. Lose it, and Chamberlain's hold would be strengthened.

It did not take long that afternoon before Chamberlain himself sealed the government's fate. Criticized, yet again, by a leading Labour man, Chamberlain, uncharacteristically impetuous, leaped to his feet, bared his teeth, and told the House, 'I accept'. He went on disastrously, 'I do not seek to evade criticism but I say this to my friends in the House—and I have friends in the House . . . I accept the challenge. I welcome it indeed . . . I call on my friends to support us in the lobby tonight.'

Chamberlain could hardly have done worse. His call to his 'friends' had reduced the debate to the level of personalities. While the House waited for the vote, Chamberlain's colleagues tried to recover lost ground.

Churchill tried his best, and emerged from the afternoon one of the few Conservatives to gain in stature. His first opportunity came when Lloyd George, speaking immediately after Chamberlain, sought to excuse Churchill from entire responsibility for the Norwegian fiasco.

Churchill leaped to his feet and snapped pugnaciously 'I take complete responsibility for everything that has been done by the Admiralty, and I take my full share of the burden'.

Lloyd George's reply was equally quick. 'The Right Honourable Gentleman must not allow himself to be converted into an air raid shelter to keep the splinters from hitting his colleagues.'

The whole House laughed at this but the remark served Churchill well. It acknowledged that Churchill had shirked no responsibility, and virtually exempted him from the attack on the government.

Churchill's own turn to speak came later that night, at the end of the debate. In a brilliant speech, full of fireworks and splendid oratory, he managed to look sincere in his defence of the government, while at the same time disassociating himself from their timid performance.

In the vote that followed 44 Conservatives went into the voting lobby with the opposition. Many others stayed in the chamber to abstain. The result was 281 for the government, 200 against—quite enough to show that Chamberlain's men had lost Parliament's confidence.

Chamberlain stood up, an erect, sombre figure. Then he picked his way over the outstretched feet of his colleagues to leave the chamber.

Straight away, he called Churchill to his room, and said he could not go on. Churchill was all for continuing the fight. They still had a good majority—he urged the PM to try to form a National Government of all parties.

At meetings all through the next day small groups of MPs talked over the next step. Then, at 4.30pm, 10 May, Chamberlain, Halifax, Churchill and the chief whip David Margesson, conferred in Chamberlain's room. Chamberlain said he could not form another government. He thought that Churchill would not command Labour support, and favoured Halifax.

Halifax, sick at the prospect, hastily declined. He sat in the House of Lords, and could see that with Churchill running defence in the House of Commons, he would rapidly become little more than an honorary Prime Minister.

Shortly after 5pm Chamberlain was on his way to Buckingham Palace to tender his resignation. At Churchill's Admiralty office a message soon arrived—his presence was requested at the Palace at 6pm.

King **George VI** himself had no desire to see Churchill Prime Minister. The King's instinct was

War Notes

CHURCHILL, Winston Leonard Spencer: Prime Minister, b. 1874 at Blenheim Palace, son of Lord Randolph Churchill. Educated at Harrow and Sandhurst. War correspondent and junior officer in colonial campaigns and Boer War 1895-1900. Conservative MP for Oldham, Lancs 1900-4. Liberal MP 1904-24. Under Secretary of State for Colonies 1905-8. As President of Board of Trade 1908-10 set up first employment exchange. Home Secretary 1910-11. First Lord of the Admiralty from 1911 but resigned 1915 over the disastrous Dardanelles (Gallipoli) campaign. Lt-Col in 6th R. Scots Fusiliers, France 1916. Returned to Cabinet under Lloyd George as Minister of Munitions July 1917. Sec of State for War, Air and Colonies 1919-22. Chancellor of Exchequer 1924-9. In political wilderness for 10 years, warning of German re-armament. Forecast second world war in 1932. Nearly lost his seat Nov 1938 because of anti-Munich stand. Among other works, published *Marlborough* (6 vols) 1933-8, selected speeches v appeasement in *While England Slept 1938, Step by Step* 1939. Visited Maginot Line Aug 1939.

COLVILLE, John Rupert: b. 1915. Educated Harrow and Trinity College, Cambridge. Page of Honour to King George V 1927-31. In Diplomatic Service as 3rd Sec 1937, Assistant private secretary to Chamberlain from 1939.

CRIPPS, Richard Stafford: Labour MP, b. 1889 youngest son of 1st Baron Parmoor. Educated as chemist at University College, London. King's Counsel 1927, then Solicitor-General 1930-1. Labour MP from 1931, he pushed for union with other left-wing parties 1936. Executive officer of Labour Party in 1937. Visited Moscow and India 1939. Appointed Ambassador to Russia 1940.

DAVIES, Clement: Liberal MP, b. 1884. King's Counsel 1926. Lib MP for Montgomeryshire from 1929 and member of Lib National Party since 1931. Interested in law reforms related to coal mining, land taxation, agriculture, titles, estate, etc. President of various literary and agricultural societies.

GEORGE VI, Albert Frederick Arthur: King of England, b. 1895 Sandringham, Norfolk, 2nd son of George V and Queen Mary. Naval training Dartmouth and air cadet Cranwell. Served in Grand Fleet at Battle of Jutland 1916. Spent short time at Trinity College, Cambridge 1919. As Duke of York 1920 showed sympathetic interest in the human problems within industry. President of Boy's Welfare Association and helped set up summer camps for boys from public schools and working class backgrounds. Played tennis at Wimbledon 1926. Married Elizabeth Bowes-Lyon, d. of Earl of Strathmore and Kinghorn April 1923. Ascended the throne upon brother Edward's abdication Dec 1936.

MACMILLAN, (Maurice) Harold: Conservative MP, b. 1894. Educated Eton and Oxford. Served in Special Reserve Grenadier Guards 1914-18, wounded 3 times. ADC to Gov-Gen of Canada 1919. Retired 1920 and married Lady Dorothy Evelyn Cavendish. Conservative MP Stockton-on-Tees 1924-9 and from 1931. Among other books, published *The Next Five Years* 1935. *Economic Aspects of Defence* 1939. Opposed Chamberlain's appeasement policy. Visited Finland Feb 1940 to arrange British aid and volunteers.

---

to side with Chamberlain, who he thought had been unfairly treated. If there had to be a change, he wanted Halifax. He was the 'obvious man', and the King was prepared to place Halifax's peerage in abeyance for the time being.

Reluctantly the King agreed on Churchill who later described his momentous audience:

'I was taken immediately to the King. His Majesty received me most graciously and bade me sit down. He looked at me searchingly and quizzically for some moments, and then said, "I suppose you don't know why I have sent for you?" Adopting his mood, I replied, "Sir, I simply couldn't imagine why." He laughed and said, "I want to ask you to form a Government." I said I would certainly do so.'

Within an hour of leaving the Palace, Labour and Liberal party leaders confirmed they would serve with him. And he had already decided the names of the leading men for his cabinet.

News of the changeover was broadcast to the nation at 9pm that night. In a dignified speech Chamberlain declared his intention of serving under Churchill as Lord President of the Council —and leader of the Conservative Party.

'I was conscious of a profound sense of relief', Churchill recalled in his memoirs, of the day's events: 'At last I had the authority to give directions over the whole scene. I felt as if I were walking with destiny, and that all my past life had been but a preparation for this hour and for this trial.'

Impatient for the morning, Churchill retired to his bed at 3am. 'I slept soundly and had no need for cheering dreams. Facts are better than dreams.'

On the day Churchill took over in Britain Hitler launched his long awaited Blitzkrieg. Here British Tommies leave for France.

FRANCE: TIME RUNS OUT

By 11.30 on the night of the disastrous 16 May, Prime Minister Reynaud had given up and gone to bed. The suitcases that his mistress had been all day packing, in readiness to flee Paris, still cluttered the floor. Reynaud was weary.

In the Chamber that afternoon he had used the last of his energy to deny the rumour that the Government was about to run away. 'We shall fight before Paris; we shall fight in Paris, if need be' he declared. It did not sound convincing.

Then there had been Churchill. For two hours he had urged counter-attacks, minimizing the German panzers as just 'so many little flags stuck in the map.' Reynaud fell into an uneasy doze. The doorbell rang. Churchill was back, waving a telegram, insisting on reading it aloud.

Reynaud listened, in his dressing gown. Churchill's news was that he had wrung the equivalent of 120 fighters out of the RAF to aid the counter-attack on the German advance. Then he insisted Daladier be roused and brought in to hear the good news. Then he harangued them until one in the morning. 'You must not lose heart!' he growled. The war had scarcely begun. If necessary they would fight it from the heart of Canada, over the ruins of a Europe laid waste by high explosive. Meanwhile there had to be a counter-attack.

Reynaud staggered back to bed. Perhaps it all still could come right. Perhaps in the morning there might yet be another Miracle of the Marne. In any case, things could hardly get worse. And, when the dawn came up, it brought the news that, surprisingly, the panzers had halted.

It had also been a bad day at **Hitler's** bleak HQ in Münstereifel. Rarely had the German High Command known the Führer in so foul a mood. 'He rages and screams that we are on the way to ruining the whole operation and risking the danger of defeat' lamented Halder to his diary. Hitler, passionate advocate of the panzer blitzkrieg, was now yelling down the phone to his commanders to put the brakes on. He feared that the racing tanks were leaving the infantry behind and that the French could now be the ones setting a trap.

The first panzer general to receive Hitler's wrath was Heinz Guderian. Von Kleist met him early on the 17th 'and without even wishing me a good morning, began in very violent terms to berate me for having disobeyed orders.' Huffily, Guderian asked to be relieved of his command. Von Kleist was taken aback, then nodded. Guderian was packed off to the rear of his panzers and their advance was limited to 'reconnaissance in force.'

That should have pinned the troublesome Guderian in his place — instead, he fixed a land-line up to his advance HQ, safe from High Command monitoring, and soon sent the tanks rolling on again.

In Paris the news that the panzers were not advancing on the capital brought the first moments of calm since the fateful 10 May. There was even talk that Colonel Charles de Gaulle was making a counter-attack.

For Paul Reynaud, news that the panzers had halted provided an opportunity to return to the

unfinished business of 9 May — the sacking of C-in-C Gamelin. Daladier was still noisy in the veteran's defence, but Reynaud was determined. Secretly he summoned two military heroes currently serving abroad. In France's darkest hour, new blood was needed.

So it was that General Maxime **Weygand**, commanding French forces in Syria, began to pack his bags for the journey home to be Gamelin's replacement. He was 73 years of age, had never commanded troops in battle and, when he saw maps of the German advances, would later say: 'If I had known the situation was so bad I would not have come.'

Recalled too, was Pétain from his embassy in Madrid to become deputy premier. There were cheers of 'At last' when Reynaud announced to the Senate that, henceforth, the 'Victor of Verdun' would be working at his side. Marshal Phillipe Pétain was now 84 and General Spears' comment was that 'he seemed dead'. Pétain's train, rumbling across the Pyrenees on 18 May, was bringing him to the tragic finale of a glorious career.

At dawn on Saturday 18 May Gamelin, still ignorant of his impending removal, was in good spirits. The news from intelligence sources was that the panzers were about to move again — but not towards Paris. They would head north, towards the Channel. Parisians breathed easier on hearing this. Perhaps Hitler was heading for England and would leave them alone.

Gamelin headed off in his car to visit General Georges at La Ferté-sous-Jouarre. If the panzers *were* going north, they would expose a long, straggling flank, ripe for attack. If only Georges could move fast enough to take advantage of this. En route, Gamelin's car halted in one of the interminable jams on the refugee-packed road.

At La Ferté, Georges was in no shape to mount a counter-attack. Gamelin surveyed the chaotic HQ with displeasure — it was so unlike the monastic calm of his own base. There were still maps of the Norwegian and Finnish campaigns on the wall. Staff officers crashed in and out. How could one work in such 'utter disorder'? Gamelin had a quiet word with Major General Joseph **Doumenc**, who agreed that the time might be near when

'We are beaten. We have lost the battle!'

Paul Reynaud, French PM, 15 May

Gamelin would have to take over Georges' command. 'Let me know the right moment' said Gamelin.

Then, after a chat with Georges, in which no decisions were made, Gamelin set off back to Vincennes. Apparently Reynaud and Pétain had something to tell him there.

So the day drifted by. The chance which Gamelin had seen had been missed. The panzer generals — unknown to Hitler — were on their way to the sea. By evening, they had captured **Saint-Quentin** and **Péronne.** The next day, Sunday 19 May, the 7 panzer divisions would rendezvous and hammer across the plains of Flanders and Picardy. Racing past those ancient battlegrounds where they had been pinned down in the dreadful trench warfare of the **Somme** lifted the spirits of any who were veterans of World War 1.

Gamelin's achievement, on the fateful Saturday, was to order some units based on the Maginot Line to head northwards to the battle. Down there, along the vast defences of France, drôle de guerre still ruled. Now, to rub salt in the nation's many wounds, the German First Army attacked and took one of the fabled fortresses. Ironically, it too was called **La Ferté**. The Maginot Line seemed as fallible as the rest of the Allied defences.

'I pity you with all my heart' said the aged Pétain, after his first meeting with Gamelin that evening. Gamelin accepted the remark as a general comment on the state of the war. Reynaud had not yet informed him that, when Weygand arrived on the morrow, he, Gamelin, would be sacked. The Commander-in-Chief ended the day by reading through the memorandum he had penned, then signed it. The next day, Sunday, he set off for La Ferté once again.

That day the confusion there was worse than usual — the news of the battle even more dire. The HQ was a babble of voices as stragglers from the front were grilled for news by interrogators. Telephones rang incessantly. The place reeked of blocked drains and, surprisingly, kitchen aromas. The chef, sensing disaster, was putting all his skill into preparing one fine, final meal.

Gamelin asked for a pen and went off to a quiet corner. For the first time, he was intervening in Georges' command of the north eastern front. Even now, he worded his 'Personal and Secret Instruction No 12' diplomatically, anxious to preserve Georges' face. 'Without wishing to interfere in the conduct of the battle' he began, he had some recommendations to make. They included the withdrawal of the French, Belgian and British armies south of the Somme.

Even as he read it out, it was plain it was all far too late. Up north, Belgium was half engulfed. The British were being cut off between the sweep of Hitler's sickle and the Channel. A telephone call around noon from Amiens revealed that General Henri Giraud of the French Ninth Army had been captured and that the army was in total disorder.

Gamelin stayed for lunch — 'a horrible memory' recalled Captain André **Beaufré**. Gamelin chatted 'of this, that and the other and made jokes'. After

coffee he left La Ferté for the last time.

Weygand flew in on that Sunday morning. By the time he had been briefed, interviewed Georges (and cancelled Gamelin's morning directive), he was both tired and depressed. He told Reynaud that he would take on the job of Commander-in-Chief, but could not promise victory — nor even give him the hope of it. Then he left. 'I shall begin by getting some sleep' he said.

At 8.55 this Sunday evening, Gamelin finally heard the news. It arrived in the form of a curt note from Reynaud, thanking him for services rendered 'in the course of a long and brilliant career' and informing him that Weygand had replaced him.

Gamelin took it hard. 'I do not see how I can be found personally responsible for the actual situation', he complained.

In nine days, 15 divisions had been lost. And a million men were now being corralled by the armies of the Reich in the north. The panzers had covered 50 miles this Sunday. From now on, whatever happened, it would be the fate of the British and the Belgians that mattered.

Refugees rest in a field to escape from enemy aircraft, while German troops (inset and below) continue their advance.

War Notes

BEAUFRE, André: French soldier, b. Neuilly sur Seine, Paris 1902. Entered Saint-Cyr Military Academy and met instructor, Charles de Gaulle 1921. Fought against the Riff in Morocco 1925. Studied at École Superieure de Guerre and École Libre des Sciences Politiques, then assigned to General Staff. Served again in Morocco 1938-9. Member of military mission to Russia April 1939 and reassigned to GHQ, Paris.

DOUMENC, Joseph: French general b. 1880. Graduate of École Polytechnique. Main French representative in futile Anglo-French-Soviet talks Aug 1939. Promoted Major-General Jan 1940. Headed admin and logistical HQ at Montry, halfway between Gamelin's command post at Vincennes, and NE Front (Georges') HQ at La Ferté-sous-Jouarre.

HITLER: gave orders on 17 May to the slower infantry divisions to catch up with panzers, which he feared were moving too fast. Conferred with OKH on 20 May about Phase 2 of French campaign.

LA FERTÉ: small fort on Maginot Line (not Georges' HQ) which was attacked on 18 May by Gen von Witzleben's 1st Army. In an awkward defensive position, it fell on 19 May. It had no strategic significance but capture was wildly acclaimed by German radio. Intention of action was to halt flow of defenders away from Maginot Line to support campaign in north. Successful in this as defence once again split on two fronts.

PÉRONNE: town in N France on R. Somme, 17 miles WNW of Saint-Quentin. An agricultural trade centre, it was virtually destroyed in WWI. Rebuilt, it was damaged in WW2.

SAINT-QUENTIN: city in Aisne Department on R. Somme and Saint-Quentin Canal. It is 80 miles NE of Paris and has textile mills and metal works. Occupied by Germans in WWI until Oct 1918 when it was burned and pillaged by them.

SOMME: Department of 2424 sq miles and 467,479 people (1936) in Picardy. Capital Amiens. Bounded by English Channel on W. Bisected E-W by canalized R. Somme. Fertile level valley with small-scale metalworkings and textiles. Entire dept ravaged by WW1 fighting 1916-18.

WEYGAND, Maxime: French general, b. 1867. Graduated from St. Cyr Miltitary Academy 1887. Became a cavalryman and instructor at cavalry school. Served as Chief of Staff to Marshal Ferdinand Foch as Colonel 1914-23. Major-General at 1918 Armistice. Headed French military advisory mission to Poland 1920. Popularly given credit for winning Battle of Warsaw. High Commissioner Syria 1923-4. Awarded Grand Croix de la Legion d'Honneur 1924. Head of French General Staff 1930, and overall army commander 1931-5. Awarded Military Medal 1932. Was main force behind a limited modernization programme and restoration of 2 year military service law. Strong right wing views and prevailing world depression made it difficult for him to gain support for comprehensive military reform. Retired 1935 aged 68 and succeeded by Gamelin. Recalled 1939 and appointed by Gamelin Commander of French Forces in Near East (Syria and Lebanon), with HQ in Beirut. C-in-C of all Theatres of Operation and Chief of Staff in the National Defence, replacing Gamelin on 19 May 1940. Aged 73, the new appointment gave him more power than Gamelin had been able to wield. One of his sons served in French Army. Publications in 1930s—*Turenne; Le 11 Novembre; Histoire militaire de Mehemet Ali; Histoire de l'armée française.*

GORT'S ARMY

Due south of Arras in the small French town of Hebuterne, the roar of revving engines shattered the morning air. After months of waiting, the 12th Royal Lancers were ready for the order to move. Seventy-five miles ahead, across the Belgian border, lay their objective —the River Dyle. It was here that the Allied commanders had decided, five months before, to halt the Blitzkrieg in its tracks.

At 10.20am, 10 May, the first Morris armoured cars—'suicide boxes' the men called them—jerked forward. At a steady 15mph they crossed the Belgian frontier at 1.30pm. Even at this speed dust blew up from the pavé roads causing the crews to squint in the dazzling white light of a glorious spring day.

Along the monotonously straight poplar-lined roads they passed through the dull towns and villages of Flanders—names familiar from the first war. Everywhere they were fêted with flags and showered with flowers, drinks and cigarettes. Everything went smoothly, according to plan. Overhead the sun shone—oddly, today, there was no sign of the Luftwaffe.

To one young war correspondent, 'Kim' Philby of *The Times*, the **BEF**'s smooth progress was too good to be true. To American colleague Drew Middleton, he remarked later that day: 'It went too damn well. With all that airpower why didn't they bother us? What is he (Hitler) up to?'

Far away in his HQ Hitler was to say this night: 'I could have wept for joy' when news of the Allied advance into Belgium reached him.

By late afternoon on the 10th, Brussels was reached. Pressing on through the Forest of Soignies, a few miles north of Waterloo, the 12th Lancers reached their forward position in front of Louvain on the River Dyle. At 6pm Lord Gort, their C-in-C, was told of their arrival.

Behind the trail-blazing Lancers came Dingo scout cars and motorcycle combinations of the 4th Royal Northumberland Fusiliers. Their task was to picket the route against enemy agents. Stories of the stab in the back by traitors and fifth columnists were widespread.

'We shall have lost practically all our trained soldiers by the next few days – unless a miracle appears to help us.'

General Ironside, CIGS

Close behind lumbered tanks and Bren gun carriers. Bringing up the rear were the men of the 44th (Home Counties) Division in full battle order, gas masks at the ready and keeping to columns of three with platoons spaced every 100 yards in the sweltering heat. It was not easy.

That same day, even before the Lancers reached the Dyle, General Walther von Reichenau's panzers were pouring across the Albert Canal, a few miles to the east. Next day, the Belgian Army in headlong retreat would clog up the roads, hampering the progress of the BEF.

By Saturday, 11 May, the BEF was well dug in along its allotted 22-mile front running along the Dyle from Louvain in the north to Wavre in the south. Though the Dyle at this point is little more than a wide stream, Gort was confident that his men could hold it.

For two days they awaited impending German onslaught. Little happened.

Joined by their CO, Lieutenant-Colonel Herbert Lumsden (he joined them fresh from London by way of cross-Channel ferry and taxi), 12th Lancers made their first contact with German armour on Whit Sunday, 12 May. But the Germans turned south towards the French. Next day was to be their baptism of fire. Coming to a small river crossing they encountered a party of mounted recce troops. The Germans, startled, turned away. The Lancers captured a horse.

At Deist an over-anxious subaltern blew a bridge over the River Denmer, thinking the Germans were near. Two Belgian divisions were left stranded on the wrong side of the river. But within minutes German motorcyclists arrived. At nightfall the Lancers withdrew 15 miles westwards, still in front of the Dyle.

Already a pattern was emerging. Hard pressed French and Belgian units to the south were retreating. To cover their flank and hold the 'line', the British were forced to retreat. At first it was orderly 'tactical withdrawal'. A few miles here and there. But by Tuesday, Louvain itself was threatened.

Louvain in flames

Refugees now flooded along the narrow open roads westwards. Bewildered, terrified and shocked they had been on the road night and day without food or rest. Mingled with them were dejected soldiers, their rifles long abandoned.

Hitler's grand plan of encirclement was ready to be sprung.

'It was a perfect spring morning and I was feeling that there was something to be said for the war after all, when suddenly out of the quietness came a faint vibration, a curious humming in the air. It gradually increased to a crescendo . . . outside, shrieks and screams announced that bombs were being dropped. Then suddenly, as suddenly as the attack had arrived, it departed' wrote Lieutenant Anthony Rhodes on the morning of Tuesday, 14 May.

Orchestrated with the air attack, German artillery now opened up a tremendous barrage. The ancient university city of Louvain was to suffer the fate of Warsaw and Rotterdam.

Rommel and his staff officers outside Cambrai in France — site of the world's first tank battle in World War 1.

Between 2.30 and 4 this Tuesday afternoon, six bridges were blown along the British sector of the Dyle. Along the west bank of the river the Tommies dug in.

Louvain itself was the hub of defence. As dusk gathered, German motorized infantry swarmed before the city. They were greeted with a deluge of fire from Vickers, Bren and Lee-Enfield rifles. Behind the infantry, field-gunners pounded the German attack with their new 25-pounders. To the north of the city, scattered among warehouses along the canal, 1st Coldstream Guards just held their positions against repeated German assaults. Again it was the gunners who smashed an attempt to launch a pontoon bridge across the Dyle.

But for divisional commander Major-General Bernard Montgomery the situation did not appear serious enough to interrupt his sleep. 'Go away and don't bother me' he snapped at an anxious staff officer. 'Tell the brigadier in Louvain to turn them out.'

At dawn on Wednesday, German artillery shelled the 2nd Royal Ulster Rifles dug in along a railway line. For two hours the battle raged from platform to platform, across the shattered remains of the station. Tracer and machine-gun bullets ripped through the air—pitched battles were fought with grenades around a signal box, but still the Germans failed to break through. Again artillery pounded the British infantry. Accuracy was not always good but Montgomery's HQ at Everburg was hit by stray shells and had to be evacuated.

With Louvain in flames, bombed from the air and pounded from the ground, Montgomery ordered an evacuation of all civilians. Taking to the roads they streamed out of the city with their pitiful possessions, not knowing where to go or in which direction to head to avoid the war. Many begged to be taken with the troops. The Inniskilling Dragoons had the heart-rending experience of 'one worn, white-faced woman dressed in rusty black implore the soldiers to take her with them—then, with a tragic gesture, she turned away and slowly made her way back, a pathetic shadow on the sunlit road'.

Along the Dyle itself, just outside Louvain, near the village of Gastuche, German infantry swept down on the 2nd Durham Light Infantry. Holding a bridge against mortar and machine-gun attacks, Second-Lieutenant Annand repeatedly drove the enemy back with grenades. Annand received the first Army VC of the war.

Then, at 11am on Wednesday the 16th, Gort issued the order to withdraw. To the men who had defended Louvain with such tenacity for two days it came as a bitter shock. But Gort had the French to consider. Their 2nd North African Division on the right had given up, and were in headlong retreat. To avoid being outflanked Gort ordered his army to retreat to the River Scheldt.

Back through the battered remains of Louvain poured Bren gun carriers, light tanks, armoured cars, field guns and infantry. For the next ten days Gort's army was to continue its long weary retreat, until it reached the English Channel.

The troops themselves were inclined to blame their allies for the retreat, not the Germans. To one British officer it seemed 'appalling to be abandoning Brussels. The Belgian troops stand round apathetically at street-corners or sit in pubs. They don't look desperately anxious to fight.'

Moving through Brussels that first night of retreat, the same eyewitness recalled: 'There was a full moon and not a cloud in the sky. Brussels was burning gaily. German bombers had started an enormous fire in a flour-mill, and the flames from it lit up the whole sky for miles around. We sat in our traffic jam, a perfect target, and wondered why nobody came and dropped bombs on us.'

The speed of the German breakthrough at Sedan left the Allies aghast. Chief of Staff to the BEF, Lieutenant-General Henry Pownall admitted to his diary 'the Germans could now drive to Amiens and Abbeville or north to Calais'.

For mile upon mile the long columns of guns, vehicles and men slowly staggered westwards. Strafed and bombed from the air, harrassed from the rear by German motorcyclists and armoured cars, the return road to the Scheldt was nothing like the advance. At Leutze the 2nd Gloucester Regiment lost 194 men in a single air raid. And everywhere along the route, towns, villages were passed in utter confusion. Rumours flew in front of the troops. Fear of spies, traitors and fifth columnists were rife. Few of these stories had any basis in fact. Often it was the local mayor, schoolmaster or doctor who was the first to depart. Stories of treason sat uneasily on their shoulders. One Burgomeister, dressed in civic splendour, gave up his town's surrender to the Sherwood

Foresters—thinking they were Germans. In Tournai, wounded elephants from a travelling circus rampaged through the burning town.

By the evening of the 19th they reached the Scheldt. The rearguard of Major-General Harold Alexander's 1st Division were forced to leave their vehicles on the wrong side of the river. Dog-tired after forced marches his men were hungry dispirited and in no condition to continue.

Gradually the hopelessness of their position dawned on Gort. French defeatism did little to help matters. Visiting Gort on the 19th, General Gaston Billotte, Gort's superior officer in the elaborate Allied chain of command, stabbed a map showing German armour near Péronne and Cambrai. 'I can do nothing against these panzers' he declared. There was nothing to be done, whined Billotte, to stop the Germans now from reaching the Channel coast. The horror of the situation struck Gort. If the Germans were to drive to the Channel along a corridor, his army would be cut off, with no escape route. The only solution, he reasoned, was to fall back to the Channel while there was time. From there the BEF could be evacuated home to England.

A staff conference settled the details. Pownall rang the War Office, twice. The Director of Military Operations 'was singularly stupid and unhelpful'. But the message registered.

London threw a fit. General Sir Edward Ironside summoned the War Cabinet to an emergency meeting at 4.30pm. The Chief of the Imperial General Staff wanted Gort to counter-attack at once. He, Ironside, would go to France himself to see it was carried out. Churchill agreed. 'The BEF would be closely invested in a bomb-trap, and its total loss would only be a matter of time.'

In fact the BEF was already in danger of extinction. To cover its wide open rear, Gort created a scratch force—Petreforce. Tunnelling, chemical warfare and pioneer troops found themselves jostling with military policemen as members of this unusual unit. With one mortar and training ammunition, 7th Royal West Kents were soon in action against German tanks on the Albert road. Three panzers were knocked out before they pulled out beyond the town.

Farther north desperate rearguard actions raged. Provost Sergeant Chambers was last seen on top of a panzer trying to prize open the hatch with his bayonet. St Pol was held to the last by a mobile bath unit. At Douellens defenders fought for seven hours, turning the approach roads into a blazing inferno by emptying petrol cans and setting light to them. Brigadier George Roupell, VC, ordered his survivors to escape to the Somme. For two years Roupell himself hid on a farm

before eventually escaping back to England by way of Spain.

Landing at Boulogne at 2am on Sunday, 20 May, Ironside lost no time in his attempt to instill aggression into the flagging Allied commanders. Gort flatly refused to turn the BEF southwards—it was impossible. He would attack tomorrow, south through Arras with two divisions, linking up with a French thrust from the south.

Ironside gave Billotte short shrift. Grabbing hold of his tunic, 6ft 4in 'Tiny' Ironside shook the despairing Frenchman and bellowed: 'You must make a plan. Attack at once to the south with all your forces on Amiens.'

Returning to GHQ, Gort told Ironside the French would never attack. The BEF must trust to its own resources. Yet another scratch force was created. Composed of two territorial army battalions and 1st Army Brigade, it was placed under the command of Major-General Harold Franklyn. 'Frankforce' was given ambitious but loosely worded orders to 'support the garrison at Arras and block the German communications from the southeast'.

By midnight it was plain that the promised French support amounted to a mere 35 tanks. British tank strength added another 74 Infantry Mark Is **(Matildas)** and Mark IIs, speed 8mph. Only 16 carried anything heavier than a machine-gun. Trained for infantry support they had no experience of armoured thrusts. Travelling through refugee-blocked roads they arrived at their start point—Vimy Ridge of 1914-18 memory—late. Infantry support failed to arrive on time. The tanks set off without them.

On the afternoon of 21 May, Major-General Giffard le Q Martel's force rumbled through fields of ripening corn blissfully unaware that they were heading for the flank of five panzer divisions. Carving their way through the German 7th Rifle Regiment they threw back much of the elite SS Totenkopft Division taking 200 prisoners.

With four German-occupied villages back in Allied hands and much of the 7th Panzer Division cracking up in panic, Major General Erwin Rommel intervened to stop the rot. 'The enemy tanks created chaos and confusion among our troops . . . We tried to create order. I brought every available gun into action against the tanks.

This rare photograph shows a German 88mm flak gun in action against British Matilda Mark 1 tanks, battle of Arras, 21 May. The tanks shown were commanded by Major King and Sergeant Doyle, 7th RTR. Inset: wounded Tommy cared for by an SS doctor.

War Notes

BOULOGNE: Seaport of 51,000 people 135 miles NNW of Paris and 30 miles SE of Folkestone. Hospital nearby evacuated to England before bombing on night of 19–20 May after BEF Adjutant-General, Sir Douglas Brownrigg, asked to evacuate 'useless mouths'. On 22nd the 20th Gds Bde (2nd Irish and 2nd Welsh Gds) arrived in 4 ships to defend the port with 1500 pioneers already there. They fought 2nd Panzer Div on a 3-mile front falling back into the town. Six RN destroyers gave gunfire support and evacuated 4368 troops as well as refugees, especially Jews and Poles. HMS *Vimeira* took 1400 people on her 2nd trip.

BRITISH EXPEDITIONARY FORCE (BEF): Consisted of 3 corps with 12 divisions plus 51st Highland Div in Maginot Line with French 10th Army till 23 May and 1st Armoured Div arriving S. of the Somme from 20 May. 9 divs had 13,600 men organized into 9 infantry battalions of 773 in 3 brigades ,3 regts with 72 field guns, 1 with 48 anti-tank guns, 4 engineer companies. The 5th and 23rd Divs only had 2 brigades. Together with the 46th they had no signals or artillery. Their bns had 6 Boyes AT rifles instead of 22, 14 Brens instead of 46. Only 25% had completed rifle training and only 50% had ever fired a Bren. Each corps had 4–5 artillery regts (2

field, 2 medium with 16×6in howitzers or 60pdrs, 1 AA , 1–3 machine-gun bns (48 Vickers), 4–5 engineer companies. GHQ controlled 6 divisional cavalry regts (each 28 lt tanks and 44 Bren carriers) 1st Army Tank Bde, 12th Royal Lancers, 1 field regt, 8 medium, 3 heavy, 3 super heavy batteries (6×12in howitzers), 8 AA regts (3.7in or Bofors 40mm guns) and 3 searchlight regts. Total manpower 394,165 of which 255,319 in divisions and other fighting units. HQs, hospitals and missions absorbed 23,545. Lines of communication 78,864.

CALAIS: Seaport of 56,102 people (1936) 145 miles N. of Paris and 27 miles ESE of Dover. Garrison of 3000 British and 800 French under Brig Claude Nicholson, half the former being Riflemen of 30th Brigade with 3rd Royal Tank Regt (48 tanks) Sent from Southampton to assist Boulogne and raid the German flank at Churchill's insistence on 23 May. Only a 4-tank patrol reached Gravelines. The rest faced 10th Panzer Div's all-out attack on the 24th. Ordered to fight to a finish, the last defenders were overrun 5pm on the 26th.

MATILDAS: Name of 2 types of British tank designed for infantry support, Mk I Protoype late 1936. In service 1939, 50 by 3 Sept Weight: 11 tons. Dimensions: 15.9 × 7.6 × 6.1ft. Engine: 70hp Ford V8. Speed: 8mph. Range: 80 miles. Armour: 10–60mm. Gun: .5in Vickers (4000 rounds), Crew: gunner and driver.
MkII (called Matilda from Aug 19 '40 when Mk I production run of 139 ended) Prototype 1940. In service March 1940, 23 arrived in France 1st week of May. Weight: 26.5 tons Dimensions: 18.4 x 8.5 x 8ft. Engines: AEC 6 cyl diesels (1st in a British tank) each 87hp. Speed: 15mph. Range: 70 miles. Armour: 20–78mm (best armoured tank in France). Guns: 2pdr (40mm) and .303in Vickers MG. Crew: cdr, gunner, loader, driver.

I personally gave each gun its target. All I cared about was to halt the enemy tanks by heavy gunfire.'

Rommel's formula worked. With 46 tanks lost and no air cover to protect them from the screaming bombs of Baron Wolfram von Richthofen's Stukas, Martel's brave counter-thrust ended. 'The chaps are absolutely shattered' wrote a Durham Light Infantry subaltern. At dawn on 23 May the massed vehicles of Petreforce and Frankforce scrambled out of Arras before the panzers closed in.

Gort's Army was now fighting back to back. Every day the ring of armour was closing tighter round them.

Unknown to Gort, at von Rundstedt's HQ at Charleville, Hitler was making a decision that saved the BEF—and it has been claimed cost Germany the war. Arriving at 10.30am on the 24th, Hitler agreed with von Rundstedt's plea to halt the panzers on the line Lens-Béthune-Aire-St Omer-Gravelines. A general halt order was telephoned to panzer commanders von Kluge and Kleist at 12.31.

Even today, 40 years on, Hitler's decision remains enigmatic. The reason given in the order was 'to conserve the armoured forces for future operations'. True, after the most energetic advance in the history of warfare, the tanks were in need of maintenance and fuel. The crews certainly were reaching exhaustion point. But the doubt still lingers that Hitler wished the BEF to escape. Certainly, later in the war Hitler was to say: 'Churchill was quite unable to appreciate the sporting spirit of which I had given proof by refraining . . . from annihilating them at Dunkirk'. But the order was revoked at 1.30pm on the 26th when panzers were allowed to move within artillery range of Dunkirk. In any case, it was assumed Göring's Luftwaffe would finish the British off on the beaches of Dunkirk.

The message for a local halt was intercepted by the British Y Service at 11.32am on the 24th. 'Can this be the turn of the tide?' asked Pownall in his diary. 'It seems almost too much to hope for. Of course these Germans are about all in.

Boulogne on the Channel coast fell on the 25th after 36 hours bitter fighting. At 5pm that day, as **Calais'** garrison fought to the end, Gort sat silent, bewildered and despondent. Nothing but an ever increasing flood of bleak reports piled up on his desk. Only one French division seemed to be available for the morrow's long planned counter-attack to the south. There were only 17 tanks left. The Belgians were on the point of collapse on a front 13 miles to the north. Then came a piece of intelligence that made grimmer reading. A captured document from a German staff officer gave details of von Bock's plan to hurl six divisions into the gap between Menin and Ypres.

At 6.30 Gort turned to his Chief of Staff and said: 'Henry, I've had a hunch. We've got to call off the 5th and 50th divisions from the attack to the south and send them over to Brookie on the left.'

In the next 36 hours these two divisions were to make possible the miracle of Dunkirk. It was a decision that saved not only the BEF, but also, it can be argued, Britain the war.

BELGIUM SURRENDERS

Paul Spaak, the Belgian Minister for Foreign Affairs, slumped deep into his armchair. He let his head roll back, his arms hung slackly down. 'Don't you understand?' he mumbled 'Belgium is lost.'

It was some time between five and six am on Saturday 25 May 1940. The five men sitting in the main room of the chateau of Wynendaele, 13 miles southwest of Bruges, cared little about the weather. Their thoughts were in the future.

Four of them, **Spaak**, the Prime Minister Hubert Pierlot and two other ministers, had driven over after an even earlier briefing at the Belgian military HQ near Bruges. At just after five they aroused the fifth member of their party King Leopold III, catching up on a few hours sleep. The **Belgian Army** was on the point of breaking. They might hold out against the German onslaught for another day — two at the most. The ministers had to know the king's plans. His decision was by no means easy to make.

On 12 May Leopold had agreed that French commander, General Gaston **Billotte** should co-ordinate the operations of the Belgian, French and British armies. In the days that followed the Germans pushed on, breaking the Allied lines at Sedan, rolling the French and British forces back towards the sea and forcing the Belgian

'I feel that my duty compels me to share the fate of my army and to stay with my people.'

King Leopold of Belgium

A German anti-tank crew enters Brussels within minutes of the surrender on 17 May. Brussels was spared the fate of Rotterdam by being declared an open city.

Army to retreat towards Ghent and the river Lys in order to keep the Allied front intact. The good weather held and two German armies kept up relentless attacks.

At this stage Leopold dissented from the battle plans of an Allied force that was increasingly tested and increasingly floundering. He sensed that the Allied armies in Belgium would soon be encircled and that Belgium's main task be merely a last resort to help the British escape.

In fact, the British commander Lord Gort was reaching the same conclusions. On 21 May he asked Leopold to retreat still further, abandoning nearly all of Belgium to the invader, and commented as he left the conference 'I do hope the Belgians don't think us awful dirty dogs.'

By now the Belgian ministers, who once thought the Army could 'march to victory through disaster', as in the first war, had turned pessimistic. They felt cut off from decisions affecting their country's future. At one point they virtually accused the King of wilfully manoeuvring the army into an impossible position with the ultimate intention of negotiating a separate peace between Belgium and Germany. The King answered them, on 22 May, after seeing the Defence Minister, General Henri Denis, the only minister with military knowledge. 'I explained my point of view with the help of maps', he wrote. 'He seemed to understand me.'

But as the situation deteriorated further, the ministers decided they should leave for France to to ensure that an independent government would survive. They felt the King should join them. That was why they drove to Wynendaele so early in the morning of 25 May.

In more normal circumstances Leopold could be a delightful person to talk to, highly-strung, maybe, and even somewhat shy, but intelligent, informal and amusing. He had always identified himself very closely with his people. Now the strain was showing as he determined to share their fate. Paul Spaak noted his appearance: 'He was dishevelled, haggard, his eyes were full of tears, his jaw was contracted.'

The ministers, too, stood while the King read them a letter he intended to send to King George VI of Britain: 'Belgium has fulfilled her engagement to maintain neutrality . . . Her powers of resistance are now on the point of being annihilated . . . I feel that my duty compels me to stay with my people.'

That was the sticking point. The ministers said that as Head of State he should join them in exile. Leopold felt that as a soldier, as C-in-C, he must remain with the Army and that, as King, his place was with the Belgian people, not with the refugees abroad. The ministers argued, collapsing into chairs with exhaustion, bursting out as they later confessed, with queries, even insults, as insinuations that the King planned to appoint a new government that would conclude its own peace with the Germans. Leopold had made up his mind: 'I intend to stay, to look after the prisoners and the economic life of the people. I am convinced that if I leave now I may never return.'

Even as the ministers drove away, soon after 6am, the German Sixth Army was launching a decisive attack against the Belgian line near Courtrai. King Leopold appreciated the new danger and issued a challenging Order of the Day: 'Soldiers, the great battle we expected has begun. It will be hard. We fight on with all our strength and with the utmost energy . . . Whatever happens, I shall share your fate.'

The Germans were threatening to break through

An ageing Belgian general receives a German general for the surrender. Thousands of Belgian prisoners, right, file into captivity in long columns.

and block the road to the sea. The Belgian ministers flew to France. By the evening, Lord Gort had decided that the British must pull out.

On 26 May the German attack intensified. As Leopold had anticipated, his army fought to protect Allied troops about to embark from Dunkirk. Yet the Belgians learned of the plans for withdrawal only from movements observed behind the British lines. No one informed them of what was happening, and they felt that they had been left to their own devices.

Belgium surrenders

At midday the Belgian told the French and British that their army had nearly reached the limits of its endurance: 'The C-in-C intends to carry on the fight as long as resources permit.'

Throughout the day, and on into the 27th, the Belgian troops slowly yielded under German assaults. Any further retreat was impossible. Three million people, half the population of Belgium, had crammed themselves between the army and the sea. Refugees blocked the roads trying to escape the enemy guns and aircraft. One British soldier remembered the poorest groups of all:

'Usually the party consisted of an elderly woman pushing the pram with a baby hidden under bedding and other packages, her daughter carrying a bigger child, and other children, according to size, either dangling miserably tired at their mother's heels or helping the granny with the pram by means of a string.'

At 12.30pm on 27 May, King Leopold dispatched a message to Lord Gort: 'The Belgian Army is losing heart. It has been fighting without a break for four days under heavy bombardment. . . . The King will be forced to surrender to avoid complete destruction.' A similar message went to the French. The King still hoped to hold out for another day but the situation was worsening. The Belgian line had broken in several places. The end had come.

At 5pm the King sent Major General Derousseaux through the lines to ask the Germans for an armistice. Messages went to the French and British telling them of the decision — but these did not reach the commanding generals until late that night. At 10pm Derousseaux returned with the German terms: 'The Führer demands that we lay down our arms unconditionally.' Leopold had to accept. 'In all conscience,' he wrote later, 'I felt I did not have the right to prolong these massacres without profit for the communal cause.' At 4am on 28 May the Belgian units ceased fire.

Leopold had chosen to stay with his Army and his people. Late on the night of 27 May he stood with Admiral Sir Roger **Keyes**, liasion officer between Leopold and Churchill, watching the crowds of refugees and said, 'It would be easier for me to go away, but even if I wished to do so, having seen this sight I could not.' Next morning, 28 May, he sent his last message to his troops: 'I shall not leave you in the misfortune which falls upon us. I wish to watch over your lives and over those of your families.'

That afternoon on the express command of the Führer, Colonel-General Walther von **Reichenau**, the commander of Sixth Army, presented himself to the King of Belgium.

The King was waiting in the 'grand salon' of the palace at Bruges. He watched Reichenau approach

and leave his vehicles in the main courtyard below. With him, to Leopold's jaded displeasure, came an entourage — an imposingly formal retinue of officers. The King sent down the commandant of the royal palaces. He did not wish any ostentatious ceremony.

The visitor of the day was hard to persuade but eventually acquiesced. He came up alone.

Right at the end of the room, behind his desk, His Majesty was standing stiffly to attention. With a ringing 'Heil Hitler' Reichenau strode towards the King, holding out his hand. Met with cold impassiveness he came awkwardly to a halt. Ten yards gaped between them. Then the King spoke: 'What will happen to my army?'

At first nonplussed, the General stammered 'I have no instructions about that your Majesty. But a conquered army must be regarded as a captive army.' After a telling silence came the reply: 'In that case General von Reichenau should consider me as his first prisoner.'

A full minute elapsed. 'Gentlemen show the General out!'

Later, the following morning, 29 May, Leopold left for the palace of **Laeken**, just north of Brussels, where Hitler now required him to stay. The American Ambassador to Belgium, Mr Cudahy, visited him there: 'He could not conceal his emotion at our meeting. Never had I seen upon a human countenance a more poignant portrayal of grief, as if the ghastly spectacle of the past 20 days had scarred his soul for ever.'

Leopold remained popular with the Belgians. They had supported the fight against the invader and very few ever welcomed the Germans; they

War Notes

BELGIUM SURRENDERS

BELGIAN ARMY: Consisted of 5 Regular Army and 2 Reserve Army Corps with 12 regular and 6 reserve infantry divisions, 2 divs of Chasseurs Ardennais, 1 brigade (bde) of Cyclist Frontier Guards, 1 Cavalry Corps of 2 divs and I bde of motorized cavalry, 2 recce regts (Gendarmerie), AA artillery regt, 4 Army artillery regts, Army Troops (Engineers, Signals, etc.), Fortress Troops and Services – a total of 650,000 men. They had 42 obsolete light tanks, were poorly equipped and, despite numbers, were therefore inferior to friend and foe. During the 18-day battle 7550 Belgians were killed and 15,850 wounded. The air force, whose 4 regts (179 aircraft) were part of the Army, lost about 30 planes on the ground and 23 in the air (10 May) including 9 Hurricanes, 15 Gladiators, 7 Fairey Foxes, 14 Fiat CR42s. Another 15 CR42s, 10 Foxes and 13 Battles fought on, moving to other airfields. On the 16th about 18 surviving planes flew to France. A Fox flew the last mission, a message drop to Ostend 26 May.

BILLOTTE, Gaston Herve Gustave: French general, b. 1875. Served 1894-1933 in French colonies. Inspector General of Colonial Troops and a member of Army Council. Made his mark as divisional commander in WW1. Assumed Command of 1st Army Group, holding the area north of the Maginot Line Sept 1939. 'He had the appearance of one whose vitality had evaporated in over-heated offices' according to Gen Spears. By 10 May 1940, his command included 4 French armies and the BEF. His 9th Army bore the brunt of the German attack. Leaving the Ypres conference on 21 May for his HQ at Lens Billotte's car skidded into a lorry – he died two days later.

KEYES, Roger John Brownlow: British admiral, b. 1872 son of a general. Joined RN 1885. Served China and as Naval attaché 1900-7. Captain 1905. CO Submarine Service 1910-4. Served Dardanelles, DSO and Legion of Honour. Rear-Admiral 1917, CO Dover Patrol and Zeebrugge Raid 1918. CO Battlecruiser Squadron 1919-21. Deputy Chief of Naval

Staff 1921-5, C-in-C Med and Portsmouth 1925-31. Retired 1935 as Admiral of the Fleet. Portsmouth's MP from 1934. Secret missions to Belgium Oct 1939-Jan 1940.

LAEKEN: Suburb of N Brussels in Brabant province. King Leopold III stayed here throughout the German occupation in the palace set in large grounds, originally built by Napoleon for Josephine.

REICHENAU, Walther von: German general, b. 1884 Karlsruhe, son of a Prussian general. Joined Ist Guards Field Artillery Regt 1903, staff officer on E. Front in WW1. Studied English in Britain 1929 and developed high regard for the British. Had frank discussions with Sq Ldr Winterbotham of M16 1934 and 1936. Reichenau became devoted to Hitler and his policies after meeting him 1932. Drafted Army's oath of allegiance while working in War Ministry 1933-4. CO 7th Corps (Munich) 1935-8 as General of Artillery. Leading role in Austrian and Sudetenland occupations. Rundstedt talked Hitler out of making him (14th in seniority) C-in-C after Fritsch's dismissal Feb 1938. Promoted to Colonel General to command 10th Army for the Polish campaign. Swam Vistula river ahead of his troops as befitted a member of the German Olympic Committee. Led the same army into Belgium – now designated 6th – consisting of 3 corps (13 divisions) and Höppner's 16th Motorized Corps (2 divisions).

SPAAK Paul-Henri: Belgian politician and lawyer b. 1899. Socialist deputy 1932. Became Minister for Foreign Affairs 1936. Strong exponent of an independent as opposed to neutral Belgium. He helped change the policy towards 'armed independence' and was much in favour of holding out against the Germans at all costs. After Leopold's capitulation Spaak went into exile in London.

accepted the decision to capitulate which prevented so much needless carnage and praised him for remaining with his people.

Outside the country the reaction was very different. Within hours of the Belgian surrender, the French Prime Minister, Paul Reynaud, broadcast a bitter attack on the King: 'In the midst of the battle, without warning, without one thought, without one word for the British and French soldiers who came to the help of his country, King Leopold III (he actually called him Leopold II in error) of the Belgians laid down his arms. It is a fact without precedent in history.' In exile, the Belgian ministers felt compelled to attack the King.

In Britain, Winston Churchill at first suspended judgment, but on 4 June he joined the attack with a speech in Parliament: 'The surrender of the Belgian Army compelled the British at the shortest notice, to cover a flank to the sea of more than 30 miles in length; otherwise all would have shared the fate to which King Leopold condemned the finest Army his country had ever formed.' Others were harsher still. Author H. G. Wells wrote: 'King Leopold has to be tried by his own people and by the world for what many of us think was his deliberate treason to them and to us . . . if he is guilty he should die. What is one life to the sweetening of the world by such an execution?'

Leopold's friends and supporters tried to make the reality known, and the King's own conduct as a prisoner impressed those who could learn of it. And then the tables turned. The fear that he would cooperate with the Germans by concluding a separate peace dropped away.

In October 1940, Sir Roger Keyes won a libel action against the *Daily Mirror* that was, in essence, a vindication of the King. Members of the Belgian Parliament, returning from France, apologized to the King for what they called 'a hasty and offensive judgement'. By the end of the year, the Belgian ministers, now in London, agreed that a grave injustice had been committed and gave their official support to the King. A few months later Paul Spaak could write: 'The King, by his obstinate refusal to collaborate with the enemy is not only the symbol of passive resistance in occupied Belgium. He is becoming an important element in the active resistance.'

Unfortunately, the effect of the initial attacks lingered on and many people still believed that somehow King Leopold had let the Allies down. Any real analysis must show that the Belgian Army was hopelessly out-matched and its surrender only a matter of time. It had in fact done well against depressing odds with a loyal King at its head. US Military Attaché, Lieutenant Colonel Brown, summed up the Army's contribution:

'The Belgians fought doggedly on successive retreat positions and at last found themselves completely cut off with their backs to the sea. Their artillery had fought with extreme brilliancy, their large units were well led. However, they were cut off and they had virtually no air power or anti-aircraft artillery protection against German air might. The Belgian King's capitulation on 28 May was the only thing King Leopold could do. Those who say otherwise didn't see the the fighting and they didn't see the German Air Force. I saw both.'

After the armistice was signed the human problem remained. Thousands of refugees remained wandering the countryside.

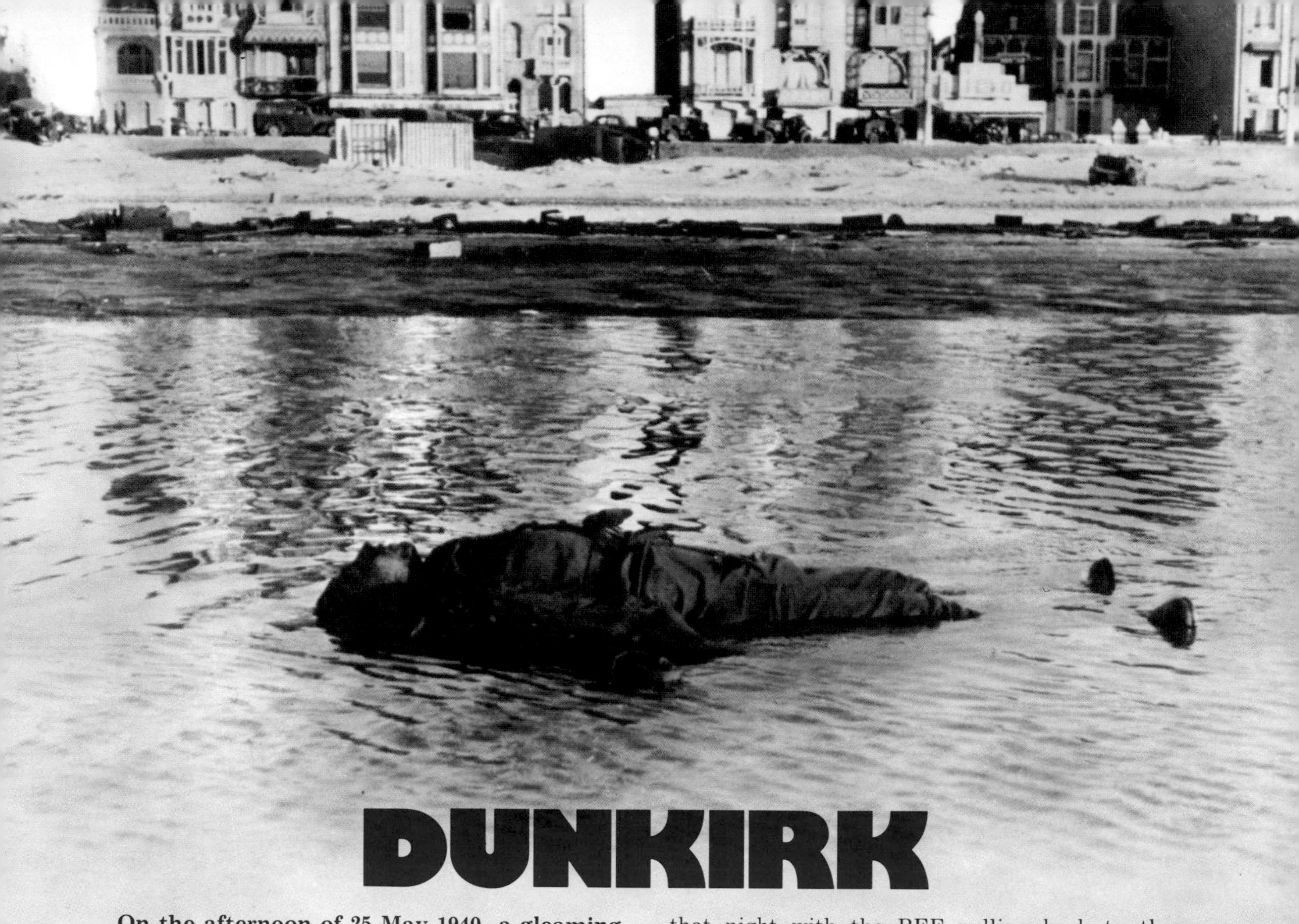

DUNKIRK

On the afternoon of 25 May 1940, a gleaming white-painted ship left Newhaven for Dunkirk. She was a hospital ship, her luxurious passenger fittings had been ripped out. Now, requisitioned by the Admiralty, the cross-channel ferry *Canterbury* bore over the calm waters to Dunkirk. She picked up 1246 wounded and was back at Newhaven by 9.30pm to sort out the dead from the dying and prepare for a second voyage. Operation Dynamo had begun.

For the next nine days the English Channel frothed with boats, large and small, packed and even bleeding with hundreds of thousands of troops of a beaten BEF and the remnants of fleeing Allied troops.

Churchill eagerly awaited news of the British counter-attack. Gort's decision to pull out left this dream standing and the French First Army were neutered on their own.

The possibility of evacuation had been preying on the minds of the War Office and BEF commanders alike for the past week. The War Office had agitated from safe corners of rooms across the Channel. Their despatches to Gort were couched in non-explicit hopes that he would stay the fight. But by 23 May Lieutenant-General Alan Brooke, commanding the 2nd Army Corps of the BEF, had confided in his diary. 'Nothing but a miracle can save the BEF now.'

Dunkirk's initial stages, however, did not seem heaven-sent. Early on 26 May Gort and Pownall visited General Georges Blanchard's HQ and drew up lines of retirement beginning that night with the BEF pulling back to the Bethune-Armentières Canal. They did not discuss going to the sea but, wrote Pownall, 'I have a strong suspicion that was in the minds of the French, as it certainly was in ours.' At 10.30am on the 26th Anthony Eden sent a telegram to Gort backing his decision to withdraw.

Gort's reply was cautious and very pessimistic '. . . I must not conceal from you that the greater part of the BEF and its equipment will inevitably be lost even in the best circumstances.' But the French were not told. Weygand himself anticipated the British evacuation and even the possibility of a French evacuation of troops. But he did not tell Blanchard or even Admiral Jean **Abrial** in charge of the Dunkirk area.

On 14 May the British people had heard this message following the BBC nine o'clock news.

'The Admiralty requisitions all self-propelled pleasure craft from 30 to 100 feet in length which haven't already been offered or requisitioned.'

The listeners were not told why. But given the mood of the country, they assumed it was part of the war effort. The response was overwhelming; within days the Admiralty had a register of practically every boat of those dimensions in the British Isles. Six of the boats were owned by women. The Admiralty told them they were not needed. The women were furious.

This announcement was considered to be the starting point of the evacuation plans. The French advanced it as one of the 'proofs' that the evacuation was decided upon early and without their consultation.

Eye Witness

'It is not the dangers and horrors of that day (1 June) which have stuck most firmly in my memory. What comes back with especial clearness is our slow movement away from the jetty. A marvellous summer night shed its magic on the waters. The sky was pure gold, the sea a mirror; and the black, rank smoke, pouring from the burning refinery, made so lovely a pattern above the low shore-line that one was cheated into forgetting its tragic origin. Even the name painted on the stern of our vessel (*Royal Daffodil*) was like something out of an Indian fairy-tale . . . We landed at Dover. Then came a whole day spent in travelling by train across southern England. That journey had left in my mind the memory of a sort of drugged exhaustion broken by chaotic sensations and images . . . the pleasure of devouring ham and cheese sandwiches handed through the windows by girls in multi-coloured dresses . . . the faint, sweet smell of cigarettes showered on us with the same generous profusion.'
Marc Bloch, French historian.

In fact the Admiralty were going about their normal administrative duties. Small craft were needed everywhere at the time and the branch known as the Small Vessels Pool was requisitioning them as an auxiliary to the Home Fleet.

The evacuation plan took shape quickly once Pownall telephoned London on the 19th. On 20 May deep in the galleries of the East Cliff below the castle at Dover, a group of Army and Navy officers gathered in a gaunt high-ceilinged chamber, one that had housed an electricity generating plant in World War 1. The 'dynamo room' they called it. The name was swiftly adopted for the operation under discussion.

At the centre of the planning was 57-year-old Vice-Admiral Bertram **Ramsay** — white haired, aloof, bluff, but a clear-thinking naval officer recalled from the retired list.

Three French ports, Calais, Boulogne and Dunkirk could be used, at this stage, to evacuate the Army. And, it was hoped, with little interference from the **Luftwaffe.** Ramsay's unit of 12 officers and 150 ratings with their 40 destroyers and 130 odd coasters and ferry boats available as troop carriers, could bring off 10,000 men each day. A total of 30,000 to 45,000 men might be rescued, it was estimated, before the panzers closed down the beachhead. There were over 500,000 troops needing rescue.

Now only Dunkirk remained. At 6.57 on the

'To my surprise I found a perfectly ordered straight column of men, about six abreast, standing as if on parade...'

Naval officer on seeing beaches of Dunkirk

Burnt-out British lorries and French medium tanks jam a street in Dunkirk.

evening of the 26th Operation Dynamo formally got under way as the first non-essential soldiers embarked in the old Liverpool to Isle of Man steamer *Mona's Isle*.

The next day a volunteer officer from Ramsay's staff, Captain William **Tennant** sailed into Dunkirk in the destroyer *Wolfhound*, confident that he could organize an orderly evacuation of non-essential troops.

The scene at Dunkirk hit him like a hammer blow. As he landed, the town was in the middle of an air raid. Bombers were droning undisturbed overhead, picking their targets with devastating precision, sending heaps of masonry crashing into the streets, and men scurrying for cover in a crouching, scurrying run. At St Pol the great oil refinery was burning, flinging billowing clouds of black smoke and smut thousands of feet into the air, so that the town looked as dark and gloomy as on a winter's day, despite the clear summer sunshine that bathed northern France to windward.

Göring's Luftwaffe was playing havoc on the scrambling Allied forces. It was four days since the weighty field marshal had received the news that the enemy in Flanders were almost surrounded. Walther Warlimont related the story. 'Göring reacted in a flash. Banging his great fist on the table, he shouted. "This is wonderful, an opportunity for the Luftwaffe. I must speak to the Führer at once." ' The Luftwaffe started their attacks on Dunkirk on the 27th.

So now, marching briskly off into the town for an inspection, Tennant found the houses and docks being systematically reduced by bombing. Corpses already littered the rubble-strewn streets. Worst of all Dunkirk harbour was useless. Oil storage tanks were blown up and the docks all bombed out of commission on one day of the

attack when 100 Heinkels had unleashed their venom on the town.

Offshore lay the **destroyers** Ramsay had sent. Seamen were manning their lifeboats, rowing into the shallows, picking up a handful of soldiers, and rowing them out to the waiting warships. Appalled by the pathetic slowness of the process, Tennant stomped from one end of Dunkirk to the other, searching for an alternative. The best prospect was the East Mole. Little more than a flimsy narrow plankway on concrete foundations, it stretched out as a breakwater 1600 yards, protecting the entrance channel to Dunkirk harbour from the racing tides.

Five men abreast could shuffle down the mole to a waiting ship — if a ship could get in without grounding. Tennant was forced to gamble, he decided to risk a ship and find out. He signalled the motorship *Queen of the Channel*, lying nearest, to come in.

Tentatively her skipper nosed in towards the mole, threw down a rope to be wrapped round a bollard, and reversed engines and rudder to bring his stern alongside. Minutes later the first of the soldiers, guided by Tennant's briskly efficient ratings, were forming up and stepping down the rickety planks. At high water 16 ships could tie up along the mole, steadily eating away at the long lines of troops.

And all the time the Luftwaffe, drawn by the tempting concentration of ships and men, did its best to obliterate the mole. They scored plenty of hits, killing men and sending lumps of concrete flashing under water to hole more than one ship. But they could not destroy the mole, and a few

Under heavy artillery fire German troops prepare to launch their rubber boats for the assault on Dunkirk. On the beaches after the armies have departed only scrap and personal belongings (inset) remain.

minutes sweating joinery soon resurfaced it.

That first day, 27 May, 7699 men were counted across the mole and onto the ships; 200,000 would escape by that route before Dynamo came to an end.

But even that was not enough. To keep the numbers moving Tennant could see that the beaches offered the best prospect. A mile wide, backed by sand dunes dotted with clumps of coarse grass, the beaches stretched out for mile after mile to form the longest continuous line of sand in Europe.

Tennant surveyed the scene around him; the red and black glow of war to landward, the destroyers lying inert, impotent and vulnerable offshore, and the growing mass of men filtering into Dunkirk to try to get back to England. The Captain gave private thanks for the foresight that had set up the register of small boats. He signalled Ramsay. 'Please send every available craft to beaches east of Dunkirk immediately. Evacuation tomorrow night is problematical.'

In England the Admiralty started gathering the small boats. From the upper Thames, its estuary, the East Coast, the Channel harbours, came millionaires' motor yachts, holiday pleasure-trip launches, tugs, fishing boats, ferry boats, a little green cockle boat from the Essex mudflats. A thousand-strong armada chugged away across the Channel. Many had never put to sea before. Few had any protection against the mines, or any weapons, or any provisions.

Mercifully, red tape was slashed. Owners put their names down, filled up with fuel, and set out. 'Aim for the gunfire,' an organizer told a skipper, 'You can't miss it. It's burning,' an incoming captain told one just setting out.

The crews were a varied bunch. A Dominican monk changed into a reefer jersey to sail with a friend. The Earl of Craven signed on as third engineer in a tugboat. The bosun of the contraband control boat *Ocean Breeze* sported a single gold ear-ring beneath a steel helmet. Stewardess Amy Goodrich defied the 'no-women' rule and told her local organizers — if nurses were sailing in a hospital ship she could sail too. She won the Dunkirk decoration. A Bank of England clerk sailed out in his pin-stripe suit and bowler hat with rolled umbrella. A chartered accountant crossed dressed in a padded gold-cap, lounge suit, and a lifebelt so thick he had to stand a foot away from the wheel.

Dark shapes on the beach

To underline the urgent need for boats, Tennant sent an officer back to London. Captain Eric **Bush** pleaded with Ramsay. Ramsay rang the Vice-Chief of the Naval Staff, Vice-Admiral Tom Phillips, and handed Bush the phone. 'How many small boats do you want? A hundred?' asked Phillips. Bush could see that London did not appreciate the scale of the problem. 'Look sir,' he answered quietly. 'Not a hundred boats. Every boat in the country should be sent if we're even to stand a chance.'

In Dunkirk, the message went out to the troops in the eastern end of town — move to the beaches, form up in groups of 50 and wait your turn. For mile after mile the men gathered in thousands. Returning to Dunkirk in a destroyer, Captain Bush was mystified by the dark shapes moving on the beach. On a clear night they couldn't be cloud shadows — his first thought. As the mists cleared he saw they were great squads of troops, winding like serpents out of the sand dunes, every few yards for nine miles along the beaches, the front ranks in each line standing up to their necks in water, waiting for the boats.

Almost every day for over a week the Luftwaffe flew over Dunkirk on bombing operations. The 27th saw a massive raid by over 300 bombers. The next day low cloud and pouring rain stopped the bombing. The following afternoon they came again, and after another day of frustration through weather, they returned again.

With no cover to run to the men dug shallow holes in the sand, they had to be shallow — too deep and you could get buried. The bombs sent cascades of sand into the air, but apart from a direct hit, did little damage as the sand muffled their blast effect. Major-General Harold Alexander was appalled to see the shapes of legless bodies being flung skywards by bomb explosions, until he realized they were just discarded overcoats. The worst effect was psychological. Battle-hardened men could not stand the thought that the screaming bombs were aimed for them, and they had nothing to reply with. Some men clutched teddy bears for comfort. One ran round in distraction crying and shouting biblical quotations. A sergeant, more angered than cowed, waved at the bombers from on top of a truck and screamed 'Come down and fight fair you bloody bastards.'

Gort comes home

On the landward side, the battle raged as Gort's army with French help threw up a protective shell round the shrinking perimeter. On 27 May, freed at last from the restrictions of Hitler's incomprehensible halt order, the panzers advanced again, aiming to complete a pincer movement that would cut off the French 1st Army and several BEF divisions in a pocket round Lille. 'Dearest Lu, I am very well. We're busy encircling the French and British in **Lille** at the moment,' wrote Erwin Rommel in a letter home. But the pincers did not close until 28 May, by which time four BEF divisions had slipped westward into the Dunkirk bridgehead.

Of the French in the pocket, five divisions were cut off and lost. General Blanchard drove to Lord Gort's HQ. There Gort read to him his latest order from London, to evacuate. Blanchard was horrified. 'So the question remains, are you going to walk out without us?' Blanchard asked. 'Yes, that is so,' replied Gort. He pleaded with Blanchard to withdraw First Army, but Blanchard, proud, his head erect, refused. His army fought on until 31 May.

On 29 May other French troops started to crowd into the beachhead. They had no orders to evacuate, but thousands were determined to do so. Gort, complaining that the French were not taking on a fair share of the naval effort, told London 'Every Frenchman embarked is at cost of one Englishman'.

Churchill was in a more co-operative mood. Knowing that most of France's navy was in the Mediterranean by Anglo-French agreement he countered an order signed by C-in-C of the **French Navy** Admiral Jean Darlan himself, that the British troops should evacuate first. He insisted that both forces moved out arm-in-arm.

On Thursday the 30th the British commanders started to leave the bridgehead. General Alan Brooke was reluctant to go. He sought out Gort and asked if it was an order. Gort said it was. But Brooke persuaded him to let him stay until he had shepherded his corps into the defence perimeter. Then on 30 May, standing in tears in the dunes, he handed his corps over to Bernard Montgomery and left for England, where he drove through the sleepy Kent countryside and was struck by the peaceful contrast with the war 39 miles and five hours away across the Channel.

Gort also received orders to leave, from Churchill himself. He stood alone in his bedroom cutting medal ribbons — his VC included — from a tunic he would have to leave behind. Always contemptous of creature comforts, he carried his own two suitcases to the destroyer, and was annoyed to be met by his military assistant in a Rolls Royce when he arrived at Dover on 1 June. The aide expressed relief at Gort's safe return. 'That I've come back safe, Huh? That isn't what matters. It's that my army gets back,' snorted Gort. In fact the havoc at Dunkirk, the soldiers grabbing at boats, pulled from the water and crowded on the beaches, was only half the story.

After Gort had left, there were still 39,000 men in the contracted area around Dunkirk. The French held a reduced sector to the west and joined up with the British on the Bergues canal. General Alexander, now the BEF's commander, conferred with Admiral Abrial. He didn't want to hold a joint front too close to Dunkirk as the rearguard action would ruin the evacuation of troops. The British held the south facing canal front joining up with the French 12th Division

'Come down and fight fair you bloody bastards!'

A British Sergeant
on the beaches of Dunkirk

and the supporting British 50th on the eastern line running to the sea. They could stay there another 24 hours if pushed, the General reckoned.

The main German attacks were at Bergues and Hoymille. With a waterlogged ground and severe enemy artillery fire, movement of the rearguard troops was almost impossible. All the counter-attacks failed but the line was held. The British troops were all withdrawn behind the French lines and by the morning of 2 June they were on the beaches awaiting the boats.

Meanwhile the Royal Navy struggled to fend off the German air, artillery and E-boat attacks.

When the planes came over there was no cover for the soldiers on the beach. Some like the Tommy above, took pot-shots with their rifles. 338,226 British and French troops were evacuated from Dunkirk in the armada of small boats sent from England. With the fall of Dunkirk 40,000 British troops were captured, and almost all their equipment.

Many ships were sunk, the destroyers *Basilisk* and *Havant*, the destroyer-leader *Keith*, the minesweeper *Skipjack* with many troops aboard, the French *Foudroyant*, the passenger ships *Brighton Queen* and *Scotia*, both heavily laden with French soldiers, the *Prague* with 3000 troops aboard. Rolls of the evacuees could not be taken in the haste of the embarkations. So the dead could not be counted.

In England there was a curious tension in the air. A carnival atmosphere at the great deliverance gave way to sober acknowledgement at the mighty defeat. Everyone was aware of the casualties. Helpers hosing down ships' decks slippery with blood knew what had happened at Dunkirk. So did the wives and mothers of the young men who woke up screaming in the night or turned pale when an aircraft flew over.

In the speech he composed to deliver in Parliament Churchill summed up the ambiguity of Operation Dynamo. 'We must be very careful not to assign to this deliverance the attributes of victory.'

Back in Blighty, Dunkirk survivors disembark from British destroyers. On the whole the evacuation was orderly and good humoured.

War Notes

ABRIAL: Jean: French admiral, b. 1879. In command of French N. Sea naval forces from late 1939 with HQ in Napoleonic Bastion 32 at Dunkirk. Left in French MTB-25 off N Goodwin lightship on 3 June. Picked up survivors but 2nd propeller damaged. Rescued by destroyer HMS *Malcolm* and landed at Dover for breakfast with Adm Ramsay.

BUSH: Eric Wheler: British sailor, b. 1888 son of Chaplain to the Forces. Educated Stoke House RN Colleges Osborne and Dartmouth. Midshipman in cruiser *Bacchante* 1914. Present at Heligoland Bight, Gallipoli landings (DSC), Jutland in battleship *Revenge*. Sub-Lieutenant 1917. Lieutenant 1920. Qualified Hindustani Interpreter 1924. Lt-Commander 1927. RN Staff College 1931. Commander 1933. Captain Auxiliary Patrol, Dover.

CASUALTIES: British Army losses including fighting 4–20 June totalled 68,111 men. Loss of equipment for the same period amounted to 2472 guns (German claimed capture of 1200 field and 1250 AA/AT guns), 63,879 vehicles (including 240 tanks with BEF), 20,548 motorcycles, 8000 Brens and 400 AT rifles, 90,000 rifles, 76,697 tons of ammo, 415,940 tons of stores, 164,929 tons of petrol.

DESTROYERS: did the lion's share of the evacuation. The 56 Allied vessels rescued 102,843 troops at a cost of 9 sunk (*Wakeful, Grenade, Grafton* on 29 May, *Bourrasque, Sirocco* 30–31 May, *Keith, Basilisk, Havant* and *Foudrouant* on 1 June.) Another 19 were damaged (2 French).

FRENCH NAVY: 6 destroyers, 3 torpedo boats and 4 sloops took part as well as 200 lesser French and Belgian rescue vessels. They embarked 48,474 Allied troops.

LILLE: Industrial city of 200,575 (1930) 130 miles NNE of Paris and France's 7th city, on R. Deule. Forms built up area of 600,000 with Tourcoing (8 miles NNE) and Roubaix (6 miles NE). Defended against 6 German divisions by dug-in French 1st Army's 4th and 5th Corps (1st Moroccan, 2nd N. African, 4th 15th and 25th Divs) from 28 May until 8pm on 31st when Gen Molinie of 25th Div surrended at third summons. Gen Waeger of German 28th Corps awarded them honours of war.

LUFTWAFFE: Luftflotten 2 and 3 committed 400 bombers and 500 fighters operating from newly captured French and Belgian bases as well as airfields in Germany. They were against the RAF on home bases, making its greatest effort of the war yet. No 11 Group put up 15 fighter squadrons with 138 Hurricanes, 86 Spitfires and 13 Defiants. They flew 2700 sorties. Losses 26 May–2 June: RAF 106, Luftwaffe 156. RAF Fighter Command lost 87 pilots killed or taken prisoner. On 31 May and 1 June Fleet Air Arm and Coastal Command squadrons were thrown into the battle. Bombing sank 72 ships and damaged at least 45. Low cloud late on 28th and morning of 29th and Channel fog on 30th delayed air attacks. Y Service in Britain jammed German bomber radios and supplied intercepts of Luftwaffe signals (via Bletchley Park) that helped to route shipping.

RAMSAY: Bertram Home: British admiral, b. 1883 son of a general. Joined RN 1898. Passed Staff College 1913. CO Monitor 25 and destroyer *Broke* in Dover Patrol 1915–9. Captain of cruisers *Weymouth* and *Danae* 1924–7. RN War College 1927–9. CO cruiser *Kent* and chief of staff, China Station 1929–31. CO Battleship *Royal Sovereign* 1933–5. Rear Admiral and Chief of Staff, Home Fleet 1935–8. Promoted Vice-Admiral. Retired 1938.

TENNANT, William: British sailor b. 1890 son of a colonel. Educated HMS *Britannia* 1905. Lieutenant 1912. Commander 1925. Captain 1932. Made a Companion of the Bath.

JUNE 1940

...WITH THE fall of Dunkirk, Hitler turns his panzers south. Swiftly, bloodlessly, they enter Paris. Desperately, a second British army is sent back to France, only to suffer the fate of another Dunkirk. Far to the north, the remains of the Allies leave Norway to her fate. In a final act of humiliation, France sues for peace in the woods of Compiègne...

1st: Dunkirk: 64,429 troops evacuated. Daytime evacuation abandoned as 10 ships badly damaged or sunk. Hitler in Brussels.

2nd: Dunkirk: 26,256 troops evacuated. Gladiator pilot shoots down 6 German bombers near Narvik.

3rd: Dunkirk: 26,746 evacuated. Bombing near Paris, 254 people killed.

4th: After last 26,175 troops evacuated Germans capture Dunkirk, 40,000 prisoners and much abandoned British equipment. French bomb Munich and Frankfurt.

5th: Germans attack on the Somme. RAF bomb Rhineland railways. French cabinet reshuffle, de Gaulle now Under-Secretary for Defence.

6th: Rommel advances 20 miles. Sir Stafford Cripps new British Ambassador in Moscow. Merchant cruiser *Carinthia* sunk by U46.

7th: Rommel advances 30 miles. French 4-engine transport Jules Verne bombs Berlin.

8th: Panzers reach R. Seine. Narvik and Harstad evacuation completed. Norwegian King and government sail for England. *Gneisenau* and *Scharnhorst* sink HMS *Glorious* and 2 destroyers.

9th: Von Rundstedt attacks on the Aisne. Panzers capture Rouen. German-Norwegian Armistice.

10th: Italy declares war on Allies. Canada declares war on Italy. Germans cross Seine.

11th: RN bombard Tobruk. 2 Italian raids on Malta. RAF bombs Turin and Genoa. French prevent Wellingtons from leaving to bomb N.Italy. Australia, N. Zealand and S. Africa declare war on Italy.

12th: Germans cross the Marne, Rheims falls. Rommel takes 20,000 Allied troops at St Valery. Japanese capture Ichang on Yangtse.

13th: Paris declared an 'open city'. Final meeting of Allied War Council.

14th: Germans enter Paris and attack Maginot Line. Churchill orders evacuation of second BEF.

15th: Germans cross Rhine and capture Verdun. Last French tank counter-attack. Soviet forces enter Lithuania.

NORWAY: THE FINAL ACT

The British and French were suffering the biggest defeat in modern history. Defending north Norway from Germans already in control of the south was a luxury that the War Office could not afford.

If this BEF did not pull out now, Britain would have even fewer troops to hold her own against the Germans massing to the shores of the English Channel. But the situation was an awkward one.

The Norwegians had struggled hard alongside General Emile Béthouart's Chasseurs Alpins and had helped the snowbound attempts of Lieutenant-General Claude **Auchinleck's** BEF. It had been messy, a battle staggering forward, wasting time and troops—a lot of valuable effort had been spent on Narvik.

On 26 May Lord Cork and Auchinleck went, grim-faced, to see Béthouart. The French commander tells his own story: 'His face (Cork's) and that of General Auchinleck wear grave expressions. Mine also, for the news from France is increasingly alarming. Cork takes a telegram from his pocket, he looks me in the eyes and offers it. I take it and read. "His Majesty's Government has decided that your forces ought to evacuate the Norwegian sector as quickly as possible." "Do you still wish to take Narvik?" Cork asked me. I hesitate for a while...at the bottom of my heart I feel that if we take Narvik, capture the Germans or push them into Sweden, the governments might change their minds. "Yes," I said, "I will attack on 28 May, as planned." '

Narvik fell. Its victory was quietly celebrated. The tiger threatened elsewhere. Ships, men, guns, morale and stamina were precious commodities to pawn on a lost cause. The British now had to maintain absolute secrecy—another rush to the coast was underway.

Sitting targets

At this stage nobody was told of the evacuation, not the Norwegian King Haakon and his cabinet, nor even RAF Coastal Command. Béthouart, Auchinleck and Cork exchanged the few names of the initiated and went back to the planning. There were 25,000 troops to be taken out, this would require 15 large troopships and only 13 were available. They would all be sitting targets for air attack, surface raider and submarine. If the Germans knew about this, the evacuation could be catastrophic.

To protect the troopships there were two aircraft carriers (themselves targets), three cruisers, the repair ship *Vindictive*—merely a token World War 1 cruiser—and, most sinister of all, only 11 destroyers. On paper, the destroyers alone would be just good enough to screen the carriers. Land-based air cover was minimal and difficult to obtain.

Even so troops and equipment had to be embarked with all eggs in one tottering basket. The equipment was especially vital now that so much was being abandoned at Dunkirk.

Priceless bonus

As for King Haakon and his government, the King, the Crown Prince, VIPs and Cabinet, would all be shipped to Britain to wave the Norwegian flag in exile. With them would come Norway's gold supply and, into the bargain, a priceless bonus—her vast merchant marine that was scattered worldwide would now join the Allies. This new-found fleet would carry millions of tons of oil and high octane spirits; whale-chasers equipped with asdic would soon vie with U-boats.

So far the theory. Before any evacuation could be effected, troops and equipment had to be concentrated from widely dispersed areas. Every hour that passed, with the BEF in France boarding at Dunkirk, made the Norway salvage operation more dangerous and more difficult. The Germans would not let them off the hook on two seaboards, once they had an inkling of what was happening.

Norwegian generals Otto Ruge and Carl Fleischer were next to be told of the British decision, a decision that meant the withdrawal of the French and Poles from Narvik and Fleischer's left flank. Ruge and his staff were

Polish troops embark for Norway (left). They were to play a key role in the capture of Narvik (above). The Germans had air superiority in Norway: the inset shows two Stuka Ju87 dive-bombers.

totally baffled. How could the British leave when General Dietl's men were already retreating towards the Swedish border, when Narvik was in Allied hands? But the Norwegian C-in-C was cut off from the reality of the military situation. He could only look around him in a narrow field of struggle and say, 'This is going well.' Contact with the **Tromso** Government was difficult at the best of times and now the official hush made it almost impossible.

The generals were asked to go with their King. The Norwegian Government wanted Fleischer and Colonel Beichmann to organize new forces from England. Ruge refused to leave on any account. His place, he said, was with his men, troops with whom he identified strongly. Their cause and their fate would be his too. Together they would stand and fall for Norway unconquered. This simple, single-minded man lived for many years after the war, reaping the rewards for his brave decision.

While the other Norwegian brass were packing their bags, the Germans were eager to blitz the northern sector. They hadn't a clue about the British plans but still intended to obliterate Narvik along with the main base and shipping at Harstad as well as Bardufoss airfield. At first, hampered by strong winds and fog, they held off. Then with better conditions on 2 June the air droned with wave after wave of Stukas, Heinkel 111s and Junkers 88s.

Each time, tired and struggling Hurricanes and Gladiators, working from Bardufoss, managed to intercept the raiding swarms and spoil their aim.

Now, too, the German Navy put to sea for the first time since the April invasion. Earlier, on 25 May they had planned to send heavy units into Westfjord to aid Dietl's defence of Narvik and to blast the convoys moving between Harstad and British ports.

Now, on 4 June Vice Admiral Wilhelm Marschall was ordered to proceed with the operation, to be codenamed 'Juno'.

The battlecruisers *Gneisenau* and *Scharnhorst* sailed from Kiel along with the cruiser *Hipper*

and four destroyers. These ships outgunned every vessel under Lord Cork's command, only Admiral Sir Charles Forbes' Home Fleet at large in the North Sea could possibly deal with them.

Marschall's orders were explicit. He was to smash all warships, transports and installations in the Harstad area. The Germans were running behind. They did not know the British evacuation was scheduled to finish on 8 June, the estimated time of Marschall's arrival on the scene. For their part the Allies were oblivious of the powerful German units heading towards the convoys.

British naval intelligence during the Norway campaign had gone from poor to scrappy with the fading out of the Norwegian Enigma in the middle of May. This said, there were still pointers persistently indicating movements of major German units which were ignored by the Admiralty, and not a glimmer of such evidence was passed on to the Home Fleet.

One Norwegian coastal station sighted the German ships. Two Norwegian telephone girls reported to Wing-Commander Dick **Atcherley** at his operations room. 'There are two German warships' one of the girls told him. He was highly amused. Atcherley, who naturally thought any mysterious warships would be well known to the Navy, recalled his last words as he embarked at Harstad: 'Look out for those bloody battleships.'

Meanwhile the evacuation was going smoothly. Destroyers embarked parties direct from the 'puffers'. These sturdy and capable little Norwegian diesel craft worked in small flotillas each in the charge of a British officer. The linking chain grew longer as destroyers then shipped the troops to troopships waiting 180 miles out at sea.

The evacuation was much helped by weather and conditions that made the convoys no easy game for German air attack. The first ships steamed out under the added cover of blanketing darkness on the night of 3/4 June. Darkness and weather between them were the strongest allies the convoys could have hoped for—armed protection was farcically small.

Vindictive alone escorted the first group of eight ships among which *Lancastria* successfully transported her share of 4700 men to safer ports. Her good luck was short-lived. She survived Norway only to be blown up and sunk off St Nazaire only two weeks later with 5000 men aboard.

No easy game

The first convoys could count their blessings. Apart from the serious lack of anti-submarine and anti-aircraft defence they were left naked to any kind of assault, thanks to a grave misadventure. On 5 June the British Q-ship *Prunella* patrolling northern waters sighted two warships. They could not be identified but even 200 miles northeast of the Faroes was close enough to worry. Forbes immediately sent two heavy cruisers, *Newcastle* and *Sussex*, along with five destroyers to intercept. It could have been a breakout by German raiders, thought Forbes. It was, in fact, a wild goose chase. Whatever was sighted by *Prunella*—certainly not warships—is still unknown. Meanwhile *Vindictive* continued as sole escort.

On 7 June with a bleak day breaking in the east Marschall, underway from Kiel, was told of ships, four large and three small, to the southeast. They are surely transports returning empty to Britain, he reckoned and kept his course. But early that evening another report changed his mind. He steered round to intercept two aircraft carriers sighted in a Luftwaffe sweep. Now he knew the British were bailing out of Norway, he told Group Command West of his plans. They approved but still didn't swallow the whole implication. 'Then go back and destroy Harstad' they briefed Marschall.

The first kills came quickly. At 6.30am the oil tanker *Oil Pioneer* was sunk along with her escort trawler *Juniper*. Reconnaissance seaplanes took wing from *Scharnhorst* and *Hipper*. They spotted British troopship *Orama* and hospital ship *Atlantis*—easy victims. *Orama* was sunk with no British troops aboard but 100

A Swordfish stands helpless on the deck of the British aircraft carrier *Glorious*, as hangars burst into flame after an 11in salvo from *Scharnhorst* and *Gneisenau*, inset.

German prisoners. *Atlantis* made no signals and passed by unmolested; her privilege of immunity was respected by the German admiral.

Marschall was now uncertain of his next move. Back towards Harstad and Narvik? Pot-luck on the seas scouted by his planes? He spread a map and carefully sifted the spatterings of information his aircraft afforded him. Yes. Narvik must be throwing out troops in thousands. Marschall sharpened his sights. The squadron altered course for Narvik.

A few hours before, the British cruiser *Devonshire* carrying King Haakon and his party, gold bullion, the British Ambassador and staff, sailed from Tromso. This was the last day. Men and booty, together with far more equipment than the British had hoped for, dashed for home. The last complement was away late that afternoon—8 June as planned.

At 4pm, about 200 miles west of Harstad a sharp-eyed midshipman in **Scharnhorst** sighted a thread of mast on the horizon. 'Suppose she's a battleship?' ventured the admiral's chief of staff, Backenholler. 'We'll get her anyway,' snapped Marschall.

'Chummy is sunk'

Soon the silhouette of the aircraft carrier **Glorious** came into view couched between two destroyers. World War 1 hero Captain Guy **D'Oyley Hughes** was in command.

The carrier's decks were cluttered with the aircraft rescued from Bardufoss. Her own Skua dive-bombers and 'string-bag' Swordfish had been reduced to make room for them. *Glorious* could not pull away—she lacked fuel, and couldn't attain the high speed that made aircraft launches possible. Nor could she turn quickly enough to avoid the enemy's superior firepower. Despite a thick smokescreen laid by the destroyers *Ardent* and **Acasta** the Germans scored the first hit. An 11in shell crashed through the vessel's thin armour, exploded a hangar and set fire to the stowed Hurricanes. Flames spread to the hangar above where crewmen struggled to prepare the Swordfish for a launch. But now it was too late.

Ardent and *Acasta* closed, without hesitation. They loosed torpedoes at the battlecruisers and missed. *Ardent*, commanded by Lieutenant-Commander J. E. Parker, was first through the smokescreen and met devastating fire that ripped her apart. She rolled over and sank.

Glorious wallowed helplessly. Another shell hit her bridge, bending metal in all directions, yet another plunged deeper into the hull. Gradually she keeled over. Throwing massive clouds of billowing red-tinged smoke skywards, she sank in a turmoil of hissing steam.

Scorning the chance to flee the inferno, Lieutenant-Commander C. E. Glasfurd sent *Acasta* streaking toward *Scharnhorst* in a flurry of spume. She veered, loosing her torpedoes and escaping a hurricane of shellfire. One torpedo hit the battlecruiser causing enough damage for the Germans to break off their sortie. A massacre of Allied troops in transit was narrowly avoided.

Acasta had another opportunity to escape but chose to resume the attack and was finally overwhelmed and sunk. According to the one survivor, Leading Seaman C. Carter, Glasfurd told his crew as they plunged through the smoke: 'Our chummy is sunk, the *Glorious* is sinking, the least we can do is make a good show. Good luck to you all.'

In her last moments *Glorious* sent off a garbled

British Guardsmen aid members of the Royal Army Medical Corps to desembark Allied wounded from Norway.

message picked up by *Devonshire*. It was not considered important enough to pass on. Other signals intercepted from a German ship by the Royal Navy, signals that indicated a sinking, were likewise ignored.

On 9 June the battleship *Valiant* came into contact with the *Atlantis* and was told about the *Orama's* fate. They met in the morning but the first that Forbes heard about it was from a German radio broadcast later that evening.

As the picture became clearer Forbes acted. That night he sailed in the 16in-gun battleship *Rodney* from Scapa Flow. Joined by the battlecruiser *Renown* and a scant screen of six destroyers, they raced towards the German marauders.

Early on the 10th *Scharnhorst* limped into Trondheim. Marschall informed the sceptical German High Command that he believed the Allies had evacuated from Norway. He was peremptorily ordered back to sea for more and greater assaults on British convoys. He went out only a few miles, returning in the evening quite convinced that he'd never catch up. Marschall was promptly dismissed and Vice-Admiral Günther Lütjens took his place.

Forbes' battleships were now adequate protection and the convoys sweated into safe waters.

Norway demobilized

When *Devonshire* arrived at Gourock on the Clyde on 10 June, there was a special train waiting for her gold shipment. On arrival in London it was dispatched across the Atlantic to follow the same hazardous route that the British gold had taken. The US—a fortress in isolation—was opening her gates to Allied bullion.

The story was by no means over for the French troops. After leaving Norway they waited a few hours off the Scottish coast then left for France where they landed in Brest and took up forlorn defensive positions in Brittany.

On 11 June Otto Ruge ordered his troops in Norway to be demobilized and sent home. 'When the orders became known,' wrote Colonel Munthe-Kaas afterwards, '...Profound anger filled the men's minds. Some wept...'

Meanwhile Forbes was unaware of the fate of *Glorious*. The 11th saw the troops safe, but the possibility of danger from *Scharnhorst*, wherever she may be, still lurked over the horizon. He was not aware of the damage *Acasta* had already done. Locating her in Trondheim the *Ark Royal* attacked *Scharnhorst* with 15 Skuas on the morning of the 12th. The single hit scored, by a 500lb bomb that failed to explode, cost the Fleet Air Arm eight of the planes.

The Norway 'sideshow' had cost the German Navy three cruisers, ten destroyers, one gunnery ship, one motorized minesweeper and numerous auxiliary craft. Its **losses** weighed almost equally with the Home Fleet's; one aircraft carrier, two cruisers, nine destroyers, five submarines and various subsidiary vessels. For the Royal Navy it was a heavy lesson in bungling intelligence and the cost of operations without adequate air support. But, like Dunkirk immediately before, it had worked—at a price.

War Notes

ACASTA: British 1350-ton destroyer. Launched Aug 1929 and completed Feb 1930. Dimensions: 323 × 32.2 × 12ft. Powered 2-shaft turbines giving 34,000shp and 35 knots. Guns: 4 × 4.7in, 2 × 2pdr pom poms, 4 × .303in AA. Torpedoes: 2 quadruple 21in tubes. Crew: 138. Sister ships: 9, the first RN destroyers with quadruple torpedo mounts.

ATCHERLEY, Richard Llewellyn Roger: British airman, b. 1904. Educated Oundle and RAF Cranwell. Served with Nos 23 and 29 Fighter Squadrons 1924-5. Central Flying School Instructor 1925-8. Schneider Trophy flying team and King's Cup Air Race 1928-9. No 14 Squadron, Amman, Jordan, 1930-4. Royal Aircraft Establishment at Farnborough 1934-7. RAF Staff College 1937, Air Staff Officer to RAF Inspector General 1938. CO 219 Night Fighter Sqdn 1939-40. Garrison commander Bardufoss, Norway.

AUCHINLECK, Claude John Eyre: British general, b. 1884 son of a colonel. Educated Wellington and Sandhurst. Joined 62nd Punjabi Regt 1904. Served Middle East 1914-18 winning DSO, Croix de Guerre and OBE. Rose to Brevet Lt-Colonel. Camberley Staff College Instructor. Asst quartermaster general, India. Imperial Defence College 1927-9. CO 1st Punjabi Regt 1929-30. Quetta Staff College Instructor 1930-3. CO Peshawar Brigade fighting Afghan tribesmen on NW Frontier 1933-6. Deputy Chief of Staff, Indian Army 1936. GOC Meerut District 1938. Recalled to Britain as Major-General to command 4th Corps. Appointed C-in-C Land Forces in Norway May 1940.

D'OYLY-HUGHES, Guy: British sailor, b. 1891. Educated RN Colleges Osborne and Dartmouth. Served in 1914-18 war winning DSC and DSO for submarine exploits in the Dardanelles. Directorate of Training, Air Ministry 1931-4. Captain of 1st Submarine Flotilla 1934-6. Chief of Staff to C-in-C Plymouth 1936-8. Captain of *Glorious* 1939. Killed in action 8 June 1940.

GLORIOUS: British 22,500-ton aircraft carrier (full-load 27,400 tons). Launched as battlecruiser April 1916, completed Jan 1917. Converted to aircraft carrier 1924-30. Given longer flight deck 1934-5. Dimensions: 786.2 × 90.5 × 24ft. Powered by 4-shaft steam turbines giving 90,000shp and 29.5 knots. Range: 4260 miles at 20 knots. Guns: 16 × 4.7in, 24 × 2pdr AA (3 mounts). Aircraft: 24 + 20 RAF fighters, 2 catapults and 2 lifts. Armour: 2-3in belt, 1-1.75in deck. Crew: 1557 (41 RAF), only 42 survivors.

LOSSES: British: 1869 troops. French and Polish: about 530. Norwegians: 1335 killed and wounded. Total Allied loss: 3734 excluding Norwegian Army surrender. German: 5296 troops. Luftwaffe: 242 planes, a third being transports. RAF and Fleet Air Arm: more than 100.

SCHARNHORST: German 38,900-ton battlecruiser. Launched Oct 1936, completed Jan 1939. Dimensions: 770.7 × 98.5 × 32.5ft. Powered by 3-shaft turbines giving 160,000shp and 32 knots. Range: 10,000 miles at 17 knots. Guns: 9 × 11in (3 turrets), 12 × 5.9in (4 twin), 7 twin 4.1in AA, 8 twin 37mm AA, 8 × 20mm. Torpedoes: 2 triple 21in tubes. Armour: 1.2–9.7in belt, 2in deck, 4–13.2in turrets. Aircraft: 2 and 2 catapults. Crew: 1840. *Acasta's* torpedo hit aft killing 48, disabling the stern turret. Starboard and middle engine rooms were flooded reducing speed to 20 knots. Sister ship: *Gneisenau* launched Dec 1936 and completed May 1938.

TROMSO: coastal town of about 10,000 in N. Norway, 95 miles NNE of Narvik. The cruiser *Glasgow* brought King Haakon and Crown Prince Olav here from Molde on 29 April.

BATTLE FOR FRANCE

'Dunkirk has fallen . . . with it has ended the greatest battle of world history.' Hitler read through his words with satisfaction. They would go out with instructions that bells should ring throughout the Reich for three days in celebration.

Meanwhile, that evening of 4 June, there was time for a rare glass of wine. 'Wonderful eventide peace, harmonious atmosphere!' Chief of Staff Franz Halder confided to his diary at the German HQ. Up on the northern coast of France the panzer crews were resting too.

But the breathing space was brief. Hitler's announcement was made at midnight. Just one hour later came the announcement that 'the second great offensive is being launched today'.

From dawn on the 5th the panzers, heralded by a massive air and artillery bombardment, would head south again. The time had come to take final revenge for all the wrongs inflicted on Germany at the fateful signing of the peace treaty in 1919. Today was the start of the Battle of France—a 'battle without hope'.

It was another clear summer day, 'Göring's weather' they were calling it now. Almost the whole strength of the German Army was assembled for the assault—143 divisions (seven more than on 10 May) confronting a French force of 49. The ten panzer divisions were now formed into five corps of two divisions each. All were massed along a 200 mile front on the north banks of the Somme, the Ailette and the Aisne.

The new French Under Secretary of State for National Defence, General of Brigade Charles de Gaulle, had a gloomy report to make to Prime Minister Paul Reynaud. 'Events are now going to move very fast,' he warned on the 6th. It would take a miracle just to be able to hold on,

Rommel's victorious 7th Panzer Division massed on the Somme. Meanwhile, French refugees (inset) move towards Paris.

let alone win. The High Command 'will not pull itself together'. The Government was sunk in 'an atmosphere of abandon'.

Desperate appeals for more aircraft had been made to Britain and the United States in the preceding days. But the British declined to send 20 fighter squadrons. Britain was looking to her own interests. Across the land old men and boys were rallying to the new Home Guard.

There seemed to be more chance of aid from the United States. Reynaud had telephoned Roosevelt on the 5th. Hopeful of winning 150 planes from the President, Reynaud's spirits were buoyant. Now the final crunch had come he was in a mood to fight on. The latest idea was that the government and all the armed forces would fall back into the ancient land of Brittany, make a redoubt there, and carry on.

Weygand, France's new C-in-C, was still wedded to the notion of making a stand on the Somme and fighting to the end. 'The battle on which the fate of the country depends will be fought without thought of retreat,' he ordained. He got to General Alphonse Georges at Les Bondons HQ at 8am on 5 June and issued a dramatic Order of the Day. 'The Battle of France has begun...the future of our sons depends on your tenacity.'

But 73-year-old Weygand was concerned. On 25 May he had warned his War Cabinet that the 'Weygand Line' could be broken through, this time. No army commander, since 1914-18, wanted to see his men slaughtered wholesale. But the pointless wasting of his troops' lives was not the only spectre that haunted Weygand's nightmares. In the streets of France, packed with drunken soldiers and shocked civilians, Weygand had seen a vision of chaos, of revolution.

'The general wants to avoid domestic troubles. Especially he wants to avoid anarchy,' commented politician Paul Baudouin. De Gaulle had the C-in-C's pessimism at first hand. 'Ah, if only I were sure the Germans would leave me the forces necessary for maintaining order,' Weygand told him.

Deployed in a series of 'hedgehog' positions and using a third of their artillery as anti-tank guns, the French were, at least, using a new kind of defence. The checkerboard system of hedgehogs, first formulated by Weygand himself on 24 May was a complete break with decades of French military thinking. Each hedgehog was a 'defence post barricaded on all sides, bristling with firearms levelled in every direction, and under a command determined not to surrender'.

A German officer wrote: 'In these ruined villages the French resisted to the last man. Some hedgehogs carried on when our infantry was 20 miles behind them.'

Dug in, round woods, villages, hills—any natural obstacle—the French were discovering, too late, the art of defence in depth. 'Trenches, machine-gun nests, concrete pillboxes, ingeniously camouflaged casements etc. have hastily been set up here, there and everywhere in the countryside around. The roads are blocked with tank barriers. And frantically in the tall grass the cricket sings,' wrote one observer.

But it could only have worked if the brave hedgehogs had friends behind them, to turn the tide back.

As it was, Major General Erwin Rommel simply took his 7th Panzer Division off the road, bypassed the defenders, and rolled on south. 'The advance went straight across country,' he wrote, 'over roadless and trackless fields, uphill, downhill, through hedges, fences and high cornfields.'

'No need to run'

On the road as they went, the Germans overtook the French civilians, fleeing south. Polly Peabody, a dauntless American socialite who had taken her 18-truck-strong American Scandinavian Field Hospital to Norway had now reached France to witness the latest horrors of the war. One refugee woman explained to her how she and her three daughters had donned four pairs of bloomers, four chemises, four slips, four dresses, two coats and carried two pairs of shoes each. 'When you have a long walk ahead of you the easiest way to carry your luggage is to wear it'.

The frightened rout angered the Germans. Rommel's men shouted to fleeing peasants, 'There's no need to run.' After all, hadn't the Germans stopped in the deserted villages of the Ardennes to relieve the agony of full-uddered

cows. The French had 'visualized the enemy as monsters who raped little girls and chopped the ears off little boys' explained Polly Peabody. 'They were gratefully surprised when this did not happen.'

It was certainly a major aid to the destruction, this throng of people now pouring south through France. From Picardy the sight of fleeing handcarts, limousines, bicycles had pushed the people from the whole Paris region into a rush south, spreading the rot of fear and confusion.

If French radio had broadcast an appeal to the French civilians to stay put the story might have been different. But the Government had not thought to do so. 'When the leaders do not set an example,' General Weygand admitted later 'it is not surprising that the masses do as they think best or go crazy.'

Within 48 hours of the start of the new battle the Weygand Line broke, as expected. By 7 June Parisians could hear the big guns firing. The sight of French soldiers trekking away from the front reminded one soldier of pictures he had seen as a boy—Napoleon's retreat from Moscow.

Daily, the telegrams went to London appealing for more planes. It was true that the **Advanced Air Striking Force** (AASF), down to 30 planes on 20 May, had 100 available by 5 June, plus the aid of some 250 bombers based in Britain. The **French Airforce** had made good its May losses of aircraft but, without organization on the ground, the Allied airforces were in a woeful plight. Of 13 French bombers that took off on the 6th to attack the Somme bridgeheads nine were lost; the force had failed to rendezvous with its fighter escort.

To French soldiers on the ground, the empty skies were depressing. 'I haven't met a single officer who has seen our airforce at work,' stated Major Daniel Barlone. The army was fighting 'like a blind man against a foe with a thousand eyes'. Britain was rapidly replacing Belgium as number one scapegoat for the ills of France. Weygand would go 'grey with rage' as he complained to Churchill's spokesman, Sir Edward Spears, about the lack of support.

On 8 June Churchill personally spelled out the position in a telegram to Reynaud. 'We are giving you all the support we can give in this great battle, short of ruining the capacity of this country to continue the war.' It was straightforward enough, and later even Reynaud would admit that Britain's hesitation came of 'a deep conviction that it would be impossible to continue the war if British fighter aircraft were gradually frittered away'.

Meanwhile, in Paris, the pessimism that had set in after the Luftwaffe Operation **Paula** on

French Colonial troops flee in fear of German soldiers as they continue their advance into France. German signallers, below, construct a line over a demolished bridge on the Oise.

3 June had, five days later, begun to turn into despair. The sound of distant guns grew louder. The restaurants were empty. On the Champs-Elysées empty buses stood parked diagonally to prevent airborne landings. In secret, this warm Saturday, 8 June, the Government began to circulate its plans to leave Paris. It was important to keep it from the press at this stage—if the population knew its leaders were planning to flee it could cause panic in the streets.

A government spokesman pledged on the 8th that the French would defend 'every stone, every clod of earth, every lamp post'.

While Rommel headed for the cool waters of the Channel, it was Colonel General Karl von Rundstedt's task to deliver the final blow with the tanks of Guderian and von Kleist. It began with the dawn on Sunday, 9 June.

Guderian had backtracked almost 150 miles down the route he had first taken north. Now his panzers fell upon Huntziger's 4th Army Group—one of the few important setbacks the Germans would encounter. The Aisne line held for 36 hours. But as the last vestige of the Weygand Line crumbled, morale disintegrated. Thrusting south the Germans reached the Seine between Rouen and the Oise, fanned out, came on again. The retreating French were marching like zombies now; panzers behind them, howling stukas above them, even death ahead of them as they came to rivers whose bridges had been blown by those retreating in front.

At General Georges' HQ at Les Bondons, a once-proud instructor from the famed academy of St Cyr 'wept openly . . . his face screwed up like a baby's.' The switchboard operators recorded the news crowding in at one minute intervals without reaction. 'Ah yes, your left has been driven in . . . oh, I see, they're behind you. I'll make a note of it!'

Heroic resistance

Weygand sent one last supreme appeal to the troops that black Sunday. 'The order remains,' he insisted, 'for each one to fight without thought of giving ground, looking straight ahead where the Command has placed him.' Desperately he searched for words of encouragement. 'The enemy has suffered considerable losses. His effort will soon reach its limit. We have come to the last quarter of an hour. Stand firm.'

But to the Government he sent a warning . . . 'complete dissolution can only be a matter of time'. While the heroic resistance of General Jean de **Lattre** de Tassigny's men of the 14th Division continued at the Aisne, the Government in Paris began packing.

Their destination was the city of Tours on the river Loire. The exodus began early on Monday morning, 10 June.

The first the press knew of it was when the Ministry of War spokesman, Colonel Thomas, failed to turn up for the usual morning briefing at the Quai d'Orsay. The public as a whole would have to wait until nightfall for the radio news that 'the government is compelled to leave the capital for imperative military reasons'. But by then everyone was in the know—and one in three civilians desperately attempted to follow their leaders south.

It was not easy to get out. A last minute change of plan had switched the government exodus from rail to road—with a wholesale commandeering of available transport. The corps diplomatique went in style, as de Gaulle witnessed. 'A convoy of luxurious, white-tyred Americans cars came sweeping along the road, with militiamen on

War Notes

ADVANCED AIR STRIKING FORCE (AASF): British airforce based in France from Sept 1939. Consisted of 10 squadrons of obsolescent Fairey Battle light bombers from No. 1 Group. They were stationed around Rheims and eastwards towards the Maginot Line in order to be within range of German industry. Reinforced by 6 squadrons of more modern Blenheim bombers and 6 squadrons of Hurricane fighters by early 1940. From 10 May 1940 AASF aircraft attacked the advancing German columns. 86 Battles were lost in 5 days especially in 12 May suicide attacks on the Maastricht bridges that won 2 posthumous VCs, the RAF's first. As the Germans advanced, AASF retreated first to the region around Troyes (16 May –3 June) and then to the area east of Le Mans (3–15 June). Operations were now flown mainly at night. AASF lost 299 aircraft in May and June 1940. Cdr, Air Vice-Marshal P. H. L. Playfair.

DENTZ, Henri Fernand: French general, b. 1881. Educated St Cyr Military Academy. Served N. Africa until 1908 when he entered the Ecole Superieure de Guerre. Served as 3rd Corps staff officer at Rouen. Captain in 39th Inf Div 1913. Served 1914-18 as battalion CO and staff officer. Served in Prague, Constantinople and Beirut 1919-26. In 1929 became chief of staff of 9th Inf Div. Promoted full Colonel 1931. CO 54th Brigade 1934. Deputy Chief of Staff to the Army 1937 as Major-General. In 1939 took command of 15th Corps (Oct) and 12th Corps (Nov).

FRENCH AIRFORCE: up to 25 May had lost over 500 aircraft (112 bombers) out of 1200 operational on 10 May. About 980 planes ready on 5 June including new Dewoitine fighters and US-built Glenn Martin bombers. By the 10th, another 100 fighters had been lost. On the 14th bomber units were ordered to S. France as preparation for flying to N. Africa. Total losses came to 892 planes (413 in air combat) with 1493 aircrew. The French claimed 585 kills and 228 probables.

LATTRE de Tassigny, Jean Joseph Marie Gabriel de: French general, b. 1889. Educated St Cyr Military Academy. By 1914 a Lieutenant in 12th Dragoons. Wounded 3 times. Served in Morocco 1921-6 and as staff officer to Gen Weygand. CO 151st Infantry Regt at Metz 1935-7. 5th Army chief of staff 1939. From Jan 1940 commanded 14th Infantry Div which took 800 prisoners on the Aisne, 9 June. On 18 June suggested that 14th Div be sent to N. Africa or Britain to continue the war, but suggestion turned down.

PAULA: Luftwaffe operation on 3 June 1940 intended to neutralize the French Air Force before the ground offensive by attacking 13 airfields and 15 aircraft factories as well as 22 rail targets near Paris. 300 bombers and 200 fighters took part flying in 3 formations. French decoding (by Equipe Z at Chateau de Vignolles) of Luftwaffe Enigma traffic since 26 May gave warning but no more than 120 fighters were ordered to intercept by Gen Vuillemin, the C-in-C. The defenders lost 17 fighters shooting down 18 raiders but the bombing destroyed only 16 aircraft on the ground, damaging 6 runways and 3 factories. Civilian losses were 254 killed and 652 wounded.

the running boards and motorcyclists surrounding the procession.' Others were less fortunate, like the guardian of a dustcart crammed with government files.

Among the procession heading south was a column of 12 vehicles, headed by a bus. Their 'load'—the 70 staff and equipment from the Chateau de Vignolles (code-named PC Bruno), centre of France's codebreaking activities, including the top secret 'Enigma' traffic. With them was British liaison officer, Captain Kenneth MacFarlan, who managed to find a British aircraft near Bordeaux to get him back to England —and Ultra.

Luckily the Germans, as in Poland, found nothing to indicate that their top secret ciphers had been broken. The team at Bletchley Park in England was able to continue unharrassed in their task to perfect their techniques.

At Paris stations crowds swarmed and crushed the barriers. Children were pressed to death against the railings. The restaurants were putting up their shutters. Taxis were mobbed in the streets. Bicycles changed hands for fabulous sums. A huge pall of smoke drifted across the frightened city, as fuel dumps were set alight. In the murk, the sun appeared as a sinister green disc. As if in a scene from a surrealist painting, cattle wandered loose in the broad thoroughfares, while firemen fled in their fire engines, ice cream men in their vans, undertakers in their hearses.

One man who would not be leaving was General

Heinkel 111s fly over Paris where over 250 people were reported killed in the first bombing raid on 3 June. German transports, right, cross a tributary of the Oise at Senlis, just 25 miles from Paris.

Fernand **Dentz,** former commander of the 12th Corps of the Army of Alsace. Weygand's decision now was to declare Paris an 'open city'. It was Dentz, against his protests, who had to stay on and hand the capital to the Germans. There could be no virtue in allowing the Wehrmacht to reduce Paris to the rubble of Warsaw.

Churchill flew in to Tours at 5pm on the 11th. He had been pushing for a meeting of the Supreme Council for several days. It would be the Allied command's last war council, and the mood was ugly.

Weygand set the tone. 'I wish to place on record,' he rasped, 'that those responsible for embarking on this war did so very lightly and without any conception of the power of German armaments.' Churchill flushed, and hunched his shoulders over the table. The French sat, eyes down, white faced. 'They looked for all the world like prisoners hauled up from some deep dungeon,' noted Sir Edward Spears. Only de Gaulle looked as if he had any fight left. On the long drive from Paris he had been urging Reynaud to battle on, to make a stand in Brittany.

Certainly there was no chance of making a stand in Paris, despite Churchill's urging. The French were obsessed with the lack of planes again. If there was to be any talk of fighting on then there had to be aircraft from Britain.

Churchill stayed adamant. 'Twenty-five squadrons must be maintained at all costs for the defence of Britain and nothing will make us give them up,' he rapped.

It ended with a dismal dinner. Churchill, sitting next to Marshal Pétain made one last attempt to raise his spirits. 'Think back,' he said. 'We went through hard times in 1918, but we got over them. We shall get over these in the same way.' Pétain roused himself from the silent daydreaming in which he was increasingly slumped. 'In 1918,' he said frostily, 'I gave you 40 divisions to save the British Army. Where are the 40 British Army divisions that we need to save ourselves today?'

Churchill went scarlet, then turned his back on Pétain and talked only with de Gaulle for the rest of the meal. Before flying back to London he had been warned by Reynaud that Pétain had already drawn up an armistice proposal. 'He was always a defeatist, even in the last war,' Churchill grumbled later.

Reynaud and de Gaulle were on their own now, so far as making a stand in Brittany was concerned. Weygand was finished with this war, had given up. Reynaud's formidable mistress, Hélène de Portes, had also decided the war was over. And, as ever, was making her opinions felt.

She was plaguing the life out of the staff at Tours, bursting into councils of war, hovering over typists' shoulders to read top level messages. One top secret telegram that went missing was eventually found in her bed. When she was frustrated in her attempts to reach Reynaud with her pleas that 'we must give up—give up.

Weary German gunners rest on a gun carriage after six weeks of campaigning. On the Champs-Elysées, below, bewildered Parisians watch alongside German soldiers as the Luftwaffe sweep overhead. A cine camera stands ready to film the victorious troops as they march in triumph through Paris, right, to the Arc de Triomphe.

We must make an end of it. There must be an armistice!' she found relief in directing traffic in the courtyard, in her red pyjamas.

Even the lofty de Gaulle was not safe from her onslaughts. Next day, 13 June, she crashed into a meeting between the general and her lover. 'What is this ridiculous joke about going to Quimper?' she demanded. 'Do you want to make a fool of yourself? I certainly don't propose to go to sleep in Breton four poster beds. If you want to go to Brittany, go by yourself!'

The 13th saw the Germans almost to the suburbs of Paris. It had to be a question of hours. On the Maginot Line soldiers in one of the fortresses watched in amazement as trucks trundled up with replacement guns, fresh from an armaments factory. They explained that there was no one left to install them. The fortresses were beginning to empty. It was time to go home.

The 13th also saw Churchill back at Tours, after one more desperate summons. This time he brought Halifax and his new Minister of Aircraft Production, Lord Beaverbrook, with him. There was only one question Reynaud wanted to discuss now. What would happen if France made a separate peace with Germany? Churchill knew it was no time for recriminations. 'If England won the war,' he pledged, 'France would be restored in her dignity and greatness.' Then he urged Reynaud to telephone Roosevelt, on behalf of both of them, and plead with him to bring America into the fight. It was Reynaud's last warlike gesture. In the small hours of the night he got through to Roosevelt. The President promised to reply as soon as possible.

The Germans marched into Paris at dawn on 14 June. After all the weeks of glorious 'invasion' weather, today started with drizzle. Only stray dogs were in the streets to see them come. There was no gunfire. From his office in Les Invalides, General Dentz watched troops march across the Pont Alexandre. A party of young German officers removed the sandbags around Napoleon's tomb, then retrieved the German flags that had stood there as trophies since 1918. Men from a propaganda company hung a large Nazi flag from the Eiffel Tower.

From their windows the French watched, silently. It was plain a new kind of life was beginning.

It was plain too, that they could not stay indoors for ever. One by one, the doors opened and Parisians ventured out. One by one the shops opened. The new customers were well behaved. They bought souvenirs, smutty postcards, pocket dictionaries. Close up, they didn't seem like monsters. They paid for their drinks.

The restaurants took down their shutters. Business is business. The new tourists presumably had appetites like anyone else. 'Ici on parle allemand' (here German is spoken) the restaurant owners wrote out on small cards to hang in the window. Other traders also began to put their wares on offer as the prostitutes ventured back to their alleys, lisping 'mein susser'. In Paris, the Occupation had begun.

LAST DITCH STAND

'The nightmares of anxiety were gone,' wrote Lieutenant-General Alan Brooke, 'roads were free from refugees, demoralization no longer surrounded me on all sides, it was another glorious English summer day' Brooke walked up the steps to the War Office. It was 1 June, the day after he had arrived back in England from France.

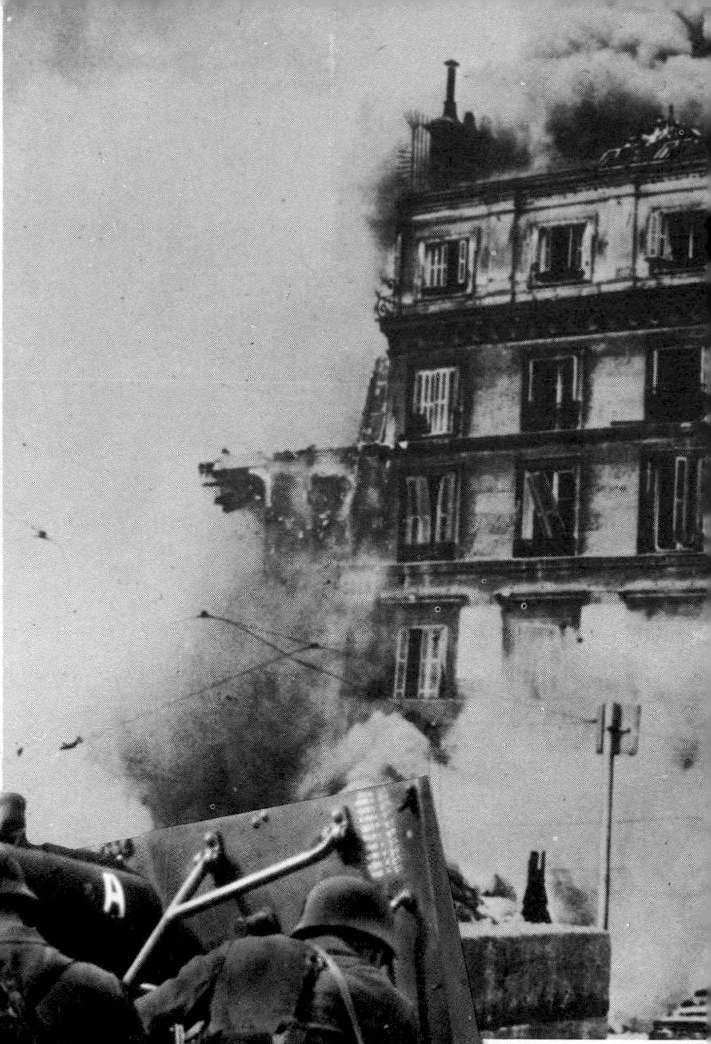

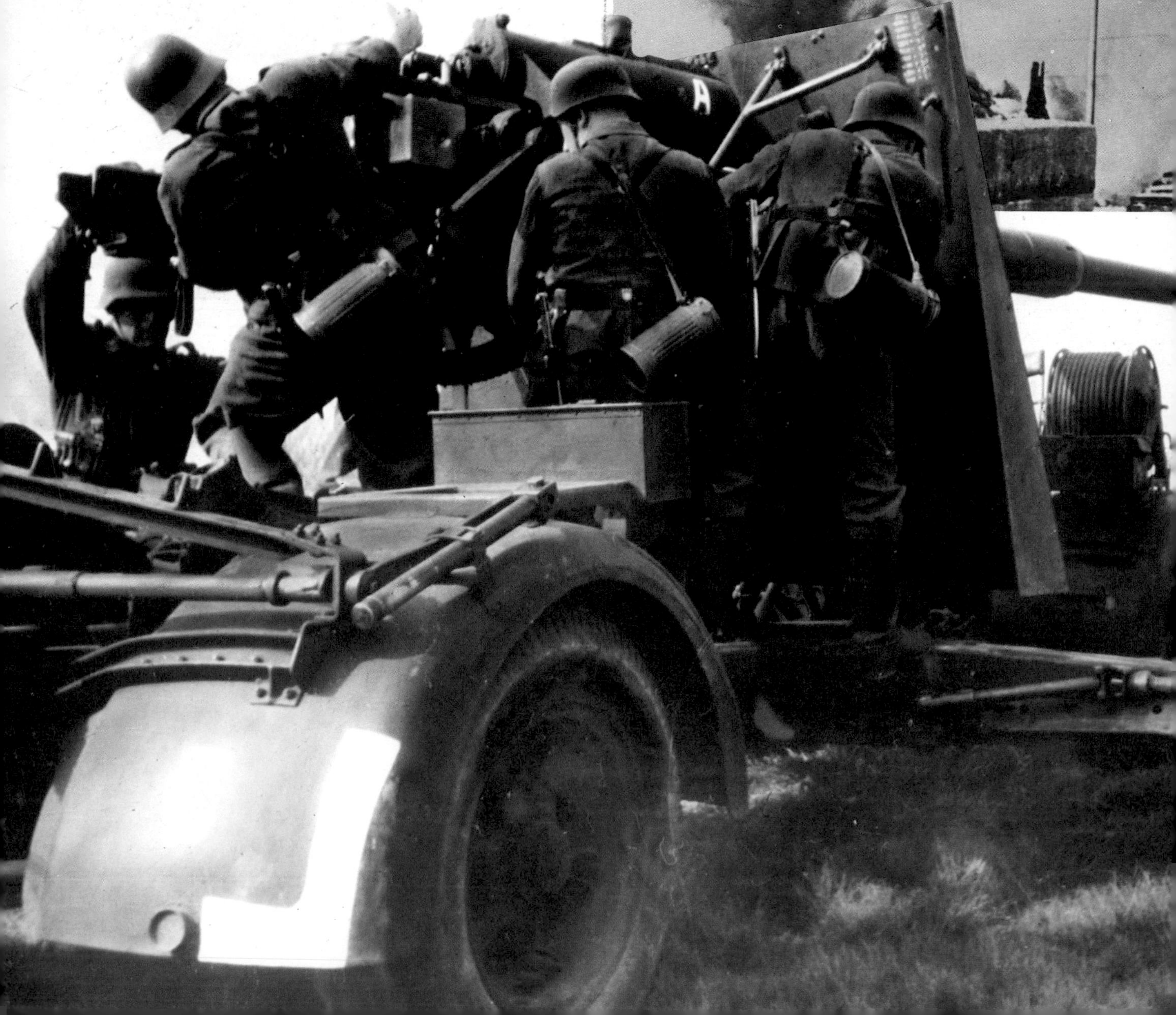

Rouen burns as the 5th Panzer Division moves into the city in captured French tanks. The makeshift British line which covered Rouen had been penetrated on 8 June. A Luftwaffe crew in action, left, manning an 88mm flak gun used as an anti-tank gun on the Channel coast.

Across the Channel men in their thousands still blocked the beaches, grabbed at boats, thigh deep in the waves—and waited. Brooke entered General John Dill's office. 'You will return to France to form a new BEF' the new Chief of The Imperial General Staff told him. Brooke was horrified. This was asking for another Dunkirk.

The commander's brief was to go back and fight alongside the French Army, the morale and the fighting value of which he knew only too well. Brooke went to see Anthony Eden and told him 'the mission I am being sent on has no value and no possibility of accomplishing anything from a military point of view . . . we've just escaped a major disaster at Dunkirk and now we're risking a second.' Eden was 'charming and sympathetic' but had to bow to Churchill's decisions.

'Last stages of disintegration'

Churchill was wary of the political repercussions of a complete evacuation from France. He wanted to show the French that his nation was not cowering behind the Channel's protection and the wings of the RAF. 'We regarded the duty of sending aid to the French as paramount' he later wrote. But he withheld the 25 air squadrons that the French demanded. Since Reynaud's visit to London on 26 May he was also aware of the possibility of a separate French armistice and had ordered secret planning for 'a certain eventuality'.

Fully realizing the fate that awaited 140,000 troops that remained in France, Brooke asked Dill to refit the 3rd and 4th Divisions so that some of the more 'seasoned' troops could be brought out. Dill told him there was no time for this. He could have the 51st Highland Division (already fighting), the 52nd, the remains of 1st **Armoured Division** and **Beauman Division**—a scattered and improvised force trying to protect depots and bases in Normandy. A fresh division, the 1st **Canadian** was perhaps a recompense for this war-weary assembly. Brooke pushed for more and Dill finally relented—Montgomery's 3rd Division would be sent out, re-equipped, as soon as possible.

Meanwhile the situation abroad was deteriorating rapidly. On 5 June the panzers began their remorseless drive west and south pushing holes into the line in every direction. The French were in what Brooke would call 'the last stages of disintegration.' Brooke himself had to measure his paces at Aldershot somewhere in the old barracks, while over the Channel, the Battle of France grew more hopeless by the hour. Fresher British forces could not be sent until the 11th and this would be difficult enough to achieve.

Major-General Victor **Fortune** and his Highlanders were under great pressure. The 51st were now on the seaward flank of the French Tenth Army in Normandy. They were trapped. Bravery was scarcely enough to keep their crucial line of defence intact. The Germans only had to break into the coastal region defended by the Argyll and Sutherland Highlanders and the rest was theirs for the taking. In one day the Argylls lost 23 officers and 500 men, killed, wounded and missing.

Fortune told Weygand he was going to retreat. The French general was livid. Every unit had retreated on the very day he told them to hold their positions. But there was nothing he could do now.

The 15th Panzer Corps drove hard into the bridgeheads forced across the Somme near Abbeville. The 51st held their ground while they could but the task was too great. Beauman tried to send up a 900-strong reinforcement brigade—'A'—from his own scant forces but most of his troops were scattered across the countryside towards Rouen to the southwest. His men had no supporting artillery, were disorganized by fleeing French troops, and got mixed up with advancing units of 1st Armoured Division.

Rommel's panzers broke through on 6 June and pushed forward 20 miles. The next day they advanced, without resistance, another 30 towards Forges-Les-Eaux.

Desperate situation

On 8 June at 10.30 in the morning, the Germans crashed through the makeshift British line covering Rouen, leaving the 51st Highlanders cut off to the north. Beauman had managed only a temporary respite for Fortune's battered battalions. The much-wanted A brigade took up 4 miles of their line east of Eu on the River Bresle.

At Sigy, to the south, the centre Pioneer battalion saw a welcome sight on the morning of the 8th. French tanks approached with pennants waving over the guns. Eager troops guided the useful machines over the minefields. Once over, the imposter vehicles opened fire. They were manned by Germans, The Pioneers fought on till 2.30pm, suffered devastating loss, then withdrew in pieces.

In the next few days from the 8th to the 11th, the panzers, with sights pointing to the south and west, swung towards **Le Havre** and Fécamp. They took Rouen. Now, the 51st Highlanders were completely cut off. Few units escaped the German drag-net to get down to **Cherbourg.**

In London Churchill pondered the dilemma. The British would possibly have to look to themselves before it was too late. He flew to France on the afternoon of the 11th, with Eden and Dill in tow. By 7.00pm they were sitting with the French—Paul Reynaud, Marshal Pétain, Weygand, Air Force C-in-C Joseph Vuillemin and the relatively junior Charles de Gaulle. Churchill again refused to send the 25 air squadrons and retorted to Weygand's outcry: 'This is not the decisive point and this is not the decisive moment. That moment will come when Hitler hurls his Luftwaffe against Britain. If we can keep command of the air, and if we can keep the seas open, and we shall keep them open, we will win it all back for you.'

The situation was desperate, the French were falling apart in every sector, the morale of the troops was worse than low; winning it all back looked unlikely. The British leaders flew back to London on the 12th convinced that collapse in France was only days away.

Brooke—now General Sir Alan Brooke—finally set out on the same day. He and a section of the 52nd Division searched on the quay for their transport. They found a dirty Dutch steamer and warily embarked on this, the 'duty boat' for the occasion. They crossed to Cherbourg.

The day before, also heading for Cherbourg, went a convoy of five Channel steamers escorted by two destroyers. The ships were packed with the advanced reinforcements, Highlanders, Royal Army Service Corps and a handful of enthusiastic Canadians. The American war correspondent, Edward **Beattie,** travelled with them.

Early on the 12th, after disembarking, Beattie watched a group of men quite unlike his travelling companions: 'down a dirt road came another sort of outfit. The men had already met the Germans and knew what sort of hell it meant.' It was a remnant of the 51st.

Beattie commandeered a car and went with the rest of the troops, through the disintegration and chaos of the French lines, towards Le Mans.

Meanwhile Brooke waited at Cherbourg having arrived in his rusty vessel on 12 June at 9.30pm. It was too dangerous to disembark straightaway. He got to shore at midnight: 'Pouring rain. Pitch dark and an air raid on, with every AA gun in Cherbourg blazing away for all it was worth . . . It was an unpleasant return to France from every point of view . . .'

Brooke headed for Le Mans where he gathered news of the fighting and issued orders to evacuate as many as possible of the 100,000 support troops still left from the original BEF. It was too late now for most of the 51st. What was left of them surrendered helpless on the evening of 12 June. Foggy conditions had prevented their rescue by the Royal Navy the night before at **St Valery.**

'I can see no hope'

Brooke went on to the French GHQ at Briare and noted the disorder and tension. He wrote that night in his diary: 'I can see no hope of the French holding out for longer than the next few days.'

At 8.30am on the 14th Brooke met up with the tired and wizened Weygand pained by a stiff neck from a car crash the evening before. 'I must be absolutely frank' the old general said.

Brooke found his worst fears confirmed. The Germans were about to enter Paris unopposed, the French armies on the verge of total breakdown.

Weygand took Brooke to see General Georges in command of the Northeast Front. There was an embarrassed silence between the two as they drove. Then Georges spoke. 'This is a terrible predicament that I am in.' Brooke then heard to his astonishment, 'Yes, I had finished my career which had been a most successful one' Brooke was struck dumb, he later wrote. 'It seemed impossible that this man destined to minister to France in her

'We never fight. We build our defence lines and get the guns into position, then when we see the Germans we hitch our guns and get out. Now we don't even hitch our guns anymore.'

French soldier fleeing to the south 14 June.

death agonies should be thinking of his military career.'

At Georges' HQ Brooke stood before a map showing a large number of red-marked sausage shaped indentations in the French lines. He pointed to them. 'They're where the Germans have got through' explained Georges. 'What about your reserves?' asked Brooke. Georges threw up his hands. 'Absolutely none, not a man, not a vehicle or gun left.'

Worse still, the French commanders told Brooke that the Inter-Allied Council now planned to hold Brittany by throwing a line of British troops across the peninsula; four divisions on an unprepared front of 95 miles where 15 divisions would not be too many.

The strain of continuous fighting day and night shows in the faces of French marines as they leave Brest for England. Allied troops withdrew after a last ditch stand in which they destroyed all that might have been of value to the enemy.

French and British troops were evacuated by Allied shipping from Cherbourg. The last ship left at 4pm on 18 June when the Germans were just 2½ miles away.

Brooke went back to Le Mans and telephoned Dill. He had to make the War Office see the impracticability of holding on in France any longer. The flurry of political decision-making continued.

Later in the evening Dill telephoned Brooke. He asked what the commander planned to do with the 52nd Division. 'Withdraw it' came the answer. 'The Prime Minister does not want you to do that.' said Dill. 'What the hell does he want?' shouted Brooke. 'He wants to speak to you.' Brooke found himself with Churchill on the other end of the phone. The Prime Minister wanted the 52nd pushed forward to block what looked like an obvious gap, the BEF should make the French feel the British were supporting them. Brooke replied that trying to block an ever-widening gap was a sure way of throwing away good troops with no hope of achieving any results.

Brooke would later criticize Churchill for trying to force a commander in the field to go against his better judgement: 'With all his wonderful qualities, interference of this nature was one of his weaknesses. The strength of his powers of persuasion had to be experienced to realize the strength that was required to counter it.' But he did end the night with the authority to stop more troops coming out from Britain and to begin the withdrawal.

Next day, 15 June, as the fighting continued, the British troops, including those who had been under French command, began moving back towards the ports, Cherbourg, St Malo, **Brest, St Nazaire.**

Brooke shifted his HQ to Vitre. By the 16th, the evacuation was underway, although the War Office had still not sanctioned a total withdrawal. The British airforces, too, were pulling out.

Brest and the other ports were jammed with British transport and the local people, according to Beattie, looked resentful and unfriendly, as though they feared the British would bring the German bombers on them.

Late that night the French politicians decided the nightmare had to end. At around 11pm Marshal Philippe Pétain formed a new government; a couple of hours later the French made the first move towards seeking an armistice.

On Monday morning, the 17th, Brooke felt that the French had abandoned his forces to their fate. 'When the end came,' he wrote, 'they never even had the decency to inform me officially that the French force had ceased fighting.' He learned from Dill, in London, that Pétain had broadcast to the French troops telling of the armistice request.

A fragmented affair

Shortly afterwards one of his French liaison officers burst into his room and collapsed into a chair, shaking from head to foot. Sobbing, he repeated the news of the broadcast. Now the War Office agreed that the only aim was to get the British forces out with all speed, saving the men, although much of the equipment, transport and guns, would be left behind. It was Dunkirk all over again, but with bigger boats.

With disintegration setting in on every side, evacuation had to be a fragmented affair but it went as smoothly as could be hoped. Rommel closed in on Cherbourg on the 17th cutting it off, but the troops who had retreated to the port still embarked successfully. The last ship left at 4pm on 18 June with the Germans just 2½ miles from the town: Rommel's 7th Panzers, the 'Ghost Division' rolled down to an empty harbour.

At Brest, on the 17th, James Hodson noted some of the rumours flying around amid the confusion: 'On quay. Soldiers are singing "South of the Border", and shouting incomprehensible phrases. Once again I'm struck by how little soldiers know of what is going on—some think America has already come in on our side; another says "Its true Russia has joined us, isn't it?" They don't know France has thrown up the sponge.' Later, on board the ship, he met a Canadian colonel with a wry sense of futility: 'We went 350 miles in one direction and then 350 miles back—got one parachutist and one wounded and that's all.'

Brooke closed down his HQ that day and went to St Nazaire to embark. As he sat out the 'Dunkirk' afternoon, news reached him of the biggest sea disaster of the war so far. Steaming out of the bay *Lancastria* had been hit by German bombers. The raid lasted 45 minutes and while she sank with 5800 troops aboard slowly and without panic, all eyes and guns were trained elsewhere. Upwards of 3000 men were killed, drowned or burnt in the flaming mat of oil that engulfed the ship as she keeled over. Over half the men were below deck.

James Hodson met some of the survivors back in England. The men were 'bespattered with oil, unshaven, wearing odd garments' he wrote. He was told how the ship had sunk: it had developed a list after the bomb had struck: '500 of our men sat on the side that stood in the air, and knowing that in a few minutes they would be plunged into the oily sea, sang "Roll out the barrel". Five minutes later, as some of them swam holding onto spares and rafts, they shouted "It's a long way to Tipperary".' But these were the lucky ones, when the flames took over, attempts to pick up the stragglers were almost impossible. One young sailor from a French trawler gripped a line between his teeth and dived 30 or 40 times from his vessel. Each time he returned with an English soldier.

'Enough disaster'

Churchill forbade the publication of this news, 'The newspapers have got quite enough disaster for today' he said. The actual losses weren't reported until weeks later.

Brooke got out later that day in an armed trawler, one of the ships that saved hundreds of men from *Lancastria*. Brooke remembered his transport well, she was covered in 'foul-smelling black treacly substance' and bundles of oil-soaked clothing which the survivors had stripped off.

Altogether three fighting divisions were brought out along with about 140,000 lines of communications troops. Whereas no transport or artillery had been saved at Dunkirk, more time and better port facilities had saved some. Close on 50,000 other Allies, French, Czechs and Poles joined the file of the evacuees. Since the beginning of Operation Dynamo at Dunkirk 558,032 men had been pulled out of France.

War Notes

ARMOURED DIVISION (1st): started arriving in France on 20 May 1940, under French command from 25 May. CO Maj-Gen Roger Evans, MC. Arrived in a depleted state without infantry or field artillery but with 150 tanks. On embarkation 17/18 June they could save only 26 tanks.

BEATTIE, Edward William: US journalist b. 1909. Educated Phillips Exeter Academy and Yale University. Joined United Press Bureau, Washington 1931 to report on the Senate. Foreign correspondent in Berlin, Ethiopian and Sino-Japanese Wars 1937-8, Germany and Czechoslovakia 1938-9. Based in London from outbreak of war.

BEAUMAN DIVISION: CO, Brig Archibald Beauman DSO, former Commander of the N. District of the BEF Lines of Communications with HQ at Rouen. His div was improvised on 31 May from various forces remaining in France during Dunkirk. The div had an irregular structure; 13 bns (only 5 of trained infantry) in A, B and C Brigades, 1 field and 3 anti-tank batteries from depot resources, Royal Engineers with 4 companies.

BREST: seaport 315 miles W. of Paris. Pop about 60,000. Chief French naval base on the Atlantic. 28,145 British Army and RAF personnel were evacuated on 16-17 June along with 4439 Allies. Occupied by 5th Panzer Div on 18 June but French Navy blew up 9 submarines and 2 warships under repair or construction.

CANADIAN DIVISION: since arrival in Britain the Canadians had missed action in Central Norway and Calais due to imminent British evacuations. The GOC Gen McNaughton landed at Calais on 23 May with a recce party of 14 only to find the Dunkirk road cut. Transport of 1st Brigade landed at Brest on 12-13 June and was sent forward by road and rail to assembly points SW of Le Mans. Ordered to withdraw on afternoon of 14th. An evacuation from Brest was over by afternoon of 17th. Ist Brigade HQ and the 48th Highlanders' train went to St Malo by mistake. Only 6 casualties (1 killed in a motorcycle crash and 5 taken prisoner) with 216 vehicles destroyed on Brest dockside.

CHERBOURG: the British 1st Armoured and 52nd Infantry Divs (30,630 men) were evacuated 15-18 June. Rommel's 'Ghost Division' chased these forces 150 miles to Cherbourg and found itself in possession of an empty port when the French forts and 30,000 men surrendered at 5pm on the 19th.

FORTUNE, Victor Morven: British general, b. 1883. Educated Winchester and Sandhurst. Served 1914-18 winning DSO. CO 1st Seaforth Highlanders 1927-9 and 5th Infantry Brigade 1932-5. Major-General 1935. CO 52nd Lowland Div 1935-6 and 51st Highland Div since 1937. PoW to 1945 with 8000 of his men.

LE HAVRE: French seaport of 161,760 (1936) 110 miles WNW of Paris and 45 miles W of Rouen. The BEF's Arkforce (2 weak brigades) was cut off from the rest of the 51st Highland Div whose retreat on Le Havre it was supposed to cover. Arkforce evacuated 11,059 troops on the night of 12-13 June with much equipment and stores. 1 transport was sunk.

ST NAZAIRE: port at mouth of R. Loire 30 miles W of Nantes. Population 37,710 (1936). BEF vehicles landed here in 1939 and in June 1940 the base area at Nantes still held 65,000 men. In the 16-18 June evacuation 57,235 were saved from the 2 ports by 6 liners, 5 destroyers and cargo ships. The unfinished battleship *Jean Bart* was towed out of St Nazaire bound for Casablanca on 18th shortly before German 11th Motorized Bde arrived.

ST VALERY: fishing port of 2000 people at Somme estuary mouth 17 miles WSW of Dieppe. Over 200 ships sent here to evacuate 51st Highland Div and French 9th Corps on night of 11-12 June. Due to fog only 2137 British and 1184 French taken off at Veules 4 miles E.

ROAD TO COMPIÈGNE

As the Germans marched into Paris on Friday 14 June under a fine drizzle, rain began to fall on the unhappy French government at Tours. Once again they were packing—this time for a flight to Bordeaux. Whether that would be the end of the road, or a staging post on the way to North Africa and a continuation of the war would depend on Roosevelt's reply to Reynaud's telephone call of the night before.

The strain of the last days had driven deep divisions between the men of Tours. **Pétain** was greatly contemptuous of Reynaud's 'immoral' life. De Gaulle had written off Pétain as a 'shipwreck'. Weygand's dislike of de Gaulle had become so extreme that lately he had threatened him with arrest. And Reynaud was exasperated by Weygand's defeatism.

Bordeaux was bursting with refugees all seeking food and shelter, and all fearful that the Germans would come in pursuit of the French Government. Arriving in ones and twos the ministers were hard put to find accommodation for the night—Léon Blum was thrown out of one shabby hotel because the proprietor said he wanted 'no Jewish warmongers' on his premises. In a local schoolroom the usually elegant corps diplomatique hung about for hours to find out where their lodgings were, while ambassadors' wives stewed in their Rolls-Royces outside.

Reynaud could not face dining in public that evening. The hostility and intrigue of Bordeaux was almost palpable. As a result it took Churchill's representative, Sir Edward Spears, quite a time to find him in the apparently empty HQ of the 8th Military Region where he was installed. 'There appeared to be no sign of life in the building,' remembered Spears. Finally Spears and Sir Ronald **Campbell**, British Ambassador, heard noises and opened a door. 'And there were Reynaud, Roland de Margerie and a couple of secretaries eating poached eggs. It looked a convivial little gathering; the participants appeared to have banished the war for the moment, and as we entered, the faces of all at that table reflected clearly that we had brought a spectre with us into the brightly lit little room. We were, in fact an awful bore.'

Spears brought with him a cable from Churchill. It was intended as a morale booster. Churchill, appalled at the news from Paris, had spent the day agonizing about the fate of the French Fleet. It was vital to keep it out of German hands, and imperative that the French fight on. 'We renew to the French Republic our pledge and resolve to continue the struggle at all costs in France, in this island, upon the oceans and in the air, wherever it may lead us . . .' Reynaud laid the cable aside. The telegram he wanted to read was Roosevelt's reply to his plea for a US declaration of war.

For that he would have to wait until the next day, Saturday 15 June. Sufficient members of the Government had reached Bordeaux by then to make up a quorum, and the decision whether

The full cycle of revenge: Hitler set the scene for the humiliation of France in the same railway carriage and clearing, above, at Compiègne, where 22 years before Germany had accepted the crushing terms of defeat at the Armistice of 1918.

German engineers cross the Rhine by pontoon bridge near Chateau Breisach.

or not to fight on could be postponed no longer. A Cabinet meeting was fixed for 4pm.

Reynaud, meanwhile, went to work on Weygand. He told him bluntly: 'I agree with you that we must stop the fighting, but the Government must carry on. Surely the best solution is a military capitulation. That would bind the army but leave the Government free to go to North Africa and rally the million troops in the French Empire.' Something like this had happened in Holland, after all.

Weygand was horrified. Such an armistice was unacceptable. 'Never,' he retorted. 'I shall always refuse, whatever may happen, to bespatter our colours with this shame.' The honour of the Army was at stake, he explained. Reynaud, well aware that hundreds of thousands of soldiers of this army were now prisoners of war, argued on, but in vain. Infuriated by Weygand's stubborness, he resolved to sack him at the first possible moment.

More telegrams landed on Roosevelt's desk in Washington—two from Churchill, one from Drexel **Biddle**, deputizing as US Ambassador in France. 'I feel that I should make it entirely clear

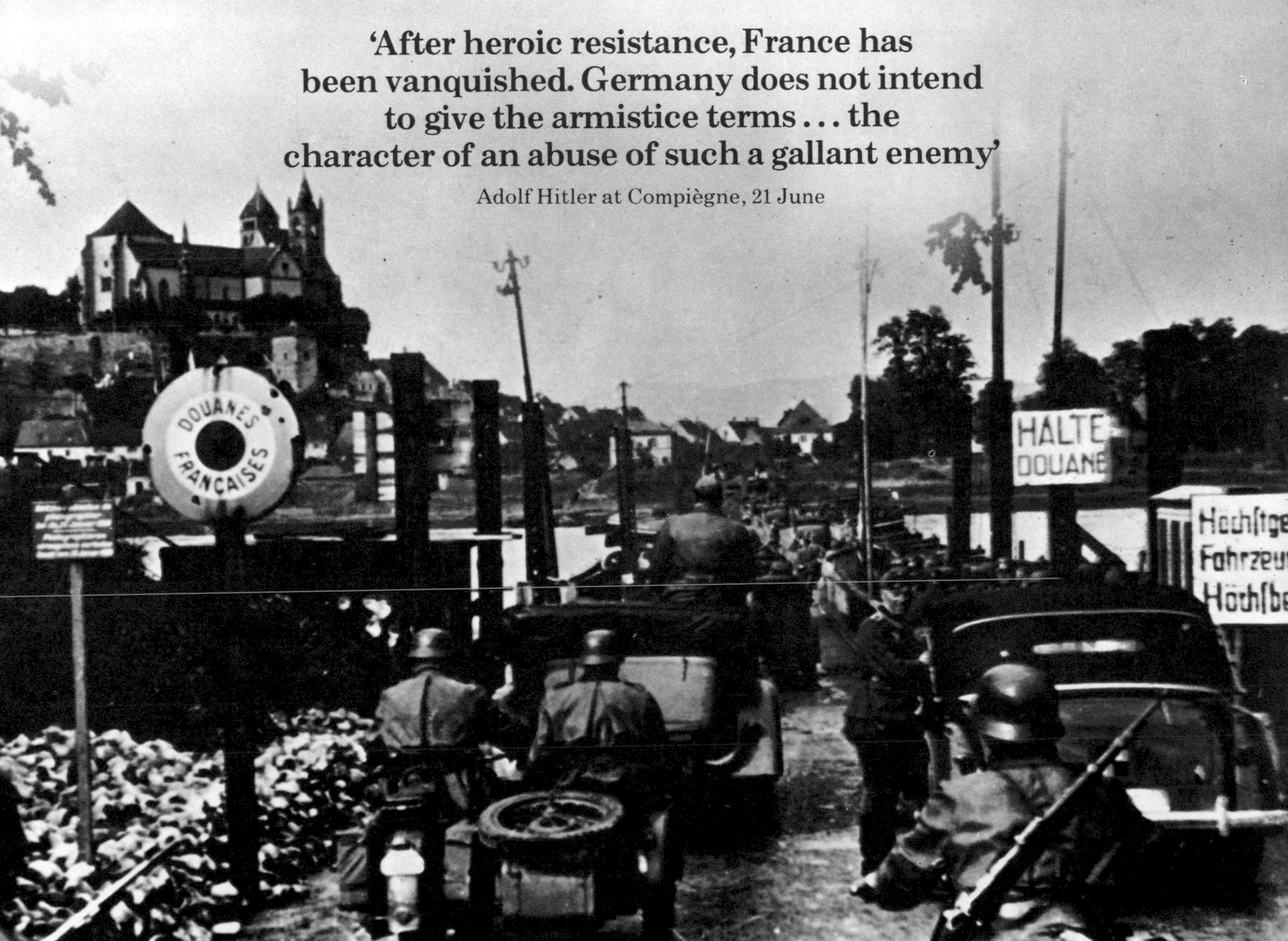

'After heroic resistance, France has been vanquished. Germany does not intend to give the armistice terms . . . the character of an abuse of such a gallant enemy'

Adolf Hitler at Compiègne, 21 June

Eye Witness

'Vercors', real name Jean Bruller, was demobilized from the defeated French Army in the summer of 1940.

'It felt strange to be at home again, in a house that was unchanged and intact, as if we had come back from holidays. The feeling didn't last. After previous homecomings I had gone straight back to work. This time I was unemployed. Voluntarily, to be sure, but quite determined. What were we going to live on? I had no idea. In the village street farther down, the shopkeepers smiled at the soldiers, chatted with those who knew a few words of French. My neighbours, a little Flemish woman, her husband a painter, a fine though modest artist with whom I had always got on well, had practically adopted as a 'filleul de guerre' a young German to whom they had given the run of their house. So I no longer went there.

This pained my painter friend who did not understand that my former desire for Franco-German friendship was, unlike his, unable to surmount my injured patriotism. Against his arguments I cited the Nazi terror, racist policy, concentration camps. He replied: 'Propaganda! We were scared stiff when they first arrived and look at them now! In a pacified Europe, humaneness will come out on top, you'll see. We must help them.'

Taken from 'The Battle of Silence' by Vercors Publishers: Collins. St James Place, London, 1968 (Translated from the French by Rita Barisse).

that the French Government is now faced with only two alternatives,' Biddle explained, 'The decision will depend on the nature of your reply.' The options were either to surrender or to adopt de Gaulle's plan for a stand in North Africa.

At 11am Washington time, Roosevelt finally wrote his reply. Once again, the answer was negative. Roosevelt, in the middle of an election campaign, knew well that he could bring neither the people nor Congress to a declaration of war.

Roosevelt's cable could promise nothing beyond all possible 'moral and material assistance ... so long as the Allies continue to resist.' Even this had to be qualified. 'These statements carry no implication of military commitments . . .'

Cabinet members filed through the sombre and colonnaded hall of the Prefect of Bordeaux's house, into his drawing room for the meeting.

Weygand sat alone in an adjoining room, still smarting at the armistice proposal being debated next door. Reynaud nominated Pétain as mediator and sent him out to try and talk Weygand into agreement. Reynaud had won the Cabinet to his side. He painted a desperate picture of the Army's present plight—ruptured in the centre, split in the east, and encircled on the Maginot Line.

After 15 minutes with Weygand, Pétain returned with the extraordinary news that he now agreed with Weygand. The military honour of the Army would be smirched if it alone surrendered. Reynaud was thunderstruck and began to argue defensively. Then Camille **Chautemps** spoke. If the Government went to Africa, the French people must see there was no other choice. So why not find out the German terms and expose them as unacceptable? The Cabinet fell silent. The proposal had had 'a deadly effect on the majority.'

Heads down—a German radio team engaged in passing news up the line. Inside the railway carriage, above, General Keitel begins to read the armistice conditions. Sitting dejected by the roadside just two of the 8 million refugees wandering through France.

Reckoning he would lose any vote taken by 6-13, Reynaud offered to resign on the spot. President Lebrun, a usually timid man, protested emotionally 'if you go, I go too'. Reynaud stayed.

The last confrontation between the Prime Minister and his C-in-C took place later that evening as the Cabinet broke up at 7.55pm.

'General,' began Reynaud. 'As we agreed earlier, I want you to seek the surrender of the Army.'

'I have never agreed to anything of the kind,' shouted Weygand.

A thwarted Reynaud went back to the conference room to write a note to Churchill. Would Britain agree to such a request being made? If not, he, Reynaud, would have to resign. It was one of the most bitter moments yet: not even a clean surrender, but a crawling request to know what surrender terms would be demanded. As he signed the note, a messenger handed him a sealed envelope. It was Roosevelt's refusal to enter the war.

Sunday, 16 June brought no relief. Reynaud was showing signs of the strain. Once again, Hélène de Portes was in full song. 'She spent an hour weeping in my office to get us to urge Reynaud to ask for an armistice,' complained Harrison **Matthews** of the US Embassy.

There were more sinister voices being raised now in favour of capitulation—at the City Hall, where politician Pierre Laval had set up office, right wingers were gathering to plot for Reynaud's removal and replacement by Pétain. In the shadow of a defeated France they still saw a political future. There would be no shortage of politicians anxious to draw a salary, by courtesy of Adolf Hitler.

The mood of collaboration spread rapidly. It found expression in one small northern town, where a party of Senegalese troops were continuing to fire at advancing Germans. The local mayor begged them to desist. The soldiers explained that, being black, they knew the Germans would shoot them out of hand. The mayor told them where to hide in the forest. He then informed the first Germans he encountered.

In London, Churchill, now with de Gaulle at his side, discussed the chances of persuading Reynaud to keep going while the Brittany front

Crowds of Berliners in the Pleasure Gardens on the 'Day of the Armed Forces' view the historic carriage from Compiègne. Below, from early May to 17 June Berliners got their news from extra editions.

was organized. From the sound of the news from Bordeaux, it would need some spectacular gesture to stiffen Reynaud's will to resist. Fortunately one lay to hand—the brainchild of a group of French exiles in London. It was a proposal for nothing less than complete union between Britain and France.

The constitution of the Union would provide for joint organs of defence, foreign, financial and economic policies. French and British citizens would become nationals of each other's country and there would be a single War Cabinet. All the forces of Britain and France would be under its direction and it would govern from wherever it could best operate.

It was an astonishing, theatrical notion which had at first won little favour with either Churchill or de Gaulle. But now they warmed to it. Swiftly, the terms of the grand offer were worked out, and de Gaulle flew back to Bordeaux with them. Churchill agreed to meet him the next day, Monday, off Brittany. They had already spoken to Reynaud on the phone, to give him the gist. He seemed delighted. 'I will die defending these proposals' he had declared.

There was excitement again in Reynaud's office as the translation of the full text was made. But when the Cabinet met the exhilaration dissolved as swiftly as it had flared.

'It would be fusion with a corpse,' commented Pétain. 'It would reduce France to the status of a dominion,' said another voice. 'Everyone I've talked to,' said Weygand, 'rejects it with indignation.' Reynaud stared at them. There was no point even in taking a vote on it, nor was there any point in pretending the war could continue. Later he said: 'It was the greatest disappointment of my life.'

With the suddenly serene expression of a man who has shed an enormous weight, Reynaud made his way to the office of President Lebrun and handed in his resignation. He emerged at 10pm. It was too late to bother with formalities. To a group of hovering ministers he simply said, 'Marshal Pétain is forming a Government.' Then he walked out.

Immediately there was a rush of ministers to the President's room, clamouring for a post in the new government. But the aged Marshal had no need for debate. Pulling a list from his briefcase he handed it to Lebrun. 'There's my government,' he said. He had no need to debate his next move either. It was to contact the German command through the Spanish Ambassador, and seek an armistice.

'End to hostilities'

Soon after 10pm Spears and Campbell went to bid Reynaud farewell. In the gloom of the almost deserted hall, Spears was approached in a stealthy manner by de Gaulle who was fearful that Weygand would soon make good his threats to arrest him.

De Gaulle reasoned that he must try to salvage the Empire and North Africa and that this could only be done from Britain.

On Monday 17 June Spears and de Gaulle went separately to the airfield so that no suspicion should be aroused, and flew to England.

Later that morning all France heard the news as Pétain's thin voice was broadcast from the Bordeaux radio station to all corners of the land. 'An old man with the voice of an old woman told us he had asked for peace,' one of the listeners recalled.

'I give to France my person,' said Pétain. 'With a heavy heart I tell you today that it is necessary to stop fighting. I addressed myself last night to the adversary to ask him if he is ready to seek with me, as soldier to soldier, after the actual fighting is over, and with honour, the means of putting an end to hostilities.'

There were some uneasy days in the interval between suing for an armistice and receiving instructions from the Germans. During this time the German advance continued. Finally at midday Pétain was asked to send an armistice delegation to meet Hitler.

Led by a reluctant General Charles Huntziger they went north to the Loire as instructed by Hitler. From there they were escorted to Paris on roads still crowded with the traffic of war. They arrived after an arduous journey at 7.30am 21 June and were allowed a few hours rest, then driven in a northeasterly direction for about 50 miles. Gradually it dawned on members of the delegation where they were being taken.

The scene chosen for the final humiliation of France was the clearing in the forest of **Compiègne** at Réthondes where Germany, 22 years earlier, had signed the 1918 Armistice. Even the old railway carriage which for years had been

Victorious German troops in France take a break from the rigours of battle.

enshrined in a museum had been dragged out and the stage had been set by Hitler for the benefit of both the French and the world press.

The granite monument in the clearing was now draped with German flags but the French, shattered by the atmosphere of the place barely glanced at it. The words carved on its rock were, in any case, engraved in their minds. 'Here on the 11th November 1918 succumbed the criminal pride of the German people.'

Marching into the clearing, Hitler strode up to the memorial, his face was 'afire with scorn, anger, hate, revenge, triumph'. Then he 'swiftly snaps his hands on his hips, arches his shoulders, plants his feet wide apart'. It was a gesture of defiance which observers later wrote would not be forgotten by anyone who had seen it.

Then striding ahead, Hitler climbed into the carriage and sat down at the green baize table in the seat that Marshal Foch had occupied in 1918. Flanked by Göring, Ribbentrop and Hess, Hitler saluted the French. They saluted in response. General Wilhelm Keitel began reading the armistice. Hitler left after the 12-minute preamble while Keitel went on with the details.

Although Hitler had intended that the French should taste the full humiliation of suing for an armistice, for strategic reasons he had tempered his terms. He realized that the purpose of this armistice was to give France no cause to fight on from North Africa. To this end he persuaded Mussolini not to press for any territorial claim on France, until a final peace treaty could be reached.

He planned to divide France and occupy only half—the area north of Tours and a strip down the Atlantic coast to the Spanish border. The rest was placed under the control of Pétain who was free to choose a seat for his government in the unoccupied zone. Hitler thought this would prevent a united France from further struggle and would deter further co-operation with Britain.

Demobilization

The French Army was to be demobilized and equipment handed over. Fortifications in the occupied zone were to be handed over in good condition. The French were allowed to keep part of the fleet to safeguard their colonial interest. The rest was to be taken out of commission.

French nationals were forbidden to fight against Germany in the service of states still at war. Merchant ships were forbidden to leave port, ships overseas were recalled or sent to neutral ports and aircraft grounded. Ports, factories, shipyards and other means of communication were to be handed over in good condition.

France was to pay the cost of occupation; French prisoners of war were to remain in Germany but all Germans held captive were to be released immediately. The French were also instructed to hand over all German subjects—this was aimed at Jews who had fled Germany and whose names were supplied by the Gestapo.

After Keitel had set out the terms in full, the French delegates spent the rest of the day in urgent discussion with the Government at Bordeaux by means of hastily rigged landlines. At midnight they were driven back to Paris and returned to Compiègne at 10.30am the following day. They relayed requests from the Government for various changes in the terms, and for the German replies to these to be attached to the armistice as a protocol.

Armistice signed

However, Keitel told the delegation on the 22nd that there were to be no negotiations and that they must sign within an hour or discussions would be broken off.

Finally at 6.50pm Keitel signed for Germany and Huntziger for France. It was all over. In a deep voice Keitel asked all to rise to honour 'all those who have bled for their Fatherland and all those who have died for the country'.

The German armistice was dependent on agreement with Italy, so the exhausted French delegates flew to Rome to bargain with Mussolini. The famous railway carriage was taken to Berlin and the French memorial, except for Foch's statue, was blown up.

The Italian armistice was signed on 24 June and both German and Italian armistices came into force at 12.35am on the 25th. A German Armistice Commission was set up, to which the French attached a delegation, to carry out the terms of Compiègne.

War Notes

BIDDLE, Anthony Joseph Drexel: US diplomat, b. 1897 into a banking family. Educated St Paul's School, Concord, New Hampshire. Married tobacco heiress Mary Duke 1915. Joined prestigious 'Squadron A' cavalry when US joined 1914-18 war. Captain by 1918. After the war was occupied by business, sport and international society. Divorced 1931 and married mining heiress Margaret Schulze. Appointed Minister to Norway July 1935. Became US Ambassador to Poland April 1937. In Sept 1939 fled Poland after his country villa was bombed, reaching France via Rumania. Became Deputy US Ambassador to France.

BORDEAUX: 4th city of France 360 miles SW of Paris. Pop 258,438 (1930). An important Atlantic port, Bordeaux is linked by rail to Paris in the north, Spain in the south and the Mediterranean town of Narbonne in the east. The first government of the Third Republic fled there when the Germans besieged Paris, 1870.

CAMPBELL, Ronald Hugh: British diplomat, b. 1883. Joined Foreign Office 1907. Served as HM Minister to France 1929-35 and to Yugoslavia 1935-9. Ambassador to France from 1939.

CHAUTEMPS, Camille: French lawyer and politician, b. 1885, Paris son of minister. Radical socialist deputy 1919. Minister of Interior 1924, of Justice 1925-6. PM 1930, 1933-4 resigning because of Stavisky affair, June 1937-March 1938 (2nd popular front government). Minister of Public Works 1936 and Minister of State 1939. Spears said his oratory 'could have made a stone weep'.

COMPIÈGNE: town with about 14,000 people on R. Oise, 45 miles NE of Paris. It became the HQ of the German Army in 1870, and was once more taken by the Germans in 1914.

MATTHEWS, Harrison Freeman: US diplomat, b. 1899. Educated Gilman Country School, Princeton University and l'Ecole Libre des Sciences Politiques in Paris. Joined Foreign Service 1923. Served Budapest 1924-6 and Bogota 1926-9. Became assistant chief of Latin American Affairs Division 1930. Visited El Salvador 1931, and became 2nd Secretary at Havana Embassy 1933. 1st Secretary Paris Embassy July 1937, and at Madrid Embassy April 1939. Returned to Paris as 1st Secretary July 1939.

PÉTAIN, Henri Philippe Benoni Omer Joseph: French marshal, b. 1856 in the Pas de Calais of peasant family. Educated St Cyr Academy, graduating as a lieutenant 1878. After attending Ecole de Guerre he served as lieutenant and captain with Chasseurs Alpins. Staff officer with 15th Corps and Military Governor of Paris. Taught at Rifle School, Chalons, as a Major 1900. Instructor at Ecole de Guerre 1901. Colonel, and CO of an infantry regiment 1914. Promoted General of Brigade Aug 1914 and commanded 6th Infantry Div on the Marne. Appointed to command 2nd Army June 1915. In charge of operations at Verdun from Feb-May 1916. His success at Verdun made him a popular hero, and he was promoted C-in-C of the French Army in May 1917 quelling a dangerous mutiny.

Marshal 1918. Appointed Inspector-General of French Army 1922. After semi-retirement recalled to command French troops in Morocco for the Riff War 1925-6. Served as vice-president of Supreme War Council and became War Minister in 1934. Appointed Ambassador to Spain (1939) after Franco's victory—he was an admirer and former teacher of Franco. Recalled to serve in War Cabinet May 1940.

JUNE 1940

'...IF they do come we shall hit them on the head with beer bottles.' Churchill's brave words are no empty gesture. Britain has little else with which to repel the invader–should he come. A question upper most in Hitler's mind as he tours World War I trenches and Paris. In Rome Mussolini admits in private the war 'will be long–not less than five years. Hitler's tree reaches as high as the sky–but it grows towards ruin.' Few would have believed him this month...

16th: Pétain forms new govt in France. 'Heavy water' leaves Gironde (W. France) aboard SS *Broompark*. R. V. Jones reports Luftwaffe 'Knickebein' beam navigation system to Air Ministry.

17th: Pétain makes armistice broadcast. Maginot Line armies encircled. Soviets occupy Estonia and Latvia. Rommel advances 150 miles. *Lancastria* sunk at St Nazaire.

18th: BEF Cherbourg and Brest evacuations completed. All large French towns to be surrendered without resistance. De Gaulle broadcasts from London. Churchill's 'finest hour' speech.

19th: German 1st Cavalry Div stopped at Loire by Saumur Cavalry School cadets. Luftwaffe bombs Bordeaux.

20th: Kleist captures Lyons. Saumur cadets surrender through lack of ammunition. Italian Riviera offensive.

21st: Hitler at Franco-German armistice talks in Forest of Compiègne. Knickebein directed at Rolls-Royce works Derby, detected by RAF Anson aircraft.

22nd: Franco-German armistice signed at Compiègne, 400,000 troops surrender in Vosges Pocket, W of Maginot Line.

23rd: Italians occupy Menton. Hitler in Paris. De Gaulle forms French National Committee in London. First British commando raid, on Boulogne.

24th: Franco-Italian Armistice signed at Villa Incisa.

25th: Ceasefire in France; day of national mourning.

26th: Soviet ultimatum to Rumania to hand over Bessarabia and N. Bukovina.

27th: Britain announces blockade of Europe from Biscay Bay to N. Norway.

28th: Luftwaffe bombs Jersey and Guernsey. Channel Islands demilitarized. Red Army occupies Bessarabia and N. Bukovina. Italians attack British garrison at Moyale, Kenya.

29th: Germans publish 'White Book' with details of Allied plans to 'invade' Low Countries.

30th: Germans land in Channel Islands. Maginot Line garrison surrenders.

A VIEW FROM FOREST MEADOW

In the early weeks of 1940, sitting with a small group round the fireplace of the Reich's Chancellery in Berlin, Hitler had told Hermann Giesler, an old friend he had nominated General Adviser on Architecture for Munich: 'As a soldier in 1914, I hoped to see Paris. As a politician after the war was lost it was not possible for me. But now I shall soon be able to have this experience.'

Giesler, a none-too-intelligent mimic, who played the role of court jester to Hitler, could not believe his ears. 'How is that possible? Does that mean peace?'

Hitler was indulgent. 'No, I have offered them peace and they just see it as a sign of weakness. They want war, and they shall have it . . . we will have beaten them in six weeks. I here and now invite you, Giesler—you will visit Paris with me.'

Now, six months later, Hitler remembered his word. On 22 June police intercepted Giesler on his way to a building site in Vienna. Told to report instead at Vienna airport, Giesler was flown to Belgium, overcome with wonder and bursting with thanks for the Führer.

'That's all right, Giesler. Of course you could not know at the time, but I was sure we would win. Naturally I remembered my invitation to you of last winter and I have invited Speer and Breker, too. I will visit Paris with my artists tomorrow early in the morning.'

For the second part of the French campaign, Hitler had set up his HQ at Brûly-de-Pesche, four miles southwest of Couvain in Belgium.

There Hitler's construction organization, headed by and named after Fritz **Todt,** prepared an extensive headquarters compound. While police detachments summarily booted local villagers and farmers out of their homes, construction teams knocked down the church tower to thwart air reconnaissance, put up six barrack buildings and a bunker for the Führer.

The concrete was still not set when the Führer moved in on 6 June. In line with his taste for the Gothic, he called his bunker 'Wolf's Gorge'. The official codename for the whole HQ had more of a pastoral ring—'Forest Meadow'. Apart from the mosquitoes that swarmed from the nearby swamp, it was an ideal place for him to contemplate his conquests, present and future.

At the beginning of June, Britain was much on his mind. On the 2nd his army commanders told him that it would only be a few days before Dunkirk fell. After that, Hitler was certain, the British would be ready for a 'reasonable peace settlement', and he could proceed to his 'great and principal task—the conflict with Bolshevism'.

The Führer wanted Britain's empire kept the white race. 'I do not want to conquer her,' he said. 'I want to come to terms with her. I want to force her to accept my friendship and to drive out the whole Jewish rabble agitating against me.'

Hitler was optimistic that he could achieve this goal. On 20 June Secretary of State Baron von **Weizsäcker** passed on a report from the Swedish Ambassador that an 'enlightened' peace party was forming within the British Cabinet, led by Lord Halifax. To Hitler, it appeared that if Britain had so far been awkward, it was largely under the influence of that 'alcoholic dilletante' Churchill.

While he waited, the fruits of victory were there for Hitler to enjoy. On 12 June the French C-in-C declared Paris an open city. Hitler also had been anxious to prevent its destruction, and had ordered his generals to by-pass Paris.

For Hitler, Paris held a magnetic attraction. As a penniless student in Vienna the young Adolf had consumed books about the city with a voracious appetite. From his studies of architecture, he knew the layout of the famous squares and boulevards.

Hitler acted as guide

The day of the visit arrived. Hitler's companions were Giesler and Albert **Speer,** both official architects of limited ability who held their appointments largely because they were sympathetic to Hitler's moods, and the sculptor Arno **Breker.** With Giesler and Breker dressed in incongruous army greatcoats that amused even the Führer, they flew to Paris. From the airport Hitler took his three 'artists' in an open car, with a driver and two adjutants.

Their first stop was the Imperial Opera House. Forewarned, the attendants had turned on the lights as if for a gala night. But it was Hitler who acted as guide, enumerating the architectural features from his profoundly detailed knowledge, and spotting instantly a feature that had changed.

On they drove through the Place de la Concorde, up the Champs-Elysées, pausing to absorb the scene, then moving off, at a wave of the Führer's hand, to the Arc de Triomphe (too small for

'We shall fall on them like wolves, with a fury they won't be able to grasp.'

Adolf Hitler, January 1940

Hitler visits the old battlefield of Vimy Ridge (in the background is a memorial to Canadian troops) where he served in World War 1 (inset, left).

Hitler's taste) and on to see the Eiffel Tower.

There Hitler revealed his thinking. In his eyes the tower represented the start of a new era of building, the beginning of a new technology based on engineering. That was the new classicism he was striving for—a co-operation between artists, architects and engineers using modern building materials and techniques. Hitler's three companions realized they were not sitting in the Führer's car just to enjoy the view. They were there to see how Hitler wanted his buildings built and his cities planned.

At the end of the tour he told the three: 'For you a hard period of work and effort lies ahead: I want to help you as much as I can.' The main aim was a new Berlin. That evening, after flying back over the deserted streets and squares for an Olympian view of Paris, Hitler drafted a decree for work to begin on rebuilding the Reich capital.

'Berlin is to be given the style commensurate with the grandeur of our victory.' The old Berlin would go. Vast processional avenues would bisect the city. The buildings, so colossal that men and women would look like insects crawling over the marble floors, would represent Germany's triumph.

He expressed the same idea in different words when they got back to Forest Meadow that afternoon. Pacing thoughtfully up and down the narrow path through the woods, he suddenly stopped, turned to Giesler, and told him with heavy emphasis: 'I want peace, and I shall do everything in my power to get peace. It is still not too late . . . I can do a lot better than make war! I only have to think of the waste of German blood —it's always the best who fall—the bravest, the most ready for sacrifice, whose task it was to be to build up the nation, to be the leaders. I don't need to make a name for myself through war, like Churchill. I want to make a name as leader of the German people.'

For the next two days Hitler toured his old World War I battlefields. He took along his old sergeant, Max Amman, now in charge of the Nazi Party press department, and his adjutants. Hitler, uncharacteristically talkative, pointed out the battleground where he had won the Iron Cross in December 1914 after being nominated for it three times. He even found the same old concrete block behind which he had crouched for cover from enemy machine-gun fire.

On 26 June he visited Bethléem Farm, where he had stayed in 1914 with Madame Crespel.

'Can I do anything for you?' Hitler asked her.

'My nephew is a prisoner. We need him for the harvest,' she replied.

Hitler signalled an adjutant to deal with it.

There was the serious matter of the war. Britain was showing no signs of moving towards the 'understanding' he had anticipated. In fact they were showing every intention of going on with the struggle. To help persuade them, Hitler authorized preparations to begin for an invasion of England. It would only be a last resort. And there were those who believed it would not take place at all. Göring's Chief of Air Staff, Major General Hans **Jeschonnek**, when asked to participate in the planning, dismissed the suggestion: 'There won't be any invasion, and I haven't time to waste planning one.'

Russian troops massing

At the same time, there were serious problems in the east—Stalin was looking greedily at his western neighbours. On 12 June Moscow issued an ultimatum to Lithuania, followed by similar ultimata to Estonia and Latvia four days later.

All three countries submitted when Soviet forces duly marched in. And intelligence reports told Hitler that Russian troops were now massing on Rumania's frontier. On the 23rd that country received the inevitable ultimatum—Russia wanted **Bessarabia**. The Rumanians gave in, and handed over northern **Bukovina** too, a province with ethnic Germans.

Hitler was deeply angered by these Russian adventures, which had swept more than 20 million people into Stalin's net. And by the last week of June his two army chiefs, Brauchitsch and Halder, were privately warning him about the build-up of Russian forces on the Reich's eastern border.

Halder in particular pointed out that the few divisions left in the east were barely enough for customs purposes. On 23 June Hitler discussed with them plans to streamline and improve the army. He decided that although the size of the army as a whole could be reduced from 155 divisions to 120 (20 divisions to be available for recall at short notice), he would double to 20 the number of armoured and mechanized divisions.

Military thinking hardens

Stationed in the east would be 17 infantry divisions and the HQ of the 18th Army.

In clear progressive steps, throughout that last week of June and the first week of July, Germany's military thinking hardened. On the 28th Halder told Brauchitsch that the purpose of the new deployment was to increase the German Army's presence, although they should avoid any attitude of open hostility. But by 3 July he had changed his tune—the eastern problem was to be examined from the point of view of how best to deliver a military blow to Russia, to extort from her a recognition of German dominance in Europe.

War Notes

BESSARABIA: a region of E. Europe stretching for about 220 miles inland from the Black Sea coast, south of Odessa. Was administered by Russia 1812-1917 and by Rumania 1917-40. The chief products are fruit, cereals and wine. After the Russians invaded in June 1940, the central part was joined to the Moldavian Soviet Socialist Republic, while the rest became part of the Ukrainian SSR.

BREKER, Arno: German sculptor, b. 1900. Dusseldorf Academy of Art, then studied in Paris. In Berlin from late 1933. Sculpted monuments for Reichschancellery. Work admired by Stalin. Exhibited at Munich House of German Art. Worked mainly on portrait busts, including Speer and Hitler.

BUKOVINA: a district of 4000sq miles NE of the Carpathian Mountains. Population 794,858 (1941). About 45% forested, 30% arable. Part of Austrian Empire until ceded to Rumania 1918. In June 1940 Russia occupied over half of the region as compensation for Rumanian 'misrule' in Bessarabia which Russia also annexed.

JESCHONNEK, Hans: Luftwaffe general, b. 1899. Served with infantry and flew a few times in WW1. Officer in Reichswehr cavalry. An ardent Nazi he transferred to Luftwaffe in 1933. Promoted colonel 1938 he played an important technical branch role in modernizing the Luftwaffe.

Göring's surprise choice as Luftwaffe Chief of Staff Feb 1939. Major General Aug 1939 and Lt-Gen July 1940. Field Marshal Milch, Göring's deputy called him 'a plucky, intelligent officer but narrow-minded and headstrong, and contemptuous of other walks of life'.

SPEER, Albert: German architect, b. 1905 Mannheim, son of an architect. Trained as architect and became assistant at Berlin Technical College. Joined the Nazi Party (No. 474,481) and the SS 1931-2 having heard Hitler speak. Organizer of a huge Nazi rally at Tempelhof Field (Berlin) on 1 May 1933. In 1934 was made responsible for the Party rallies at Nuremberg. Their success brought Speer to Hitler's attention. Showing well-judged enthusiasm for the Führer's grandiose architectural ideas for a new Berlin, Speer became a section leader of the German Labour Front and a member of the Deputy Führer's staff. Architectural Inspector of the Reich 1937, and in 1938 awarded the Party's Golden Badge of Honour. Built the New Chancellery 1938-9. His planning work to turn Berlin into a fitting capital for the German Reich was interrupted by the outbreak of war.

TODT, Fritz: German engineer, b. 1891 Pforzheim, Baden, son of a jewelry factory owner. Educated Pforzheim Humanist High School and Munich Technical College. Served on the W. Front 1914-16 before joining airforce as observer. Wounded in air battle. In 1920s worked as civil engineer, joining the Nazi Party in 1923. He became a colonel on the staff of Heinrich Himmler's SS 1931. In 1933 became head of a semi-military government department called 'Organization Todt' which was responsible for building 1850 miles of autobahns, the West Wall and numerous military installations. Kept aloof from Party functions and Hitler's receptions. Reich Minister for Armament and Munitions 20 March 1940. A friend of Speer who shared his dislike of Bormann.

WEIZSÄCKER, Ernst Freiherr von: German diplomat, b. 1882 Stuttgart. Joined Imperial Navy 1910 and served 1914-18. Left navy with rank of commander. Entered Foreign Office 1920. Through 1920s served abroad in various diplomatic posts. Appointed Minister to Norway 1931 and Minister to Switzerland 1933. Member of Nazi Party and SS. In 1938 became Secretary of State to the new Foreign Minister, von Ribbentrop.

STAB IN THE BACK

It was, as usual, a scene from Grand Opera. On the balcony of the Palazzo Venezia in Rome the soloist, Benito Mussolini, was in top voice. Below, the faithful chorus of Fascist plainclothes policemen waited their cue. Il Duce was telling them that, at last, Italy was in the war.

Expanding his chest beneath the resplendent black uniform, Mussolini roared out the message. 'Italian people, rush to arms' he declaimed. 'Show your tenacity, your courage, your valour' he exhorted. The chorus went into action: 'Guerra! Guerra!' they cried. But today, at 6pm on 10 June 1940, it seemed that there were two choruses in the square. Cries of 'Crepa! Crepa!' ('Drop dead') rivalled the 'Guerras'. Yells of 'Pace' struggled with the shouts of 'Duce'.

In the cities of Genoa and Turin the crowds in the piazzas heard the proceedings by radio relay and listened in silence. In Milan, in front of the cathedral, they wept.

'Suicide', had been the stunned comment of Marshal Pietro **Badoglio**, 68-year-old army chief of staff, when Mussolini summoned him on 26 May to announce 'Yesterday I sent Hitler a statement in writing. On 5 June I shall be ready to declare war.' Mussolini had been shouting on that occasion too—as if sheer noise would cancel out

'Marshal, all I need is a few thousand dead to be able to sit down as a belligerent at a peace conference.'

Mussolini to Marshal Badoglio

the facts of Italy's unpreparedness for aggression.

The facts were grim. 'We haven't even enough shirts for the **Army**—how is it possible to declare war?' Badoglio had protested on 26 May. And that was the least of the shortages. Though Mussolini had boasted to Hitler in 1939 that he had 12 million bayonets the sober truth was that he had only 1.3 million rifles to stick them on—and those rifles were a model perfected in 1891.

There was a month's supply of ammunition. The **Air Force** had fuel for no more than 40 sorties. The standard army tank, the pitifully small 3.4-ton **L3**, was so lightly armoured that rifle fire could pierce it—the men called them 'sardine tins'. Transport was in such short supply that, for big parades, the Army had to borrow police cars and paint them khaki. The police insisted they be repainted before getting them back. In Africa, on the outposts of the ramshackle Roman Empire, things were yet worse. In **Libya** the guns dated from the 1870s and were mounted on garbage trucks.

At sea, Italy's war prospects looked brighter. On paper, the Navy looked impressive. It included no fewer than eight battleships—though in June 1940 only four were ready for sea. The ships were extremely fast, but they had been designed more for display than for war and their impressive speed was achieved only at the expense of reduced armour and range—many had to keep within about 500 miles of base. There were no aircraft carriers. The submarine fleet appeared strong—80 vessels had surfaced simultaneously in a spectacular display watched by Hitler—but once again there were fundamental weaknesses. Though the sanitation arrangements were impressive, the subs could only carry a relatively small number of torpedoes, scarcely more than half as many as their German counterparts—and they took twice as long to submerge.

Mussolini enjoyed making theatrical speeches. The declaration of war, in front of Rome's Palazzo Venezia (inset), was a carefully stage-managed affair.

On the brink of war

Behind the weaknesses of Italian equipment lay yet more fundamental flaws in the whole economy. Fascists had talked war—but sold arms abroad to pay for food. No less than 25 million tons of food had been imported in 1939. Even after the European war began Mussolini was still exporting war material—Britain was due to take delivery of 400 aircraft in early 1940. They were never delivered, but 23 other countries figured on the list of Italian arms sales in 1940, from Finland to Japan, from Brazil to China. Other arms had simply been given away—Franco had been supplied with some 800 heavy guns for his war in Spain. They had not been returned.

But perhaps the most fatal flaw of all was deep in the Italian character itself. Mussolini had once told his son-in-law, Foreign Minister Count Ciano, 'the Italian race is a race of sheep. Eighteen years is not enough to change them . . . We must keep them disciplined and in uniform from morning to night. Beat them and beat them and beat them . . . . To make a people great it is necessary to send them into battle even if you have to kick them in the pants. That is what I shall do.'

Added together, these weaknesses of men and materials had kept Mussolini teetering on the brink of the final decision. Certainly his friend Hitler had no desire to see Italy plunge into the fray. On 26 August 1939 Mussolini had sent Hitler a shopping list of supplies he needed for war, with a suitably apologetic covering note: 'Führer, I would not have sent you this list if I had had the time . . . to accumulate a stockpile and to accelerate the growth of self-sufficiency.' The list asked for 1.75 million tons of petrol, coal, steel, wood and anti-aircraft batteries. The supplies were not forthcoming. Hitler saved Mussolini the embarrassment of a direct refusal by agreeing that Italy should, for the time being, remain neutral.

So from the beginning of the war in September 1939, Italy had remained a bystander, a non-belligerent ('neutral' was not an acceptable word in the Fascist vocabulary). Mussolini's enthusiasm for war, however, was unabated, and he vacillated dizzily between declaring war at once and waiting prudently until Italy had gathered strength. In successive messages to Hitler he promised Italian support, and even Italian rescue.

Hitler sent back messages of thanks, but was prepared to wage war without Mussolini's help. 'I offer my heartiest thanks for the diplomatic and political assistance that you have recently given to Germany and to her just cause . . . I do not expect to need Italy's military aid.'

'I am forced to declare war' Mussolini had ex-

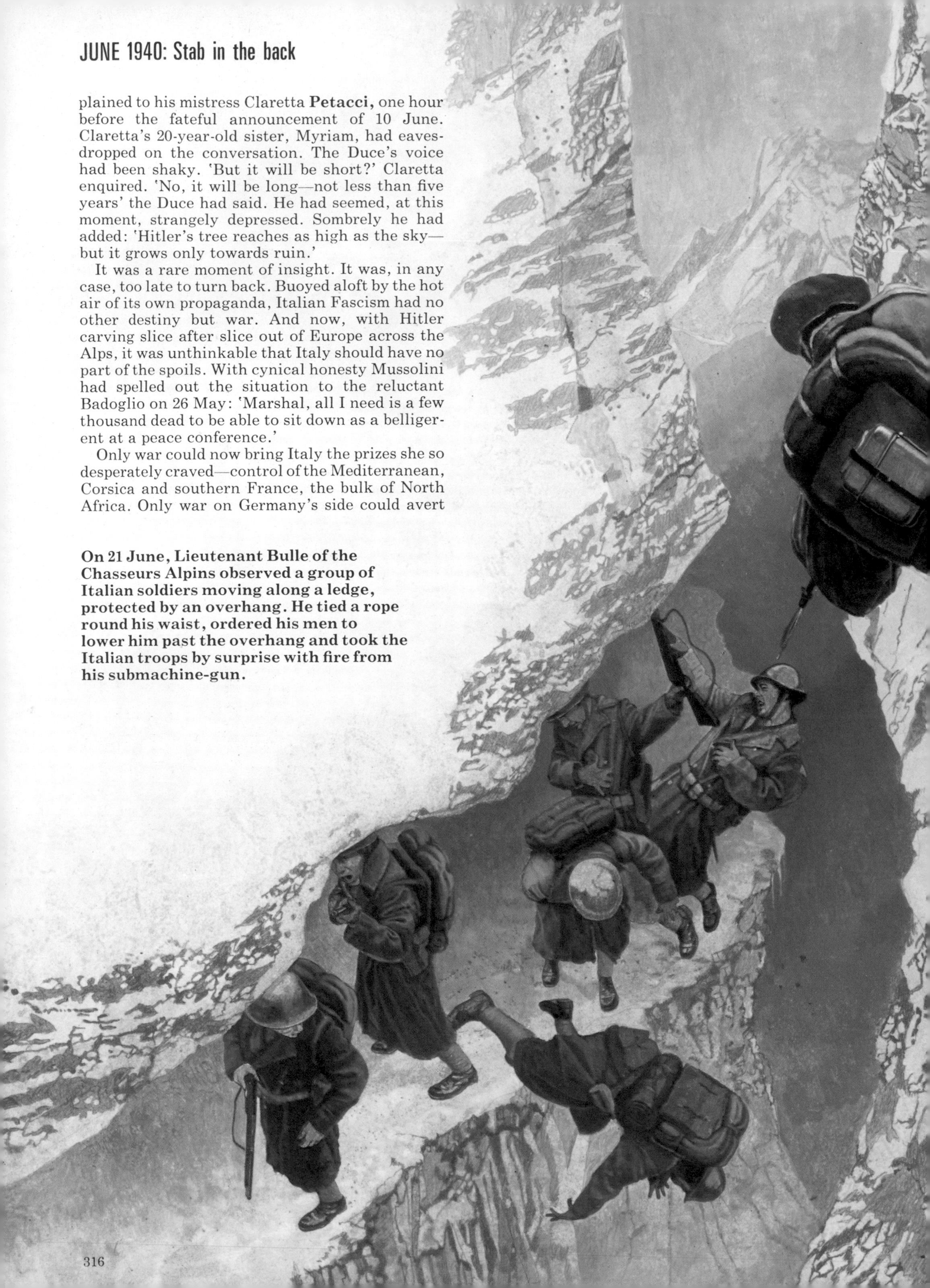

plained to his mistress Claretta **Petacci,** one hour before the fateful announcement of 10 June. Claretta's 20-year-old sister, Myriam, had eavesdropped on the conversation. The Duce's voice had been shaky. 'But it will be short?' Claretta enquired. 'No, it will be long—not less than five years' the Duce had said. He had seemed, at this moment, strangely depressed. Sombrely he had added: 'Hitler's tree reaches as high as the sky—but it grows only towards ruin.'

It was a rare moment of insight. It was, in any case, too late to turn back. Buoyed aloft by the hot air of its own propaganda, Italian Fascism had no other destiny but war. And now, with Hitler carving slice after slice out of Europe across the Alps, it was unthinkable that Italy should have no part of the spoils. With cynical honesty Mussolini had spelled out the situation to the reluctant Badoglio on 26 May: 'Marshal, all I need is a few thousand dead to be able to sit down as a belligerent at a peace conference.'

Only war could now bring Italy the prizes she so desperately craved—control of the Mediterranean, Corsica and southern France, the bulk of North Africa. Only war on Germany's side could avert

On 21 June, Lieutenant Bulle of the Chasseurs Alpins observed a group of Italian soldiers moving along a ledge, protected by an overhang. He tied a rope round his waist, ordered his men to lower him past the overhang and took the Italian troops by surprise with fire from his submachine-gun.

In the Alpine campaign, over 500,000 Italian soldiers made little progress against the French. For the gain of just 13 small villages, 631 Italian soldiers died. The French lost only 37 men.

the ultimate nightmare—that Hitler, having dealt with the rest of Europe, might next turn on Italy too . . .

At least Italian industrialists, robbed of export markets when Italy turned down a British order for £20 million worth of arms and equipment, favoured opening new markets by conquest. And as Hitler's panzers rolled through France, even some of the Italian generals dared hope the gamble might succeed.

On 8 June General Giacomo Carboni tried to persuade Marshal Badoglio to resign as chief of staff to try to stop Mussolini declaring war. Badoglio refused: 'I believe there is really no more to be done. Besides, who knows? Perhaps Mussolini is right. Certainly the Germans are extremely strong, and they might be able to win a quick victory.'

The codeword that flashed the news to Britain's embassies in Europe after the announcement of 10 June was 'Duplicity'.

In London's Soho district, as the first dawn of Italy's war came up on the 11th, the small army of Italian waiters who staffed the many restaurants of the quarter wondered uneasily whether to stay home for the day. They had good reason. A blistering denunciation of Italy from Churchill would inflame normally phlegmatic Londoners. Fists flew in the street before the day was out. Rounded up, the waiters were interned.

Worldwide, criticism of Italy's action was just as violent. Roosevelt denounced the 'stab in the back'. Berliners were no less hostile. Plainly, Italy was riding on Hitler's coat-tails for a share of the spoils.

Italy too late for glory

From the outset, it was plain that Mussolini was getting little glory from his new adventure. On the night of 11 June Rolls-Royce armoured cars of the 11th Hussars drove smoothly across the Egyptian frontier into Libya and took 70 prisoners, to the amazement of Italian troops who had not been informed they were at war. In the Mediterranean that same day one aircraft carrier, 11 cruisers and 12 destroyers began a sweep of the sea that would rout the numerically superior Italians. Genoa and the Libyan coastal towns suffered Anglo-French naval bombardments despite lavish minefields laid to protect them. Before June was over, seven submarines had been lost. Inexperienced, without radar or air reconnaissance or training in night operations the Italian Navy began to regret their Duce's hastiness. So did the sailors on some 200 merchant ships that the sudden declaration of war had left stranded abroad.

Had Mussolini concentrated his attack on Malta, the story might have been different. But his main aim was northwards—across the Alps into France. It would prove to be the most abject mistake of all.

France, in mid-June, was already plainly a broken country. By 17 June she was suing for armistice. It looked as if Italy would, after all, be too late for the fray and any reward.

But three Italian armies, amounting to 34 divisions or more than half a million men, advanced on

Italian troops during the Alpine campaign. Most had inadequate combat gear and cardboard boots—a far cry from the 'crack troops' of the propaganda picture (inset).

three separate lines through the Alpine passes. A total of 175,000 soldiers in the grandly titled but already reduced Army of the Alps opposed them.

The best of French resistance came from Alpine troops who occupied the heights above the mountain passes. Outnumbered five to one by the Italian troops advancing against them, they knew they could not repel an attack, but at least they could hold it.

'My section will continue to prevent a passage through the Col d'Enclave,' wrote Lieutenant Bulle, commanding a unit of the 7th Battalion of Chasseurs Alpins. 'We do not have many men, but we shall hold on. As long as we have a single bullet left, no enemy soldier will break through the Col. Long live eternal France!'

Sending the message off in the hands of a corporal on skis, Bulle and his section prepared to sell their lives. The Italians, frozen in their flimsy combat gear and cardboard boots, struggled across the snow into the curtain of bullets from Bulle's section. Soon the snow ran red with Italian blood and frightened chamois goats hurtled around aimlessly among the bodies.

All along the Alpine front, small groups of French troops like these held off massive Italian forces. The Italians penetrated only as far as **Menton**. Italian newspapers had already printed headlines announcing the capture of **Nice**. The propaganda machine was ready with announcements that the Alpine campaign was among the 'most titanic enterprises of all time', and French resistance—keener, they said, in the Alps than against the Germans on the northern front—had produced enormous casualties.

In fact 631 Italian soldiers died, according to Italian figures. The French admitted 37 fatalities. And the Italian gain totalled 13 small villages.

On the evening of 23 June the French delegates arrived at the Villa Incisa on the Cassia Road to ask formally for an armistice.

Even Mussolini wanted the meeting kept secret. Because there had been no struggle, there would be no theatrical display. And to avoid offending Hitler by disrupting the negotiations, Mussolini limited his claims to the small sector of territory his armies had captured, and to a demilitarized zone 30 miles deep.

Mussolini blamed his own armies for letting him down. Even Michelangelo with only clay would have been nothing more than a potter.

Then, in yet another of his amazing emotional swings, Mussolini changed his approach once more. On 30 June he visited the Alpine front and persuaded himself that his soldiers had performed brilliantly. Back in Rome he ordered the propaganda machine to mobilize, and soon the Italian people were learning that they were masters of the Mediterranean and exercised control as far as the Indian Ocean. Their air force was the strongest in the world, considerably better than Britain's RAF. And Italy had all the raw materials needed for a war. Above all, Fascism had produced a new style of fighting.

War Notes

AIR FORCE: was divided into 2 branches: Independent Air Force with 2 air corps, 4 air divisions, 1 air brigade with a total of 166 squadrons. And Army Air Forces with 3 regiments and 4 independent groups with total of 24 squadrons. Strength 84,000 men, 3296 aircraft (1284 modern).

ARMY: strength on 10 June 1940 53,000 officers and 1,379,000 men in Italy, Libya and Albania plus 250,955 troops and Militia in Italian E. Africa. A total of 73 divisions: 57 infantry, 5 Alpini, 3 Rapid, 2 motorized, 3 armoured (only 2 with tanks), 2 Blackshirt divs. Generally not too well equipped especially in transport, severe problems through lack of lorries particularly in N. Africa. Artillery fairly obsolete but competently employed mostly dating from WWI. Italian National Militia formed 29 reinforcement battalions, used mostly for territorial defence and training.

BADOGLIO, Pietro: Italian marshal, b.1871 Grazzano Monferrato, Alessandra. First prominent in Libyan war 1911-12. Served as an officer from 1914; planned and carried out capture of Monte Sabotini 1916. Negotiated armistice for Italy at end of war. Promoted General and succeeded Diaz as Chief of General Staff 1919-21. Against Mussolini's Fascist regime but eventually came to accept it and was again C-in-C 1925. Made a Marshal 1926. Colonizing Governor of Libya 1928-33. Led Italian forces in war against Ethiopia and ruled the country as viceroy after conquest 1936. Re-appointed C-in-C Sept 1939.

L3: Italian light tank based on a 1929 Carden-Loyd design bought from Britain. Fiat produced the enclosed Carro Veloce or CV33, followed by the CV35 in 1936. By 1940 2500 built with 500 used in Ethiopia 1935-6 and 2 battalions sent to Spanish Civil War. Organized into 70-tank cavalry recce groups or infantry support battalions. Weight: 3.4 tons. Dimensions: 10.4 × 4 × 4.2ft. Engine 43hp Fiat SPA CV3 4cyl liquid cooled. Speed: 26mph. Range: 75 miles. Guns: 2 × 8mm Breda Model 38s of limited traverse, also a flamethrower version with 100 yard range and 520 litres of fuel in trailer. Armour: 6-13.5mm. Crew: driver and gunner. Outclassed by the tanks of other powers.

LIBYA: colony of Italian empire comprising 4 provinces: Tripoli (capital), Misurata, Benghazi and Derna, covering an area of 810,000 sq miles. Population: 1 million. About 16,000 Genoan immigrants arrived in Libya under colonization scheme 1938. Occupied by Italy 1911-12 after war with Turkey. Boundaries established after WW1, but not effectively occupied until 1931. Italians established agricultural settlement during '30s contributing greatly to local food supply. Revenue and expenditure balanced at 600m lire 1939-40. Italian forces in Libya: 221,395 men; 1885 guns; 340 tanks; 315 aircraft (151 effective); 44 anti-tank guns.

MENTON: town on Mediterranean and Italian border 13 miles ENE Nice and 5 miles WSW Ventimiglia. Population 11,079. Part of Monaco until 1848, when it was seized by Sardinia and ceded to France 1860. From 20 June 1940 the Italian 1st Army overran 60% of the town but was halted by 472 guns supporting French 15th Corps. Post at Pont-St. Louis held by 2nd Lt Gros and 9 men until ceasefire.

NICE: city 420 miles SE Paris nr Italian border, dominated by Maritime Alps. Population: 181,984. After plebiscite in 1860, ceded for 2nd time to France (1st time 1796-1814) by Sardinia. Mild winter climate makes it leading resort of French Riviera.

PETACCI, Claretta (Clara): Mussolini's mistress, b. 1912. Within a short time of meeting him in 1936, she was virtually Mussolini's wife and had a certain amount of influence over him. Despite his frequent attempts to finish the relationship and mistreatment, her affection for him never wavered.

JUNE 1940

CHURCHILL RALLIES THE NATION

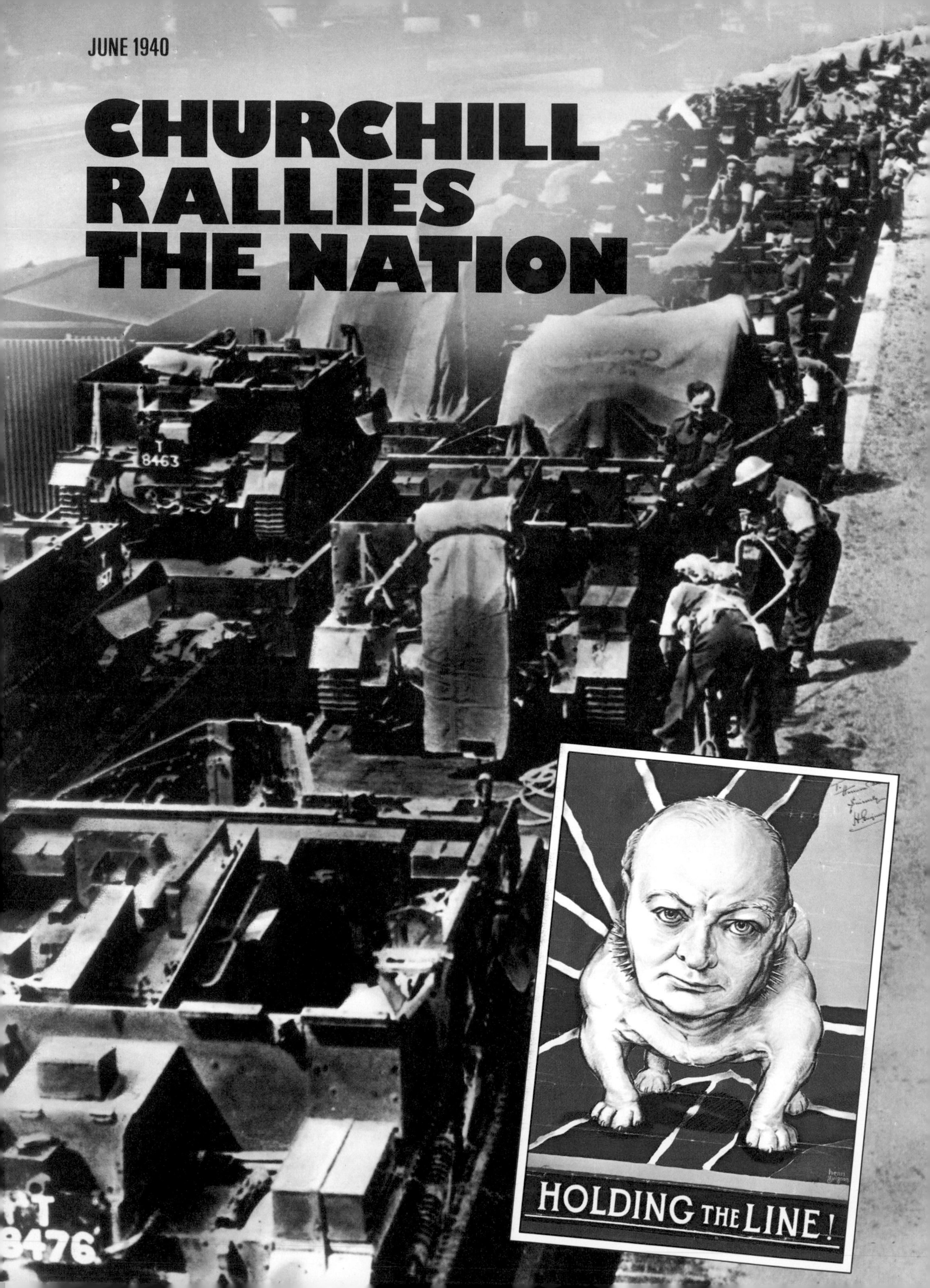

'Of course, whatever happens at Dunkirk, we shall fight on.'

Winston Churchill

In the wake of the Dunkirk evacuation, slowly like a lumbering animal waking from a deep sleep, the British government—and the people with it—were beginning to gear themselves for the invasion that appeared inevitable.

The nation experienced both a sense of relief and of anger as the bulk of the British army narrowly escaped annihilation. In Dorset, men back from Dunkirk were not grateful for their deliverance. Packed in quiet country towns, they shocked respectable citizens with blasphemous anger at what had happened. A sergeant, cursing his junior officers for taking the last transport and leaving the men to fend for themselves, found angry agreement among his audience.

Mass-Observation, the organization that tested British public opinion, reported army morale as 'zero in many places'. On 3 June, the Ministry of Information recorded at six of its 13 centres, that the returning troops were voicing strong criticisms—aimed mainly at the politicians responsible for the disaster.

Many civilians felt the same. 'This is not our war. This is a war of the high-up people who use long words and have different feelings' was a typical comment. The people did not seem to care, could not grasp the impending danger. Only 50 per cent of the population expected Britain to go on fighting alone. 'Everyone is going around looking as if they want to put their heads in a gas oven' recorded Mass-Observation. It was describing a nation suffering more from confusion than despair.

American Ambassador, Joseph Kennedy, commented after Dunkirk, 'To suppose the Allies have much to fight with except courage is fallacious.'

Ernest **Bevin,** newly appointed Minister of Labour, summed up the ordinary Englishman's mood. 'If one could judge by the feelings of the people, it was not so much that this or that person had let them down. But that the system based on monopoly and big business has failed to deliver the goods in the hour of trial.'

What the British people were asking for now was leadership. They wanted to know what was going on. They saw the appointment of the new Prime Minister on 10 May as a good sign. But in political circles there was still widespread hostility towards Winston Churchill. When he entered the chamber of the House of Commons, it was the Labour members who cheered him. Neville Chamberlain's old supporters pointedly sat on their hands. 'Old Neville was still the best of the lot,' thought Alexander Cadogan. In his view Churchill was 'too rambling and remote and sentimental'.

But it was these critical politicians who were out of touch with the people. Duff **Cooper,** Minister of Information, demonstrated as much when he berated Hitler as 'not a gentleman because he doesn't drink wine or eat grapefruit'. Most of the people of Britain had never been able to afford either.

Churchill was closer to the mood of the ordinary people. Not that he had anything in common with them. As Mrs Clementine Churchill had pointed out to Churchill's doctor, Charles **Moran,** 'You probably don't realize, Charles, that he knows nothing of the life of ordinary people. He's never been in a bus and only once on the Underground.'

Churchill himself commented: 'I don't know about oratory, but I do know what is in people's minds and how to speak to them.'

Even so, it took time before he began to win their complete respect and affection. It was the uncompromising phrases like 'I have nothing to offer but blood, toil, tears and sweat' he used in speeches such as that of 13 May, that would serve to rally the nation's morale.

But there was nothing spontaneous about his speeches. He worked hard to hit the right tone, testing out his colourful words on friends and colleagues, and composing in simple solid phrases that contrasted vividly with the bland oratory of other politicians.

'We shall not flag or fail'

Before he rose to speak, Churchill would sit hunched up with his head sunk in his shoulders, his mouth set in a bulldog grimace. When he stood up he invariably went through the same routine, first patting his chest, then smoothing his palm across his stomach, finally folding his hands over his groin.

Then he would begin to speak. His voice, impeded by a distinct lisp, was, according to experienced Parliamentarians like Lord Halifax, lacking all charm with 'no facility of gesture'.

But the content, the product of an imaginative mind, overcame the deficiencies of its delivery. On 4 June he announced to the House of Commons the rescue of the BEF from Dunkirk, and told the world of the government's resolve to fight on. His words would echo through history.

'Even though large tracts of Europe and many old and famous States have fallen or may fall into the grip of the Gestapo and all the odious apparatus of Nazi rule, we shall not flag or fail. We shall go on to the end. We shall fight in France, we shall fight in the seas and oceans, we shall fight with growing confidence and growing strength in the air; we shall defend our Island, whatever the cost may be. We shall fight on the beaches, we shall fight on the landing-grounds, we shall fight in the fields and in the streets, we shall fight in the hills; we shall never surrender . . .'

From Kent—the inevitable front line if Germany invaded—a correspondent wrote to *The Times:* '. . . Let Hitler come and see. Let us hope that he will come: for the slow temper of the English is hot now, and like dirt from a shovel, his duped and

New bren gun carriers are entrained for delivery to their units. And Churchill's determination that Britain would stand firm against the Nazis is graphically shown in a US poster (inset).

doped, half baked and wholly bestial hordes would be flung from our coasts.'

Down in Cornwall, a mother cycled home to listen to Churchill's speech, broadcast on the evening of the 4th, thinking as she pedalled through the countryside on that lovely summer evening, 'Far worse than death would be for the children to grow up Nazis, so if they landed I must be prepared to shoot the children and myself.'

And with Churchill's speech they realized that they were playing a new game, with new rules. It was a game they took seriously. Overnight, Mass-Observation reported, people carrying their gas masks leaped from nil to 30 per cent.

There were many less encouraging manifestations of the new mood. The least attractive was the internment of aliens. The programme began on 12 May, when a coastal belt from Inverness to Dorset became a 'Protected area'. The police, often backed up by trucks of armed soldiers, arrested all male Germans and Austrians between 16 and 60 years of age. The first 'bag' amounted to 2000.

The Home Office announced that the special measures applied 'for the time being'. They intended to mitigate the rigour of the measures as soon as circumstances permitted. Four days later the police rounded up another 2000 for internment. At the end of May women were to be included and 3000 woke up to a new life behind bars. On 3 June the protected areas were extended. At the same time all foreigners, except the French, over the age of 16 found they were subject to a curfew from 10.30pm (midnight in London) until 6am.

Internment was a brutal business. Police were not obliged to give any reason for an arrest, and the government did not bother to publish the names of those interned. On 11 June the Home Secretary's department told the House of Commons that publication would be 'impracticable, and a waste of paper involving considerable expenditure'.

All strangers were suspect

By 11 June more than 10,000 'aliens' had been interned. Many were refugees who had come to Britain to escape barbed wire in Europe. Now they found themselves behind it in Britain, on racecourses and sports grounds, in tents, military barracks, half-finished housing estates—even in the winter quarters of the Bertram Mills Circus at Ascot.

In most camps the ground was wet. Censorship deprived them of newspapers and radio, and Jews found themselves interned with Nazi sympathizers. Conditions were appalling. As one commandant said: 'I can do nothing more than keep you from starvation.' Some committed suicide at the prospect of indefinite internment. Some were more fortunate, and were soon released from the camps to work as scientists and technicians.

Stirred by internment, the British public suffered a brief period of 'fifth column' hysteria. When Churchill encouraged them with a reference in his 4 June speech to 'this malignancy in our midst', everybody thought any stranger must be a saboteur.

With all the street and village names removed, it was hard enough moving about the countryside. Now it became even worse. One traveller who stopped to ask directions from a woman in Sussex got nothing more than an icy stare. In Winchester a clergyman's daughter reported the officer billeted with her family at the vicarage. He could not be British, she thought. He had used the lavatory and failed to pull the chain afterwards.

This brand of overreaction became official. Sir John **Anderson,** as Home Secretary, responsible for public morale, introduced fines and prison for spreading 'alarm and despondency'. A woman who told soldiers: 'You're bloody fools for wearing

A soldier on leave says goodbye to his young son. On 3 June some 50,000 evacuees left East Coast towns after German air raids—the inset shows a wrecked school.

JUNE 1940: Churchill rallies the nation

Help from overseas. Canadian airmen arrive in Britain in June 1940.

those uniforms' got three months jail and a £20 fine. Another culprit found himself in jail for declaring: 'It will be a good thing when the British Empire is finished.'

More usefully, as people realized the extent of their own peril, they at last began to prepare to meet it. On 3 June a new wave of evacuation saw 50,000 bewildered children leave the East Coast towns. They travelled in 97 special trains to the supposedly safe havens in the rural counties of western Britain. On 14 June 120,000 more followed them from the London area.

Volunteers flocked to farms to work on the land, many of them schoolboys and students, many others, recruits to the Woman's Land Army.

In Whitehall sleepy civil servants appeared to be injected with a new wonder energy drug. Some even broke into a gentle run in the dusty corridors. Part of the reason was the volley of memos Churchill sent out with a red slip of paper attached, printed with the instructions ACTION THIS DAY. Within days of the beaches of Dunkirk being evacuated Churchill, in his capacity as Minister of Defence, was already writing a stream of memoranda about landing craft, **striking companies** 'to raid the coast of occupied Europe', the recruitment of 5000 paratroops and the installation of 15in guns to fire across the Channel.

Churchill had brought two important men into his cabinet—Lord **Beaverbrook** and Ernest Bevin.

Lord Beaverbrook, a fiery Canadian newspaper proprietor, at first refused Churchill's proffered appointment as Minister of Aircraft Production. Others were also against his appointment. Lloyd George summed up their objections: 'No one in any party trusts Max.'

But Churchill persisted, and won. 'I felt sure that our life depended on the flow of new aircraft, I needed his vital and vibrant energy.'

The result was a revolution in the aircraft industry. When Beaverbrook took over, fighter reserves amounted to five Spitfires and Hurricanes. He put all aircraft factories on a 24-hour, seven day a week basis for four weeks. 'Any firm unable to follow this advice . . . should send me a telegram explaining the difficulties and I will do what I can to smooth them out.' He appealed to the public for pots and pans to melt down to make Spitfires, and started a Spitfire fund. Freed from the feeling of impotence they had suffered under the preceding administration, the public responded warmly.

Ernest Bevin, a new discovery, had no Parliamentary experience. But as General Secretary of Britain's second biggest trade union, the Transport and General Workers', he understood the working man and the part labour would play in the war. He was not an economist, but saw clearly that if the country took no steps to remedy unemployment, it was neglecting its most precious resource—manpower. He was also a born fighter.

Armed with the Emergency Powers Act of 22 May, Bevin had virtually dictatorial control over the movements of men into war industries. He could institute retraining schemes, direct the men to wherever industry needed them, even lay down their wages and working conditions.

Like Beaverbrook, Bevin was a man you either loved or hated. And Beaverbrook was one of the men who hated him. But Churchill needed them both: 'I was in such harmony with both Beaverbrook and Bevin in the white hot weeks.'

They knew—everybody knew—that they had a new leader, one who took a firm and determined view of what needed doing. On 18 June, in the fourth of his famous 1940 speeches, Churchill confirmed his leadership.

'What General Weygand called the "Battle of France" is over. I expect that the Battle of Britain is about to begin . . . Let us therefore brace ourselves to our duties, and so bear ourselves that, if the British Empire and its commonwealth last for a thousand years, men will still say "this was their finest hour".'

'No more bloody Allies'

Delivered in the House of Commons, Churchill's speech was impressive. But when he broadcast to the nation later that evening, it was a far poorer effort. Diarist Harold Nicolson, recorded: 'How I wish Winston would not talk on the wireless unless he is feeling in good form. He hates the microphone, and when we bullied him into speaking last night, he just sulked and read his House of Commons speech over again. Now, as delivered in the House of Commons, that speech was magnificent, especially the concluding sentences. But it sounded ghastly on the wireless. All the great vigour he put into it seemed to evaporate.'

Cecil **King** in his seldom complimentary diary described the speech as 'a few stumbling sentences to the effect that the situation was disastrous, but all right. Whether he was drunk or all-in from sheer fatigue, I don't know, but it was the poorest possible effort.'

But again these judgements were from Churchill's close associates. The public heard it differently. They felt more reassured by the half dozen sentences which the Prime Minister barked into the microphone than they would have been by any lengthy prepared oration.

Above all they were happy to have a leader, and proud to be alone. A tug boat skipper hailed a friend across the Thames: 'Now we know where we are! No more bloody Allies.' King George VI, more sedately, wrote to his mother: 'Personally I feel happier now that we have no allies to be polite to and to pamper.'

In Churchill's own words 'their blood was up', and the British revealed one of the convictions they instinctively felt—it was better to be dead than defeated.

War Notes

ANDERSON, John: Home Secretary, b. 1882. Educated Edinburgh University as mathematician. Entered Colonial Office 1905. Permanent under secretary, Home Office 1922-32 and Governor of Bengal 1932-7. MP 1938 and as Lord Privy Seal 1938-9 responsible for civil defence, developed the family bomb shelter which later bore his name. Home Secretary and Minister of Home Security 1939. Started pressing for internment on 15 May 1940. On 18th asked that all Italians resident for less than 20 years be interned. On 22nd Cabinet agreed. Next day Sir Oswald Mosley and up to 80 of his British Union of Fascists were arrested. By the end of June 747 were interned.

BEAVERBROOK, William Maxwell Aitken, 1st Baron: British newspaper publisher and politician, b. 1879 Maple, Ontario, son of a Presbyterian minister. After minimal education took a variety of jobs, before becoming a promoter with the help of wealthy financier. Organized mergers of banks and other companies; made his fortune by selling his holdings following merger of cement companies. Went to London and became private secretary to Tory MP Bonar Law. Elected MP 1910 and was government representative at W. Front 1914-18, responsible for Canadian war records. Made a peer and bought *Daily Express* 1917. Minister of Information and Chancellor of Duchy of Lancaster 1918.

BEVIN, Ernest: British politician, b. 1881 Somerset. After working as farm labourer, moved to Bristol as carter. Joined Dockers' Union 1910, becoming Assistant General Secretary by 1920. Led Council of Action against British support for Poland in her war with Russia 1920. Formed Transport and General Workers' Union by merging 32 unions, 1922, and became its general secretary. A member of TUC General Council 1925, he was largely instrumental in bringing about the General Strike of 1926 and for negotiating its conclusion. Served on Macmillan Committee of Finance and Industry 1930. Resisted Communist influence in trade unions and led Labour Party's support for sanctions and rearmament.

COOPER, Alfred Duff: British politician, b. 1890. Educated Oxford. Entered Foreign Office 1913. Joined Household Brigade Officers Cadet Battalion 1917 and served on W. Front. Married Lady Diana Manners 1919. MP 1924. Financial Secretary at War Office 1928-9, 1931-4; at Treasury 1934-5. Secretary of State for War 1935-7. First Lord of the Admiralty 1937-8. Denounced Munich Agreement as meaningless and unworkable and resigned from Cabinet 1938. Commissioned by Beaverbrook to write weekly article for *Evening Standard*. US lecture tour 1939.

KING, Cecil Harmsworth: British newspaper director, b.1901, son of Sir Lucas White King. Educated Winchester and Christ Church Oxford. Director of *Daily Mirror* from 1929.

MASS-OBSERVATION: British social research organization founded by Tom Harrisson and Charles Madge 1937 and financed by Secret Service funds. Employed to produce report on public's opinion of the war Sept 1939. Results served as basis for *War Begins at Home* published 1940.

MORAN, Charles McMoran Wilson: British doctor, b. 1882 Skipton-in-Craven, Yorks. Medical Officer (MO) with 1st Bn Royal Fusiliers 1914-17 then MO with 7th Stationary Hospital, Boulogne, 1917-18. Major Royal Army Medical Corps awarded MC. Dean of St Mary's Hospital Medical School from 1920.

STRIKING COMPANIES: units of men specially recruited and organized for raiding enemy coast. Brainchild of Lt-Col Dudley Clarke, whose idea was submitted on 5 June and given the go-ahead on the 8th. The 1st 'Commando' (name was taken from mobile Boer units) raid took place from 6 RAF air-sea rescue craft on night of 23-24 June at Boulogne and Le Touquet under Major Ronnie Tod. The raiders, armed with 20 of the 40 Tommy guns in Britain, killed 2 sentries and threw grenades into a military building.

'I, GENERAL DE GAULLE....'

As the hyper-efficient German war machine carved swathes through France's disintegrating armies, and as France's political and military leadership stumbled towards confused defeatism, one man stood above his country's sad decline like a beacon.

At 6ft 4in, with a tiny head on top of a shapeless body, Charles André Joseph Marie **de Gaulle** had earned the nickname 'La grande asperge'—the tall asparagus—at the **St Cyr** Military Academy. His height had proved a handicap during World War 1. It made him too noticeable as a prisoner after capture at Verdun and frustrated five separate escape attempts.

But for any disadvantages that arose from his odd appearance, de Gaulle made up with a lofty independence of mind—and an outstanding military brain.

With the exception of Paul Reynaud, who championed de Gaulle, French politicians took little notice of the young soldier's writings, but by 1934 both Hitler and Ribbentrop noted their respect for de Gaulle as France's expert in modern warfare. In that year he had published *Vers l' armée de métier* (Towards a Professional Army) in which he pressed his ideas for a small, highly mechanized force. Sales in Germany were 1000 copies, in France 100.

By the time war broke out, Colonel de Gaulle had won command of a tank brigade, in Alsace with the Fifth Army. But the tank was still far from enjoying the role in France that de Gaulle had dreamed of. Instead of the 500-strong tank divisions he had advocated, the Higher War Council was developing divisions of 120 tanks apiece. These were spread throughout the Army as infantry support, and not used as independent strike forces.

In March 1940 the Daladier government fell and Paul Reynaud took over. De Gaulle was delighted. Reynaud supported de Gaulle, and wanted him as Under-Secretary of State in his war cabinet. But the partisan nature of French politics soon killed that idea. To gain the support of Daladier's Radical Party, Reynaud had to give the defeatist Paul Baudouin the key post instead.

French troops on parade in London. On 28 June the British Government recognized General de Gaulle as 'Chief of all the Free French wherever they may be'.

In June 1940 de Gaulle had a second chance to join the government. Paul Reynaud shuffled his cabinet and brought in de Gaulle as Under-Secretary of State for National Defence.

The problem for de Gaulle was that he had virtually no support. Even Reynaud was losing ground as the group gathering round his mistress, Hélène de Portes, was pressing him to seek an armistice. De Gaulle was not popular with his fellow officers who thought him arrogant, and his old mentor Marshal Pétain complained: 'His vanity leads him to believe that he knows every secret about the art of war. He could have invented it. I know all about him. He belonged to my staff. Not only is he vain, but he is an ingrate and has few friends in the Army.'

De Gaulle's first job was to fly to London to persuade the British that Reynaud was resolved to fight on and ask them for aid—specifically for 20 squadrons of fighters. Churchill insisted on the squadrons staying at home for the defence of Britain, so in material terms de Gaulle's mission failed. But he opened up valuable connections with the British government, and also with French groups in London.

That night, 10 June, de Gaulle returned to Paris, where the situation was rapidly deteriorating. The government was packing up and moving out to Bordeaux.

Three days later Churchill and his entourage paid another visit to France, for a conference at Tours. There Churchill said that Britain would not object to a French armistice, so long as the

'France has lost a battle! But France has not lost the war!'

General de Gaulle

French troops rescued from Dunkirk. Only a few were to join de Gaulle's Free French—most returned to France.

French undertook not to hand over their fleet to the Germans. De Gaulle was shocked. He found Reynaud and asked him bluntly if he meant to request an armistice. 'Of course not,' Reynaud replied. 'But one must make an impression on the British in order to obtain from them a wider co-operation.'

Back in Bordeaux the next day, 14 June, pressure among government figures for an armistice was growing. The atmosphere was rife with defeatism and intrigue. De Gaulle told Reynaud: 'I refuse to submit to an armistice.' He pressed Reynaud to go to Algiers: 'Are you—yes or no—resolved on that?'

'Yes,' Reynaud replied.

So de Gaulle set off to London the next day to arrange for British help with transport. The two men expected to meet again in Algiers.

A surprising move

Sailing from Brest by destroyer to Plymouth, de Gaulle took a train to London, and installed himself in the Hyde Park Hotel. There two momentous pieces of news awaited him. One he expected. The other was a surprise.

The obvious news was that the government in France was moving towards formally requesting an armistice.

Less expected was the announcement of a plan for France and Britain to unite as one nation. Drafted by Sir Robert **Vansittart,** British Under-Secretary of State at the Foreign Office, and a group of Frenchmen including Jean **Monnet,** the scheme called for an 'indispensable Franco-British union'.

British and French citizens would share a common citizenship. There would be one war cabinet, and the new country would create 'common organisms' for defence, foreign policy, finance and economic affairs.

The architects of the scheme had not yet put it to the British government. That was to be de Gaulle's next task.

That afternoon Churchill put the plan before the British cabinet. After two hours of discussion he came out and told de Gaulle: 'We are agreed.'

De Gaulle telephoned Reynaud at Bordeaux, then gave Churchill the receiver so that the two leaders could confirm their agreement.

Then de Gaulle rushed back to Bordeaux in a plane Churchill made available. He landed at 9.30 that evening. That afternoon Reynaud had put the Anglo-French union idea before his own cabinet. They had heard him out in stony silence, then threw out the idea. Reynaud resigned.

Immediately, de Gaulle made up his mind to leave France the next morning. With Reynaud gone, President Lebrun had called on Marshal Pétain to form a government. And that meant capitulation.

As his last gesture in office, Reynaud gave de Gaulle one million francs to finance a small French force from London and a letter sending him on a mission, still as Under-Secretary of State. It might help him past awkward border guards.

Edward Spears was still in Bordeaux. Together with the Ambassador, Sir Ronald Campbell, he went to Reynaud's residence later that night. There, walking through the hall, Spears heard someone whisper his name. He looked up and saw a tall figure standing in the shadows, his back against a large column. It was de Gaulle.

'I must speak to you. It is extremely urgent,' whispered de Gaulle.

'But I can't now. The Ambassador and I are going to see the Premier,' Spears whispered back.

'You must,' de Gaulle insisted. 'I have good reason to believe Weygand intends arresting me.'

Spears told de Gaulle to wait where he was. When they emerged from the interview with Reynaud de Gaulle was still there, standing tall and straight against the column, and out of view from the front entrance. He had turned several shades whiter with the strain of his wait.

Anxious not to talk in the Premier's hall, the two men made their way to the Hotel Montré where Spears was staying. There de Gaulle repeated that he faced arrest, or a posting that would deliberately keep him out of England. Spears, depressed by the 'nauseating stench of defeat' in Bordeaux, also wanted to see de Gaulle keep alive the flame of resistance in England.

The problem was that de Gaulle no longer had the slightest authority. With no government post, he was merely an acting brigadier general in the Army, and the youngest of them. The military hierarchy would not support his challenge to Pétain's authority. He did not even have any right to leave the country.

Undeterred, Spears hatched a plot to take de Gaulle back to England with him. Aware of the risks of arrest, he made a number of appointments for de Gaulle the next morning to confuse anybody trying to track him down. With the Frenchman's luggage hidden under overcoats, they drove to the airport. Once there, they saw aircraft stacked wing to wing the length of the airport—ready, Spears presumed, to fly to Morocco.

Hasty exit

As the pilot worked through the take-off preparations, de Gaulle and Spears continued their deception. Among the many figures on the crowded airfield there could be some whose job it was to see de Gaulle did not leave. So Spears arranged to board the plane, while de Gaulle stood around pretending to see him off. When the plane was rolling for take-off, Spears planned to pull de Gaulle on board.

All was ready. Then the pilot said that he could not take off unless de Gaulle's luggage (it contained important papers so could not be left behind) was lashed down. Nobody carried string, so an aide, Lieutenant de Courcel, set off in search. After ten minutes—packed with excruciating anxiety that they would be discovered—de Courcel reappeared with a ball of string and the luggage was secured.

At last the aircraft began to roll. Spears hooked his hands together and hauled de Gaulle on board. De Courcel, more nimble, nipped in behind him. With the chauffeur and others gaping incredulous behind them, the pilot taxied through the maze of aircraft to a runway and, after a short taxi through the congestion, they were airborne.

Churchill later wrote—'De Gaulle carried with him, in this small airplane, the honour of France.'

That afternoon Spears escorted de Gaulle into the garden of 10 Downing Street, where Churchill was sitting enjoying the sunshine. After a short talk Churchill arranged for de Gaulle to broadcast on the BBC the next day.

Churchill was opposing the views of his own Foreign Office in letting de Gaulle broadcast. They thought it would only impair relations with the French government in Bordeaux. But Churchill saw in de Gaulle a focus of French resistance, bringing support—however small—for the Allied war effort now based in Britain.

De Gaulle himself had loftier ideals. He did not see his undertaking merely as aid given by a handful of exiled Frenchmen to the British Empire. He saw himself now as the embodiment of France.

'As for me, with a hill like that to climb? I was starting from scratch. Not a shadow of force or of an organization at my side. In France no following and no reputation. Abroad, neither credit nor standing. But this very destitution showed me my line of conduct. It was by adopting without compromise the cause of national recovery that I could

Writing home. French soldiers at Dover docks after evacuation from Dunkirk.

acquire authority . . . In short, limited and alone though I was, and precisely because I was so, I had to climb to the heights and never come down.'

After working for the rest of that day and most of the next over the text of his speech at a small flat in Seymour Place, de Gaulle sat down in studio B2 at Broadcasting House for the French Service bulletin at 6pm on 18 June. Reading from two sheets of paper propped up on a makeshift lectern, he boomed into the microphone. An engineer clutched at the dials to bring the sound down to normal.

'France is not alone'

De Gaulle felt himself beginning a new life. 'As I heard the irrevocable words come forth, I felt within myself that one life was ending, the life I had led within the framework of a solid France and an indivisible army. At the age of 49, I had become an adventurer, a man whom destiny had plucked from the line and made unique.'

De Gaulle refused to accept defeat: '. . . but has the last word been said? Must we abandon all hope? Is our defeat final and irremediable? To these questions I answer—No!

'Speaking in full knowledge of the facts, I ask you to believe me when I say that the cause of France is not lost . . . . For remember this, France does not stand alone. She is not isolated. Behind her is a vast Empire and she can make common cause with the British Empire, which commands the seas and is continuing the struggle. Like England, she can draw unreservedly on the immense industrial resources of the United States.

'The war is not limited to our unfortunate country. The outcome of the struggle has not been decided by the Battle of France. This is a world war . . . I, General de Gaulle, now in London, call on all French officers and men who are at present on British soil, or may be in the future, with or without their arms; I call on all engineers and skilled workmen from the armament factories who are at present on British soil, or may be in the future, to get in touch with me.

'Whatever happens, the flames of French resistance must not and shall not die.'

Historic words—heard by few

It was a stirring speech. The problem was—few heard it. The BBC had hardly heard of de Gaulle. With no idea that his speech might be important in history, no recording was made of it.

The Times next day gave it a brief mention: the *Daily Express* buried it on page eight. In France most homes were suffering a power failure that night, so had no electricity to drive their wireless sets. Those that still worked were tuned to Bordeaux, where news of the armistice was still the main story. The few French troops in Britain missed it—nobody had told them de Gaulle would broadcast.

The important Frenchmen in Britain, diplomats and officials, had too strong a career loyalty to throw in their lot with a self-appointed dissident. Jean Monnet, who had so strongly promoted the Anglo-French Union a few days earlier, did not

Senegalese troops in England after Dunkirk. Senegal, in West Africa, was part of the French Empire.

approve of de Gaulle's conception of resistance. He and other leading Frenchmen left for home or the United States. A series of telegrams from de Gaulle to **French Empire** Governors, pleading with them to form a committee to continue the war, had no effect.

But then, slowly, the movement started to grow. Spears arranged a new office for de Gaulle, conveniently located across the road from the House of Commons. The furniture was little more than a telephone, a few hard chairs, and naked light bulbs. But Spears' secretary, Miss Morris, managed to get hold of a barrel of wine and stood it in the corridor, so that supporters could toast their future with de Gaulle.

'Chief of all Free French'

By the end of June the Free French had grown to dozens. A few pilots who escaped from a military airfield near Bordeaux joined him. General Béthouart, a Narvik veteran currently stationed in England, permitted de Gaulle to address his men. As a result parts of two Foreign Legion battalions, 200 Chasseurs Alpins, and sundry tankmen, engineers and signallers pledged their support. After de Gaulle had gone, two British officers sent by the War Office carefully warned the troops that they would be rebelling against their own government if they joined.

De Gaulle tried to visit a thousand French soldiers in camp at Aintree, Liverpool. The British admiral in charge turned him away, because his visit might prejudice order. At Haydock Park he was luckier, and the first of a stream of sailors joined him. Isolated volunteers, many having escaped through Spain, arrived in London via Gibraltar. Groups of merchant seamen heard of de Gaulle and asked to enroll. A flotilla of fishing boats crossed from the Breton island of Sein and reached Cornwall.

On 28 June the British government announced that they recognized de Gaulle, as 'Chief of all the Free French wherever they may be, who rally to him for the defence of the Allied cause'.

By that time de Gaulle had turned down several orders from the Pétain government to return home. They responded by demoting him to the rank of Colonel and placing him on the retired list.

On 2 August they put him on trial in his absence. The variety of charges including supporting the interests of England against those of France, inciting French soldiers and sailors to place themselves in the service of England, making broadcasts which would persuade the enemy that the terms of the Armistice would not be met, and defecting abroad in time of war.

The court found de Gaulle guilty of five of the six charges against him.

The penalty was death, military degradation, and confiscation of all property and personal effects. He was also ordered to pay costs.

It was rumoured that when the judgement arrived on Marshal Pétain's desk, the old hero who had once told students at a de Gaulle lecture 'Listen to him attentively, for the day will come when France in gratitude will call for him,' scrawled across the paper: 'Will not execute.'

War Notes

DE GAULLE, Charles André Joseph Marie: French soldier, b. 1890, Lille. Educated College Stanislas, Paris and St Cyr military academy. Lieutenant in Pétain's 33rd Infantry Regt 1914-16, seeing action in Belgium and Champagne; 2 wounds. Promoted Captain 1915. Wounded and captured 1916. Member French Mission to Poland 1920. Taught military history at St Cyr 1920-1. Served under Marshal Pétain at Ecole Superieure de Guerre 1921-7. Commanded 19th Infantry Battalion attached to Rhine Army 1927-9. Served in Middle East 1929-32. Appointed General Secretary of the Defence Council 1932. Promoted to Lt-Colonel 1933 and full Colonel in 1937 when he took command of 507th Armoured Regiment at Metz. Wrote *Towards a Professional Army* 1934 and *France and her Army* 1938. Promoted to Brigadier-General 11 May 1940 and took command of the hastily forming 4th Armoured Div at Laon. Led it in 3 local counter-attacks, Montcornet 17 May, La Fère 19th and Abbeville 27th-31st. Lack of infantry, air and artillery support, training and fuel hampered all 3. The first two proved a minor worry to Guderian's flank, inflicting 230 casualties at Montcornet for less than 200 and about 10 tanks (out of 150). A 120-mile march to Abbeville cost 30 tank breakdowns. The attack over unfavourable terrain failed to eradicate the German Somme bridgehead and left the division with 34 tanks but took 500 PoWs.

FRENCH EMPIRE: in 1940 it included Algeria, Morocco, Tunisia, French Somaliland, Madagascar, French Equatorial Africa (Central African Republic, Chad, Congo Republic and Gabon), French West Africa (Senegal, Mauritania, French Sudan, Upper Volta, Niger, Guinea, Ivory Coast), French Indochina (Laos, Cambodia and Vietnam), French Antilles (Guadeloupe and Martinique), French Guiana and a number of Pacific islands including New Caledonia and Tahiti. Total area of 3.7 million sq miles and population of 65.5 million (1936). Technically Algeria was an integral part of France, sending deputies to Paris.

MONNET, Jean: French economist, b. 1888. Left school at 16 to enter family brandy business. Took charge of its export side and travelled widely. Visited Britain, US, Canada and Egypt where he remained for several years. Served in the supply division of French Army in 1914, being rejected as unfit for active service. Appointed liaison officer for Ministry of Trade in London end 1914. Obtained 100 million franc loan for French Government from Canadian Hudson Bay Company. Served on committees responsible for Allies food, raw materials and arms. Co-founder of Interallied Executive to Supreme Economic Council by Clemenceau. Deputy Secretary-General League of Nations 1919. In 1923 returned to now ailing family business, which he soon revived. Went to China to advise on financial matters 1933. On return he formed New York partnership to arrange loans for China and reorganize US companies. Recalled from US in 1938 by Daladier to join French purchasing commission. By spring 1940 he was chairman of Anglo-French Co-ordinating Commitee concerned with supplies for the two countries.

ST CYR: top French military academy at St Cyr d'Ecole near Versailles. Founded by Napoleon in 1803. Full name is Ecole Speciale Militaire de Saint-Cyr.

VANSITTART, Robert Gilbert: British diplomat, b. 1881. Educated Eton. Joined Foreign Office (FO) 1902 as attaché. Served Paris 1903-7. Became 3rd secretary 1905. Served Teheran 1907-9, Cairo 1909 and Stockholm 1915. Returned Paris 1919 as 1st secretary. Took part in peace negotiations. Private secretary to Foreign Secretary, Lord Curzon, 1920-4. Head of FO American Section 1924-8. Principal private secretary to PMs Stanley Baldwin and Ramsay MacDonald. Appointed Under-Secretary of State for Foreign Affairs 1930. Highly influential on British foreign policy in 1930s. In 1937 his retirement announced, but in 1938 he returned as 'chief diplomatic adviser to the FO'. Directed British anti-Nazi propaganda abroad.

BROOMSTICK ARMY

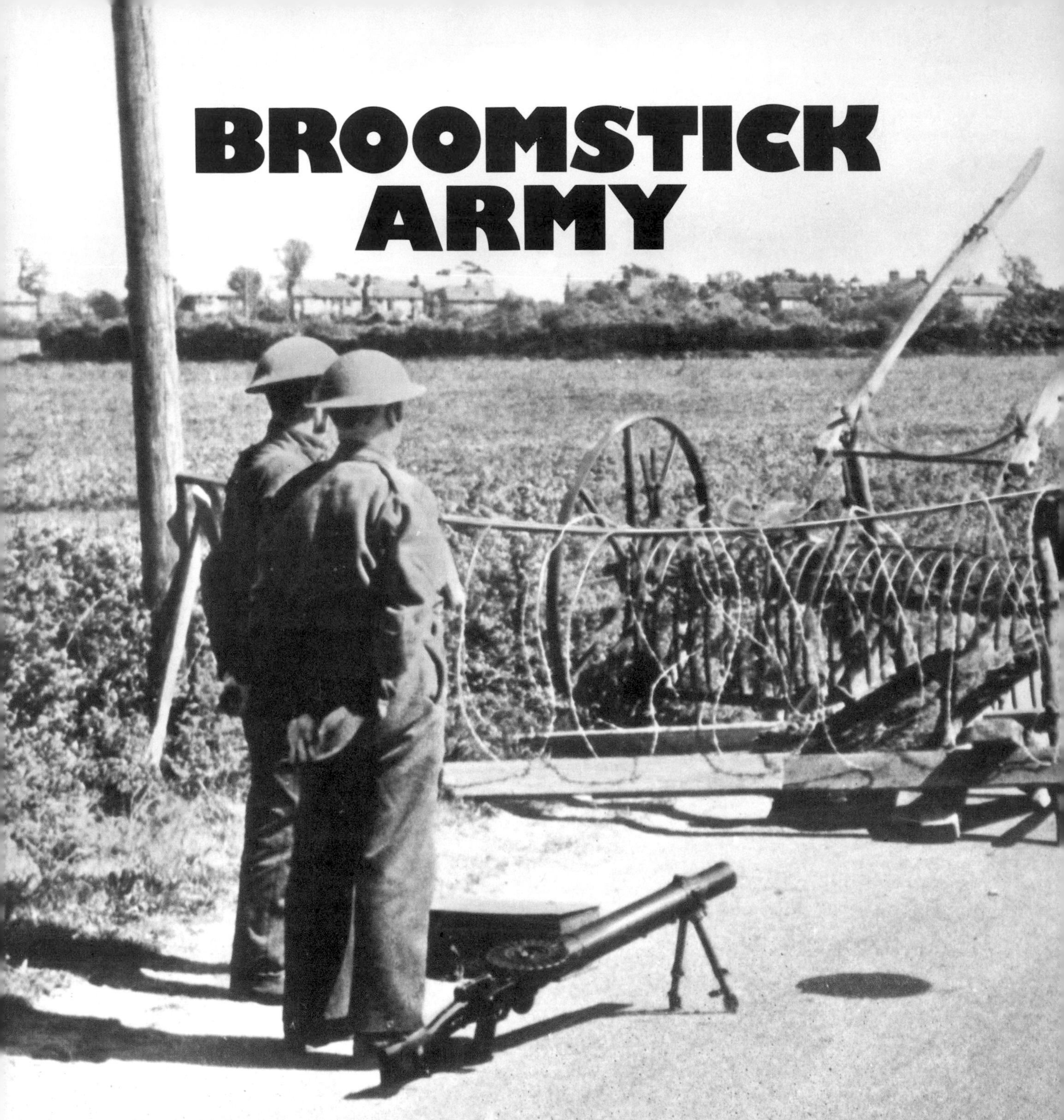

In his familiar calm, dignified voice Anthony Eden, Secretary of State for War, broadcast to the men of Britain on 14 May a call to volunteer for a new defence force. Within 24 hours a quarter of a million men were enlisted. Before June the number had doubled.

'We are going to ask you to help in a manner which I know will be welcome to thousands of you. The Government has received inquiries from all over the Kingdom from men who wish to do something for the defence of their country. Now is your opportunity. We want large numbers of such men, between the ages of 17 and 65, to come forward now and offer their services. The name of the new force will be Local Defence Volunteers. In order to volunteer what you have to do is to give your name in at your local police station.'

Even before Eden had finished speaking, men were striding round to police stations throughout the country. Overworked station sergeants, many of them not yet issued with the right forms, made lists of names. The queuing went on until after midnight.

It was no sudden rush of enthusiasm. Before the official call people had got together to form small defence units. In Churchill's words 'All over the country, in every town and village, bands of determined men came together armed with shot-

'They were most of them elderley, with kind, careworn faces . . . They had done their job in the last war.'

Wife of Home Guard major

guns, sporting rifles, clubs and spears.'

The new Local Defence Volunteer force was the formal structure which expressed the long standing determination of Britons to defend their homes. In particular the volunteers force was designed to defeat the tactics of Hitler's victory in Scandinavia and northwest Europe.

Churchill was sure that 'a country where every street and every village bristles with loyal, resolute, armed men is a country against which the kind of tactics which destroyed Dutch resistance—tactics of parachutists or airborne troops in carriers or gliders, Fifth Column activities . . . would prove wholly ineffective. A country so defended would not be liable to be overthrown by such tactics.'

Men from all walks of life who were unable to join the regular forces flocked to enrol in the new service. Officially, 65 was the upper age limit, but hundreds gave false ages, and every unit had a proportion of 70 and 80-year-olds. Some turned up at recruiting stations with walking sticks—some stumped along on crutches, and had tactfully to be turned away. Once back in uniform, the years seemed irrelevant. A Berkshire volunteer remembered: 'I think that none of us will forget our first LDV route march. On it a quarter of a century slipped away in a flash . . . There were few youngsters in that first platoon of ours.'

Many men wore a chest-full of ribbons that showed they had served before. Most of the recruits in the first wave, up to November 1940, had served in World War 1; some in the Boer War.

For the new conflict, they all cheerfully abandoned their previous ranks. Retired lieutenant-generals fell in alongside corporals. Admirals became privates in the ranks. Old class distinctions disappeared, as businessmen and lawyers drilled shoulder to shoulder with farm workers, clerks, and factory hands.

Armed with a rifle and an obsolete Lewis machine-gun, Home Guard soldiers man a roadblock to check driver identification. Modern rifles were scarce: some units only had one for every 25 men.

Most had put in a full day's work in their ordinary jobs, many of them in war industries, before they pulled on their boots and set out again for training on two or three evenings a week. At weekends there were more parades. Ten hours a week they undertook to give to soldiering.

Of their keenness there was no doubt. Their efficiency was another matter. In the early days they had few weapons, and practically no equipment. They had to improvize. Instead of a rifle, they drilled with broomsticks. Eden viewed his force with a sidelong glance and called it 'my broomstick army'.

For roadblocks they rescued old iron bedsteads from scrap-heaps. They pressed any vehicles they could find into service as army transport, often using vans owned by local farmers and tradesmen. If they needed wire to decapitate enemy motor cyclists, they used washing line. Appeals to local sources produced much of the equipment which the Government could not supply.

Like national guerilla movements all over Europe they produced home-made bombs—**Molotov cocktails**—from tin cans and beer bottles. Churchill was not far wrong when he observed, on the point of France's surrender, 'Well, now we shall have to fight them alone.'

'Yes sir, but what with?' he was asked.

'With bottles, my boy, empty bottles.'

One unit produced their own makeshift tank by welding steel plates on to an old car chassis. A group of miners concocted an anti-tank weapon. They attached an anti-tank mine to a broomstave, and blocked off one end of a boiler tube. Firing the missile electrically out of the end of the tube, they worked up enough accuracy to stop a 35mph car at a considerable range.

Modern rifles were in short supply. In Kent the standard allocation during June was one rifle between ten men. In Berkshire they were even worse off. They started with a rifle and ten rounds between every 25 men, then had to give up their rifles to the regular army coming home from Dunkirk.

'An army of Blimps'

The Government appealed to the public for arms. Eager to help, 20,000 owners handed in shotguns, and pistols of various kinds. Then many of those weapons went to the regular army.

Gradually, the equipment situation improved. Out of the **Imperial War Museum** came a stock of rifles, World War 1 models and not fired in a lifetime, but serviceable with some attention. They were better than the weapons carried by a patrol in Somerset—pikes from HMS *Victory*, last used at the Battle of Trafalgar.

The United States helped with a shipment of half a million .300in rifles. Women volunteers worked day and night to shift the coating of thick yellow grease that had protected the rifles for 20 years since their manufacture. Private citizens in America also sent over shotguns and sporting rifles, often with messages attached: 'To help you in England in your hour of need, from Mrs and Mr J. B. Harrison and family.'

Inevitably, with a fair number of pot-bellied veterans and men unfit for front-line service, the LDVs became the target for critics, including cartoonists like David **Low**, who invented the Colonel Blimp character, and the novelist George **Orwell**, who called the LDVs a 'people's army officered by Blimps.'

In June the movement began to settle down and take on a measure of efficiency. Winston Churchill had a hand in it. He suggested that the organization should change its name. 'I do not think very much of the name Local Defence Volunteers,' he wrote to Anthony Eden. Minister of Supply, Herbert **Morrison**, suggested they should change it to 'Civic Guard'. Churchill turned down any idea that sounded like town hall bureaucracy. His favourite was Home Guard, a name he first dreamed up in October 1939. So the name changed.

Gradually, they also evolved a training programme. Individual units were responsible for their own training. But in June a magazine publisher, Edward **Hulton** of *Picture Post*,

sponsored a training school at Osterley Park in West London. Run by the Spanish Civil War veteran Tom **Wintringham**, its tutors included three Spanish miners who taught the art of destroying tanks with explosives, and became Home Guard idols. Home Guard officers and NCOs crammed a lot into the two-day Osterley Park course. They did weapon training, and learned the confidence and cunning of guerilla warfare.

The Osterley gospel spread rapidly, as its students took the ideas back to their units at home. But when political capital was made out of the school's success, the War Office stepped in to take it over officially.

Was it effective?

No one ever found out whether the Home Guard would have been effective or not. They were never intended for the role of first line troops. If it came to a war on British soil, they were designed primarily as back up for the regular army. The one exception was the role first conceived for them, to meet and deal with invasion by enemy paratroops. The Home Guard would be on the spot to deal with them as they landed. This original conception led to the inelegant name they first took—parashots.

By the time they were formed, the role the Government envisaged for them had expanded. First they were to warn of enemy landings. By energetic patrolling, and setting up outlying observation posts, the Home Guard would in theory cover the country with an infallible observation

The Home Guard prepares for an invasion: elaborate camouflage precautions (left), and making Molotov cocktails to use against German tanks (above).

network that would rule out secret landings.

If a parachute force did land, the Home Guard was supposed to wipe it out, or at least hold it. By guarding key points like road junctions and bridges with carefully prepared defensive positions, and by blocking roads with felled trees and trenches, they could hamper enemy units, stop them destroying communications and spreading the kind of panic that had cost northwest Europeans their freedom.

Their job also was to protect sensitive installations such as factories, and in a 'scorched earth' operation to remove food stocks, and even cut off water supplies that the enemy might use. Once the street and village names had been obliterated on 28 May, they were also to use their local knowledge to guide the regular army into battle.

If the invading forces still established themselves, the Home Guard had a harassing role. Their task was to reduce panzer crews to a state of nervous hysteria by shooting at them whenever they tried to get out of the tank.

The Home Guard might appear to have taken themselves less than fully seriously; some cheerfully referred to themselves as the 'Look, Duck, and Vanish Brigade'. But they dedicated themselves to their work with the knowledge that they would be fighting for their own homes.

Some critics have described the Home Guard as the biggest bluff in history because Hitler himself took them seriously. He had this warning broadcast over German radio.

'The British Government is committing the worst crime of all. Evidently it permits open preparations for the formation of murder bands. The preparations which are being made all over England to arm the civilian population for guerilla warfare are contrary to the rules of international law. German official quarters warn the misled British public and remind them of the fate of the Polish 'franc-tireurs' and gangs of murderers. Civilians who take up arms against German soldiers are, under international law, no better than murderers, whether they are priests or bank clerks. British people, you will do well to heed our warning.'

The British people were not impressed, like the farmer who politely dismissed the idea of any training. He told the officer how he had gone out against a mad bull and killed it with his first shot. He was quite capable of dealing with any Jerry who turned up.

Local Defence Volunteers on parade in a Berkshire town. The volunteers, in full time employment during the day, would give up two or three evenings a week and part of the weekend for training.

War Notes

HOME GUARD

HULTON, Edward: British barrister and publisher, b. 1906 Harrogate, son of Sir Edward Hulton, former proprietor of *Evening Standard.* Educated at Harrow and Brasenose College, Oxford. Contested Leek Division, Staffs as Unionist 1929 and Harwich Div 1931. Called to Bar, Inner Temple. Practised on SE Circuit. Chairman and Managing Director of Hulton Publications Ltd from 1938. Bought *Lilliput* from Stefan Lorant who became Editor of *Picture Post* which Hulton set up.

IMPERIAL WAR MUSEUM: founded by War Cabinet 1917. It was established by Act of Parliament 1920 in the old Bethlehem Hospital, Lambeth Road (London). World War 1 memorial to effort and sacrifice made by men and women of the Empire.

LOW, David: British cartoonist and caricaturist b. 1891 Dunedin, New Zealand. Worked on *The Bulletin,* Sydney 1911, *Star,* London 1919 and *Evening Standard* 1927. Cartoons collected in various publications including *Europe Since Versailles* 1939, *Europe at War* 1940.

MOLOTOV COCKTAIL: primitive but effective against vehicles and buildings if used fearlessly. First employed in Spanish Civil War 1936-39 but given nickname by Finns to mock Soviet foreign minister. During Winter War 40,000 bottles provided for the purpose by Finland's State Liquor Board. Early cocktails were lit with a petrol-soaked rag in neck of bottle. Casualty rates for throwers were 60-70%. At Osterley Park the mixer of Molotov Cocktails and dispenser of explosives was Wilfred Vernon.

MORRISON, Herbert: British politician b. 1891. Educated Queen's College, Galway and Trinity College Cambridge. Entered Secretary's Department, Admiralty 1921. Became Private Secretary to Civil Lord 1925, and a Principal in Secretary's Dept 1930. Was Director of Greenwich Hospital 1934-8 and became Asst Sec, Admiralty 1939. Became Minister for Supplies in Churchill's War Cabinet of 11 May 1940.

ORWELL, George: British writer b. 1903 Motihari. Educated Eton 1917-21. Was Asst. District Superintendent of India Imperial Police in Burma 1922-7. Rebelled against imperial background and became an anarchist. Later changed to become a Socialist. Disillusioned with Communism after fighting in Spanish Civil War. Publications: *Down and Out in Paris and London* 1933, *The Road to Wigan Pier* 1937, *Homage to Catalonia* 1938.

WINTRINGHAM, Tom: British soldier and writer b. 1898 Grimsby. Served in airforce, France 1916-18. Was in Spain as a correspondent 1937 and became British battalion CO in the International Brigade. On return to England advocated the formation of a people's army. Publications: *English Captain* 1939, *New Ways of War, Armies of Freemen* 1940.

JULY 1940

...KNOWING he must smash the RAF before any invasion can succeed, Hitler throws the Luftwaffe against British targets... the Battle of Britain has begun. Meanwhile France has been hacked into two parts–the German-occupied north and the so-called 'Free Zone' in the south–and must learn to live with the enemy. This is the month that Hitler's troops invade the Channel Islands and the Royal Navy sinks French warships at Oran in North Africa...

1st: French Government moves from Bordeaux to Vichy. German occupation of Channel Is completed.
2nd: Hitler asks for Britain invasion plan.
3rd: Operation Catapult, RN moves against French Fleet.
4th: Italians capture Kassala and Galabat in the Sudan.
5th: Vichy breaks off relations with Britain.
6th: Hitler returns to Berlin for victory celebrations.
7th: Italians bomb Alexandria.
8th: British tea rationing begins. Fleet Air Arm disables battleship *Richelieu* at Dakar.
9th: British and Italian Fleets clash off Calabria.
10th: First RAF Czech squadron formed.
11th: Pétain proclaims himself 'Head of French State'.
12th: Aberdeen, Cardiff bombed.
13th: British paratroop training begins.
14th: Roosevelt sends Colonel Donovan to assess Britain's chances of survival.
15th: Home Office bans fireworks, kite and balloon flying.
16th: Hitler orders Sealion invasion preparations.
17th: Britain agrees to close Burma Road for 3 months.
18th: Roosevelt nominated for third term.
19th: Hitler makes 'last appeal to reason'.
20th: Göring sets up first Luftwaffe night fighter unit.
21st: Baltic State assemblies vote for union with USSR.
22nd: British War Cabinet approves SOE.
23rd: Local Defence Volunteers renamed Home Guard, 3rd War Budget raises income tax to 7s 6d (38p) in £.
24th: French liner *Meknès* repatriating 1277 sailors, sunk by E-boat, 383 dead.
25th: Stukas and E-boats sink 8 coasters.
26th: RAF daylight raid on Dortmund power station.
27th: RN destroyers *Codrington* (Dover) and *Wren* (off Suffolk) sunk by Luftwaffe.
28th: First U-boats operate from Bergen, Norway.
29th: Vichy forms court to try ex-French leaders.
30th: Luftwaffe attacks E. Coast shipping.
31st: Hitler fixes invasion of Russia for May 1941. Battle of Britain July losses: Luftwaffe 216, RAF 77.

BRITAIN INVADED

An air raid warning at dusk on Sunday, 30 June, sent the inhabitants of the Channel Island of Guernsey scurrying for shelter. Two hours later they heard the 'all clear'.

During those hours a German force had landed. The island had been taken without any show of resistance.

Earlier that afternoon, Captain Liebe-Pieteritz on routine reconnaissance, had seen **Guernsey** airfield completely deserted and decided to land. Leaving three planes in the air to cover him, he touched down on the runway completely unmolested. He took off again to rejoin his companions when three Bristol Blenheims appeared in the sky. They shot down two of the Blenheims before returning to their base.

When he reported the incident to Luftflotte 3, it fully convinced them that the Islands were undefended. Just a platoon of Luftwaffe soldiers would be sent to occupy the island. Later that evening the unit of steel-helmeted, black-booted soldiers were deposited by four Junkers 52 transports. Armed with rifle, machine pistol and hand grenade, they stood silently, waiting.

Within minutes, Inspector W. R. Schulpher, head of the island's police force, arrived with a letter addressed to the 'Officer Commanding German troops in Guernsey'. He handed it to the senior officer, Major Albrecht Lanz.

Written in English and signed by the Bailiff of Guernsey, it declared Guernsey an 'open island' with 'no armed forces of any description'. Major Lanz, who did not understand English, simply indicated that he wished to be taken to the 'chief-man' of the island.

They drove to Guernsey's largest hotel, the Royal, where they were joined by the Bailiff, Victor Gosselin **Carey,** and several senior officials.

Through an interpreter, Major Lanz announced that the island was now under German occupation. He dictated a number of regulations and instructions for the people of Guernsey which he ordered to be published on the front page of the following day's *Star*. The issue would be distributed to the people free of charge.

Jersey surrenders

Early the following morning, Monday, 1 July, German planes flying low over the island of **Jersey** dropped copies of an ultimatum addressed to the Chief of Military and Civil Authorities. Jersey was being advised to surrender peacefully. White flags should be displayed and white crosses painted in prominent places. In return the Germans guaranteed continued life, liberty and property.

The Bailiff of Jersey, Alexander **Coutanche**, read the ultimatum to the people in Royal Square. He finished by saying that they had no option but to surrender. As he instructed the people to go home and hang white sheets and pillowslips from their houses, a voice in the crowd called out 'We've got men. We've got our fists'. But it was quickly shushed.

The tokens of surrender were displayed.

Later that afternoon a company of 396th Infantry Regiment accompanied by a light flak unit was met at Jersey Airport by Bailiff Coutanehe, Attorney General C. W. Duret Aubin and the Government Secretary. The occupation had begun.

Forty-eight hours later, the Military Commander Major Lanz and his Chief of Staff Dr Maas travelled the eight miles from **St Peter Port,** Jersey, to the tiny island of **Sark.**

The island's charming despot, La Dame de Sark, Mrs Robert **Hathaway**, had already set her tone. 'We stay and see this island through,' she said. And the 471 Sarkese stayed put. Only the British residents left.

The Seneschal (Bailiff) William Carré, had been requested by Mrs Hathaway to meet the Germans and act as guide.

Mrs Hathaway's servants had been briefed. 'Show them in,' La Dame had told them, 'as if I am used to receiving enemy officers every day of my life.' She addressed them in perfect German, and offered them lunch. Issued with the same rules as the other islands Sark was left under the occupation of 11 soldiers.

The Channel Islands had remained loyal to the British Crown for centuries. But in the ominous summer of 1940, when the invading German Army was only hours away, they were abandoned to their fate. The entire episode was one of Britain's greatest blunders of the war. But whether it was merely inefficiency and confusion or deliberate collusion remains a mystery to this day.

When war broke out in September 1939, Lieutenant-Governors Major-General J. M. R. Harrison of Jersey and Major-General A. P. D. Telfer-Smollet of Guernsey had decided on 2 September, without instruction from London, to call up all ranks of their militias. Speed was vital. The order from London would come.

But the War Office and Home Office between them were in a quandary as to the proper procedures to follow. Should the War Office deal direct with the Lieutenant-Governors or should communications be sent through the Home Office? It was 11 September before it was decided that the War Office could inform the Islands that the militias should be embodied.

Volunteers for the fight

The men of the Channel Islands, as they had in World War 1, volunteered to fight with the British. On 16 September the States of Jersey passed a law placing all their resources at the disposal of the crown. By the 27th the States of Guernsey had passed a resolution that 'for the period of the duration of the war . . . our constitutional rights and privileges in respect of military services overseas . . . should be waived'.

For centuries the men of the Islands had been exempt from military service. Virtually self-governing, the acts and laws of the United Kingdom could be applied only by express provision. To allow enlistment, a special bill was drawn up. But the National Service (Channel Islands) Bill remained unsigned by the King until

Signs of the occupation: Guernsey's British flag is flown to Germany (left) and the German documentary 'Victory in the West' is shown at the local cinema.

An He111 bomber crew on a French airfield. It was three weeks before the Luftwaffe was deployed for the assault on Britain. One fighter base would be on Guernsey.

On the evening of 28 June, a squadron of Heinkel 111s bombed St Peter Port in Guernsey. People ran for their lives. The only resistance came from a light anti-aircraft gun on the ferry 'Isle of Sark'.

two days before the Germans arrived.

This unexplained delay suspended all the islanders' attempts to prepare for war. There was only time to intern aliens and remove signposts, but there were no arrangements for defence, nor emergency evacuation plans. Whitehall was seemingly indifferent to their plight, and refused a request for guns on the grounds of the acute shortage of weapons in Britain.

By 13 June the French Normandy coast opposite was clearly going to be in German hands. Despite bitter protests from Prime Minister Churchill, who called it a 'repugnant decision', the War Cabinet finally agreed to withdraw troops from the Channel Islands. Strategically unimportant, their defence would certainly be expensive and probably unsuccessful. Telegrams informed the Lieutenant-Governors of Jersey and Guernsey of demilitarization.

If the two larger islands had almost no information from Whitehall, **Alderney** had even less. On 16 June the Chief Administrator J. G. French (Judge of Alderney) was given two hours' notice to ship out a thousand men. Horror-struck islanders watched as soldiers smashed up equipment and covered the airfield in barbed wire.

By 19 June all British troops had left Normandy, and by midday on the 20th the last of the troops had been taken by ship from the Channel Islands. With them went 3000 young men, eligible for service, and 500 Irish labourers who had been lifting potatoes.

The withdrawal of troops had been carried out secretly which left the Germans with the impression that the Channel Islands were still heavily manned garrisons—the first line of Britain's defence.

But the Channel Islanders thought demilitarization had been announced to the world. They believed their safety lay in two facts. The first was that the British would protect them, if only to ensure the security of the newly completed Post Office cable that provided Britain with a vital communications link with Europe. The second was that the Hague Convention of 1907 prohibited the bombardment of undefended ports or towns.

So when, on 19 June, the British Government announced the evacuation of women and children, and men of an age to fight, the immediate result was panic. As rumours mounted, banks were besieged, shops and offices were locked up. People rushing to register their names for embarkation shot their pets as they left—over 5000 dogs and cats were destroyed.

It was on Guernsey that fear was greatest. Only a few people knew of the decision to disarm, and the headline in the local paper on 20 June 'Island Evacuation. All children being sent to the mainland today' precipitated chaos.

Those who managed to get aboard the small craft normally used for mail, potatoes and coal suffered real hardship. After queuing in their hundreds in the sweltering sun for hours, many spent two days on the sea without food or water. On landing they were given a hasty meal and taken to start a new life in Scotland, Yorkshire or Lancashire.

In Alderney it was somewhat simpler. Some

'...the drone of approaching aircraft was heard. In seconds the peaceful summer evening became a horrible nightmare...'

Frank Falla, Channel Islands journalist

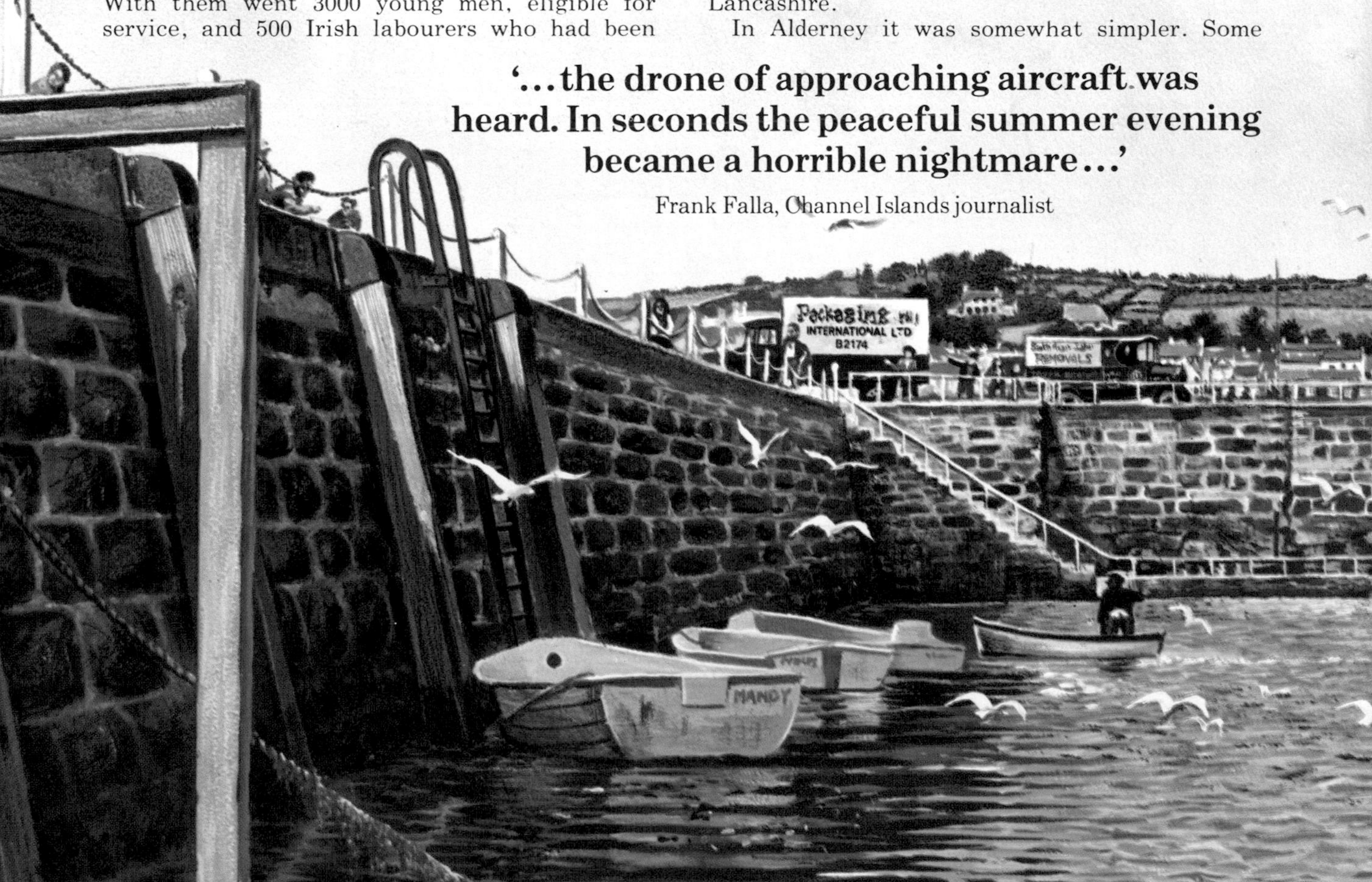

people had already left. Panicked by the arrival of fishing boats loaded with refugees from Boulogne and St Valéry, on 12 and 13 June, islanders had already begun to hire boats to take them across to Guernsey. Eventually on 23 June six ships arrived to evacuate as many of the remaining inhabitants as wanted to go. Only 20 people of the 1100 still on the island remained. On Sark, headed by La Dame, calm reigned. Barely a handful left.

On 24 June the Bailiffs of Jersey and Guernsey received a message from the King, speaking of 'resolute fortitude' and 'the reward of victory'. With these words came a note from the Home Secretary. It warned against widespread publication, lest the Germans be alerted to the withdrawal of troops. And later that day, RAF planes dropped heartening pamphlets to the islanders, promising the British would come to their relief 'with all our rapidly and enormously increasing strength'.

Even then, the Channel Islands' authorities apparently failed to realize that the world was still unaware of their demilitarization. It seems obvious now that the dropping of the pamphlets was the only way of encouraging the islanders without telling the Germans that the Islands were theirs for the taking. And yet no one queried the meaning of the Home Secretary's note, or asked the Home Office just what was going on.

The real reason for the official silence seems now to have been based on a mistake. The Chiefs of Staff assumed the Germans would be kept informed of troop movements by their secret agents in the Islands. It was felt that knowing of the withdrawal, they would be unlikely to waste resources in attacking.

This turned out to be a terrible error. The Germans did not learn of the removal of troops until 30 June. When flight after reconnaissance flight was made without retaliation, it simply made them more suspicious. Admiral Karlgeorg **Schuster** was of the opinion that the three main Islands had defence installations.

Decision to invade

But by 18 June the Germans had decided to take the Islands. Their preparations were meticulous—even French fisherman who knew the Islands were questioned. This was the first move on to British territory, and defeat would be a disaster.

First, squadrons of Heinkel 111s would make an armed raid to test the Islands' defences. If there was no retaliation the invasion would begin. The assault, codenamed 'Green Arrow', would be carried out by naval assault troops supported by the Army and Luftwaffe. The combined operation would be commanded by Admiral Eugen Lindau.

But while final arrangements for 'Green Arrow' were being made by Admiral Lindau and Luftflotte 3 in Paris on the 30th, the initiative of Liebe-Pieteritz had already made them redundant.

On 28 June, in the cool of early evening, the harbour of St Peter Port in Guernsey was crowded with people leaving and those seeing them off. Lorries and horse-drawn carts from the country queued patiently to unload tomatoes into cargo boats. The mailboat *Isle of Sark*, carrying people who had been lucky enough to get a berth, was on the point of sailing.

At 6.55 pm the bustle was stilled by the angry hum of many planes. A squadron of Heinkel 111s appeared out of the sky. They dropped 180 bombs.

There was no defence for the milling, screaming crowd—the only scant shelter was beneath the pier. On the mailboat, a man sank down, blood pouring from his groin. Beside him a small boy screamed as the light anti-aircraft gun on board was fired over his head. People panicked down the gangway, attempting to reach the shelter of the warehouses on the wharves, but were flung down by bursts of machine-gun fire from the planes. The shrieks of the injured were lost in the crackle of flames as sheds caught fire. On the gangway, the uniformed policeman collecting tickets disappeared as another bomb burst beside him.

Shortly after, three more Heinkels swooped on La Rocque in Jersey, dropping two huge bombs. In all 44 civilians—including a young boy and an old woman—died needlessly and without warning.

The telegram reporting the raids was the last communication the Channel Islands had with Britain until the end of the war. And on its receipt, finally, two hours afterwards, the BBC announced on the nine o'clock news on 28 June

that the Channel Islands had been demilitarized and all forces and equipment withdrawn.

The islanders still could not believe they would be occupied. The Guernsey *Star* next day argued that the Nazis could not hold the Islands, and back in England the Home Secretary was insisting on evacuating the entire population.

But it was too late.

By the following Wednesday, 3 July, four of the Channel Islands were occupied. Albrecht Lanz, the first German Military Commandant, had moved into the house of the Lieutenant-Governer in one of Guernsey's best residential districts, and soldiers had been billeted around him. Hundreds of soldiers were brought in, taking over hotels, clubs and schools. They bought every cigarette, emptied the bicycle shops and tried to pick up local girls.

The aftermath

The Germans introduced European time, to accord with Germany, allowed petrol only for essential services and requisitioned all cars, which they painted grey. Food was rationed and curfews imposed. When a man cycling home late at night was found to be called Churchill he was promptly arrested.

The Germans allowed the National Anthem to be played, but only with permission, and prayers could be said for the Royal Family in church. They behaved immaculately. In Jersey an Irishman was prosecuted for striking one of the King's enemies—he punched a German soldier on the nose in a café brawl. The prosecutor said that because of the consideration and courtesy shown by the Germans 'it is intolerable that any member of these forces should be treated with less consideration or courtesy'.

After the horror of the air raid—for which Dr Maas, Chief of Staff to the Military Commandant apologized, saying it was 'quite a mistake'—the people of the Islands realized just how isolated they were. Drawn together as never before by the common enemy, they felt a real relief at knowing their fate.

Churchill, humiliated by events and the harping of German radio on the easy victory, ordered a secret landing of commandos. The plan, code named 'Anger Ambassador', failed—due to bad weather and fear of German reprisals. However detestable they found the task, the islanders would have had to report anyone landing clandestinely. The Lieutenant-Governor of Guernsey begged the Home Office to leave the Islands in peace; such operations could only 'result in loss of life among the civilian population'.

The Channel Islanders knew that they could survive only if they accepted the yoke upon them. It was to be five long years before Churchill's prophetic words would come true, and the day dawned when 'the shadow of the bully will be lifted from you . . .'

A German officer and a policeman on Jersey in July 1940. Most of the islanders gradually came to accept the presence of the invader—it was hard to remain permanently hostile.

War Notes

ALDERNEY: island $3\frac{1}{2} \times 1\frac{1}{2}$ miles, comprising 2000 acres. Population 1500. Part of Bailiwick of Guernsey but with representative assembly, States of Alderney, to deal with local affairs. Separated from Normandy by the 10-mile Race of Alderney. Nearest English coast is 55 miles to N. Heavily fortified by British until garrison withdrawn 1930.

CAREY, Victor Gosselin: Bailiff of Guernsey, b. 1871 son of Maj-Gen de Vic F. Carey of Le Vallon, Guernsey. Educated Elisabeth College, Guernsey, Marlborough and Caen University. Called to Guernsey Bar 1898. Receiver-General of Guernsey 1912–35. Bailiff of Guernsey from 1935. Hon Doctor of Law, Caen University 1938.

COUTANCHE, Alexander Moncrieff: Bailiff of Jersey, b. 1892, son of Jersey notary Adolphus Arnold Coutanche. Educated Victoria College Jersey, then privately. Entered Middle Temple 1912. Called to Jersey Bar 1913; English Bar 1915. Claims Commission 1917–20. Staff Captain 1919. Deputy St. Helier, States of Jersey 1922–5. Solicitor-General of Jersey 1925–31. Attorney-General 1931–5. Bailiff of Jersey from 1935. Honorary Doctor of Law, Caen University 1938.

GUERNSEY: 2nd largest of Channel Islands, 30 miles W. of Normandy, comprising 30 sq miles. Population 41,000. Capital, St Peter Port. Local governing body, States of Deliberation, is presided over by the Bailiff. Bailiwick of Guernsey also responsible for Alderney and Sark, and 4 small adjacent islands (34–230 acres) of Brechou, Herm, Jethou and Lihou. Lt-Governor is personal representative of the Crown. Day-to-day management of the States' affairs is carried out by permanent civil servants. A British infantry battalion stationed here until 1939 when 1st Royal Irish Fusiliers left.

HATHAWAY, Dame Sibyl Mary: Dame of Sark, b. 1884 daughter of William F. Collings. Married Dudley Beaumont 1901; widowed 1918. Married American Robert Woodward Hathaway 1929. Became 21st Seigneur of Sark on father's death 1927.

JERSEY: largest of Channel Islands, 12 miles W. of France, 10×5 miles comprising 45 sq miles. Capital St Helier on S. coast. Population 50,000. Local governing body, Assembly of the States, similar to States of Guernsey. The Ecrehous Rocks 6 miles NW and Les Miniquiers 12 miles S. are part of Jersey bailiwick.

ST PETER PORT: capital of Guernsey on E. coast. Population 18,250. Its well-protected anchorage and position in English Channel made it a refuge and port of call for smugglers and privateers. Harbour built 1853–74.

SARK: island 7 miles E. of Guernsey, comprising 1000 acres. Great Sark (N) and Little Sark (S) are connected by a 100yd isthmus just 6ft wide at its top. Population 600. Part of Bailiwick of Guernsey but Chief Pleas (body of 40 tenants and 12 deputies) regulate local affairs. The Pleas were presided over by Seneschal (appointed by the Seigneur).

SCHUSTER, Karlgeorg: German admiral, b. 1887. Joined Navy 1905. Appointed Chief of Staff for commercial and economic warfare, OKW late Sept 1939. Promoted Admiral Commanding France, June 1940.

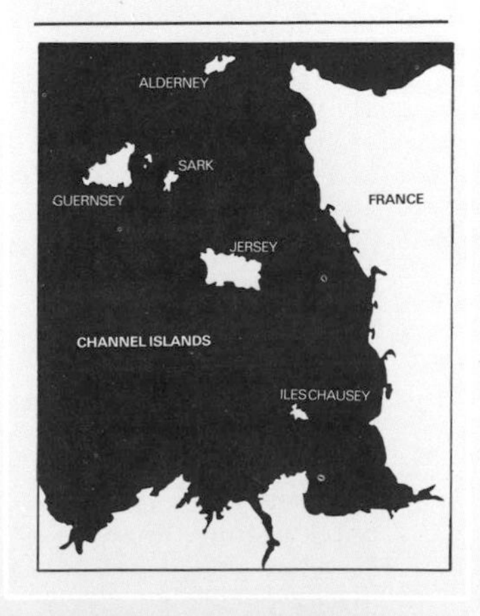

LAST APPEAL TO REASON

As the train pulled into Berlin's Anhalt station at 3pm on 6 July the band played the Badenweiler March. Stepping briskly into the sunlight Adolf Hitler crossed the platform and slumped into the back of a waiting car. Cautiously it edged its way through the mass of humanity lining the streets. A million swastikas hung from buildings, roses lay on the road leading to the Chancellery for the cavalcade of cars to crush. The return of the Führer triumphant from two months campaigning in the West was marked by a victory parade through the capital.

But the flags and flowers were carefully stage-managed. Few Berliners seemed to care about the war. The fact that France and most of Europe had been defeated in six short weeks seemed to leave many Germans apprehensive for the future.

No one was less certain of the future than Adolf Hitler himself. What to do next was a question that had preoccupied him since the fall of France. Nothing was settled. Britain seemed reluctant to conclude peace. And the spectre of Communist Russia loomed in the East. The old fear of enemies on two fronts seemed to haunt Hitler whatever he did. How to break out and secure his newly won possessions? That was the burning question in Hitler's mind on his return to the German capital.

Peace feelers put out to Britain during June had come to nothing, despite the ever confident predictions of Foreign Minister Ribbentrop. There really was no reason at all for Britain to continue the war. Germany has no quarrel with Britain. Their interests were mutual. Everything pointed to co-operation, not war. But the British under Churchill seemed impervious to appeals to reason. Perhaps Göring was right. The Luftwaffe would have to bomb the British to the conference table.

Who would stop Russia?

But uppermost in the Führer's mind on his return was not the problem of Britain, but Russia. Maybe not this year, or even in ten years time, perhaps not for a hundred years, but sooner or later Russia would unleash her millions into Western Europe. Who was there to stop her but he, Adolf Hitler? Plans for the invasion of Russia began.

For public consumption there was talk of peace. But this too worried Hitler. Gestapo reports had shown since the beginning of the war in 1939 that peace not war was what the German people wanted. And Hitler, as ever, was sensitive to popular opinion. But the people must not be allowed to get soft.

As the month continued alarming reports of Russian diplomatic activity reached Hitler. Returning to Berlin on the 18th from his **Berghof** mountain retreat Hitler read several dispatches intercepted by the ever efficient **Forschungsamt.**

From Ankara came a report of a conversation between Mikhail Ivanovich Kalinin, President of the Supreme Soviet, and the new British Ambassador to Moscow, Sir Stafford Cripps. According to the report, Cripps suggested that Britain had interests in common with Russia. From the Italians came a decoded Greek telegram sent to Athens by the Greek legation in Moscow. The Russians, according to Cripps, were making feverish war preparations. If the war continued, argued Cripps, the Russians would inevitably join in on Britain's side.

In the Balkans too the Russians appeared to be setting everyone at Germany's throat. To the Yugoslav minister in Moscow, Kalinin cast aspersions on German business practices in Yugoslavia. 'This is no way for the Germans to safeguard the peace', Kalinin asserted. 'They always demand more and more. No, you must struggle against it . . .'

Possibility of peace

Now, the time had come to make a final appeal to the British. If they persisted in waging war against Germany then they would get what was coming to them. Plans for an invasion went ahead.

Hitler had good reason for thinking that the British might be persuaded to conclude a peace settlement. Rumour had it that certain members of Churchill's war cabinet, principally Lord Halifax, were in favour of peace. Even Churchill himself seemed to be encouraging 'peace feelers'.

Certainly the ex-King of England, the Duke of **Windsor,** seemed receptive to National Socialist thinking. Perhaps he could be used to further the aims of peace? From Madrid came a report of a conversation between the Duke and the American Ambassador to Spain: 'The most important thing now to be done', said the Duke, 'is to end the war before thousands more are killed or maimed just to save the face of a few politicians'.

Meeting the Duke back in 1937, Hitler had warmed to the man's social conscience—and his radical solutions. If the Duke and Duchess could be seduced from their home at the Estoril Palace near Lisbon and conscripted to the Nazi cause, anything might happen. Ribbentrop was charged with the mission.

Ribbentrop threw himself into the intrigue. Walther Schellenberg, hero of Venlo, now chief of Reinhard Heydrich's Intelligence, flew to Madrid to mastermind the Duke's kidnapping.

In Madrid Schellenberg found the story of the Duke's willingness to be abducted a little improb-

A LAST APPEAL TO REASON
BY
ADOLF HITLER

Back from France: a German armoured division is welcomed in Munich. Hitler makes his 'appeal to reason' speech, and translations are dropped over Britain (left).

able. Certainly the story that the Duke was to make a hunting trip to Spain—giving Schellenberg his opportunity—proved to be false. Schellenberg decided to fly on to Lisbon to get nearer the truth.

Through a network of friends and contacts Schellenberg was able to establish the size of the Portuguese and British guard at the Estoril, the number of rooms, servants and the geography of the place. He even managed to infiltrate the official police guard with his own people. But it was clear that the Duke had no intention of going to Spain, for hunting or any other reason. True, he did not like the cordon of police security vetting his every move. Nor was he happy at the prospect of being shipped out to the Bahamas as Governor-General as Churchill insisted. But, significantly, he had no intention of living in a neutral country, let alone Germany.

From Ribbentrop came the message: 'The Führer orders that an abduction is to be organized at once!' Schellenberg rightly suspected the source of this order. Surely the Führer could not be so misinformed? Schellenberg decided to circumvent the 'order'.

With little trouble he managed to make the British suspect that the Duke's safety was threatened. The Portuguese guard on the Estoril was doubled. The British followed suit. Schellenberg informed Berlin: the situation was too dangerous. Came the laconic reply: 'You are responsible for measures suitable to the situation.' Schellenberg was relieved.

In Berlin the message from Britain was at last becoming clear: no talks, no deals and no peace. But despite the mass of evidence plain for all to see, Hitler still believed that there existed a 'peace party' in Britain able to come to their senses and realize that there was no good reason for the war between Britain and Germany to continue. Perhaps a last appeal to reason would work. Preparations went ahead for an important Führer speech. Booked for 19 July it was to be held at the Kroll Opera House in Berlin, amidst a welter of publicity. Journalists from all over the world were invited. German radio stations made preparations to broadcast the speech live throughout the Reich and occupied Europe.

It was fast approaching 7pm on Friday 19 July. Nervous coughs resounded throughout the packed, flower-decked Kroll Opera House. In the orchestra pit, serious-faced Reich Deputies waited for the Führer's entry. Master of the theatrical, Hitler waited until tension reached fever pitch. There was heavy silence. Suddenly, without announcement, Hitler strode up to the rostrum. He thumbed through his papers and looked up. 'Members of the Reichstag, I have summoned you all in the midst of our tremendous struggle for the freedom and future of the German nation. I have done so first because I have considered it imperative to give our people an insight into the events unique in history . . . secondly because I wish to express my gratitude to our magnificent soldiers, and, thirdly, with the intention of appealing once more and for the last time to common sense.'

Calmly, with care and precision, Hitler went through the catalogue of accusations. Germany had never wanted war. That had been thrust upon her by Capitalists and Jews. Now, with the power of Germany firmly established, there was no reason, no reason at all, for war to continue. One man and one man alone was responsible for its

'Mr Churchill ought perhaps for once to believe me, when I prophesy that a great empire will be destroyed.'

Adolf Hitler, July 1940

continuation—Winston Churchill. 'Believe me, gentlemen, I feel deep disgust for this type of unscrupulous politician who wrecks whole nations and states . . . It never has been my intention to wage war, but rather to build up a state with a new social order and the finest possible standard of culture'.

Accusing Churchill of ordering the bombing of civilians Hitler promised that he would repay with a vengeance. Not upon Churchill himself 'for he no doubt will already be in Canada' but upon 'millions of other people'.

Never had it been his intention to harm or destroy the great British Empire. But if Churchill refused to listen to the dictates of common sense then 'this struggle . . . can end only with the annihilation of one or other of the two adversaries. Mr Churchill may believe that this will be Germany. I know that it will be Britain.'

Even now, at this late hour, asserted Hitler, in a final flourish of rhetoric, the 'sacrifices of millions' could be averted. 'I feel it my duty before my own conscience to appeal once more to reason and common sense, in Great Britain as much as elsewhere. I consider myself in a position to make this appeal since I am not the vanquished begging favours, but the victor speaking in the name of reason.'

Over 500 miles away, across the 'German Ocean', the speech made little impact. Churchill remained unmoved and made no public response or allusion to the speech. Members of his government granted it was 'diabolically clever' but remained steadfast. Curiously, those whom Hitler had believed might respond to 'reason' hardened in their determination to continue ,the war. Harold Nicolson considered the next move. 'I think Hitler will probably invade us within the next few days. He has 6000 aeroplanes ready for the job.'

A new mood swept the country. Where there had been doubt, uncertainty and indecision, there was now resolution and a determination to 'see the thing through'. The writer George Orwell, no admirer of the English establishment, noted that 'the English were like a family, with many skeletons in the closet, but united in trouble'.

The formal reply to Hitler's speech came three days later from Foreign Secretary Lord Halifax. He rejected Hitler's appeal unconditionally.

Yet Harold Nicolson was wrong in thinking Hitler was about to invade Britain. The doubts he had suffered as to what to do next had been resolved. Leaving the Kroll after his speech he confided to Field Marshal von Rundstedt that he had no intention of invading Britain.

Back at his mountain retreat at the Berghof on the last day of the month the Führer gathered his senior commanders for a momentous announcement. 'England's hope is Russia and America. If hope on Russia is eliminated, America is also eliminated.' Hitler ordered his generals to regroup their forces to the east within six weeks.

Victorious German troops parade in front of Berlin's Brandenburg Gate as Hitler (inset), flanked by Göring and Raeder, gives the Nazi salute.

War Notes

BERGHOF: Hitler's estate of 3.8 square miles on the Obersalzberg mountain above town of Berchtesgaden, Bavaria. Designed and planned by Hitler himself, after buying the original Wachenfeld cottage on the site 1928, the Berghof had underground facilities to an average depth of 100ft. Main feature of the house was the Great Hall: 60ft long with a red marble table and panoramic window.

FORSCHUNGSAMT (FA): 'research office' set up 1933 under Hermann Göring, had monopoly of all wiretapping operations. Moved to secret compound in Berlin's Charlottenburg district 1935. Its operations were vital to Hitler's police state, developed a highly efficient decoding department with 240 cryptanalysts using Hollerith punch-card computers able to decode 3000 intercepted foreign messages a month.

WINDSOR, Edward, Duke of: born in 1894, the eldest son of George V and Queen Mary. Succeeded 20 Jan 1936 as Edward VIII, first bachelor King in 176 years. Caused constitutional crisis over proposed marriage to Mrs Wallis Simpson, American commoner pending 2nd divorce. Abdicated 11 Dec 1936. Visited Germany in 1937 to study social and housing conditions and met Hitler. Major-General attached to staff of BEF 1939.

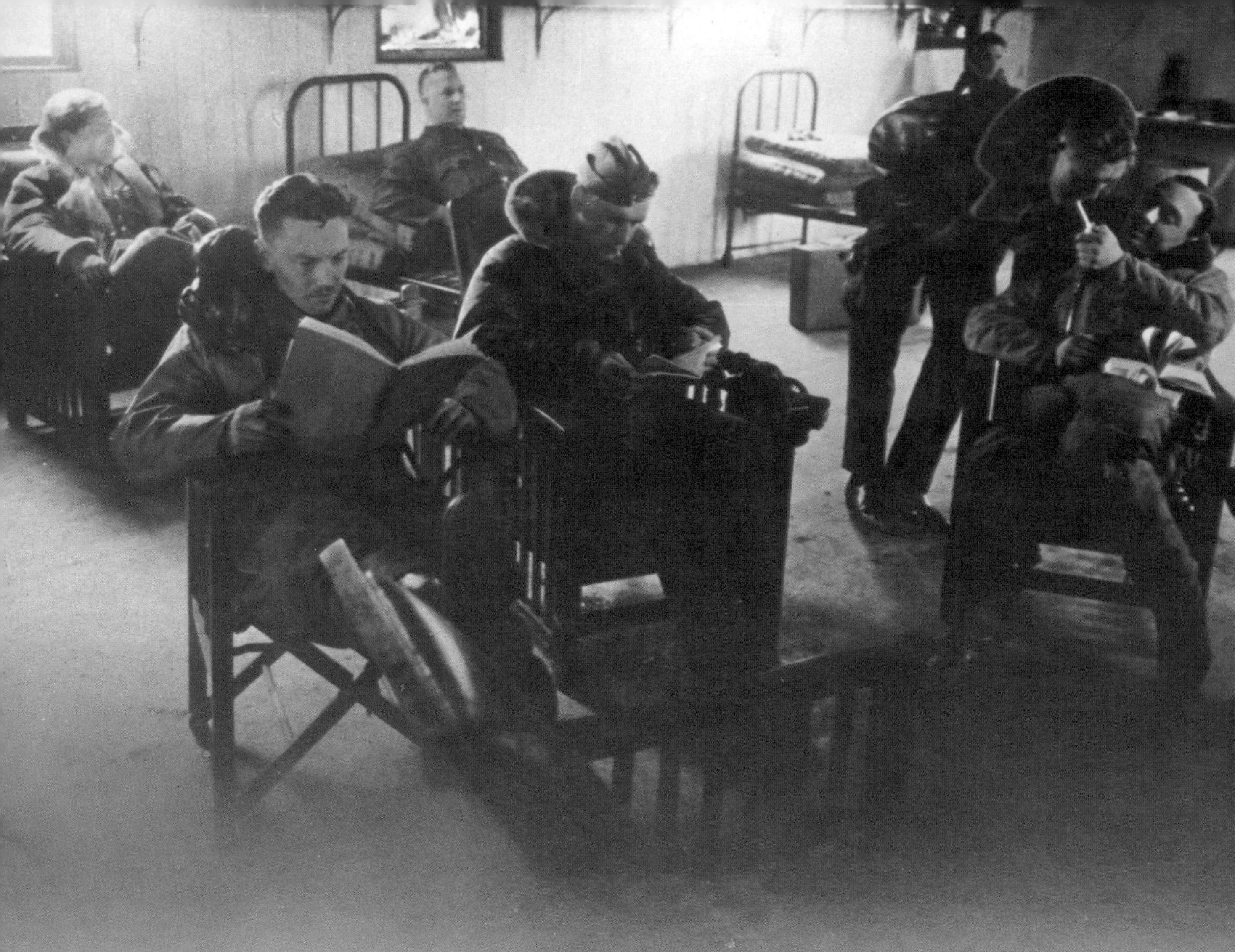

GLADIATORS OF HELLFIRE CORNER

'The Führer has decided that under certain circumstances—the most important of which is achieving air superiority—a landing in England may take place,' read War Directive 15 on 2 July. It was Hitler's tentative beginning to what Churchill had envisaged as The Battle of Britain four weeks earlier.

The essentials for the successful launching of a German invasion were the reduction of the RAF to impotence, weakening of the Royal Navy by denying it the use of ports in Southern England, and softening-up coastal areas marked as objectives for the landing forces. The inducing of war nerves and panic among the civilian population would be a useful spin-off.

Hermann Göring was confident that he could achieve a success in the air 'that might even rule out the necessity of a German invasion.'

Attacking convoys and coastal installations, and 'free chase' fighters roving Kent and Sussex, would lure Britain's aircraft forward from inland bases to within lethal reach of the **Messerschmitt 109** which, with an endurance of about 80 minutes, could spend only 20 minutes over England.

Colonel Johannes Fink was grandly titled Kanalkampfführer (Channel battleleader) and given 75 bombers, 60 Stukas and Theo Osterkamp's 200 fighters for the task. With a fine sense of occasion he parked his command bus near the statue of Louis Blériot, first man to fly the Channel.

But when instead of allowing them 'free chase', Göring tethered his fighters to escorting the slower bombers, the famous German fighter ace, Adolf Galland, complained bitterly, 'the Germans found themselves in a similar predicament of a dog on a chain which wants to attack the foe, but cannot because of its limited orbit.'

Air Chief Marshal Sir Hugh **Dowding,** commanding Fighter Command, well aware of the purpose of the German coat-trailing tactics, permitted his pilots to respond, in the main, only to dangerous attacks on shipping and coastal installations. However, when dogfights did develop further inland the Luftwaffe, more often than not, got more than it gave. Although alarmingly real to those who felt its results, the deadly attrition the Germans hoped for was not apparent.

For the attack against Britain, Göring was redeploying and re-equipping the three Air Fleets that had dominated the skies of Western Europe since 10 May. Luftflotte 2, under Colonel General Albert Kesselring, in the Low Countries and northeast France; Luftflotte 3, under Hugo Sperrle, in northeast France; and Luftflotte 5, under Colonel General Hans-Jürgen Stumpff, in Norway and Denmark. By 20 July their combined operational strength had been doubled to 1315 bombers, 280 dive-bombers, 1055 fighters, and 170 reconnaissance planes.

Against the Luftwaffe

Opposing the Luftwaffe was Dowding's Fighter Command comprising 1250 fighter pilots and 591 fighters on 1 July. The Command was divided into four operational Groups—Nos. 10, 11, 12 and 13—of which, at the time, No. 11 and No. 12 were strategically the most important.

Between Dowding and Air Vice-Marshal Sir Keith Park, who commanded 11 Group defending London and the southeast along the English Channel, there was a complete rapport. Neither man worked particularly well with Air Vice-Marshal Trafford Leigh-Mallory. He commanded 12 Group which defended the Eastern Counties from Hull southwards, and the industrial complexes around Birmingham and Coventry.

Mallory was a dogmatic advocate of multiple squadron tactics—the big wing formation—which, although it was to come into its own later in the war, Dowding knew to be unsuitable for the air struggle now developing over Southern England.

Two of Fighter Command's most valuable assets were Ultra and Radiolocation. Ultra was Intelligence of the highest order, derived from the secret ability of the British to decode, rapidly, intercepts through the German Enigma cipher machine system, especially the codes used by the Luftwaffe. On 4 July for example Dowding knew that most of its units would have refitted by the middle of the month. The work already done at Bletchley Park caused Air Intelligence to make a drastic revision of German bomber strength from 2500 to 1250, the daily bomb load estimate from 4800 to 1800 tons.

Nevertheless, because the Luftwaffe made increasing use of landlines in Occupied France, Dowding was not in regular receipt of detailed daily operational orders. Sometimes targets and forces despatched would reach him but often too late to be used, either because of last-minute Luftwaffe changes or because the deciphering took too long.

Radiolocation, the contemporary name for **radar,** covered the entire South and East Coasts down to about 600ft at up to 40 miles range. As soon as Luftwaffe planes were airborne over France they became liable to detection by the chain of 29 radiolocation stations around the British coast, which were known as 'Chain Home'

Britain gets ready for the onslaught: RAF pilots (left) wait to be called into action while the crew of a 3in anti-aircraft gun perfect their technique.

or CH. At the start it baffled the Germans that they were confronted by RAF fighters whenever they approached Britain.

Aircraft flying within sight of the shore or cross-country were reported by Observer Corps posts manned by highly trained aircraft spotters. The jumble of information, telephoned by CH and observers, went directly to the Group Filter rooms, was plotted on map tables, and resolved by Filter officers into a single plot for each raid. A Group Controller had to make an immediate assessment of priorities before the filtered plots were passed to Sector Operations rooms by earnest young WAAFs.

A Sector Operations room provided fighter pilots with an early warning system. A huge plotting table on a sunken floor ringed with WAAFs and airmen, wearing head-and-breast sets, received information from the Group Filter room. Using long rakes like those of croupiers they moved coloured arrows across a giant gridded map to indicate the progress of each raid. Friendly fighters appeared with a prefix 'F' in red on a white ground. Hostiles had a black 'H' on yellow. On average the plot was only four minutes behind the real events.

On 1 July an attack on the coastal ports of Wick and Hull, and the dive-bombing of a convoy off Plymouth, in which the raiders got off scot free, might have been an indication that ports and shipping were the Luftwaffe's next objectives.

If there were any doubts, few could have remained after Thursday, 4 July. A force of 33 Ju87s swooped out of a misty morning sky and plastered Portland Naval Base, Dorset, with bombs. Four ships sank and nine were damaged. During the four minutes the raid lasted no British fighters arrived, but aboard the repeatedly hit HMS *Foyle Bank*, an auxiliary anti-aircraft ship, was Acting Seaman Jack Foreman Mantle. Mortally wounded by a bomb which shattered his left leg, Mantle stuck by his gun and shot down a Stuka. His VC, awarded posthumously, was the first of the Battle of Britain.

On the same day a nine-ship convoy passing through the Strait of Dover was attacked. One ship was beached and a Hurricane shot down.

The Hawker **Hurricane,** although inferior to the Spitfire in terms of speed and climb, was manoeuvrable and could take a lot of combat damage. It was the Hurricane that bore the brunt of the Battle of Britain, shooting down 80 per cent of all German aircraft lost.

To the Luftwaffe, as yet unaware of CH, it

'The fighter pilot's emotions are those of the duellist – cool, precise, impersonal.'

Flight Lieutenant Richard Hillary

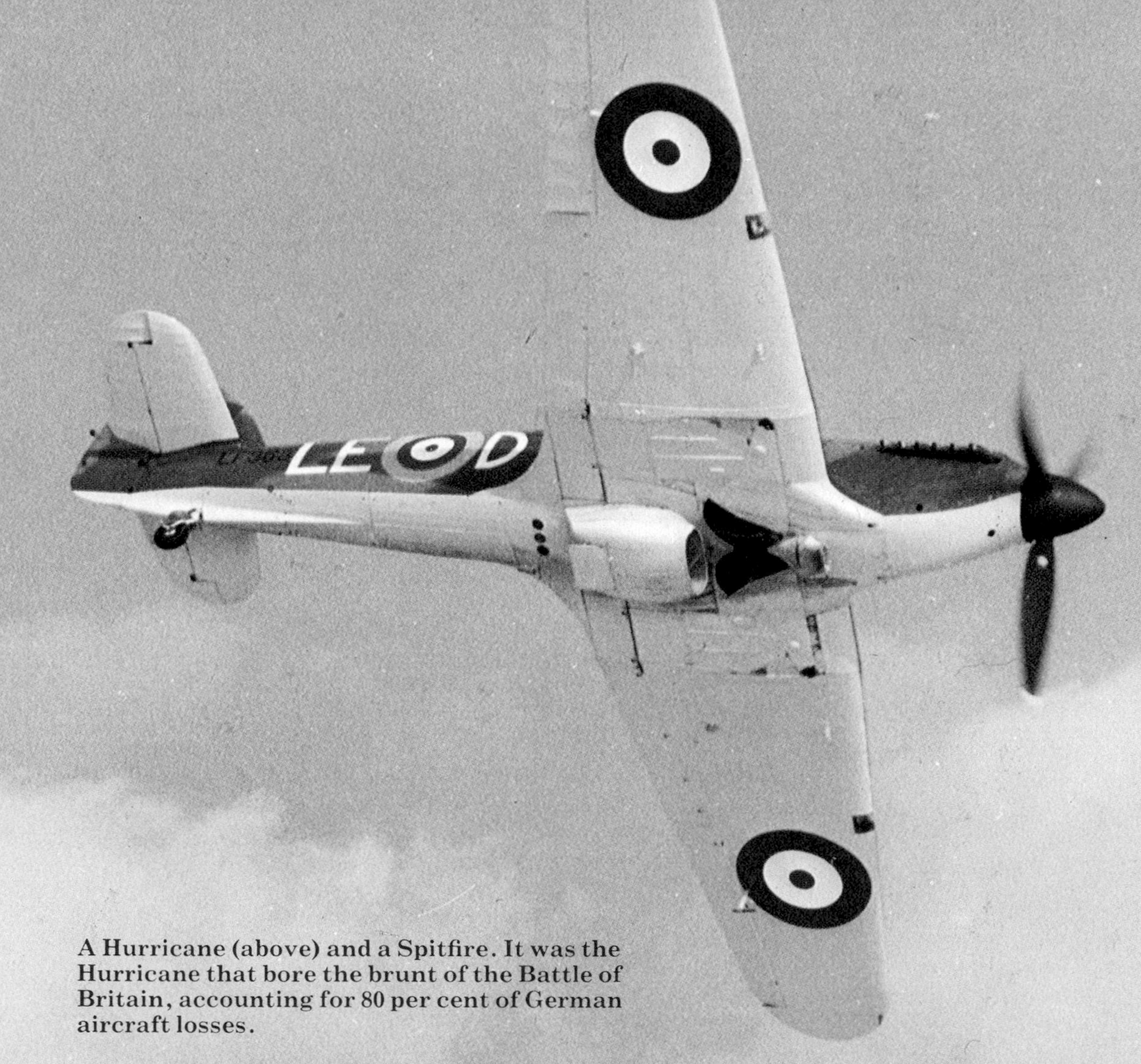

A Hurricane (above) and a Spitfire. It was the Hurricane that bore the brunt of the Battle of Britain, accounting for 80 per cent of German aircraft losses.

seemed that the RAF were adopting the wasteful and exhausting policy of standing patrols. How else did they achieve such swift and accurate interceptions? They pressed home their Channel attacks.

On Sunday 7 July a concentrated attack on a convoy was made by 45 Dornier Do17Zs, least prominent of the trio of twin-engine aircraft that made up the Luftwaffe's bomber strength. Meanwhile, a 'free chase' by Me109s drew off British interceptors. No. 65 Squadron lost three Spitfires and their pilots; of the convoy, one ship was sunk and three damaged. Again it was just the type of wasteful action Fink wanted and Dowding feared would sap Fighter Command's strength before the main battle was joined.

Dowding's worst fears were confirmed next day when another four fighters were lost in dogfights over convoys from Bristol to the Thames Estuary. However, there was some consolation for No. 11 Group, 'to whom the scourge of free-chasing was already causing some apprehension'. The RAF downed four Me109s.

Fighting on the 9th involved over 200 aircraft as the RAF broke up two attacks on convoys, and intervened in the dive-bombing of Portland. Flying Officer David Crook shot down a Stuka flown by Hauptmann Freiherr von Dalwigk, holder of the Knight's Cross. One of several

Heinkel He59 ambulance seaplanes, searching for ditched German airmen, was set upon by Spitfires and forced down. Tackling the fighter escort, New Zealand ace Al Deere survived a collision with a Me109, in a head-on attack when neither pilot would give way.

As the next day dawned in thick cloud there were eight convoys creeping across the sea in British coastal waters. It was the large convoy, codenamed Bread, that attracted the heaviest raid to date culminating in massive dogfights involving over 100 planes wheeling and weaving an aerial dance of death. Nine Hurricanes of No. 11 Squadron flew head-on in a shallow V, unnerving the bomber pilots causing them to veer away and lose formation. It was a risky manoeuvre. A Hurricane and a Dornier Do17Z collided—fatally. Only two other aircraft fell and the solitary bomb hit sank a 700-ton sloop.

Hurricanes hit

The *Daily Herald's* front page announced on the 13th that cocktail sausages would be going up to 5¾d per lb. In the afternoon Ju87s attacking a convoy off Dover were jumped by Hurricanes of No. 56 Squadron before the Me109 escort could intervene. When they did they found the British so preoccupied that two Hurricanes fell to their guns in minutes. To make matters worse, a Hurricane was hit by Dover ack-ack. Fortunately the pilot landed unhurt. The British claimed seven Stukas, but in fact they all returned home.

On the 16th Hitler issued his Directive 16 which began: 'Since England, despite the hopelessness of her military position, shows no sign of willingness to come to terms, I have decided to prepare, and if necessary carry out, a landing operation against her and, if necessary, to carry it out.'

Göring still stood by his stated aims of luring Fighter Command into a battle of attrition over Southern England; devastating airfields in Kent and Sussex, and dominating the Channel.

Warned of the passage of a convoy through the Strait of Dover on the 18th, after a four-day spell of poor flying weather, and aware now of the British ability to detect his formations building up over France, Kesselring laid a trap. A fighter squadron simulated a bomber force forming up. When 12 Spitfires arrived over the convoy there were no bombers—just unfettered Me109s waiting to pounce. Only Pilot Officer P. Litchfield and his Spitfire fell victim, yet looking back, had RAF losses continued to rise at the rate apparent since the beginning of the month, Fighter Command would have ceased to exist as an effective force before the end of August.

The 19th saw nine convoys off the coast. The strong fighter forces, ready in forward airfields, included 12 Bolton Paul Defiants of No. 141 Squadron. These two-seat turret fighters mounted no forward guns. No. 264 Squadron, Fighter Command's only other Defiant Squadron, had apparently achieved spectacular success over Dunkirk six weeks previously. Mistaking them for Hurricanes, which they resembled superficially, 17 Messerschmitts attacked and fell victims to the Defiant's rear-gunners. According to Luftwaffe records losses totalled 14 for the day.

But this time, without warning from the controller, nine Defiants of No. 141 Squadron were

In July 1940 the Luftwaffe attacked coastal installations and shipping to lure British fighters from their inland bases.

attacked south of Folkestone by 15 Me109s from the Richthofen Geschwader. Immediately recognizing the Defiants for what they were, the Germans came in from below and astern. Six luckless Defiants were blasted out of the sky in less than 60 seconds: of the three surviving aircraft that limped home, one was a write-off. Only the arrival of 12 Hurricanes saved the squadron.

Churchill was with Dowding at Bentley Priory, Fighter Command HQ, when the news came in. The Prime Minister was 'inclined to accept the bad news as the fortunes of war'.

'That may be so,' Dowding replied, 'but what I am conscious of is that so many of my men have died.' The tally read: RAF—five pilots and 11 fighters lost; Luftwaffe—five planes and 13 airmen, none fighter pilots. The British claim was 13 aircraft. It had been altogether a black day for Fighter Command.

Yet the following day resulted in a big boost for the Command's morale when Ju87s escorted by 50 Messerschmitt fighters approached convoy Bosom off Kent. The Germans were surprised by a powerful Hurricane escort hurtling out of the evening sun. In the ensuing half hour dogfight the 28 RAF fighters shot down two Stukas and four Me109s for the loss of a Spitfire and Hurricane. The Luftwaffe now stepped up minelaying all round the British coast.

Hell's Angels

On 29 July Dover itself was raided by 48 Stukas and 80 Me109s. Dogfights above the town were watched by hundreds of servicemen and civilians, oblivious of the falling debris—spent cartridges, unexploded cannon shells, and fragments of exploded aircraft and anti-aircraft shells. An observer remarked, 'It is like watching *Hell's Angels* come to life.' *Hell's Angels* was a popular Hollywood film which featured spectacular air fighting of World War 1.

Throughout the confused fighting in which four Ju87s and a Spitfire fell, Dover's ack-ack persisted in putting up a heavy, indiscriminate, barrage angering the 28 RAF pilots. They had already formed a low opinion of the gunners' aircraft recognition.

North and west of Dover the shipping strikes continued. Off Portland the destroyer *Delight* was sunk by Stukas. New German 'Freya' radar 60 miles away on the Cherbourg Peninsula had vectored in the bombers. An Enigma message was one clue for Air Scientific Intelligence in its long hunt to work out how the system worked.

The month closed with the Germans strafing Dover's balloon barrage. It had been a gruelling experimental month of thrust and parry in which the southeastern corner of coast between Folkestone and Margate had undergone its baptism of fire and been christened 'Hellfire Corner'.

Weaknesses in the British defences had been exposed, but due to immediate remedial steps taken by Dowding and his Group Commanders, the Luftwaffe had been unable to exploit them. But the Me109 still posed the biggest threat to the continued survival of British air defence. And the real trial of strength was yet to come.

War Notes

DOWDING, Hugh Casswall Tremenheere: British air marshal, b. 1882 son of Scottish schoolmaster. Educated Winchester and RMA Woolwich. Commissioned into Garrison Artillery 1899. Served in Far East earning nickname of 'Stuffy'. As Captain learnt to fly 1913 and joined Royal Flying Corps 1914. Set up Wireless Experimental Establishment at Brooklands 1915 and heard first radio messages from the air. Flight commander No. 9 Squadron and CO 16 Sqdn July 1915. Lt-Colonel Feb 1916. Brigadier-General 1918. Sacked by Trenchard and returned to artillery but then reinstated. Chief Staff Officer, Iraq 1920. Air Commodore 1922. Air Marshal and Director of Training, Air Ministry, 1926-9. AOC Transjordan and Palestine 1929. AOC Fighting Area, Air Defence of Great Britain 1929-30. Air Council Member for Research and Development 1930-6. Air Marshal and knighted 1933. Backed radar, Hurricane and Spitfire development. C-in-C Fighter Command from July 1936. Brought in all-weather runways, operations rooms and expanded the Observer Corps. Addressed War Cabinet on 15 May 1940, and by 19th had stopped further fighter squadrons going to France. A teetotal, reserved widower, Dowding shared a house with his sister Hilda down the hill from his HQ. His son was a Spitfire pilot with 74 Squadron.

HURRICANE: British fighter. Designed by Sydney Camm of Hawker. First flew Nov 1935. In service as first 8-gun monoplane fighter in world Dec 1937, 5 squadrons equipped Sept 1938, 18 by Sept 1939 with 497 built. During French campaign 11 squadrons lost 75 Hurricanes in combat and 120 on the ground. Mk 1 data. Weight: 6440lb. Length: 31.5ft. Wingspan: 40ft. Engine: Rolls Royce Merlin III 12-cylinder liquid cooled giving 1030 hp at 16,250ft. Max speed: 328 mph at 16,250ft, cruising speed 230mph. Ceiling: 34,200ft. Range: 505 miles. Guns: 8 × .303 in Browning MGs with 334 rounds each, 14 seconds firing.

MESSERSCHMITT (Me) 109: German single-engine fighter. First flew Sept 1935. In service Jan 1937. About 2300 built by the end of 1939, 1056 in Luftwaffe on 1 Sept. Me 109E was in service from April 1939 largely replacing Bs and Cs in front-line units by end of year. Data for E3 variant which gave the pilot 8mm armour. Weight: 5523lb. Wingspan: 32.3 ft. Length: 28.3ft. Engine: Daimler-Benz DB601Aa liquid-cooled inverted V-12, 1175hp. Max speed: 348mph at 14,560ft, top cruising speed 300mph. Ceiling: 34,450ft. Guns: 2 × 20 mm cannon in wings (60 shells each), 2 × 7·9mm machine-guns in nose (500 rounds each). On 10 May 1940 the Luftwaffe used 1016 of its 1346 Me109s losing 235 by end of June. By 20 July Luftflotte 2 and 3 had 809 Me109s (656 serviceable). Production was only 155 a month. The RAF forced down an undamaged E3 at Amiens on 2 May 1940.

RADAR: a word of US origin coined in 1943. The original British term was radio direction finding or RDF. In 1932 the Scottish scientist Robert Watson-Watt wrote a Post Office report that aircraft re-radiated radio signals. In Feb 1935 he gave a practical demonstration to the Air Ministry Defence Committee using a BBC transmitter and RAF Heyford bomber. He received £100,000 grant rowards research at Orfordness, setting up a 70ft mast in June. The first radar station was set up at the Bawdsey research centre near Felixstowe and handed over to the RAF May 1937. Compulsory purchase got more sites in 1938 to set up a chain of 350ft steel aerial masts from the Solent to the Tay that would detect planes flying at 5000ft 40 miles away. Five tracked Chamberlain's flight to Munich. The recce airship *Graf Zeppelin* failed to detect the growing system in May and Aug 1939. It cost £10 million to build. Chain Home worked on a long 10-13·5 metre wavelength with 200 kilowatt transmitters for a range of 120 miles. Chain Home Low for low-flying aircraft detection had a 1·5 metre wavelength from scanners on a 185ft tower.

FRANCE DIVIDED

On 25 June 1940, France's 'day of mourning', when what remained of the French Army ceased fire, a young lieutenant pulled his armoured car to the side of a lonely road, scribbled a note: 'France is defeated. I have no wish to live under a German occupation,' put his pistol to his head and shot himself.

Not all French people however reacted so violently to the prospect of occupation. For a while, people were too stunned by the sheer size of the catastrophe to do anything at all. Nobody knew for sure what the Germans intended to do. Perhaps France the country would become a vassal state.

Hitler however had other plans. Convinced that the war in Europe was over, he saw the armistice as a temporary measure which would give way eventually to a re-drawn map of Europe. He therefore divided **France** into an occupied zone and a free zone.

The Occupied Zone was by far the larger and more prosperous. It accounted for 60 per cent of the country. The demarcation line started near the middle of the Spanish frontier, ran north towards Tours and then east towards Dijon and the Swiss frontier. All the main industrial areas were thus denied to the South; 97 per cent of the fishing industry, 75 per cent of mining, 66 per cent of cultivated land, 62 per cent of cereals and 70 per cent of potato, milk, butter and meat production were in Occupied France.

Almost from the start, the South, which was known as the Free Zone faced a serious shortage of food and industrial goods. The position was

'News-stand vendors offer them maps... buses pour them out in unending waves... *these are not tourists.* They are conquerors.'

Advice to the Occupied, underground news-sheet

aggravated by the presence of 300,000 refugees and large numbers of Jews who had no wish to remain in Occupied France.

Hitler's reasons for creating two Frances were simple: he hoped to prevent the creation of an exiled French Government and to retain indirect control of both the French Fleet and the French Empire.

Life in Occupied France came back to 'normal' very quickly. In Paris, the shops began from the very beginning of July to show 'Business as usual' signs. Fraternization was actively encouraged. The newspapers were already boasting of the benefits of defeat, and announcing that France was rid of her real enemies such as politicians like Edouard Daladier and Léon Blum. Posters began to appear on the walls of Paris and other major cities showing a smiling German soldier, bareheaded, his tunic unbuttoned, holding and feeding a French child while two other children look up at him in awe. The caption ran: 'Abandoned population, have confidence in the German soldier!'

In country areas the German soldiers were noticeable for their scarcity. Even close to the demarcation line, a corporal and section would control a huge area. Charles Trenchant, a tenant farmer to an English family, recalled that when the armistice came, he buried all evidence of the English family's presence (they had returned to Britain to enlist) so that when the inevitable German patrol turned up at the farm, he was able to say 'This is mine' and continue to bring in the wheat harvest.

But things were very different in the Free Zone, which was not only poor and sparsely inhabited, but had to contend with the formation of a completely new government.

Its head was the 84-year-old idolized Marshal of France Philippe Pétain, the 'Saviour of Verdun'. He was a small erect man with piercing blue eyes and a snowy white moustache. His tenacious defence of Verdun in 1916—'They shall not pass'—had turned him into a living legend. When Paul Reynaud, the French Prime Minister, refused to negotiate the armistice, Pétain had taken over. Now it was assumed that this sprightly old man would soon take over the running of what was left of France from the President, Albert Lebrun.

And then there was Pierre **Laval.** He came from the Auvergne which formed a great part of the new state. The Auvergnards had a reputation for meanness, and Laval was certainly tight-fisted. He was 57 at the time of the armistice, a small swarthy man, often depicted as a toad by cartoonists. His jowls sagged and his small face was round and yellow; his black hair greasy. His thick lips almost always held a Gauloise cigarette which stained his moustache nicotine yellow. He had a brilliant mind and studied at the famous

Relaxing in a Brussels café, German soldiers read of their successes in France. And (below) civilians queue to cross from the 'free' zone to the occupied zone.

Lycée Saint-Louis in Paris, but always retained his love of the country and held all his life to the peasant belief that a 'sou remained a sou whether it belonged to him or the state'. He had a passionate hatred of Britain.

The first problem the new state had to solve was where to have its capital. Laval was in favour of the Auvergne city of **Clermont-Ferrand**; but it soon became obvious that it was far too cramped and there just wasn't enough room for all the government offices. **Lyons**, on the Rhône was then suggested, but this was the city of Edouard **Herriot**, the radical deputy and speaker of the Chamber of Deputies, and neither Pétain nor Laval wanted to be in a place where Herriot was so powerful.

As a compromise **Vichy** was suggested, Vichy that popular watering place, famous for its elegant hotels and villas, its mineral waters and its hot springs—the greatest in France. President Lebrun was horrified at the choice: 'If we go to Vichy,' he said, 'they will say in France and abroad that we are a Casino Government.' But in this, as in much else, the President of the Third Republic was overruled. So Vichy it was.

Arriving at Vichy

The Marshal arrived on the morning of 1 July. Laval followed in the afternoon. The clutch on his car gave up just outside the town, so he had to finish the journey on foot, a squat figure in a black suit, a grey Homburg on his head and the inevitable white tie at his throat.

The seat of Government was the Hotel du Parc. There was the Casino that Lebrun so dreaded on the right and a covered hall containing three mineral springs on the left. In front was the Old Park. Laval had an office on the second floor; Pétain had his suite on the floor above. Offices were housed in the hotels and villas around.

Conditions were chaotic. The workmen were still in the building trying to make the awkward shaped rooms into reasonable offices. Connecting doors were taken away in order to make the rooms larger. A stream of orderlies carried files, personal luggage and office equipment from one floor to another. Tables complete with typewriters were wedged between wardrobes and washbasins. The whole place looked like a hurried and badly organized business convention.

Yet Pétain and Laval knew exactly what they wanted to do. These two very different men—the Marshal slow-minded but logical, Laval quick-witted and intuitive—nevertheless shared one identical political belief: a distrust of the Parliamentary system. Pétain had told Raymond Poincaré, France's President during World War 1, that he didn't give a damn for the French Constitution. Laval had always been a rebel. As a Socialist deputy for the working class Aubervilliers suburb of Paris in 1914 he was almost arrested as a potential saboteur. Now, in 1940, he was convinced that he had been right all along. Parliamentary democracy was to blame for France's entry into the war against Nazism and Fascism. Parliamentary democracy must disappear and be replaced by a French form of Nazism.

The problem was how to achieve this. The Third Republic was still technically in existence. Lebrun was still President, although as Laval told Pétain 'I undertake to obtain Albert Lebrun's full agreement to his disappearance'. But constitutional change could only be achieved by the vote of the deputies and senators; and this could only happen if 480 voted themselves out of existence.

Laval, who liked to look upon himself as a good working-class lawyer, set to work to cajole and frighten the parliamentarians. He reminded them how close the German Army was and told them that if they did not agree to their own dissolution, the Germans would enforce it. He claimed that Britain was no real friend of France. France indeed was 'nothing but a toy in the hands of England who had exploited us to ensure her own safety'. The Royal Navy's shelling of the French Fleet on 3 July off Mérs-el-Kebir near Oran strengthened his argument: Britain was the real enemy, Germany and Italy were France's friends.

At 9.30 on Tuesday 9 July Herriot took the

A few of the 1,900,000 prisoners taken by Germany during the invasion of France. And a Renault armoured tractor (right) helps to plough a field in France.

chair for the first formal meeting of the Chamber of Deputies since 16 May. It was a beautiful day with a cloudless blue sky.

Laval spoke again about the great need for a change in the Constitution. He described the declaration of war as 'the greatest crime which has been perpetrated in our country for a long time'. He attacked Britain in vitriolic terms and spoke of the need to revive old-fashioned virtues of discipline. 'It is,' he declared, 'the excess of liberty that has led us to where we are.'

When the Government's bill was put to the vote, it was carried by 569 votes to 80. The deputies had agreed to commit political suicide. Laval said: 'Gentlemen, in the name of Marshal Pétain, I thank you on behalf of France'. The Third Republic was ended by legal and constitutional methods. Albert Lebrun was quietly obliged to retire. Pétain was installed instead as Head of State. He was given full authority except for the power to declare war. As he himself said later: 'They have given me power, in fact all power. More than Louis XIV ever had.'

Léon Blum, the old socialist Popular Front leader passed judgement: 'During those two days I saw men change and become corrupt as though they had been plunged into a poisonous bath.'

By the second week of July, Hitler could feel extremely pleased at the way events had turned out, at least as far as France was concerned. The two Frances had settled down remarkably quickly. In the Occupied Zone, people were back at work as if nothing had happened. One farmer said: 'It's like the summer of 1939, except there isn't the fear of war any more.' In the South, the gamble to allow the French Government to choose its own form had paid off. The Head of State, Pétain, was seen as a patriarchal Messiah bent on creating a New Gaul, while the Chief Minister Laval was whole-heartedly committed to following the policies of Hitler and Mussolini.

Yet even at this early stage, the first flickering of French resistance was discernable. Rumours, carefully fanned by the BBC, began to circulate: Britain was not going to sue for peace after all, despite what the Germans might say. Churchill made that only too clear. Not that the French thought Britain had much chance of succeeding where France had failed. But it was a gesture.

Then there was the question of the French general who had escaped from France and set himself up in London as the real head of the French state. He had made a stirring speech reminding his listeners that France had lost a battle but not a war and calling upon Frenchmen everywhere to rally to his and France's cause. His name had a symbolic and prophetic ring: Charles de Gaulle.

July 14th had long been kept as a celebration for the storming of the Bastille in 1789, a day of pride in Republicanism and of the Frenchman's wish for liberty. The 1939 Fête Nationale, the 150th anniversary of the date, had been particularly splendid. A huge army, with a detachment of the Brigade of Guards from London, had

A poster in occupied Paris appeals for Franco-German friendship as French citizens (bottom) eagerly study lists of prisoners for news of missing relatives.

marched down the Champs-Elysées to the roaring applause of the crowds. The parade had ended with a fly-past of 400 fighters and bombers.

Now there was nothing but a pathetic ceremony at the Vichy war memorial. The Marshal had put on his old Verdun uniform and took the march past of the few hundred soldiers Vichy could muster. Paul **Baudouin,** one of the deputies, sadly recorded in his diary: 'Mass at 9am. At the elevation of the Host the Marshal knelt. It is a long time since the Head of State did this. We went on foot to a meagre review, the first since the disaster, and I came away very upset at the miserable appearance of the few companies which marched past. The men were sickly, yellow and small, while most of them wore glasses. Have we fallen so low?'

'Advice to the Occupied'

But in Paris a different ceremony was performed: the very first clandestine broadsheet appeared. It was written by Jean Texier and was privately distributed by his friends. Entitled *Advice to the Occupied*, it had this to say about the thousands of German 'tourists' who now visited the capital: 'The news-stand dealers offer them maps of Paris and conversation manuals: the buses pour them out in unending waves in front of Notre Dame and the Pantheon; there is not one of them who does not have his little camera screwed to his eye. However, have no illusions about them: *these are not tourists*. They are conquerors . . .'

There was advice to those who could speak German, 'If one speaks to you in German, shrug helplessly and walk on . . .' There was whimsical encouragement to those who wanted to forget the bitterness of defeat: 'I know a philosopher who has found a curious way of consoling himself: "We have taken too many prisoners," he sighs.'

There was humour too: 'You grumble because they make you return home precisely at 9pm . . . Don't you understand that that is to allow you to listen to the English radio?'

Finally there was advice to those who wanted to give the broadsheet a wider circulation: 'It is useless telling your friends to buy *Advice to the Occupied* at bookshops. No doubt you only have one copy and wish to keep it. All right, make some copies and your friends may copy theirs in turn. It's a good occupation for the Occupied. . .'

But all this was still some way from the real movement which did not begin in earnest until the publication of the first underground newspaper *Resistance* in December 1940. All that was possible in July were these gentle verbal exercises, and the posting of 'Vive de Gaulle' stickers on walls.

These efforts were confined to Paris and one or two other large cities in the Occupied Zone. None appeared, in July at least, in the Zone Sud, for the movement was anti-German not anti-Vichy. It was, in fact, whispered that Pétain and Laval were playing a subtle game of 'double-bluff' yielding as little as possible to German demands and awaiting an opportunity to bring France back into the fight. It would be some months before this illusion was finally dispelled and the active Resistance would be really formed.

War Notes

BAUDOUIN, Paul: French banker and politician, b. 1894. A director of the Bank of Indochina. Approved by Blum to manage Exchange Equalization Fund 1937. Special envoy to Rome 1939. Under Secretary of State for War in Reynaud Government March 1940. Pétain's foreign minister until Oct.

CLERMONT-FERRAND: city 210 miles SSE of Paris. Pop 101,128 (1930). Large industrial centre situated at foot of a range of extinct volcanoes.

FRANCE, Fall of: since 10 May French Army losses totalled 90,000–92,000 dead, 200,000–250,000 wounded and 1.45–1.9 million prisoners (no accurate figures have ever been published). Officer casualties totalled 40,000 including 130 generals. By 25 June, apart from the Army of the Alps and the Maginot Line's 220,000 defenders (who did not surrender their forts until 30 June), France only had 65,000 troops still fighting as units. French Air Force losses came to 892 planes (413 in air combat) with 1493 aircrew killed, wounded and missing. Some 1705 fighters (550 overseas) and 1136 bomber/recce planes (590 overseas) survived the armistice. German campaign losses were 27,074 killed 111,034 wounded and 18,384 captured and missing. Of these 95,330 were suffered after 4 June or a daily loss rate double May's. Luftwaffe admitted 534 planes lost in combat from all causes out of 1469 (635 bombers and 457 fighters). Anglo-French claims came to 1735, 210 by flak. France was to be fought over again in 1944–5 but it is significant that financial and economic costs have been estimated as twice those of 1914–18.

HERRIOT, Edouard: French politician, b. 1872 Troyes. Mayor of Lyons from 1905, and member of Chamber of Deputies from 1919. Became leader of Radical Socialist Party 1919. Prime Minister 1924–5, Minister for Public Instruction 1926–8. He was once again premier June–Dec 1932. Became Minister of State 1934–6 and President of Chamber of Deputies 1936. Before France fell he and Jeanneney, leader of the Senate, were opposed to an armistice. On 16 June begged Lebrun to support Reynaud's decision to fight on from N. Africa. But ordered French engineers to remove demolition charges from Lyons' bridges.

LAVAL, Pierre: French politician, b. 1883 Chateldon, Central France. Lawyer who joined Socialist Party 1903. He entered parliament as Deputy for Aubervilliers (Paris) in 1914. Opposed World War 1. Became independent Senator for Seine in 1926. He held numerous ministerial posts: Public Works 1925, Justice 1926, Labour 1930 and 1932, PM and Foreign Minister 1931–2 and 1935–6 (signing treaties with Italy and USSR to oppose Hitler), Colonies 1934 and Foreign Minister 1934–5. In 1939 was alone in condemning the declaration of war against Germany. Nominated Minister of State by Pétain and was vice-premier in Vichy Government July–Dec 1940.

LYONS: 3rd largest French city, with 1936 pop of 546,683. At confluence of Rhône and Saône rivers. Known for silk industry, textiles and chemical industries, 240 miles SSE of Paris and 170 miles N of Marseilles. Entered by Kleist's tanks on 22 June after declared 'an open city'.

VICHY: town of 29.000 in central France, 28 miles NNE of Clermont-Ferrand. It is a leading health resort with a luxurious spa made up of hotels, the normal establishments, places of entertainment and parks. Vichy water is exported. Captured and given up by the Germans in June.

MAPS

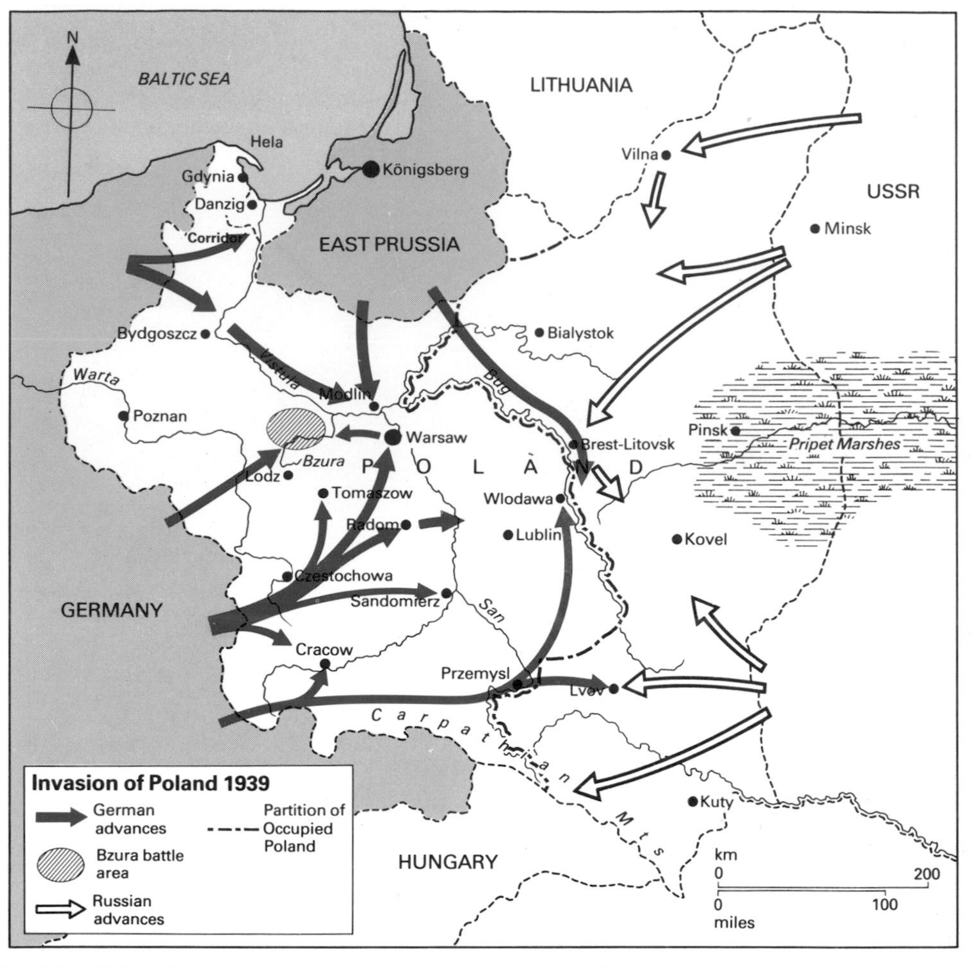

Invasion of Poland 1939
German advances
Bzura battle area
Russian advances
Partition of Occupied Poland
BALTIC SEA
LITHUANIA
USSR
EAST PRUSSIA
GERMANY
HUNGARY
POLAND
Hela
Gdynia
Danzig
Corridor
Königsberg
Vilna
Minsk
Bydgoszcz
Bialystok
Warta
Vistula
Bug
Modlin
Poznan
Warsaw
Brest-Litovsk
Pinsk
Pripet Marshes
Bzura
Lodz
Tomaszow
Wlodawa
Radom
Lublin
Kovel
Czestochowa
Sandomierz
San
Cracow
Przemysl
Lvov
Carpathian Mts
Kuty
km
0
200
0
100
miles

Campaign in the West May–June 1940
German advance
Allied moves
German airborne attacks 10 May
miles
0
50
100
0
50
100
Km
ENGLAND
HOLLAND
GERMANY
BELGIUM
LUXEMBOURG
FRANCE
Channel
Fortress Holland
Grebbe Line
The Hague
Rotterdam
Zeeland
Walcheren
Peel Line
Middleburg
Beveland
Breda
Tilburg
Zeebrugge
Ostend
Bruges
Antwerp
Nieuport
Dunkirk
Ypres
Scheldt
Albert Canal
Meuse
Rhine
Munchen Gladbach
Ruhr
Gravelines
Ghent
Dyle
Menin
Le Paradis
Courtrai
Eben-Emael
Cologne
Aachen
Boulogne
Brussels
Tirlemont
Aa
Oudenarde
Lille
Tournai
Louvain
Noyelles
Valenciennes
Namur
Sambre
Mauberge
Arras
Dinant
Somme
Cambrai
Givet
Abbeville
Péronne
Berlaimont
Montherme
Siegfried Line
Charleville
Amiens
St Quentin
Mézières
Ardennes
Montcornet
Sedan
Laon
Semois
Aisne
Maginot Line
Paris

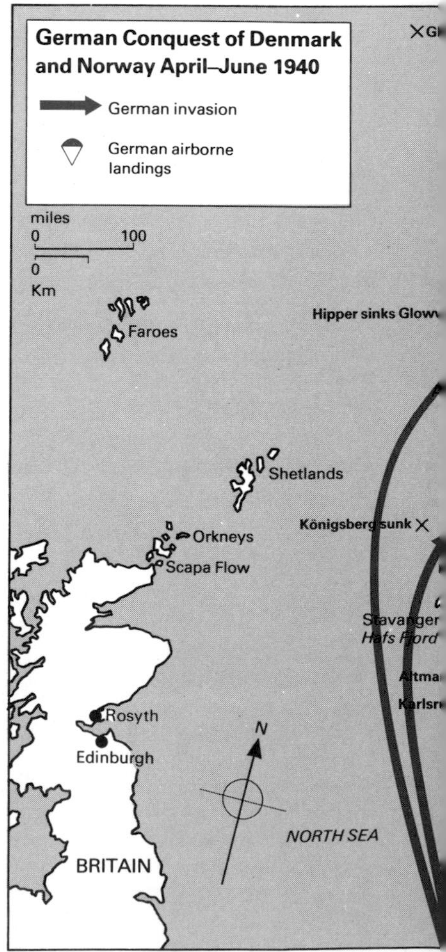

German Conquest of Denmark and Norway April–June 1940
German invasion
German airborne landings
miles
0
100
0
Km
Hipper sinks Glowworm
Faroes
Shetlands
Königsberg sunk
Orkneys
Scapa Flow
Stavanger
Hafs Fjord
Rosyth
Edinburgh
NORTH SEA
BRITAIN

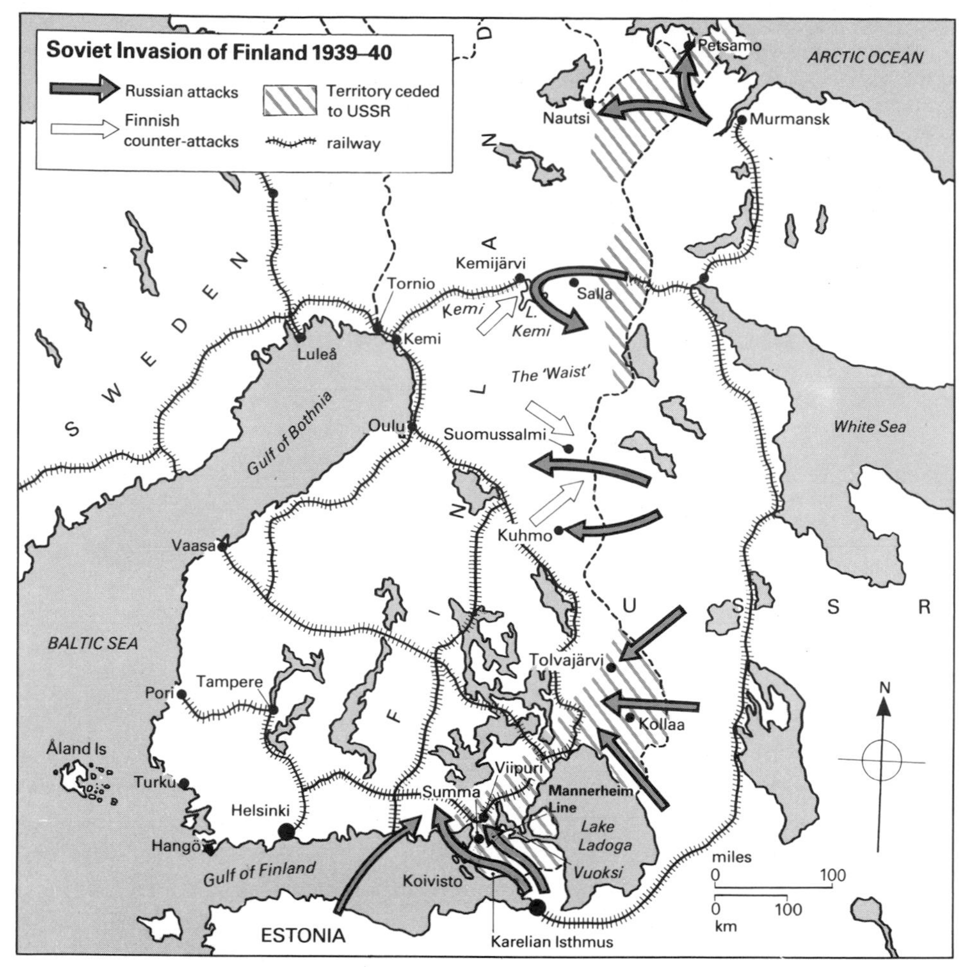
Soviet Invasion of Finland 1939–40
Russian attacks
Finnish counter-attacks
Territory ceded to USSR
railway
Petsamo
ARCTIC OCEAN
Nautsi
Murmansk
Kemijärvi
Salla
Tornio
Kemi
L. Kemi
Kemi
Luleå
The 'Waist'
SWEDEN
Gulf of Bothnia
Oulu
Suomussalmi
White Sea
Kuhmo
Vaasa
FINLAND
USSR
BALTIC SEA
Tolvajärvi
Tampere
Pori
Kollaa
Åland Is
Turku
Viipuri
Summa
Mannerheim Line
Helsinki
Lake Ladoga
Hangö
Vuoksi
Gulf of Finland
Koivisto
ESTONIA
Karelian Isthmus
miles
0
100
0
100
km
N

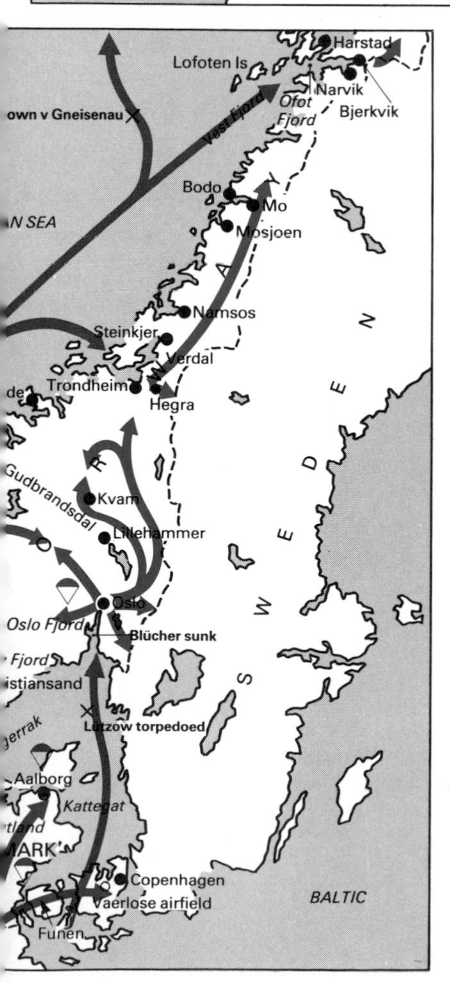
Harstad
Lofoten Is
Narvik
Ofot Fjord
Bjerkvik
Vest Fjord
own v Gneisenau
Bodo
Mo
N SEA
Mosjoen
Namsos
Steinkjer
Verdal
Trondheim
Hegra
Gudbrandsdal
Kvam
Lillehammer
SWEDEN
Oslo
Oslo Fjord
Blücher sunk
Fjord
istiansand
Lützow torpedoed
Aalborg
Kattegat
Copenhagen
Vaerlose airfield
Funen
BALTIC

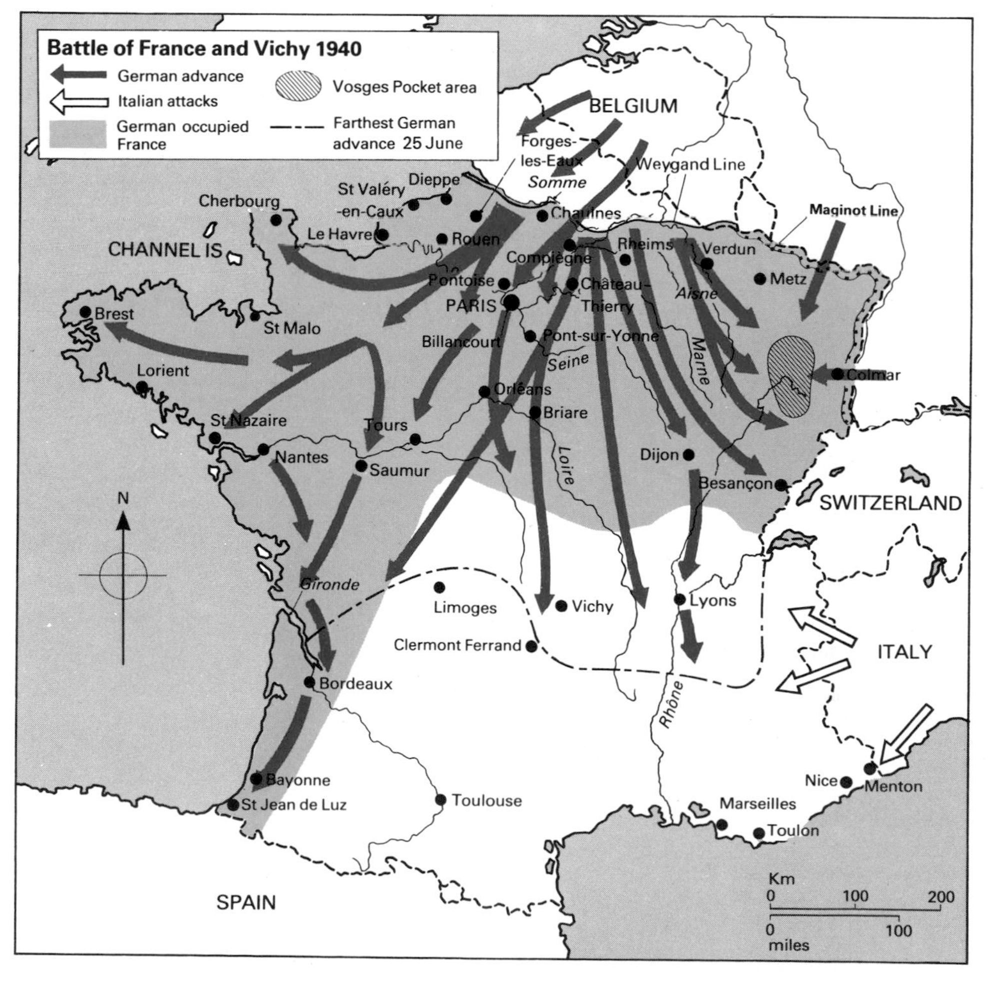
Battle of France and Vichy 1940
German advance
Italian attacks
German occupied France
Vosges Pocket area
Farthest German advance 25 June
BELGIUM
Forges-les-Eaux
Somme
Weygand Line
Dieppe
St Valéry-en-Caux
Cherbourg
Chaulnes
Maginot Line
Le Havre
Rouen
Rheims
Verdun
CHANNEL IS
Compiègne
Metz
Pontoise
Château-Thierry
Aisne
PARIS
Brest
St Malo
Billancourt
Pont-sur-Yonne
Marne
Seine
Lorient
Colmar
Orléans
Briare
St Nazaire
Tours
Nantes
Saumur
Dijon
Loire
Besançon
SWITZERLAND
N
Gironde
Limoges
Vichy
Lyons
Clermont Ferrand
ITALY
Bordeaux
Rhône
Nice
Menton
Bayonne
St Jean de Luz
Toulouse
Marseilles
Toulon
SPAIN
Km
0
100
200
0
100
miles

INDEX

123 = italic: indicates picture

123 = bold: indicates war notes entry

EYE WITNESS = small caps: eye witness boxes

B

C

D

E

I

J

K

L

M

N

O

P

Q

R

S

T

U

V

W

Y

Z